Readings in the Psychology of Adjustment

READINGS IN THE PSYCHOLOGY OF ADJUSTMENT

Edited by

Leon Gorlow, Ph.D.
ASSOCIATE PROFESSOR OF PSYCHOLOGY
THE PENNSYLVANIA STATE UNIVERSITY

and

Walter Katkovsky, Ph.D.
RESEARCH ASSOCIATE, THE FELS RESEARCH INSTITUTE
ASSISTANT PROFESSOR OF PSYCHOLOGY, ANTIOCH COLLEGE

McGRAW-HILL BOOK COMPANY, INC.
1959   New York   Toronto   London

Preface

One of the heavy demands upon departments of psychology is providing instruction in the area of personal adjustment and mental hygiene. The demand comes from a wide variety of sources: students who require a general introduction to the study of human behavior; students who are seeking a better understanding of their own problems; and students who seek an orientation to the area of adjustment as a basis for advanced training in psychology. The first of these includes persons who are entering fields which necessitate an understanding of personal relationships, such as teaching, school administration, guidance and counseling, business and personnel work, and nursing. The second group includes students having difficulty in adjusting to college work, students seeking aid with personal problems, and those who need guides to more effective living. The third group consists of undergraduate students who are entertaining the idea of pursuing advanced training in the behavioral sciences.

The content of the study of adjustment is vast. It includes material from many other disciplines and overlaps other areas of psychological inquiry. Consequently the courses of instruction and textbooks variously labeled with the terms "mental hygiene" or "adjustment" generally are limited in the amount of material they are able to encompass. There is a justified need for a more comprehensive presentation of material relating to human adjustment than is provided by most texts. We believe the student's interests are served by a presentation of varied issues and argument in the field. Our hope is that we have produced a book of readings which will serve this purpose.

A volume which introduces the reader to the main currents of thought in the psychology of adjustment would seem to be useful in several ways. The book may be exceedingly useful as a supplementary text which offers rich material for discussion. In addition, since the readings have been structured in an orderly fashion, the book may be useful as a basic text in courses called "mental hygiene," "the psychology of adjustment," "personal adjustment," "mental health and education," etc. Finally the general reader who is interested in the contributions of psychology to the pressing social problems concerning psychological health and illness will find it rewarding.

We should like to acknowledge the kindness of the authors, editors, and publishers whose permissions to reproduce the reading selections made this volume possible. Specific permission citations are noted at the bottom of the first page of each selection. We hope that the organization, editing, and introductory materials, which have been prepared jointly by the editors, facilitate the understanding of the ideas presented by the authors of the papers.

Leon Gorlow
Walter Katkovsky

Contents

Introduction

An attempt has been made to organize the contributions from many fields to the psychology of adjustment and mental hygiene. Rather than being a discipline in its own right, the psychology of adjustment borrows its content from many areas of investigation. An inspection of the total field brings the reviewer to a consideration of such things as the scientific method, theories of personality, clinical and abnormal psychology, and the psychology of learning and development. In addition, the study of adjustment draws upon content from such fields as psychiatry, sociology, cultural anthropology, and genetics.

The first section of the readings is devoted to a number of selections about science and the scientific method. The intention is to provide the reader with some understanding of the demands of scientific inquiry. This presentation is followed by a set of readings which illustrate the various methods used in psychological research. Readings are provided which illustrate natural observation, the clinical case study method, correlational and experimental analysis.

The second section deals with the concept of adjustment, the various definitions given it, and their implications. In this section there are presentations which illustrate both relativistic and nonrelativistic statements about psychological health and psychological distress. It is apparent from the different points of view presented that controversy exists about adequate criteria for mental health.

Since definitions of adjustment are inevitably related to theories of personality, the next section presents a set of readings which define some of the current personality theories. Readings in trait theory, orthodox psychoanalysis, neopsychoanalysis, phenomenology, and learning theory comprise the material.

The fourth section contains the broad scope of material which deals with the process of adjustment. The first group of readings in the section provides a consideration of determinants or conditions of adjustment. More specifically such variables as constitutional and ecological factors, parent-child relationships, and cultural influences are discussed. The second group of readings presents the ideas of such persons as Horney, Adler, Fromm, Riesman, and Mowrer, who have written extensively about dynamic personality processes. The final group in this section deals with pathological modes of adjustment and their consequences.

The fifth section is concerned with adjustment from the point of view of developmental psychology, where adjustment within the different life stages is discussed. Attention is given to childhood, adolescence, and old age, and the problems and behavioral characteristics peculiar to each stage are considered.

Behavioral change and psychotherapy are the topics which comprise the next section. While an extensive elaboration of the various positions dealing with psychotherapy is not attempted, illustrations of major contributions are provided. The views of psychoanalysis, client-centered therapy, and learning theory are represented. In addition, specific techniques such as group and play therapy are discussed.

The volume ends with a group of selections which depict problems of widespread social concern. The community needs to be involved with such issues as quackery in psychological services, with the problems inherent in the control of human behavior, and with the influence of psychological thinking on criminal law.

It is apparent in the readings and comments throughout this volume that numerous questions, problems, and controversies exist in the area of adjustment. These have been emphasized intentionally, since it is the belief of the editors that the controversial issues and the unsolved problems define the study of adjustment as it exists today and will determine its future developments. In addition, the editors hope that by bringing varied and opposing points of view to the attention of the reader, this volume will promote greater involvement with, and a realistic perception of, the total field of study.

The Philosophy of Science and Methods of Inquiry

The psychology of adjustment is concerned with the total range of psychological adjustments involved in human experience. It seeks to give a full understanding of a person's mode of dealing with both internal and external sources of stimulation. It inquires into basic sources of motivation; it studies the transformation of motives by learning; it studies the variability in response to experience; and it seeks to define the conditions under which people alter their behavior. It is clear then that the scope of inquiry is extremely broad, and consequently it is essential that the method of inquiry be a disciplined one.

In its attempt to order human experience, psychology, in common with many other disciplines, shares a fundamental commitment to the method of science. It is important to acknowledge that science is not a set of facts, a set of laws, or a set of relationships. These are rather the fruits of science; they are the consequences of *behaving* scientifically. Science is controlled operations and procedures designed to answer questions pertaining to a specific area of inquiry. Since investigators in the psychology of adjustment for the most part adhere to the scientific method, the first section of readings is devoted to an elaboration of the meaning of science and the various approaches which are used by the scientist. We have divided these readings into two groups: the first deals with the meaning of science abstractly, while the second illustrates some of the procedures as they apply to specific problems in the area of adjustment.

A. Philosophy of science

The first selection is taken from Churchman and Ackoff's *Methods of Inquiry*. It is a volume in the philosophy of science and its title suggests appropriately that science is foremost a way of behaving, a method. The selection provides a general definition of science as *controlled inquiry*, and it is this element of control which distinguishes scientific work from work of a nonscientific nature. Intuition, for example, does not constitute scientific inquiry inasmuch as it lacks conscious efforts at control. The selection is extremely pointed in defining the behavior of scientists. The distinction which the authors draw between scientific inquiry and common-sense inquiry is worthy of note. Rather than being completely antithetical, the two methods are viewed as different in degree only. The scientist is more aware of the possibility of error and strives for increased precision in his operations.

A section from a paper by Feigl on the scientific outlook is next reprinted. It may be approached as an elaboration in some detail of the view presented by Churchman and Ackoff. Feigl leads us through a carefully stated discussion of the general criteria of the scientific method, indicating that scientific inquiry may be formulated as ideals to be approximated but never fully attained. In order to approximate an ideal, the successive elimination of error is necessary. Thus we again see that precision is one of the key attributes of the scientific method. Such concepts as testability, reliability, and comprehensiveness are used to further define the field of inquiry, and the paper closes with an extremely valuable and well-considered critique of some common misconceptions about science.

The section ends with a selection from Brown and Ghiselli's book *Scientific Method in Psychology*. The content here is more directly related to the field of human behavior, and our attention is narrowed to the concern of psychology. Brown and Ghiselli begin their exposition by specifying four questions which may be asked with respect to any phenomenon: (1) Is it so? (2) To what extent is it so? (3) Why is it so? (4) What are the conditions that bring it about? These questions lead quite naturally to a discussion of description, explanation, prediction, and theorizing. Their discussion of the conditions necessary for scientific inquiry suggests again that science is a *method* which seeks as much control as it can muster over its operations and procedures.

THE MEANING OF SCIENCE *

⟦ C. West Churchman and R. L. Ackoff

Science has come to play such an important part in our lives that it is often difficult for us to realize that its pursuit and products have only become major factors in society in the last few hundred years. It has become so important that one could not hope today to understand our culture without understanding the role science plays in it. Science has come to mean "efficient inquiry" to us. It has a fundamental role to play in the basic activities of the people who make decisions and try to solve problems. Many of our critical social problems today hinge on the nature and role of science. We often hear such questions asked as, Can and should science investigate such and such an area? Can and should science tell us how to live? Can science save us? We are all anxious to know what science can do now, what it will eventually be able to do, and what it ought to do. Consequently, an understanding of science is no longer the exclusive concern of the scientist, though it may be his primary concern.

What do we mean by "science"? It is usually defined as "an organized body of knowledge." But this is too "passive" a definition to lead to an understanding of it. Science is not a mere state or accumulation; it is an activity as well as the products of that activity. Science is inquiry; but not all inquiry is scientific. This fact gives us a clue to how we may go about defining it. Science as a kind of inquiry must differ from other types of inquiry either by virtue of *what* it inquires into, or *how* it inquires; that is, on the basis of either its content, or its method—or perhaps both.

Let us call "common sense" inquiry the kind of inquiry we indulge in as laymen in our everyday lives. First we want to ask whether scientific and common sense inquiry differ with respect to subject matter, that is, content. It is sometimes said that common sense deals only with immediate and practical problems, whereas science is restricted to long-run, and not immediately practical problems. It is easy to see the inadequacy of this assertion on the basis of the types of inquiry with which we commonly observe common sense and science to be concerned. Science certainly inquires into immediately practical problems: applied sciences like engineering are no less scientific for their applications. Nor is common sense restricted to the immediate, for such general inquiries as have produced the wisdom contained in proverbs have been performed on a common sense basis.

* From C. West Churchman and R. L. Ackoff, *Methods of Inquiry*, 1st ed., pp. 9–11, Educational Publishers, Inc., St. Louis, 1950. Reprinted by permission of Dr. Churchman and the publisher.

No, it seems more fruitful to look for difference between scientific and common sense inquiry in terms of their method. Common sense itself immediately suggests a distinction: science is *controlled* inquiry, and common sense is not. This suggestion is not, of course, a solution for at best it only gives the problem a name. What is meant by control? Before seeking an answer, however, it is worth noting the conformity of the suggestions with normal usage. We are inclined to say, among other things, not so much that science is an organized body of knowledge, as an organized way of obtaining knowledge. To be sure, science organizes its results, but so does philosophy. Scientists create systems, but so do poets. But science uses an organized and systematic method of inquiry, in some sense a *controlled* method, which makes it unique.

Now again to the question: What is control? We say a man has his automobile under control if he can use it efficiently as an instrument for the pursuit of his objective, say, safe and rapid transportation. In effect, he controls his car when he leads it; but he loses control when it leads him. By analogy we would say that a method of inquiry is under control if the inquirer can use it efficiently in solving the problems that force him into the inquiry in the first place. The *degree* of that efficiency will be a measure of the degree of his control. But we still have to find out what is involved in saying that the inquirer can "use his method efficiently," or that he can lead it rather than have it lead him.

Suppose a scientist is forced to take a certain step in his inquiry for which he has no alternative. Then this step "leads him," he does not lead it—or analogously, he does not have it under control. Practically in science, this means that he cannot investigate the advisability of his step. In so far as the scientist can examine the adequacy of his steps and make an efficient selection, then he leads or controls his steps, and they do not lead him.

We often say that common sense takes a lot for granted; science is more sceptical since it wants to examine everything. This contains in simple language the essence of the notion of control. Common sense inquiry is led by habits of inquiry, by things and methods it takes for granted. Science seeks to test every aspect of its procedure and its assumptions. It is this that differentiates between common sense and science. A method of inquiry, then, is under complete control when every aspect of the activity is itself subject to inquiry with respect to its adequacy for the problematic purpose.

Of course, complete control is something we do not have, or ever expect to have. It represents, however, something we seek. Nor do we ever completely lack control. Complete lack or presence of control are the extreme values of a continuous scale. Science and common sense represent the upper and lower portions of the scale, respectively.

To say a method of inquiry is not under control is not to say that the conclusion it reaches must be wrong. On the contrary, we know that common sense, or the most primitive kind of inquiry, might give us a correct answer to a question. But in the long run we are not confident about the solutions of common sense. Here is the critical point in our high evaluation of science: we believe a controlled method of inquiry is *more apt* to produce correct answers than uncontrolled methods.

We can see now why an understanding of scientific *method* is so critical to an understanding of science. It is its method which provides the essential difference between science and common sense. To know what science can, will, and ought to do, we must know what the method of science is, i.e., the nature of its controls, and what is controlled by it.

THE SCIENTIFIC OUTLOOK *

⟮ HERBERT FEIGL

Criteria of the Scientific Method

What . . . are the basic characteristics of the scientific method? The often alleged difficulties of an adequate definition of science seem to me mainly a matter of terminology. We must first distinguish between pure mathematics as an exclusively formal-conceptual discipline, and the factual (or empirical, that is, the natural and the social-cultural) sciences. The certainty, complete exactitude, and necessity of pure mathematics depends precisely on its detachment from empirical fact. Mathematics as applied in the factual sciences merely lends its forms and deductive structures to the contents furnished by experience. But no matter how predominant mathematics may be in the formulations and derivations of empirical facts, factual knowledge cannot attain either the absolute precision or necessity of pure mathematics. The knowledge claimed in the natural and the social sciences is a matter of successive approximations and of increasing degrees of confirmation. Warranted assertibility or probability is all that we can conceivably secure in the sciences that deal with the facts of experience. It is empirical science, thus conceived as an unending quest (its truths claim to be held only "until further notice"), which is under consideration here. Science in this sense differs only in degree from the knowledge accumulated throughout the ages by sound and common sense.

The aims of science are description, explanation, and prediction. The first aim is basic and indispensable, the second and third (closely related to each other) arise as the most desirable fruits of scientific labors whenever

* From Herbert Feigl, "The Scientific Outlook: Naturalism and Humanism," *Amer. Quart.*, *1*, 135–148. Pages 138–148 reprinted by permission of the author and the Editor, *American Quarterly*.

inquiry rises beyond the mere fact-gathering stage. History, often and nowadays quite fashionably declared an art, is scientific to the extent that it ascertains its facts concerning past events by a meticulous scrutiny of present evidence. Causal interpretation of these facts (in history, but similarly also in psychology, sociology, cultural anthropology, and economics) is usually much more difficult than, but in principle not logically different from, causal interpretation (that is, explanation) in the natural sciences. The aims of the pure (empirical) sciences are then essentially the same throughout the whole field. What the scientists are seeking are descriptions, explanations, and predictions which are as adequate and accurate as possible in the given context of research.

The quest for scientific knowledge is therefore regulated by certain standards or criteria which may best be formulated in the form of ideals to be approximated, but perhaps never fully attained. The most important of these regulative ideals are:

1. *Intersubjective testability.* This is only a more adequate formulation of what is generally meant by the "objectivity" of science. What is here involved is not only the freedom from personal or cultural bias or partiality, but—even more fundamentally—the requirement that the knowledge claims of science be in principle capable of test (confirmation or disconfirmation, at the least indirectly and to some degree) on the part of any person properly equipped with intelligence and the technical devices of observation or experimentation. The term *intersubjective* stresses the social nature of the scientific enterprise. If there be any "truths" that are accessible only to privileged individuals, such as mystics or visionaries—that is, knowledge-claims which by their very nature cannot independently be checked by anyone else—then such "truths" are not of the kind that we seek in the sciences. The criterion of intersubjective testability thus delimits the scientific from the nonscientific activities of man.

Religious ecstasy, the elations of love, the inspiration of the artist, yes, even the flash of insight on the part of a scientific genius are not in themselves scientific activities. All these processes may eventually become subject matter for scientific study. But in themselves they do not validate knowledge-claims. They may, as in the case of the scientific intuition (or empathy in the psychological-cultural field) be instrumental in the generation of knowledge-claims. But it is these knowledge-claims which have to be, first, formulated in an intersubjectively intelligible (or communicable) manner, and, second, subjected to the appropriate kind of tests in order to ascertain their validity. Beliefs transcending all possible tests by observation, self-observation, experiment, measurement, or statistical analysis are recognized as theological or metaphysical and therefore devoid of the type of meaning that we all associate with the knowledge-claims of common sense or factual science. From the point of view of the scientific outlook in philosophy it may be suggested that the sort of significance with which the in-principleunconfirmable assertions of transcendent theology and metaphysics impress so many people is largely emotive. The pictorial, emotional, and motivational appeals of language, no matter how indispensable or valuable in the contexts of practical life, art, education, persuasion, and propaganda, must, however, not be confused with the cognitive meanings (purely formal- and/or factual-empirical) that are of the essence of science. Each type of significance has its function, and in most uses of language both are combined or even fused. The only point stressed here is that they must not be *confused*, that is, mistaken for one another, if we wish to be clear as to what we are about.

2. *Reliability, or a sufficient degree of confirmation.* This second criterion of scientific knowledge enables us to distinguish what is generally called "mere opinion" (or worse still, "superstition") from knowledge (well-substantiated belief). It may be considered as the delimitation of the scientific from the unscientific knowledge-claims. Clearly, in contrast to the first criterion, we face here a distinction of degree. There is no sharp line of demarcation between the well-confirmed laws, theories, or hypotheses of science, and the only poorly substantiated hunches and ideas-on-trial which may ultimately either be included in the corpus of scientific knowledge or else rejected as unconfirmed. Truth-claims which we repudiate as "superstition," and, quite generally, as judgments based upon hasty generalization or weak analogy (if they fulfill the criterion of testability), differ from what we accept as "scientific truth" in the extremely low degree of probability to which they are supported by the available evidence. Astrology or alchemy, for example, are not factually meaningless, but they are considered false to fact in that all available evidence speaks overwhelmingly against them. Modern techniques of experimentation and of statistical analysis are the most powerful tools we have in the discernment between chance and law and hence the best means of enhancing the reliability of knowledge.

3. *Definiteness and precision.* This obvious standard of scientific method requires that the concepts used in the formulation of scientific knowledge-claims be as definitely delimited as possible. On the level of the qualitative-classificatory sciences this amounts to the attempt to reduce all border-zone vagueness to a minimum. On the level of quantitative science the exactitude of the concepts is enormously enhanced through the application of the techniques of measurement. The mensurational devices usually also increase the degree of objectivity. This is especially clear when they are contrasted with purely impressionistic ways of estimating magnitudes. Of course, there is no point in sharpening precision to a higher degree than the problem in hand requires. (You need no razor to cut butter.)

4. *Coherence or systematic structure.* This is what T. H. Huxley had in mind when he defined science as "organized common-sense." Not a mere collection of miscellaneous items of information, but a well-connected account of the facts is what we seek in science. On the descriptive level

this results, for example, in systems of classification or division, in diagrams, statistical charts, and the like. On the explanatory levels of science sets of laws, or theoretical assumptions, are utilized. Explanation in science consists in the hypothetico-deductive procedure. The laws, theories, or hypotheses form the premises from which we derive logically, or logico-mathematically, the observed or observable facts. These facts, often belonging to heterogeneous domains, thus become integrated into a coherent, unifying structure. (Theological and metaphysical systems have, frequently enough, ambitiously tried to imitate this feature of science; but even if they succeeded in proceeding *more geometrico*, the important difference from science remains: they either lack testability or else reliability in the senses specified in our previous points.)

5. *Comprehensiveness or scope of knowledge.* This final point in our enumeration of criteria of science also characterizes scientific knowledge as different in degree (often enormously) from common-sense knowledge. Not only through bold and sweeping hypotheses, but especially through the ingenious devices by means of which they are tested, science acquires a reach far beyond the limits of our unaided senses. With telescopes, microscopes, spectroscopes, Geiger counters, lie detectors, and the thousands of other contrivances of modern science we manage to amplify our senses and thus open up avenues of at least indirect access to the worlds of the very distant, the very large, the extremely small, or the disguised and concealed. The resulting increase in the completeness of our knowledge is, of course, popularly the most impressive feature of science. It must be kept in mind, however, that the scope thus achieved is a product of hard labor, and not to be confused with the sham completeness metaphysicians procure for their world pictures by verbal magic. Instead of presenting a finished account of the world, the genuine scientist keeps his unifying hypotheses open to revision and is always ready to modify or abandon them if evidence should render them doubtful. This self-corrective aspect of science has rightly been stressed as its most important characteristic and must always be kept in mind when we refer to the comprehensiveness or the unification achieved by the scientific account of the universe. It is a sign of one's maturity to be able to live with an unfinished world view.

The foregoing outline of the criteria of science has been set down in a somewhat dogmatic tone. But this was done only for the sake of brevity.[1] The spirit behind it is that of a humble account of what, I think, an impartial and elaborate study of the history of thought from magic to science would reveal. In any case, these criteria seem unquestionably the guiding ideals of present-day empirical science. They may therefore be used in a definition of science as we understand this term today. It seems rather use-

[1] A thorough discussion of the logical, epistemological, methodological, and historical issues connected with the criteria would require a whole book, not just another essay.

less to speculate about just what this term, by a change of meaning, might come to connote in the future.

It should be remembered that the criteria listed characterize the *pure* factual (empirical) sciences. The aims of the *applied* sciences—the technologies, medicine, social and economic planning, and others—are practical control, production, guidance, therapy, reform, and so forth. Responsible activity in the application of science clearly presupposes information which is fairly well substantiated by the methods of the pure sciences. (These remarks intend to draw merely a logically important distinction. The obvious practical interpenetration and important mutual fertilization of the pure and the applied disciplines is of course not denied here.)

Critique of Misconceptions

Having indicated at least in broad outline the nature of scientific method we may now turn to the critique of some of the misconceptions to which it is all too commonly exposed. In what follows, a dozen typical charges against science are stated and answered consecutively.[2]

Science arises exclusively out of practical and social needs and has its only value in serving them in turn. (Dialectical Materialism and Vocationalism)

While this is important it does not tell the whole story. Science has always also been the pursuit of knowledge, the satisfaction of a deep-rooted curiosity. It should be recognized as one of the cultural values along with art, literature, and music. Better teaching of the sciences and their history can redress the balance. Fuller utilization of results and suggestions from the history and the philosophy of science would give the student a deeper appreciation of the evolution of scientific knowledge and of the scientific point of view. Through proper instruction, the student could be led to rediscover some of the important results of science. The intellectual gratification that comes with a grasp of the order of nature, with the understanding of its processes by means of laws and theories, is one of the most powerful incentives in the pursuit of pure knowledge.

Science cannot furnish a secure basis for human affairs since it is unstable. It changes its views continually. (Traditionalism)

While there is constant evolution, and occasionally a revolution, in the scientific outlook, the charge is a superficial (usually journalistic) exaggeration. The typical progress of science reveals that later views often contain

---

[2] These charges are not straw men. In more than twenty years of reading, listening, teaching, and argument I have encountered them again and again in Europe and just as frequently in this country. If space permitted and time were less valuable, I could quote many well-known writers in connection with each charge.

much of the earlier views (to the extent that these have stood the test of repeated examination). The more radical or revolutionary changes usually amount to a revision of the conceptual frame of a scientific discipline. The criticism often also presupposes other sources of certainty which will simply not bear critical scrutiny. The quest for absolute certainty is an immature, if not infantile, trait of thinking. The best knowledge we have can be established only by the method of trial and error. It is of the essence of science to make such knowledge as reliable as is humanly and technically possible.

Science rests on uncritical and uncriticized presuppositions. It validates its outlook by its own standards. It therefore begs the question as regards alternative approaches for settling problems of knowledge and action.

Science has been clarifying and revising its basic assumptions throughout its development. Particularly since the beginning of the modern age and still more intensively since the beginning of our century, an increasing awareness of, and critical attitude toward, the fundamental presuppositions has been most fruitfully applied in the repudiation of dogmatic prejudices and in the articulation of the conceptual frame of scientific method. It can be shown (through logical analysis) that the procedure of science is the only one we are *certain* will yield the results (reliable knowledge, that is, valid explanation and predictions) *if* such results can at all be achieved. Any alleged rival method—theology, metaphysics, mysticism, intuition, dialectics—if it made any contributions at all could not be examined and appraised on any basis other than the usual inductive criteria of science. Generally, it seems that these alleged alternatives do not even aim primarily at knowledge but, like the arts, at the enrichment of experience. They may therefore more properly be said to be *non*scientific, rather than *un*scientific.

Science distorts the facts of reality. In its Procrustean manner it introduces discontinuities where there is continuity (and vice versa). The abstractions and idealizations used in science can never do justice to the richness and complexities of experience.

Since the task of science is to discover as reliable and precise a knowledge of what happens under what conditions, it always tries to approximate the facts as closely as the problem on hand requires and permits. Both continuity and discontinuity can be formulated mathematically and be given an adequate formulation only with the help of modern mathematics.

Science can deal only with the measurable and therefore tends to "explain away" that which it cannot measure.

While measurement is eminently desirable in order to enhance the precision and objectivity of knowledge, it is not indispensable in many branches of science or, at least, on their more qualitative levels of analysis. Science does not explain away the qualities of experience. It aims at, and often succeeds in, making these qualities more predictable.

Science never explains, it merely describes the phenomena of experience. The reality beyond the appearances is also beyond the reach of science.

This is partly a terminological issue and partly a result of the (traditional but most misleading and useless) metaphysical distinction between appearance and reality. In the sense in which the word *explaining* is used in common life, science *does* explain facts—it deduces them from laws or theoretical assumptions. Questions which are in principle incapable of being answered by the scientific method turn out, on closer analysis, not to be questions of knowledge. They are expressions of emotional tensions or of the wish for soothing (or exciting) experience.

Science and the scientific attitude are incompatible with religion and the religious attitude.

If by religion one refers to an explanation of the universe and a derivation of moral norms from theological premises, then indeed there is logical incompatibility with the results, methods, and general outlook of science. But if religion means an attitude of sincere devotion to human values, such as justice, peace, relief from suffering, there is not only no conflict between religion and science but rather a need for mutual supplementation.

Science is responsible for the evils and maladjustments of our civilization. It is creating ever more powerful weapons of destruction. The employment of scientific techniques in the machine age has contributed to the misery, physical and mental, of the multitudes. Moreover, the biological facts of evolution imply the negation of all morality: the law of the jungle.

These are particularly superficial charges. It is the social-political-economic structure of a society that is responsible for these various evils. Scientific knowledge itself is socially and morally neutral. But the manner in which it is applied, whether for the benefit or to the detriment of humanity, depends entirely on ourselves. Scientists are becoming increasingly aware that they, even more than the average citizen, have to work for enlightenment toward the proper use of knowledge. The facts and theories of evolution have been construed in many ways as regards their implications for ethics. Julian Huxley reads them very differently from the way his grandfather Thomas Henry did.[3] It should be easy to see that the forces active on the level of human civilization and intelligent communal life are not completely reducible to those involved in the ruthless struggle for survival.

[3] Compare Julian Huxley, *Touchstone for Ethics* (Harper, 1947); but see also C. D. Broad, "Review of Julian S. Huxley's Evolutionary Ethics" (*Mind* 53, 1949), reprinted in H. Feigl and W. Sellars, *Readings in Philosophical Analysis* (New York, 1949).

The ethical neutrality of scientific truth and the ivory tower situation of the pure researcher is apt to generate an attitude of indifference toward the pressing problems of humanity.

Only maladjusted individuals are unable to combine the detachment necessary for the pursuit of truth with an ardent interest in the improvement of the condition of humanity.

Scientific method, while eminently successful in the explanation, prediction, and control of physical phenomena, is distinctly less successful in regard to the facts of organic life and almost altogether hopeless in the mental and social realm. The methods of the physical sciences are essentially mechanistic (if not materialistic) and therefore reductionistic; they cannot do justice to the complex organismic, teleological, and emergent features of life and mind.

"Scientism" as a slogan of criticism and reproach is very fashionable these days. It is true that some scientists and especially some of the popularizers of science have indulged in reductive fallacies of various sorts. But the true scientific spirit as exemplified in some of the foremost researchers is free from that impatience and simple-mindedness that tries to finish the unfinished business of science by hasty speculation. Admittedly, there are tremendous problems yet to be solved. On the other hand what method is there but the method of science to solve them? Explanations of the mechanistic type (in *one* sense of the term) have been abandoned even in physics. But mechanistic explanation in a wider sense of a search for law (deterministic or statistical) is still the indispensable procedure of all sciences that have gone beyond the purely classificatory level. Organic wholeness, teleology, and emergence can be understood, if at all, only by causal analysis on the usual empirical basis. Purposiveness and freedom of choice, far from being incompatible with causality, presuppose causal order.

The methods of science can never replace the intuitive insight or empathic understanding of the practical psychologist, psychiatrist, cultural anthropologist, or historian. This claim is made particularly wherever the object of knowledge is the individual, the unique and unrepeatable.

It is only through the scientific method that the validity and reliability of the intuitive approach can be gauged. There is, on this ground, some doubt as to its more exaggerated claims. However, there is nothing in the principles of scientific method that would deny the occasional, or even frequent, efficacy of intuitive judgments based, as they must be, on a rich (but often not articulated) background of experience in the given field. Aside from the mere artistic contemplation of the unique and individual, knowledge, in the proper sense of the word, always means the subsumption of the specific case under general concepts or laws. This holds in the social sciences just as much as in the natural sciences.

Science cannot determine values. Since scientific knowledge can (at best) find out only what is the case, it can, by its very nature, never tell what ought to be.

This final challenge often comes from theology or metaphysics. It usually maintains that questions of aims, goals, and ideals cannot be settled by the methods of science but rather require recourse either to divine revelation, the voice of conscience, or some metaphysical a priori truths. The answer to this in a scientific age would seem to be that a mature mankind should be able to determine its own value standards on the basis of its needs, wants, and the facts of the social condition of man. But it is true that science cannot dictate value standards. It can, as in social psychology, ascertain the actual evaluations of groups and individuals, study their compatibilities and incompatibilities, and recommend (that is *applied* science!) ways and means of harmonizing conflicting evaluations. True enough, in many of the urgent issues that confront us, we do not possess enough scientific knowledge to warrant a course of action. This means that we have to act, as so often in life, on the highest probabilities available even if these probabilities be low in themselves. But such estimates of probabilities will still be made most reliable by the scientific method. Common life experience and wisdom, when freed from its adherence to prescientific thought patterns, is not fundamentally different from scientific knowledge. In both we find the procedure of self-correction, so essentially needed if knowledge is to be a guide for action. There is an important common element in mature thinking (as we find it in science) and mature social action (as we find it in democracy): progress arises out of the peaceful competition of ideas as they are put to intersubjective test. Cooperative planning on the basis of the best and fullest knowledge available is the only path left to an awakened humanity that has embarked on the adventure of science and civilization.

The scientific view of the world that we have characterized and defended against criticisms from various quarters may with historical and terminological justice be called Naturalism.[4] It differs from mechanistic materialism (too often a mere straw man put up by theologians or idealistic metaphysicians) in that it steers clear of reductive fallacies. If uninformed persons insist on viewing science as essentially materialistic and the humanities as essentially idealistic (not to say spiritualistic) the hopes of fruitful collaboration of both fields in education are slim indeed. But science, properly interpreted, is not dependent on any sort of metaphysics. It merely attempts to cover a maximum of facts by a minimum of laws. On the other side, a mature humanism requires no longer a theological or metaphysical

---

[4] It should scarcely need mentioning that this meaning of naturalism has only a distant and tenuous relation to the other meaning in which it is applied to a certain type of literature.

frame either. Human nature and human history become progressively understood in the light of advancing science. It is therefore no longer justifiable to speak of science *versus* the humanities. Naturalism *and* humanism should be our maxim in philosophy and in education. A Scientific Humanism emerges as a philosophy holding considerable promise for mankind—*if* mankind will at all succeed in growing up.

THE GENERAL AIMS AND METHODS
OF SCIENCE *

❪ C. W. Brown and Edwin E. Ghiselli

The objective of the scientist is to understand the phenomenon with which he is working. He considers that he understands it when he can successfully predict its expressions under circumstances somewhat different from those used in studying it, or when his knowledge enables him to control its expressions to achieve certain ends.

Four Fundamental Questions

The scientist asks himself four questions. In connection with any phenomenon he may query: Is it so? He is here concerned with the existence of the phenomenon, that is, whether or not what he has experienced has any degree of permanence. He wants to know if he can experience it repeatedly and if other observers can also experience it, or if the phenomenon is an illusion, a fantasy, or a delusion. A second and closely related question is: To what extent is it so? This requires an estimate of the magnitude, amount, frequency, or some other quantitative characteristic of the phenomenon. These two questions fall primarily in the province of description.

Having satisfied himself on these questions, the scientist then asks: Why is it so? He is now required to do some "speculating," to reason beyond the facts that he has collected; to get behind the facts, so to speak. Related to this third question is a further one, viz., What are the conditions that bring about the phenomenon? In certain respects, the answering of this question provides some of the necessary information for answering the third question; that is, to determine the conditions that bring about a phenomenon is to take a first step toward understanding why it is so. These last two questions fall primarily in the realm of explanation and theory.

* From C. W. Brown and Edwin E. Ghiselli, *Scientific Method in Psychology*, pp. 35–55, McGraw-Hill Book Company, Inc., New York, 1955. Reprinted by permission of the authors and the publisher.

Understanding as the General Aim of Science

Understanding and the search for truth. One of the most general state-ments of the aim of science is: to discover truth about natural events. To do this requires knowledge about the events, and this knowledge comes from the experiencing of the events. Experiencing natural phenomena gives the scientist his facts, and his aim is to discover, accumulate, and interpret facts and relationships among facts.

Facts about the natural universe are not isolated events but are patterned and related in diverse ways that in most instances are unknown to the scientist. Sometimes facts are initially experienced in ways that are mean-ingful, but most of the time the scientist's effort is expended in arranging the known facts in new patterns in an effort to discover unknown meanings and relationships. Through rational analysis he organizes the facts into more and more abstract and general systems. The end result is the formula-tion of general principles or laws under which all of the facts and relation-ships within some restricted domain of experience can be subsumed. The word understanding best expresses the end result of this "search for truth," and it expresses more accurately than any other word the general aim of all scientific work.

A continuum of understanding. Experience, knowledge, and understand-ing are closely related. They should be placed on a common continuum with experience at the beginning and understanding at the end. From ex-perience we pass through knowledge on our way to attaining understanding. There are no sharp lines of demarcation between them. They are really three different points or levels on a common axis.

It is obvious that understanding is more than experiencing. Sometimes, having experienced a phenomenon on several occasions, an individual will declare that he understands it. He may be in error, and this type of error frequently occurs in everyday life. Mere repetition of the experience of an event does not necessarily result in an understanding of the event. We all can recall having experienced some phenomenon many times, and of know-ing little more about it after the last experience than we knew after the first one. Most housewives do not understand electricity although they have used it in many ways over many years. Experience is a first step, and an important step, toward understanding—but it is not understanding.

Understanding is more than knowledge. Knowledge is a second step toward understanding. By manipulation of experience through the thought processes old meanings are reinterpreted and new meanings are discovered. The end result is knowledge. This knowledge is then further enlarged, organized, and systematized, and the end result is understanding. Knowl-edge, then, must be integrated and ordered before we have understanding.

The continuous expansion of understanding. Understanding is character-ized as continuously growing and expanding. At the beginning it waits upon experience and knowledge, but after it comes into being in its own right it does not remain static. Additional experiences and further knowledge increase understanding, so it is continuously evolving. Gaining understanding is a never-ending process, because with each increment of understanding further doubt arises, and this doubt, in turn, creates a need for more experience and knowledge. In some individuals, understanding begets complacency; in others, uncertainty. If we were forced to classify the scientist, we would, of course, place him among those whose understanding causes them continually to question the *status quo* and thus to seek further experience and knowledge.

Prediction as an Aim of Science

The meaning of prediction. No scientist is content to stop after he has made a discovery, confirmed a hypothesis, or explained a complex phenomenon. He wants to make some use of his results. He therefore projects his generalizations to situations in which he believes they will hold; he makes predictions concerning the way the principles he develops will operate in new situations.

Suppose that in studying the intelligence of a class of eighth-grade children we learn that the brightest child obtains a score twice the amount of the lowest score achieved. Such a large discrepancy might lead us to conclude that the progress in school attainable by the children getting the highest and lowest scores would differ considerably if differences in intelligence were reflected in school achievement. We might predict that the brightest child could progress faster if given more work, or that the social adjustment of the dullest child would improve if he were not forced to compete with the brightest child. Thus on the basis of this present knowledge we are forecasting what would take place if we used this knowledge in a given specific way.

Prediction and understanding. Prediction is based on understanding. Understanding forms the springboard from which prediction into the unknown is made. In turn, prediction contributes toward the further testing and verification of understanding. One check we can apply to our understanding of a phenomenon is the success with which we can use that understanding in new situations. If our prediction is unsuccessful, then our understanding of the phenomenon is to be questioned and challenged in reference to the particular predicted situation.

In the aforementioned example, our predictions concerning the improvement in the rate of progress of the brightest child or the improvement in social adjustment of the dullest child might turn out to be successful, thus verifying the application of our findings. We might then recommend the segregation of students in school in terms of their intelligence-test scores. We could make a broad prediction that the school progress and social adjustment of all children would be improved if they were allowed to work with children of their own intelligence level. Our prediction might then be found in error. The social adjustment of children might be more closely associated with their ages than with their intelligence-test scores. Equalizing the children in terms of intelligence would exaggerate differences in the ages of the children occupying the same classroom. If there were a very close relation between age and social adjustment, we would have to revise our notion about segregating all of the children in terms of their intelligence. Regardless of whether our prediction turned out to be correct or incorrect, the result of our prediction would have a direct effect upon our understanding of the problem involved.

Tentative nature of a prediction. The predicted situation always differs from the predictor situation. Sometimes the difference is small, as when a given situation is being duplicated with a minimum of change. For example, having determined the learning scores of rats in an alley maze, we might predict a similar distribution of scores for these rats on an elevated maze. Sometimes the difference is large, as when several factors are allowed to vary between the predictor and predicted situations. Having determined the distribution of scores of some rats on a brightness-discrimination problem, we might then destroy different parts of the visual areas of the brain and predict that the brightness-discrimination function would be lost. In this instance the brain damage may produce differences in health and differences in motivation as well as differences in learning ability, and consequently our prediction has more likelihood of failure than if only differences in learning ability were present.

Regardless of whether the difference between the predictor and predicted situations is large or small, in a prediction we set up a relationship which cannot be completely verified by a utilization of knowledge from the past. The unknown factors that are present force us to accept the prediction as only tentatively correct. Our confidence in the prediction will, of course, vary with the degree to which the predicted situation corresponds to the predictor situation. The wider the discrepancies between the two situations, the less confidence we shall have that the prediction will turn out successfully.

The testing of predictions. We must include a testing situation as part of prediction. A prediction that cannot be tested is of no value. It forever remains an unknown.

The test may be either rational or empirical in nature. In a rational test we may show, through reasoning, that the outcome of our particular explanation or theory ought to be of a certain kind or have particular characteristics. If our prediction concerns relationships that are only partially understood, we may be able, through reasoning, to increase this understanding by introducing into the relationships additional meanings that at first were thought to be irrelevant.

Suppose we are interested in explaining how we see color. We recall that there are two kinds of retinal structures, the rods and the cones, and that the latter are color-sensitive. We also know from our color-mixing experiments that the spectral colors can be obtained from variations in the mixture of three colors, viz., a certain red, a certain yellow, and a certain blue. Associating these facts together might lead us to the notion that there are three color-sensitive structures in the retina, one for each of these colors. We now can explain how we see color by stating that the light rays differentially activate one or more of these three color-sensitive structures in the retina. With this explanation we can now proceed to predict what might happen if there were radical changes in these structures. We might, for instance, predict that if a person were born without any one of them he would be color-blind to certain hues. Or again, if the color-sensitive structures were not evenly and uniformly distributed in the retina, a person might see certain hues and fail to see certain other hues in some given part of the visual field. We are pleased with our explanation because it enables us to give plausible predictions about other events in which we are interested.

Tests of the rational kind are one of the most valuable tools of the theoretical scientist. Although he may not be interested in knowing if his ideas have practical value in everyday-life situations, he nevertheless is concerned with any forward reference that his data, explanations, or theories may have. Consequently, he finds prediction a valuable aid in forecasting in "conceptual space" what can be expected from his ideas.

In an empirical test, the prediction is applied to conditions in the natural world. The relationships stipulated in the findings are projected to natural phenomena and these phenomena are then carefully observed to determine if these relationships occur according to the demands of the prediction.

Let us consider again the example of the predictive value of our explanation of how we see color. After having predicted that if people were born without one of these sensitive color processes in their retina they would be blind to certain particular colors, we could then explore the possibility that there are color-blind persons who fit our predicted descriptions. We would first describe (predict) the types of color blindness that would occur, depending on which color process or combinations of color processes were absent in the retina. For example, if the retina contained no red-sensitive process the person should not see red hues, or if all three sensitive processes were absent the person should be totally color-blind. Having calculated the various types of blindness, we would then study color-blind people and learn if their actual blindness corresponded to the blindness predicted by our color-vision explanation. If we found a relatively high correspondence, we would have empirical evidence supporting our explanation.

Eventually, all predictions should be brought to some kind of empirical test. Empirical conditions offer the most easily understood types of situation. They usually allow for the coincident observation of the phenomena by many individuals, and therefore increase the probability of reaching agreement among different investigators.

Control as an Aim of Science

The meaning of control. As an aim of science, control refers to the manipulation of the conditions determining a phenomenon in order to achieve some desired end. In utilizing present understanding to control the functioning of any factor, we are thus testing and verifying this understanding.

Ready examples of the use of control are to be found in the area of vocational guidance. Aptitude-test scores have been found to correlate rather highly with success in college. From this finding we can now exercise a more intelligent control over the admission of students to college training. We can advise an individual who has very low aptitude scores that he should not attempt college work. In such an instance we might save the person from many serious frustrations and direct his activities to areas where he would achieve marked success. We would be exercising control over his behavior, and the resulting achievement would serve to verify the understanding gained concerning the relation between aptitude-test scores and college success.

Control and prediction. Control is a corollary aim to prediction. Actually, the two are inseparable when interpreted as general aims of science. To achieve any prediction, regardless of how simple it might be, some control of the determinants of the behavior is required. In the problem of predicting college success from aptitude-test scores, we have exercised control by permitting only certain kinds of behavior to be expressed, i.e., those behaviors that are elicited by the particular tests used. Likewise, regardless of the behavior we desire to control, there is always an uncertainty about the end result, so whether we consciously make a prediction or not the conditions characteristic of prediction are present. When we speak of the relationship between aptitude and college success in connection with the advice we give a high school graduate who is considering going to college, there is implied a predictive relation between the two types of variables.

Control and application. Sometimes the term control is restricted to situations of a practical nature, such as the example of segregating school children in terms of their intelligence-test scores. This is a narrow interpretation of the term. Control serves equally well at the abstract and theoretical levels on which the "pure" scientist works. His task is to form inferences from his theory and to devise new conceptual situations to which the theory can be applied. He must logically show how an end result of a given kind can be produced by controlling the conceptual situations according to the implications of his theory. For example, the concept of control can be found throughout Einstein's theory of relativity, although what Einstein did can in no sense be construed to be control of practical situations.

The Empirical and Rational Phases of Science

The scientist capitalizes on any type of approach that he thinks will enhance his chances of gaining knowledge. Some of these involve the direct manipulation of the natural phenomena he is studying, whereas some of them involve the use of the higher mental processes by which he thinks about these phenomena. There are then both empirical and rational phases, and the scientific method is an intelligent combination of these two types of procedures.

The empirical phases of science. The meaning of empirical should not be restricted to the meaning of "that which is sensed." Experiences of natural phenomena are the first facts the scientist collects. The original experiences he gains in collecting the facts are of great significance because they are the "stock" with which he "sets up housekeeping."

In addition to the sensory experiences themselves, empirical refers to the techniques and procedures in which sensory experience plays an important role. Beyond the original observations, empirical features are to be found in all of the subsequent steps in which sensory experience is present. For example, the experimentalist, in the designing, constructing, and operating of apparatus, depends heavily upon empirical procedures. This is also true for various types of analysis of the data. Frequently the scientist reduces his data to graphic form and through the examination of diagrams, figures, and drawings he discovers many new meanings. These are empirical procedures.

Empirical facts are the point of origin of evidence. The scientist tests his ideas under natural conditions. These tests thus provide the means for confirming and justifying all of his work. They are the court of final appeal where he must be content to rest his case.

In the realm of the production of hunches, ideas, and hypotheses, empirical procedures by themselves are strictly limited in scope. Alone, raw sensory experience provides us with only a rather elemental type of meaning. Mere awareness of an object is very limited. We add little to knowledge if we terminate our activity at this point. The full import and significance of an experience results from various intellectual manipulations of the sensed data gained in the experience. Rational phases, then, are essential to higher-order meanings.

The rational phases of science. Whether or not the facts of experience eventually add significantly to our knowledge depends upon the kind of rational manipulations we perform and the accuracy with which we perform these manipulations. We can study the data statistically or logically; we can analyze them into more elemental structures or combine them into complex patterns; we can note their similarities or their differences. These rational manipulations of sensory and inferential meanings are the "heart" processes of our descriptions, explanations, generalizations, and theories. Through these manipulations we learn about the relationships between other variables and the phenomena under study and the significance that these relationships have for future understanding.

The rational phases of the scientific method include all procedures in which higher-order meanings are involved and include such individual processes as memory, abstraction, inference, reasoning, generalization, judgment, and the like.

Certainly, as scientists, we must use rational procedures from the beginning of an investigation right through to the end. Science particularly requires rational processes in the setting up of the problem, in the analysis of the results, and in the interpretation of the findings.

The rational procedures of formal logic are a valuable part of the scientific method. As indicated earlier, scientists must practice "straight" or "sound" reasoning. Logic sets up patterns of reasoning for us to follow, patterns which, if followed, will lead us to what are considered logically correct conclusions. Logic aids in the accurate formulation of propositions so they can be evaluated against other possible alternatives. It enables us to state our postulates so their full implications can be developed through further reasoning. "Straight" thinking is required in every stage of a scientific inquiry, and therefore we should not depreciate or ignore a procedure that has as its fundamental purpose the description of the conditions for accurate thinking.

The Major Methods of Science

In an earlier discussion it was pointed out that science can be interpreted as a very general method composed of many important but less general procedures. Some of these procedures deserve separate treatment because they form the solid core of the scientific method. These major methods are symbolization, description, explanation, and theorizing.

Symbolization as a Method of Science

The meaning of symbolizing. Symbolization has to do with translating experience into symbols. Experience is fleeting; it is here, then gone. There is little time for pondering its nature while its sensory components are still manifest. If we are to deal with an experience after its disappearance, some change caused by the experience must be carried over in time and must be of such a nature that it can be rearoused in memory and manipulated by means of various thought processes. This is accomplished through symbols or words. Experiences are given names. Every event, and every characteristic of every event, is given a symbol or word-tag by which it is known from that time forward. It is this word-tag that, so to speak, makes the experience "immortal."

Symbolization includes the assignment of names to objectively observed events, e.g., tables, rocks, houses; the assignment of names to subjective events, e.g., joys, pains, thoughts; and the assignment of words and other symbols to conceptual events created through the thought processes, e.g., infinity, purposes, theories, relativity.

Language is stressed in symbolization because it is the most widely used type of sign. It is not sufficient for all purposes, however, and an investigator may need to adopt or invent some other forms of symbolization. Two other systems of signs that are of great service are mathematics and symbolic logic.

The characteristic of correspondence in symbolizing. The most important characteristic of symbolization concerns the degree of accuracy with which the symbols represent the facts they stand for. The objective in science is to develop symbols which can accurately substitute for the particular aspects of the events we want to represent; that is, to devise symbols that will faithfully signify the meanings of these events. It is important, then, that there be some form of correspondence between the world of events, on the one hand, and the system of symbols, on the other. An ideal arrangement is one in which there is a distinct symbol for each of the attributes, phases, qualities, aspects, elements, etc., that can be found in a given class of events. Actually we must be content with much less than this perfect "co-relationship."

Symbolizing in science. We find that symbolization contributes to the scientist's work in two very significant ways; namely, (1) it makes possible a permanent record of experience, and (2) it furnishes a vehicle or mechanism for the rational manipulation of past experience.

By means of symbols, experiences are retained in varying degrees by the individual, so that through his memory he can later reproduce them for further examination and use. Experiences also are retained through written records. Both of these methods enable the scientist to call back again the meanings of a previous experience. He thus gains an unlimited number of opportunities to study the experience.

It will be recalled that the manipulation of symbols in thinking is one of the essential procedures in science. The scientist, by mentally manipulating the word that stands for an event, is doing the next best thing to manipulating the event itself. In fact, dealing with an event in thought by manipulating its word meanings is in some respects superior to manipulating the event as an experience. The actual experienced event occupies a single precise point in time and space; the recalled event does not, and can therefore be manipulated indefinitely without respect to temporal and spatial contexts.

The demands to be met by symbolization. It will help us to understand what we should expect from symbolization as a method in science if we briefly review three characteristics of natural phenomena that set the demands that must be met by a successful system of symbols.

The tremendous complexity of natural phenomena sets the most severe demand. There is no apparent limitation to the extent to which natural phenomena can be subdivided and differentiated. Each event studied, upon closer examination, is found to be composed of parts, and, similarly, each part is found to be composed of other parts, ad infinitum. Truly, on the face of it, we are here confronted with what we can call an infinite progression. To be successful, our system of symbolization must have unlimited possibilities in regard to the number of signs it can supply.

A second demand to be met by our system of symbols is referable to the characteristic of change. Never is the "same" event exactly the same. It is merely treated as constant in order to fulfill some particular purpose. Our system of symbols must be flexible enough to accommodate itself to changes in meanings occurring in time.

A third characteristic is summed up in the word relationship. Not only is an object found to be divisible into parts, and the object and its parts found to undergo continuous change, but the object and its subdivisions are found to be related in very complex ways with each other and with other objects and their subdivisions. For the want of exact knowledge and a more precise symbol, we shall use the word infinite to characterize both the number and diversity of the relationships that exist among natural phenomena. We must make our symbols accurately express the nature and degree of these relationships.

The deficiency of words as symbols of natural phenomena. Keeping in mind the foregoing demands placed upon symbolization, let us consider the handicap under which we are working in trying to force natural phenomena into the system of signs called language—a system that we have poorly mastered even at best. We need not question the fact that language is one of the most valuable tools that man has invented, but there is need for questioning man's failure to make a more accurate use of the language he possesses. In meeting the demand for increased numbers of meanings, we have not exploited language to the fullest. We have been content to allow the same word to do double duty—actually, many times more than double duty. We also have been negligent in another way; we have assigned the same meaning to more than one word. Certainly, when we are in need of accurate representation of such a tremendous number of meanings, it is most inefficient to use the same word to stand for several meanings and to make several words function as representatives of the same meaning.

Language is deficient in representing changes in time. In many instances natural phenomena change faster than the words with which we describe them. Much of our language is still in the "horse-and-buggy" era. In fact, we persist in refusing to accept the innovations that crowd in upon us, and even ridicule the individual who dares to "coin" a new word.

Language, in the strict meaning of the term, is most deficient in regard to the symbolization of relationships. Here there is a severe limitation on the number of words that are available, so the scientist has had to look elsewhere to find a more exact and comprehensive system. This he has found in the symbolization of mathematics. Seldom does a scientist nowadays rely solely upon words for representing the relationships he wishes to describe. Numbers and their relationships are now a prime necessity in science.

Science has demonstrated through its use of mathematics and tabular and pictorial techniques that meanings can be represented with precision. It likewise has improved the precision of its descriptions through a more careful use of language as a vehicle for meanings. Some of this increased precision has come from the invention of new words, but much has been achieved through correct choice and use of familiar words. This is a step we all can take to achieve greater accuracy in our language. We are not expected to invent a new term every time we encounter difficulty in expression. It can be expected, however, that we shall exercise increasingly greater care in the selection of the words we use.

Description as a Method of Science

The meaning of description. As already noted, the function of symbolization is to assign word meanings to experiences of natural phenomena. But word meanings left as isolated events serve no useful purpose. Description is a systematic attempt to symbolize the obvious relationships that are found among the natural phenomena under study. By manipulating the name-tags, description creates a word picture of the orders that are readily observable among the phenomena. The term description, then, is usually applied to the ordering of natural events in ways that issue immediately and directly from the facts themselves. The organizations and relationships dealt with are of a simple nature. An important feature of the new meanings formed in description is that the characteristics and relationships evolved can be readily traced to sensory experiences and involve little or no abstraction from these experiences.

Description serves a bookkeeping function. At the time of the occurrence of an experience, there is never time for us to analyze it into its constituent determiners and to note all of the relationships it bears with other experiences. Through description, an account of the experience is put in a more or less permanent written form. With the written record available, we are able to examine the data at will. The written record does not consist merely of a listing of symbols; rather, the patterns and arrangements experienced in the data are recorded. It is then that description as a simple rational process comes into play.

Description as classification. Classification has to do with the discovery of relatively stable associations among properties or characteristics and with the symbolizing of these associations. Classificatory schemes serve the purpose of organizing and grouping large numbers of facts into smaller numbers of divisions which then can be manipulated as units in further analyses. Events or processes that have the same characteristics are grouped together and these groups or categories are given names. Classes of familiar common objects are exemplified by ants, people, buildings, books, games, etc. The tendency is to make the classificatory categories as specific and precise as possible. Highly abstract classes which tend to go far beyond the empirical facts are not considered description. Some examples of these are categories of reason, *n*-dimensions of space, brain models, types of personality organizations, and the like.

The classification assigned a given event or process is to be considered as somewhat tentative in nature. Classificatory schemes gradually undergo change as more and more knowledge is gained about the events or processes being classified. What appears on first inspection to be a certain kind of property upon a more thorough examination may turn out to be quite a different kind of property.

Description as seriating. A second form of description is called simple ordering or seriating. Seriating requires more knowledge about the events than does classification. It requires not only some common characteristic or feature in all of the events but that this characteristic or feature be known to exist in degrees or amounts, or be arrangeable on some form of continuum in a consistent way. If we are studying the reading ability of individuals then we can arrange our subjects in an order according to their speed of reading. The subjects are not only classified as being capable of reading, but are arranged in order on a continuum of reading speed. Another example, in which the ordering is of a little different kind, is the arrangement of geometric figures constructed from straight lines. We can arrange the following figures on a continuum in terms of the number of their sides: triangle, quadrangle, pentagon, hexagon, heptagon, and octagon. When the characteristic being described is a magnitude and is measurable, a basis is available for accurately determining differences between the objects or events and thus a more precise classification scheme can be developed.

Description as correlation. A third application of description is called correlation. In examining a group of objects it is sometimes noted that two different characteristics are associated in such a way that when one is present the other is present and when one is absent the other is also absent. The two characteristics are said to occur concomitantly and such a relationship is referred to as correlation. As an example, the concomitant variation of eye color and hair color in man can be cited. In the case of individuals with blond hair, the eyes are more frequently light in color than dark, while the reverse of this tends to be true for individuals possessing brown or black hair.

Quantitative characteristics may also be found correlated, as in the relationship between the variables of height and weight. Such a correlation can be expressed in numerical terms, and thus its variation in degree or amount can be expressed quantitatively.

It will be noted that, in general, the correlation form of description goes somewhat beyond classification and seriating; that is, the facts are first classified and arranged in order of magnitude before an attempt is made to correlate them.

In the forms of description discussed above, it is to be remembered that the feature or characteristic used as a basis for classifying, seriating, or correlating must be discoverable in the facts or events themselves. What actually can be observed or what can be empirically demonstrated becomes the basis on which the description proceeds. No recourse is made to knowledge that lies beyond the events or to inferences or theories that transcend the knowledge gained directly from the events.

Explanation as a Method of Science

The meaning of explanation. As already stated, one of the fundamental objectives of science is to find the reasons for the occurrence of events. The scarcity of facts may compel us to resort to higher-order conceptual meanings in order to account for the phenomena we are studying. In searching for the possible conditions giving rise to an event, we are trying to answer the question: Why is it so? Explanation is the fundamental method through which we discover the answer to this type of question.

Explanation proceeds to the discovery of higher-order meanings by means of the manipulation of concepts. Symbolization, then, is necessary for explanation. The sensed experiences and the meanings derived from them must be symbolically represented in verbal or other form and thus made available for mental manipulation.

Explanation involves abstraction. Conceptual meanings depend upon the process of abstraction. As we attempt to create new patterns and relationships among the facts, reasoning takes us further and further away from the factual meanings of description to meanings at higher and higher levels of abstraction and generalization. Meanings in the form of postulated entities, processes, or relations, which the scientist conceptually invents to account for his results, are called logical constructs.

At higher levels of abstraction, explanation becomes theorizing. When an explanation effects a pattern of logical constructs as a conceptual framework into which all the facts relevant to some phenomenon can be fitted, it is usually called a theory.

Let us again refer to the example of explaining how we see color. The three most important empirical meanings are that we see variations in color, that the retina of the eye is not structurally uniform but contains at least two structures, namely, the rods and cones, and that the cones are the sensitive structures responding when colors are seen. Explanation now enters in the postulation that there are three color-sensitive retinal structures, each sensitive to a different band of wave length. These three structures are not distinguishable in the retina and therefore are conceptual in nature. They are at least one step removed, through abstraction, from the observable structures of rods and cones. They are conceptually devised to supplement our knowledge about the responses of rods and cones. In attempting to learn about the various kinds of color blindness, we manipulate these conceptualized retinal structures. They are logical constructs that we use to push beyond the empirical facts that we now possess about color seeing.

Explanation and description. There is general agreement that there is no sharp dividing line between description and explanation. Explanation begins where description leaves off. Both have the fundamental function of discovering the meanings of experienced events through the manipulation of symbols. The primary feature that distinguishes the two is the relative amount of conceptualizing involved. As already pointed out, the purpose of description is to discover the meanings that are observable in the sensed data themselves. The manipulation of the data is done in ways that issue directly from an observation of the facts available to experience. In explanation, the meanings are less observable in the data and are discovered through some process of mental manipulation of the data. The meanings derived at the descriptive level are further manipulated in explanation in an attempt to discover additional meanings. In our example of color vision, the empirical meanings about the functions of rods and cones were manipulated and gave rise to the postulation of three different retinal structures sensitive to color stimuli. The meanings of these three conceptual structures were then further manipulated to discover additional meanings about how we see colors.

Compared to the meanings of description, the meanings of explanation are more flexible, that is, they can be more easily changed to suit the purposes of the investigator. As a consequence, the meanings of explanation are more controversial. Procedures of mental manipulation are private to each thinker, and it is often difficult to get these manipulatory processes sufficiently similar in two or more individuals to achieve correspondence in the final meanings devised. In the experiencing of concepts, individuals do not see eye to eye as readily as in the experiencing of percepts.

Referring again to our example, the exact colors which presumably result from the activation of the three postulated retinal structures cannot be established to everyone's satisfaction. Different investigators postulate different structures because they use different criteria for defining them. One investigator may define the retinal structures in terms of the three colors which, through mixture, give only the spectral colors. Another may use as his criterion the three colors which, when mixed, give both spectral and nonspectral colors. In these two instances the three postulated color structures would not be exactly the same.

The meanings of explanation are subject to less control than the meanings of description. Being removed by several steps from the empirical facts, explanatory meanings also are further removed from the controlling influence of experience. This is apparent in the explanations of the chemical changes in the cone and rod responses. We know that in rod stimulation there is a bleaching of a substance called rhodopsin. In cone response we are not certain about the existence of a similar substance and therefore our explanations of cone response are more variable. Broad explanations of behavior, like the instinct hypothesis, are difficult to dislodge from the layman's thinking because they are far removed from the actual concrete facts known about behavior.

Compared to descriptive meanings, explanations are more tentative in nature. In general, an explanation contains so much meaning that is guessed that it must be accepted only as a possible truth. As it receives verification through logic and experience it can be expressed as a probable truth, and sometimes the degree of probability can be accurately stated, depending on the amount and accuracy of the empirical data available.

The purposes served by explanation. Explanation is directed toward increasing our understanding of natural phenomena. It is like description in that it results in the formation of classificatory schemes into which sensed data may be meaningfully organized, but the schemes of explanation are not readily observable in the data and depend primarily upon the reasoning processes. Through manipulation of their conceptual meanings, explanation relates variables in terms of their less obvious features. It results in the discovery of the more subtle orders that characterize the relations among natural phenomena.

Explanation enables us to carry knowledge forward. Explanation reveals the gaps existing in our understanding and sets about to devise the necessary conditions that will bridge these gaps. Explanations built on past experiences make easier the understanding of present and future experiences. Knowledge from the past has to be put on trial. Through postulation, this knowledge is modified and formed into explanation, which then is subjected to empirical testing. Knowledge is then carried forward in time through explanation and is thus used in the gaining of further knowledge.

Theorizing as a Method of Science

In his attempt to understand nature, man has never been content with merely gathering and ordering existential facts. He seems always to have a burning curiosity to discover some supposed "final explanation." An examination of the explanations that he has conjured up to account for his behavior will show that he has run the full gamut of the explanatory continuum, from the factual at one end to the highly imaginary at the other. What he has lacked in fact he has readily made up with fiction. The suppositions used by older generations seem a bit incredible to us today, but in our own ways we "moderns" continue to call upon little understood postulated entities or principles—pixies—to fill in the gaps of knowledge, thus giving the appearance that our intellectual armor is impervious.

Older fallacious theories of behavior. One of the earlier explanations of the behavior of the feebleminded and insane is illustrative of the prescientific theories man has held. The early diagnosticians believed that a mentally deficient person was possessed of an evil spirit or of a good spirit, according to the nature of his behavior. If the diagnosis was of an evil spirit, all manner of exorcisms, magic rituals, physical punishments, and the like were practiced in an effort to banish the supposed demon. More fortunate was the person who was judged possessed of a saintly spirit, as he was considered a messenger of the Deity, and his every want was administered to by those who curried his favor.

Another example of this fallacious explanation of abnormal behavior is seen in the early New England conceptions of witchcraft. Hysterical symptoms in the form of anesthesias were declared to be of the devil and merited the harshest of treatment. Many persons displaying such symptoms were put to death by hanging.

Fairy tales are rich in the use of personified concepts as determiners of events. Giants, dwarfs, brownies, elves, goblins, and similar imaginary persons, who have all of the traits of human beings, are conjured up as explanatory devices to allay the questioning fears of children or to free the parent of the task of giving valid explanations to the thousand-and-one questions of his offspring.

Current fallacious theories of behavior. Modern man has not freed himself of the use of imaginary entities in his attempts to account for his behavior. Modern pixies, however, are not always personified, and they are more abstract in nature. But they are still products of the imagination constructed to serve as ready answers for difficult questions, and often serve in the same uncritical way as did the pixies of earlier generations. For many individuals, these modern pixies satisfactorily account for behavior, and, after all, that is their function.

Fate is a modern pixy frequently used to explain behavior. If a person has come through several dangerous situations unscathed when others have been injured or killed, his good fortune is attributed to fate—it "just wasn't his time to go." *Lady Luck* is another explanation offered to account for the nature of results. If the individual has good fortune, Lady Luck is on his side; if he experiences ill fortune, then the "Good Lady" has forsaken him.

One of the current overworked pixies of uncritical psychological thinking is *human nature*. This concept has had wide application in the explanation of group behavior. For example, war is a form of social behavior that has never been adequately explained. It can readily be dismissed from the minds of some thinkers, however, by being attributed to human nature. *Instinct* is another tired, overworked old pixy. It seems that every type of behavior of which man is capable has at one time or another been attributed to instinct. *Heredity* and *environment* are always available as explanatory devices and are frequently called in to settle disputes about the determination of behavior. The *unconscious* is another modern pixy of questionable repute, seemingly charged with about every function that the human individual possesses.

We must recognize that these latter concepts are in use today, some of them playing a prominent role in current explanations of behavior. Thus the censor mechanism of psychoanalysis has become the "little man" who guards the portals to the dungeons of the unconscious. This pixy is most mortal in his behavior; and his frailties, so humanlike, explain in turn the behavior of the individual in which he dwells. To characterize concepts such as these as modern pixies is to bring into relief their uncritical use as end explanations of human response. It is to level criticism against those users of concepts who, when they announce that a given concept is applicable to some behavior, consider that thereby they have fully accounted for that behavior. We do not suggest that their concepts are entirely useless to psychology. Rather, we wish to indicate the need for clearer thinking with regard to the manner in which their concepts are formulated, interpreted, and used.

Scientific pixies. A scientist devises theories to understand better that which he observes. He does not engage in theorizing merely to satisfy some intellectual curiosity. By the use of logical reasoning he deduces and formulates from present knowledge postulates through which common features and relationships or underlying principles and laws can be discovered, thereby rendering more understandable the phenomena he is investigating. He devises a rule that states the common conditions of a group of events, and then under this rule he subsumes the new event to be explained. This step of bringing forward knowledge in the form of hypotheses to be verified is an essential step in his program to discover truth. He makes progress because the insufficiency of old explanations stimulates him to evolve new hypotheses. These, in turn, lead to new modes of experiment and analysis and thus to the discovery of additional knowledge.

The thalamic theory of emotion is a good illustration of this procedure. The familiar association between physiological changes in the body and emotional experiences required explanation. If the physiological changes were to be accepted as components of emotion, then the widespread occurrence of these physiological changes in emotion had to be explained. Furthermore, what is called emotional control, by which is meant the simple fact that the individual can develop means for preventing impulsive, explosive, and intense emotional expressions, needed to be explained. In the thalamic theory the physiological changes are considered a bona fide part of the emotional experience. The thalamic region of the brain was postulated as a controlling center from which issued the nervous impulses that evoked the emotion. Impulses from the thalamus excite the sympathetic nervous system and through it elicit widespread bodily changes. The cortex of the brain was postulated as containing the higher centers through which the thalamic region was kept under control. The cortex of the brain is involved in the reasoning and evaluative processes by which emotion-provoking situations are assessed. Through these processes the thalamus is brought under control. Following the enunciation of this theory a large number of experiments were conducted that have greatly increased our knowledge concerning the nature of emotional responses.

Scientific compared with nonscientific pixies. It is interesting to note that the pixies of the scientist and the nonscientist are alike in one point; namely, they are born of the imagination—they are beyond apprehension by the senses. By the process of assumption, these imaginary factors are assigned explanatory powers. The scientist postulates entities, structures, relations, mechanisms, and the like, which he cannot sense, that is, see, hear, or feel. He employs constructs that do not refer to things that are actually observable or that are representative duplications of former sensory experiences. These constructs refer to entities or relationships the existence of which he postulates in order to understand better the things that he actually observes. In a similar way, through his imagination, the nonscientific individual postulates his ghosts, spirits, elves, and gremlins.

More important for our consideration are the points on which the pixies of the scientist differ from those of the nonscientist. To begin with, scientific theories are not personified. They are not imaginary people, big or little, good or evil. They do not have the characteristics of people. They do not have desires, feelings, or intentions. They do not have to be placated as do the gods of primitive tribes.

Theories of science are not reified concepts. They do not come alive and act, working toward ends and accomplishing purposes. For example, in the hands of some psychoanalysts the concept of the unconscious has been reified. In their thinking it is no longer a simple rational idea that helps to explain man's behavior. It is described as if it were another person on the inside of the individual, a person with desires and ambitions at variance with those of the individual. Such an interpretation is not far removed from ghosts and demons.

Scientific theories stem from facts. Although a theory involves entities or constructs that are not observable, the propositions through which the theory was devised stem from facts. The scientist defines his theories very carefully, assigning them the characteristics that they have in order that they may explain the observed events. He is aware that they are products of his imagination which he projects into reality. The nonscientist is usually unaware of the linkages through which his pixies have evolved from empirical situations.

To the scientist, a theory is a tool of research. It is not an end in itself but a means to further understanding, a form of lever by means of which he can pry loose more facts. A theory to him is something to be tested. It provides various postulates, and from these postulates the scientist is able to devise theorems for empirical testing. If he is unable to devise testable theorems the theory is abandoned as unproductive. The pixies of the nonscientist are accepted uncritically; they are accepted without challenge. He does not feel the need of questioning them and sees no need of subjecting them to any analysis or test. They do not serve as useful tools because they do not lend themselves to investigation.

A scientific theory has a predictive character through which the scientist seeks to improve his control over new phenomena. The pixies of the nonscientist offer hindsight, not foresight. They are conjured up to account for past events and are used by the witch doctor and his modern counterparts as portents of the future. They are unpredictable. For example, the censor of the Freudian psychoanalyst has its own whims to satisfy and its "behavior" cannot be foreseen. Being unpredictable, such pixies offer no control over future events.

The scientist controls his theory. He keeps it subservient to his problems and purposes and makes it work for him. In many respects the pixies of the nonscientist control him much as the rabbit's foot controls the behavior of the superstitious person. They function to stifle and channelize thought, facilitating the acceptance of stereotypes, and discouraging the entertainment of new ideas.

Selected Readings

Feigl, H.: Operationism and Scientific Method, in H. Feigl and W. Sellars (eds.), "Readings in Philosophical Analysis," pp. 498–509, Appleton-Century-Crofts, Inc., 1949. This article considers the problem of definition and argues that the meaning of "operational" should be confined to the definition of empirical concepts. Operationism is considered to be "a set of regulative or critical standards" that may be used in appraising the meaningfulness of scientific concepts.

Feigl, H.: Some Remarks on the Meaning of Scientific Explanation, ibid., pp. 510–514. Description is restricted to "singular statements representing fully specific facts, events or situations." Explanation is defined as "a procedure of inference." Several levels of explanation are described.

Marx, M. H.: The General Nature of Theory Construction, in M. H. Marx (ed.), "Psychological Theory: Contemporary Readings," chap. 1, The Macmillan Company, 1951. The basic assumptions and elements of theory construction are discussed as these are found in the science of psychology. Both reductive and constructive types of explanations are considered.

B. Methods of inquiry

In the next group of readings we turn to an examination of the specific methods which psychology employs in its research in the study of adjustment. The previous readings provide us with a criterion for the evaluation of research. We need to obseive the extent to which the investigator has been able to exert control over his operations and procedures. The less control involved in his methods, the less confidence we have in his conclusions.

Psychology would prefer to seek answers to its questions through experimentation. It is with this method that we can have the greatest amount of confidence in the conclusions which are yielded. Experiments, by definition, involve the controlled manipulation of human behavior. However, the systematic manipulation of human behavior is sometimes impractical and often repugnant to us. For example, in order to test experimentally some hypothesis about the effects of punishment upon an aspect of child behavior, the investigator would need to instruct a group of mothers to follow a controlled regimen in punishing their children. The consequences for children subjected to this planned pain would be sought in comparison with children of a group of mothers who were instructed in not providing this pain. Such an experiment may well violate our ethical standards. It is for reasons such as this that psychology, in studying adjustment, needs to resort to other methods of investigation than direct experimentation.

The first selection, whose author is anonymous, describes a schizophrenic experience. This selection is meant to illustrate the *case report* as a method of investigation. This category of study involves an effort to account for the behavior *of an individual* by describing the history of his experience which presumably operated to cause the behavior under study. The disadvantages of this method reside in the serious lack of control. The observer can, in fact, discover any historical antecedents he wishes to discover. Freud will discover psychosexual difficulty; Adler will discover the early experiencing of inferiority; and Sullivan will almost surely discover anxiety experienced in an empathic relationship with the mothering one. In other words, the method is open to serious bias on the part of the observer. In addition, the case study method is based on a single individual and limits the degree of generality from the findings on that person to others. It is, however, a fruitful method for generating hypotheses about behavior which may be amenable to more

33

controlled investigation. It is also the method which psychologists, psychiatrists, social workers, teachers, guidance counselors, etc., find valuable when they attempt to understand a given individual's behavior difficulty.

The Henderson article, which follows, provides an example of the *field study* method of investigating human behavior. Essentially this method consists in the investigator's immersion in a given context and his subsequent narrative account of the phenomena under study. This approach is fruitful in widening our view of human behavior to include the effects of sociocultural institutions upon human actions. For example, Margaret Mead has studied the cultures of the South Pacific; the Lynds have studied Middletown; and Henderson has studied the mass-produced suburbs. The field study method, however, relies heavily on the interpretations of the observer. Has he been biased in his observations? Has his personal experience led to a distortion of the data? All observations are necessarily selective, and we must ask: Has his selection led to an accurate portrayal? On the other hand, we feel some confidence in his analysis when similar accounts are provided us by other independent observers. And the method again is fruitful in suggesting hypotheses for more controlled study.

There have been some attempts to control the bias of the observer by pursuing a course of recording everything that takes place within a given context and in a defined and limited time span. *One Boy's Day* [1] by Barker and Wright represents such an effort. It is a straightforward account of the experience of one boy from the moment his mother wakes him in the morning to the moment he goes to bed that night. This approach results in a voluminous amount of material even for the relatively simple experience of one boy's day. The reader is soon lost in a mass of data over which it is difficult to achieve some meaningful integration.

The next selection illustrates the method which has been called *natural experiment*. Owing to our reluctance over performing controlled experiments with human beings where there is some danger of harm, psychology leans heavily on analyzing the consequences of events which occur naturally. In lieu of administering a planned regimen of pain to children in some systematic fashion, psychological researchers have simply identified children whose day-to-day experience has involved pain. That is, children with known histories involving pain are compared with children whose known histories involve little or no pain. Note, however, that in this procedure the experimenter, or we may better call him the researcher,

---

[1] Roger G. Barker and Herbert F. Wright, *One Boy's Day*, Harper & Brothers, New York, 1951.

has not been able to control the condition of pain. For us, the lack of control suggests caution about the conclusion that he reaches.

By using the method of natural experiment, or perhaps we need to say that by taking advantage of nature's experiments, Dennis is able to seek out the differences in praise which children of different ethnic groups experience. He is able to isolate four groups of children, each of which has experienced a known and different history, i.e., a history of having been reared as an American, an Arab, an Armenian, a Near East Jew. This classification makes possible an analysis of differences in the experience of praise among them. Note again that he has taken children as he has found them; he has not imposed conditions upon their rearing. The method of natural experimentation is widely used wherever it is impractical or hurtful to conduct a controlled experiment.

The final selection illustrates the *experimental method*. We have already suggested that an important and essential feature of the method resides in the fact that the investigator *imposes* known conditions upon his subjects. He is able to control the history of his subjects with respect to the issues under view: he does not accept their history; he imposes a history which he has carefully defined. In the case of Scott's paper on changing attitudes, the experimenter consciously and systematically manipulates the experience of his subjects by proclaiming half of them "better debaters" while proclaiming the remaining half "poor debaters." Note that a control group of individuals is also included in the analysis; this enables Scott to compare the effect of manipulating conditions of reward or punishment with the effects of a condition in which neither reward nor punishment is present. The control which he has utilized in this experiment warrants our placing a relatively high degree of confidence in his findings.

CASE REPORT:

AN AUTOBIOGRAPHY

OF A SCHIZOPHRENIC EXPERIENCE *

⟨ Anonymous

Most of what follows is based on an unpublished autobiography written in the spring of 1951, shortly after I had returned home from the second of the three episodes of my schizophrenic experience. My disorder was diagnosed as catatonic schizophrenia.[1] The three episodes occurred over a four-year period. I am concentrating here chiefly on a description of the first episode. This occurred after I had received a year and a half of psychotherapy consisting of weekly contacts with a psychiatric social worker at a child guidance clinic. I had gone for this help when I had come to feel unable to deal with the problems that had arisen in my relations with my children. The disorder was coincidental with processes of personality change which had started some time before I went to the child guidance clinic for help and which continued after recovery from the acute illness.

Background

Social position. When I first went to the child guidance clinic, I was, in terms of our social structure, the wife of a professional man and I had come from a professional, middle-class background. I had myself been trained as a social caseworker after I completed college.

I was married when I was 21 years old. During the following 10 years, I had three children. At the time I experienced the first schizophrenic episode, I was 36 years old.

Ever since my college days, I had been an active member in groups interested in political and social reform and world peace. I had done organiza-

* From Anonymous, "Case Report: An Autobiography of a Schizophrenic Experience," *J. abnorm. soc. Psychol.*, 51, 677–689. Reprinted by permission of the Managing Editor, the American Psychological Association.

[1] The writer was confined at Sheppard Pratt Hospital from November, 1948 through April, 1949. The diagnosis was catatonic schizophrenia. Remission occurred after three weeks under sodium amytal. The second confinement was at the same hospital from November, 1949 through January, 1950. Remission was spontaneous. The third confinement was at St. Elizabeths Hospital, and again the diagnosis was catatonic schizophrenia. It lasted from July, 1951 through September, 1952. Remission occurred after a series of seven electric shock treatments which were administered in July of 1952.

tional work and publicity for the C.I.O. union, to which I belonged, and later for the women's auxiliary. I became active for a time in a cooperative nursery school which my youngest child attended, and during the year before my illness had served as president of the organization. I had also been a collector for the Community Chest in my neighborhood. As a family we lived in our own home and were stable and settled in a particular locality.

In my personal relations I had always had an adequate number of friends and had never had any difficulty in making close friends. I had, however, been under the strain of steadily increasing anxiety at the time I consulted the clinic, and had also reached an impasse in which I felt incompetent as a mother. One of the chief problems I presented was my feeling that I lacked sufficient warmth in my relations to my two oldest children. My relation to my youngest child was secure and satisfying.

Marital and sexual adjustment. I was faced during the period of psychotherapy with a crisis in my marital relationship and just before illness had decided upon divorce, which I finally obtained several years later after recovery from the schizophrenic disorder. Most of the clinical work was focused at first on the difficulties I had about asserting myself in personal relationships, and as I obtained emotional support from the therapist I began to be more self-confident. I began to use a greater amount of independent initiative and judgment in my daily life, and my relations to the children began to improve. The need for greater decisiveness and assertiveness in my relation with my children made it impossible for me to continue long-established relations of over-dependency and over-identification which I had maintained in relation to my mother and my husband. There was a simultaneous break with both identifications. My long-suppressed negative reactions to certain aspects of my husband's personality finally came to the forefront. I had previously related to my husband both in a semimaternal and managerial as well as a submissive way. Hostility had been breaking through openly in dreams before I went for help, but generally I had been able to keep hostility and derogatory feelings out of consciousness so that I was able to maintain an adequate amount of warmth and tenderness in the relationship. The final break with my husband therefore constituted a severe emotional deprivation for me. It deprived me of physical and emotional closeness to which I had been accustomed for many years.

I sought compensations for this increasing isolation. I became involved in an intense love affair which aroused a feeling of semicompulsive dependency on this relationship. I seemed to be torn from my moorings and alienated from my former self, because I had temporarily lost my normal investment in other interests. Intense feelings about childhood frustrations and disappointments in relation to my father were stirred up at this time and I seemed to feel these early deprivations more keenly in retrospect than I had during my childhood.

My dependency needs were acute at this time but an over-investment in the extramarital relationship was causing me to lose powers of moral control and to disregard the interests of my children. I made desperate efforts to break the over-attachment, and thought finally that I had succeeded. I found the best corrective was writing poetry and intellectual work which enabled me to fight off feelings of incipient depression. Creative activity was intensified but finally became compulsive and over-absorbing. I was not able to maintain a normal extraverted relation to my children, or to switch my attention at will to practical details of living. I experienced a sudden feeling of creative release before my illness, was convinced that I was rapidly attaining the height of my intellectual powers, and that for the first time in my life, I would be able to function up to the level of my ability in this direction.

During my entire married life I had been semifrigid, i.e., I had been unable to attain orgasm except occasionally during sleep. I had, however, enjoyed sexual relationships, found them relaxing and emotionally renewing, and had seldom been bothered by residual tension. Capacity for sexual response increased gradually during the years of marriage but I remained semifrigid even in the extramarital relation described above. Divorce was finally necessary because I no longer felt attracted to my husband sexually after the emotional break was made.

I attained adequate capacity for vaginal orgasm during the recovery phase after the third episode of illness. The increase in sexuality that was associated with loss of inhibition had a terrifying impact during the early phases of psychosis and was expressed symbolically in the experience of "hell-fire" described below and in other ways. During the recovery phases, increased sexuality posed severe problems of control. The situation was aggravated at times by my isolation and by intense religious emotions which stimulated the entire body and increased the need for sex. For a while, casual relations with men were both intensely pleasurable and emotionally satisfying, since they were associated with a mystical and religious type of nonpersonal love and acceptance of other people. This phase wore off gradually and I returned to my usual needs for personal intimacy and personal love, lack of which increased my frustration and unhappiness in casual relations.

Changes in self-perception. The new self-confidence I was obtaining from the relation with my therapist enabled me to see more clearly certain aspects of myself which I had seen before only dimly, outside of full awareness. To these aspects of my personality I had a strong negative reaction. My new perceptions disturbed the picture I had long held of myself as being primarily a highly social person, interested in community problems, and in the welfare of others. Later, during some periods of illness, I saw myself also as cold, indifferent to others, withdrawn, and at times as impulsively cruel. I became aware of the strength of my competitive ambitious feelings which had, however, largely been kept in check by my actual preoccupation with more highly social interests. I had expressed feelings of social distance and status by maintaining subdued but occasionally con-scious attitudes of impatience and contempt for other people who did not seem to be as quick or competent as myself.

I also felt just before illness that I had failed to give an adequate amount of love to my two older children, and that I had not had full interest in their development as individuals after they had outgrown the stage of early childhood. The extramarital affair intensified insight and self-rejection because I felt that there were limiting and egotistical elements in my love, that I was giving no more than I was receiving, and that I still had an insufficient degree of love for my children.

Loss of ego-support. Throughout most of the period of therapy I had a desire to impress my therapist and to win her approval. I went out of my way to take pains with my dress and personal appearance when I saw her. Later on, I began to feel that my point of view was changing, that my values were different from hers, and that there was no longer as much common ground for discussion. I also felt I knew myself better than she knew me. I was failing to communicate a good many of my half-formed thoughts about myself, partly because of limitations of time, and partly because these thoughts were not fully clear even to myself. At this point I was no longer able to obtain emotional support from the transference relationship.

In addition to increased loneliness caused by my marital problem, I was also conscious of an increasing intellectual isolation. I was losing a previ-ously established sense of close group identification with organizations to which I had formerly belonged as I become aware that my views were be-ginning to differ from those of others which I had once accepted. I had pre-viously had a sense of "we-ness" both in regard to family and other group associations. This was being replaced by a sense of personal separateness.

The Illness

The onset stage. A few weeks before my illness I began to regress into success daydreams somewhat similar to, though not quite as naive and grandiose, as those I had had during early adolescence. I was puzzled by this tendency, though not greatly alarmed because it hardly seemed that my daydreaming self was a part of my adult ethical self. At the onset of panic, I was suddenly confronted with an overwhelming conviction that I had discovered the secrets of the universe, which were being rapidly made plain with incredible lucidity. The truths discovered seemed to be known immediately and directly, with absolute certainty. I had no sense of doubt or awareness of the possibility of doubt. In spite of former atheism and strong antireligious sentiments, I was suddenly convinced that it was possible to prove rationally the existence of God. I remember at the time trying to write an essay on cognition. I began to write compulsively and at the same time was aware that I was developing schizophrenia. I found later among the disorganized notes which I had carefully hidden away, a number of passages that were quite lucid as well as others that were incoherent and full of symbolic sexual content. I also felt that I was embarking on a great Promethean adventure. I was filled with an audacious and unconquerable spirit. As panic mounted, I grew afraid of being alone, had an intense desire to communicate. I had for a short time a sense of exclusive mission but was able to struggle consciously against messianic delusions. These tendencies were replaced by a sense of burdensome and exclusive responsibility, which continued throughout the entire several years of illness.

Some special characteristics of the first episode. During the first episode I was hyperactive and extremely tense. Feelings of guilt and self-rejection which I had started to have before onset were in evidence during the acute phase of illness only to a very minor degree and were expressed symbolically and nonrationally. It was only later on, during more rational and integrated periods of disturbance, that I developed an intense guilt consciousness and conscious self-repudiation. These guilt feelings were finally resolved and dissipated during periods of comparative rationality. I shall not discuss here the emotional functions of the guilt experience.

I did not feel especially isolated or actively lonely during the projective, fear-ridden first episode. I had little or no desire to communicate with real people, although I talked extensively with an imaginary companion. I felt painfully lonely during later phases of disturbance when I was more rational and in relatively normal contact with other people.

The world disaster experience. Shortly after I was taken to the hospital for the first time in a rigid catatonic condition, I was plunged into the horror of a world catastrophe. I was being caught up in a cataclysm and totally dislocated. I myself had been responsible for setting the destructive forces into motion, although I had acted with no intent to harm, and defended myself with healthy indignation against the accusations of others. If I had done something wrong, I certainly was suffering the consequences along with everyone else. Part of the time I was exploring a new planet (a marvelous and breath-taking adventure) but it was too lonely, I could persuade no one to settle there, and I had to get back to the earth somehow. The earth, however, had been devastated by atomic bombs and most of its inhabitants killed. Only a few people—myself and the dimly perceived nursing staff—had escaped. At other times, I felt totally alone on the new planet.

The issue of world salvation was of predominant importance and I was trying to tell people how to go back to the abandoned earth. All personal matters relating to my family were forgotten. At times when the universe was collapsing, I was not sure that things would turn out all right. I thought I might have to stay in the endless hell-fire of atomic destruction. The chief horror consisted in the fact that I would never be able to die. I thought I would either have to figure out some form of suicide or else get a lobotomy.

During some of the time that I was dislocated in interplanetary space, I was also having vivid fantasies in connection with water, and these afforded me considerable relief. Water represented conservation of life, in contrast to its destruction by fire.

Water fantasies had started one or two days after admission to the hospital. I suddenly felt I had been plunged into a sea, was drowning and struggling for breath. At that point I realized that I was in a sedative tub. I saw that I was strapped in such a way that I was in no danger of drowning. I knew that as long as I was awake I would not need the straps because I would be careful not to drown, but I continued to feel terrified.

Water fantasies returned at times when I was given wet-pack treatments. I clearly remember reciting to myself some lines of Swinburne. I recalled only the first stanza of the poem and falsely interpolated at the end a line belonging to the second, thus skipping all parts in which the poet expressed a longing for death:

> I will go back to the great sweet mother
> Mother and lover of men, the sea.
> I will go down to her, I and none other,
> Close with her, kiss her, and mix her with me;
> Cling to her, strive with her, hold her fast;
> O fair white mother, in days long past
> Born without sister, born without brother,
> Wrought without hand in a world without stain.

It was not I who wanted to go back to the sea, because I myself was the sea, or maternal principle. The haunting recollection of this poem was followed by a vivid pleasurable hallucination of rape, by which I became pregnant. The entire illness after that was emotionally identified with childbirth, that is, with productive suffering. The baby had been too difficult to deliver, there had been a Caesarian operation, but vaguely in some way the symbolic child could be saved though there was no actual child.

It was only at times when I was plunged directly into hell-fire that I felt there was no effort I could make except in the direction of death. At other times, though I seemed to be almost pulled apart in a disintegrating universe, I felt there must be some way I could hold things together. I was somehow an indispensable link in preventing total collapse. I was unable to think coherently or plan any action, but I had to use my poetic imagination instead, for poetry could be counted on not to lead me astray. As soon as I struggled into a little more coherence, I tried to think of other things I must do. What about "know thyself"? This did not seem to be helpful. Then I hit upon Polonius' lines:

> This above all: to thine own self be true,
> And it must follow as the night the day,
> Thou canst not then be false to any man.

After I remembered this, I was also able to feel that I was involved in the struggle for world peace and progress. The universe stopped whirling about so drastically and I felt more like my old self.

Quite frequently, during the following months, I kept coming back to Shakespeare's advice, which gave me some reassurance. I had, however, seen Laurence Olivier's *Hamlet* a few weeks before becoming sick, and had thought at the time that the statement would only apply to persons who had trustworthy social selves to begin with. This was my problem in a nutshell. There was a part of myself that had not been trustworthy, attributes which I had not liked, and which had to be eradicated. I was by no means rejecting myself completely, for incorporated into that self were all the values I cherished most. My feeling for nature, art, and science, and my general love of life seemd to be entirely in harmony with my value-system and inseparable from it. I became aware during my first illness of the tremendous debt which I owed to the past.

During the first three weeks of hospitalization, I saw visions at various times. The capacity to see visions did not return after this period. These visions could be divided into two categories. The first type had no relation to and was not suggested by surrounding objects in the material environment, but were entirely projections of inner states of consciousness and appeared before my eyes in the same way that a motion picture is presented to the eye of the observer. The second type did not constitute true visions, but could rather be called visual hallucinations and distortions, sometimes suggested by the play of light and shadow, etc. acting upon an overwrought imagination. The true visions had definite but rather complex content and my attention was focused on grasping their meaning.

Occasionally during subsequent periods of disturbance there was some distortion of vision and some degree of hallucination. On several occasions my eyes became markedly oversensitive to light. Ordinary colors appeared to be much too bright, and sunlight seemed dazzling in intensity. When this happened, ordinary reading was impossible, and print seemed excessively black.

The formation of the delusional system. After the first few weeks of extreme disorganization, I began to acquire some relatively stable paranoid delusions. These delusions were accompanied by fear, and were based in part on erroneous perceptions and hallucinations, as well as on erroneous inferences from accurate perception. I also had a sense of discovery, creative excitement, and intense, at times mystical, inspiration in intervals when there was relief from fear.

During the paranoid period I thought I was being persecuted for my beliefs, that my enemies were actively trying to interfere with my activities, were trying to harm me, and at times even to kill me. I was primarily a citizen of the larger community. I was trying to persuade people who did not agree with me, but whom I felt could be won over, of the correctness of my beliefs. The only trouble was that it was difficult to get people to listen to me.

The picture of myself which I had at this time was much the same as that which I had always carried around with me during most of my adult life before I had become ethically self-conscious. I was a worthy citizen and was not afflicted with a sense of failure as a mother. I had regained a sense of inner control. I was once more a mature competent adult with great reserves of strength, and this was how I had almost always felt. I did, however, feel different from normal to the extent that I was in the midst of a bewildering and terrifying situation unlike anything I had ever encountered before. I was being compelled to focus attention on a new set of facts. Because of the continuously unpredictable nature of the delusional occurrences in the ward, the sense of routine and habit was almost entirely absent, I was dealing with novelty, consciousness was much more narrowly and sharply focused than normally, and a large mass of my previous memories and life reactions were inaccessible to me.

At no time during the first episode did I entirely lose feelings of personal guilt, and I retained some capacity for ethical awareness. In this situation, however, too great a preoccupation with problems of self-valuation would have impeded the fulfillment of my social mission. For the most part, my attention was directed toward problems in external reality, as it appeared to me. I was extraverted, not introverted, in spite of what might have been appearances to the contrary.

In order to carry through the task which had been imposed upon me, and to defend myself against the terrifying and bewildering dangers of my external situation, I was endowed in my imagination with truly cosmic powers. The sense of power was not always purely defensive but was also connected with a strong sense of valid inspiration. I felt that I had power to determine the weather which responded to my inner moods, and even to control the movement of the sun in relation to other astronomical bodies. None of these powers gave me feelings of competence or satisfaction. They had been given to me to cope with an emergency. I did not know how I obtained them and I derived no feeling of special importance from them. Whatever "magical" powers I did have were directed solely to the control of nonhuman forces, and I did not feel that I had any control over people. I was, on the contrary, acutely aware that in relation to the nursing staff, doctors, etc., I was singularly helpless and unable to make my wants known. Sometimes I did feel that I was able to acquire added power or psychic force which I was able to use in a defensive way to keep other people from getting control of me. I was also afraid that other people had power to read my mind, and thought I must develop ways of blocking my thoughts from other people.

I was carrying through a predominantly maternal role when I was not preoccupied with the more neutral role of world citizen. I was the one who must protect other people, and I was doing so to the best of my ability. I had never been more conscious of being a woman and a mother. Every once in a while an "inner voice" would say to me "Think of the children first and you will be all right." I clung desperately to this advice, even though it was far from sufficient to ward off fear.

I actually thought very little about my own children. I was convinced that my two older children were safe and well taken care of by relatives and had no wish to see them, but from time to time I did have a strong desire to take my youngest child in my arms. I was also convinced, most of the time, that he was dead, a delusion which will be discussed further below. Occasionally I had an intense longing for another baby, a longing so great that it amounted to a physical ache in the breasts. . .[2]

Conflict about life sacrifice. I felt serious anxiety about my capacity to surrender my life voluntarily in any and all circumstances when required in the interests of another individual. Included in the notes which I had written during the initial phase of panic, I found the following statement:

> The instinct of the individual to survive is the strongest instinct of all, and we know very well that this is so. Our first impulse is to save ourselves. Any other reaction to a personal danger situation is routed through devious channels. The race can survive only through the individual. Thus though we appear to be working against our own interests, we are not. This is the basic riddle of the universe on a feeling level. Inability to solve it has created a racial neurosis on the subject.

It would have been more correct to say that I had a long-standing personal neurosis on the subject. When I was about twelve or thirteen years old I had heard that persons (both men and women) were sometimes decorated for bravery because of heroic actions in which the life of another person was saved. I wondered at the time whether I would have the courage to act in this way. I was afraid I would be paralyzed by fear, that I would stop too long to calculate risks, and that I would not act to help the other person if there were a serious chance that I might lose my own life. I pictured myself as totally alone and unobserved with the unknown person who was in danger. I shoved aside the question and forgot about it during adult life, although I think it did cross my mind occasionally when I read about heroic rescues in the newspaper.

It was this long-buried fear of failure in such a type of "cold" isolated situation that was for me one of the sources of greatest anxiety in the early catatonic state of disorganization. This fear was not conscious during acute disturbance. I was, however, being accused of treachery by the entire social group. For a brief time (just before the world catastrophe described

---

[2] In the omitted section, Anonymous goes on to describe intense and overwhelming feelings of anger, aggression, fear, and sympathy directed toward individuals (fellow patients, nurses, her children, etc.) in her environment. She also reports on a set of religious confusions. Ed.

above) I felt I was being ostracized by all my friends and relatives. No such person as myself had ever existed. I alone knew that I existed, but could convince no one of this fact.

The fear about my own cowardice and my excessively strong self-protective impulses did not become conscious until a good while after recovery from the second episode, when self-confidence about other types of performance had been restored, and I felt myself to be a normally adequate mother. I had a great resistance to bringing the matter into full awareness, but when I was finally able to do so I realized that I would never dare to say that I would not have failed in a situation of this type. If there had been real danger, perhaps I would have thought "Why lose two lives rather than one?," while actually there might have been some chance of successful action. Perhaps, on the other hand, I would have become so immediately identified with the person who needed help that I would have been able to act impulsivly. There was also the not too pleasant thought that I might have acted differently if under observation by others than if I had been alone. I would never know what I would have done.

In finally thinking through the issue, I recognized that I would never feel justified in risking my life in this way as long as I had children dependent on me, but that if I no longer had such responsibilities the rule would apply. I also felt that a man who failed to act in this way toward a neighbor or member of his fraternal in-group would be considered a weakling by others, and would consider himself a weakling provided he accepted the standard as morally valid or socially necessary. A childless woman might not have been so strongly condemned in the past in this respect, but new mores are being evolved because of the emancipation of women. Girls are taught first-aid and life-saving techniques along with boys. Just before the second period of hospitalization I planned to join a volunteer rescue and fire-fighting squad in my local community and was upset when I learned that women were not eligible for membership.

Rules regarding life sacrifice are enforced by group opinion as well as by individual acquiescence in their validity. The penalty for violation is loss of "social face" if caught by others, and loss of self-respect if caught by the self. I certainly had not been born with an instinct to act in this way, yet bravery of this type was a vital component of my ego-ideal. . . .

Chief personality changes. The chief personality changes which I consider took place in myself during the period of six or seven years which included the psychosis can be summarized as follows: (1) I lost a chronic, diffused anxiety which I had long carried around in adult life; (2) I grew more capable of self-assertion without anxiety; I acquired a more secure sense of adult authority in my relation with my children. These changes also included a shift from the masochistic to a nonmasochistic emotional orientation; (3) I lost a sense of excessive dependency on other adults; a sense of personal separateness and isolation replaced a former capacity for identification with other individuals and with groups; (4) My relations with people generally became easier and more relaxed; I acquired a greater capacity for warmth and outgoing interest in all sorts of people; (5) I acquired a deeper sense of human equality and of the potential dignity of every human being; (6) My interest in competitive evaluations of myself and others was decreased to a marked degree; (7) There were changes in psychosexual adjustment, including a change from a chronic state of semifrigidity to a state of sexual adequacy; (8) My intellectual capacities functioned more freely and more efficiently than before; (9) I changed from a nonreligious to a religious type of orientation, acquiring a sense of religious dependency and a capacity for religious communication.

A FIELD STUDY OF AMERICAN SUBURBS *

(HARRY HENDERSON

Since World War II, whole new towns and small cities, consisting of acres of near-identical Cape Cod and ranch-type houses, have been bulldozed into existence on the outskirts of America's major cities. Begun as "veterans' housing," and still commonly called "projects," these new communities differ radically from the older urban areas whose slow, cumulative growth depended on rivers and railroads, raw materials or markets, industries and aavilable labor. They also differ from the older suburbs which were built around eisting villages. These new communities are of necessity built on open farmland—to house people quickly, cheaply, and profitably. They reflect not only the increased number of young American families, but an enormous expansion of the middle class via the easy credit extended to veterans.

The best known of these communities, Levittown, Long Island, is also the largest; its population is now estimated at 70,000. Lakewood, near Long Beach in the Los Angeles area, is a close second. Park Forest, some thirty miles south of Chicago—which has significant qualitative differences from the others, in that its social character was as conscientiously planned as its physical layout—now has 20,000 people and will have 30,000 when completed. No one knows exactly how many of these postwar communities exist in all. The Federal Home and Housing Authority, which insured mortgages for nearly all the houses, has no records in terms of communities or even large developments. However, one can safely assume that their combined population totals several million people.

* From Harry Henderson, "The Mass-produced Suburbs," Harper's Magazine, 207, 25–32. Copyright, 1953, by Harper & Brothers. Reprinted by permission of the author.

These communities have none of the long-festering social problems of older towns, such as slums, crowded streets, vacant lots that are both neighborhood dumps and playgrounds, or sagging, neon-fronted business districts that sprawl in all directions. Instead everything is new. Dangerous traffic intersections are almost unknown. Grassy play areas abound. Shops are centrally located and under one roof, at least theoretically, with adjacent off-street parking.

Socially, these communities have neither history, tradition, nor established structure—no inherited customs, institutions, "socially important" families, or "big houses." Everybody lives in a "good neighborhood"; there is, to use that classic American euphemism, no "wrong side of the tracks." Outwardly, there are neither rich nor poor, and initially there were no older people, teen-agers, in-laws, family doctors, "big shots," churches, organizations, schools, or local governments. Since the builder required a large cheap site, the mass-produced suburbs are usually located at the extreme edge of the commuting radius. This means they are economically dependent on the big city, without local industry to provide employment and share tax burdens.

Three years ago I began a series of extensive visits to these new communities to learn what effect this kind of housing and social organization has on people. I was particularly interested in what customs developed, what groups became important, what attitudes and ways of handling problems were created. I wanted to know, for instance, how people made friends, how you became a "big shot," and how life in these towns differed from that of our older towns.

The notes below are an attempt to describe what I found out, a reporter's report on a new generation's version of the "American way." They are based on interviews and my own observations in six such communities, including Levittown and Park Forest. While each community is different, certain common patterns exist, although their strength varies in accordance with two factors: screening and size.

Screening—or the selection of people by fixed criteria—obviously affects the economic, social, and cultural life. Where screening is based on something more than the ability to make a down payment, the population tends to become a narrow, specialized, upper stratum of the middle class. Size affects the community in another way. The construction of fifty or a hundred new homes on a common plot immediately beside a suburb of 5,000 merely results in their becoming part of that community, adopting its social structure. But when the number of new homes is many times larger than the old, both problems and new ways of living emerge with greater force. (However, even in small projects some new patterns are present.)

These notes are, of course, subjective and as such liable to personal distortion. Valid statistical data—because of the short time people stay put in these towns, plus a host of other factors—are simply beyond the reach of one man. But, for whatever they are worth, here they are:

At first glance, regardless of variations in trim, color, and position of the houses, they seem monotonous; nothing rises above two stories, there are no full-grown trees, and the horizon is an endless picket fence of telephone poles and television aerials. (The mass builder seeks flat land because it cuts his construction costs.)

However one may feel about it aesthetically, this puts the emphasis on people and their activities. One rarely hears complaints about the identical character of the houses. "You don't feel it when you live here," most people say. One mother, a Midwestern college graduate with two children, told me: "We're not peas in a pod. I thought it would be like that, especially because incomes are nearly the same. But it's amazing how different and varied people are, likes and dislikes, attitudes and wants. I never really knew what people were like until I came here."

Since no one can acquire prestige through an imposing house, or inherited position, activity—the participation in community or group affairs—becomes the basis of prestige. In addition, it is the quickest way to meet people and make friends. In communities of strangers, where everybody realizes his need for companionship, the first year is apt to witness almost frantic participation in all kinds of activities. Later, as friends are made, this tapers off somewhat.

The standardized house also creates an emphasis on interior decorating. Most people try hard to achieve "something different." In hundreds of houses I never saw two interiors that matched—and I saw my first tiger-striped wallpaper. (The only item that is endlessly repeated is a brass skillet hung on a red brick wall.) Yet two styles predominate: Early American and Modern. What is rarely seen, except in homes of older-than-average people, is a family heirloom.

Taste levels are high. My interviews with wives revealed that their models and ideas came primarily from pictures of rooms in national magazines. Nobody copies an entire room, but they take different items from different pictures. At first most women said, "Well, moving into a new house, you want everything new." Later some altered this explanation, saying, "Nearly everybody is new. . . . I mean, they are newly married and new to the community. They don't feel too certain about things, especially moving into a place where everyone is a stranger. If you've seen something in a magazine—well, people will nearly always like it." So many times were remarks of this character repeated that I concluded that what many sought in their furniture was a kind of "approval insurance."

Asked whom they missed most, women usually replied, "My mother." Men's answers were scattered, apt to be old friends, neighbors, relatives. Many women said, "I wish there was some place close by to walk to, like the candy store in the city. Just some place to take the kids to buy a cone or newspaper in the afternoon. It helps break up the monontony of the day." They considered the centrally located shopping centers too distant for such outings.

Because these communities were built from scratch, they afforded a degree of planning impossible in our older cities, and—depending on the builder's foresight and awareness of social problems—advantage was taken of this. Planners solved complex problems in traffic flow, space arrangement, play areas, heating problems, site locations to provide sunlight, and kitchen traffic. But nobody thought about dogs.

The people in these communities have generally escaped from crowded city apartments. Their 50 x 100-foot plot seems to them to be the size of a ranch. One of their first acts is to buy a dog, on the theory that "it's good for the children," an old idea in American family folklore, and to turn the dog loose. Usually the people know nothing about dogs or their training. Theoretically, the dog is the children's responsibility; generally they are too young to handle it.

The result is that the dogs form great packs which race through the area, knocking down small boys and girls, wrecking gardens and flower beds, and raising general hell. Then people try tying them up; the dogs howl and bark until no one can stand it. Locked up inside the house, they are a constant worry, and charge out to bite mailmen and delivery-men. In one community thirteen mailmen were bitten in one summer.

Dogs, along with children, are the greatest cause of tension within a block. In Park Forest, outside Chicago, dogs were finally voted out of the 3,000-unit rental area in the bitterest, hottest, meanest, most tearful fight in that community's history. But they are permitted in the private-home area because our conception of private property includes the right to own a dog even though he may be the damnedest nuisance in the world. One can hardly describe the emotions aroused by dogs in these communities. One man told me he had bought his dog simply "because I am damn sick and tired of my neighbor's dog yapping all night. I just want to give them a taste of what it's like."

II

The populations differ strikingly from those of the older towns. The men's ages average 31 years; the women's about 26. Incomes fall somewhere between $4,000 and $7,000 yearly, although incomes in excess of this can be found everywhere. Their homes cost between $7,000 and $12,000. Roughly 90 per cent of the men are veterans. Their major occupational classifications are managers, professionals, salesmen, skilled workers, and small business men. Most communities also have sizable numbers of transient army families.

Buying or renting a home in one of these communities is, of course, a form of economic and personal screening. As a result, there are no poor, no Negroes; and, as communities, these contain the best educated people in America. In Park Forest, where the screening was intensive, more than 50 per cent of the men and 25 per cent of the women are college graduates; the local movie theater survives by showing Westerns for the kids in the afternoon and foreign "art films" for the adults in the evening.

Initially, city-bred women, accustomed to the constant sights and sounds of other people, suffer greatly from loneliness, especially if their children are as yet unborn. One woman expressed it this way: "Your husband gets up and goes off in the morning—and you're left with the day to spend. The housework is a matter of minutes. I used to think I had been brought to the end of the earth and deserted." Another said, "I used to sit by the window . . . just wishing someone would go by."

Generally this disappears as friends are made and children appear. Today most communities have "older" (by several years) residents who make real efforts to help newcomers overcome their "newness."

Hardware stores report their biggest selling item year-round is floor wax. "Honest to God," said one store manager, "I think they eat the stuff."

The daily pattern of household life is governed by the husband's commuting schedule. It is entirely a woman's day because virtually every male commutes. Usually the men must leave between 7:00 and 8:00 A.M.; therefore they rise between 6:00 and 7:00 A.M. In most cases the wife rises with her husband, makes his breakfast while he shaves, and has a cup of coffee with him. Then she often returns to bed until the children get up. The husband is not likely to be back before 7:00 or 7:30 P.M.

This leaves the woman alone all day to cope with the needs of the children, her housekeeping, and shopping. (Servants, needless to say, are unknown.) When the husband returns, he is generally tired, both from his work and his traveling. (Three hours a day is not uncommon; perhaps the most widespread dream of the men is a job nearer the community, and they often make earnest efforts to find it.) Often by the time the husband returns the children are ready for bed. The husband helps put them to bed; as they grow older, they are allowed to stay up later. Then he and his wife eat their supper and wash the dishes. By 10:00 P.M. most lights are out.

For the women this is a long, monotonous daily proposition. Generally the men, once home, do not want to leave. They want to "relax" or "improve the property"—putter around the lawn or shrubbery. However, the women want a "change." Thus, groups of women often go to the movies together.

Usually both husband and wife are involved in some group activity and have meetings to go to. A frequent complaint is: "We never get time to see each other"; or, "We merely pass coming and going." On the one occasion when I was refused an interview, the husband said, "Gee, I'd like to help, but I so seldom get a chance to see my wife for a whole evening. . . . I'd rather not have the interruption."

Many couples credit television, which simultaneously eased baby-sitting, entertainment, and financial problems, with having brought them closer. Their favorites are comedy shows, especially those about young couples, such as "I Love Lucy." Though often contemptuous of many programs, they speak of TV gratefully as "something we can share," as "bringing romance back." Some even credit it with having "saved our marriage." One wife said: "Until we got that TV set, I thought my husband had forgotten how to neck."

These are the first towns in America where the impact of TV is so concentrated that it literally affects everyone's life. Organizations dare not hold meetings at hours when popular shows are on. In addition, it tends to bind people together, giving the whole community a common experience.

The Coffee Klatsch is an institution everywhere. A kind of floating, day-long talkfest, shifting from house to house, it has developed among young women to help fill their need for adult conversation and companionship. The conversation is strictly chitchat. One woman described it as "Just small talk . . . about what's new . . . about whose kid is sick . . . and then about who is apt to get sick." Yet many women complain there is "too much talk," and some are very critical of the gregariousness.

III

When people moved into these communities, they shed many of their parents' and their home-town customs. For instance, slacks or shorts are standard wear for both men and women at all times, including trips to the shopping center. Visiting grandparents invariably are shocked and whisper: "Why, nobody dresses around here!"

Children, regardless of sex, wear dungarees or shorts and a cotton T-shirt until puberty. One mother expressed the attitude of most: "Kids don't wear anything you bother with. It cuts down on the time needed for dressing, washing, and ironing." Parents who started raising their children in older communities are shocked to find "nobody dresses their kids for school."

Gone also are most rituals and ceremonies. If you want to know someone, you introduce yourself; there is no waiting for the "right people." You "drop in" without phoning. If you have an idea that will solve some problem, you immediately call up everybody concerned. One result is that, generally speaking, there is less lag than elsewhere between an idea and "getting something done," which may be anything from organizing a dance to getting a stop sign for your corner.

The attitude toward pregnancy is unusually casual. Because it is so common, pregnancy is regarded more objectively and referred to in terms that would seem outlandish in older communities. It is often called "our major industry"; or someone will say, "That's the Levittown Look," or, "It must be the water; you don't see any men around." Nearly every place has its own unofficial name stressing its fecundity; Park Foresters call it "Fertile Acres." And when pregnancy is discussed seriously, it is referred to in practically sociological terms: "We have a three-year pregnancy cycle here that is terrific."

Pregnancies are generally planned and the considerations shown are based on real needs. Women with romantic ideas, or those accustomed to being surrounded by doting relatives, sometimes feel that they are being neglected. As one woman put it, "I had Jane in the city. My mother and sisters used to call up daily just to see how I was. Out here you are nothing special. At first, when I was pregnant with Arleen, I really missed the attention."

A marked feeling of transience pervades everything from shopping to friendships. This feeling reflects both optimism and uncertainty, and it encourages a tendency to seek expedient solutions. For instance, the question of whether or not one plans to spend his life there is shunted aside—optimistically. This has serious effects on school and town government problems.

The uncertainty stems, as one young salesman expressed it, from the fact that "you just don't know—whether you'll make the grade, whether the company will transfer you, whether you'll be getting along with your wife five years from now, whether the neighbors will move out and monsters will move in. So you hesitate to sink deep roots." In general, optimism prevails over uncertainty. Many—a majority, I would say—consider this merely their "first" house. They insist that they are young, and they confidently look forward to owning a $15,000 to $20,000 house some day.

Interestingly, while most look upon their present house as a "temporary deal," because "under the GI-Bill owning is cheaper than renting," the most orthodox and conservative views prevail concerning property and home ownership. There is more talk about property values than you would hear in older towns and much effort is put into "making the place look like something." This may mean the addition of fences, garage, patio, etc. A standard proud comment is: "We could walk out of this place with $1,000 profit tomorrow."

Actual transience is high. Business transfers and increased incomes are its major causes. As a result, there is a flourishing business in the resale of houses. In one community where I interviewed twelve families in one block there years ago, all but four have since moved. From the remaining families I learned that the removals had nearly all been due to increased incomes which permitted more expensive homes. Others had moved to cut commuting time or because of company transfers. Unfortunately, no over-all statistics on transience exist.

The replacements for departed families are often older, 45 to 50 being the average age of the men. Their goal is the $7,000 to $12,000 house. More certain of what they can and will do, they are less anxious about "success," and financially not so hard pressed. Having resided in older towns, they like these new communities because of their friendliness and optimism. "The older towns are dead," said one small business man who is typical of this group.

Usually these "second generation" people have teen-age children and, in interviews, they emphasized the absence of "bad neighborhoods" and ample play areas as reasons for moving. Many also liked the idea that economically everyone is in the same class. One father, a skilled aviation worker, said, "Where we used to live we had both rich and very poor. Our girls were caught in the middle because the rich kids dressed better and hung out together, and the poor kids dressed poorer and hung out together. They were nobody's friend, while here they are everybody's friend. I'd say they are happier than they ever were."

Except for Park Forest,* none of the communities I visited has a local police force. Yet crime can hardly be said to exist—probably the most spectacular aspect of these new towns. In one community with 15,000 people the crime record amounted, in two years, to 6 burglary cases, 35 larceny cases, 13 assault cases (husband-wife rows), and 6 disorderly conduct cases. Typically, the communities are patrolled by existing county and township police, who report their only major problems are traffic and lost children.

Even Levittown, with 70,000 people not far from New York's turbulent, scheming underworld, has virtually no crime. According to the Nassau County police, who studied one year's record, it had no murders, robberies, or auto thefts during that period; an average city of that size during the same period would have had 4 murders, 3 robberies, and 149 auto thefts.

Levittown had 3 assault cases, 16 burglaries, and 200 larceny cases while comparable cities averaged 73 assault cases, 362 burglaries, and 942 larcenies. Larceny in Levittown was mainly bicycle stealing. (Since these statistics were gathered, the FBI has caught a Levittowner who planned a payroll robbery and a young mother, later adjudged insane, has asphyxiated her two small children.)

* This small city, the work of Phillip Klutznick and Jerrold Loebl (to name its principal creators) is based on the planning principle that, if a builder creates a market for building a city, he can afford to make less money on housing—and make up for it on the rental of shopping space. Because this is a long-term proposition, the builder must therefore assume a greater degree of social responsibility for community assets like schools, churches, and town government than the builders who sell everything at a profit and get out fast, like hit-and-run drivers.—H.H.

Police attribute this lack of crime to the fact that nearly all the men were honorably discharged from the armed services and subjected to a credit screening. This, they say, "eliminated the criminal element and riff-raff." Some police officials included the absence of slums and disreputable hang-outs as causes. Personally, I felt many more factors were involved, including the absence of real poverty; the strong ties of family, religious, and organizational activities; steady employment; and the absence of a restrictive, frustrating social structure.

IV

Every family operates, or tries to operate, under a budget plan. Most families report their living standards have been raised by moving into the community. There is almost constant self-scolding because living costs outrun the budget. The shining goal: economic security. The word "success" is on everyone's lips and "successful people" are those who advance economically.

Most families report it costs a minimum of between $100 or $150 a month to live in these communities. While the rent or mortgage payment may come to only $65 or $75 monthly, other expenses—commuting, garbage, water, utilities—push the total much higher. In addition, distances to the shopping center and commuting stations virtually require a car and all its expenses.

If the axiom, "a week's pay for a month's rent," is applied, it is obvious that many families are barely making ends meet and some are having real difficulty. Typical comments on their economic situation: "We're just like everybody else here—broke," or, "We're all in the same boat, economically. Just getting by, I'd say." I estimated the average man's income from his regular job to be under $100 a week.

Where screening was based only on the ability to make the down payment rather than ability to pay, you often find a sizable number of men seeking supplementary work: weekend clerking in stores; finishing attics; door-to-door selling. In one community a man who acts as a clearing house for jobs told me: "I'd say that 50 per cent of these people are running on their nerve. One winter of sickness would knock them out." A great number of women whose children have reached school age seek work, but it is hard to find and pays less than they were used to earning in the city. I talked to a night taxi-driver in one community whose job stemmed from his children's illnesses. This supplementary work left him only six hours between jobs. It was rough, he admitted, ". . . but I figure it's worth it to have the kids here. I couldn't stand taking them back to the city. I'll get these bills cleaned up yet."

In addition, the economic pinch is relieved in some families by subsidies from parents. "There are a fair percentage of them who are still leaning on Mama and Papa," one store proprietor said. "I know because I cash their checks." In other cases the pressure is relieved by "doubling up." This seldom means two young families in one house; usually the "doubling up" is with in-laws, who share expenses. Technically this produces substandard housing; the people involved regard this as nonsense. No stigma is attached to the practice and many women expressed the wish to have their parents live with them, mainly because they wanted companionship and guidance on child-raising.

Shopping habits reflect the tight economic situation. Food is widely purchased with an eye on the penny. Store managers complain that the "trade is transient; you can't build up personal service." (New brides are sometimes astonishingly ignorant; one confessed she had almost bought a hundred pounds of coffee from a door-to-door salesman who told her, "It'll be a long cold winter, you'll have friends dropping in and will need lots of hot coffee.") Slacks, retailing at $6, are the biggest items in both men's and women's clothing. A $20 "cocktail dress" is the leading item in women's apparel. Beer, rather than whisky, is bought for parties; the biggest selling whisky is a blend retailing for $3.75. Men's suits are often selected by the man and the wife together; she generally picks hard-wearing fabrics. In some communities "suit clubs," reminiscent of the Depression, are in operation; in a "suit club" everybody pays $1.50 a week and a weekly drawing is held, the winner immediately getting a suit regardless of how much he has paid.

Both the individual and the community face these economic stresses with a powerful, deep-seated optimism based on the conviction that they are just starting their careers. The men sometimes say with a grin: "After all, this is only the first wife, first car, first house, first kids—wait till we get going." Though, in the long run, they measure success in economic terms, people are frank about "being broke" and there is no stigma attached to it by anyone, including families with larger incomes. "Money just doesn't cut any ice around here," said one young engineer whose earnings put him in the $8,000-a-year class. "We've all been broke at one time or another. The important thing is, nobody expects to stay broke."

Usually one couple "trades nights" for baby-sitting with a nearby couple. In addition, they may belong to a baby-sitting "co-op," which involves a larger group. In these groups one mother "keeps the book"—a record of how many hours you sit as well as how many you use. You are allowed to "go into debt" fifteen hours or "get ahead" fifteen hours. The only clear-cut case of ostracism I encountered involved a women who had "gone into debt" some seventy hours to her "co-op."

Socially, the outstanding characteristic of these people is their friendliness, warmth, and lack of pretentious snobbery. Outgoing and buoyant, they are quick to recognize common problems and the need for co-operation; one does not find the indifference, coldness, and "closed doors" of a long-established community. There is much casual "dropping in" and visiting from house to house which results in the sharing of many problems and pleasures. Often the discussion of a few women over supper plans will end up with four or five families eating together. This may then lead to "fun," which may be anything from cards to "just talk" or "everybody trying to roller-skate, acting like a bunch of kids." Nobody goes "out" often. Many report that, as a result of this pattern of living, they "drink more often but get high less" than they used to. Drinking, it seemed to me, had become much more of a social amenity and less of an emotional safety valve than it is elsewhere.

This generalized, informal friendliness assumes so many forms that it is a very real part of everyone's life, replacing the thousand-skeined social structure of older American towns. It explains why the people who live in these communities are for the most part enthusiastic about them. "Here, for the first time in my life," one salesman said, "I don't worry about my family when on the road. Here at least a dozen families are constantly in touch with them and ready to help if anything goes wrong, whether it's the car, the oil heater, or one of the kids getting sick. In Pittsburgh I had to rely on scattered relatives who weren't in touch with my family more than once a week."

This is the big cushion which, while making life more enjoyable, protects the inhabitants of the new suburbs and solves their minor problems. It absorbs innumerable small transportation needs, puts up TV aerials, repairs cars, finishes attics, and carries the load of sudden emergencies. Nothing in these communities, to me, is more impressive than this uniform pattern of casual but warm friendliness and co-operation.

A CROSS–CULTURAL STUDY OF THE REINFORCEMENT OF CHILD BEHAVIOR *

(WAYNE DENNIS [1]

Few psychologists reject the proposition that the rewarding of an act increases the frequency, vigor and promptness with which it will recur. That the strength of a response can be increased by reward has probably been recognized from an early human period. It is likely that parents and other

* From Wayne Dennis, "A Cross-cultural Study of the Reinforcement of Child Behavior," Child Develpm., 28, 431–438. Reprinted by permission of the author and the Editor, Child Development.

[1] The research here reported was done during 1955–1956 while the author was a visiting professor at the American University of Beirut, Lebanon. The writer wishes to express his gratitude to the University for making the study possible, and to the Rocke-

adults—without benefit of Thorndike, Skinner and others—early found that reward was an effective means of social control. It goes almost without saying that they rewarded those acts of which they approved, and hence rewards had the effect of transmitting and inculcating social values.

It follows that if one knew what child behaviors were being rewarded in a society one could formulate hypotheses concerning both the values of the adults and the future behavior of the children. But in a "field situation" it is difficult to know what is being rewarded. The approval of child behavior often occurs in the home, or in some other setting in which it cannot readily be observed. We wish to report some data obtained with a method which we believe will enable a researcher to investigate in nearly any society those reinforcements which probably play a major part in the socialization of the child.

Method

The method consists in using the critical incident technique developed by Flanagan and his associates (1). In general, this technique involves asking the subject to describe one or more instances of behavior of a specified kind. In the present connection this means that the subject is asked to describe instances of behavior on his part for which he has been praised. The subject is not asked to give generalizations. Instead the investigator derives generalizations from the analysis of many specific incidents.

In the present investigation all data were gathered by means of individual interviews of school children. Specifically, the procedure is as follows: The child is taken from his classroom to the interviewing room by the interviewer. After preliminary remarks to establish rapport the interviewer obtains from the subject his name and his age at his last birthday. He then says: "I am interested in knowing what things boys and girls do that cause people to praise them. Do you remember a time lately when you did something for which someone praised you? Tell me about a particular time when someone praised you."

If the response does not indicate in detail what the child did, or just who was involved or just who gave the praise, appropriate supplementary questions are asked. The interviewer records the responses as nearly verbatim as is possible. In each case, the interview is conducted in the native language of the child. In the present study the answers of children whose primary language was not English were translated by the interviewer and recorded in English.

feller Brothers Fund for a grant to the University which defrayed the costs of the investigation. He wishes also to express his appreciation to those who served as research assistants in the study (Mrs. Adele Hamdan Taky Din, Miss Leila Biksmati, Mrs. Yvonne Sayyegh, and Mrs. Marie Therese Broussalian) and to the principals, teachers and pupils who so generously cooperated.

After the first incident is recorded, the interviewer says, "Now tell me about another time when you were praised." In the study here reported only two responses were requested from each child.

Subjects

All subjects were attending schools in Beirut, Lebanon, and were between 5.0 and 10.99 years of age. The groups were as follows:

Americans. These were pupils at the American Community School in Beirut. In the main they were children of parents employed in Lebanon by American government agencies, by the American University of Beirut, or by American oil companies and other business concerns. By most standards of classification, the majority of the subjects came from middle class well-educated parents. At the time they were tested (March–April, 1956) each child had been in Lebanon a minimum of six months. Many had resided in Lebanon two or more years. Some non-Americans attend this school; their responses were excluded from the results. The pupils of this school constituted the majority of American children of school age residing in Beirut in 1955–1956. There is no assumption that this group is typical of American children in the United States, but it is believed that many American children would give responses similar to those which we obtained. The American subjects totalled 120 children. There was approximately equal representation of the two sexes, and of the various age levels.

Arabs. This group consisted of 240 children chosen so that they could be conveniently subdivided in various ways. The subgroups were boys and girls (120 of each), Moslems and Arab Christians (120 of each), pupils of private schools and pupils of public schools (120 of each) and three age groups, 5- to 6-year-olds, 7- to 8-year-olds and 9- to 10-year-olds (80 of each).

Armenians. Children of this group attended a private Armenian school which is one of the best Armenian schools in Beirut. They belong primarily to the middle class. In most cases, their families emigrated to Lebanon following World War I. In this group there were 60 subjects equally divided as to age and sex.

Jews. These subjects came from a school which is attended by the majority of the children of the Jewish colony in Beirut. All social classes are represented, but it is believed that few parents fall into the unskilled labor classification. The majority of the families of these children have lived in the Near East for several centuries. Arabic is their primary tongue and they were questioned in this language. This group contained 60 subjects approximately equally distributed in regard to age and sex.

Categorization of Incidents

The incidents reported fell into certain categories. These categories, which are listed in Tables 1 and 2, are as follows:

1. *Academic.* This class includes all incidents relating to academic performance, such as being praised for doing lessons, for doing them well, for grades, for improvement, etc. Assisting teacher, however, falls in category 8, and doing unassigned creative or constructive work whether associated with the school or not is placed in category 13.

2–8. *Assistance.* These items are differentiated from each other in terms of the person to whom assistance is given. Sample items are: helped mother wash dishes, ran out and bought groceries for my aunt, etc. Item 6, assisting unfortunates, includes helping a blind man across the street, helping someone who has been injured, giving alms to the poor or to beggars, etc.

9–11. The titles of these categories shown in Table 1 are self-explanatory. "Being quiet" includes refraining from activity as well as refraining from making noise.

12. *Giving or sharing.* This heading indicates voluntarily offering a present to others, giving food, sharing a toy, etc. It does not include almsgiving, which in included under item 6.

13. *Creative work.* Under this class is included such items as unassigned art work, making a dress, making a boat or a kite, constructing toys or models, and organizing a group activity.

Categorization of Rewarding Persons

As shown by Table 3, the persons doing the praising were classified according to their relationship to the child. These persons were mother, father, teacher, adult relatives, and other children. Some persons who were reported as praising did not fall into one of these categories; they were omitted from the tabulations. For this reason the percentages in Table 3 do not total 100 per cent.

Results

Table 1 indicates the frequency of each kind of incident in each of the four main groups. Table 2 gives the same information for the various subdivisions of the Arab group. The other groups are not large enough to justify such subdivision. Table 3 compares the groups in regard to the persons who did the praising. Each set of results will be briefly discussed below.

Table 1 demonstrates that the relative frequencies of various kinds of rewarded behavior vary greatly between groups. For example, there is a large difference between the American group and the other groups in regard to the per cent of incidents which involve academic performance (item 1 of Table 1). In the American group praise for academic performance constitutes only 5 per cent of the total. In other groups it makes up from 28 to 41 per cent of the total (p of difference of 5 to 28 per cent $< .001$). This difference may be due to the fact that the American school is a "progressive" one which, between ages 5 and 10, puts very little pressure upon the pupil. By and large, the parents seem to approve of the permissive atmosphere of the school. In contrast the majority of the Lebanese schools stress academic achievement, even among 5-year-olds, and the parents, too, stress school performance.

TABLE 1. GROUP COMPARISONS OF INCIDENTS REPORTED: PERCENTAGE OF
RESPONSES IN EACH CATEGORY

	American	Arab	Armenian	Jewish
1. Academic performance	5%	28%	31%	41%
2. Assist mother	25	26	15	22
3. Assist father	6	2	0	2
4. Assist sibling	9	4	3	5
5. Assist relatives	0	2	3	0
6. Assist unfortunate	0	9	12	3
7. Assist peers	8	0	1	2
8. Assist others	7	5	3	3
9. Being quiet	1	3	5	2
10. Being polite, obedient	5	11	7	7
11. Sports and games	6	2	3	2
12. Giving or sharing	9	2	8	3
13. Creative work	13	2	8	3
14. Miscellaneous	6	5	4	7
Number of children	120	240	60	60
Number of responses	240	440	120	116

While item 1 of Table 2 shows a decline with age in the relative importance of academic achievement among the Lebanese subjects, this is probably due to the fact that other forms of praised behavior, such as assisting others, increase with age. The introduction of new behavior reduces the *proportion* of incidents concerned with praise for academic performance but does not indicate that academic work becomes less important in an absolute sense.

Among the Lebanese groups, the Jewish group is highest in respect to the emphasis placed upon academic achievement. The p of the Arab-Jewish difference is .01. The Armenian group, which is second, is not significantly different from the Arab group. Table 2 shows that within the Arab group Christians and Moslems do not differ in giving praise for school performance. But boys receive more praise for academic items than do girls.

Attention is next directed to the categories which deal with assisting or helping others (item 2–8). In all groups the child is praised for helping the mother more often than for helping other individuals. It will be noted that the values for assisting father, assisting siblings, assisting peers, and assisting "others" are appreciably greater for the American group than for any other group. Apparently American children are encouraged to enter into cooperative activities rather widely, whereas the Lebanese child's helpfulness centers chiefly upon the mother. An exception to this generalization arises in the case of assisting unfortunates, the majority of whom are street beggars who are blind or crippled or otherwise handicapped. The Near Eastern custom of giving alms to such people is engaged in by children as

TABLE 2. COMPARISONS OF SUBDIVISIONS WITHIN THE ARAB GROUP: PERCENTAGE OF INCIDENTS IN EACH CATEGORY

	Religion		Sex		School		CA		
	Christ.	Moslem	M	F	Priv.	Gov't	5,6	7,8	9,10
1. Academic performance	26	30	35	21	29	27	46	21	17
2. Assist mother	26	26	18	33	21	31	19	33	25
3. Assist father	2	2	2	2	0	4	2	1	3
4. Assist sibling	3	5	2	5	6	2	1	4	6
5. Assist relatives	2	2	2	3	1	3	1	3	3
6. Assist unfortunate ...	8	9	10	8	10	7	1	7	18
7. Assist peers	0	0	0	0	0	0	0	1	0
8. Assist others	7	3	5	5	5	5	2	4	9
9. Being quiet	3	2	1	4	4	2	5	1	3
10. Being polite & obedient	12	9	11	10	9	12	14	12	6
11. Sports & games	1	3	2	1	3	1	1	1	3
12. Giving or sharing	1	2	2	1	2	1	0	3	2
13. Creative work	2	1	2	1	2	1	3	2	0
14. Miscellaneous	7	4	7	5	6	4	6	7	5
Number of children	120	120	120	120	120	120	80	80	80
Number of responses	225	215	215	225	221	219	149	147	146

well as by adults, and children are praised for their almsgiving. This kind of charity seems to be almost absent among the American and among the Jewish children. At any rate, they report no praise for almsgiving.

It will be noted that the American children are seldom praised for being quiet or for being polite and obedient (item 9). The Lebanese parents and the Lebanese teachers, on the other hand, frequently praise the child for sitting still and making no noise. The American-Arab difference in this respect is significant at the 1 per cent level of confidence.

Praise for performance in sports and games (item 11) has three times the frequency among Americans as among the Arab and Jewish groups. The p value of the American-Arab difference is .02.

Giving and sharing (item 12; this item does not include almsgiving) is approximately three times as frequent in the American group as in the Arab and Jewish groups (p of American-Arab difference is .001). Creative work, such as constructing things and initiating projects, is highest among the American children. The American frequency (13 per cent) is 6½ times the Arab frequency (2 per cent) ($p < .001$). The Armenian group is second highest (8 per cent).

Table 3 shows the relative frequency with which children are praised by various persons. The three Near Eastern groups resemble each other in that the major portion of the praise is administered by adults, chiefly by parents and teachers. Near Eastern children appear not to be rewarded by other children, the amounts of praise received from children being only 1, 4, and 12 per cent in the three groups. The difference between the

TABLE 3. PERSONS GIVING PRAISE: PERCENTAGE OF INCIDENTS IN EACH CATEGORY

Persons praising	Americans	Arabs	Armenians	Jews
Mother	37	44	32	34
Father	13	17	7	11
Teacher	5	15	24	28
Adult relatives	0	9	9	8
Children	25	4	12	1
Number of children	120	240	60	60
Number of responses	240	440	120	116

American group and each of the other groups has a p of .001 or less. These facts are in accord with the earlier finding that there is only infrequent reference in these groups to assisting peers. Among the Americans, however, approval by other children makes up 25 per cent of the total. For the Americans, teachers are responsible for only 5 per cent of the praise incidents, whereas for the Jews and the Armenians the corresponding figures are respectively 28 and 24 per cent (p of difference between 5 and 24 per cent $< .001$). The Americans appear to relate much more to their peers; the Lebanese child relates predominantly to adults.

In summary, the American children are distinguished from the other groups as follows: They receive a larger portion of their praise for assisting persons other than unfortunates (with proportionally less assistance given to the mother by the Americans than by the others). They also exceed the groups in rewards for performance in sports and games, giving and sharing, and in creativity. The Near Eastern groups receive relatively more praise than the Americans for academic achievement, for assisting unfortunates and for being quiet, polite and obedient.

It will be noted that while there are some differences among the three Near Eastern groups, there is a considerable degree of agreement among them. There is a generalized Near Eastern pattern of child approval which differs considerably from the American pattern. This is shown by Table 4, which contains the correlations between the rank orders of the categories for each pair of groups. It will be noted that the intercorrelations of the

Lebanese groups are between .67 and .83, whereas the correlations between each of these and the American group range from —.11 to .32.

If adequate data on values were available, we believe it could be shown that praise is bestowed in accordance with the prevailing values of each group. For example, Near Eastern society is known to be very strongly family-centered. Accordingly we find that children are frequently rewarded for assisting relatives but seldom rewarded for assisting peers or other non-relatives. The exception to this rule is the giving of alms. Arab children are praised for giving alms; American children are not. This difference too accords with adult values. The well-known interest in sports shown by the

TABLE 4. CORRELATIONS BETWEEN THE RELATIVE FREQUENCIES
OF CATEGORIES

	Arab	Armenian	Jewish
American	−.11	.06	.32
Arab		.67	.83
Armenian			.68

American adult is paralleled by rewards for participation in games in child-hood. Near Eastern interest in sports is slight in comparison with the interest in America; we find Near Eastern children are seldom rewarded for achievement in sports. To give further examples from our data of the probable congruence between adult values and the rewarding of child behavior would unnecessarily repeat material previously presented. While our data do not *prove* that values and habits are inculcated by reward, they seem entirely consonant with this interpretation.

Summary

The critical incident technique was used to investigate the relative frequency with which different kinds of behavior are rewarded in three Near Eastern groups of children and in an American group. Highly significant differences were found between the American group and the Near Eastern groups. While some differences exist among the Near Eastern groups, they have a considerable degree of similarity.

It is suggested that rewarding behavior by praise, and by other means, is an important method of transmitting and inculcating social norms and values. On the basis of our experience the critical incident technique is recommended to psychologists, anthropologists and others as a useful tool in making cross-cultural comparisons. Its usefulness, of course, is not limited to the study of praise.

Reference

1. Flanagan, J. C. The critical incident technique. *Psychol. Bull.*, 1954, *51*, 327–358.

AN EXPERIMENT IN ATTITUDE CHANGE *

⟮ WILLIAM ABBOTT SCOTT [1]

Public opinion researchers are familiar, through anecdote if not personal acquaintance, with the woman who, when asked her opinion on social security, replied that she didn't know because no one had ever asked her, and she never knew what her opinions were until she opened her mouth and expressed them. Perhaps this apocryphal respondent was displaying more insight into the psychological processes underlying her attitude than is readily apparent. Though cognitive approaches to attitude development are more flattering in their emphasis on the rationally cognized relation of an object to the person's goals (1, 3, 8, 9), nonrational determiners may be equally important in the acquisition of attitudes.

According to Doob (4) an attitude may be regarded, like a habit, as an implicit anticipatory response which mediates overt behaviors, and arises out of them through response reinforcement. Thus, it is conceivable that an opinion be expressed initially, in the absence of a supporting attitude, but if the verbal behavior is rewarded, the corresponding attitude may develop and mediate subsequent opinion expressions in the presence of similar cues. This response reinforcement formulation thus focuses more on reward of verbal expressions than on cognized means-end relationships as critical factors in attitude development.

The two formulations, and the sets of variables they employ, are by no means incompatible. It is reasonable to suggest, for instance, that lacking a well structured and salient set of cognitive associations regarding an object, a person may be more readily induced to respond to it in nonlogical fashion, the outcome of his response then contributing to a nascent cognitive structure; but given a set of values and cognitions that can readily be applied to a new object, these will influence the person's attitudinal set and thus produce a response consistent with the pre-existing cognitive structure. It is not the purpose of this paper to propose a systematically inclusive formulation of these two classes of determinants, but rather to offer evidence concerning the efficacy of response reinforcement in the determination of attitudes.

* From William Abbott Scott, "Attitude Change through Reward of Verbal Behavior," *J. abnorm. soc. Psychol.*, 55, 72–75. Reprinted by permission of the author and the Managing Editor, the American Psychological Association.

[1] The author is indebted to Prof. Maurice P. Smith for his suggestions regarding design and report of the study, and to the following graduate teaching fellows who assisted in the collection of data: H. Hess, P. Khanna, A. Matthews, and I. Richardson.

Other studies (2, 5, 10) have demonstrated the influence of social approval and disapproval on the modification of verbal behavior, but they provide no information about their effects on the underlying attitudes. The present study was designed to explore, in a controlled fashion, the effects on attitudes of reward and punishment of expressed opinions. Specifically, it was predicted that subjects (Ss) rewarded by group approval for expressing opinions opposite from their initial attitudes would show a change in the direction of the expressed opinions, while Ss punished by group disapproval for expressing contrary opinions would not show such a change. This prediction implies that reward of a new behavior increases the relative strength of the underlying predisposition, while punishment of a new behavior leads the S to revert to his formerly preferred response disposition.

Method

All students in 29 general psychology discussion sections were administered free-response questions on mimeographed sheets to assess their attitudes toward three controversial issues:

1. *Universal military training.* It has been proposed that all physically able males between the ages of 18 and 25 be required to spend two years in the armed forces so that they will be trained and ready for armed service in the event of a national emergency. How do you feel about this proposal?

2. *Night hours for women students.* Senior women at the University are not required to be back in their dorms or houses by any set time at night. Some students are requesting that all women be given the same freedom of hours. How do you feel about this?

3. *De-emphasis of football.* It has been suggested that too much emphasis is placed on football at the University, in scholarships and special treatment for players. How do you feel about this?

Each of the classes was assigned, in systematic fashion, one of the three issues for debate. The instructor read the class members' opinions on the designated issue and selected from each class two which appeared definitely favorable and two definitely unfavorable. The four students were contacted outside of class and their cooperation requested in an "experiment to see how much they could affect the opinions of class members" by debating the particular issue; but each student would take the side opposite to his own opinion. Two pairs of debaters were formed for each class, members with "pro" opinions taking the "con" side of the argument, and vice versa. It was explained that, following the debate, the quality of performance would be assessed in two ways: first, by a class vote on which member of each pair did the better job; and second, by a retest of the class' opinions on the issue, "to see in which direction opinions are influenced."

The debaters were counseled to avoid mentioning to anyone that they didn't really believe what they were to say. (This was intended to help prevent the occurrence of interfering responses [see 7] which might negate the effect of the experimental stimulus.) In pairing the debaters, an attempt was made to equate their verbal abilities, as evidenced in their written opinions, in order that a subsequent false report of the vote would appear valid.

The debates were held two weeks after the original assessment of attitudes. One pair of opponents was called into the classroom, while the other pair waited in an adjoining room. The "pro" debater spoke first, for three minutes, followed by a three-minute presentation from the "con" debater. Then each had a two-minute rebuttal period, in reverse order. The first pair left the room, and the second pair of opponents entered for a similar performance. Then, with all four debaters present, voting instructions were given to the class ("On the first ballot write which side—pro or con—did a better job on the first debate. On the second ballot write which side—pro or con—did a better job on the second debate").

The ballots were handed in, and the instructor made a pretense of counting them, while one of the students tallied votes (as read by the instructor) on the blackboard, under the name of each debater. It had been determined in advance for each pair of debaters in all classes who would "win." "Winners" and "losers" were assigned alternately through the pairs of debaters, so that half the time the "pros" won, and half the time the "cons" won.

The instructor then repeated the implications of the vote, mentioning the names of the "winners" and "losers," and explained that the next step in the judgment would be to see how the class's attitudes had been affected. All class members were given sheets of paper on which were printed the statement of the issue that had been debated—exactly like the first opinion assessment, except that only one issue appeared on the sheet. Debaters were also asked to write their present opinions, "to see if there was any change in them."

After the opinion retest forms were collected, the nature and purpose of the experiment were explained, the pre- and postopinions of the debaters were read, and an attempt made to reduce the threat of the situation for the "losers" and for those debaters whose opinions had ostensibly shifted.

The pre- and postopinions of the debaters were subsequently typed on cards, after the deletion of certain passages that might indicate which were postopinions (such as "I still feel that . . ."). The cards were identified only by numbers, duplicated on the original opinion questionnaires, and the numbers assigned in "random" fashion, so as to prevent contamination in coding. Opinions on the cards were coded on a seven-point scale: 1—very pro; 2—pro; 3—pro, qualified; 4—neutral or balanced pro and con; 5—con, qualified; 6—con; 7—very con. Then, by reference to the original questionnaires, each card was identified as a pre- or postopinion of a "winner" or "loser."

Of the 58 pairs of debaters initially designated, only 36 finally produced complete data. Twenty-one pairs failed to debate, due either to absences or to rescheduling of classes; the postopinion of one member of the final pair was not codeable. The 36 debates took place in 19 different classes, with six different instructors. From these classes a sample of 36 students whose original opinions were definitely pro or con, but who did not debate, was selected as a control group. Their pre- and postopinions were similarly transferred to cards with random identification by numbers, and coded on the same seven-point scale.

Results

It was predicted that debaters who "won" would show an average change in the direction of their debate greater than the corresponding change shown by "losers" and greater than the average change of the control group. Data bearing on this prediction are presented in Table 1. Winners changed

TABLE 1. CHANGES OF WINNERS, LOSERS, AND CONTROLS FROM
PRE- TO POSTTEST
(Positive sign indicates mean change in direction opposite to Ss' original opinions)

	Winners, (N = 36)	Losers, (N = 36)	Controls, (N = 36)
Number of changers (either direction)	24	16	18
Number of changers (toward opp. direction)	21	7	11
Mean change	+1.25	−0.17	+0.31
SD of change	1.77	1.17	1.37

Difference in mean changes:
    Winners vs. losers: $t = 3.97$; $p < .001$.
    Winners vs. controls: $t = 2.49$; $p < .02$.
    Losers vs. controls: $t = 1.58$; $p > .10$.

an average of 1.25 points (in the direction of debate) on the seven-point scale, while losers changed an average of 0.17 points in the opposite direction (more extreme than their original positions). The control group changed an average of 0.31 points toward the opinion opposite from their original one.

The difference between mean changes of winners and losers is significant beyond the .001 level of confidence, and the difference between winners and controls is significant beyond the .02 level of confidence. The difference between losers and controls is not significant.

An analysis of mean changes for the three issues separately, and for original pros versus original cons showed no significant differences among these groups, so the prediction was confirmed regardless of the issue and regardless of which extreme opinion the debater started with. When the *proportions of changers* in the three groups are compared, results are consistent with those for mean changes. More winning individuals shifted toward the opposite opinion than either losers or controls.

Discussion

The experiment was designed to give both winners and losers equivalent contact with arguments for the opposite side, and to give both the experience of verbalizing these arguments as if they were their own. What distinguished the two groups was the brief experience of either group approval or group disapproval for their performances. These performances involved principally the oral presentation of arguments—verbal behavior to which they were unaccustomed. The vote of "win" is presumed to have reinforced the verbal behavior and with it the accompanying implicit responses —attitudes and cognitive support for them. The vote of "lose" presumably weakened whatever response tendencies had been established by the overt behavior or by cognitive contact with the opposite side, so that Ss reverted to their pre-existing attitudes.

If the opinion posttests be regarded as valid reflection of Ss' attitudes following the experimental stimulus, then one may conclude that social reward for expressing a new opinion tends to reinforce the concomitant attitudes, whereas social disapproval of the new behavior tends to lead to nonreinforcement of the accompanying attitudes. It appears that, in the present experiment, the brief experience of reward or punishment was a significant factor in accounting for attitude change, rather than the more prolonged experience of cognitive contact with opposing arguments.

This finding is, however, subject to at least two interpretations. It may be that reward of a new behavior was the crucial factor, while cognitive contact in and of itself had no effect. Or it may be that contact with opposing arguments produced a change in attitude, which was then reinforced or extinguished depending on whether the first overt expressions were rewarded or punished. Since Janis and King (6) showed that contact with the opposite side tended, by itself, to produce some change, the latter interpretation appears more plausible. In order to help determine the relative importance of these two influences—cognitive contact and reinforcement —in this situation, it would have been necessary to have some Ss debate without a subsequent "winning" or "losing" experience. This experiment did not provide for such a condition. Regardless of whether one accepts a single-factor or a two-factor interpretation of the results, it appears that they speak clearly for the significance of reward in producing attitude change in this type of situation.

It should be noted that very few of the changes in opinion were of a spectacular sort. (Only seven of the rewarded Ss reversed the direction of their opinions; the other fourteen changers merely showed some weakening of their initial opinions, as indicated by a shift along the seven-point scale toward the neutral position.) Although the experience of success or failure was made as strong as possible under these restricted conditions, it was nevertheless a brief and perhaps not too potent one. Between the announcement of the "class vote" and the posttest of opinion no more than five minutes elapsed.

The degree to which the new opinions persisted was not assessed in this study. It is reasonable to suppose that effects of the experimental situation were transitory, since the Ss' initial attitudes presumably found considerable social support in their current friendship groups. In order to produce enduring attitude changes, it would probably be necessary to so change the Ss' social environments that the new behaviors would receive continued reinforcement. But transitory or enduring, the principles of attitude change illustrated in this experiment would appear to be applicable.

Summary

An experiment in attitude change was suggested by Doob's learning theory of attitude development. Seventy-two Ss were induced to engage in debates on three different issues, taking sides opposite to those which they had indicated as their own in an opinion pretest. Half of the Ss were rewarded, in predetermined order, by a purported vote which proclaimed them the better debaters, while the other half were punished by presumably losing the debate. Posttests of Ss' opinions showed a tendency of the "winners" to change their opinions in the direction of their debates, while the "losers" did not change significantly. A control group of nondebaters likewise showed no significant change in opinions.

References

1. Carlson, E. Attitude change through modification of attitude structure. *J. abnorm. soc. Psychol.*, 1956, 52, 256–261.
2. Cohen, B. D., et al. Experimental manipulation of verbal behavior. *J. exp. Psychol.*, 1954, 47, 106–110.
3. Crockett, W. H. Attitude change as a function of cognitive differentiation and affect under conditions of norm-presentation with and without counter-arguments. Unpublished doctor's dissertation, Univer. of Michigan, 1952.
4. Doob, L. W. The behavior of attitudes. *Psychol. Rev.*, 1947, 54, 135–156.
5. Hildrum, D. C., & Brown, R. W. Verbal reinforcement and interviewer bias. *J. abnorm. soc. Psychol.*, 1956, 53, 108–111.
6. Janis, I. L., & King, B. T. The influence of role playing on opinion change. *J. abnorm. soc. Psychol.*, 1954, 49, 211–218.
7. Kelman, H. C. Attitude change as a function of response restriction. *Hum. Rel.*, 1953, 6, 185–214.
8. Krech, D., & Crutchfield, R. S. *Theory and problems of social psychology.* New York: McGraw-Hill, 1948. Chaps. 5–6.
9. Rosenberg, M. J. Cognitive structure and attitudinal affect. *J. abnorm. soc. Psychol.*, 1956, 53, 367–372.
10. Verplanck, W. S. The control of the content of conversation: reinforcement of statements of opinion. *J. abnorm. soc. Psychol.*, 1955, 51, 668–676.

The Concept of Adjustment

Perhaps no psychological concept in our everyday language is as popular as the term *adjustment*. Whether one happens to be describing the state of mind of a given individual, the repairing or resetting of a watch, or balancing a financial ledger, the concept of adjustment is likely to creep into our conversation. In everyday discourse the term may be used to convey a variety of different ideas. Yet we seldom find it necessary to stop and question the precise meaning of the word; rather, we hopefully rely on the context in which it is used to make the meaning clear to us. For example, we may speak of the need to *adjust* to something that is inevitable in order to express the idea that we must *accept* things over which we have no control. Or we may refer to adjusting as *growing accustomed* to a particular condition, such as adjusting to the seasonal changes in the weather. We may debate the importance of adjusting our behavior and opinions to those of others, or, in other words, *conforming* to the ways of the majority. Still other examples occur: We speak of adjusting our differences of opinion (*settling* them), adjusting our ideas to fit the facts (*making them more accurate*), adjusting our daily schedules (*regulating* them), and adjusting our wishes to those of others (*harmonizing* or *compromising* them).

This variety of meaning to which the concept of adjustment applies constitutes both an advantage and a limitation. On the one hand, the multiple meaning may act as a stimulant to our thinking more carefully and more broadly about a particular issue. Various associations with the word compel us to qualify and elaborate the idea we wish to express. In this way the generality of the concept may enhance clarity of thought and expression. On the other hand, we find ourselves using the term in an unclear and imprecise fashion. For example, we are prone to speak of someone's poor adjustment to a given set of circumstances, meaning no more than that we are dissatisfied with his behavior. When we speak of adjustment in a general way, without specifying our particular meaning, the idea communicated to our listener may be quite different from the one which we intended.

While the concept of adjustment in a psychological sense is less broad than in its everyday usage, it is nonetheless beset by many of the same complexities and difficulties that accompany its everyday usage. When we speak in psychological terms and refer to something about the individual—his state of mind, his manner of interacting with others, his mental health, or the degree to which he seems normal or abnormal—difficulties in communication are still present. In the readings that follow some of the problems associated with the psychological definitions of "adjustment" are considered together with suggested approaches for dealing with the problems.

The first selection by Wile deals with the meaning and criteria of normality-abnormality [1] and aptly expresses much of the confusion centering on the definitions of these concepts. Wile's proposal for mitigating the difficulties in communication that result from the diverse meanings and standards of mental health is that we supplement our terms with descriptive elaborations. For example, if we wish to indicate that an individual's behavior departs from the norm, it is necessary to do more than merely label him as abnormal or maladjusted; we must use additional words such as "unusual," "atypical," "deviant," or "idiosyncratic," in order to convey our specific meaning about his behavior.

The process of elaboration and qualification suggested by Wile undoubtedly aids communication. Its use in conveying a meaningful assessment of an individual in a psychological report or diagnostic evaluation is helpful. We might, however, question the utility of a term which fails to communicate clearly without additional elaboration. While such a procedure may be useful in formulating a general descriptive analysis of a person, its scientific utility is seriously limited. If we cannot eliminate the ambiguity concerning maladjustment, how can the factors which promote it be predicted and controlled?

The second selection again presents a discussion of the diverse meanings associated with adjustment or mental health, but here the focus is on research definitions of mental health and illness. In summarizing many of the definitions and methods of measuring mental health which have been reported in the psychological literature, Scott raises a number of cogent issues and problems. One

[1] While significant distinctions may be made between a normal and a well-adjusted person, and also between an abnormal and a maladjusted person, for purposes of the present discussion the concepts of normality and abnormality are considered synonymous with adjustment and maladjustment.

issue of particular significance is the extent to which the various criteria which have been proposed for mental health are interrelated. If the varied criteria for mental health used in research are not highly related, or are incompatible with one another, we must question the practice of thinking of these criteria as parts of a whole which we call maladjustment, abnormality, or mental illness. Scott appropriately points to the need for further research to investigate the relationships among the various criteria of mental health.

Tindall's research project represents an attempt congruent with Scott's suggestion. Tindall selected measures of adjustment which sample those commonly used for diagnostic and research purposes and compared each with the other. While many of the intercorrelations are beyond what might be expected by chance, his over-all findings indicate that it is reasonable to question the usefulness of the concept of adjustment as one global personality characteristic and to seek more than one measure for diagnostic and predictive purposes. We might wonder whether or not different relationships would be found with populations other than the one used in this study (perhaps with older or noninstitutionalized subjects) but this possibility only points to the need for further research along the lines of Tindall's work.

The two selections which follow represent more theoretical approaches to the study of adjustment than the previous ones. Both authors present their ideas about the criteria which define normality or adjustment, and while they differ radically from one another, each position stems from certain theoretical assumptions. Focusing on the abnormal or pathological, Slotkin takes the view that since most of man's behavior is learned within a cultural context, pathological behavior is influenced strongly by the particular setting in which the learning occurs. It follows that the nature of the abnormality varies from culture to culture, and further, that the criteria of what constitutes abnormality vary as well. Slotkin illustrates clearly that behavior which is considered pathological or maladjusted in one culture may be quite acceptable and customary in another. While he demonstrates the importance of cultural considerations in defining adjustment, his adoption of a cultural or relativistic definition of adjustment or maladjustment is less extreme than that proposed by others. Some investigators have argued that pathology by necessity must be relativistic since it represents an evaluative judgment made about an individual's behavior for which no absolute standards exist. Slotkin does not argue against the logic or possibility of making cultural comparisons or developing universal standards. He believes that similarities between cultures may promote similarities in the forms of pathology, and that broad concepts concerning adjustment will be developed which will enable us to make cross-cultural comparisons. Those theorists who adopt a more extreme relativistic position question the utility of developing concepts so broad that their use necessitates ignoring differences between cultures.

In sharp contrast with the relativistic position, Shoben presents a theoretical discussion of "the normal personality" and lists a number of characteristics which he regards as possible universal criteria for good adjustment. Underlying his thinking is the assumption that man by nature (regardless of the culture, society, or group to which he belongs) has certain "unique potentialities." The development of these potentialities is regarded as the broad criterion for mental health and the more an individual actualizes his potentialities, the better adjusted he is considered. Shoben's position may be termed an *idealistic* conception of adjustment since it stresses what man *could* be. If we were able to agree that all of mankind has the same direction or goal, we would be able to evaluate individuals or groups with respect to that goal. The task then, according to this reasoning, is to determine the goal or the specific unique potentialities or ideals of mankind. As Shoben indicates, psychology's efforts along these lines must be considered quite tentative.

The diversity of meaning and the problems associated with adjustment cited in the readings in this section by no means exhaust the issues involved. Additional questions certainly may be asked: If we accept the notion that an idealistic conception of adjustment is possible, how might we know when we have discovered it? On the other hand, if specific cultures define what constitutes adjustment, should we be content with the criteria voted by our culture? Should we attempt to influence it, and if so, how and according to what standards? When confronted with practical decisions, such as committing persons to institutions, initiating or terminating psychological treatment, or attempting to establish programs to promote mental health, to which of the various criteria of adjustment should we subscribe? How should we handle inconsistencies among the criteria which might lead us to make different decisions? But there is no need to expand on the problems involved; these undoubtedly will be apparent to the reader.

When considering the controversy and problems associated with the study of adjustment, the reader may respond in one of a number of ways. He may decide upon a definition which he finds suitable to his own purposes. He may question the fruitfulness of the entire argument and conclude that since we can never come to any agreement about the nature of adjustment, we therefore should discard the concept. A third response is to recognize that we can mean many things when we speak of adjustment or maladjustment, and that the selection of one criterion over another is quite arbitrary and depends on the individual making the judgment and his purpose. Thus rather than debate the merits of each criterion as to which *really* means adjustment, we can think in terms of the specific questions we wish to ask: How effective are this person's actions in enabling him to satisfy his needs? How well does he get along with others? How atypical or unconventional are his thoughts and actions, and what are their consequences? How happy is he? In asking these more specific questions we are likely to communicate more clearly with one another and reach greater agreement in our evaluations.

WHAT CONSTITUTES ABNORMALITY? *

(IRA S. WILE

What constitutes abnormality? It depends upon what constitutes normality. The all or none principle does not apply, since the same reaction may be sometimes normal and sometimes abnormal. Ill health is not the opposite of health, nor is insanity the opposite of sanity. "What is a really sane man? Most of us think of someone like ourselves which, perhaps, only goes to show how vague and how very various are our notions of the essentials of sanity and insanity" (1).

This idea is presented thus by Moss and Hunt (2): "We look at people or we observe conditions and too often call them normal or abnormal in accordance with the extent to which they fit in with our preconceived notions of what they should be. We make 'normal' correspond to 'desirable,' from our personal point of view—an attitude, alas, that leaves very little in the world that is universally called 'normal.'" This idea Hyslop (3) termed "Our own self-opinionated standards of mentality."

Abnormality varies according to the frame of reference—personal, familial, state, civil, economic, social or religious. Normality and abnormality are based upon prevailing concepts concerning physical, intellectual, ethical and moral elements with judgments concerning their social, asocial or antisocial implications.

Beliefs constantly change; wherefore subjective wishes, desires, opinions, judgments and their overt expression, reflect temporal emphases. The time

* From Ira S. Wile, "What Constitutes Abnormality?" *Amer. J. Orthopsychiat.*, 10, 216–228. Reprinted by permission of the Editor, *American Journal of Orthopsychiatry*.

factor affects the concepts of abnormality. One need but think of the once prevailing belief in witchcraft, ghosts, visions, in the efficacy of the royal touch, in the doctrine of signatures, in the power of asafoetida to ward off disease, in the Victorian values of feminine behavior or in the status of lynch law in frontier days.

The normal opinion may become abnormal as science grows, while ideas of abnormality are modified by spatial factors. Note the normal shifts in personal habits, such as eating with one's fingers, wearing wigs, spitting on the floor, scarring or painting the body. What is normal to one culture may be abnormal to another.

What are normal heredity and environment? What are normal income, companionships, interests? What are normal occupations, sleep, incompatibility? What is normal church-going, abnormal movie-going, normal school behavior, abnormal practices? What are the criteria for evaluation? Do they lie in the nature of the act or in the value to the actor? Are they based upon the functional meaning to the organism or the functional worth to society? Is crying normal or abnormal when it results from pain or from a desire for attention? When is corporal punishment normal or abnormal? Is the judgment concerning this value to be related to its potentially useful related service to the child or to society? Either way, why is it then so lacking in the culture of the American Indians?

In law the judge or jury make decisions according to the sanctioned subjective or objective standards. This view differs from that of the psychiatrist and psychologist.

There are numerous bases for judging abnormality. The subjective basis is undependable because of the variability of self-reference; the statistical is concerned with objective, but not equally measurable, deviations from an assumed standard; the materialistic seeks to pass judgment upon specific behaviors and their underlying causes. The hazard of self-reference depends upon the degree to which one's personal judgment fits in with that of his own or other groups. In terms of group ideas and mores the reformer, genius, and leaders in science, politics or religion, are among the abnormal.

Statistical extremes are readily differentiated, but there are borderlands where normality and abnormality are not readily separable. The child with IQ 70 and one with IQ 130 are equally distant from the median, but they are not considered equally abnormal because desirability beclouds statistical interpretation. Nonetheless, the high IQ group is more susceptible than the inferiors to severe functional mental disorders. What are the statistical differentials for abnormality of introversion, extraversion, truth, honesty, of memory and the forgettery, of sexual urge and mental conflict?

Specific differences of behavior are difficult to define. Some are definite as, for example, the presence or absence of the Widal, or the Wassermann reaction; the existence of bacilli-carriers, the presence of drug addiction. Classification of underlying causes or the nature of disturbances based upon degree of overt activity is difficult. Alcohol in excess and tea drinking in moderation are not readily defined because they are personal reactions. The use of hasheesh, the betal nut, chewing tobacco and chewing gum, like lying, stealing and sexual activity, offer problems in diagnosing abnormality from normality.

Is abnormality merely a variation and, if so, variation from what? If it is merely departure from type, then progress becomes possible only through abnormality. Is it wide variance from the average? If so, what are the normal limits of variation? Is the deviation from a factual or average type, or from an ideal or normative type? Abnormality, thus considered, means "distinctly deviating from a more or less precisely determined norm, standard or type."

The criterion, according to the *Dictionary of Philosophy and Psychology* (4), "applies more definitely to the process of judgment; it is the rule or mode of control as employed to assist judgment in making proper discriminations. The standard is the principle used to measure value, and to lay off a scale of values."

If the criterion is the deciding principle in forming judgments, and if the standard is the principle giving content to the adequate judgment, the norm —which regulates the value of the facts—may be the standard by which their relative worth is measured, and the criterion by which the individual is guided to a correct apprehension of these worths. Thus the norm is related to a criterion and a standard and yet norms help to determine the validity of criteria and standards. If one says, "A normal person is one who is not like the average person," the average person becomes the norm, but what criteria determine the validity of the norm?

What are the standards employed in devising the norm? Shall we support Knight's statement (5) ". . . a study of abnormal psychology (the futile, the wrong, and the inadequate) contributes to a dynamic understanding of normal behavior (the successful, the right, the adequate)." Does the abnormal determine the normal, or the normal the abnormal?

Shall we consider the normative position and view the normal as "an authoritative standard" representing an ideal with high, even religious, sanction? Or shall we use a negative concept of pathology and define as normal anyone "who has no unusual condition serious enough to be considered abnormal?" Shall we regard as abnormal the pathological and morbid or that which is undesirable? Bridges (6) emphasized the value of the normative and statistical conceptions. "According to the normative view the normal is regarded as the ideal function or the best possible adaptation," and then he frankly admits that it is impossible to give a definition of "best possible adaptation."

Reckless and Smith (7) emphasize the normal as the favorable or ideal and they interpret abnormality by the statistical approach as "the amount of deviation of a case from the degree of the factor possessed by the average person of the general population." This would make the average the normal, which is invalid, since a group average only localizes a group trend which varies among groups. The average may deviate greatly from the normative. The average number of physical defects among New York school children is approximately 3½ defects per child, hence a child without reported defect would be abnormal, because of marked deviation from the average.

If the principle of deviation is joined with the idea of favorable or unfavorable, one might refer to the supernormal or subnormal on the basis of beneficial or handicapping degrees of deviation from the average.

The median, rather than the average, deals with a central mathematical measurement, but medians are not static for identical data. They vary in cities of different size and for the same nationalities in different countries as, for example, the Japanese in California and Japan, or the Italians in New York and Rome. The median applies only to the group measured. Height and weight tables, presenting central tendencies for different ages at different heights, are not equally applicable in Minnesota and Louisiana, nor to races of pygmies and giants. If we regard abnormal as deviation from the norm or central tendency, the definite median is less valuable for determining abnormality. The mean and the median are less distinctive than the mode, but all are jeopardized by the fact that judgments based upon general statistics ignore the specific elements operative in the single individual as opposed to those which may have been at work in the group.

If there is no definite line separating the normal from the abnormal, should one depend upon some degree of the abnormal as represented by qualitative deviation from the median? Our desire for a hard and fast line leads us to build objective standards into which so much of the subjective enters that difficult problems arise in the use of various tables and scales. In the last analysis, abnormality involves a judgment dependent upon, and with reference to, the cause, the nature and the effect of the extent of variation from the locus of reference, whether it be the mean, median or mode. These judgments become difficult because numerous social and environmental differences do not appear in the statistical variation, nor may they be susceptible to quantitative measure. This is obvious when it is necessary to substitute qualitative descriptions in our scales and to find a numerical symbol to indicate the degree of fear, disobedience, gentleness, cruelty or dishonesty in behavior. The weakness is exemplified in the study of differences of behavior at various age levels, when the traits listed and evaluated are not possessed by 60 per cent of the group. If 5 per cent of six year olds desire to be fed and 5 per cent refuse to eat, both represent abnormal behavior. This would be equally true for the percentages of children who never have tantrums and the corresponding group who have them at a high frequency rate. What certainty is there of the abnormality of these types of behavior with reference to nervous tensions, emotional insecurity or adaptation in later life? Figures concerning habits, for example, may be more related to exposure to habit formation than to the presence or non-presence of the behavior studied in terms of normality or abnormality.

If abnormality is marked deviation from a dominant norm, i.e., non-conformity with a group type, is a white man abnormal in the black belt, and an Irish Catholic at a Russian Jewish Center, or a woman without goitre in a Swiss village? Are all our leaders, agitators, inventors, creators of new philosophical ideas, protagonists for special therapies, to be regarded as abnormal? The idea of abnormality implies a deviating relationship of the individual from some group. Abnormality includes super-normality, hence genius is as abnormal as dullness; a precocious memory as a facile forgettery; and hyper- as hypo-emotionalism.

The word *abnormal* would apply to individuals whose general or special reactions exhibit slight deviation from expectancy. This term carries none of the implications of *abnormality*, but would require social localization because of the variations of mores in space and time. The concept of abnormality in economics is sensed from the statement: "The course of action which might be expected under certain conditions from the members of an industrial group is the normal action of the members of that group." This implies that norms vary in expression because there are groups within groups. The reactions of a person vary if he is at the same time a member of a religious sect, a communist cell, an athletic club, a co-educational high school and a fraternity. His patterns of action are delimited by his several participations, and judgments concerning their normality would depend upon the varied group patterns and the differing judgments of each group upon particular behaviors.

Abnormality requires reference, whether to economics, disease, education or sex activity. Why over-emphasize sex, if sex behavior is a constant factor and, if masturbation is as prevalent as alleged, why treat it as an abnormality? It is difficult to evaluate experiences involving habits and mores because personal or familial reference may reflect a complete normality which is rejected by the community. This applies to such behavior as the practice of nudism in the home, or emphasis upon the stork story of birth.

In considering relationships it is necessary to know what follows a reaction, which is non-existent in the absence of that reaction. Once all mental defectives were regarded as potential criminals. Is mental deficiency provocative of juvenile delinquency? Are most mental defectives delinquent? Does juvenile delinquency occur in children who are non-defective? Many children who are from broken homes reach the Juvenile Courts, but how many children from such homes do not? What factors operate when there are two or more variables in the background? Which is the abnormal one or the one that conduces to abnormality? What factors are incidental to multiple causation as opposed to direct or precipitant causation? Which factor constitutes the urge or stimulus to deviate behavior, of whatever degree? Such questions are not readily answerable.

Recognizing the distinction between normal and normative, is abnormality determined by utility values? This might hold true for myopia and color blindness, polydactyly and degenerating third molars. The utility values of lying, stealing and truancy cannot be clearly stated. Are values determinable on the basis of Southard's (8) division of evils into the medical, educational, moral, legal and economic factors? The duration of breast feeding by Italian women differs in the United States and in Italy. If utility is the reference point, is the decline normal or abnormal in the light of maternal occupation and the infant mortality rate for artificially fed infants? To whom shall the utility be referred—to the individual, his group, his city, state, nation, world or the cosmos?

Esthetic values may attach to utility values. How far are leanness and fleshiness abnormal? Is a moderate naevus on the face viewed with the same feeling of abnormality as a similar naevus on the less exposed part of the anatomy? Is not extreme beauty as abnormal as ugliness? And are standards of beauty constant among nations, regardless of endocrine theories? Abnormality is a relative term indicating some deviation from a theoretic standard which practically is not constant. The idea of a norm is static but the norm itself is dynamic. A tall person among the short, the redheaded among the black, an albino among the white, show the labile norm as easily as Gulliver's variation in deviation among the Lilliputians and the Brobdingnagians.

In judging abnormality one considers norms of variables whose interacting relations demand evaluation. In estimating physical health the individual is judged as a whole, but different parts and systems of his organization are also evaluated. The weakness in the physical field appears when one asks what is an abnormal tonsil and what constitutes malnutrition. A variety of theoretic evidences of physical fitness exist but they must find unity. The concept of unity is helpful because the use of any one as a basis of judgment would be as meaningless as one or two Lombrosian stigmata.

Disease is a relative matter and abnormal behavior may be deemed disease. Can we differentiate an occasional or acute abnormality, an habitual or chronic abnormality, an episodic or sub-acute abnormality? A single event may reveal a highly significant deviation that suggests abnormality, while a series of events may not establish it. Shall the standards of normality and abnormality be based upon conscious, purposeful behavior or that due to irresponsible urges and unconscious conflicts? Disease disregards both criteria.

What conscious and unconscious factors determine beliefs in devils and witchcraft, in duppies and voodooism? Cotton Mather was regarded as normal in his acceptance of witchcraft and as abnormal in his espousal of vaccination. Protecting against the evil eye, the wearing of amulets, the use of flagellation, the exhibition of hysteria, the mob spirit in action, the jitterbug, social hypocrisy, the pursuit of power, pressures for social reform, the intolerant totalitarian states, the urged reform of marriage and divorce, are behaviors concerning which one might ask, are they essentially morbid? Are they sufficiently pathological to require treatment? Does normal behavior always represent the wholesome and the beneficial; if not, should it be regarded as normal? Clearly the norm is not static—the same behavior may be normal or abnormal. A dry mouth is not normal under many conditions, but it is in a state of fear or fever. Lying is differentiated from pathological lying, phantasy and imagination are not far apart. The normal style of today is abnormal tomorrow and the absolutes of yesterday appear to be the relatives of today.

Discussions of abnormality depend upon established, though variable, criteria. Some give pronouncements of abnormality based upon their own interests. The factors, elements or characteristics of criteria are diverse for various disciplines. Abnormal, as deviation from the customary or usual, calls for a reconciliation with the doctrine of individual differences. How far does the behavior of an individual depart from its customary expression? To what extent does it differ from the customary practice of his group or groups? Much depends on whether the frame of reference is the norm of the self or the norm of a group of which the self is a member. What is normal for one person may appear abnormal when he is compared with his or another group. The reactions of the homosexual, sadistic, post-encephalitic, neurotic or paranoid person illustrate this. Statistics present facts numerically. The meaning lies not in the statistical table or graph but in its interpretation, following some accepted criteria. What are the criteria for departures from anatomic norms? Asthenic and pyknic are useful concepts, but how are they to be interpreted as isolated types? Is an age-height-weight chart a satisfactory norm for evaluating an individual's deviation? What is the normal developmental level of an individual uncompared with others? When is the extent of carpal ossification proof of normality? What is the normal size of the sella turcica? A club foot, intrauterine amputations or congenital cataract are better defined as anomalies, malformations or structural changes—terms which, like hypertrophy, dystrophy and atrophy do not emphasize abnormality.

Ritter wisely comments (9): "Normality, both in function and in structure, consists not in rigid, invariable activities and organs but in a ceaseless play of constitutionally antagonistic forces and structures." This becomes evident in discussing deviations from physiological norms. In fear, are rapid pulse rate and heightened blood pressure normal or abnormal? Is the polycythaemia of congenital heart disease not normal? Is not fever a normal defensive responsive reaction? Is a limp, to save a cut foot, abnormal? In metabolic rates, as in the chemistry of blood and urine, wide degrees of variation characterize normality. The physiological criteria for purely physical phenomena tend to establish distinction on the basis of the pathological rather than the abnormal. The criteria in the field of mental health also deal with the pathological, which is often termed the abnormal, with a relative rather than an absolute meaning. Abnormality is thus recognized as one of degree rather than of kind. When does a neurotic become the victim of a neurosis; when are the prepsychotic pronounced psychotic?

There is no psychology abnormal *per se*. An organ, including the brain, may offer symptomatic responses that differ from customary expectancy. If the organ itself is weakened, diseased, or congenitally inadequate, its functional activity would be the normal for such an organ, although called an abnormal reaction. If behavior arises from a combination of organic activities, is the behavior itself abnormal when it follows deviated function? There may be abnormal organs or brains yielding stimuli which are pathological as deviations from accepted or standardized structural and functional norms.

Normality and abnormality appear to be related to function rather than to structure. Burnham (10) writes: "The normal mind is not one that is perfectly integrated and free from defects, arrests of development, or even from attitudes and habits of thought similar to those of pathological conditions, but rather it is a mind that can compensate for its defects and for its weaknesses, that can correct its own errors and is able to control its pathological tendencies, or, in a single word, a mind that under ordinary conditions can function normally." While he begs the question by leaving in doubt what he means by "function normally," the basic concept is one of adjustment. The essential factor in judgment concerning abnormality becomes the degree of non-adjustment of an organ, or an organism, in the light of its capacity and the demands made upon it.

The criterion for intellectual variations is usually some standard scale or test. The total content of intelligence is not yet measurable. There are definite talents and there are partial plus and minus values for specific functions. Plus values are as abnormal as equal minus values, but they receive different social sanctions. The criteria for intellectual activity, as measured in terms of initiative, judgment, imagination, aggression and submission, depend upon inconstant factors of time, place, group and external pressures. With the best of standards interpretations vary. Is school failure abnormal when the school demands more than a student can produce? Is truancy as a response to a sense of failure normal or abnormal? Is mental incompetence abnormal or normal as the response of an inadequate mechanism? Disregarding IQ standards, who is feebleminded? The answer involves not merely the mental level but an inability to get along in the world, an inability to manage one's own affairs with ordinary prudence and to compete with one's normal fellows. Intellectual abnormality is more than an IQ below 70 or 90 or above 110 or 150. There is a distinction between the inferior who is incomplete in structure and the abnormal who may be inadequate, although superior in mental organization. The problem of abnormality in the broader mental field depends largely upon the concepts of those who sit in judgment.

The criteria for emotional deviations are more difficult. There is the distinction between potential and kinetic emotion. Adequacy or inadequacy is largely interpreted with relation to the occasion. What are normal emotional reactions in marital relations; normal and abnormal emotional reactions in parent-child relationships; what is normal and abnormal in righteous moral indignation and emotional revolt? What is the normality and abnormality of the emotional factors involved in the Inquisition, the Reformation, the religious ecstasy and secular enthusiasm? There are no standards, but there are definite opinions on a basis of the desirable and the wholesome.

Analyses of children's behavior in terms of the frequency rates of particular types of emotional reaction usually fail to indicate the degree of reaction. They cannot indicate the degree of the eliciting stimulus nor show that the reaction is proper, proportionate, wholesome or desirable. There is reason in McDougall's apology (11): "I ask the reader to pardon my use of the expression 'abnormal psychology' in the restricted sense of psychology of functional disorders." What is the standard of intensity, duration or frequency for fear, rage or love? What is the normal or abnormal expression of an emotion in terms of a specific personality?

Is Rosanoff correct in stating that a normal person is characterized by "inhibitions, emotional control, a superior durability of mind, rational balance and nervous stability?" If this be true, at what age is normality reached? Is a normal person always inhibited, and what is meant by rational balance and nervous stability?

If one compares specific traits among psychotic and non-psychotic children, what is learned depends upon the traits selected. Michaels and Goodman (12), for example, found thumb sucking present to the extent of 5.8 per cent among psychotics and 24.5 per cent among normals; temper tantrums, 29.5 per cent among psychotics and 14.5 per cent among normals; fears, 8.9 per cent among psychotics and 45 per cent among normals; nail biting, 21.4 per cent among psychotics and 51.3 per cent among normals. Are the traits normal or abnormal? They found enuresis persistent after age ten significantly more frequent in the psychotic group, but was it any more abnormal for them than for a normal group? In their psychotic subjects they found no tendency to a positive correlation between enuresis and the presence or absence of 41 various factors, nor did they find any relation between enuresis and any type of psychosis. Was the psychosis one form of abnormality and the enuresis another, or were they related, and if so, how were they related as abnormalities?

Abnormality concerns departures from social, cultural standards. In the light of mores, behavior is amoral, moral or immoral; in terms of social desirability, behavior is social, asocial or anti-social. Ideas of ethics make behavior right or wrong. Social law creates the categories of delinquent and criminal behavior. Social standards are not fixed, even though they are temporal and arbitrary and social judgments vary with time, place and circumstance. If variation from socially accepted norms *de facto* is abnormality, then all minorities and all unwonted or uncomfortable situations are abnormal, and all efforts at social reorganization or disorganization would be thus categorized. Dance manias, tarantism and jitter-bugs, belief in devils with cloven hoofs, horns and tails, are no more abnormal than escape from epidemic diseases attacking a majority of the population. Was surviving the black plague or smallpox an abnormal reaction?

Crime is a social phenomenon and there is no natural line separating the criminal and non-criminal. The difference between diplomacy and duplicity lies in social values. As Comte suggested, "The social side of man's mental life determines his content far more than does his biology." Delinquency is an arbitrary legal demarcation, a social rather than a psychological concept—a problem of degree in reaction, complicated by apprehension and social attitude.

Any definition of abnormality should involve the three categories Alexander claims enter into personality (*13*). Recognizing that their relational quantitative significance cannot be determined, he said, "There are three categories of factors affecting personality, all interrelated yet distinct: (1) *hereditary* factors, (2) early high individual *emotional experiences in the family situation* which are not typical for a race or a culture but only for one specific family and (3) finally, those *cultural influences* to which all members of a particular social group are equally exposed." Zilboorg (*14*) notes that it is impossible to establish specific relationships "unless we first establish a proper yard stick by which personality traits and cultural characteristics can be measured equitably."

The implications of social standards create difficulties because judgment cannot rest merely upon that which is desirable. Some extreme deviations from the mediocrity of the norm are desirable and others are undesirable. The world needs the genius and the superlative artist, but also those who are willing to fight against the *status quo* and to oppose the comfortable smugness of a non-progressive majority. Unfortunately poverty, disease, frustration are not called abnormal.

Evidently there is no acceptable norm for most of our psychological reactions. If behavior is harmful to the individual, it is usually considered abnormal, but the connotation changes if the harmfulness results from service to others. Social approbation largely defines the nature and extent of abnormality. In the language of Dorcus and Schaffer (*15*) "Social approbation of actions determines to a considerable degree the classification of an individual as 'normal' or 'abnormal.' We do not mean that social approbation itself is necessarily the determining factor, but that the person who cannot distinguish between what is socially approved and what is not, probably lacks in observation or in reasoning ability. Deficiency in one of its aspects is a primary basis for his 'abnormal' behavior." This concept is supportive of Hollingsworth's (*16*) suggestion that a norm is "a rule or authoritative standard" which tells us how we ought to think or act. This is normative rather than statistical.

The abnormal is not always undesirable, for example, high IQ or selfless sacrifice. Society is more troubled, however, by responses less effective than those of the average individual, regardless of whether the behavior is personally dysgenic. There is a confusion among ideas of average performance, standards of excellence and standards of inadequacy. A central tendency principle establishes normality as mediocrity. Group facts measured in terms of desirability or in terms of thoroughness possess different values of normality and abnormality. There is a distinction between the successive records of an individual's actions and of those of his group. The behavior of members of the Ku Klux Klan, of the religious sect of Thugs, or of members of Unions or Employer's Associations, involve different standards of normality in terms of each group and in terms of the society in which they operate. Judgments differ concerning encephalitis and schizophrenia, because of differences in origin. Insanity is more likely to be called abnormality than most sequelae of physical disease. Is insanity more abnormal than arthritis deformans or brain tumor, because socially less desirable?

Allowance must be made for shifts in social outlook and their relation to changing goals and practices. An active pacifist during war is condemned as anti-social although during peace he is rated social. The bases of rightness or wrongness, normality or abnormality, are found in social judgments, although individuals maintain their own opinions. To use magnetism in therapy today would appear abnormal; hypnotism is now a selective procedure; psychoanalysis as a panacea is as abnormal as the use af amulets, incantations and magic, which once were deemed normal. Treatment by means of sacred objects continues to be accepted as normal by large communions.

Altering ideas challenge concepts of abnormality. Many opinions concerning incompetence are wholly irrational. Average minds are affected by the opinions of those they call abnormal. Present accepted forms of music once were hissed as perverting all music. Art norms shift from classicism to surrealism. Each introduction of the strange brings forth the cry that it is abnormal. May not normality itself be dysgenic in that it limits variation? Is there not a difference between the normality of abnormals and the abnormality of normals? Jastrow (17) wrote, "Logically considered 'abnormal psychology' is the proper name for the entire body of doctrine, the system of interpretation, the development of concepts, under which the mental expert of to-day proceeds, whatever his direct or indirect purpose." This makes abnormal what the expert considers abnormal because "a fertile principle of abnormal psychology is that all the distinctive abnormal tendencies, many of which may be viewed as temperamental issues or liabilities, appear in the normal mind in restrained form, active on a smaller scale, a counterpart in miniature" (18). The abnormal then is latent in the normal, but what constitutes it in the abnormal?

Abnormality is also classed as primary or secondary. Thus congenital deafness would be primary and deafness following otitis secondary. It is also distinguished as organic and functional. Is it not also important to indicate whether an activity arises from the conscious or the unconscious level? Personal idiosyncrasy, individual difference, pure individualism, as such, involve abnormality, while the common factors of action would constitute normality. Deviations, however, are not abnormal, if a wide range of variation is accepted in the concept of normality. The hypothetical average is unsafe for diagnosis.

Individual or group intolerance may create the idea of abnormality for minor deviations. The projection of one's personal inadequacies upon others may lead to a designation as abnormal of the trends one desires to forget or resist. Considering individuals in terms of their potentials leads to the conclusion that everyone is abnormal in some respects, but this does not mean that everyone is pathological or undesirable. Science leaves many traits and functions still unmeasured, such as temperament, character, emotionality and primary urges. A regular curve of distribution for each and all traits does not localize any particular person nor indicate which traits are temporary or permanent, remediable or irremediable.

Behavior, as response, might be assumed always to be a normal reaction, particularly as there is no method of measuring the intensity of all stimuli. It is difficult to hold that overt behavior is abnormal unless it is due to conscious action. Behavior determined by unconscious conflicts cannot be called abnormal until some norm for behavior acceptable under the impact of unconscious mechanisms is accepted. What is the normal human response toward the Oedipus complex, the inferiority complex, and when do the reactions to such complexes become abnormality? If the Oedipus complex is universal, it is normal; but this does not define its normal form of expression. It is as unwise to generalize about normality of unconscious function as it is to accept statistical evaluations as reliable beyond indicating the frequency rate. If one can escape rationalization only by continued psychoanalysis, then rationalization is normal. If acceptance of a procedure by the mass is normative, then all psychogenetic doctrine may possibly be abnormal. Again, progress in theory and therapy depends upon variation.

Socrates, with his spirit voice, Caesar with his seizures, tempestuous Edward I of England, the bibulous Henry the Eighth, Ivan the Terrible and Catherine the Great, along with Peter the Hermit and his crusaders, Pope Innocent VIII and his "witch-finders," Paracelsus and the Alchemists, Mohammed, Swedenborg and Joan of Arc and their visions, Luther and his Devil, even Columbus and his voice, and "Toms o'Bedlams," all have their counterpart in the deviates of today. We have our Blakes and our Turners, our wise and our stupid, our warriors, pacifists, philosophers and explorers, saints, sinners and materialists, who are as abnormal as rapists or kidnapers. We have those who would prohibit and those who should inhibit, as man struggles to meet the demands of his day, or to challenge his environment. The abnormals comprise those who threaten human rights and those who right human wrongs. The former are rejected as unworthy, the latter accepted as worthy. Both types serve the continuity and development of society under the stress of changing ideas and ideals. Whether or not they are always deemed abnormal depends upon the moving locus of judgment.

Dogmatism is dangerous when a questioning attitude is essential for judgment. I believe we should relegate the term abnormal to lay usage. We should set forth impressions and judgments by scientific definition or accurate description. There is no dichotomy of good and bad, right and wrong, health and disease, sane and insane, normal and abnormal. We should formulate possible frames of reference for diagnostic judgments; we should depend less upon figures of incidence and frequency, as though they revealed the existence of identical stimulus and response mechanisms in all people. This is contrary to probability, if one accepts the principle of individual and cultural differences which must include diversities in susceptibility to stimuli and capability of response.

Knowing the tendency to project the normal against the background of the abnormal, we should admit that we lack a sufficiently definite background of abnormality to enable us to define normality in terms of the abnormal. The term abnormal interpreted liberally should carry no connotation of opprobrium, nor should it be regarded as the equivalent of morbidity or disease, the unpleasant or undesirable. The abnormal is not synonymous with the pathological or morbid. Many abnormalities are not pathological deviations, such as various idiosyncrasies or marked individual differences of a wholly benign nature.

I agree with Jastrow (19): "Its underlying connotation is that of pronounced or significant variation from rather well defined accepted norms. . . . The mere uncommonness of a phenomenon has little relation to its significance as an abnormal variation. The abnormal is not the monstrous. . . . It is not the mere fact of difference, but of a difference that yields in analyses a knowledge of its nature, that gives to the abnormal its true significance."

The term abnormal should be supplanted in orthopsychiatry by a more specific and informative terminology. The semantic problem involved in normal and abnormal can be solved by employing terms which indicate specifically what it is desired to express. We should employ such terms as legal and illegal, wilfully culpable, inadvertently culpable and non-culpable. We might use such expressions as hereditary and acquired; inferior, average and superior; reasonable and unreasonable; conscious, subconscious and unconscious; customary and anomalous; purposeful, incidental and accidental; usual and unusual; slight, marked and great deviation; desirable and undesirable; healthful and pathological; benign and malignant; disordered, diseased and morbid; social, asocial and anti-social; distinctive and non-distinctive; significant, insignificant and pathognomonic; relative and absolute; temporary or occasional, permanent or habitual; adjusted and maladjusted; endogenous and exogenous; correct and incorrect; right and wrong; remediable and irremediable.

By this procedure we would receive specific impressions upon which to base rational interpretations.

Bibliography

1. Robert, Harry, and Nelson, M. G. *The Troubled Mind*. New York: E. P. Dutton & Co., 1939, p. 120.
2. Moss, F. A., and Hunt, T. *Foundations of Abnormal Psychology*. New York: Prentice-Hall, 1932.
3. Hyslop, Theodore B. *The Great Abnormals*. London: Philip Allan & Co., 1925.
4. *Dictionary of Philosophy and Psychology*. Edited by James M. Baldwin. New York: The Macmillan Co., 1928.
5. Knight, F. B. Introduction to *The Psychology of Abnormal People* by J. J. B. Morgan. New York: Longmans, Green, 1928.
6. Bridges, James W. *Psychology, Normal and Abnormal*. New York: D. Appleton & Co., 1930, p. 14.
7. Reckless, W. C., and Smith, M. *Juvenile Delinquency*. New York: McGraw-Hill Book Co., 1932.
8. Southard, E. E., and Jarrett, Mary C. *The Kingdom of Evils*. London: George Allen & Unwin, Ltd. New York: The Macmillan Co.
9. Ritter, William E. *The Unity of the Organism*. Boston: Richard G. Badger, 1919.
10. Burnham, William E. *The Normal Mind*. New York: D. Appleton & Co., 1925.
11. McDougall, William. *Outline of Abnormal Psychology*. New York: Charles Scribner's Sons, 1926, p. 1.
12. Michaels, J. J., and Goodman, Sylvia E. *Arch. Neurol. and Psychiat.* 40 (4): pp. 698–706.
13. Alexander, Franz. "A Tentative Analysis of the Variables in Personality Development," *Am. J. Orthopsychiatry*, 8 (4): 589, 1938.
14. Zilboorg, Gregory. *Ibid.*, p. 596.
15. Dorcus, Roger, and Schaffer, G. Wilson. *Textbook of Abnormal Psychology*. Baltimore: The Williams & Wilkins Co., 1934.
16. Hollingsworth, H. L. *Abnormal Psychology*. New York: Ronald Press Co., 1930.
17. Jastrow, Joseph. Introduction to *Readings in Abnormal Psychology and Mental Hygiene*. Edited by W. S. Taylor. New York: D. Appleton & Co., 1926, p. 20.
18. *Ibid.*, p. 28.
19. Jastrow, Joseph. *The Subconscious*. New York: Houghton Mifflin, 1906.

DEFINITIONS OF MENTAL HEALTH
AND ILLNESS *

(WILLIAM ABBOTT SCOTT [1]

A serious obstacle to research in the area of mental illness lies in the lack of a clear definition of the phenomenon to be studied. The term "mental ill health" has been used by different researchers to refer to such diverse manifestations as schizophrenia, suicide, unhappiness, juvenile delinquency, and passive acceptance of an intolerable environment. Whether some or all of these various reactions should be included in a single category of "mental illness" is not clear from a survey of the current literature. Theories describing the nature and antecedents of one sort of disturbance rarely relate it to another, and there is a paucity of research evidence indicating the extent to which such manifestations are empirically intercorrelated.

In the face of such ambiguity it would appear useful to attempt an organized review of the various definitions of mental illness which are explicit or implicit in recent research, with a view toward highlighting their commonalities and discrepancies on both a theoretical and an empirical level. Such a presentation might help students concerned with causative factors to assess the comparability of previous research findings on correlates of "mental illness," and also point toward some next steps in research to discover the degree to which these diverse phenomena represent either unitary, or multifold, psychological processes.

The research criteria for mental illness to be reviewed here are subsumed under the following categories: (1) exposure to psychiatric treatment; (2) social maladjustment; (3) psychiatric diagnosis; (4) subjective unhappiness; (5) objective psychological symptoms; and (6) failure of positive adaptation. For each category we shall review studies which appear to

* From William Abbott Scott, "Research Definitions in Mental Health and Mental Illness," *Psychol. Bull.*, 55, 29–45. Reprinted by permission of the author and the Managing Editor, the American Psychological Association.

[1] This review was prepared for the Survey Research Center, University of Michigan, as background material for that organization's national survey of mental health, sponsored by the Joint Commission on Mental Illness and Health. The writer is indebted to Dr. Gerald Gurin of the Survey Research Center, and to Dr. Fillmore Sanford, formerly of the Joint Commission, for their contributions to the ideas presented here. Also appreciation is due the following researchers for their suggestions and for data from current studies which they provided: Harry Beilin, John Clausen, Benjamin Darsky, John Glidewell, Marie Jahoda, Morton Kramer, Thomas Langner, Charles Metzner, M. Brewster Smith, and Shirley Star.

have employed the definition, either explicitly or implicitly. This will be accompanied by a critical discussion of the adequacy of each definition, together with an assessment, based on empirical data where possible, of the relation between this and other definitions. Finally, we shall attempt to summarize the differences among the definitions, by indicating their divergent approaches to certain basic problems in the conceptualization of mental illness and health.

Mental Illness as Exposure to Psychiatric Treatment

The most frequently used operational definition of mental illness, at least in terms of the number of studies employing it, is simply the fact of a person's being under psychiatric treatment. And this definition is usually restricted to hospital treatment, rather than outpatient service. Nearly all the ecological studies (e.g., 3, 16, 22, 30, 35, 50) and most of the studies correlating mental illness with demographic characteristics (e.g., 5, 19, 29, 41, 47) use this as a criterion. They obtain their information from hospital records or, in unusual instances (e.g., 28), from psychiatrists in the area who furnish information about persons treated on an outpatient basis.

Such a definition of mental illness is operational rather than conceptual, but its implicit meaning for the interpretation of research results is that anyone who is regarded by someone (hospital authorities, relatives, neighbors, or himself) as disturbed enough to require hospitalization or outpatient treatment is mentally ill, and people who do not fit into such diagnoses are mentally healthy. Use of hospital records, moreover, requires that the criterion of the nature of the mental illness be the diagnosis which appears on the record.

Shortcomings of such an operational definition are recognized by no one better than its users. The reliability of psychiatric diagnosis is of course open to question, and any attempt to determine correlates of particular kinds of mental disturbance must take into account the large error inherent in the measuring process. (One study of the association between diagnosis at Boston Psychopathic Hospital and previous diagnoses of the patients at other hospitals showed only 51 per cent above-chance agreement between the two [cf. 15, pp. 42–43].)

If "under the care of a psychiatrist" is to be regarded as the criterion of mental illness, one must realize the automatic limitation on the size of the mentally ill population that such a definition imposes. Kramer (34, p. 124) has estimated that the maximum possible number of mentally ill, under such a definition, would be less than 7,000,000, given the present number of available psychiatrists.

It has been suggested by both sociologists (7, 10) and physicians (17) that different rates of hospital admissions for different geographical areas may indicate more than anything else about the areas the relative degree

to which the communities tolerate or reject persons with deviant behavior
(11). Or as the Chief of the National Institute of Mental Health puts it:
researchers using hospital records are dependent on the public's rather un-
even willingness to give up its mentally ill members and to support them
in institutions (17); this in addition to the admittedly unstandardized and
often substandard methods of record-keeping used by the various hospitals
is likely to render incomparable prevalence and incidence data from various
geographical areas.

The effects of such differential thresholds for admission in various communities are difficult to estimate, since they cannot be uniform from study
to study. In 1938 a house-to-house survey in Williamson County, Tennessee,
yielded nearly one person diagnosed as psychotic, but never having been in
a mental hospital, for every hospitalized psychotic from the county (48).
By contrast, Eaton found in his study of the Hutterites (14) that more intensive canvassing by psychiatrists did not yield a larger number of persons
deemed psychotic than did a more superficial count based on community
reports.

Eaton's study *did* yield higher proportions of neurotic diagnoses the more
intensive the case finding procedure became, and this observation relates
to the finding in New Haven that neurotics under outpatient treatment
came disproportionately from the upper socioeconomic strata (28). At first
consideration, such differential rates seem readily attributable to the cost of
psychiatric treatment, but Hollingshead and Redlich prefer to seek an explanation in the greater social distance between lower-class neurotics and
the psychiatrists than in the case of middle- and upper-class neurotics.
Whatever the sources of rate differences, it is clear that such correlations
as have been reported make one wary of the hospital admissions or outpatient figures as indicative of the "true" incidence of psychiatric disorders.
Thus the criterion of exposure to psychiatric treatment is at best a rough
indicator of any underlying conceptual definition of mental illness.

Maladjustment as Mental Illness

Adjustment is necessarily determined with reference to norms of the
total society or of some more restricted community within the society.
Accordingly, one may conceptually define adjustment as adherence to
social norms. Such a definition of mental health has an advantage over
the preceding in encompassing a range of more-or-less healthy, more-or-less
ill behavior, rather than posing a forced dichotomy. The operation for assessing mental health by this criterion might ideally be a community (or other
relevant group) consensus concerning a given subject's degree of adjustment. This has been approximated by at least one set of studies (1, 2).

Rather than assess consensus by pooling many divergent individual
opinions, it is possible to assume that a law or other visible sign of social

norms constitutes the criterion against which adjustment is determined. Such reference is employed in studies of suicide (12, 26) or juvenile delinquency (25) or divorce (39, 53) as indicants of maladjustment. While the operational criterion may become dichotomous in such cases (whether or not the person comes in contact with the law), this is not necessarily so. Gordon (21) has suggested considering the "biologic gradient" of suicide, extending from contemplation of the act to its actual accomplishment.

Finally, it would be possible to assess degree of adjustment with reference to some externally defined set of requirements for a given social system. Thus a work situation might be seen as demanding a high level of productivity from all its members, and the degree of adherence to this standard becomes the criterion of adjustment, without reference to the individual opinions of the group members or to the manifest norms of the group. This criterion of conformity to the requirements of a given social structure has not been explicitly employed by any of the researchers covered in the present review, but it has been hinted at (37) and remains a possibility, provided that the structural requirements of a social system can be determined independently of the members' behaviors.

Theory of social structure suggests that these three criteria of adjustment would tend toward congruence: The demands of a particular social system lead to the development of social norms, which are expressed in laws or customs and also in the individual participants' notions of what is acceptable behavior. Lack of congruence may be taken as evidence of cultural lag, of poor correspondence between manifest and latent function within the social structure, or of defensive psychological processes within the participating individuals. Since all of these factors supporting discrepancy do occur within most social systems, the criteria may be expected to yield somewhat different results.

When maladjustment is assessed by community consensus, one finds considerable divergence of opinion among various segments of the public regarding what constitutes good and poor adjustment. The Minnesota Child Welfare studies (1) showed differences in criteria for assessing adjustment among different occupational groups in the community. Teachers tended to emphasize standards different from those emphasized by ministers, who in turn displayed some differences from a more heterogeneous group of community adults. Beilin concludes that it is meaningless to discuss "adjustment" in the abstract or to contemplate the prediction of "adjustment" in general. One must specify *adjustment to what, adjustment to whose standards* (2). Lindemann reflects this relativistic conception of mental health when he states: "We find it preferable not to talk about a 'case' in psychiatry—rather we try to assess functional impairment in specific situations as viewed by different professional groups in the community. So a 'case' is really a relationship of possibly pathogenic situation and appropriate or inappropriate behavior to that situation. It is often a matter of arbitrary choice whether such a person becomes an object of psychiatric care" (38, p. 130).

Thus, though adjustment appears a more conceptually adequate criterion of mental health than does exposure to treatment, the necessity for considering different personal frames of reference and the demands of different social structures poses seemingly insurmountable obstacles to the establishment of mutually consistent operational definitions. All such difficulties which lie "hidden," as it were, under the psychiatric treatment criterion, come to the fore to plague the researcher trying to establish a criterion for adjustment which applies to the treated and nontreated alike.

Psychiatric Diagnosis as Criterion for Mental Illness

There have been a few studies in which entire communities or samples of them have been systematically screened, either by direct examination (44, 48) or by evidence from community records or hearsay (13, 14, 54). Here the criterion for mental illness or health need not be dichotomous, but can be divided into several gradations. Such intensive case-finding can be expected to increase the yield of persons classified as neurotic (34, p. 124) over that provided by the criterion of exposure to treatment, but whether the psychotic group is thereby increased will depend on the community (34, p. 124; 48) and, of course, on the standards for diagnosis employed by the particular investigator.

The lack of standardization of diagnostic procedures and criteria contributes to the incomparability of mental illness rates derived from such studies (34, p. 139; 55). So long as the criterion of assessment is largely dependent on the psychiatrist's subjective integration of a different set of facts for each subject, nonuniform results can be anticipated. Expensive and unreliable though the method may be, it at least places the judgment regarding mental illness or health in the hands of professionals, which is not the case when adjustment is the criterion. And though hospitalization is in part determined by the judgment of professionals, who is sent to the hospitals for psychiatric diagnosis is, for the most part, out of the hands of the psychiatrists. As Felix and Bowers (17) have observed, it is the community rather than the clinician that operates the case-finding process today, and this will continue to be so until diagnostic examinations are given regularly to all people.

Mental Illness Defined Subjectively

It has been maintained by some that a major indication of need for psychotherapy is the person's own feeling of unhappiness or inadequacy. Conversely, the degree of mental health may be assessed by manifestations of subjective happiness, self-confidence, and morale. Lewis (36) quotes Ernest Jones to the effect that the main criterion for effect of therapy is the patient's subjective sense of strength, confidence, and well-being. Terman (52, 53) has used a "marriage happiness" test, composed largely of subjective items, and Pollak (43) has suggested that old-age adjustment be assessed in terms of the person's degree of happiness or well-being in various areas of his life.

That such criteria of mental health correlate somewhat with independent diagnoses by physicians has been indicated in two sorts of studies. In the Baltimore Eastern Health District (9), cases diagnosed psychoneurotic were found to express complaints about their own physical health; it is suggested that persons who report chronic nervousness can be classified as suffering from a psychiatric condition. Rogers has maintained that a marked discrepancy between one's "perceived self" and "ideal self" constitutes evidence of psychiatric disturbance (45), and some empirical studies lend support to this position. When Q sorts of subjects' self concepts are compared with Q sorts of their ideal selves, it is possible to distinguish psychiatric groups from nonpsychiatric groups on the basis of the degree of discrepancy between these two measures (4). Furthermore, progress in therapy (as judged by the therapist) tends to be associated with increasing similarity between the patient's self concept and ideal self (46).

Though subjective well-being is an appealing criterion for mental health in ordinary daily living, it might be presumed that under some circumstances psychological defense mechanisms could operate to prevent the person's reporting, or becoming aware of, his own underlying unhappiness and disturbance. Jahoda (33) has rejected happiness as a criterion for mental health on somewhat different grounds: Happiness, she says, is a function not only of the person's behavior patterns, but of the environment in which he moves. If one wants to relate mental health to characteristics of the environment, then one must not take as a criterion of mental health something that already presupposes a benign environment. "There are certain circumstances in which to be happy would make it necessary first to be completely sick" (33, p. 105).

Such objections to this criteria imply that it is possible to find persons who are mentally ill by some other criterion, yet who nevertheless report themselves as happy or self-satisfied. Empirical demonstration of this implication is not available at present. In fact, while one study predicted defensively high Q sorts for the self concept of paranoid psychotics, they were found to have a greater discrepancy between self- and ideal-sorts than normals, and no less discrepancy between these measures than psychoneurotics (4).

Mental Illness Defined by Objective Psychological Symptoms

It is generally accepted almost by definition that mental illness entails both a disordering of psychological processes and a deviation of behavior from social norms (6). The latter aspect of disturbance may be assessed as maladjustment to one's social environment (discussed above); the former aspect can presumably be assessed by psychological inventories aimed at the assumedly critical processes. The distinction between the psychological inventory approach and the subjective assessment procedure discussed above is not really a clear one. Subjective well-being may be regarded as one of the psychological processes which becomes disordered. Yet more "objective" measures of psychological process, which do not require the subject's verbal report of his degree of happiness, are frequently preferred, both to guard against purposeful distortion and to tap areas of disorder which may not be accompanied by subjective counterparts.

Such "objective" psychological inventories may represent various degrees of manifest purpose. For some, the objective of assessment is transparent, and the only reason they are not classed as devices for subjective report is that they stop just short of requiring the subject to report his over-all level of well-being. Such a manifest-level inventory is Halmos' questionnaire concerning the respondent's difficulties in social relations (24).

At a somewhat less obvious level are such inventories as the MMPI, the War Department Neuropsychiatric Screening Battery, and the Cornell Medical Index, which require subjects to check the presence of various subjective and objective symptoms (e.g., "I smoke too much."). Once validated against an accepted criterion, such as psychiatric diagnosis, these are frequently used as criteria themselves. Rennie constructed a composite instrument of this type to assess his respondents' levels of mental health in the Yorkville study (44); at the same time, a validity analysis of the index was undertaken, by correlating each item with independent psychiatric diagnosis on a subsample of the respondents. On the basis of their experience with such a composite instrument, one of Rennie's colleagues (Langner, personal communication, August 1956) suggests caution in abstracting parts of previously validated batteries, since the item validities are sometimes not maintained when they are used out of context of the total instrument.

An adaptation of the psychiatric screening battery approach for use with children is suggested in the work of the St. Louis County Public Health Department (20). It involves obtaining information about symptoms from the children's mothers rather than from the children themselves. Naturally, the symptoms covered must be of the "objective" type ("Does Johnny wet the bed?") rather than the "subjective" type ("Does Johnny worry a lot?"). As validated by an outside criterion (teachers' and psychiatric social workers' ratings of the child's level of adjustment), the number of symptoms reported by the mothers appears to be a promising index of the child's mental health.

A general characteristic of the types of psychological inventories reviewed so far is that each item in the battery is assumed, a priori, to involve a "directional" quality, such that one type of answer (e.g., "yes" to "Are you troubled with nightmares?") may be taken as indicative of psychological disorder, and the opposite answer as indicative of normal functioning. Thus the index of disturbance is computed by adding all the positive indicators, weighted equally. That alternative methods of test construction may yield equally, or more, valid indices of mental illness is indicated by the extensive investigations of McQuitty (40).

McQuitty proposes several different methods of diagnostic test scoring, each based on explicit assumptions about the diagnostic procedure which the test is supposed to represent. One of the simplest assumptions, for example, is that an individual is mentally ill to the extent that his psychological processes deviate from the culturally modal processes. Thus, any type of multiple-alternative test may be administered to a group of subjects representing a "normal" population. Each alternative of each item is then scored for its "popularity." The score for a subject is then computed by adding the popularity scores of the items he checks (McQuitty calls this the T method of scoring); a high popularity score is taken as evidence of mental health (by this "typicality" criterion).

An alternative assumption proposed by McQuitty as underlying the diagnostic procedure might be that mental health is manifest to the degree that the subject's responses conform to *any* pattern of answers represented by a significant number of community people, regardless of whether that pattern is the most popular one. Such an assumption leads to a scoring procedure (H method) whereby a subject's index of "cultural harmony" is based on the degree to which his responses to different questions "go together" in the same manner as do the responses of all people in the sample who check the same alternatives he does.

Elaborations on these basic procedures provide for differential weighting of responses depending on their degree of deviance (WH method), and correction for "linkage" between successive pairs of items (WHc method).

The Bernreuter Personality Test and the Strong Vocational Interest Inventory were administered by McQuitty to a group of mental patients and to a group of university students; they were scored by different methods, the scores for the two tests were correlated, and the mean scores of the two groups compared. Results of the comparisons indicate that: (1) when appropriately scored, the Strong can discriminate mental patients from normals, though not so well as the Bernreuter; (2) better results are obtained if, instead of treating each answer as a separate, independent measure, it is evaluated in terms of the pattern of other answers with which it occurs (WHc scoring method); (3) within the Bernreuter, those items which correlated best with the total score (McQuitty's WHc method of scoring) and provided the best discrimination between patients and normals tended to be of the "subjective" type (i.e., they depended on the subject's introspection, as in "Do you often have disturbing thoughts?") rather than the "objective" (items which an observer could report, such as "Do you talk very much?"); (4) different scoring procedures appeared differentially appropriate for the "subjective" and "objective" items; (5) when the "subjective" items were scored by the method most appropriate to them (i.e., the method which best discriminated patients from normals), and the "objective" items by their most appropriate method, the correlation between the two scores on the same group of subjects was about zero, indicating that two independent dimensions of mental health were being tapped by these two sets of items.

A separate study reported by McQuitty (40) indicated that the simple T method of scoring (based on the popularity of the subject's responses) both subjective and objective items significantly discriminated groups of school children classified on the basis of independent criteria of mental health. There is considerable evidence from these studies that, especially with respect to those traits measured by the "objective" items, the person may be regarded as mentally ill to the extent that he deviates from the dominant community pattern.

The foregoing studies provide a certain amount of evidence that measures of mental illness according to psychometric criteria relate to two of the criteria discussed earlier—maladjustment and psychiatric diagnosis. That such concurrent validation may yield somewhat different results from studies of predictive validity is indicated in Beilin's report of the Nobles County study (2). Two indices of student adjustment predictors were constructed, one (the "pupil index") based on students' responses to five different instruments, and the other (the "teacher index") based on teacher ratings. Both were concurrently validated against juvenile court judges' nominations of delinquent youngsters and against teachers' descriptions of the youngsters. Four years later the mental health of the youth was assessed by a number of different criteria—community reputation, interviewers' ratings, self-assessment, and an adaptation of the Rundquist-Sletto morale scale. The predictors correlated significantly with only some of the subsequent criteria, and all of the correlations were at best moderate. The "pupil index" correlated better with the interviewer's rating than with the community reputation criterion; while the "teacher index" correlated better with the subject's subsequent community reputation than with the interviewer's rating. Or, stated more generally, the psychologist's predictor predicted better to a psychologist's criterion, and a community predictor predicted better to a community criterion. Though the time span (four years) between the predictor and criterion measures may have been such as to allow for considerable change in the subjects, one is nevertheless reminded by these results that various criteria for mental health are not necessarily highly correlated.

In summarizing the various studies of mental health and illness defined by psychological testing batteries, we may note that many of them lack an underlying conception of the nature of mental illness from which to derive items and scoring procedures (a notable exception being McQuitty's measures), that some of them challenge the notion of the unidimensional nature of mental health, and that their degree of correlation with other criteria, such as adjustment or psychiatric diagnosis, depends on the nature of the criterion.

Mental Health as Positive Striving

A radically different approach to the assessment of mental health is indicated in the definitions proposed by some writers with a mental hygiene orientation. Gruenberg suggests that, though failure to live up to the expectations of those around him may constitute mental illness, one should also consider the person's failure to live up to his own potentialities (23, p. 131). Frank speaks of the "positive" aspect of mental health—healthy personalities are those who "continue to grow, develop, and mature through life, accepting responsibilities, finding fulfillments, without paying too high a cost personally or socially, as they participate in maintaining the social order and carrying on our culture" (18). In a less exhortative tone, Henry (27) discusses successful adaptation of the person in the "normal stressful situation." He sees many normal situations as situations of inherent stress. Some individuals in them develop mental disease, while others may develop out of them a more complex, but more successful, personality. It is this successful coping with the "normal stressful situation" that Henry regards as indicative of mental health.

Jahoda has translated this kind of emphasis on the positive, striving aspects of behavior into a set of criteria amenable to empirical research. She proposes three basic features of mental health (31): (1) The person displays active adjustment, or attempts at mastery of his environment, in contrast to lack of adjustment or indiscriminate adjustment through passive acceptance of social conditions. (2) The person manifests unity of personality—the maintenance of a stable integration which remains intact in spite of the flexibility of behavior which derives from active adjustment. (3) The person perceives the world and himself correctly, independent of his personal needs.

Active mastery of the environment, according to Jahoda, presupposes a deliberate choice of what one does and does not conform to, and consists of the deliberate modification of environmental conditions. "In a society in which regimentation prevails, active adjustment will hardly be possible; in a society where overt regimentation is replaced by the invisible compulsiveness of conformity pressures, active adjustment will be equally rare. Only where there exists social recognition of alternative forms of behavior is there a chance for the individual to master his surroundings and attain mental health" (31, p. 563).

Such an approach is quite at odds with the subjective criterion of personal happiness, and with the conformity criterion referred to above as "adjustment." Attempted adjustment does not necessarily result in success, for success is dependent on the environment. The best mode of adjustment only maximizes the chances of success. It is mentally healthy behavior even if the environment does not permit a solution of the problem (33). Jahoda proposes that the criterion of happiness be replaced with some more "objective" definition of mental health, based on an explicit set of values.

In an unpublished community study, Jahoda apparently attempted to assess only two of the aspects of mental health incorporated in her definition. Veridicality of perception (actually, of judgment) was determined by asking respondents to estimate certain characteristics of their communities concerning which objective data were available (e.g., proportion of people with only grade-school education), and at the same time inferring needs to distort reality from the respondent's evaluative statements about the problem (e.g., how important R believed education to be). This method of assessing need-free perception was regarded as something less than satisfactory (Jahoda, personal communication, August 1956), since the need was so difficult to determine, and it was difficult to establish unambiguously that distortion of judgment was due to the operation of a need rather than simply to lack of valid information.

The degree of attempted active adjustment was assessed by first asking a respondent to mention a particular problem in the community, then determining what he had done, or tried to do, about it, and how he felt about the problem at the time of interview (33). Three aspects of respondents' reactions were coded from their replies (32): (1) the stage of problem solution—mere consideration of the problem, consideration of solutions, or actual implementation; (2) the feeling tone associated with the problem—continued worry or improvement in feeling (either through partial solution or through passive acceptance); (3) the directness or indirectness of the approach—i.e., whether R went to the heart of the problem in his attempted solution or merely dealt temporarily with recurrent nuisances.

In her analysis Jahoda relates her measures of problem-solving and need-free perception to various characteristics of the respondents and of the communities in which they live. The relationships are interesting (e.g., in one of the communities the level of problem-solving was related to the degree of community participation of the respondent), but they appear to leave unanswered a basic question about the appropriateness of the criteria. If one accepts Jahoda's definition of mental health as involving the two components assessed in the study, then the results can be interpreted as showing what patterns of social interaction are associated with mental health. But if one is skeptical about the meaningfulness of the definition, then he is impelled to search for correlations between her two measures and other, more commonly accepted, criteria of mental health. These are not reported, although it would appear to be a fair question to ask about the relation of her concepts to those employed by other researchers.

If one is wedded to the happiness criterion of mental health, for example, one may speculate about the possibility of a negative relation between it and those provided by Jahoda. Unhappiness could conceivably lead to excessive coping behavior (attempted adjustment), or excessive coping behavior might elicit negative reactions from others which, in turn, would increase one's unhappiness. In like fashion, it could be that need-free perception would lead to increased unhappiness, since psychological defenses are not available to bolster one's self image. Though Jahoda might reject the suggestion that happiness is even relevant to her criteria, it would appear useful to explore, both conceptually and empirically, the interrelations among other measures of mental health and the novel one proposed by her.

Clausen (6) has maintained that researchers must ultimately face the task of relating mental health defined in positive terms to the individual's ability to resist mental illness under stress. At present it is not known whether they represent a common factor or are independent characteristics. Jahoda (personal communication, August 1956) suspects that positive mental health, as she defines it, may indeed represent a dimension orthogonal to that represented by the conventional psychological symptoms of mental illness. Thus, from a different approach than that employed by McQuitty comes the suggestion that mental health and illness may be a multidimensional phenomenon.

In employing these particular criteria, especially that of active adaptation, Jahoda seems willing to defend the evaluative standards implicit in it. And it may well be that values relating to attempted mastery of problems are every bit as defensible as the values of conformity implied in the adjustment criteria discussed above. Nevertheless, the former appear to exemplify the application of the Protestant ethic to the mental health movement in a manner which might introduce culture and class biases into one's conclusions. Miller and Swanson (42) have hypothesized that lower-class children will show more defeatism than middle-class children, as a result of different interpersonal and environmental experiences. Would they thereby be less mentally healthy by any standards besides those of the middle class? Truly, the problems posed in setting up absolute values from which to judge mental health and illness are perplexing.

Basic Problems in the Definition of Mental Health and Illness

Underlying the diversities in definition of mental illness one can discern certain basic differences of viewpoint concerning how the phenomena should be conceptualized. We may abstract certain foci of disagreement by posing the following four points of contention: (1) Does mental illness refer to a unitary concept or to an artificial grouping of basically different specific disorders? (2) Is mental illness an acute or chronic state of the organism? (3) Is maladjustment (or deviance from social norms) an essential concomitant of mental illness? (4) Should mental illness be explicitly defined according to values other than social conformity?

Each of the proposed definitions takes a stand, either explicitly or implicitly, on one or more of these issues. It is likely that resolution of disagreements will depend in part on the outcome of future empirical research. But at least some of the divergence inheres in the theoretical formulation of the problem, and is more a matter of conceptual predilection than of empirical fact. In either case, if one is to arrive at consistent theoretical and operational definitions of mental illness, it would be well to make explicit one's bias concerning each of these issues, and attempt to rationalize it in terms of his conception of the causes of disturbance.

The Unitary or Specific Nature of Mental Illness

The position that mental illness is manifest in some rather general form, regardless of the specific diagnostic category in which the patient is placed, would appear to be implicit in the subjective definition of the phenomenon. If the person's feeling of happiness or adequacy is regarded as the crucial indicator of his mental state, this would appear to imply that over-all health or illness can be assessed for a particular person, regardless of the area of functioning referred to. Likewise, the definition of mental health in terms of purposeful striving or active adjustment tends to ignore differences in the underlying bases for such striving or lack thereof. Such a position has been stated explicitly by Stieglitz: "The mensuration of health . . . closely parallels the measurement of biological age as contrasted to chronological age. . . . We are no longer seeking to discover specific disease entities, or even clinical syndromes, but attempting to measure biological effectiveness in adaptation" (51, p. 79). And such a unitary view of the phenomenon is implied in Schneider's comment: "The major 'cause' of mental disease is seen as some form of disorientation between the personality and society" (49, p. 31).

By contrast, the specific view of mental illness is taken by Gordon: "What we choose to call mental disease is an artificial grouping of many morbid processes. The first essential, in my opinion, is to separate the various entities, and in the approach to an epidemiology of mental diseases, to center attention on some one condition, or a few selected conditions, which have functions in common with other mass diseases well understood in their group relationships" (15, p. 107). McQuitty offers empirical evidence in favor of a specific view, in his isolation of two quite independent measures of mental illness (by psychological testing), both of which correlate with external diagnostic criteria. And he further speculates that the number of areas in which the degree of personality integration varies rather independently is probably greater than the two which he has isolated. "One might expect that mental illness might develop within any one of more patterns. In order to understand the mental illness of a particular subject, we must isolate the pattern, or patterns, of characteristics to which his mental illness pertains" (40, p. 22).

While the weight of opinion and evidence appears to favor the multidimensional view, this may simply be a function of the operational definitions employed (e.g., mental health defined by responses to a battery of tests is bound to turn out multidimensional to the extent that intercorrelations among the test items are low). But there are yet insufficient empirical data collected from the unitary point of view to test whether its assumption is correct. Indeed, it seems quite plausible that both happiness and active adaptation may be partially a function of the situation; hence the concept of mental health implied by them must become multidimensional to the extent that they allow for intersituational variability.

The Acute or Chronic Nature of Mental Illness

The psychologist's testing approach to assessing mental illness inclines him toward a view of the condition as chronic. That is, the predisposing conditions within the organism are generally presumed to be relatively enduring, though perhaps triggered off into an actual psychotic break by excessively stressful situations. The epidemiological approach, on the other hand, is usually concerned with the counting of actual hospitalized cases, and this may incline one toward a view of mental illness as predominantly acute. Felix has espoused this position explicitly: "Unless the kinds of mental illness are specified, I can't conceive that mental illness is a chronic disease. More mental illnesses by far are acute and even short term than there are mental illnesses which are chronic and long term" (15, p. 163). Of course, the epidemiological approach traditionally considers characteristics of the host, as well as characteristics of the agent and the environment. But the predisposing factors within the organism seem to be regarded, like "low resistance," not as a subliminal state of the disease, but rather as a general susceptibility to any acute attack precipitated by external factors.

It is easier to regard a psychosis as acute than it is similarly to regard a neurosis, since in the former disorder the break with normal behavior appears more precipitate. However, such a judgment, based on easily observable external behaviors, may be unduly superficial. Even in the case of such a discrete disturbance as suicide, at least one writer (21) recommends considering the biologic gradient of the disorder. He distinguishes varying degrees of suicide, with successful accomplishment as merely a possible end product. Where such continuity between morbid and nonmorbid states can be discerned, the possibility of chronic disturbance might well be considered.

The Problem of Mental Health as Conformity to Social Norms

The criterion of mental health based on adjustment clearly implies that conformity to the social situation in which the individual is permanently imbedded is a healthy response. And such an assumption would appear to be lurking, in various shapes, behind nearly all of the other definitions considered (with the possible exception of some of the "positive striving" criteria, which stress conformity to a set of standards independent of the person's immediate social group). In fact, McQuitty's methods of scoring psychological inventories are all explicitly based on the assumption that conformity (either to the total community or to a significant subgroup) is healthy.

If the stability of the larger social system be regarded as the final good, or if human development be seen as demanding harmony in relation to that social system, then such an assumption would appear basic and defensible. But one is still impelled to consider the possibility that the social system, or even an entire society, may be sick, and conformity to its norms would constitute mental illness, in some more absolute sense. If any particular behavior pattern is considered both from the standpoint of its adaptability within the social structure to which the individual maintains primary allegiance and from the standpoint of its relation to certain external ideal standards imposed by the observer, perhaps a comparison of the two discrepancy measures would yield information about the degree to which the social system approaches the ideal. On the other hand, such a comparison might be interpreted as merely indicating the degree to which the researcher who sets the external standards is himself adapted to the social system which he is studying. The dilemma appears insoluble.

The Problem of Values in Criteria for Mental Health

The mental hygiene movement has traditionally been identified with one or another set of values—ideal standards from which behavior could be assessed as appropriate or inappropriate. The particular set of values adopted probably depends to a considerable degree on who is doing the judging. Such a diversity of evaluative judgments leads to chaos in the popular literature and to considerable confusion in the usage of the term "mental health" in scientific research. Kingsley Davis (8) presented a rather strong case for the proposition that mental hygiene, being a social movement and source of advice concerning personal conduct, has inevitably been influenced by the Protestant ethic inherent in our culture. The main features of this Protestant ethic, as seen by him, are its democratic, worldly, ascetic, individualistic, rationalistic, and utilitarian orientations.

To the extent that research on mental health is based on criteria devolved from such an ideology, it is middle-class-Protestant biased. To the extent that it is based on some other set of "absolute" norms for behavior, it is probably biased toward some other cultural configuration. At least one researcher, Jahoda (33), has clearly taken the position that mental health criteria must be based on an explicit set of values. There is some advantage in allowing the assumptions to come into full view, but in this case the resulting criteria appear to be rather specialized and not comparable with those used by other researchers. Perhaps the difficulty lies not so much in the existence of explicit assumptions as in their level of generality. If a more basic set of assumptions could be found, from which the diverse criteria for mental health and illness can be derived, then comparability among researches might better be achieved. One would be in a better position to state when mental illness, as defined by psychological tests or by absence of active adjustment, is likely to be displayed in mental illness defined by psychiatric diagnosis or deviance from community standards.

Summary

The various categories of definitions of mental illness discussed here have been distinguished primarily on the basis of their differing operational definitions: the dependent variables employed in empirical research on the phenomena are clearly different. Moreover the conceptualizations of mental illness explicit or implicit in the empirical criteria are often quite divergent —viz., the radically different viewpoints underlying the "maladjustment," "subjective unhappiness," and "lack of positive striving" definitions.

Certain conceptual and methodological difficulties in each of these types of definition have been noted: "Exposure to treatment" is deficient in that only a limited proportion of those diagnosable as mentally ill ever reach psychiatric treatment. "Social maladjustment" is open to question because of the varying requirements of different social systems and the diversity of criteria for adjustment employed by community members. "Psychiatric diagnosis" provides an expensive, and often unreliable, method of assessing the state of mental health. "Subjective unhappiness" can be criticized as a criterion since it may be a function of intolerable environmental conditions as well as the psychological state of the person, and is subject to distortion by defense mechanisms. The validity of "objective testing procedures" appears to depend considerably on the method by which they are scored, and there is strong evidence that a major component of their score may simply be the degree of conformity of the person to the community average. Finally, criteria included under the heading of "positive striving" are subject to question in that they are inevitably based on disputable value systems of their proponents.

While many of these difficulties would not be considered damaging from the point of view of certain of the definitions of mental illness, they run into conflict with others. Also they suggest certain basic incompatibilities among the various approaches to conceptualization of mental illness. Whether these incompatibilities should be reconciled by further theoretical and empirical exploration, or whether they should be regarded as valid indicators that mental health and illness constitute multidimensional phenomena is still a moot question. We can only note that various studies employing two or more of these different categories of criteria have tended to yield moderate, but not impressive, interrelations.

The criterion of "exposure to psychiatric treatment" has been related to "maladjustment," "psychiatric diagnosis," "subjective unhappiness," and "objective psychometrics." Also "maladjustment" has been related to "psychiatric diagnosis" and to certain "objective" measures; and "psychiatric diagnosis" has been related to both "subjective" and "objective" measures of mental illness. The areas of interrelationship for which no empirical studies have been found are between "subjective" measures and both "maladjustment" and "objective" assessment; also between the "positive striving" criteria and all of the other types of measures.

Two directions for future theory and research are indicated by these results. First, more investigations are needed of the extent of relationship among the various criteria, and of the conditions under which the magnitudes of the intercorrelations vary. Second, assuming absence of high intercorrelations under many conditions, it would be worthwhile to explore the implications of poor congruence between one measure and another—implications both for the person and for the social system in which he lives.

References

1. Beilin, H. The effects of social (occupational) role and age upon the criteria of mental health. *J. soc. Psychol.*, in press.
2. Beilin, H. The prediction of adjustment over a four year interval. *J. clin. Psychol.*, 1957, 13, 270–274.
3. Belknap, I. V., & Jaco, E. G. The epidemiology of mental disorders in a political-type city, 1946–1952. In *Interrelations between the social environment and psychiatric disorders*. N.Y.: Milbank Memorial Fund, 1953.
4. Chase, P. Concepts of self and concepts of others in adjusted and maladjusted hospital patients. Unpublished doctor's dissertation, Univer. of Colorado, 1956.
5. Clark, R. E. Psychoses, income and occupational prestige. *Amer. J. Sociol.*, 1949, 54, 433–440.
6. Clausen, J. A. *Sociology and the field of mental health*. N.Y.: Russell Sage Foundation, 1956.
7. Clausen, J. A., & Kohn, M. L. The ecological approach in social psychiatry. *Amer. J. Sociol.*, 1954, 60, 140–151.
8. Davis, K. Mental hygiene and the class structure. *Psychiatry*, 1938, 1, 55–65.

9. Downes, Jean, & Simon, Katherine. Characteristics of psychoneurotic patients and their families as revealed in a general morbidity study. *Milbank Memorial Fund Quarterly*, 1954, 32, 42–64.
10. Dunham, H. W. Current status of ecological research in mental disorder. *Social Forces*, 1947, 25, 321–326.
11. Dunham, H. W. Some persistent problems in the epidemiology of mental disorders. *Amer. J. Psychiat.*, 1953, 109, 567–575.
12. Durkheim, E. *Le suicide*. Paris: F. Alcan, 1897. (English translation, Glencoe, Ill.: Free Press, 1951.)
13. Eaton, J. W. *Culture and mental disorders*. Glencoe, Ill.: Free Press, 1955.
14. Eaton, J. W., & Weil, R. J. The mental health of the Hutterites. In A. M. Rose (Ed.), *Mental health and mental disorder*. N.Y.: Norton, 1955.
15. *Epidemiology of mental disorder*. N.Y.: Milbank Memorial Fund, 1950.
16. Faris, R. E. L., & Dunham, H. W. *Mental disorders in urban areas*. Chicago: Chicago Univer. Press, 1939.
17. Felix, R. H., & Bowers, R. V. Mental hygiene and socio-environmental factors. *Milbank Memorial Fund Quarterly*, 1948, 26, 125–147.
18. Frank, L. K. The promotion of mental health. *Ann. Amer. Acad. of Pol. Soc. Sci.*, 1953, 286, 167–174.
19. Frumkin, R. M. Occupation and major mental disorders. In A. M. Rose (Ed.), *Mental health and mental disorder*. N.Y.: Norton, 1955.
20. Glidewell, J. C., et al. Behavior symptoms in children and degree of sickness. *Amer. J. Psychiat.*, 1957, 114, 47–53.
21. Gordon, J. E., et al. An epidemiologic analysis of suicide. In *Epidemiology of mental disorder*. N.Y.: Milbank Memorial Fund, 1950.
22. Gruenberg, E. M. Community conditions and psychoses of the elderly. *Amer. J. Psychiat.*, 1954, 110, 888–896.
23. Gruenberg, E. M. Comment in *Interrelations between the social environment and psychiatric disorders*. N.Y.: Milbank Memorial Fund, 1953.
24. Halmos, P. *Solitude and privacy*. London: Routledge and Kegan Paul, 1952.
25. Hathaway, S. R., & Monachesi, E. D. The Minnesota Multiphasic Personality Inventory in the study of juvenile delinquents. In A. M. Rose (Ed.), *Mental health and mental disorder*. N.Y.: Norton, 1955.
26. Henry, A. F., & Short, J. *Suicide and homicide*. Glencoe, Ill.: Free Press, 1954.
27. Henry, W. E. Psychology. In *Interrelations between the social environment and psychiatric disorders*. N.Y.: Milbank Memorial Fund, 1953.
28. Hollingshead, A. B., & Redlich, F. C. Social stratification and psychiatric disorders. *Amer. sociol. Rev.*, 1953, 18, 163–169.
29. Hyde, P. W., & Kingsley, L. V. Studies in medical sociology. I: The relation of mental disorders to the community socio-economic level. *New England J. Med.*, 1944, 231, 543–548.
30. Jaco, E. G. The social isolation hypothesis and schizophrenia. *Amer. sociol. Rev.*, 1954, 19, 567–577.
31. Jahoda, Marie. Toward a social psychology of mental health. In A. M. Rose (Ed.), *Mental health and mental disorder*. N.Y.: Norton, 1955.
32. Jahoda, Marie. The meaning of psychological health. *Soc. Casewk*, 1953, 34, 349–354.
33. Jahoda, Marie. Social psychology. In *Interrelations between the social environment and psychiatric disorders*. N.Y.: Milbank Memorial Fund, 1953.
34. Kramer, M. Comment in *Interrelations between the social environment and psychiatric disorders*. N.Y.: Milbank Memorial Fund, 1953.
35. Lemert, E. M. An exploratory study of mental disorders in a rural problem area. *Rural Sociol.*, 1948, 13, 48–64.

36. Lewis, A. Social aspects of psychiatry. *Edinburgh med. J.*, 1951, *58*, 241–247.
37. Lindemann, E., et al. Minor disorders. In *Epidemiology of mental disorders*. N.Y.: Milbank Memorial Fund, 1950.
38. Lindemann, E. Comment in *Interrelations between the social environment and psychiatric disorders*. N.Y.: Milbank Memorial Fund, 1953.
39. Locke, H. *Predicting adjustment in marriage: a comparison of a divorced and a happily married group*. N.Y.: Holt, 1951.
40. McQuitty, L. L. Theories and methods in some objective assessments of psychological well-being. *Psychol. Monogr.*, 1954, *68*, No. 14.
41. Malzberg, B. *Social and biological aspects of mental disease*. Utica: State Hosp. Press, 1940.
42. Miller, D. R., & Swanson, G. E. A proposed study of the learning of techniques for resolving conflicts of impulses. In *Interrelations between the social environment and psychiatric disorders*. N.Y.: Milbank Memorial Fund, 1953.
43. Pollak, O. Social adjustment in old age. *Soc. Sci. Res. Council Bull.* No. 59, 1948.
44. Rennie, T. A. C. The Yorkville community mental health research study. In *Interrelations between the social environment and psychiatric disorders*. N.Y.: Milbank Memorial Fund, 1953.
45. Rogers, C. *Client-centered therapy*. Boston: Houghton Mifflin, 1951.
46. Rogers, C., & Dymond, Rosalind. *Psychotherapy and personality change*. Chicago: Univer. of Chicago Press, 1954.
47. Rose, A. M., & Stub, H. R. Summary of studies on the incidence of mental disorders. In A. M. Rose (Ed.), *Mental health and mental disorder*. N.Y.: Norton, 1955.
48. Roth, W. F., & Luton, F. H. The mental health program in Tennessee. *Amer. J. Psychiat.*, 1943, *99*, 662–675.
49. Schneider, E. V. Sociological concepts and psychiatric research. In *Interrelations between the social environment and psychiatric disorders*. N.Y.: Milbank Memorial Fund, 1953.
50. Schroeder, C. W. Mental disorders in cities. *Amer. J. Sociol.*, 1942, *48*, 40–47.
51. Stieglitz, E. J. The integration of clinical and social medicine. In I. Galdston (Ed.), *Social medicine—its derivations and objectives*. N.Y. Acad. of Med., 1947. N.Y.: Commonwealth Fund, 1949.
52. Terman, L. M., et al. *Psychological factors in marital happiness*. N.Y.: McGraw-Hill, 1938.
53. Terman, L. M., & Wallin, P. The validity of marriage prediction and marital adjustment tests. *Amer. sociol. Rev.*, 1949, *14*, 497–505.
54. Tietze, C., et al. Personal disorder and spatial mobility. *Amer. J. Sociol.*, 1942, *48*, 29–39.
55. Tietze, C., et al. A survey of statistical studies on the prevalence and incidence of mental disorders in sample populations. *Publ. Hlth. Rep.*, 1943, *58*, 1909–1927.

RELATIONSHIPS AMONG MEASURES
OF ADJUSTMENT *

⟨ Ralph H. Tindall

Many specific tests and devices have been used to establish overall adjustment indices. They imply that there is an entity labeled adjustment which can be legitimately assessed (1). A review of psychological literature dealing with diagnostic or therapeutic efforts shows that groups or individuals have been labeled relatively well adjusted on the basis of a single, or, at the best, a few indices purporting to measure adjustment status. This has occurred and continues to occur in spite of summaries, such as that of Ellis (4), which point out the weaknesses of using certain of these indices as independent criteria. Claims for the validity of various personality appraisal devices have usually been based upon their agreement with results obtained from using some other established technique. Frequently this comparison has been only with a test of similar type, e.g., comparing a self inventory with another self inventory; few studies have attempted to compare representative measures from all of the modes of measuring so-called adjustment. Such a study would indicate the extent to which these various types of measures are getting at something in common which might be labeled "adjustment"; an analysis of subareas of agreement and disagreement should help point up next possible steps in this measurement area. In brief, it is proposed to categorize existing techniques which purport to measure adjustment, select representative devices under each category, administer these carefully to a select population, and then analyze the nature of their interrelationships.

Methods

As a basis both for selecting and for constructing adequate measures of adjustment, it seemed an important first step to study definitions of adjustment commonly used in order to find aspects covered and areas of agreement. A review of representative writings dealing with the concept of adjustment disclosed that while there were differences in expression and terminology there was general agreement as to the general nature of adjust-

* From Ralph H. Tindall, "Relationships among Indices of Adjustment Status," Educ. Psychol. Measmt., 15, 152–162. Reprinted by permission of the author and the Editor, Educational and Psychological Measurement.

ment (3, 6, 7, 8, 9). In brief, adjustment is usually described as a process that covers the individual life span, operating within a complex environmental field. The process is goal directed behavior instituted by a need which may arise at any level within a hierarchy of needs ranging from elementary physiological tissue needs through the most complicated psychological symbolizations. The process is sustained when this goal directed behavior meets, in a complex environmental setting, thwarting circumstances which serve to heighten tensions producing varied responses in the organism. One, or a combination of these varied responses, eventually leads to a solution response which enables the organism to attain a transitory goal that results in the reduction of that particular tension (2, p. 35). The very process of obtaining the transitory goal, against a complex environmental setting, frequently establishes the circumstances for the arousal of new tensions, thus perpetuating the process.

Seven characteristics or facets of adjustment were generally described as desirable by the majority of writers in the field. There was no implication in their writings, nor is there such implication here, that these facets are independent or mutually exclusive. Rather, these descriptive terms frequently coexist and complement each other in the behavior of individuals judged well adjusted. These seven facets briefly reviewed are:

1. *Maintaining an integrated personality.* This involves the coordination of one's needs and goal seeking behavior into smoothly functioning interaction with the environment.

2. *Conforming to social demands.* Emphasis here is upon harmony with the standards of the cultural group without surrendering individual spontaneity.

3. *Adapting to reality conditions.* This facet is characteristic of the ability to expose oneself to present hardship conditions in order to make gains toward long range goals.

4. *Maintaining consistency.* A qualitative facet which makes possible prediction for behavior and permits hopes for the assessment of adjustment.

5. *Maturing with age.* Allowance is made for maturation and development of the individual with concomitant growth of more complex adjustment processes.

6. *Maintaining an optimal emotional tone.* In the face of emotionally loaded situations the well adjusted person is neither constricted in emotional involvement nor overwhelmed by his reactions.

7. *Contributing optimally to society through an increasing efficiency.* Here is an insurance that adjustive behavior reaches beyond self-centered goals.

In the course of developing a concept of adjustment, various commonly used mechanisms of adjustment were recognized. It was found that while the mechanisms themselves were well recognized (i.e., withdrawal, projection, introjection, direct attack, sublimation, etc.), there was disagreement as to a mechanism's classification *per se* along the adjustment continuum. Establishing the existence of a particular mechanism in operation would not automatically label the behavior as maladjustment or good adjustment. It was necessary to take into consideration the complex environmental circumstances in which the behavior occurred. Since the process of adjustment is a continuous one, since it exhibits itself against a complicated environmental background, and since it may occur at any level of a complex physiological-psychological hierarchy, the inherent difficulties of measurement were recognized. Despite these difficulties, techniques purporting to measure adjustment exist and enjoy relatively wide usage. It is these very attempts to appraise adjustment that make this study a legitimate project.

Into what categories of approach can commonly used measures of adjustment be placed? What actual measurement devices were considered representative of these categories and used in this study? It is believed that present day measures are of five major types: (1) questionnaires and inventories; (2) ratings by adult judges; (3) ratings by peers using sociometric techniques; (4) adjustment indices secured by means of projective techniques; and (5) systematized direct observation. Representative techniques were chosen in each category in accordance with criteria that took into account suitability of use with the age group selected, systems of scoring resulting in a numerical index of adjustment, practicability of application, and differences of approach within the major type.

The type (1) approach, i.e., questionnaires and inventories, was represented by the *California Test of Personality*, which gave two indices of adjustment, self adjustment and social adjustment. The *Heston Personal Adjustment Inventory* was also selected under type (1) as representing an inventory built through the process of factor analysis. This inventory gave six indices of adjustment: analytical thinking, sociability, emotional stability, confidence, personal relations, and home satisfaction.

Three indices were used for the type (2) approach, ratings by adult judges. One was the average global rating of adjustment, made independently by two teachers and one cottage supervisor who had had experience with each boy in the selected population, in which variation in each of the seven facets of adjustment was taken into account. The second index under type (2) was secured by using the average rating of the two men in the Dean of Boys' office, secured by independent rating of each boy on the *Haggerty-Olson-Wickman Behavior Rating Schedule B*. The third index in type (2) was secured by having the psychologist make an overall adjustment rating of each boy on the basis of case history material, close acquaintanceship, and a semi-structured interview.

Type (3), sociometric techniques, was represented by a "Guess Who" index and a "Companionship Choice" index. The "Guess Who" index was secured by presenting an opportunity for nominating boys for characteristics shown by Tryon (10) to be most and least admired in adolescent societies. The "Companionship Choice" index was determined through opportunity to choose and to reject companions for desirable activities.

Type (4), projective techniques, was represented by an index secured through the use of the *Rotter Incomplete Sentence Test* and through the use of *Munroe's Rorschach Check List*.

Type (5), systematized direct observation, was exemplified by a Time Sample of behavior. Three well defined categories of generally considered maladaptive behavior were checked for occurrence in ten five minute periods. These periods were selected so as to sample representative daily activity.

Since the study was designed to examine the relationships among various techniques purporting to measure adjustment, it was necessary to select a relatively stable and well known population upon which to apply the various techniques. The writer was serving as resident psychologist at the Ohio Soldiers' and Sailors' Orphans' Home at the time. Within the larger population at the Home (over four hundred children), a population consisting of all the white boys who had reached their fourteenth birthday as of April 1, 1950, who had been in residence for at least six months, and who were not being immediately discharged, appeared to be the most appropriate. The resulting population consisted of sixty-six adolescent boys, who were known to vary in their adjustment status. They were found to be within the average range of ability, but to be retarded slightly by school placement standards. They would have rated low on a scale of family stability. Approximately five per cent of these boys were orphans, while the majority were children whose homes had been broken by reason of divorce, desertion of a parent, etc. The cultural background was somewhat below that usually considered middle class. The boys had lived in the orphanage an average of approximately six years. While an atypical group in some respects, the immediate environmental field was similar; they were well known, and they were available for study and follow-up. Since the emphasis of the study was on techniques, this population lent itself well to the study.

In addition to the sixteen indices of adjustment used, it was felt necessary to measure the effect of three extraneous variables on adjustment status. These were: chronological age, mental age, and months of residence in the institution.

In order to secure these various arrays of indices, each technique was applied to the population with utmost care taken to prevent bias in scoring. All protocols were identified by code numbers during the application and scoring process. Where published techniques were used, there was strict adherence to administrative directions. All techniques were applied in the time between April, 1950, and September, 1950. Raw scores were transmuted so that high scores indicated relatively good adjustment while low scores indicated maladjustment.

Results

Characteristics of the data. The nineteen resulting arrays were inspected for normalcy of distribution and other characteristics. Means, standard deviations, and reliabilities for each technique were computed. One of the outstanding characteristics of the data secured from the chosen population was that on several measures, e.g., the *California Test of Personality*, the *Heston Personal Adjustment Inventory*, the *Haggerty-Olson-Wickman Behavior Rating Schedule B*, and the *Munroe Rorschach Check List*, the mean score of this population was considerably below the mean score of the standardization group. This implies that, while the scores of the population chosen were normally distributed as a group, they gave evidence of more maladjustment than was found in the standardization populations. This is the situation we would expect to exist with such an institutional group. It was also found that the reliability coefficient of the average teacher-supervisor rating (T and S Rating), .58, was too low to assure confidence in this particular index. The data showed that the Time Sample technique supplied a range of scores too narrow to be considered very discriminating.

Relationships of adjustment indices with extraneous variables. Correlations were found between each of the sixteen arrays of adjustment indices and each of the three arrays secured from measuring the extraneous variables of chronological age, mental age, and length of residence. In general it was found that very few of these relationships were at a statistically significant level and there were logical explanations for the few instances found. Thus, the index of adjustment established through the use of the *Haggerty-Olson-Wickman Behavior Schedule B* was significantly related to mental age, i.e., .26, but the former rating technique devotes one area to scales concerning ability status. In fact it offers validating evidence for that particular area of the scale. The "Guess Who" index was found to be significantly related to months in residence at the orphanage, i.e., .26, but with continued group living one would expect behavior modification in accordance with group standards. The Time Sample index was related to both chronological age and months in residence at a significant level, i.e., .47 and .30, respectively. This may be partially accounted for by a tendency for the behavior observed to become more covert with age. Since the Time Sample index was also discovered to be rather poor in discriminating between persons in the population, little significance should be attached to relationships found with this measure.

Intercorrelations among adjustment indices. The resulting intercorrelations are reported in Table 1. In general, there is a positive but low correlation among the various arrays of adjustment indices. The median intercorrelation coefficient is .228. This is sufficient to indicate just a thread of relationship among these common approaches to measurement of adjustment. The results are insufficient to support strongly a global concept of adjustment.

An examination of Table 1 reveals that forty-one of the one hundred and twenty intercorrelations were significant at the .01 level or better, or about one-third of the possible correlations found (5, p. 209). In addition, seventeen more of these intercorrelations were significant at the .05 level. Thus, a number of the techniques used were tapping related processes; this lends some support to a global concept of adjustment. However, the lowness of these relationships and the infrequency of their occurrence detract from the usefulness of this global concept.

Certain factors appeared present which could account for some of the relationships found. These factors may have influenced the amount of relationship found above and beyond that contributed by adjustment. Relationships among techniques within each of these major groupings were at a higher level than most of those relationships found among the various types. For example, the median r between self ratings was .33, and between peer ratings was .30. Thus, the bias of a particular rater affects the results irrespective of the device used. There was also more relationship among three of the major groupings of techniques than among the others. Questionnaires and inventories, ratings by adults, and ratings by peers using sociometric techniques had a median r of .30 with each other; all are established by some form of personal report, based perhaps on character reputation, which could plausibly account for some of the relationship found. Several of the tests provide ratings of self adjustment and social adjustment. Conceivably, these two aspects are inextricably bound together in a particular individual, and when attempts are made to measure them separately related results are obtained. In brief, then, while some generality of relationship was obtained, some of this is attributable to factors other than adjustment of the individual.

It will be noted that the two projective techniques are unrelated to each other and to other indices established by other techniques. On the other hand, in the intensive case studies these projective techniques were found useful in constructing hypotheses in regard to individual behavior dynamics.

It is interesting at this point to note that the rating of the psychologist, which is frequently used as the criterion measure when validation studies are made of an adjustment assessing technique, was related at a significant level to eight of the fifteen other indices, six of them at the one per cent level. These correlations were not high, the highest being .58 with the index established by averaging the ratings of the two deans.

In addition to studying the relationships among arrays of various adjustment indices, a detailed study of five individual cases was made. These cases were selected according to several criteria, the most important being that two of them evidence relatively high scores in the self adjustment area as measured by the *California Test of Personality*, and in the social adjustment

TABLE 1. INTERCORRELATIONS OF ADJUSTMENT INDICES
(r <.24 below .05 level; r > .32 above .01 level; N = 66)

Indices	Self adjustment	Social adjustment	Analytical thinking	Confidence	Sociability	Personal relations	Emotional stability	Home satis.	"T & S" rating	Deans' rating	Psych. rating	Guess who	Companion choice	Rorschach	Incomplete sentences	Time sample
Self-adjustment		.66	.24	.53	.20	.62	.48	.33	.71	.26	.40	.50	.32	.26	.32	.27
Soc. adjustment			.11	.35	.15	.46	.33	.38	.42	.27	.47	.28	.27	.35	.32	.12
Anal. th'k'g				.33	.31	.17	.30	-.13	-.04	.13	.07	.20	.07	.11	-.04	-.09
Confidence					.50	.76	.81	.33	.03	.17	.21	.30	.22	.14	.15	.01
Sociability						.29	.32	.02	-.09	-.06	.04	.33	-.04	.11	.08	.03
Pers. relations							.79	.38	.16	.25	.31	.27	.37	.18	.21	.12
Emot. stability								.43	.01	.07	.16	.22	.24	.18	.09	.07
Home satis.									.21	-.02	.20	-.05	.13	.20	.03	.10
"T & S" rating										.55	.49	.53	.60	.29	.10	.46
Deans' rating											.58	.37	.63	.19	.10	.17
Psych. rating												.30	.49	.11	.36	.19
Guess who													.63	.25	.13	.29
Comp. choice														.32	.11	.22
Rorschach															.09	-.09
Inc. sentences																-.10
Mean	57.0	66.2	20.8	24.9	22.1	21.6	26.4	37.2	97.5	82.6	93.8	.8	.1	15.6	125.5	6.5
S.D.	11.3	11.9	4.5	7.0	6.8	6.1	7.6	7.6	33.1	18.5	16.2	25.8	27.6	4.8	16.3	2.9

area as measured by the *Companionship Choice Test.* Similarly, two were to evidence low scores in these areas while the fifth was to show discrepancy between scores in these areas. By using standard scores it was possible to compare all indices with behavioral, psychological, and historical data. This individual case study supported the hypothesis that reported self adjustment and social acceptance reported by peers were fruitful screening devices. Individual discrepancy among the various techniques for measuring adjustment could, in the majority of cases, be explained on the basis of the detailed case history. It was clearly indicated in these five cases that no one score taken alone could be depended upon to assess adjustment adequately in an individual case.

While such a correlation matrix as this would permit a factor analysis study, the very low relationships would not make such a study fruitful. The area known as adjustment apparently needs more careful definition. If meaningful concepts could be delineated, then more valid measuring devices might be constructed. More refined statistical techniques might then be applied.

Conclusions

1. The data secured in this study indicate that techniques purporting to appraise adjustment status when applied to the same population do not produce results that are closely related. This would imply that a global concept of adjustment, based on present day tests, is limited in usefulness. Assessment of adjustment by one technique has little predictive value in terms of results which might be secured by using another technique.

2. Evaluative studies, where claims are made in regard to change in adjustment status, should report several indices of adjustment. If it can be shown that there has been a significant change brought about in adjustment as measured by various techniques, more confidence can be placed in those results.

3. There is a need for clearer definitions within the concept of adjustment. We suggest that in our culture there should be certain common situations that should lend themselves to definition in terms of behavior that could be agreed upon as to position on an adjustment-maladjustment continuum.

4. Differences among techniques, within the same general type of adjustment assessing measures, point out the need for refinement of present techniques. The addition of more and more varieties of adjustment assessing techniques, validated through comparison of results established by existing techniques, serves to complicate rather than clarify the existing situation.

5. For the best use of existing techniques, the results of this study appear to indicate using many instead of one or a few indices before general

conclusions in regard to adjustment status are drawn. Results secured should be checked with actual behavior manifestations as well as historical data. If it is desired to screen out those whose adjustment status is questionable in groups such as the one used in this study, a score indicating the subject's feelings in regard to self adjustment and a score based upon peer acceptance indicating social adjustment are useful.

Finally, one further caution may be added. After over two years of follow up on the individual cases making up this population, where fairly complete biographical, psychological, and educational data exist, there is yet to be in evidence any one clear-cut measure which would predict in more than a general way the course of individual adjustment.

References

1. Buros, O. K. *The Third Mental Measurements Yearbook.* New Brunswick, N.J.: Rutgers Press, 1949.
2. Dashiell, J. F. *Fundamentals of General Psychology.* Chicago: Houghton Mifflin, 1937.
3. Dysinger, D. W. "Signs of Personality Disintegration." In Pennington, L. A., and Berg, I. A. *An Introduction to Clinical Psychology.* New York: Ronald Press, 1948.
4. Ellis, Albert. "The Validity of Personality Questionnaires." *Psychological Bulletin,* XLII (1946), 385–440.
5. Fisher, R. A. *Statistical Methods for Research Workers.* New York: Hafner Publishing Company, 1950.
6. Krech, David, and Crutchfield, R. S. *Theory and Problems of Social Psychology.* New York: McGraw-Hill, 1948.
7. Shaffer, L. F. *The Psychology of Adjustment.* Chicago: Houghton Mifflin, 1936.
8. Symonds, P. M. *The Dynamics of Human Adjustment.* New York: Appleton-Century-Croft, 1946.
9. Traxler, A. E. *Techniques of Guidance.* New York: Harper & Brothers, 1945.
10. Tryon, C. M. *Evaluation of Adolescent Personality by Adolescents.* Monograph of the Society for Research in Child Development, No. 4, 1939.

CULTURE AND PSYCHOPATHOLOGY *

(J. S. SLOTKIN

A social scientist dealing with psychopathological phenomena may take either a social or cultural approach to his problem, or, of course, a combination of both approaches. At the outset, I want to distinguish between these two methods of attack because they are significantly different. In the

* From J. S. Slotkin, "Culture and Psychopathology," *J. abnorm. soc. Psychol.,* 51, 269–275. Reprinted by permission of Mrs. J. S. Slotkin and the Managing Editor, the American Psychological Association.

former, the investigator is interested primarily in the relations between social interaction ("interpersonal relations") and personality disorder; this tends to be the province of social psychopathology (44). In the latter, the investigator is interested primarily in the relation between customs (or culture) and personality disorder; this might be said to be the province of cultural psychopathology. In terms of this distinction, the present paper deals with cultural psychopathology. More specifically, it is concerned with the contributions of anthropology to symptomatology and psychodynamics.

Symptomatology

In my opinion, the major contribution of anthropology to symptomatology is the opportunity it offers for reducing the ethnocentrism of the diagnostician. He usually participates in the white, middle-class, urban subculture of Western culture. When his patients come from the same milieu, he may have little difficulty. But when his patients participate in other subcultures, or entirely different cultures, there is often trouble. A few cases from my own experience will illustrate this.

A Menomini Indian was said by a psychiatrist to be suffering from phobias because he was afraid of snakes and night time. When I explained to the psychiatrist that, to the Menomini, all but one species of snakes are believed to be evil spirits, and that evil spirits, ghosts, and witches come out at night, he changed his diagnosis of the case.

The same psychiatrist told me that the least acculturated Menomini seemed to be "a bunch of psychopaths" with the exception of one normal woman. But these Menomini's mores require that the people treat each other as members of one family. All are supposed to be on a par; there should be no aggression, acquisitiveness on one's own behalf, or individual aggrandisement. The so-called "normal" woman is really a severe neurotic whose drives lead her to thinly sublimated aggressiveness, attempts at personal acquisition, and individual aggrandisement; behavior which fits in with our own standards. Therefore, when judged in terms of the white middle class subculture, her behavior seems normal, while that of the other Menomini seems abnormal.

A Negro from a rural south-eastern community was diagnosed as a psychopath because he had lived with a succession of women, each of whom he had deserted after she had borne some children. When I was asked my opinion (this man was a patient in a public psychiatric hospital) I was able to show that this was customary in the man's subsociety, and suggested that the psychiatrists read Frazier's *Negro Family in the United States*. After doing so, they discharged the man.

In an isolated rural area of the Ozark Mountains a man received a revelation from God, and a "call" to preach that revelation to his neighbors. He did so successfully. Later he was "called" to preach in the neighboring communities, and with equal success. He soon achieved great prestige in the area as a highly respected charismatic leader. But then he received a "call" to go to the city. Soon after arriving in St. Louis he was arrested for preaching on the street in the business district during the rush hour. Subsequently he was diagnosed by psychiatrists as a paranoid schizophrene, because he had delusions of grandeur and hallucinations. Here a man who conforms to a rural, lower class subculture, seems to be a deviant from the point of view of an urban, middle-class subculture.

A social worker was disturbed because she had just discovered that an entire family of clients was paranoid. That morning she had called at their home and found a bloody bedsheet hanging on a line. The family said that a daughter had been married the day before, and the sheet was exposed so that all the neighbors could see she had been a virgin. I asked if the family came from the Balkans. Startled, she replied they did. I then explained that this was a Balkan marriage custom.

The fact is that most distinctions between the fundamental symptomatological concepts in psychiatry have implicit or explicit social or cultural reference. This can be demonstrated by a critical analysis of a few basic concepts.

Let us begin with the difference between the normal and the abnormal. Four kinds of distinctions are usually made:

1. The normal individual seems to have a relatively well-organized personality; the abnormal, a relatively disorganized personality (20). However, in paranoia the personality becomes relatively well organized, but psychotic; almost invariably beliefs are diagnosed as a delusional system because they markedly deviate from customary beliefs. So in spite of the seemingly intrapersonal character of this distinction between the normal and abnormal, it has a cultural reference.

2. The normal individual seems to be able to gratify his motives effectively by means of his behavior; the abnormal engages in ineffective behavior (33, pp. 8, 21). However, a psychopath gratifies his motives effectively, but by violating customs. Also those who conform to inadequate customs are, by definition, engaging in ineffective behavior. Thus the criteria of effectiveness and ineffectiveness tend to be culturally conditioned.

3. The normal individual has a personality approximating the average of his social group; the abnormal has an aberrant personality (12). However, it is at least theoretically possible that most members of a group may be neurotic or psychotic, in which case the aberrant personality may be neither. This is temporarily the case in mass hysterias (25, 37).

4. The normal individual conforms to the customs of his group; the abnormal individual is a deviant (2). However, in order to engage in effective behavior it is necessary to violate inadequate customs (6, 31, 32). Also, a group may have social roles which the neurotic or psychotic can assume satisfactorily; in which case he is a conformist. Thus, in our own society neurotic aggression can be channelized in certain areas of our economy, and the neurotic, as a result, may become a successful and respected business man. Or, among the Tembu, certain types of schizophrenes gain high prestige as shamans (29, chap. 10). Finally, conformity itself can be a neurotic symptom, as we see in the case of many ultraconservatives in our own society.

Next, let us consider the difference between neurosis and psychosis. Three kinds of distinctions are usually made:

1. The neurotic may engage in deviant behavior, but it is limited to violation of the folkways; the psychotic and psychopath [1] violate the mores for seemingly incomprehensible reasons. This is the common-sense distinction, translated into anthropological language. It was on this basis that the Balkan family discussed above was termed psychotic.

2. The neurotic suffers from inner conflict but still adheres to reality; the psychotic distorts or rejects reality (16). However, reality is culturally defined. Thus, the revelation and calls of the Ozarkian mentioned above are "real" in his own subculture, but "unreal" in ours.

3. The neurotic has insight into his disorganization; the psychotic has none. But if insight is taken to mean that the patient is aware of his abnormality, one does not have to have much clinical experience to come across neurotics who have no insight, and psychotics who do (e.g., for a psychotic, see 39, p. 355). In such cases the patient usually makes his judgment in reference to the customs of his group. If he realizes that his symptoms include deviant behavior, he has "insight"; if he believes his behavior conforms, he has no "insight."

An inspection of the distinctions made above will show that most of them have social and/or cultural reference. Two conclusions seem to follow from this.

The first conclusion is that many fundamental psychopathological concepts implicitly depend upon certain social or cultural notions. Almost invariably, these notions have been derived from the theoretician's own cultural milieu, and may be inadequate when applied to psychiatric disorders found in other societies.

The second conclusion is that when confronted by a patient, the clinician's (be he psychiatrist, clinical psychologist, or psychiatric caseworker) determination of normality versus abnormality, and, in the latter case, between neurosis, psychosis, or psychopathy, is often, if not usually, made in terms of his judgment as to the nature of the patient's culture. The fact that the clinician's ethnocentrism may lead him to a wrong diagnosis emphasizes the importance of the anthropological contribution to his work when he is dealing with patients from subcultures other than his own, or with people from wholly different cultures.

It follows that a valid diagnosis cannot be based upon symptomatology alone, but must be derived from a study of the psychodynamics of the individual patient in relation to his social and cultural milieu. In this, the cultural point of view agrees with what is usually considered to be the best of modern clinical practice.

Now we turn to the syndromes themselves. They may be considered from two points of view, namely content and form.

---

[1] My own interpretation of psychopathy is social rather than cultural, and therefore falls outside the province of this paper (41, pp. 50–54).

It is obvious that the content of a syndrome is influenced by the patient's culture. For instance, a Menomini paranoid schizophrene states that her behavior is controlled by a witch; a middle-class white paranoid schizophrene, that his behavior is controlled from a radio station.

Of great theoretical as well as practical interest is the problem of whether the form of a syndrome is also influenced by culture. Freud raised the question in relation to a case of devil possession (15). Some literature dealing with abnormalities in exotic groups suggests the possibility of cultural differences in forms of personality disorder, though this literature is usually written by people untrained in either anthropology or psychiatry, and their data are fragmentary (e.g., 26, 45). My own case study of a Menomini paranoid schizophrene did not reveal any difference in the form of the psychosis; but unfortunately the case is inconclusive because the patient is somewhat acculturated (40).

Finally, there is some evidence that the incidence of the various syndromes found in a group is influenced by cultural factors. Thus, in the United States, studies have shown that there are ecological (10) and class (22) differences in the incidence of syndromes. Hysteria seems to have been more common in the Western middle-class subsociety during the nineteenth century than it is in the twentieth century. And among the Menomini, the only psychosis I found was paranoid schizophrenia (42; cf. for Kenya, 4). Though there is a high incidence of syphilis among the Menomini, I never saw or heard of a case of general paresis; I have no idea whether this is due to genetic or cultural factors.

Psychodynamics

As I see it, the major contribution of anthropology to psychodynamics is in providing comparative material by which to test the universality of psychodynamic theory. Two major areas will be considered here, namely, etiology and defense mechanisms.

In regard to etiology, some believe that the sheer complexity of civilization contributes to personality disorganization (17, but cf. 1). It has been suggested that insofar as the individual adopts the customs of a disorganized culture, cultural disorganization will lead to personality disorganization (41, pp. 334-336). Also, in heterogeneous cultures, as an individual shifts from one culture to another, his personality tends to become disorganized (41, pp. 326-334); in this connection, particular attention has been paid to the effects of acculturation (4, 5, 34, 35, 38).

Another cultural approach to etiology has been taken. No culture provides adequate gratification for all the motives of its participants. As cultures vary in their areas of inadequacy, the latter are correspondingly reflected in the areas of personality breakdown (23, 41, pp. 336-341). Thus, while the early studies of Freud showed that at that time, in the Western white middle class, breakdowns resulted from the repression of sexual motives

(13), among the Menomini breakdowns result from the repression of social competition and conflict (42).

The etiological influences of particular aspects of culture have been investigated. The classic case is Malinowski's demonstration that the Oedipus complex need not be focused on the parents, but varies with the kinship structure (30; cf. 11). Freud's hypothesis about the effect of successive social roles constituting the cultural life cycle (14) has also been modified in the light of anthropological knowledge (3).

Finally, the culture influences the individual's perception of a situation; most pertinently, by defining it as one which does or does not threaten his ego security (18, 21). Thus, an average member of our middle class feels inadequate when he cannot afford to buy such symbols of his status as clothing and automobiles of a particular quality. A Menomini will exhibit anxiety if he has to go out alone at night. Neither will feel insecure in the situation deemed threatening by the other.

The situation regarding defense mechanisms is similar to that concerning syndromes. They may be considered from two points of view, namely, content and form.

It is easy to see that the content of defense mechanisms is influenced by culture (41, pp. 346–368). Thus, the motives which are repressed by patients depend upon the mores of their groups, as was stated above. Also, Devereux has shown that negativism has reference to the culture of the patient's group, and is to be understood in terms of this relation (7).

The problem of the form of defense mechanisms can be put in this way: Are there different kinds of defense mechanisms in various cultures? Again, as in the case of syndromes, there is some material in the ethnographic literature which suggests the possibility that this may be so. But I did not find any new forms of defense mechanisms in my own investigations among the Menomini; though here too the evidence is inconclusive because of acculturation. Similar results, subject to the same limitations, were reached by Dorothy Eggan in her study of a Hopi's dreams (9).

Finally, I would like to suggest the hypothesis that the incidence of the various defense mechanisms found in a group is influenced by its culture (e.g., 8, p. 55).

Case Study

In order to illustrate some of the preceding remarks, I will present an instance of a typical neurosis among the least acculturated Menomini Indians of Wisconsin. This group believes that all serious physical and mental disorders are the result of witchcraft.

When projection is used as a defense mechanism, some part of the personality which greatly conflicts with the individual's concept of himself is cut off and referred to the environment. This permits him to respond to the projected impulses as if they were forced upon him from the outside. Such a defense reduces the damage to his ego ideal; he can take a relatively impersonal approach to the repressed material, and his conscious guilt feelings are minimized.

In our own white middle-class subsociety, this kind of projection tends to result in some psychotic syndromes: paranoia, paranoid state, or paranoid schizophrenia. Among the Menomini, however, such projection tends to result in a neurotic syndrome because of the belief in witchcraft. (In passing, I might also suggest that our own psychotherapy, in one of its aspects, has a function analogous to the Menomini belief. By teaching the patient that repressed material is due to amoral "natural causes," rather than to his own immoral volition, the patient is reassured and his guilt feelings minimized.)

The following case deals with a married woman born in 1912 who told me, "One time I had a lot of trouble with my head." The data are transcribed from tape-recorded interviews. The people spoke English by preference; it is the language usually employed by persons of their age. The woman first gave her own account of the episode, which I later supplemented through interrogation. Relevant excerpts from the interrogation have been interpolated into her account:

[During World War II her husband was drafted, and she and her children went to live with her stepmother.] I remember the time when I was staying with my stepmother; I used to stay with her, anyway, after my father died. And those people [2] used to come here quite a bit, you know; the people there, the woman. And she was a big friend to my stepmother.

And one time—I don't know; I guess about the third or fourth time they came there—well, I used to get them dizzy spells; I used to get them headaches. And all of a sudden, anyway, while I'd be doing something, working around— and for a while I was wondering what that was—I used to have awful pains in my head here, and have them dizzy spells. Sometimes I'd sit down, and get up and all of a sudden I'd be dizzy. So finally, later on, I was getting worse; finally I couldn't even stand it. So, after, I asked my stepmother to give me something; try to doctor me up; anyway, she'd give me some kind of a sneezing powder that they use, the Indians, to cure their headaches and all that. That didn't do me any good. And she'd have some kind of a—I don't know how it looks; she'd get some coals in a little coal shovel, and sprinkle some kind of a medicine in there, and that makes that smoke, and they make you cover your head. Well, she done that too; but then that didn't do me any good.

Yet—well, I was getting worse, anyway. I didn't know what that was, first. But I used to hear from the different people, you know, how that love powder [3]

[2] The E. family, in which the husband is Menomini and the wife Chippewa; they live on one of the Chippewa reservations. The Menomini are fearful of witchcraft; particularly from members of other tribes who visit them, or among whom they visit.

[3] Among the Menomini, "love powder," a form of sexual magic, is the most common form of magic.

works, and all that. And they say that, even when a person uses that [love powder] too much on one person, it makes them go crazy or something, and out of their head. So I was getting scared, for a while. And I know that fellow [i.e., the E.'s son, who came with his parents] used to be—used to always want to talk to me, and take me out, or something like that.[4] But I always used to turn him down; I really didn't care for that fellow. But I knew his mother was right in with him, and I suppose she might have told him to try and talk to me, or something like that.

Well, finally, one time, anyway, they were gone. Then a funny thing used to happen. Every time I'd wake up, you know, [I would] think about that fellow; seem like I had him in my mind all the time. And I thought about that right away, "Say! It couldn't be that they're using [love] medicine on me!" Gosh! I got scared, anyway.

Q: When you say dizzy spells, what were they like?
A: . . . Just like when you whirl around some place, and then you stop, [it] seemed like. . . . That just started gradually. . . . I never was that way before. . . . I'd be the same all the time [i.e., the dizziness persisted], until towards about—oh, one time, when they left; and that's when it got worse, after they left.
Q: When did you think of this fellow; before you became dizzy, while you were dizzy, or afterwards?
A: Before.
Q: You would think of this man, and then you would become dizzy?
A: Yes.
Q: What sort of ideas would you have about him?
A: Just like I wanted to see him, or something.
Q: Would you dream about him at night, too?
A: No, I never used to dream about him. (Pause) I don't remember; I sup- pose I did; I don't know; I don't remember that part, if I used to dream about him or not. But I know I used to just wish to see him, or something like that. . . .
Q: Did you ever dream of loving [i.e., copulating with] him, too?
A: Yes . . .
Q: Did you ever think of [i.e., fantasy] loving him, too?
A: Yes. . . . It seemed like every time I'd wake up in the morning—well, that [i.e., the man] was the first thing I'd think about, just as soon as I'd wake up.

And my aunt [the most important medicine woman in the tribe] lived just a little ways there, right where she's living now; my stepmother used to live just down this side there, in a log house she used to stay. So one time I was getting worse. I just about made it over to my aunt's. I don't know which one of these I had—of these two [older children] here; it was small, anyway. I took one of them—I don't know which one it was—took my baby; I wrapped him up; and I started out. I couldn't even stay on that trail [a distance of about 100 yards]; it was like as if I was drunk or something; I was just dizzy; I just about made it over to my aunt's there. I got over there; well, I laid down right away, and told my aunt about it. She asked me what was the matter; I told her all about it; how I'd been feeling, and the rest of it, you know. Well, I [also] told the old man, my uncle [5] . . . he knew quite a few medicines. And there was one old lady

---

[4] Except when in the company of her closest male kin, no married woman is supposed to be alone with a man; she is always to be accompanied by a chaperon.

[5] A Potawatomi married to her aunt.

happening to be visiting there [6]. . . . and I guess she knew quite a few medicines. And she must have been some kind of a relation to me on my father's side; my father was part Potawatomi. Well, after they heard me—I told them how I felt, and all that—the old lady said, "Well, I think by now [I know] just what's wrong, and I think I know what I could do for her." So she went to work and she start doctoring me. In just about four days there [I was cured] [7]. . . . While I was using the medicine, she told me to try not to put that guy in my mind; I [was] supposed to keep him off my mind and have something else on my mind. So I done that for three days; fourth day I was all right.

Q: What sort of medicines did the medicine woman use?
A: That's what I don't know.
Q: What did she do to you?
A: Well, I don't know what she done. She cut me four times up here . . . [the top of the head] right about in the middle. Then she—I don't know what she put on there; some kind of medicine; right on each side [of the temples]; right on here. Then she put some medicine on there; she sprinkled some. She got a piece of buckskin, and [it was] round; and she sprinkled some kind of medicine on there; and she put it on there after she cut me four times a little bit. That was about all. Then she wrapped something around my head, and then she used some kind of smoke, or something—that medicine what they sprinkle on coals, hot coals. That's all she done.
Q: And then she told you to think of something else; what sort of things were you told to think of?
A: To think of the future, or something like that.
Q: What kind of ideas did you try to have?
A: Well, that medicine would help me out, and something like that, and I'd be all right after.
Q: What did you think of the whole experience?
A: I don't know what to say about it. I think that's just no good. (Laughs) And I wasn't sure, either, if I was being that [i.e., subjected to love magic] . . . That love powder, well, I don't really know how that works, and all that. I used to hear different people say that, you know; how a person would feel used on [i.e., on whom was used] that medicine. Now the people [the E. family] don't—when that woman—she still comes around here for these [ritual] doings; she don't look at me so much, you know; she's not so friendly to me any more. . . .
Q: What did your stepmother [now dead] think of it?
A: She thought that wasn't so good, either; she didn't like it, either. I noticed, after, that she wasn't so friendly with that woman.

Chaperonage of married women, as well as other data, suggests that married men are jealous of their wives. Therefore, in order to verify that the Menomini accept this woman's form of projection, I interviewed the husband in order to determine his attitude toward the matter. Though I have seen him exhibit jealousy in other situations, he was matter-of-fact in relating his version of the incident. The relevant excerpts follow:

I know there's a medicine that was used on my wife, one time. . . . They [i.e., the E.'s] used that [love powder] on her. They was staying right in the same

[6] A Potawatomi relative of her uncle's.
[7] Everything goes by fours in the culture.

house there; this fellow was there. And when that medicine started to work on her . . . [it] seemed like that fellow was always on her mind, you know; she couldn't get him out of her mind; she wanted to do something, thinking about him all the time. Finally, she said, it started acting on her too much, you know, and she started to go crazy, you might as well say. . . . So finally she got scared [went to her aunt, and was cured].

Conclusion

This paper has been written from a culturally relativistic point of view in regard to diagnostic problems, the material being almost exclusively based upon empirical data. But even the briefest consideration will demonstrate the theoretical validity of this position. Man inherits a limited repertory of responses. Most of his responses are learned; and the majority of these are learned from others, i.e., culturally acquired. Consequently, it is to be expected that the individual's responses, abnormal as well as normal, are greatly influenced by his cultural milieu. And cultures vary tremendously.

I have deliberately emphasized the psychopathological implications of cultural variability, rather than cultural similarity, in order to drive home the importance of a cultural approach to diagnostic problems. We are now aware of the problem; much remains to be done before we have a satisfactory solution. Psychodynamic generalizations are needed which have universal validity from a comparative (cross-cultural) point of view. These are to be differentiated from findings which have particular validity, that is, are relative to individual cultures or aggregates of cultures. This goal can be achieved only through the close collaboration of psychiatrists, clinical psychologists, and anthropologists; and especially by students who have been trained in both the clinical and cultural fields.

References

1. Beaglehole, E. Cultural complexity and psychological problems. *Psychiatry*, 1940, 3, 329–339.
2. Benedict, Ruth. Anthropology and the abnormal. *J. gen. Psychol.*, 1934, 10, 59–82.
3. Benedict, Ruth. Continuities and discontinuities in cultural conditioning. *Psychiatry*, 1938, 1, 161–167.
4. Carothers, J. C. A study of mental derangement in Africans, etc. *J. ment. Sci.*, 1947, 93, 548–597. (Reprinted: *Psychiatry*, 1948, 11, 47–86.)
5. Devereux, G. A sociological theory of schizophrenia. *Psychoanal. Rev.*, 1939, 28, 315–342.
6. Devereux, G. Maladjustment and social neurosis. *Amer. sociol. Rev.*, 1939, 4, 844–851.
7. Devereux, G. Social negativism and criminal psychopathology. *J. crim. Psychopath.*, 1940, 1, 323–338.
8. Devereux, G. *Reality and dream.* New York: International Universities Press, 1951.
9. Eggan, Dorothy. The significance of dreams for anthropological research. *Amer. Anthropologist*, 1949, 51, 177–198.
10. Faris, R. E. L., & Dunham, H. W. Mental disorders in urban areas. Chicago: Univer. of Chicago Press, 1939.

11. Ferenczi, S., *et al.* Psycho-analysis and the war neurosis. Anonymous (Tr.). Vienna: International Psycho-Analytical Press, 1921.

12. Foley, J. P. The criterion of abnormality. *J. abnorm. soc. Psychol.*, 1936, 30, 279–291.

13. Freud, S. *Studies in hysteria*, A. A. Brill (Tr.), New York: Nervous and Mental Disease Publ., 1936.

14. Freud, S. "Civilized" sexual morality and modern nervousness. In J. Riviere (Ed., Trans.), *Collected papers of*. . . . Vol. 2. London: Hogarth, 1924–50. Pp. 16–99.

15. Freud, S. A neurosis of demoniacal possession in the seventeenth century. In J. Riviere (Ed., Trans.), *Collected papers of*. . . . Vol. 4. London: Hogarth, 1924–50. Pp. 436–472.

16. Freud, S. Neurosis and psychosis. In J. Riviere (Ed., Trans.), *Collected papers of*. . . . Vol. 2. London: Hogarth, 1924–50. Pp. 250–254.

17. Freud, S. *Civilization and its discontents*. J. Riviere (Tr.). London: Hogarth, 1930.

18. Gillin, J. Magical fright. *Psychiatry*, 1948, 11, 387–400.

19. Green, A. W. Culture, normality, and personality conflict. *Amer. Anthropologist*, 1948, 50, 225–237.

20. Hacker, F. J. The concept of normality and its practical significance. *Amer. J. Orthopsychiatry*, 1945, 15, 47–64.

21. Hallowell, A. I. Fear and anxiety as cultural and individual variables in a primitive society. *J. soc. Psychol.*, 1938, 9, 25–47.

22. Hollingshead, A. B., & Redlich, F. C. Social stratification and psychiatric disorders. *Amer. sociol. Rev.*, 1953, 18, 163–169.

23. Holmberg, A. R. *Nomads of the long bow*. Publ. No. 10. Washington: Institute of Social Anthropology, Smithsonian Institution, 1950.

24. Honigmann, J. J. Toward a distinction between psychiatric and social abnormality. *Soc. Forces*, 1953, 31, 274–277.

25. Johnson, D. M. The "phantom anesthetist" of Mattoon: A field study of mass hysteria. *J. abnorm. soc. Psychol.*, 1945, 40, 175–186.

26. Koritschoner, H. Ngoma ya sheitani. *J. Roy. Anthropol. Inst.*, 1934, 66, 209–219.

27. Kroeber, A. L. Cultural anthropology. In M. Bentley and E. V. Cowdry (Eds.), *The Problem of Mental Disorder*. New York: McGraw-Hill, 1934. Pp. 346–353.

28. La Barre, W. A classified bibliography of the literature on culture and personality. 1948 (Mimeographed).

29. Laubscher, B. T. F. *Sex, custom and psychopathology*. London: Routledge, 1937.

30. Malinowski, B. *Sex and repression in savage society*. London: Kegan Paul, Trench, Trubner, 1927.

31. Maslow, A. H. Self-actualizing people: A study of psychological health. *Personality*, symposium, 1950, 1, 11–34.

32. Maslow, A. H. Resistance to acculturation. *J. soc. Issues*, 7, 1951, 4, 26–29.

33. Masserman, J. H. *Behavior and neurosis*. Chicago: Univer. of Chicago Press, 1943.

34. Park, R. E. Personality and cultural conflict. In E. C. Hughes (Ed.), *Race and culture*, Glencoe, Ill.: Free Press, 1950. Pp. 357–371.

35. Sachs, W. *Black anger*. Boston: Little Brown, 1947.

36. Sapir, E. Cultural anthropology and psychiatry. In D. G. Mandelbaum (Ed.), *Selected writings of* . . . Berkeley: Univer. of California Press, 1949. Pp. 509–521.

37. Schuler, E. A., & Parenton, V. J. A recent epidemic of hysteria in a Louisiana high school. *J. soc. Psychol.*, 1943, 17, 221–235.

38. Seligman, C. G. Temperament, conflict and psychosis in a stone-age population. *Brit. J. med. Psychol.*, 1929, 9, 187–202.

39. Slotkin, J. S. The nature and effects of social interaction in schizophrenia. *J. abnorm. soc. Psychol.*, 1942, 37, 345–368.

40. Slotkin, J. S. A case of paranoid schizophrenia among the Menomini Indians. Unpublished ms., 1951.
41. Slotkin, J. S. *Personality development*. New York: Harper, 1952.
42. Slotkin, J. S. Social psychiatry of a Menomini community. *J. abnorm. soc. Psychol.*, 1953, *48*, 10–16.
43. Wegrocki, H. J. A critique of cultural and statistical concepts of abnormality. *J. abnorm. soc. Psychol.*, 1939, *34*, 166–178.
44. Weinberg, S. K. *Society and personality disorders*. New York: Prentice-Hall, 1952.
45. Yap, P. M. The Latah reaction. *J. ment. Sci.*, 1952, *98*, 515–564.

TOWARD A CONCEPT

OF THE NORMAL PERSONALITY *

《 EDWARD JOSEPH SHOBEN, JR.

Clinical practice and the behavioral sciences alike have typically focused on the pathological in their studies of personality and behavior dynamics. While much of crucial importance remains to be learned, there is an abundant empirical knowledge and an impressive body of theory concerning the deviant and the diseased, the anxious and the neurotic, the disturbed and the maladjusted. In contrast, there is little information and even less conceptual clarity about the nature of psychological normality. Indeed, there are even those (5, 13) who argue that there is no such thing as a normal man; there are only those who manage their inter-personal relationships in such a way that others are strongly motivated to avoid them, even by committing them to a mental hospital or a prison, as opposed to those who do not incite such degrees of social ostracism.

This argument has two characteristics. First, it appears to dispose of the problem by simply distributing people along a dimension of pathology. All men are a little queer, but some are much more so than others. Second, it has affinities with the two major ideas that have been brought to bear on the question of what constitutes normal or abnormal behavior: the statistical conception of the usual or the average and the notion of cultural relativism. If pathology is conceived as the extent to which one is tolerated by

* From Edward J. Shoben, Jr., "Toward a Concept of the Normal Personality," *Amer. Psychologist*, 12, 183–189. Reprinted by permission of the author and the Managing Editor, the American Psychological Association. This paper is revised from versions read on March 26, 1956, at the convention of the American Personnel and Guidance Association in Washington, D.C., and on November 16, 1956, at a conference on mental health research at Catholic University in Washington, D.C., under the joint sponsorship of Catholic University, the University of Maryland, and the U.S. Veterans Administration.

one's fellows, than any individual can theoretically be described in terms of some index number that reflects the degree of acceptability accorded him. The resulting distribution would effectively amount to an ordering of people from the least to the most pathological. Similarly, if the positions on this continuum are thought of as functions of one's acceptance or avoidance by others, then they can only be defined by reference to some group. The implications here are twofold. First, the conception of pathology is necessarily relativistic, varying from group to group or culture to culture. Second, the degree of pathology is defined as the obverse of the degree of conformity to group norms. The more one's behavior conforms to the standards of the group, the less is he likely to be subject to social avoidance; whereas the more one's behavior deviates from the rules, the greater is the probability of ostracism to the point of institutional commitment.

Statistical and Relativistic Concepts of Normality

Yet the issues are fully clarified by these statistical or culturally relativistic ideas. Is it most fruitful to regard normality or integrative behavior as merely reflecting a minimal degree of pathology, or may there be a certain merit in considering the asset side of personality, the positive aspects of human development? This question becomes particularly relevant when one is concerned with the socialization process or with the goals and outcomes of psychotherapy or various rehabilitative efforts.

It seems most improbable that the family, the church, and the school, the main agents of socialization, exist for the minimizing of inevitable pathological traits in the developing members of the community. Rather, parents, priests, and educators are likely to insist that their function is that of facilitating some sort of positive growth, the progressive acquisition of those characteristics, including skills, knowledge, and attitudes, which permit more productive, contributory, and satisfying ways of life. Similarly, while psychotherapists may sometimes accept the limited goals of simply trying to inhibit pathological processes, there are certainly those (11, 16) who take the position that therapy is to be judged more in terms of how much it contributes to a patient's ability to achieve adult gratifications rather than its sheer efficiency in reducing symptoms or shoring up pathological defenses.

A general concern for such a point of view seems to be emerging in the field of public mental health (26). Beginning with an emphasis on treatment, the concept of community mental health swung to a preventive phase with the main interest focused on identifying the antecedents of mental disease and on reducing morbidity rates by attacking their determinants. The vogue of eugenics was one illustrative feature of this stage. More recently, there has been a considerable dissatisfaction with the whole notion of interpreting psychological states in terms of disease analogues

(15, 23). Maladjustive behavior patterns, the neuroses, and—perhaps to a lesser extent—the psychoses may possibly be better understood as disordered, ineffective, and defensive styles of life than as forms of sickness. In consequence, there seems to be a growing tendency to conceive of the public mental health enterprise as emphasizing positive development with the prevention and treatment of pathology regarded as vital but secondary.

But in what does positive development consist? The statistical concept of the average is not very helpful. Tiegs and Katz (27), for example, reported a study of college students who had been rated for fourteen different evidences of "nervousness." By and large, these traits were normally distributed, suggesting that those subjects rated low must be considered just as "abnormal" (unusual) as those rated high. This conception seems to provide a superficial quantitative model only at the expense of hopeless self contradiction and violence to the ordinary categories of communication. Even in a case that at first blush seems to cause no difficulty, the problem remains. Criminal behavior, for example, is distributed in a J-shaped fashion with most cases concentrated at the point of zero offenses, ranging to a relatively few instances of many-time offenders. Few would argue that the usual behavior here is not also the most "positive." But one suspects that the sheer frequency of law-abiding behavior has little to do with its acknowledged integrative character. If conformity to social rules is generally considered more desirable than criminality, it is not because of its rate of occurrence but because of its consequences for both society and the individual.

Thus, a statistical emphasis on the usual as the criterion of positive adjustment or normality shades into a socially relativistic concept with an implied criterion of conformity. The terms "usual" or "most frequent" or "average" are meaningless without reference to some group, and this state of affairs poses two problems. First, conformity in itself, as history abundantly demonstrates, is a dubious guide to conduct. Innovation is as necessary to a culture's survival as are tradition and conservation, and conformity has frequently meant acquiescence in conditions undermining the maturity and positive development of human beings rather than their enhancement. On more personal levels, conformity sometimes seems related in some degree to personality processes that can quite properly be called pathological (2, 24). Second, relativistic conceptions of normality pose serious questions as to the reference group against which any individual is to be assessed. Benedict (3), for example, has made it quite clear that behavior which is considered abnormal in one culture is quite acceptable in others, that certain forms of abnormalities which occur in some societies are absent in others, and that conduct which is thought completely normal in one group may be regarded as intensely pathological in another. Such observations, while descriptively sound, can lead readily to two troublesome inferences. One is that the storm trooper must be considered as the prototype of integrative adjustment in Nazi culture, the members of the Politburo as best representing human normality Soviet style, and the cruelest adolescent in a delinquent gang as its most positively developed member. The other is that any evaluative judgment of cultures and societies must be regarded as inappropriate. Since normality is conceived only in terms of conformity to group standards, the group itself must be beyond appraisal. Thus, the suspicion and mistrust of Dobu (10), the sense of resigned futility that permeates Alor (6), and the regimentation that characterizes totalitarian nations can logically only be taken as norms in terms of which individual behavior may be interpreted, not as indications of abnormal tendencies in the cultures themselves.

Wegrocki (28), in criticizing such relativistic notions, argues that it is not the form of behavior, the actual acts themselves, that defines its normal or pathological character. Rather, it is its function. What he calls the "quintessence of abnormality" lies in reactions which represent an escape from conflicts and problems rather than a facing of them. This formulation, implying that integrative adjustments are those which most directly confront conflicts and problems, seems essentially free of the difficulties inherent in statistical conceptions and the idea of cultural relativism. But it presents troubles of its own. For instance, what does it mean to "face" a problem or conflict? On what ground, other than the most arbitrarily moralistic one, can such confrontations be defended as more positive than escape? Finally, does this facing of one's problems have any relationship to the matter of conformity in the sense of helping to clarify decisions regarding the acceptance or rejection of group standards?

To deal with such questions requires coming to grips with certain problems of value. It is at this point that the behavioral sciences and ethics meet and merge, and it seems unlikely that any conception of normality can be developed apart from some general considerations that are fundamentally moral. Once the purely relativistic ideas of normality are swept away, it becomes difficult to avoid some concern for the issues of happiness and right conduct, i.e., conduct leading to the greatest degree of human satisfaction, that are the traditional province of the literary interpreter of human experience, the theologian, and the moral philosopher. A primary challenge here is that of providing a rational and naturalistic basis for a concept of integrative adjustment that is at once consistent with the stance and contributions of empirical science and in harmony with whatever wisdom mankind has accumulated through its history.

Symbolic and Social Aspects of Human Nature

One way to meet this challenge is by frankly postulating a basic principle of value. The fundamental contention advanced here is that behavior is "positive" or "integrative" to the extent that it reflects the unique attributes of the human animal. There are undoubtedly other ways of approaching a fruitful concept of normality. Nevertheless, this assertion is consistent with the implications of organic evolution, escapes the fallacy of the survival-of-the-fittest doctrine in its various forms, and permits a derivation of more specific criteria of positive adjustment from the distinctive characteristics of man. No discontinuity within the phylogenetic scale need be assumed. It seems clear, however, that man, while certainly an animal, can hardly be described as "nothing but" an animal; and his normality or integration seems much more likely to consist in the fulfillment of his unique potentialities than in the development of those he shares with infrahuman organisms.

Foremost among these uniquely human potentialities, as Cassirer (4) and Langer (14) make clear, is the enormous capacity for symbolization. What is most characteristic of men is their pervasive employment of *propositional* language. While other organisms, especially dogs (22) and the higher apes (29), react to symbols, their faculty for doing so indicates only an ability to respond to mediate or representative as well as direct stimuli. Man, on the other hand, uses symbols designatively, as a vehicle for recollecting past events, for dealing with things which are not physically present, and for projecting experience into the future. Goldstein (12) makes the same point in his discussion of the "attitude toward the merely possible," the ability to deal with things that are only imagined or which are not part of an immediate, concrete situation. In patients whose speech has been impaired because of brain damage, this attitude toward the possible is disrupted. Thus, aphasics are typically unable to say such things as, "The snow is black" or "The moon shines in the daytime"; similarly, they are incapable of *pretending* to comb their hair or to take a drink of water although they can actually *perform* these acts. Such patients appear to have lost the uniquely human capacity for thinking *about* things as well as directly "thinking things."

It is his symbolic ability, then, that makes man the only creature who can "look before and after and pine for what is not." Propositional speech makes it possible for him to learn from not only his own personal experience but from that of other men in other times and places, to forecast the consequences of his own behavior, and to have ideals. These three symbol-given attributes—the aptitude for capitalizing on experience, including the experience of others over time, the capacity for foresight and the self-imposed control of behavior through the anticipation of its outcomes, and the ability to envision worlds closer than the present one to the heart's desire—constitute a basic set of distinctively human potentialities.

A second set of such potentialities seems related to the long period of helpless dependence that characterizes infancy and childhood. Made mandatory by the relative biological incompleteness of the human body, this phase of development is likely to be lengthened as cultures become more complex. Thus, in such simpler societies as the Samoan (18), children can achieve a higher degree of independence at an earlier age than in the civilizations of the West, for example, where the necessity for learning complicated and specialized economic skills extends the period of dependence through adolescence and even into chronological young adulthood. The central point, however, is that unlike the young of any other species, human children in *all* cultural settings must spend a long time during which the gratification of their most basic needs is mediated by somebody else and is dependent on their relationship to somebody else.

This state of affairs exposes youngsters during their earliest and most formative stages of development to two fundamental conditions of human life. The first is that one's survival, contentment, and need fulfillment involve an inevitable element of reliance on other people. The second is that the relative autonomy, authority, and power that characterize the parent figures and others on whom one relies in childhood are always perceived to a greater or lesser extent in association with responsibility and a kind of altruism. This is, the enjoyment of adult privileges and status tends to occur in conjunction with the acceptance in some degree of the task of in some way mediating the need-gratifications of others. Mowrer and Kluckhohn (20) seem to be speaking of a similar pattern when they describe the socialization process as progressing from childhood *dependency* through *independence* to adult *dependability*.

Moreover, this reciprocal relationship between reliance and responsibility seems to obtain on adult levels as well as between children and parents, with the degree of reciprocity a partial function of the complexity of the culture. In simpler societies, a relatively small number of persons may assume primary responsibility for virtually all of the needs of the group in excess of its bare subsistence demands. Under civilized conditions, however, the specialization made necessary by technology and the pattern of urban living means that each adult is dependent on some other adult in some way and that, conversely, he is responsible in some fashion for the welfare of some other adult. The difference between the simpler and the more complex cultures, however, is only one of degree. The crucial point is that throughout human society, men are in one way or another dependent on each other both in the familiar situation of parents and children and in the course of adult living. This pattern of interdependency gives to human life a social character to be found nowhere else in the animal kingdom. Even among the remarkable social insects, the patterns of symbiosis found there seem to be a result of a genetically determined division of labor rather than the fulfillment of a potentiality for the mutual sharing of responsibilities for each other.

It is in this notion of the fulfillment of distinctively human potentialities that a fruitful conception of positive adjustment may have its roots. From the symbolic and peculiarly social character of human life, it may be possible to derive a set of potential attributes the cultivation of which results in something different from the mere absence of pathology and which forms a standard against which to assess the degree of integration in individual persons. To accept this task is to attempt the construction of a normative or ideal model of a normal, positively developed, or integratively adjusted human being.

A Model of Integrative Adjustment

In the first place, it would seem that as the symbolic capacity that endows man with foresight develops in an individual, there is a concomitant increase in his ability to control his own behavior by anticipating its probable long-range consequences. The normal person is, first of all, one who has learned that in many situations his greatest satisfaction is gained by foregoing the immediate opportunities for comfort and pleasure in the interest of more remote rewards. He lives according to what Paul Elmer More, the Anglican theologian, calls "the law of costingness":

. . . the simple and tyrannical fact that, whether in the world physical, or in the world intellectual, or in the world spiritual, we can get nothing without paying an exacted price. The fool is he who ignores, and the villain is he who thinks he can outwit, the vigilance of the nemesis guarding this law of costingness . . . all (one's) progress is dependent on surrendering one interest or value for a higher interest or value. (19, p. 158).

Mowrer and Ullman (21) have made the same point in arguing, from the results of an ingenious experiment, that normality results in large part from the acquired ability to subject impulses to control through the symbolic cues one presents to oneself in the course of estimating the consequences of one's own behavior. Through symbolization, the future outcomes of one's actions are drawn into the psychological present; the strength of more remote rewards or punishments is consequently increased; and a long-range inhibitory or facilitating effect on incipient conduct is thereby exercised.

This increase in self-control means a lessened need for control by external authority, and conformity consequently becomes a relatively unimportant issue. The integratively adjusted person either conforms to the standards of his group because their acceptance leads to the most rewarding long-range consequences for him, or he rebels against authority, whether of persons or of law or custom, on *considered* grounds. This considered form of revolt implies two things. The first is an honest conviction that rules or the ruler are somehow unjust and that the implementation of his own values is likely to lead to a more broadly satisfying state of affairs. Such an attack on authority is very different from revolts that occur out of sheer needs for self-assertion or desires for power or as expressions of displaced hostility. The main dimension of difference is that of honesty as opposed to deception. The normal person is relatively well aware of his motives in either conforming or rebelling. The pathological rebel, on the other hand, tends to deceive himself and others about his goals. His reasons for nonconformity amount to rationalizations, and his justifications are typically projections. This kind of self-defeating and socially disruptive deceptiveness is seen daily in clinical practice.

The second characteristic of nonconformity in the normal person is that it is undertaken with an essential acceptance of the possible consequences. Having considered the risks beforehand, he is inclined neither to whine nor to ask that his rebellious conduct be overlooked if he runs afoul of trouble. In keeping with the "law of costingness," he is willing to pay the price for behaving in accordance with his own idiosyncratic values. "We have the right to lead our own lives," John Erskine (8) makes Helen of Troy say to her daughter Hermione, "but that right implies another—to suffer the consequences. . . . Do your best, and if it's a mistake, hide nothing and be glad to suffer for it. That's morality." A psychological paraphrase of this bit of belletristic wisdom is not inappropriate: The assumption of responsibility * for one's actions is one of the attributes of personal integration.

But if personal responsibility and self-control through foresight can be derived as aspects of integrative adjustment from man's symbolic capacity, a third characteristic of interpersonal responsibility can be deduced from his social nature. If interdependency is an essential part of human social life, then the normal person becomes one who can act dependably in relation to others and at the same time acknowledge his need for others. The roots of the former probably lie, as McClelland (17) has pointed out, in the role perceptions which developing children form of parent figures and other agents of the socialization process. By conceiving of such people as at least in some degree the nurturant guides of others and through identification with them, the integratively adjusted individual "wants to be" himself trustworthy and altruistic in the sense of being dependable and acting out of a genuine concern for the welfare of others as he can best conceive it. Altruism in this context, therefore, means nothing sentimental. It certainly includes the making and enforcement of disciplinary rules and the imposition of behavioral limits, but only if these steps are motivated by an interest in helping others and express concern and affection rather than mere personal annoyance or the power conferred by a superior status.

Similarly, the acknowledgment of one's needs for others implies a learned

---

* This conception of responsibility is by no means antideterministic. As Fingarette (8) points out, one can *understand* his own or another's behavior, in the sense of accounting for it or rationally explaining it, by the retrospective process of examining the past. Responsibility, on the other hand, is neither retrospective in orientation nor explanatory in function. It is future oriented and refers to the *act* of proclaiming oneself as answerable for one's own conduct and its consequences. Thus, "responsibility," in this context, is not a logical term, implying causation, but a behavioral and attitudinal one, descriptive of a class of human actions.

capacity for forming and maintaining intimate interpersonal relationships. Erikson (7) refers to this aspect of the normal personality as the attitude of "basic trust," and it is not far from what can be meaningfully styled in plain language as the ability to love. One suspects that the origins of this ability lie in the long experience during childhood of having need gratifications frequently associated with the presence of another person, typically a parent figure. By this association and the process of generalization, one comes to attach a positive affect to others. But as the youngster develops, he gradually learns that the need-mediating behavior of others is maintained only by his reciprocating, by his entering into a relationship of mutuality with others. If this kind of mutuality is not required of him, he is likely to perpetuate his dependency beyond the period his biological level of development and the complexity of his culture define as appropriate; whereas if he is required to demonstrate this mutuality too soon, he is likely to form the schema that interpersonal relationships are essentially matters of traded favors and that instead of basic trust, the proper attitude is one of getting as much as possible while giving no more than necessary. The pursuit in research and thought of such hypotheses as these might shed a good deal of light on the determinants of friendship, marital happiness, and effective parenthood, the relational expressions of effective personal integration.

But there is still another interpersonal attitude relevant to a positive conception of adjustment that is somewhat different from that bound up with relationships of an intimate and personal kind. There is a sense in which each individual, even if he regards himself as unfortunate and unhappy, owes his essential humanity to the group which enabled him to survive his helpless infancy. As studies of feral children (25) have shown, even the humanly distinctive and enormously adaptive trait of propositional speech does not become usable without the stimulation and nurture of other people. A kind of obligation is therefore created for the person to be an asset rather than a burden to society. It is partly to the discharging of this obligation that Adler (1) referred in developing his concept of social interest as a mark of normality. While the notion certainly implies the learning of local loyalties and personal affections, it also transcends the provincial limits of group and era. Because man's symbolic capacity enables him to benefit from the record of human history and to anticipate the future, and because his pattern of social interdependency, especially in civilized societies, reaches across the boundaries of political units and parochial affiliations, it seems reasonable to expect the positively developed person to behave in such a fashion as to contribute, according to his own particular lights, to the general welfare of humanity, to take as his frame of reference mankind at large as best he understands it rather than his own group or clan.

Ideologies are at issue here, but there need be neither embarrassment nor a lack of room for debate regarding the specifics of policy and values in the hypothesis that democratic attitudes are closely bound up with personality integration. After all, democracy in psychological terms implies only a concern about others, a valuing of persons above things, and a willingness to participate in mutually gratifying relationships with many categories of persons, including those of which one has only vicarious knowledge. Departures from democratic attitudes in this psychological sense mean a restriction on the potentiality for friendship and imply both a fear of others and a valuation of such things as power over people, thus endangering the interpersonal rewards that come from acting on the attitude of basic trust. Democratic social interest, then, means simply the most direct route to the fulfillment of a distinctively human capacity derived from man's symbolic character and the inevitability of his social life.

Finally, man's ability to assume an attitude toward the "merely possible" suggests that the normal person has ideals and standards that he tries to live up to even though they often exceed his grasp. For an integrative adjustment does not consist in the attainment of perfection but in a striving to act in accordance with the best principles of conduct that one can conceive. Operationally, this notion implies that there is an optimum discrepancy between one's self-concept and one's ego-ideal. Those for whom this discrepancy is too large (in favor, of course, of the ideal) are likely to condemn themselves to the frustration of never approximating their goals and to an almost perpetually low self-esteem. Those whose discrepancies are too low, on the other hand, are probably less than integratively adjusted either because they are failing to fulfill their human capacity to envision themselves as they could be or because they are self-deceptively overestimating themselves.

This model of integrative adjustment as characterized by self-control, personal responsibility, social responsibility, democratic social interest, and ideals must be regarded only in the most tentative fashion. Nevertheless, it does seem to take into account some realistic considerations. It avoids the impossible conception of the normal person as one who is always happy, free from conflict, and without problems. Rather, it suggests that he may often fall short of his ideals; and because of ignorance, the limitations under which an individual lives in a complex world, or the strength of immediate pressures, he may sometimes behave in ways that prove to be shortsighted or self-defeating. Consequently, he knows something of the experience of guilt at times, and because he tries to be fully aware of the risks he takes, he can hardly be entirely free from fear and worry. On the other hand, a person who is congruent to the model is likely to be one who enjoys a relatively consistent and high degree of self-respect and who elicits a predominantly positive and warm reaction from others. Moreover, it is such a person who seems to learn wisdom rather than hostile bitterness or pathologically frightened withdrawal from whatever disappointments or

2 3 4 5 6 7 8 9

suffering may be his lot. Guilt, for example, becomes a challenge to his honesty, especially with himself but also with others; and it signalizes for him the desirability of modifying his behavior, or greater effort to live up to his ideals, rather than the need to defend himself by such mechanisms as rationalization or projection. Finally, the model permits a wide variation in the actual behaviors in which normal people may engage and even makes allowance for a wide range of disagreements among them. Integrative adjustment does not consist in the individual's fitting a preconceived behavioral mold. It may well consist in the degree to which his efforts fulfill the symbolic and social potentialities that are distinctively human.

References

1. Adler, A. Social interest: A challenge to mankind. London: Faber & Faber, 1938.
2. Adorno, T. W., Frenkel-Brunswik, Else, Levinson, D. J., & Sanford, R. N. The authoritarian personality. New York: Harper, 1950.
3. Benedict, Ruth. Anthropology and the abnormal. J. gen. Psychol., 1934, 10, 59–82.
4. Cassirer, E. An essay on man. New Haven: Yale Univer. Press, 1944.
5. Darrah, L. W. The difficulty of being normal. J. nerv. ment. Dis., 1939, 90, 730–739.
6. DuBois, Cora. The people of Alor. Minneapolis: Univer. Minnesota Press, 1944.
7. Erikson, E. H. Childhood and society. New York: Norton, 1950.
8. Erskine, J. The private life of Helen of Troy. New York: Bobbs-Merrill Co., 1925.
9. Fingarette, H. Psychoanalytic perspectives on moral guilt and responsibility: A re-evaluation. Phil. phenomenol Res., 1955, 16, 18–36.
10. Fortune, R. F. Sorcerers of Dobu. London: Routledge, 1932.
11. Fromm, E. The sane society. New York: Rinehart, 1955.
12. Goldstein, K. Human nature in the light of psychopathology. Cambridge, Mass.: Harvard Univer. Press, 1940.
13. Hacker, F. H. The concept of normality and its practical significance. Amer. J. Orthopsychiat., 1945, 15, 47–64.
14. Langer, Susanne K. Philosophy in a new key. Cambridge, Mass.: Harvard Univer. Press, 1942.
15. Marzolf, S. S. The disease concept in psychology. Psychol. Rev., 1947, 54, 211–221.
16. May, R. Man's search for himself. New York: Norton, 1953.
17. McClelland, D. Personality. New York: William Sloane Associates, 1951.
18. Mead, Margaret. Coming of age in Samoa. New York: William Morrow, 1928.
19. More, P. E. The Catholic faith. Princeton: Princeton Univer. Press, 1931.
20. Mowrer, O. H., & Kluckhohn, C. A dynamic theory of personality. In Hunt, J. McV. (Ed.), Personality and the behavior disorders. New York: Ronald Press, 1944. Pp. 69–135.
21. Mowrer, O. H., & Ullman, A. D. Time as a determinant in integrative learning. Psychol. Rev., 1945, 52, 61–90.
22. Pavlov, I. P. Conditioned reflexes. London: Oxford Univer. Press, 1927.
23. Riese, W. The conception of disease. New York: Philosophical Library, 1953.
24. Riesman, D. The lonely crowd. New Haven: Yale Univer. Press, 1950.
25. Singh, J. A. L., & Zingg, R. M. Wolf-children and feral man. New York: Harper, 1942.
26. Subcommittee on Evaluation of Mental Health Activities. Evaluation in mental health. Bethesda, Md.: Public Health Service, 1955.

27. Tiegs, E. W., & Katz, B. *Mental hygiene in education.* New York: Ronald Press, 1941.
28. Wegrocki, H. J. A critique of cultural and statistical concepts of abnormality. *J. abnorm. soc. Psychol.,* 1939, 34, 166–178.
29. Yerkes, R. M. *Chimpanzees: A laboratory colony.* New Haven: Yale Univer. Press, 1943.

Theories of Personality

When we observe the behavior of human beings, the rich complexity of behavior and the puzzling differences among individuals are apparent. In order that behavior can be viewed with systematic understanding, it is necessary to impose organization. Individual A loves his children when individual B does not; individual C seems to us to defeat himself while D achieves his goals; E appears to live in a world of fantasy, unfamiliar to most of us; F is happy while G is depressed. How are we to comprehend the differences? Most of us entertain some set of implicit or explicit notions which define, somewhat to our satisfaction, human behavior. Most of us feel, more or less in a vague way, that we can account for the behavior of the persons who interact with us. Our private systems, however, are incomplete and do not share widespread acknowledgment.

There have been formal attempts to comprehend man in all his complexity. The history of thought in philosophy and religion, literature and art, biology, economics, and psychology is replete with more or less fundamental analyses of human behavior and man's ultimate nature. The concern has been with stating basic considerations about the fundamental characteristics of man.

In this section of readings, we are concerned with illustrating the variety of ways in which contemporary psychology approaches the problem of the nature of man. How does the clinical psychologist understand the individual who is in distress? What does the research psychologist investigate? To pursue answers to these questions is to be made aware that there is a variety of systematic ways of understanding people, and that these separate conceptualizations lead to differences in research attack. We shall see that there is disagreement rather than fundamentally shared views. We shall see that psychology, in common with the other physical and behavioral sciences, argues and speculates in diverse ways.

The efforts which are illustrated below belong to the domain of what has come to be known as *personality theory*. We are here concerned with providing accounts of some of the major theories or sets of speculative hypotheses which guide psychologists in their search for explanation and control.

If we are to consider speculations about the nature of *personality*, we need to come to some more or less convenient definition of the term. Since different theories define the word differently, it is no easy task to find a definition acceptable to all psychologists. In 1937, Gordon W. Allport published *Personality: A Psychological Interpretation*, which is extremely valuable for its report of his scholarly search for definitions of personality in a variety of settings.[1] Allport discovered forty-eight definitions or meanings which the term had acquired in sociology, law, philosophy, theology, psychology, and literature. It became clear to Allport that there were two fundamentally opposed meanings. One meaning defined personality in terms of outward appearance while the other defined personality in terms of inner experience. That is, throughout history we find definitions where distinctions are made between what an individual offers for public consumption and what he is *really* like. Allport proposed a forty-ninth definition for psychology, *what a man really is*, which he elaborated in the following formal statement: "Personality is the dynamic organization within the individual of those psychophysical systems that determine his unique adjustment to his environment." For Allport, his definition is sufficiently broad to represent a "synthesis of contemporary psychological usage." While its generality involves limitations, it serves as a useful and convenient orientation to this section. All the personality theories to be considered involve postulating an *organization* of *systems* (habits, traits, attitudes, needs, self-concepts, etc.) which *determine* (lie in back of specific acts) adjustment.

Before we turn to the specific personality theories, we need to give some consideration to theories in a formal sense. When can we say that we have a theory? Neal E. Miller, in commenting upon theoretical models, gives an unequivocal reply. He writes that "a system can properly be called a model or theory if, and only if, one can use it to make rigorous deductions about some of the consequences of different sets of conditions. High school geometry is a familiar example." [2] We have a theory here because we can deduce the consequences of a *great* number of different conditions from a *limited* set of definitions and axioms. In addition we can

[1] Gordon W. Allport, *Personality: A Psychological Interpretation*, Henry Holt and Company, Inc., New York, 1937.

[2] Neal E. Miller, Comments on theoretical models in *Theoretical Models and Personality Theory*, David Krech and George S. Klein (eds.), Duke University Press, Durham, N.C., 1952.

turn to recent analyses in the philosophy of science for the formal properties of theories. The considerations of philosophers of science have led to the view that a formal theory should contain *basic terms, defined terms, formation rules, transformation rules, postulates* and *theorems.*[3]

According to the criteria given above, a good many psychological theories are properly not theories at all but points of view or notions. Miller calls them "articles of faith or intuition." We shall, however, not utilize any formal definition of theory to preclude a point of view from consideration. Still it is worth noting that most personality theories do not share in the properties which Miller and various philosophers of science have called to our attention.

It is important to indicate that the theories will vary in many respects. Some will appear to be more scientifically rigorous than others, the scope of inquiry will differ in ambition, and the evidence available to support each will vary in its character. Eysenck's work, for example, will appear to be more rigorous than Jung's; Jung will surely appear to be more ambitious in his undertaking than Maslow; the evidence adduced in support of a learning theory approach by Shaffer and Shoben will be different from the evidence offered by Freud.

The section opens with selections relating to the theories of Freud, Jung, and Sullivan grouped together because they all belong to the tradition of psychoanalytic theory. Jung, however, withdrew from association with psychoanalysis when he could no longer accept Freud's theory of sexuality, and Sullivan has been identified as *neo-Freudian,* which involves major revisions of Freudian theory.

The selection from Freud is drawn from the last publication before his death. His professed aim was to provide an outline of his theory. The passage which is reprinted here provides the reader with the three fundamental aspects of his total scheme. There is an account of his *theory of mind,* his *theory of infantile sexuality,* and his *theory of unconscious determinism.* Taken together, they summarize a large share of his total contribution, which has had a significant impact on our view of the nature of man. His influence has been felt strongly not only in psychology and psychiatry, but in other disciplines as well. Literature, anthropology, sociology, education, art, law, theology, philosophy, political science, economics, etc., have all felt his persuasive force.

Freud's attempt to account for human behavior is the most ambitious theory of those considered. His concern is with the

[3] An elaboration of this view is given in William C. Schutz, *FIRO: A Three-dimensional Theory of Interpersonal Behavior,* Rinehart & Company, Inc., New York, 1958.

totality of human experience. While the scope of psychoanalytic theory enables us to speculate about a wide variety of human behavior, his method of validating his generalizations, which consists of the careful examination in a treatment situation of the life history of the individual, leaves a good deal to be desired in rigor. All of the limitations which relate to the case study method apply. Contemporary psychology, however, is continuing to find ways of subjecting Freudian hypotheses to controlled investigation and experimentation.

Similar evaluations may be applied to Jung's personality theory. Again there is lack of rigor in defining concepts and pursuing evidence; again there is the richest speculation with respect to the totality of human existence. Jung's basic unit of investigation is the *psyche*. With this concept he refers to the psychological structure of the human being. He thinks of the psyche as a kind of nonphysical space wherein psychic phenomena occur. In order to describe these phenomena, Jung has found it necessary to develop a vocabulary which is not widely shared and which includes such concepts as *persona, personal unconscious, collective unconscious, anima, animus,* and *archetypes*. The selection from Progoff relates Jung's considerations of the nature of the psyche. While this represents a small part of his total theory, it has been selected as typical of his best known formulations.

Sullivan's theory of personality is represented by a selection from the writings of Patrick Mullahy, who has been his chief interpreter. According to the theory which has become known as the *interpersonal theory of psychiatry*, personality is "the relatively enduring pattern of recurrent interpersonal situations which characterize a human life." The proper field of investigation is the interpersonal situation; the individual does not and cannot exist apart from his transactions with other people. Sullivan's fundamental hypothesis, therefore, led him away from preoccupation with biological drives and Freudian instinctual urges to the study of social interactions, mother and child, doctor and patient, etc. Mullahy's selection gives an account of Sullivan's view with respect to the goals of behavior, the modes of human experience, and the evolving of the self through interaction with others.

A selection from Shaffer and Shoben is given next. It is included here because it represents one attempt to apply learning theory to the complex behavior of human beings. Formal learning theory was initiated in an attempt to develop the principles by which learning occurs, and until recently efforts have been concerned with the learning of relatively simple tasks. It is possible, however, to view the totality of human experience with the theoretical notions and rigorous procedures of learning theorists. Dollard and Miller, in *Personality and Psychotherapy*, for example, have translated Freud into a set of words familiar to an experimental psychology of learning.[4] The words "drive," "cue," "response," "reward," "drive reduction" recur throughout their discussion of complex human behavior. Similarly, Shaffer and Shoben define two types of learning, associative learning and drive-reduction learning, which, they feel, are sufficient to account for the elaboration of motives and the stabilization of modes of response. Learning theorists achieve rigor in definitions and procedure; their operations are public and replicable; their method is experimentation. Their experimental subjects, however, are largely infrahuman and their experiments too often represent an oversimplified model of the hypothesis under test.

Rogers's theory of the self or of self-regarding attitudes follows. Since his theory of personality developed concurrently with a theory of psychotherapy, it is heavily flavored with observations about the therapeutic process. The paper which is reproduced here gives an account of his carefully ordered observations about attitudes toward the self and attitudes toward others which he has developed from his therapeutic experience. These observations form the basis for a theory of personality which uses as its major construct the *self-concept*. This term refers to the totality of attitudes the individual holds with reference to himself. The self-concept is learned in evaluational transactions with others (notably, important others such as mother and father), and it influences behavior whether or not it is in accord with reality. The program of extensive research which the theory has encouraged testifies to its heuristic value.

The remaining papers by Eysenck and Maslow represent hierarchical models of personality organization. Maslow formulates a theory of motivation which explicitly orders physiological needs, the needs for safety, love, esteem, and self-actualization into a heirarchy of prepotency; and Eysenck describes a procedure for discovering relatively pure, psychological factors which are denotable, measurable, and lie in back of the specific acts of human beings. Maslow's approach is therefore speculative and "derives most directly, however, from clinical experience"; Eysenck's contribution is methodological in that he outlines a limited and careful experimental procedure. The two papers are important in that they represent current concerns: Maslow for a theory of personality that emphasizes the striving, self-actualizing, healthy aspect of the in-

[4] John Dollard and Neal E. Miller, *Personality and Psychotherapy*, McGraw-Hill Book Company, Inc., New York, 1950.

dividual; Eysenck for the application of a methodology which he feels will ultimately lead to a clarification of the entire field of inquiry in personality theory.

PSYCHOANALYTIC THEORY *

[SIGMUND FREUD

The Psychical Apparatus

Psychoanalysis makes a basic assumption,[1] the discussion of which falls within the sphere of philosophical thought, but the justification of which lies in its results. We know two things concerning what we call our psyche or mental life: firstly, its bodily organ and scene of action, the brain (or nervous system), and secondly, our acts of consciousness, which are immediate data and cannot be more fully explained by any kind of description. Everything that lies between these two terminal points is unknown to us and, so far as we are aware, there is no direct relation between them. If it existed, it would at the most afford an exact localization of the processes of consciousness and would give us no help toward understanding them.

Our two hypotheses start out from these ends or beginnings of our knowledge. The first is concerned with localization. We assume that mental life is the function of an apparatus to which we ascribe the characteristics of being extended in space and of being made up of several portions—which we imagine, that is, as being like a telescope or microscope or something of the sort. The consistent carrying through of a conception of this kind is a scientific novelty, even though some attempts in that direction have been made previously.

We have arrived at our knowledge of this psychical apparatus by studying the individual development of human beings. To the oldest of these mental provinces or agencies we give the name of *id*. It contains everything that is inherited, that is present at birth, that is fixed in the constitution—above all, therefore, the instincts, which originate in the somatic organization and which find their first mental expression in the id in forms unknown to us.[2]

* From Sigmund Freud, *An Outline of Psychoanalysis*, pp. 13–45, W. W. Norton & Company, Inc., New York. Copyright 1949. Reprinted by the permission of the publisher.

[1] [It will be seen that this basic assumption is a double-barrelled one and is sometimes referred to by the author as two separate hypotheses. So, for instance, in the next paragraph. . . .—*Trans.*]

[2] This oldest portion of the mental apparatus remains the most important throughout life, and it was the first subject of the investigations of psychoanalysis. [Throughout

Under the influence of the real external world which surrounds us, one portion of the id has undergone a special development. From what was originally a cortical layer, provided with organs for receiving stimuli and with apparatus for protection against excessive stimulation, a special organization has arisen which henceforward acts as an intermediary between the id and the external world. This region of our mental life has been given the name of *ego*.

The principal characteristics of the ego are these. In consequence of the relation which was already established between sensory perception and muscular action, the ego is in control of voluntary movement. It has the task of self-preservation. As regards *external* events, it performs that task by becoming aware of the stimuli from without, by storing up experiences of them (in the memory), by avoiding excessive stimuli (through flight), by dealing with moderate stimuli (through adaptation) and, finally, by learning to bring about appropriate modifications in the external world to its own advantage (through activity). As regards *internal* events, in relation to the id, it performs that task by gaining control over the demands of the instincts, by deciding whether they shall be allowed to obtain satisfaction, by postponing that satisfaction to times and circumstances favorable in the external world or by suppressing their excitations completely. Its activities are governed by consideration of the tensions produced by stimuli present within it or introduced into it. The raising of these tensions is in general felt as *unpleasure* and their lowering as *pleasure*. It is probable, however, that what is felt as pleasure or unpleasure is not the *absolute* degree of the tensions but something in the rhythm of their changes. The ego pursues pleasure and seeks to avoid unpleasure. An increase in unpleasure which is expected and foreseen is met by a *signal of anxiety*; the occasion of this increase, whether it threatens from without or within, is called a *danger*. From time to time the ego gives up its connection with the external world and withdraws into the state of sleep, in which its organization undergoes far-reaching changes. It may be inferred from the state of sleep that that organization consists in a particular distribution of mental energy.

The long period of childhood, during which the growing human being lives in dependence upon his parents, leaves behind it a precipitate, which forms within his ego a special agency in which this parental influence is prolonged. It has received the name of *superego*. In so far as the superego is differentiated from the ego or opposed to it, it constitutes a third force which the ego must take into account.

Thus, an action by the ego is as it should be if it satisfies simultaneously the demands of the id, of the superego and of reality, that is to say if it is

---

. . . the English word "instinct" is, with some misgivings, used to render the German "*Trieb*." The sense in which Freud uses the term is, in any case, made clear in the following pages.—*Trans.*]

able to reconcile their demands with one another. The details of the relation between the ego and the superego become completely intelligible if they are carried back to the child's attitude toward his parents. The parents' influence naturally includes not merely the personalities of the parents themselves but also the racial, national, and family traditions handed on through them as well as the demands of the immediate social *milieu* which they represent. In the same way, an individual's superego in the course of his development takes over contributions from later successors and substitutes of his parents, such as teachers, admired figures in public life, or high social ideals. It will be seen that, in spite of their fundamental difference, the id and the superego have one thing in common: they both represent the influences of the past (the id the influence of heredity, the superego essentially the influence of what is taken over from other people), whereas the ego is principally determined by the individual's own experience, that is to say by accidental and current events.

This general pattern of a psychical apparatus may be supposed to apply equally to the higher animals which resemble man mentally. A superego must be presumed to be present wherever, as in the case of man, there is a long period of dependence in childhood. The assumption of a distinction between ego and id cannot be avoided.

Animal psychology has not yet taken in hand the interesting problem which is here presented.

The Theory of the Instincts

The power of the id expresses the true purpose of the individual organism's life. This consists in the satisfaction of its innate needs. No such purpose as that of keeping itself alive or of protecting itself from dangers by means of anxiety can be attributed to the id. That is the business of the ego, which is also concerned with discovering the most favorable and least perilous method of obtaining satisfaction, taking the external world into account. The superego may bring fresh needs to the fore, but its chief function remains the *limitation* of satisfactions.

The forces which we assume to exist behind the tensions caused by the needs of the id are called *instincts*. They represent the somatic demands upon mental life. Though they are the ultimate cause of all activity, they are by nature conservative; the state, whatever it may be, which a living thing has reached, gives rise to a tendency to re-establish that state so soon as it has been abandoned. It is possible to distinguish an indeterminate number of instincts and in common practice this is in fact done. For us, however, the important question arises whether we may not be able to derive all of these various instincts from a few fundamental ones. We have found that instincts can change their aim (by displacement) and also that they can replace one another—the energy of one instinct passing over to another. This latter process is still insufficiently understood. After long doubts and vacillations we have decided to assume the existence of only two basic instincts, *Eros* and *the destructive instinct*. (The contrast between the instincts of self-preservation and of the preservation of the species, as well as the contrast between ego-love and object-love, fall within the bounds of Eros.) The aim of the first of these basic instincts is to establish ever greater unities and to preserve them thus—in short, to bind together; the aim of the second, on the contrary, is to undo connections and so to destroy things. We may suppose that the final aim of the destructive instinct is to reduce living things to an inorganic state. For this reason we also call it the *death instinct*. If we suppose that living things appeared later than inanimate ones and arose out of them, then the death instinct agrees with the formula that we have stated, to the effect that instincts tend toward a return to an earlier state. We are unable to apply the formula to Eros (the love instinct). That would be to imply that living substance had once been a unity but had subsequently been torn apart and was now tending toward re-union.[3]

In biological functions the two basic instincts work against each other or combine with each other. Thus, the act of eating is a destruction of the object with the final aim of incorporating it, and the sexual act is an act of aggression having as its purpose the most intimate union. This interaction of the two basic instincts with and against each other gives rise to the whole variegation of the phenomena of life. The analogy of our two basic instincts extends from the region of animate things to the pair of opposing forces—attraction and repulsion—which rule in the inorganic world.[4]

Modifications in the proportions of the fusion between the instincts have the most noticeable results. A surplus of sexual aggressiveness will change a lover into a sexual murderer, while a sharp diminution in the aggressive factor will lead to shyness or impotence.

There can be no question of restricting one or the other of the basic instincts to a single region of the mind. They are necessarily present everywhere. We may picture an initial state of things by supposing that the whole available energy of Eros, to which we shall henceforward give the name of *libido*, is present in the as yet undifferentiated ego-id and serves to neutralize the destructive impulses which are simultaneously present. (There is no term analogous to "libido" for describing the energy of the destructive instinct.) It becomes relatively easy for us to follow the later vicissitudes of the libido; but this is more difficult with the destructive instinct.

So long as that instinct operates internally, as a death instinct, it remains

---

[3] Something of the sort has been imagined by poets, but nothing like it is known to us from the actual history of living substance.

[4] This picture of the basic forces or instincts, which still arouses much opposition among analysts, was already a familiar one to the philosopher Empedocles of Acragas.

silent; we only come across it after it has become diverted outward as an instinct of destruction. That that diversion should occur seems essential for the preservation of the individual; the musculature is employed for the purpose. When the superego begins to be formed, considerable amounts of the aggressive instinct become fixated within the ego and operate there in a self-destructive fashion. This is one of the dangers to health to which mankind become subject on the path to cultural development. The holding back of aggressiveness is in general unhealthy and leads to illness. A person in a fit of rage often demonstrates how the transition from restrained aggressiveness to self-destructiveness is effected, by turning his aggressiveness against himself: he tears his hair or beats his face with his fists—treatment which he would evidently have preferred to apply to someone else. Some portion of self-destructiveness remains permanently within, until it at length succeeds in doing the individual to death, not, perhaps, until his libido has been used up or has become fixated in some disadvantageous way. Thus it may in general be suspected that the *individual* dies of his internal conflicts but that the *species* dies of its unsuccessful struggle against the external world, when the latter undergoes changes of a kind that cannot be dealt with by the adaptations which the species has acquired.

It is difficult to say anything of the behavior of the libido in the id and in the superego. Everything that we know about it relates to the ego, in which the whole available amount of libido is at first stored up. We call this state of things absolute, primary *narcissism*. It continues until the ego begins to cathect [5] the presentations of objects with libido—to change narcissistic libido into *object libido*. Throughout life the ego remains the great reservoir from which libidinal cathexes [5] are sent out on to objects and into which they are also once more withdrawn, like the pseudopodia of a body of protoplasm. It is only when someone is completely in love that the main quantity of libido is transferred on to the object and the object to some extent takes the place of the ego. A characteristic of libido which is important in life is its *mobility*, the ease with which it passes from one object to another. This must be contrasted with the *fixation* of libido to particular objects, which often persists through life.

There can be no question that the libido has somatic sources, that it streams into the ego from various organs and parts of the body. This is most clearly seen in the case of the portion of the libido which, from its instinctual aim, is known as sexual excitation. The most prominent of the parts of the body from which this libido arises are described by the name of *erotogenic zones*, though strictly speaking the whole body is an ero-

[5] [The words "cathexis" and "to cathect" are used as renderings of the German "Besetzung" and "besetzen." These are the terms with which Freud expresses the idea of psychical energy being lodged in or attaching itself to mental structures or processes, somewhat on the analogy of an electric charge.—*Trans.*]

togenic zone. The greater part of what we know about Eros—that is, about its exponent, the libido—has been gained from the study of the sexual function, which, indeed, in the popular view, if not in our theory, coincides with Eros. We have been able to form a picture of the way in which the sexual impulse, which is destined to exercise a decisive influence on our life, gradually develops out of successive contributions from a number of component instincts, which represent particular erotogenic zones.

The Development of the Sexual Function

According to the popular view, human sexual life consists essentially in the impulse to bring one's own genitals into contact with those of someone of the opposite sex. With this are associated, as accessory phenomena and introductory acts, kissing this extraneous body, looking at and touching it. This impulse is supposed to make its appearance at puberty, that is, at the age of sexual maturity, and to serve the purposes of reproduction. Nevertheless, certain facts have always been known that fail to fit into the narrow framework of this view. (1) It is a remarkable fact that there are people who are only attracted by the persons and genitals of members of their own sex. (2) It is equally remarkable that there are people whose desires behave in every way like sexual ones, but who at the same time entirely disregard the sexual organs or their normal use; people of this kind are known as "perverts." (3) And finally it is striking that many children (who are on that account regarded as degenerates) take a very early interest in their genitals and show signs of excitation in them.

It may well be believed that psychoanalysis provoked astonishment and denials when, partly upon the basis of these three neglected facts, it contradicted all the popular opinions upon sexuality. Its principal findings are as follows:

1. Sexual life does not begin only at puberty, but starts with clear manifestations soon after birth.

2. It is necessary to distinguish sharply between the concepts of "sexual" and "genital." The former is the wider concept and includes many activities that have nothing to do with the genitals.

3. Sexual life comprises the function of obtaining pleasure from zones of the body—a function which is subsequently brought into the service of that of reproduction. The two functions often fail to coincide completely.

The chief interest is naturally focused upon the first of these assertions, the most unexpected of all. It has been found that in early childhood there are signs of bodily activity to which only ancient prejudice could deny the name of sexual, and which are connected with mental phenomena that we come across later in adult love, such as fixation to a particular object, jealousy, and so on. It is further found that these phenomena which emerge in early childhood form part of a regular process of development, that they undergo a steady increase and reach a climax toward the end of the fifth year, after which there follows a lull. During this lull, progress is at a standstill and much is unlearned and undone. After the end of this period of latency, as it is called, sexual life is resumed with puberty, or, as we might say, it has a second efflorescence. Here we come upon the fact that the onset of sexual life is *diphasic*, that it occurs in two waves; this is unknown except in man and evidently has an important bearing upon his genesis.[6] It is not a matter of indifference that, with few exceptions, the events of the early period of sexuality fall a victim to *infantile amnesia*. Our understanding of the etiology of the neuroses and the technique of analytic therapy are derived from these views; and the tracing of the process of development in this early period has also provided evidence for yet other conclusions.

The first organ to make its appearance as an erotogenic zone and to make libidinal demands upon the mind is, from the time of birth onward, the mouth. To begin with, all mental activity is centered upon the task of providing satisfaction for the needs of that zone. In the first instance, of course, the latter serves the purposes of self-preservation by means of nourishment; but physiology should not be confused with psychology. The baby's obstinate persistence in sucking gives evidence at an early stage of a need for satisfaction which, although it originates from and is stimulated by the taking of nourishment, nevertheless seeks to obtain pleasure independently of nourishment and for that reason may and should be described as "sexual."

Sadistic impulses already begin to occur sporadically during the oral phase along with the appearance of the teeth. Their extent increases greatly during the second phase, which we describe as the sadistic-anal phase, because satisfaction is then sought in aggression and in the excretory function. We justify our inclusion of aggressive impulses in the libido by supposing that sadism is an instinctual fusion of purely libidinal and purely destructive impulses, a fusion which thenceforward persists without interruption.[7]

The third phase is the so-called phallic one, which is, as it were, a forerunner of the final shape of sexual life, and already greatly resembles it. It is

---

[6] Cf. the hypothesis that man is descended from a mammal which reached sexual maturity at the age of five, but that some great external influence was brought to bear upon the species and interrupted the straight line of development of sexuality. This may also have been related to some other transformations in the sexual life of man as compared with that of animals, such as the suppression of the periodicity of the libido and the exploitation of the part played by menstruation in the relation between the sexes.

[7] The question arises whether satisfaction of purely destructive instinctual impulses can be felt as pleasure, whether pure destructiveness without any libidinal component occurs. Satisfaction of what remains in the ego of the death instinct seems not to produce feelings of pleasure, although masochism represents a fusion which is precisely analogous to sadism.

to be noted that what comes in question at this stage is not the genitals of both sexes but only those of the male (the phallus). The female genitals long remain unknown: in the child's attempt at understanding sexual processes, he pays homage to the venerable cloacal theory—a theory which has a genetic justification.[8]

With the phallic phase and in the course of it the sexuality of early childhood reaches its height and approaches its decline. Thenceforward boys and girls have different histories. To begin with, both place their intellectual activity at the service of sexual research; both start off from the presumption of the universal presence of the penis. But now the paths of the sexes divide. The boy enter the Œdipus phase; he begins to manipulate his penis, and simultaneously has phantasies of carrying out some sort of activity with it in relation to his mother; but at last, owing to the combined effect of a threat of castration and the spectacle of women's lack of a penis, he experiences the greatest trauma of his life, and this introduces the period of latency with all its attendant consequences. The girl, after vainly attempting to do the same as the boy, comes to recognize her lack of a penis or rather the inferiority of her clitoris, with permanent effects upon the development of her character; and, as a result of this first disappointment in rivalry, she often turns away altogether from sexual life.

It would be a mistake to suppose that these three phases succeed one another in a clear-cut fashion: one of them may appear in addition to another, they may overlap one another, they may be present simultaneously.

In the earlier phases the separate component instincts set about their pursuit of pleasure independently of one another; in the phallic phase there are the first signs of an organization which subordinates the other trends to the primacy of the genitals and signifies the beginning of a co-ordination of the general pursuit of pleasure into the sexual function. The complete organization is not attained until puberty, in a fourth, or genital, phase. A state of affairs is then established in which (1) many earlier libidinal cathexes are retained, (2) others are included in the sexual function as preparatory or auxiliary acts, their satisfaction producing what is known as fore-pleasure, and (3) other tendencies are excluded from the organization, and are either entirely suppressed (repressed) or are employed in the ego in some other way, forming character-traits or undergoing sublimation with a displacement of their aims.

This process is not always carried out perfectly. Inhibitions in the course of its development manifest themselves as the various disturbances of sexual life. Fixations of the libido to conditions at earlier phases are then found, the trend of which, moving independently of the normal sexual aim, is described as *perversion*. One example of an inhibition in development of

---

[8] The occurrence of early vaginal excitations is often asserted. But it is most probably a question of excitations in the clitoris, that is, in an organ analogous to the penis, so that this fact would not preclude us from describing the phase as phallic.

this kind is homosexuality, if it is manifest. Analysis shows that in every case a homosexual attachment to an object has at one time been present and in most cases has persisted in a latent condition. The situation is complicated by the fact that the processes necessary for bringing about a normal outcome are not for the most part either completely present or completely absent; they are as a rule *partially* present, so that the final result remains dependent upon *quantitative* relations. Thus genital organization will be attained, but will be weakened in respect of those portions of the libido which have not proceeded so far but have remained fixated to pregenital objects and aims. Such weakening shows itself in a tendency, if there is an absence of genital satisfaction or if there are difficulties in the real world, for the libido to return to its earliest pregenital cathexes (*i.e.*, to *regress*).

During the study of the sexual functions it has been possible to gain a first, preliminary conviction, or rather suspicion, of two pieces of knowledge which will later be found to be important over the whole of our field. Firstly, the normal and abnormal phenomena that we observe (that is, the phenomenology of the subject) require to be described from the point of view of dynamics and of economics (*i.e.*, in this connection, from the point of view of the quantitative distribution of the libido). And secondly, the etiology of the disturbances which we are studying is to be found in the developmental history of the individual, that is to say, in the early part of his life.

Mental Qualities

We have described the structure of the psychical apparatus and the energies or forces which are active in it, and we have followed in a striking example the way in which those energies (and principally the libido) organize themselves into a physiological function which serves the purpose of the preservation of the species. There was nothing in all this to exemplify the quite peculiar character of what is mental, apart, of course, from the empirical fact that this apparatus and these energies underlie the functions which we call our mental life. We will now turn to something which is a unique characteristic of what is mental, and which, in fact, according to a widely held opinion, actually coincides with it to the exclusion of all else.

The starting point for this investigation is provided by a fact without parallel, which defies all explanation or description—the fact of consciousness. Nevertheless, if anyone speaks of consciousness, we know immediately and from our own most personal experience what is meant by it.[9] Many people, both inside and outside the science of psychology, are

[9] Extreme lines of thought, such as the American doctrine of behaviorism, think it possible to construct a psychology which disregards this fundamental fact.

satisfied with the assumption that consciousness alone is mental, and nothing then remains for psychology but to discriminate in the phenomenology of the mind between perceptions, feelings, intellective processes and volitions. It is generally agreed, however, that these conscious processes do not form unbroken series which are complete in themselves; so that there is no alternative to assuming that there are physical or somatic processes which accompany the mental ones and which must admittedly be more complete than the mental series, since some of them have conscious processes parallel to them but others have not. It thus seems natural to lay the stress in psychology upon these somatic processes, to see in *them* the true essence of what is mental and to try to arrive at some other assessment of the conscious processes. The majority of philosophers, however, as well as many other people, dispute this position and declare that the notion of a mental thing being unconscious is self-contradictory.

But it is precisely this that psychoanalysis is obliged to assert, and this is its second fundamental hypothesis. It explains the supposed somatic accessory processes as being what is essentially mental and disregards for the moment the quality of consciousness. It does not stand alone in this opinion. Many thinkers (such as Theodor Lipps, for instance) have made the same assertion in the same words. And the general dissatisfaction with the usual view of what is mental has resulted in an ever more urgent demand for the inclusion in psychological thought of a concept of the unconscious, though the demand has been of such an indefinite and vague nature that it could have no influence upon science.

Now it might appear as though this dispute between psychoanalysis and philosophy was only concerned with a trifling matter of definition—the question whether the name "mental" should be applied to one or another series of phenomena. Actually, however, this step has been of the greatest importance. Whereas the psychology of consciousness never went beyond this broken sequence of events which was obviously dependent upon something else, the other view, which held that what is mental is in itself unconscious, enabled psychology to take its place as a natural science like any other. The processes with which it is concerned are in themselves just as unknowable as those dealt with by the other sciences, by chemistry or physics, for example; but it is possible to establish the laws which those processes obey and to follow over long and unbroken stretches their mutual relations and interdependences—in short, to gain what is known as an "understanding" of the sphere of natural phenomena in question. This cannot be effected without framing fresh hypotheses and creating fresh concepts; but these are not to be despised as evidence of our embarrassment but must on the contrary be valued as enriching science. We can claim for them the same value as approximations as belongs to the corresponding intellectual scaffolding found in other natural sciences, and we look forward to their being modified, corrected and more precisely determined as more experience is accumulated and sifted. So too it will be entirely in accordance with our expectations if the basic concepts and principles of the new science (instinct, nervous energy, etc.) remain for a considerable time no less indeterminate than those of the older sciences (force, mass, attraction, etc.).

Every science is based upon observations and experiences arrived at through the medium of our psychical apparatus. But since *our* science has as its subject that apparatus itself, the analogy ends here. We make our observations through the medium of the same perceptual apparatus, precisely by the help of the breaks in the series of [conscious] mental events, since we fill in the omissions by plausible inferences and translate them into conscious material. In this way we construct, as it were, a series of conscious events complementary to the unconscious mental processes. The relative certainty of our mental science rests upon the binding force of these inferences. Anyone who goes deeply into the subject will find that our technique holds its ground against every criticism.

In the course of our work the distinctions which we denote as *mental qualities* force themselves on our attention. There is no need to characterize what we call *conscious:* it is the same as the consciousness of philosophers and of everyday opinion. Everything else that is mental is in our view *unconscious.* We are soon led to make an important division in this unconscious. Some processes become conscious easily; they may then cease to be conscious, but can become conscious once more without any trouble: as people say, they can be reproduced or remembered. This reminds us that consciousness is in general a very highly fugitive condition. What is conscious is conscious only for a moment. If our perceptions do not confirm this, the contradiction is merely an apparent one. It is explained by the fact that the stimuli of perception can persist for some time, so that in the course of it the perception of them can be repeated. The whole position can be clearly seen from the conscious perception of our intellective processes; it is true that these may persist, but they may just as easily pass in a flash. Everything unconscious that behaves in this way, that can easily exchange the unconscious condition for the conscious one, is therefore better described as "capable of entering consciousness," or as *preconscious.* Experience has taught us that there are hardly any mental processes, even of the most complicated kind, which cannot on occasion remain preconscious, although as a rule they press forward, as we say, into consciousness. There are other mental processes or mental material which have no such easy access to consciousness, but which must be inferred, discovered, and translated into conscious form in the manner that has been described. It is for such material that we reserve the name of the unconscious proper.

Thus we have attributed three qualities to mental processes: they are either conscious, preconscious, or unconscious. The division between the three classes of material which have these qualities is neither absolute nor permanent. What is preconscious becomes conscious, as we have seen, without any activity on our part; what is unconscious can, as a result of our efforts, be made conscious, though in the process we may have an impression that we are overcoming what are often very strong resistances. When we make an attempt of this kind upon someone else, we ought not to forget that the conscious filling up of the breaks in his perceptions—the construction which we are offering him—does not so far mean that we have made conscious in him the unconscious material in question. All that is so far true is that the material is present in his mind in two versions, first in the conscious reconstruction that he has just received and secondly in its original unconscious condition. By persistent efforts we usually succeed in bringing it about that this unconscious material too becomes conscious to him, as a result of which the two versions come to coincide. The amount of effort needed, by which we estimate the resistance against the material becoming conscious, varies in magnitude in each individual case. For instance, what comes about in an analytic treatment as the result of our efforts can also occur spontaneously: material which is ordinarily unconscious can transform itself into preconscious and then into conscious material—a thing that happens upon a large scale in psychotic states. From this we may infer that the maintenance of certain internal resistances is a *sine qua non* of normality. A lowering of resistances of this sort, with a consequent pressing forward of unconscious material, takes place regularly in the state of sleep and thus brings about a necessary precondition for the formation of dreams. On the other hand, preconscious material can become temporarily inaccessible and cut off by resistances, as on occasions of passing forgetfulness, or a preconscious thought can actually be temporarily pushed back into the unconscious condition, as seems to be necessary in the case of jokes. We shall see that a similar reversion of preconscious material or processes to the unconscious condition plays a great part in the causation of neurotic disorders.

The theory of the three qualities of mental events, as described in this generalized and simplified manner, seems likely to be a source of endless confusion rather than a help to clarification. But it must not be forgotten that it is properly not a theory at all, but a first attempt at a stock-taking of the facts of our observation, that it keeps as close as possible to those facts and does not seek to explain them. The complications which it reveals may bring into relief the peculiar difficulties with which our investigation has to contend. It seems likely however that we shall learn more about the subject if we follow out the relations between the mental qualities and the provinces or agencies which we have postulated in the mental apparatus—though these relations too are far from being simple.

The process of a thing becoming conscious is above all linked with the perceptions which our sense organs receive from the external world. From the topographical point of view, therefore, it is a phenomenon which occurs in the outermost cortex of the ego. It is true that we also receive conscious information from the inside of the body—the feelings, which actually exercise a more peremptory influence upon our mental life than external perceptions; moreover, in certain circumstances the sense organs themselves transmit feelings, sensations of pain, in addition to the perceptions which are specific to them. Since, however, these feelings (as we call them, in contrast to conscious perceptions) also emanate from the terminal organs, and since we regard all of those organs as prolongations or offshoots of the cortex, it is still possible to maintain the assertion made at the beginning of this paragraph. It need only be said by way of distinction that, as regards the terminal organs of *feeling*, the body itself takes the place of the external world.

Conscious processes on the periphery of the ego and everything else in the ego unconscious—such would be the simplest state of affairs that we might picture. And such may in fact be the conditions prevailing in animals. But in men there is an added complication owing to which internal processes in the ego may also acquire the quality of consciousness. This complication is produced by the function of speech, which brings the material in the ego into a firm connection with the memory-traces of visual and more particularly of auditory perceptions. Thenceforward the perceptual periphery of the cortex of the ego can be stimulated to a much greater extent from inside as well; internal events such as sequences of ideas and intellective processes can become conscious; and a special apparatus becomes necessary in order to distinguish between the two possibilities—that is, what is known as *reality-testing*. The equation "perception = reality (external world)" no longer holds. Errors, which can now easily arise and do in fact habitually arise in dreams, are called *hallucinations*.

The inside of the ego, which comprises above all the intellective processes, has the quality of being preconscious. This is characteristic of the ego and belongs to it alone. It would not be right, however, to assert that a connection with the memory-traces of speech is a prerequisite of the preconscious condition. On the contrary, that condition does not depend upon any such prerequisite, although the presence of speech gives a safe clue to the preconscious nature of a process. The preconscious condition, which is characterized on the one hand by having access to consciousness and on the other hand by being linked with the verbal residues, is nevertheless something peculiar, the nature of which is not exhausted by these two characteristics. The proof of this is that large portions of the ego, and in particular of the superego, which cannot be denied the characteristic of being preconscious, none the less remain for the most part unconscious in the phenomenological sense of the word. We do not know why this must be so. We shall attempt later on to attack the problem of the true nature of the preconscious.

The sole quality that rules in the id is that of being unconscious. Id and unconscious are as intimately united as ego and preconscious; indeed, the former connection is even more exclusive. If we look back at the developmental history of the individual and of his psychical apparatus, we shall be able to make an important distinction in the id. Originally, of course, everything was id; the ego was developed out of the id by the continual influence of the external world. In the course of this slow development certain material in the id was transformed into the preconscious condition and was thus taken into the ego. Other material remained unaltered in the id, as its hardly accessible nucleus. But during this development the young and feeble ego dropped and pushed back into the unconscious condition certain material which it had already taken in, and behaved similarly in regard to many new impressions which it *might* have taken in, so that these were rejected and were able to leave traces in the id only. In consideration of its origin, we term this portion of the id *the repressed*. It is of little importance that we are not always able to draw a sharp distinction between these two categories of material in the id. They coincide approximately with the division between what was originally present and what was acquired during the development of the ego.

Having now decided upon the topographical division of the mental apparatus into an ego and an id, with which the difference in quality between preconscious and unconscious runs parallel, and having agreed that this quality is only an *indication* of the distinction and does not constitute its essence, we are faced by a further question. What is the true nature of the condition which is disclosed in the case of the id by the quality of being unconscious and in the case of the ego by that of being preconscious, and in what does the distinction between them consist?

But of this we know nothing; and the profound obscurity of our ignorance is scarcely illuminated by a glimmer or two of light. For here we have approached the still shrouded secret of the nature of what is mental. We assume, as the other natural sciences have taught us to expect, that in mental life some kind of energy is at work; but we have no data which enable us to come nearer to a knowledge of it by an analogy with other forms of energy. We seem to recognize that nervous or psychical energy exists in two forms, one freely mobile and the other, by contrast, bound; we speak of cathexes and hypercathexes of the material of the mind and even venture to suppose that a hypercathexis brings about a sort of synthesis of different processes—a synthesis in the course of which free energy is transformed into bound energy. Further than this we have been unable to go. Nevertheless, we hold firmly to the view that the distinction between the unconscious and the preconscious condition also lies in dynamic relations of this same kind, which would explain how it is that, whether spontaneously or with our assistance, the one can be changed into the other.

But behind all of these uncertainties there lies one new fact, the discovery of which we owe to psychoanalytic research. We have learned that processes in the unconscious or in the id obey different laws from those in the preconscious ego. We name these laws in their totality the *primary process*, in contrast to the *secondary process* which regulates events in the preconscious or ego. Thus the study of mental qualities has after all proved not unfruitful in the end.

JUNG'S THEORY OF PSYCHOLOGICAL TYPES *

[IRA PROGOFF

The Context of the Theory of Types

The terms "introvert" and "extravert," which Jung developed, have become part of everyday speech. In the process of being popularized, however, they have come to be used in a loose and generalized way that deprives them of the specific analytical insights which belong with the conception of "psychological types." The meaning of the terms "introvert" and "extravert" depends on the context of Jung's theory of "types," and their significance can be grasped adequately only when they are understood in terms of the total structure of Jung's thought.

Contrary to the simple tests that appear in the "psychology" columns of the newspapers, the theory of types is not a convenient way to classify people into neat little pigeonholes. It is not a basis for saying to each in his turn: you're an extravert; you're an introvert; you're a thinking type; you're a feeling type; and so on. There are psychologists who look for a set of handy categories which they can use to explain people away and then file them in a tidy compartment of their minds. Jung offers no such principle. Instead, he has developed a rather involved system by which to focus, in a tentative and hypothetical way, on the more important factors in the personality of the individual. . . .

The thinking by which Jung develops the theory of types runs somewhat as follows. His study of the individual has to focus on the movement of libidinal energy in the psyche and on its manifestations in psychic phenomena. That is the basic material with which he works. If we follow the expression of libido as the individual makes his adjustment to experience, we find that certain aspects of this movement tend to follow similar

* From Ira Progoff, *Jung's Psychology and Its Social Meaning*, pp. 98–115, Julian Press, Inc., New York, 1953. Reprinted by permission of the author and the publisher.

patterns within particular individuals. To this extent, it can be said that there are necessary steps in the expression of libido, and this provides certain criteria with which to study the development of the personality in daily life. It does not give any absolute standard of measurement; but it does provide a starting point on which at least to construct some hypotheses. Jung's theory of "psychological types" must be kept within this limiting context; it is an effort merely to find something to work with in tackling the problem of individual differences.

The Four Functions

The first point at which the individual meets the outside world is through the senses. He must first establish "the fact that something is there." Jung terms this "Sensation."

The individual must go further than mere sensation, to the point where he can understand the meaning of the things with which his senses have come in contact. He must assimilate them into consciousness. This second step, which "gives the interpretation of that which is perceived," Jung calls "Thinking."

After the object has been given a meaning, it must be evaluated. The individual judges whether the new sensation is pleasant or unpleasant in terms of his psychic orientation. The function which "establishes the value of the object" Jung calls "Feeling."

Finally, there is an aspect of experience which eludes consciousness. There are things that the individual knows directly, intuitively, we should say; these are the implications and overtones of experience which cannot be known in any other way. The "immediate awareness of relationships" Jung calls "Intuition." [1]

The libido has thus made four stops. At each point, psychic energy was expressed in a different way toward experience, and yet in a necessary way. Each one of the four phenomena which occurred when the libido met the object of experience must occur in some degree in every experience the individual has in life. Each is an expression of libido, and Jung terms them the four "functions" of the psyche. "By psychological function," Jung says, "I understand a certain form of psychic activity that remains theoretically the same under varying circumstances. From the energic standpoint a function is a phenomenal form of libido which theoretically remains constant in much the same way as physical force can be considered as the form or momentary manifestation of physical energy." [2]

[1] For these four definitions see C. G. Jung, *Factors Determining Human Behavior*, Harvard Tercentenary Conference on Arts and Sciences, Harvard University Press, Cambridge, 1937, pp. 60, 61.

[2] C. G. Jung, *Psychological Types*, translated by H. G. Baynes, Harcourt, Brace, New York, 1923, p. 547.

Rational and Non-rational Functions

There are, thus, four psychological functions in which libido is constantly expressed: Sensation, Thinking, Feeling and Intuition. Of these, Jung terms two "rational" and two "non-rational." He terms thinking and feeling as "rational functions" because they involve a deliberate attitude and action on the part of the individual toward the object. In thinking, the individual interprets the object; in feeling he judges it. Jung therefore describes them as "rational," in the sense that they are purposive functions from the individual's point of view. In sensation, the relation is more passive; the object is only experienced by the individual. In intuition, the very nature of the process is that the individual does not purposively or rationally seek to understand the object; it "comes to him," as the saying is. Sensation and intuition are, therefore, termed the two "non-rational" functions in man.

Jung postulates it as a matter of his own experience and observation that there is, in general, a compensatory relation within each pair of functions. In the rational set, thinking and feeling act as opposites and tend to balance each other, while sensation and intuition are in the same relationship in the non-rational set. Consequently, if we set the four functions down on paper so that they would form a circle in terms of these relationships, thinking would be opposite feeling, and sensation would be opposite intuition.

The Purpose of the Function-Compass

At this point, the conception of the four functions can begin to be useful. Jung likes to think of them as a compass which he can use as a guide in interpreting a psychological condition. Certainly the psyche is enough of a wilderness when we approach it, not knowing where to begin or what to look for first. Jung intends the compass of the four functions to give a sense of direction and to serve as a means of orientating the study of personality. It is certainly a flexible compass, for it can be used with any one of the four points taken as "north," according to the psychological qualities of the individual. The function-compass may be set to fit the dominant function of the individual to whom it is being applied.

The main point to keep in mind in the theory of types is that all four of the functions are experienced by every individual to some degree, and although one is more highly developed in each individual than the others, the other three remain. Each individual, according to his nature, tends to specialize in one of the functions. It may be any one of the four; but whichever one it is, whether rational or non-rational, the individual raises it to a conscious level in keeping with other aspects of his psychological development. Most important is the fact that the individual uses his leading or dominant function not merely as a means of experiencing the world, but as the basis around which he organizes his personality. The individual uses the dominant function as a focus for orientating and for building his psychic life. If, for example, it is his nature to make thinking his dominant function, he does not merely use his thinking process as a means of interpreting experience; everyone uses "thinking" for this purpose. But, as a "thinking type" he makes of thinking more than a means; it is to him a goal in itself. Thinking becomes his "nature"; he approaches life in its terms, and other people come to classify him in their minds in terms of the characteristics that follow from the dominant use of the thinking process.

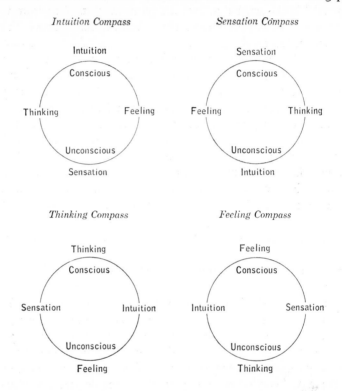

An individual can have any one of the four functions dominant in his psyche, and he then orientates his personality around it. Whichever one is dominant for him is "north" on his particular function-compass. The other functions move around correspondingly. The dominant function is at the peak of the individual's consciousness, since it is the most highly developed in his psyche. If thinking is dominant, it is fully in consciousness under normal conditions and feeling is in the unconscious; the other two functions waver in between, depending on other factors in the psyche. If sensation is dominant, it is conscious while intuition is unconscious. The [above] diagrams illustrate the way the function-compass looks for each individual, depending on his dominant function.

The function-compass is, of course, only a conceptual representation of the situation in the psyche. Actually there is a great deal of variation and all the functions overlap. The value of the compass is that it gives a starting-point for thinking about the functions, and it is a way of visualizing how the opposites balance one another and maintain their constant interrelationship.

Differentiation and the Dominant Function

The main characteristic of the dominant function, whichever it happens to be, is that it is well developed in the field of consciousness. It becomes this way only by virtue of the fact that unconsciously the individual favors it over the other functions. It receives a greater intensity of psychic energy and is able to rise from the unconscious to consciousness. Once on the higher level, its manner of operation is transformed. It is clearer, in sharper focus, and its contents are more finely differentiated. The explanation is difficult to give, but it seems that while the function was in the unconscious, there was a tendency for its contents to have a generalized, uncertain nature, and to appear indirectly or in symbols, as is characteristic of the unconscious. While a function is below in the unconscious, it has a tendency to be amalgamated, and to fuse its contents in an undifferentiated way. There is a tendency, for example, for thinking to be mixed with feeling in such a way that neither feeling nor thinking can be clear or efficient, since each is contaminated by its opposite and cannot operate with clarity in its own terms. As Jung phrases it, "Just so far as a function is wholly or mainly unconscious is it also undifferentiated, i.e., it is not only fused together in its parts, but also merged with other functions." [3]

When the function is carried up by the forward movement of libido into the realm of consciousness, it is separated from its opposite (differentiated, in Jung's terms) and becomes keen, aware, specialized and increasingly competent as it becomes increasingly differentiated. In coming into consciousness it has left its inferior aspects behind. It is free to develop itself in its own terms and, depending on outer circumstances, the conscious ego is inclined to give the dominant function full freedom to do this. In due course, the Ego and the dominant function may be fused, and the entire Persona—that is, the conscious appearance that is displayed to the outside world—may come to be nothing more than the dominant function. We see this very often in the case of men who make their professions their whole lives.

In moving out of the unconscious, the dominant function leaves behind the characteristics of the unconscious. If, however, it ever returns to the unconscious because of a change in the equilibrium of the psyche, it recovers all the impediments it once owned. It is only while it is in the field of the conscious that it is gifted with strong abilities and is able to lead the

[3] *Ibid.*, p. 539.

personality. This process of differentiation is indeed important to the psyche. "Differentiation consists in the separation of the selected functions from other functions, and in the separation of its individual parts from each other. Without differentiation direction is impossible, since the direction of a function is dependent upon the isolation and exclusion of the irrelevant. Through fusion with what is irrelevant, direction becomes impossible; only a differentiated function proves itself capable of direction." [4]

In primitive societies, the specializations of life are less rigid, and the less intense development of consciousness permits a fairly low degree of differentiation to be sufficient. It is possible in a society with a moderately low degree of differentiation for the individual to have all four of the functions in consciousness, though one will necessarily be more highly developed than the others. In modern times, however, a man who wishes to build a socially acceptable Persona needs to specialize in one of the functions at the expense of the others. "The very conditions of society force a man to apply himself first and foremost to the differentiation of that function with which he is either most gifted by nature, or which provides his most effective means for social success. Very frequently, indeed as a general rule, a man identifies himself more or less completely with the most favored, hence the most developed, function. It is this circumstance which gives rise to psychological types." [5]

The Inferior Function and the Shadow Side

In specializing in this way under the press of modern social competition, the individual must make a particular effort to suppress his weaker functions. He deliberately cuts them out of consciousness so that he can concentrate on the strongest function, that is, the function on which he can "capitalize." In doing this, however, he creates a very dangerous situation within his psyche, a situation of unbalance. Originally, the differentiated function rose from the unconscious to consciousness because it received a greater supply of psychic energy. As its development is intensified now, it receives increasing quantities of libido until finally it begins to be overcharged. This energy has to come from somewhere, and necessarily it is withdrawn from the other functions, especially from the opposite of the dominant function. At first nothing unfavorable happens, and the condition may continue for some time, especially if the other functions have some degree of consciousness. But as the draining of libido continues, the weakest function drops below the threshold of consciousness and goes steadily deeper into the unconscious. Whatever energy content it retains then ceases to belong to itself alone, but is transferred to the unconscious, where it activates dormant elements.

[4] *Ibid.,* pp. 539, 540.
[5] *Ibid.,* p. 564.

Now the danger signals begin to reach consciousness. Strange manifestations of the unconscious burst in on the conscious attitude which the dominant function maintains in the Persona. Moods and weaknesses of every sort break through the conscious veneer. The weakest and least adapted function is taken over by the Shadow complex and becomes identified with the negative, unpleasant side of the personality. The opposite of the conscious attitude reaches the surface, breaking in on consciousness as an autonomous "partial system." Based on the opposite of the dominant function, the complex operates with a power of its own, and acts to embarrass the Ego by foolish and tactless errors. When a group of psychic contents possesses enough libido to move up from the unconscious and disturb consciousness in this way, a neurosis is in full swing. The individual realizes that something is amiss, that his weaker side is taking over his personality. He strains all the harder to assert his dominant function, but in doing this, he only intensifies the one-sidedness and worsens his condition. Jung has often observed that when "the patient seeks to compensate the unconsciously disturbing influence by means of special performance of the directed function . . . the chase continues even, on occasion, to the point of nervous collapse." [6]

The condition of neurosis which develops in this way indicates the dangerous effects of the over-differentiation of any function. The very quality which is the strength of a psychological type may turn out to be its weakness if it is carried to the point of over-balance.

Introversion and Extraversion

Up to this point, our discussion of types has been in terms only of the psychological functions. We have noted four types, one for each of the dominant functions. The dominant function develops as an aspect of the progression movement of the libido, and the conscious attitude it creates decays when a regression movement sets in. There is, however, another type of libido movement. "The libido moves not only forward and backward, but also outward and inward." [7]

This additional direction of the libido adds a new aspect to the psyche. When we discuss the forward movement of the libido, we must specify whether it is a forward movement *inward* or a forward movement *outward*. That is to say, the progression movement of the libido may be directed out into the environment, toward concrete objects of the objective world; or it may be directed inward down into the person. Similarly, the regression movement of libido can be a retreat to the inner world, or a retreat from the inner world to the world of objects.

[6] *Ibid.*, pp. 370, 371.
[7] C. G. Jung, *Contributions to Analytical Psychology*, translated by H. G. and C. F. Baynes, Harcourt, Brace, New York, 1928, p. 45.

Jung describes the general direction of the libido movement under the terms Introversion and Extraversion. The movement toward the outer world is Extraversion; the movement toward the inner world is Introversion. Every person has both tendencies in his nature. Just as everyone goes through a time when the libido moves forward and a time when the libido regresses, so everyone must experience movements in an outward direction and in an inward direction. Jung's analysis here, however, is based on his observation that there is a tendency for the conscious personality to concentrate on either one of the directions. Regardless of his other psychological qualities, the individual seems, at least to his neighbors, to be "by nature" an open, friendly, casual, externalizing personality, that is, an extravert; or else he seems to be reserved and withdrawn and preconcerned, and they think of him as "by nature" an introvert. It is these common sense observations, made by people in their daily relations, that led to the easy acceptance of Jung's two terms.

The reason a person gives the impression of being either an introvert or an extravert is that his dominant function has come to be associated with that particular type of libido movement. In each personality there are parts that are extraverted and parts that are introverted. It depends on which function—dominant or inferior—and also on which autonomous complex the libido has become identified with. An individual who is a thinking type may be extraverted in his dominant function, but introverted in his inferior function of feeling. Introversion or extraversion in itself means nothing; it is merely a direction of libido movement. But everything depends on what is being moved.

Jung himself remarked that the terms introvert and extravert by themselves mean as little as when "Molière's *bourgeois gentilhomme* discovered that he ordinarily spoke in prose. These distinctions attain meaning and value only when we realize all the other characteristics that go with the type." [8]

Libido Movement and the Variety of Types

There is really no such person as an introvert or an extravert *per se*. The syndicated newspaper strips which ask, "Are you an introvert? Are you an extravert?" are asking impossible questions. They have taken the words from Jung and missed the meaning. There are, however, extravert types who have identified extraversion with their dominant function, with thinking, feeling, sensation, or intuition, as the case may be. There are, thus, extravert thinking types, extravert feeling types, and so on. Similarly, for those who have identified their introverted libido movement with their dominant function, there are introverted thinking types, introverted feeling types, and

[8] C. G. Jung, *Modern Man in Search of a Soul*, translated by W. S. Dell and C. F. Baynes, Harcourt, Brace, New York, 1933, p. 28.

so on. All in all, Jung has named two psychological types for each of the four functions, one for each of the directions of libido movement. Of these eight general psychological types, however—though many of their charac- teristics are definite and specific—there are really as many variations as the discerning eye can find. The eight psychological types serve the same pur- pose as the function-compasses; they are guiding principles, tools of analysis, to help the psychologist orient himself. Moreover, the introversion-extra- version concept gives the function-compass a second dimension, considering the individual's relation to the outer world in terms of his dominant and inferior functions.

Jung has made some interesting observations on the personality traits that tend to be found among the various psychological types. He has contrasted Immanuel Kant, the introverted thinking type, with Charles Darwin, the extraverted thinking type. One can readily see the basis of difference here. Both have differentiated thinking as their dominant function, but one turned thinking outward and the other turned thinking inward. "Darwin ranges over the wide fields of objective facts, while Kant restricts himself to a critique of knowledge in general." [9] Jung remarked also, on how prevalent the feeling type is among women, though, of course, not exclusively. The extraverted feeling woman is the easy-going, companionable mother and wife, while the introverted feeling type is devoted to her family in a quiet way. Jung points out that she is the type of whom it may be said that "still water runs deep," and then he adds, "They are mostly silent, inaccessible and hard to understand; often they hide behind a childish or banal mask and not infrequently their temperament is melancholic." [10]

Of the introverted intuitive type Jung says, "Had this type not existed, there would have been no prophets in Israel." [11] But many an eccentric may also be discovered among those who have a strongly introverted intuition function.

Significance of the Type Theory

The important point to keep in mind is that the characteristics of the types are not, in themselves, of primary significance. Jung was not inter- ested in building up a descriptive typology with definite qualities assigned to each of the eight types, neatly defined and categorized. That would be pedantic and artificial. He merely sought some clues with which to ap- proach the psychic processes of the individual. The infinite varieties of in- dividual differences are the external result of the combinations of libido movement and psychological function. The specific value of Jung's con- cepts is that they do not operate on the surface. When, for example, Jung

[9] *Psychological Types*, p. 484.
[10] *Ibid.*, p. 492.
[11] *Ibid.*, p. 307.

describes a man as an extraverted feeling type, he is not calling him a name. He is describing the nature of the libido movement in the individual and the psychological function to which this movement is attached, in so far as these facts are observable from the analysis of conscious and unconscious contents. In understanding Jung's theories on types, it is not important to remember the names of the types or their superficial qualities. What is important is to be aware of the dual nature of libido movement, inward and outward, forward and backward, and the way these movements are related to the dominant and inferior functions, to the creation and destruction of the conscious attitude.

The theory of types is inextricably connected with the principle of opposites. In the function-compass, the opposite of the dominant function remains in the unconscious, or is the first function to return to the unconscious when the conscious attitude grows weak. This balancing includes the introvert-extravert concept. If the person is an extraverted feeling type, the dominant function is feeling and the inferior function is its opposite, the other of the two rational functions, thinking. The feeling function is expressed in an extraverted way; the thinking function in an introverted way. When both are conscious and under control, there is no danger. But when the weaker thinking function slides back into the unconscious, it slides back into the Shadow side, and in such a condition, the thinking function tends to be especially tactless. If the conscious attitude breaks down—if the Persona can no longer hold itself together in society—the introverted thinking attitude may very possibly take over the personality of the extraverted feeling type—but in a weak, inferior form.

We should keep in mind that the dominant function and its corresponding type are aspects of the libido in its progression; in regression the libido leaves the psyche open to the incompetence of the inferior function and also to the weird and overwhelming effects of the reactivated unconscious contents. "The superior function is always the expression of the conscious personality, its aim, its will, and its achievement, while the inferior functions belong to the things that happen to one. Not that they merely beget blunders, e.g., *lapsus linguae* and *lapsus calami*, but they may also breed half or three-quarter resolves, since the inferior functions also possess a slight degree of consciousness. The extraverted feeling type is a classical example of this, for he enjoys an excellent feeling rapport with his entourage, yet occasionally opinions of an incomparable tactlessness will just happen to him. These opinions have their source in his inferior or unconscious thinking, which is only partly subject to control and is insufficiently related to the object; to a large extent, therefore, it can operate without consideration of responsibility." [12]

As a descriptive analysis, Jung's theory of psychological types is very in-

[12] *Ibid.*, pp. 426, 427.

teresting. As a series of concepts to be used for classifying individuals, it can be the basis for a great variety of "tests" to be worked out and graded and reduced to charts and statistics. But the real value of the type analysis for Jung is that it gives him some tools to work with. The concept of "type" means nothing in itself. There is no such thing as a pure type, and it doesn't matter at all. The balancing of the principle of opposites and the ever wandering libido, inward and outward, backwards and frontwards, while the conscious and unconscious press each other in a never ending tension, is the basis for the study of the psyche. The difficulty has been in finding a way to think of those movements in specific terms without losing the essential sense of psychic dynamics. Jung offered his theory of psychological types as an effort to meet this need.[13]

SOME ASPECTS OF SULLIVAN'S THEORY OF INTERPERSONAL RELATIONS *

⟨ PATRICK MULLAHY

The Goals of Human Behavior

We begin our exposition of Sullivan with some preliminary distinctions and assumptions. He differentiates "human performances," which include revery processes, such as day dreaming, and thought, into a two-part classification. In more popular language, the purposes, the goals or end states of human behavior are divided into two actually interrelated classes. These two classes refer to the pursuit of satisfactions and the pursuit of security. Satisfactions include sleep and rest, food and drink, sexual fulfillment (the satisfaction of lust). Loneliness is also listed as a "middling example." These satisfactions are closely connected with the bodily organization of man. Hence, loneliness is included by Sullivan because, among other things, we have a desire to touch one another and to be physically close.

The class of pursuits pertaining to security refer more directly to man's cultural equipment than to bodily organization. The concept of security, in Sullivan's sense, is not easy to explain. Roughly, it refers to the state of well-being, of "good feeling," of euphoria. All "those movements, actions, speech, thoughts, reveries and so on which pertain more to the culture which has been imbedded in a particular individual than to the organization of

[13] *Modern Man in Search of a Soul*, p. 108.
* From Patrick Mullahy, *Oedipus: Myth and Complex*, pp. 280–301, Thomas Nelson & Sons, New York, 1948. Reprinted by the permission of the author and publisher.

his tissues and glands, is apt to belong in this classification of the pursuit of security." [1]

The process of becoming a human being, for Sullivan, is synonymous with the process of acculturation or socialization. The need for security arises from the fact that every person undergoes this process of acculturation which begins at birth. From the very beginning of life in this world, everyone, at first through "empathy," which we discuss below, is made to feel some of the effects of the culture by the attitudes of the significant person or persons who take care of him: mother, nurse, or their surrogates. The attitudes of those who take care of the child are themselves socially conditioned. Because of empathy, long before the infant can understand what is happening, he experiences something of the attitudes of the significant people around him. Later he is deliberately taught what is right and wrong, "good" and "bad." In this way, the impulses, the biological strivings of the infant are socially "conditioned," that is, moulded, both as to form of expression and fulfillment, according to the culturally approved patterns. As we shall see, because of the experiences of approval and disapproval from the parents or their surrogates, the achievement of satisfactions according to the culturally "correct" or approved patterns causes a profound feeling of well-being, of good feeling, of security. When, for certain reasons, the felt needs of a person, the biological strivings, cannot be fulfilled according to culturally approved patterns, which he learned in early life, he feels intense and painful uneasiness and discomfort, insecurity, or *anxiety*.

It is not very difficult to see that the distinction between the pursuit of satisfactions and the pursuit of security and their attainment is logical or conceptual. The two are inextricably bound up together. But these two broad classifications are helpful for preliminary discussion. In general terms they explain what one is after in any situation with other persons, whether real or "fantastic" or a blend of both ("eidetic"). Hence, they represent "integrating tendencies." They explain why a situation in which two or more people—"all but one of which may be illusory" (or eidetic)—are involved or "integrated" becomes an interpersonal situation. It is because of these needs that one cannot live and be human except in communal existence with others.

The Concept of Tension

Because of the great role which anxiety and tension play in Sullivan's theories, we need first to mention some of his ideas about the latter. The achievement of satisfactions causes a decrease of tonus, tension, of the unstriped, involuntary muscles. But the effort at warding off anxiety (in-

[1] Harry Stack Sullivan, *Conceptions of Modern Psychiatry*, The William Alanson White Psychiatric Foundation, Washington, D.C., 1947, p. 6.

security) is accompanied by heightened tonus, often of the striped, skeletal muscles, often of the unstriped, visceral muscles.

The facts seem to indicate that tonic changes in the unstriped, involuntary muscles of the viscera—the internal organs of the body—are, from birth onward, intimately related to the experiencing of desires, needs for satisfaction. Heightened tone of the stomach wall is called out by depletion of our chemical supplies and the occurrence of vigorous contractions in these tense muscles gives rise to the "pangs of hunger." The taking of food—the ingestion of which probably leads to a release of nutritive substance stored in the liver—promptly relieves the excess tone and the contractions quiet down to the churning of the stomach contents. Hunger, in a way of speaking, is from the first influx of food, more a matter of the oral dynamism than of the stomach. In infants, at least, once this dynamism has discharged itself, alertness disappears, vigilance is withdrawn from circumambient reality, and sleep supervenes. Throughout life the pursuit of satisfactions is physiologically provoked by increased tone in some unstriped muscles; and the securing of the satisfactions is a relaxation of this tone, with a tendency towards the diminution of attention, alertness, and vigilance, and an approach to sleep.[2]

In the securing of satisfaction, the striped, skeletal muscles are "of relatively instrumental value" in very early infancy. They are said to do what is necessary—we are not told what that is—and then relax. But as soon as the mother begins to include prohibitions and disapprovals in educating the youngster, things get complicated. He develops a need for security against primarily "noxious emotional states empathized from the personal environment." Here the skeletal muscles take on a new function.

This function is to get rid of empathized discomfort and painful tension of various origins.

The oral dynamism [the respiratory apparatus, the food-taking apparatus, from which the speaking apparatus is evolved] has been the channel for performances needed to appease hunger—and pain and other discomforts. It may be presumed that its function in emitting the cry has been quite automatic. This may not have worked too well, and delayed response to the cry may be one of the first experiences that tend to focus alertness. But in any case, the oral dynamism is not now effective in securing relief from the discomfort set up by empathy; on some occasions, it is simply ineffectual, and on other occasions, its activity is accompanied by increase of the empathized discomfort. This leads gradually to a differentiation of empathized from other discomforts, and to the *inhibition* of the cry as a universal tool. The inhibiting of a complex pattern of behavior is not as simple as was its automatic initiation. Some of the movements are cut off, but the increase of tone in the appropriate muscles may not be inhibited. The experience of emphathized hostility or unfriendly prohibition or, as it later comes to be observed, a forbidding gesture becomes colored by and associated with heightened tone in some striped muscles—at first those concerned with the cry.

The course of acculturation, in so far as it pertains to toilet habits, is also a learning to suffer increasing tension in the bladder and rectum, and to resist

[2] *Op. cit.*, p. 43.

the automatic relaxation of the sphincter muscles concerned in retaining the urine and feces. Failures in this are often accompanied by empathized discomfort [due to parental disapproval], and success is often the occasion of empathized comfort which is added to the satisfaction from relief of the tension.[3]

Action which avoids or relieves any of these tensions is experienced as continued or enhanced *self-respect* or self-esteem. Thus a person who has become tense at an expression of hostility from someone he is talking to may subsequently, let us say, be made to laugh heartily at some remark or occurrence. When this happens, he suddenly feels a relief from tension; he "feels better" about himself and others. While the effort to ward off anxiety involves an increase of tension, the relief from anxiety is associated with actions which, among other things, decrease muscle tension.

Anxiety is not synonymous with muscle tension, but the latter is a necessary condition for its experience. As we shall see, *anxiety is always related to interpersonal relations.*

The Power Motive

Even more important and logically more fundamental than the impulses resulting from a feeling of hunger or thirst is the "power motive," the impulse to obtain and maintain a feeling of ability. To be able to obtain satisfactions and security is to have power in interpersonal relations; not to be able to do so is to be powerless, helpless. According to Sullivan, the development of actions, thoughts, foresights, etc., which are "calculated" to protect one from insecurity, is based on and springs from the disappointments and frustrations of early infancy. When one achieves power or ability in interpersonal relations, one respects oneself and therefore others. While the attitude toward the self is first determined by the attitude of those who take care of the child, his subsequent attitude toward others is determined by the attitude he has toward himself. "If there is a valid and real attitude toward the self, that attitude will manifest as valid and real toward others." [4]

Empathy

There is said to be "a peculiar emotional relationship" between the infant and those who take care of him. Long before he can understand what is happening to him, this "emotional contagion or communion" between him and the significant adult, the mother or nurse, exists. Sullivan surmises its greatest importance is between the ages of six and twenty-seven months. For example if a mother looks with disfavor on her offspring or she suffers

---

[3] *Op. cit.*, p. 44. Sullivan has changed his mind about empathizing comfort before the epoch of childhood, feeling that there is no certain evidence of its existence before then. (Personal communication to the writer.)

[4] *Op. cit.*, p. 7.

a fright around feeding time, there may be great feeding difficulties. This unclear mode of emotional communication is thought to be biological, for certain animals are said to exhibit a similar phenomenon. Since the attitudes of the mother or nurse are socially conditioned, this mode of emotional communication, which does not seem to occur, in Sullivan's view, through ordinary sensory channels, is very important for understanding acculturation. In later years, however, empathy is not much in evidence.

Three Modes of Experience

All experience occurs in one or more of three "modes"—the prototaxic, parataxic, and syntaxic. As the Greek roots of this horrendous term indicate, the prototaxic mode refers to the first kind of experience the infant has and the order or arrangement in which it occurs. As grown-ups, we experience things in terms of time and space, of here and "out there," of before and after. We break up our experience, so to speak, into constituent elements for the purposes of getting along in the world. Furthermore, our experience, or at least much of it, is referable to a self who does the experiencing, the self being a center of reference. "I went for a walk in the park at four o'clock." These are examples of every day distinctions we make. Others, of course, are much more subtle and refined.

Now in the beginning, the infant, Sullivan hypothecates, makes no such distinctions for a variety of reasons. Aside from structural and functional limitations, the organism at birth has had, of course, no direct experience with the cultural heritage. We shall avoid saying he has no mind as yet— for we shall not deal here with the problem of the nature of mind nor with the problem of what he inherits from his life in the womb, concerning which apparently not a great deal is known, at least regarding mind.

According to Sullivan's hypothesis all that the infant "knows" are momentary states, the distinction of before and after being a later acquirement. The infant vaguely feels or "prehends" earlier and later states without realizing any serial connection between them. He has no ego in any distinctive sense because the self has not yet developed. For such reasons, he has no awareness of himself as an entity separate from the rest of the world. In other words, his felt experience is all of a piece, undifferentiated, without definite limits. It is as if his experiences were "cosmic." This mode of experience is often marked in certain schizophrenic states.

The terms "parataxic" and "syntaxic" [5] also are etymologically related to the order and arrangement of experience. At the risk of confusion, we shall remind the reader that parataxic (like syntaxic) is a grammatical term as well, which refers to the ranging of clauses or propositions one after another without connectives such as "and," "or," "since," etc., to show the relations between them.

[5] Or "syntactic."

Gradually the infant learns to make some discrimination between himself and the rest of the world. As Sullivan puts it, he no longer reaches out to touch the moon. In other words he gradually learns to make elementary differentiations in his experience.

We learn in infancy that objects which our distance receptors, our eyes and ears, for example, encounter, are of a quite different order of relationship from things which our tactile or our gustatory receptors encounter. That which one has in one's mouth so that one can taste it, while it may be regurgitated to the distress of everyone is still in a very different relationship than is the full moon which one encounters through one's eye but can in no sense manage.[6]

As the infant develops and maturation proceeds, the original undifferentiated wholeness of experience is broken. However, the "parts," the diverse aspects, the various kinds of experience are not related or connected in a logical fashion. They "just happen" together, or they do not, depending on circumstances. In other words, various experiences are felt as concomitant, not recognized as connected in an orderly way. The child cannot yet relate them to one another or make logical distinctions among them. What is experienced is assumed to be the "natural" way of such occurrences, without reflection and comparison. Since no connections or relations are established, there is no logical movement of "thought" from one idea to the next. The parataxic mode is not a step by step process. Experience is undergone as momentary, unconnected states of being.

The parataxic mode of organizing experience occurs mainly through visual and auditory channels. Dreams are often examples of this mode of experiencing. But it occurs a good deal of the time in waking life. In other words, we do not—and cannot—always organize our experience into a logically connected, related totality, in which the various elements are compared, contrasted, and ordered in a precise fashion. Ordinarily we do not indulge in careful ratiocination as we dress in the morning, proceed to work, and so on. It is not necessary, and in any case there is not enough time.

As the infant learns the rudiments of language, he is said to pass into the "epoch" of childhood. And here we introduce another term, the "autistic." The autistic is a verbal manifestation of the parataxic. But the capacity for verbal communication is just beginning to be manifested, and the tools, vocabulary, grammar, etc., are scarcely formed and learned. Because of the child's limited equipment and experience with the symbol activity and experience of others, his own symbol activity is arbitrary, highly personal, unchecked and untested. Hence his imagination is not curbed to conform to everyday "reality." Autistic symbols, however, are useful in recall and foresight.

Let us take an example of a child who has been given a picture book also containing words, say, to name or describe the pictures. It will have a pic-

[6] *Op. cit.*, p. 16.

ture of a cat, and below or above or somewhere on the page there is written what the child eventually learns is c-a-t. Then, too, to complete the example, the animal who runs around the house also is referred to by the same name as that of the colored or black and white pattern in the book. Sullivan comments on the significance of such a frequent phenomenon in our culture as follows:

I am sure no child who can learn has not noticed an enormous discrepancy between this immobile representation in the book which, perhaps, resembles one of the momentary states that kitty has been in on some occasion. I am certain that every child knows that there is something very strange in this printed representation being so closely connected with the same word that seems to cover adequately the troublesome, amusing, and very active pet. Yet, because of unnumbered, sometimes subtle, sometimes crude experiences with the carrier of culture, the parent, the child finally comes to accept as valid and useful a reference to the picture as "kitty" and to the creature as "kitty."

The child thus learns some of the more complicated implications of a symbol in contradistinction to the actuality to which the symbol refers, which is its referent; in other words, the distinction between the symbol and that which is symbolized. This occurs, however, before verbal formulation is possible.

From the picture book and the spoken word in this culture one progresses to the printed word and finally discovers that the combination of signs, c-a-t, includes "kitty" in some miraculous fashion, and that it always works. There is nothing like consistent experience to impress one with the validity of an idea. So one comes to a point where printed words, with or without consensually valid meaning, come to be very important in one's growth of acquaintance with the world.

There was first the visually and otherwise impressive pet, which was called "kitty" (an associated vocalization): then came the picture of the kitten; now comes the generic *c a t* which includes kitty, picture of kitten, a kitten doll, and alley cats seen from the windows. And all this is learnt so easily that— since no one troubles to point it out—there is no lucid understanding of the sundry types of reality and reference that are being experienced. Familiarity breeds indifference in this case. The possibilities for confusion in handling the various kinds of symbols, naturally, remain quite considerable.[7]

The child gradually begins to catch on to patterns of relationships, to the grammatical structure of the language, and to the usual relationships and distinctions obtaining in his society. There is a more discriminating realization of the other fellow, the responder. The child now more clearly realizes that, for example, when he cries "dada," the other person responds in a more or less characteristic fashion. And so the child learns to anticipate the responses of others. These responses become associated with the use of certain words and gestures. In other words, the characteristic reactions of the other people give meaning to the language, a meaning that is thus implicitly agreed upon. Of course, the child does not set out systematically to learn the everyday meaning of the language. He learns by the trial and error method. Hence, he also learns that not only one's own experience is impor-

[7] *Op. cit.*, p. 16.

tant, but that of others. He also learns to use verbal symbols as an economical way to get a lot to happen in a short time, with little use of energy.

Of course, there is a great deal more than this to be said about the learning process, but this sketch may indicate some of the ways by which, according to Sullivan, a child learns to use language with an interpersonal reference.

In any case, the child gradually learns the "consensually validated" meaning of language—in the widest sense of language. These meanings have been acquired from group activities, interpersonal activities, social experience. Consensually validated symbol activity involves an appeal to principles which are accepted as true by the hearer. And when this happens, the youngster has acquired or learned the syntaxic mode of experience.

But the learning process is not always consistent—because the significant others are not always consistent in their behavior. Furthermore, as we know, people do not always take the trouble to teach the child the distinctions between various symbols and that to which they refer. The trial and error method by which a good deal of learning necessarily occurs is not ideally suited for acquiring precise distinctions. For such reasons, language thus comes to have a double meaning—a personal meaning and a consensually validated meaning or a blend of both. In this way, among others, people come to maintain a wide margin of misinformation and illusion about others, themselves, and the world.

Tension, when it occurs in connection with needs, such as those of food and sex, is experienced in the syntaxic and parataxic modes. The tension of anxiety, however, is experienced by grown-ups mainly in the parataxic mode.[8]

The Meaning of Dynamism

Before taking up an exposition of the self dynamism (or self system or, simply, self), we must try to indicate what the term "dynamism" means. It has been defined as "a relatively enduring configuration of energy which manifests itself in characterizable processes in interpersonal relations." [9] In other words dynamism refers to the way energy is organized and channeled in the human organism. Dynamism implies only a relatively enduring capacity to bring about change. It is analogous to any structure or organization of processes which always contains numerous sub-structures.

For Sullivan energy always means physical energy. He rejects the notion of "psychic energy."

[8] Anxiety is always *felt*. Contrary to previous formulations, Sullivan now is convinced it never occurs in the prototaxic mode but that it occurs mainly in the parataxic. (Personal communication to the writer.)

[9] Harry Stack Sullivan, "Introduction to the Study of Interpersonal Relations," *Psychiatry*, vol. 1, p. 123, footnote, 1938.

The Evolution of the Self

As everyone knows, certain restraints are put on the young offspring's freedom which are or are considered to be necessary for his socialization, for training him and making him the sort of person considered right and desirable in the society in which he will live and have his being. These restraints, above everything else, bring about the evolution of the self dynamism. In this evolution, other aspects of the personality, such as *the selectively inattended* and *disassociated* processes, those which occur outside of self-awareness, are also developed.

We shall begin our exposition of Sullivan's theories concerning the evolution of personality with the "epoch" of infancy. Infancy refers to the period from birth to the maturation of the capacity for language behavior. During this period certain of the attitudes of the parent or nurse are said to be conveyed empathically. Suppose the mother is tired or upset or angry when she is in close contact with the infant, let us say, when she nurses or bathes him. Something of her attitude is then conveyed to him. His sense of well-being, his euphoria, is markedly decreased. The mother who observes or at least senses this gets anxious, which state is then communicated to the infant, further lowering his feeling of well-being, further increasing his insecurity. And so the process goes on. It is "dynamic."

Euphoria and anxiety are, conceptually, direct opposites, "polar constructs." In actuality there is no such thing as "pure" euphoria, in which there is no tension and therefore no action, something like an empty state of bliss. Perhaps the nearest approximation to euphoria in the "ideal" sense is deepest sleep. Nor is there any actual state of absolute anxiety. In the state of terror—in which there is a complete but temporary disorganization of personality—the most extreme degree of tension ordinarily observable occurs. Euphoria and anxiety are inversely related.

It is not difficult to see that a chronically hostile mother will induce an intense and more or less chronic anxiety in the offspring. Furthermore, such a mother will deprive him of the experience of tenderness—a deprivation which will have fateful consequences for his future well-being and happiness.

One of the characteristics of anxiety is that it interferes with observation and analysis, with the acquisition of information and understanding and with recall and foresight. It interferes with alertness to the factors in a situation that are relevant to its occurrence. Therefore it interferes with effective action.

Sooner or later the infant is recognized as educable. And when this happens, there is said to be a restriction of tender cooperation. The exhibition of tenderness by the parents tends to be modified so that it will be used more on "suitable" occasions. The mother, for example, begins to train the child in the "proper" toilet habits, those considered proper in the society in which she lives. She will express or withhold tenderness and approval as the child learns to conform or not to her desires and methods in this matter. Thus, training involves the expression of tenderness and approval for some acts and disapproval and the withholding of tenderness for others. In other words, some performances bring tenderness and approval with the consequent increase of euphoria, while others bring disapproval and hence anxiety. These experiences of rewards and punishments come to be regarded as something special. Gradually the child catches on to the fact that they are related to his feelings of euphoria and anxiety. The more or less abrupt supervention of anxiety gradually teaches or forces him to focus awareness on the performances which bring approval and disapproval. He learns, for example, to recall incidents occurring before anxiety. After a while a forbidding gesture will be sufficient to change his behavior. In other words, as his observation improves, his grasp on the patterns of approval and disapproval becomes more refined. He learns that when anxiety is present and something is done which brings tenderness and approval, the painful discomfort is assuaged or banished.

Hence, the child gradually learns to focus attention on behavior which brings approval and disapproval in order to win rewards, tenderness and approval, and escape punishment, disapproval and disapprobation.

In infancy a vague idea of "my" body arises. From the sentience of the body as a basis, there gradually evolve three "personifications" of "me"— "good me," "bad me," and "not-me." The "good me" is an organization of experiences of approval, tenderness, and general good feeling. The "bad me" is an organization of experiences related to increasing anxiety states. The "rudimentary personification" of "not-me" evolves very gradually. The processes labeled "not-me" belong to the most poorly grasped aspects of living and refer to "uncanny" experiences like horror, dread, loathing, awe. What these uncanny experiences are about is not known, but they seem to originate in the experiences of anxiety in infancy, "primitive anxiety." They occur in the parataxic mode. The personification, "not-me," is not constituted by communicative processes and hence not much can be said about it. Nightmares and certain schizophrenic experiences are examples of uncanny experiences of the "not-me."

The "personifications" of "good me" and "bad me" belong to the self system. In other words, to put this crudely, there are times when "I" am "good me" and times when "I" am "bad me." Whether or not the self is predominantly one or the other depends on the course of experience, especially in early life. But the "good me" is essentially desirable, for it is organized on the basis of experiences of security. Hence "I" shall tend to regard "my" self as essentially the "good me"—at least unless my life experience has been extraordinarily unfortunate.

We can now state in general terms the origin, nature, and function of the self dynamism. It has its basis in the need for alertness to approval, tenderness and disapproval. We should like, too, to call attention to its *restrictive* function.

The self-dynamism is built up out of this experience of approbation and disapproval, of reward and punishment. The peculiarity of the self-dynamism is that as it grows it functions, in accordance with its state of development, right from the start. As it develops, it becomes more and more related to a microscope in its function. Since the approbation of the important person is very valuable, since disapprobation denies satisfaction and gives anxiety, the self becomes extremely important. It permits a minute focus on those performances of the child which are the cause of approbation and disapprobation, but, very much like a microscope, it interferes with noticing the rest of the world. When you are staring through your microscope, you don't see much except what comes through that channel. So with the self-dynamism. It has a tendency to focus attention on performances with the significant other person which get approbation or disfavor. And that peculiarity, closely connected with anxiety, persists thenceforth through life. It comes about that the self, that to which we refer when we say 'I,' is the only thing which has alertness, which notices what goes on, and, needless to say, notices what goes on in its own field. The rest of the personality gets along outside awareness. Its impulses, its performances are not noted.[10]

Among the peculiarities of anxiety is the fact that it is always "at 180° to any other tension with which it coincides." [11] In other words, it directly opposes the tensions of somatic needs and thereby prevents or hinders the satisfaction of somatic needs. An extremely anxious person cannot obtain proper sexual satisfaction or may be prevented from enjoying food by nausea, vomiting, etc. While all other tensions are followed by activities, either overt or covert, which resolve the tensions and satisfy needs, the tension of anxiety, in Sullivan's language, does not result in energy transformations directed to its relief by the removal of the situational factors obviously concerned in its provocation. The tension of fear, on the other hand, is often manifested in activities which remove the situational factors provoking fear, escapes them, neutralizes their importance or defers being afraid until the near future when the real or apparent danger is over.

As one grows, one learns, if only in a dim way, how to avoid most situations which provoke intense anxiety, but the capacity for it remains. And it will manifest itself throughout life. In this respect, the difference between the "normal" person and the "neurotic" is only one of degree.

Because experiences of approbation and disapproval occur long before one can think, long before one can discriminate what occurs, the earliest attitudes, and the most "deep seated" and pervasive, are acquired unthinkingly, with little or no discrimination. Furthermore, the infant, and to a large extent also, the child, is biologically and psychologically helpless. Not only does he depend on the parents for the necessities of life itself, but he

[10] *Conceptions of Modern Psychiatry*, pp. 9–10.

[11] Harry Stack Sullivan, "The Meaning of Anxiety in Psychiatry and in Life," *Psychiatry*, vol. 11, no. 1, p. 4, 1948.

has no or only an incipient ability to think and no or insufficient social experience. Hence, in earliest years the attitudes, codes, and behavior of the parents and their surrogates are necessarily accepted without criticism or discrimination. In Sullivan's language he is still pretty much restricted to the parataxic mode of experience. Later, at least to some degree, he will develop the ability to question, compare and relate his experiences.

The "facilitations and deprivations," that which is approved and disapproved by the parents and others close to the child, becomes the source of the material built into the self dynamism. By and large their behavior will be sufficiently consistent to give the self-system a form and direction which it will maintain throughout life. Any experience which promises to threaten the form and direction of the self will provoke anxiety. When this happens, the person will not clearly notice what is happening; its significance will not be realized. And he will usually, without being aware of it, indulge in behavior calculated to nullify the experience or its importance.

Thus, anxiety is the instrumentality by which the self limits and restricts awareness. It functions so as to maintain its own form and direction.

Even when the self is a derogatory and hateful system it will inhibit and misinterpret any disassociated feeling or experience of friendliness towards others; and it will misinterpret any gestures of friendliness from others. The direction and characteristics given to the self in infancy and childhood are maintained year after year, at an extraordinary cost, so that most people in this culture, and presumably in any other, because of inadequate and unfortunate experience in early life, become "inferior caricatures of what they might have been." Not only the family, but various other cultural institutions less directly, all combine, more or less unwittingly, to produce this effect.[12]

Actions, including thinking, phantasy, and emotions and feelings, if they are to occur within self-awareness, must conform to the characteristics of the self. Otherwise they are "disassociated" or "selectively inattended."

The self may be said to be made up of or at least circumscribed by *reflected appraisals*. The child lacks the equipment and experience necessary for a careful and unclouded evaluation of himself. The only guide he has is that of the significant adults who take care of him, and who treat and regard him in accordance with the way in which they have developed from their own life experience. Hence, the child experiences himself and appraises himself in terms of what the parents and others close to him manifest. By empathy, facial expression, gestures, words, deeds they convey to him the attitudes they hold toward him and their regard or lack of it for him.

These he "naturally" accepts because he is not yet a questioning, evaluating being. If the significant people express a respecting, loving attitude toward him, he acquires a respecting, loving attitude toward himself. If

[12] Patrick Mullahy, "A Theory of Interpersonal Relations and the Evolution of Personality," *Psychiatry*, vol. 8, no. 2, p. 191, 1945.

they are derogatory and hateful, then he will acquire a derogatory and hateful attitude toward himself. Throughout life, save perhaps for the intervention of extraordinary circumstances and allowing for some modification through later experience, he will carry the attitude toward himself he learned in early life around with him just as surely as he will carry his skin.

Sullivan suggests, however, that the controlling limiting function of the self is not absolute. Certain impelling needs, such as the need of sexual satisfaction, if thwarted, may prove too powerful even for the self system. Fortunately children retain a capacity for change. A loving teacher may undo somewhat the effects of a destructive parent, but a hateful destructive teacher may limit or slow up the effects of the loving care of tender parents.

To the extent to which limitations and peculiarities of the self interfere with biologically necessary satisfactions and security, then to that extent a person is mentally ill.

The self-dynamism is not synonymous with momentary self-awareness. It is a more or less stable organization or configuration of interpersonal processes, past, present, and of the prospective future. The self has a before and after. Since it merges with other processes occurring outside discriminating awareness, it has "background," it shades imperceptibly into marginal processes of awareness. These marginal processes of awareness may often be noted just before one "drops off" to sleep. Because the self also manifests itself in focal awareness, it has a "foreground."

Selective Inattention and Disassociation

It does not seem necessary to emphasize the fact that much of human experience and behavior occurs outside self-awareness. Freud formulated phenomena occurring outside self-awareness in terms of the "preconscious" and "unconscious." But for Freud these concepts have "topographical" and other features which are foreign to Sullivan's thought. Hence the latter usually avoids the use of such terms because they are "loaded" with meaning to which he does not subscribe.

The concepts by which he tries to formulate his thoughts on such matters are labeled "selective inattention" and "disassociation." The difference between the two is one of degree, measured by the difficulty of access to discriminating awareness.

The child gradually learns to pay close attention to behavior which is approved and disapproved. He must in order to maintain security and avoid anxiety. His attention becomes focused on these performances. This process is analogous to what goes on when, say, a music lover is present at a thrilling concert. Such a person becomes absorbed in the music, "wrapped up" in it. His attention will be entirely focused on the performance and enjoyment of it. To everything else he will pay little heed. In fact, he will not be conscious of anything else, such as the people around him, the passage of time, and so on. For the child his security is at issue, which of course is vitally important, and he will pay close attention to what goes on when approval or disapproval is involved. Certain other experiences either of himself or others will not be so clearly noticed because they entail no particular approval and tenderness or disapproval. Hence, his attention and inattention become selective. To some of his experience and behavior he will be inattentive, and this will then not be carefully discriminated. It will go on outside of discriminated awareness.

Some of these processes can more easily become the object of careful awareness than others. Thus, a friend may call attention to some of them, point them out, and in this case they then become subject to the person's awareness. Such processes are said to be selectively inattended. They can be accepted by the self.

But there are other processes which, when pointed out, do not get careful attention and scrutiny. In spite of the friend's efforts, they will not be clearly noticed. On the contrary, the person will not be able to become consciously aware of them. He will deny their existence, perhaps becoming tense and angry at the efforts of his friend. Nor will he, usually, be able to recall any experience of them. Such experiences are said to be disassociated. The self refuses to grant them awareness.

Motivational systems or dynamisms existing in disassociation are not necessarily "abnormal." And they may find expression in an interpersonal situation without those who participate becoming consciously aware of what is going on. In general, disassociated tendencies are expressed in dreams, phantasies and in unnoticed everyday behavior. In fact, if this were not so, the self system of "normal" people would disintegrate. In other words, the disassociated tendencies would prove too powerful for the inhibitions of the self, thus causing unbearable anxiety, and the person would "go to pieces."

The Meaning of Interpersonal

There is a final point to be mentioned. The term "interpersonal" refers not only to real people existing in space and time but also to "fantastic personifications" or to people who exist physically but who serve rather as "potent representations" of other people once significant in a person's past, say, one's mother or father. In general, any frame of reference, whether constituted by real people, imaginary people existing only in story books, illusory personifications of real people (eidetic persons), or any idea or object given traits or characteristics possessed by human beings, along with one other real person, can serve to make up an interpersonal situation. We can personify and become "integrated" with almost anything, including cultural entities like the government, the church, the school, who "have their being and their manifestation so far as any particular person is concerned in other people who are significant for one reason or another to him. . . ." [13]

A LEARNING APPROACH TO PERSONALITY *

(LAURANCE F. SHAFFER AND EDWARD JOSEPH SHOBEN, JR.

Once a strong motive is aroused, it tends to keep a person or an animal in a state of continued activity. Thwarting of behavior by frustration or by conflict delays the fulfillment of the motive temporarily, but does not abolish the drive. In fact, a thwarted motive is usually strengthened. The original drive that initiated the behavior sequence continues to stimulate. In addition, a person's total drive is increased by emotional tensions, such as the anger-type drives which frustration usually arouses, or the anxiety which results from conflict. The organism has a strong urge to be active, and something has to happen.

Resolving Conflicts and Frustrations

Varied responses. Confronted with an unsatisfied need or an unavoided annoyance, an organism makes *varied responses,* one after another, until at length some act is discovered that will reduce the drive. This exploratory activity which begins when a drive is aroused and ends when the drive is reduced is one of the most general patterns of human and animal behavior. It is shown by organisms very low in the evolutionary scale.

The very simple organism *Stentor* has a repertory of several adjustive responses that it can make to a noxious chemical stimulus in its environment. *Stentor,* a tiny protozoan, is attached to the substratum at the lower end of its tube (Fig. 1). At the top of the tube are cilia or hairs that draw water containing food particles down into it. If a few drops of red ink are introduced into the water near the animal, a series of responses is initiated. First, the *Stentor* bends to one side, avoiding the ink. If several bendings do not bring relief, the movement of the cilia is reversed, pushing the water away instead of drawing it in. If further adjustment is necessary a third response is made, of contracting into its tube. Finally, when all these responses prove unavailing, the *Stentor* releases itself from its support and floats away. Even a single-celled animal can adjust to an injurious stimulus,

---

[13] *Conceptions of Modern Psychiatry,* p. 23.

* From Laurance F. Shaffer and Edward Joseph Shoben, Jr., *The Psychology of Adjustment,* 2d ed., pp. 124–138, Houghton Mifflin Company, Boston, 1956. Reprinted by permission of Professor Shaffer and the publisher.

and has a sequence or hierarchy of responses that it makes in a preferred order until readjustment is achieved.

One of the classic descriptions of behavior when thwarted was made by E. L. Thorndike, from observations in some of his earliest experiments with animals.[1] Thorndike placed cats in puzzle boxes (Fig. 2), which were cages constructed so that the performance of acts such as pulling loops of string or stepping on pedals would cause the door to open, releasing the confined

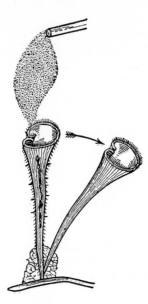

Fig. 1. Adjustive behavior of stentor. Ink is introduced near the mouth of the tiny simple organism. The first response is bending away from the source of the noxious stimulation. (H. S. Jennings, *Behavior of the lower organisms.* New York: Columbia University Press, 1906. Reprinted here by permission from Columbia University Press.)

animal. Young, hungry, and rather untamed cats were used as subjects, since they had enough drive to stir them to activity. Food was placed outside the box where the animal could see it. The cats reacted vigorously to the situation. They tried to squeeze through the bars; they clawed and bit at portions of the cage; they struck at various parts of the apparatus. In the course of such varied activities, a cat would in time pull the string, press the latch, or step on the pedal that released the door. The problem was then solved and the animal got out, reducing the drives induced by its hunger and confinement.

Similar experiments have been performed with human subjects. If a problem is very difficult in relation to one's ability, or if it is of a very novel sort so that previously acquired habits are not serviceable, varied motor activity similar to that of the lower animals will result. Mechanical puzzles, assemblies of wire and metal pieces that will come apart if manipulated correctly, have been used to study human adjustments to unfamiliar and

[1] E. L. Thorndike, "Animal Intelligence," *Psychol. Rev. Monogr. Sup.,* 1898, 2, No. 4 (Whole No. 8).

difficult tasks.[2] Most people respond to the puzzles by moving the pieces at random, pulling here and pushing there. In fact, varied movements are about the only way to gain success. One of the common causes of failure is the continued repetition of the same useless movement. When easier or more familiar problem-solving tasks are given to human subjects, the amount of varied activity may be reduced, and a solution sometimes is reached in one exploratory trial.

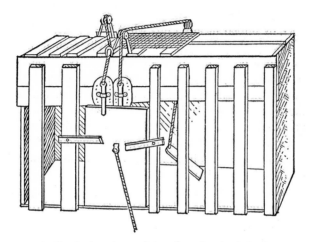

FIG. 2. Puzzle box for studying the adjustive behavior of cats. The apparatus shown is the very difficult puzzle box K, which required three responses for its solution: stepping on a pedal, pulling a loop of cord, and turning a latch on the door. Other easier boxes required only one response. (E. L. Thorndike, Animal intelligence. *Psychol. Rev. Monogr. Sup.*, 1898, 2, No. 4. Reprinted here by permission from the Managing Editor, the American Psychological Association.)

We do not have to go to the psychological laboratory to find evidence of varied responses in the adjustment process. The pattern can be found in innumerable real-life situations. Let us suppose that a boy has kicked his football into the branches of a tree. He may first try to jump from the ground to reach the ball, but it is too high. Then he tries to climb the tree, but there are no low limbs to offer a suitable foothold. He tries to shake the tree, but it is too solid. If the motive to get the ball is sufficiently persistent and if the boy has enough ingenuity he may at length arrive at a solution, such as throwing stones to hit the ball or getting a ladder. If all attempts fail the boy may kick the tree in anger, or blame others for the loss of the ball, or just sit down and cry. These last reactions are not

[2] H. A. Ruger, "The Psychology of Efficiency," *Arch. Psychol.*, New York, 1910, No. 15.

directed realistically to the solution of the problem, but are responses to the boy's own emotional tension.

The varied responses to a thwarted drive are often called *trial and error* behavior. The "trials" that will be attempted in any new situation depend on past experience and previously learned solutions. A cat in a puzzle box has a large number of possible alternative forms of response. When first placed in the box, it scratches, claws, and tries to squeeze through the bars, which are very natural and sensible things for a cat to do under the circumstances. In the past it has escaped from confinement, as when caught behind a fence by similar means. Only when these habits fail to be effective does a cat show the less directed random activity seen in the experiment. Men behave similarly. At first they are likely to try rational adjustments. If these are thwarted by external obstacles, or inhibited by a man's own conflicts, subsequent trials are likely to become overmotivated, excessively emotional, and hence less effective.

Tension reduction. What brings to an end the series of varied responses aroused by a drive? From the psychological viewpoint there is only one answer: the solution of an adjustment is *tension reduction*. Any response that reduces the drive tension brings activity to a close because it removes the stimulus that maintained the behavior. When a hungry animal eats, the visceral state that acted as a drive ceases to exist, and the source of the animal's activity is removed. Similarly, when a person is motivated by an emotional tension or by a social motive derived from emotion, any activity that reduces the emotional state is to him a successful response. It terminates the sequence that began with the appearance of the drive.

Various responses may differ in the degree of their effectiveness as reducers of tension. An unattractive girl may experience conflict between her need for masculine attention and her fear of being rebuffed. Her anxiety will be reduced most effectively by actual success in attracting men. But it will also be reduced to some extent by becoming a man-hater, by competing with men in their own occupational fields, or by becoming emotionally attached to members of her own sex. The direct solution is usually most effectively tension reducing, but various substitute solutions also have utility from the point of view of the individual, to the extent that they reduce the drive that initiated the adjustment.

Quite fortunately, most behavior that reduces your drives also serves your long-range welfare. When you are hungry, you eat; when in real danger, you guard yourself or run away. But some very effective reducers of tensions may have ultimately harmful effects. Eating a poisoned food will stay your hunger, but you will become ill later. Fleeing from imagined dangers may prevent you from gaining other legitimate satisfactions. The word *adjustment* does not carry any connotations of goodness or badness, or of ultimate welfare or disaster. Adjustments do vary in quality, an important and complicated issue. . . . Meanwhile, it is important to remember that adjustment means immediate tension reduction. Some responses to thwarting are inadequate, substitute, or unreal, but if they reduce drives they are adjustments nonetheless.

Learning in Adjustment

So far, the adjustment process has been described as a sequence of behavior by which organisms overcome obstructions and resolve conflicts.

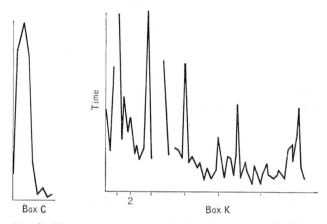

Fig. 3. Time improvement in adjustive learning. At the left is shown the sudden decrease in time taken to escape from a simple and easy puzzle box C. At the right is a record of the times of escape from the difficult box K, showing gradual and irregular improvement. The first may be taken to represent learning with "insight," the second, "blind" learning in adjustment. (E. L. Thorndike, Animal intelligence. *Psychol. Rev. Monogr. Sup.*, 1898, 2, No. 4. Reprinted here by permission from the Managing Editor, the American Psychological Association.)

Attention has been directed to the process by which the first solution of a problem is achieved. This approach is very practical, for many problems are met once, solved, and never encountered again.

When you observe a series of solutions of the same problem, however, another important phenomenon is discovered. In his experiments with cats, Thorndike placed an animal in the same problem box again and again and noted the time required for escape on each successive trial. The results of some of these experiments are shown in Fig. 3. In the series of trials, the animal *learns* to escape from the box. The early trials are characterized by the varied responses previously described. In the later attempts the animal goes directly to the latch, operates it, and escapes at once. In some way or another, the successful solution is selected and perpetuated; the unsuccessful trials tend to drop out and be eliminated.

What is the cause of learning—of this progressive increase in the probability of making the "successful" response? An easy answer that satisfies many laymen is to say that the animal "remembers" the correct solution. However, memory is no more satisfactory an explanation for this problem of learning than it was for the conditioned reaction. In many instances of learning, the words and images that we call memory may not be present at all. A golfer improves from novice to expert by learning processes in which good responses are selected and inefficient ones eliminated, yet if he tries to remember just how to make a stroke nothing but confusion results. In the case of learning by lower animals no evidence of memory is possible except the observation that the animal does learn, and so the explanation turns out to be circular.

The Law of Effect. The explanation of learning by trial, error, and success proposed by Thorndike was that the successful responses were "stamped in" by the satisfaction resulting from the escape and the food. Later, he formalized this principle as the *Law of Effect:*

. . . when a modifiable connection between a situation and a response is made and is accompanied or followed by a satisfying state of affairs, that connection's strength is increased. . . . By a satisfying state of affairs is meant one which the animal does nothing to avoid, often doing things which maintain or renew it.*

The Law of Effect has been a useful practical principle. Most of the economic processes of our culture and most of our educational methods are based on the observation that people will repeat and learn acts that have satisfying end-results. In the laboratories, countless hungry animals from insects to apes have been induced to learn mazes and to solve other problems when rewarded with food.

The exact processes underlying the Law of Effect have raised many doubts. Some of the earliest statements of the principle implied that the *pleasure* resulting from certain responses tends to strengthen those responses directly. It is hard to conceive how a subjective experience of pleasure can make the changes in the nervous system that must happen when learning takes place. It is more likely that pleasure is the result of certain successful adjustments than that it is a cause. Furthermore, a pleasure-oriented theory of learning fails to account for the observation, especially evident in complex human learning, that many painful responses are selected and learned as efficiently as immediately pleasurable ones. Thorndike avoided the pleasure theory by defining a satisfying state as "one which the animal does nothing to avoid, often doing things which maintain or renew it." Such a theory almost says that an animal *learns* what it *performs*, and eliminates the concept of pleasure at the risk of approaching

* E. L. Thorndike, *Educational Psychology.* Vol. II. *The Psychology of Learning.* New York: Teachers College, Columbia University, 1913. Pp. 4 and 2.

circularity. It is evident that further serious consideration must be given to the definition of what is meant by "satisfying."

Reward and punishment. The original statement of the Law of Effect made it both a law of reward and a law of punishment. In addition to the generalization about the results of satisfaction, Thorndike stated that when a connection is accompanied or followed by an annoying state of affairs, its strength is decreased. Further experiments have led to a re-examination of the effectiveness of punishment in "weakening connections" directly. In a

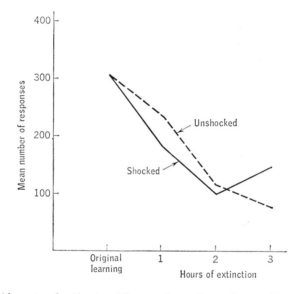

Fig. 4. Punishment and extinction. The experiment shows that punishment suppresses a response but does not extinguish it. Two groups, each of 3 rats, learned a bar-pressing response with food reward. Then the *shocked* rats (solid line) were shocked an average of 9 times when they pressed the bar during a 15-minute period in the first extinction hour. The *unshocked* rats (broken line) were not. During the first and second hours of unrewarded extinction, the unshocked rats made more responses. During the third hour, the shocked rats responded more often. The total number of responses made by the shocked and unshocked rats during the three hours was almost exactly equal. [Data of Experiment A, adjusted for differences in performance before extinction, from W. K. Estes, An experimental study of punishment. *Psychol. Monogr.,* 1944, 57, No. 3 (Whole No. 263). Reprinted here by permission from the Managing Editor, the American Psychological Association.]

series of human learning experiments with verbal material, Thorndike [3] found that the learning of a correct response word was indeed strengthened by the experimenter saying "Right!" On the other hand, saying "Wrong!" when the subject gave an incorrect word did not appreciably decrease the likelihood of the subject giving that response again on the subsequent trial. Even when the mild punishment of saying "Wrong!" was accompanied by

[3] E. L. Thorndike, *Human Learning.* New York: Century, 1931.

a slight electric shock or by a small monetary fine, it proved not to be a dependable way to eliminate a response. As a result of this experiment, Thorndike abandoned his earlier proposition about the effect of "annoying states of affairs."

In an important experiment with rats, W. K. Estes further clarified the relationships of reward and punishment to learning.[4] The rats first learned to press a small bar projecting into their cage when each pressing of the bar was rewarded with a food pellet. Then one group of rats was punished by being given an electric shock when they pressed the bar, while another group was unpunished. Subsequently, both groups were placed in the apparatus for successive periods, and the number of bar-pressings was recorded under conditions involving neither reward nor punishment. As might be expected, the unshocked rats showed a gradual extinction of the unrewarded response until they no longer pressed the bar at all (Fig. 4). A comparison of the behavior of the shocked rats with the unshocked ones was instructive. In the *earlier* extinction trials, the shocked rats made fewer bar-pressing responses; in the *later* trials they made *more* responses than the unshocked rats. They "made up for" their slower rate of responding in the earlier tests. In the end, the shocked rats made just as great a total number of responses before the habit was extinguished as did the unshocked animals. The punishment *suppressed* the bar-pressing response temporarily, but did not *weaken* it in the long run.

Some other experiments have shown that a painful effect accompanying a response may even strengthen it under certain conditions.[5] In a study of adult human learning by Peterson,[6] the subjects learned a "mental maze," in which they acquired the ability to recite a sequence of numbers which were presented in successive pairs, one of each pair being "right" and the other "wrong." Subjects learned by three procedures: (1) with only verbal promptings of right and wrong given by the experimenter; (2) with, in addition, an electric shock accompanying each wrong response; and (3) with an electric shock accompanying each *right* response. Far from

[4] W. K. Estes, "An Experimental Study of Punishment," *Psychol. Monogr.*, 1944, 57, No. 3 (Whole No. 263).

[5] K. F. Muenzinger, "Motivation in Learning: I. Electric Shock for Correct Response in the Visual Discrimination Habit," *J. comp. Psychol.*, 1934, 17, 267–277; K. F. Muenzinger, "Concerning the Effect of Shock for Right Responses in Visual Discrimination Learning," *J. exp. Psychol.*, 1948, 38, 201–203; K. F. Muenzinger, et al., "Motivation in Learning: VIII. Equivalent Amounts of Electric Shock for Right and Wrong Responses in a Visual Discrimination Habit," *J. comp. Psychol.*, 1938, 26, 117–186. G. J. Wischner, "The Effect of Punishment on Discrimination Learning in a Non-correction Situation," *J. exp. Psychol.*, 1947, 37, 271–284; G. J. Wischner, "A Reply to Dr. Muenzinger on the Effect of Punishment on Discrimination Learning in a Non-correction Situation," *J. exp. Psychol.*, 1948, 38, 203–204.

[6] J. Peterson, "Learning when Frequency and Recency Factors are Negative and Right Responses are Painful," *Psychol. Bull.*, 1931, 28, 207–208.

preventing learning, the painful result of giving the right answer became a positive aid for reaching the goal, and the subjects so shocked learned more quickly than those who received only verbal prompting. In both the animal and the human experiments, reaching a motivated goal was the important determiner of learning. The mild shock served only to signal or emphasize success and therefore was an aid to learning, not a hindrance.

Common observation seems to find some instances in which punishment is related to learning. The once-burned child avoids the fire, and parental punishment sometimes seems to deter a child from disapproved behavior. The best interpretation is that such punishments do not weaken responses directly, but that they set up new drives. A child burned by a hot stove acquires a conditioned fear of it. In the future the sight of the stove will arouse this drive, which can then be reduced by avoiding the stove. Escape from pain is a reward and the child learns from satisfying that need, not directly from the punishment.

The learning situation that occurs when a child is punished by his parent is more complicated.[7] Presumably the child has a motive to perform the forbidden act. Punishment evokes a conflicting drive stemming from the anxiety aroused by the parents' displeasure. The child has to resolve his approach-avoidance conflict as best he can, and does not always solve it in the same way. When the forbidden act is fulfilling a very strong drive, the child may continue it in spite of repeated and severe punishment, to the dismay of his uncomprehending parents. Or he may suppress the punished response, as did the rats in Estes' experiment, without really weakening the tendency. In that case, the conflict continues. Finally, the child may reduce his anxiety by adopting a response that pleases his parents. The punishment seems to work, but the real cause of the learning is the reduction of his anxiety.

The analyses and experiments point to a need for reformulating the Law of Effect. Learning is not determined directly by pleasure or pain, but by the reduction of drives and the achievement of adjustment. The revised Law of Effect is substantially the same as the Law of Primary Reinforcement described by C. L. Hull.[8] It may be stated: *Organisms tend to repeat and learn responses that lead to tension reduction and to the completion of motivated activity.*

Closure and insight. Other theories of learning have been proposed that are not inharmonious with the interpretation of adjustive learning just stated, although they differ somewhat in their assumptions and implications. The *Gestalt* school of psychology would define the puzzle-box problem in terms of the animal's perception of the total situation, includ-

---

[7] O. H. Mowrer, "A Stimulus-Response Analysis of Anxiety and Its Role as a Reinforcing Agent," *Psychol. Rev.,* 1939, 46, 553–565.

[8] C. L. Hull, *Principles of Behavior,* New York: Appleton-Century, 1943.

ing the needs, the obstructions, and the goal.[9] The situation is described as an "open" system that is incomplete or out of equilibrium from the point of view of the animal. The successful act brings about a *closure* or restoration of equilibrium. Learning proceeds by an improvement of the perception of the situation. At first the latch is part of the perceptual *ground*, while the food is the *figure* or portion of the total field of which the animal is acutely aware. Learning consists of the enlargement of this figure to include the latch as well as the food, which in the end are "seen together" as the significant factors in the attainment of the goal.

Since the Gestalt view of learning is based on perception, the school objects to the notions that definite movements are learned, and that progress in learning is gradual. Their experiments, performed chiefly with chimpanzees, seem to support both these contentions. Typically, the apes learned by a suddenly effective movement preceded by relatively inactive periods. In one experiment a large box was placed in front of a cage so as to make it impossible for the ape to reach a piece of fruit placed outside. After regarding the situation for about two hours the ape suddenly picked up the box, moved it aside, and reached for the fruit. No random responses that in any way concerned the box had been made previous to the final movement. In many experiments learning occurred in one trial. After one successful attempt, the task was performed immediately when presented again. This sudden learning has been ascribed to a *perceptual reorganization* or "insight" that makes the total situation suddenly clearer to the learner. If insight is defined objectively in terms of an abrupt drop in the time taken to solve a problem, it can be found in the learning of animals much lower than apes. Some of Thorndike's learning curves for cats (Fig. 3) showed quick drops when the problem was "simple, obvious and clearly defined," consisting only of pressing a single latch. Other experiments have found evidence of insight in rats.[10] When human subjects solve mechanical puzzles, sudden improvement after long periods of random activity is typical rather than exceptional.

The Gestalt approach has made a valuable contribution by emphasizing that perceptions can be learned as well as movements. People do learn by perceptual reorganization and insight, and the experiments show that lower animals can also learn in that manner. Some Gestalt concepts are useful in describing the processes of psychotherapy through which disturbed people learn to improve their life adjustments. The chief criticism of the

[9] K. Kofka, *The Growth of the Mind.* New York: Harcourt, Brace, 1925; K. Kofka, *Principles of Gestalt Psychology.* New York: Harcourt, Brace, 1935; W. Kohler, *The Mentality of Apes.* New York: Harcourt, Brace, 1925; W. Kohler, *Gestalt Psychology.* (Rev. ed.) New York: Liveright, 1947.

[10] E. C. Tolman, "Cognitive Maps in Rats and Men," *Psychol. Rev.* 1948, 55, 189–208; E. C. Tolman, and C. H. Honzik, " 'Insight' in Rats," *Univ. Calif. Publ. Psychol.,* 1930, 4, 215–232.

Gestalt theory arises from its stress on intellectual understanding as the basis of all learning. The salient fact about maladjustment is that people often learn blindly and stupidly in response to strong thwarted drives. Perceptual theories supplement but cannot entirely replace the principle of learning by tension reduction.

More than one kind of learning. Will the Law of Effect account for all learning? It does indeed seem to explain adjustive learning quite adequately, but there is another type of learning that does not conform to this principle. Tension reduction describes how you learn to adjust to a fear. You can, however, learn to *have* a fear as well as learn to *reduce* it.[11] A child not previously afraid of dogs can learn to fear them through an injurious experience. That is *tension-producing* learning and certainly cannot be covered by a principle of tension reduction.

We have already encountered a law of learning that can be applied to the acquisition of fears and other tensions. The conditioned reaction shows that learning occurs through the *simultaneous occurrence* of a previously neutral stimulus with the response to which it is to be conditioned. To learn a fear of a new situation it is only necessary for that situation to occur at the same time that the fear response is evoked. Through conditioning you learn to have drives in the face of certain situations; through trial-and-error or adjustive learning you learn to reduce these drives by effective behavior.

The experimental evidence about conditioning confirms the hypothesis that it is a form of learning applying particularly to emotion and drive. Emotional responses and particular aspects of emotion such as the sweating of the palms of the hands are very readily conditioned. Motor responses such as eyelid blinking and finger retraction have also been conditioned, but the resulting learned reactions are usually weak and unstable, quite in contrast with the strength and dependability of emotional conditioning. Many supposed instances of motor conditioning can be reinterpreted in terms of adjustive learning. In numerous experiments, dogs have been "conditioned" to lift a paw upon receiving a light or sound stimulus, the learning being reinforced by the administration of an electric shock as an unconditioned stimulus. These results can be explained more clearly as tension-reduction learning. The real conditioning is that the dog learns to fear the signal that forewarns of the shock. Lifting his paw is an adjustive response by which he avoids the shock and thereby reduces his fear tension.

A number of theorists have attempted to reduce all learning to one principle. Several would explain all learning in terms of drive reduction,[12] while others have tried to reduce trial and error to a special case of con-

---

[11] O. H. Mowrer, "On the Dual Nature of Learning: A Re-interpretation of 'Conditioning' and 'Problem-solving,'" *Harvard educ. Rev.*, 1947, 17, 102–148.

[12] C. L. Hull, *Principles of Behavior*. New York: Appleton-Century, 1943; J. Dollard, and N. E. Miller, *Personality and Psychotherapy*. New York: McGraw-Hill, 1950.

ditioning.[13] Scientific parsimony would indeed be grateful for a single law, but not at the expense of ignoring pertinent contrary evidence. Many psychologists today prefer to have several sets of laws each of which applies to clearly defined cases of learning.[14] There is at least associative learning (conditioning), trial-and-error learning (tension reduction), and possibly also the perceptual-organization learning advocated by the Gestalt theory.

Learning in human adjustments. Theories of learning have been described at length because of the importance of learning in the acquisition of human adjustive responses. The *personality* of an individual consists of his persistent tendencies to make certain kinds of adjustments rather than other kinds. Some earlier psychological theories assigned the basis of personality to heredity, to constitutional and unmodifiable aspects of temperament, or to an inevitable "growth" process that unfolded as a person matured. None of these explanations have proved very fruitful for understanding, predicting, or modifying personality. Learning theories are more promising.

The formation of personality is a vastly more complicated process than is the acquisition of the habits that have been investigated experimentally. It proceeds over a longer period of time and is the result of a person's adjustments to many situations. It is wrong to oversimplify the problems involved in the acquisition of adjustive habits; it is equally wrong to fail to recognize their origins from simple processes of adjustive learning. If a thwarted child has reduced his tension successfully by withdrawing, he is predisposed to withdraw on other occasions when thwarting occurs. If he has effectively reduced a tension by overaggressive behavior, by a tantrum, or by developing a headache, these successful solutions are learned and are likely to be tried in all future situations of a similar nature.

"Abnormal" personality habits are learned in the same way as normal ones. An experiment reported by Skinner illustrates this quite clearly.[15] A hungry pigeon was placed in a cage constructed so that it received food from a swinging hopper at regular intervals of fifteen seconds. Six of eight birds used as experimental subjects developed extraordinary behavior. One acquired a habit of turning counterclockwise about the cage, making two or three turns between feedings. Another developed a "tossing" response, as if repeatedly lifting up an invisible bar with its head. Two birds showed a pendular swinging of the head and body. The other responses were

[13] E. B. Holt, *Animal Drive and the Learning Process.* New York: Holt, 1931; E. R. Guthrie, *The Psychology of Learning.* New York: Harper, 1935.

[14] H. Schlosberg, "The Relationship between Success and the Laws of Conditioning," *Psychol. Rev.*, 1937, *44*, 379–394; B. F. Skinner, *The Behavior of Organisms.* New York: Appleton-Century-Crofts, 1938; E. C. Tolman, "There Is More than One Kind of Learning," *Psychol. Rev.*, 1949, *56*, 144–155; O. H. Mowrer, *op. cit.* p. 311; O. H. Mowrer, *Learning Theory and Personality Dynamics.* New York: Ronald Press, 1950.

[15] B. F. Skinner, " 'Superstition' in the Pigeon," *J. exp. Psychol.*, 1948, *38*, 168–172.

equally bizarre. The learning process had an obvious source. Each bird happened to be making some movement just before the food was given. The "rewarded" response was repeated immediately, and the reinforcements came at such short intervals that other behavior did not have time to intervene and interfere with the response before it was "rewarded" again. The experimental behavior is analogous to superstitions seen in people who perform rituals "to change their luck." It is also like the repetitious and really useless behavior of some neurotic persons whose responses, however irrelevant, have been reinforced by the reduction of their anxiety.

An example of human learning very much like that of the pigeons is shown in a case that E. B. Holt quoted from Preyer with comments of his own.

Two children suffered, during their first six months of infancy, from eruptions of the skin. At first, their arm movements were too uncoordinated to enable them to scratch the affected parts. But they soon learned to reach up to their faces, which were accessible because uncovered, and then, "At every moment when they were not watched the hands went up to the head, and the skin, even where healthy, was rubbed and scratched. These scratching movements cannot be inborn and must be acquired. An accidental contact of hand and head resulting in a decrease of the itching sensation must necessarily induce a preference for the hand-to-head motion, over all other movements." That is, the restlessness produced by a mild annoyer led to trial-and-error learning and alleviation of the annoyance. "Now this reflex reaching toward the head led, as a further consequence, to a peculiar association in one of the two cases. (Observations on the other child are lacking.) As, namely, the eczema healed and finally disappeared, the habit of lifting the arms and carrying the hands to the head persisted, and reappeared whenever the child met anything disagreeable or whenever it manifested opposition, as when it did not wish to play or did wish to stop playing. . . . In this way peculiar expressive movements originate from acquired reflexes." *

Here a personality characteristic of an unusual sort has been caught in the making. To a less acute observer the tendency of the child to put his hands to his face whenever in need of adjustment would have been inexplicable, or perhaps would have been considered "instinctive." In the same manner other persons acquire tendencies to go away alone, to fight, to pout, to lie, or to twiddle their fingers whenever they are thwarted. These personality and character traits are the residuals of the individual's past experiences and of his past tension-reducing solutions of problems.

* E. B. Holt, *Animal Drive and the Learning Process.* New York: Henry Holt and Company, Inc., 1931. Pp. 225–226. Reprinted by permission of the publisher.

THE SIGNIFICANCE OF THE SELF–REGARDING ATTITUDES AND PERCEPTIONS *

⟨ CARL R. ROGERS

One of the elements which was noted from the first in clinical experience in client-centered psychotherapy was that attitudes of the client toward himself, often heavily laden with affect, not only were prominent in all phases of therapy, but seemed to undergo marked fluctuations and changes. Whether this was a secondary and insignificant phenomenon or an evidence of a basic personality process was uncertain. As a variety of research studies in therapy have been added to a growing body of clinical experience, we have pursued this question. It has led us to recognize that not only are feelings about the self involved in therapy, but the way the self is perceived. We have also begun to study the ways in which these self-regarding attitudes and self-perceptions are related to behavior and personality. Out of this complex study there have begun to develop certain theoretical formulations regarding the self and its function in personality. It is the purpose of this paper to give a broad overview of the evidence accumulated regarding the self-regarding attitudes and perceptions, and to suggest a conceptual framework into which this evidence may fit.

Inasmuch as some of the studies upon which this paper is primarily based are as yet unpublished,[1] a word is in order in regard to them. They are all studies based upon small numbers of cases. In several instances the analysis has been made of the hundreds of responses in but one electrically recorded series of interviews. In all instances the reliability of the objective procedures used in analyzing the material has been determined, and while these reliability measures are sufficient to warrant considerable confidence in the results, they are not so high as might be desired. In general the studies bear the marks of their pioneering nature, being more satisfactorily objective than previous investigations in this field, but being still less rigorously objective than is desirable. It has been our experience in opening up the area of psychotherapy to objective scrutiny that fully satisfactory scientific methodology must develop with experience.

* From Carl R. Rogers, "The Significance of the Self-regarding Attitudes and Perceptions," in *Feelings and Emotions*, Martin L., Reymert (ed.), pp. 374–382, McGraw-Hill Book Company, Inc., New York, 1950. Reprinted by permission of the author and publisher.

[1] The complete list is included in the bibliography. Any of the unpublished studies may be obtained or borrowed from the Counseling Center, University of Chicago, Chicago 37, Ill.

It is hoped that these remarks will indicate that the evidence summarized in this paper should be approached with skepticism. It is tentative and suggestive, certainly not definitive or final. It is presented because its coherence and relatedness appear to give it some weight.

The Emotionalized Attitudes toward the Self in Therapy

There is now considerable evidence from various studies regarding the emotionalized attitudes and feelings directed toward the self during the course of therapy, as these attitudes and feelings are determinable from the verbal material of the interviews. We may summarize the main trend of this evidence quite simply. In cases where there is any indication that change took place or that therapy was to some degree "successful" (whether the criterion is client judgment, counselor judgment, or rating by a judge), the following statements would be true.

There is a trend toward an increasing number and proportion of positively toned self-references and self-regarding attitudes as therapy progresses (12, 20, 26, 28, 30, 31).

There is a trend toward a decreasing number and proportion of self-references and self-regarding attitudes which are negative in emotional tone (12, 20, 26, 28, 30, 31).

Attitudes of ambivalence toward the self, in which positive and negative feelings are expressed together, tend to increase slightly until somewhat beyond the midpoint of therapy, and then to decrease slightly. At no period are ambivalent attitudes a frequent expression (1, 20, 26).

At the conclusion of therapy there are more positively toned self-references than negative (1, 12, 20, 26, 28, 30, 31).

These trends are not found, or are found in lesser degree, in cases regarded as unsuccessful (20, 29).

There are certain other findings, less general in their nature, which tend to qualify these statements.

The sharpest and clearest measure of the above trends is in terms of positive and negative feelings toward the self which are expressed as being currently held. The elimination of past attitudes from consideration heightens the slope of both curves (26).

In the individual case, though the general trends are as described, there may be wide fluctuations from interview to interview in the self-regarding attitudes. After a slow rise in positive attitudes, negative attitudes may become sharply predominant for a time, etc. (10, 20).

Within the general trends described there is more variability in self-regarding attitudes in the later stages of therapy than in the early stages (26).

There is often an initial decrease in the positively toned self-regarding attitudes, before the general upward trend becomes evident (20, 26).

The "unsuccessful" case may remain consistently high in negative feelings about the self or consistently high in positive self-attitudes (20, 29).

One feels tempted to launch at once into possible clinical explanations of these findings. I would prefer, however, to focus our attention solely on the objective facts for the moment—the evidence of change in feelings about the self, the evidence of a general trend which includes wide fluctuations, and the evidence that positive self-references alone do not seem to spell whatever is included in the vague concept of "successful therapy."

The Changing Perception of Self in Therapy

In addition to the studies of feelings about the self, there is more scattered evidence regarding the changes in the perception of the self during therapy. The individual comes to perceive himself differently, to form different conceptualizations about himself, and these alterations in perception appear to be concomitant with the alteration in emotionalized attitudes already described. Though more studies are needed in this area, investigating other aspects of the perceptual change and utilizing larger numbers of cases, it may be useful to summarize the evidence now available. Again our knowledge is largely limited to those cases in which, by common sense, general criteria, some "success" or change appears to have occurred. Again the studies are based upon electrically recorded and transcribed cases.

There is a tendency for the "acceptance of self," operationally defined, to increase during therapy. Acceptance of self, according to the definition used, means that the client tends:

To perceive himself as a person of worth, worthy of respect rather than condemnation.

To perceive his standards as being based upon his own experience, rather than upon the attitudes or desires of others.

To perceive his own feelings, motives, social and personal experiences, without distortion of the basic sensory data (27).

The study upon which these statements are based is confirmed by others, most of them less rigorous in nature. From these other studies it would appear that the individual in "successful" therapy tends:

To perceive his abilities and characteristics with more objectivity and with greater comfort (24).

To perceive all aspects of self and self-in-relationship with less emotion and more objectivity (30).

To perceive himself as more independent and more able to cope with life problems (18, 24).

To perceive himself as more able to be spontaneous and genuine (18).

To perceive himself as the evaluator of experience, rather than regarding himself as existing in a world where the values are inherent in and attached to the objects of his perception (17).

To perceive himself as more integrated, less divided (18, 24).

How may we summarize these changes in self-perception? The essential elements would appear to be that the individual changes in three general ways. He perceives himself as a more adequate person, with more worth and more possibility of meeting life. He permits more experiential data to enter awareness, and thus achieves a more realistic appraisal of himself, his relationships, and his environment. He tends to place the basis of standards within himself, recognizing that the "goodness" or "badness" of any experience of perceptual object is not something inherent in that object, but is a value placed on it by himself.

Thus far, then, we may say, on the basis of the evidence, that the feelings and emotions regarding the self tend to change in therapy, and likewise the ways in which the self is perceived. These changes are not random, but appear to have commonality of trend. There is a definite and marked correlation between the degree of positive feelings about the self and the degree to which the self is perceived as adequate, as related realistically to experience, and as capable of evaluating experience (21). These statements are based primarily upon studies of cases in which some progress took place, and experience suggests that they require modification in "unsuccessful" cases.

But thus far these changes are all within the phenomenal field of the client. He feels differently about himself, he sees himself differently, but in the inelegant vernacular, "So what?" There has been a strong tendency in psychology to regard these self-feelings and self-perceptions as notoriously inaccurate, and as an inadequate basis for scientific thinking. Even if these changes occur, does this mean any essential alteration in the behavior or personality of the client? Are these self-attitudes significant of change that is externally observable, or are they merely introspective fluff which must be brushed off before we can see the hard facts underneath? Let us turn to this point.

Attitudinal, Physiological, and Behavioral Correlates

Our objective knowledge regarding the correlates of these changes in the attitudes toward and perceptions of the self is very meager, considering the practical and theoretical importance of the issue. Yet some evidence exists, and it is generally consistent in nature. We may at the present time say that in client-centered therapy the trends which have been described in self-regarding feelings and self-perceptions are correlated with certain other findings bearing upon the attitudes, physiological reactions, and behavior of the individual. The described changes in self-attitudes and self-perceptions are positively correlated with:

A decrease in psychological tension as verbally expressed (2, 15, 25, 33).
A decrease in objectively measured physiological tensions in a frustrating situation. This may be termed heightened frustration-tolerance (32).
A decrease in current defensive behavior, operationally defined and objectively measured in the interview (11, 13).
A decrease in negatively toned attitudes toward others (21, 26, 30).
An increase in attitudes of acceptance of and respect for others (27).

An increase in the maturity of reported behavior (12).

Improvement in adjustment on the job and in job training, as rated by impartial observers (4).

Alteration in personality structure as measured by projective and objective tests, this change being in the direction of lessened anxiety, greater personal integration, greater emotional stability and control, increased adaptability, lessened neurotic and introvertive tendencies, increased sociability and self-confidence (6, 9, 14, 19, 22).

There are two other directions in which there is some evidence. There is scattered and inconclusive evidence that increased functional intelligence and functional learning are correlated with the described changes in self-attitudes and self-perceptions (3, 5, 7, 8). There is also evidence that social adjustment in the community over a two-year period is correlated significantly with the degree of objectivity and realism of perception of self and self-in-relationship-to-environment (23). The research on which this statement is based is a study of self-appraisal in a group of delinquents and is not a study of therapy. It is therefore somewhat different in kind from the other researches cited. The inference is of this order: there is evidence to show that the experience of client-centered therapy is associated with an increase in objectivity of self-appraisal; there is evidence to show that objectivity of self-appraisal is associated, in delinquents, with a prognosis of more satisfactory family, school, and community adjustment; there appears to be a possibility that the experience of therapy may be associated with a prognosis of improved social adjustment. Obviously, until a satisfactory follow-up study of social adjustment in therapy cases is completed, the evidence is inconclusive.

Pulling together the threads from the three lines of inquiry we have followed, it may be said that within the limitations set by the fairly large probable error of the studies thus far completed, there is some evidence for the following statement. Characteristic changes occur in the emotionalized self-regarding attitudes during client-centered psychotherapy; these changes are correlated with characteristic alterations in the perceptions of self; both of these trends appear to be correlated with changes in physiological tensions, psychological discomfort, social attitudes, defensive behavior, maturity of behavior, personality structure, and social adjustment.

Some Theoretical Formulations Regarding the Self

It is a consideration of such evidence which has led us to attempt to formulate a theory to include these facts, a theory which involves the use of the theoretical construct, the self. Some of the propositions of that theory will be briefly presented in this paper without the amplification which they perhaps deserve. The aim is not to present a complete and closed theory, but to indicate some lines of thought which may appear profitable in the building of theory.

The central construct of our theory would be the concept of self, or the self as a perceived object in the phenomenal field. Drawing upon the evidence and upon clinical experience, it would appear that the most useful definition of the self-concept, or self-structure, would be along these lines. The self-structure is an organized configuration of perceptions of the self which are admissible to awareness. It is composed of such elements as the perceptions of one's characteristics and abilities; the percepts and concepts of the self in relation to others and to environment; the value qualities which are perceived as associated with experiences and objects; and the goals and ideals which are perceived as having positive or negative valence. It is, then, the organized picture, existing in awareness either as figure or ground, of the self and the self-in-relationship, together with the positive or negative values which are associated with those qualities and relationships, as they are perceived as existing in the past, present, or future.

There is no necessary close relationship between the elements of the structure of self and the elements of sensory experience. Thus an individual of average appearance may perceive himself as ugly, distorting the evidence of his senses. He may have the sensory experience of anger at his wife, and perceive himself as feeling only an unruffled affection, denying to awareness his visceral reactions. These phenomena of distortion and denial of sensory experience appear to come about because of his perception of certain attitudes of others toward him. As the structure of self becomes thus formed in part upon a distortion or denial of the relevant sensory evidence, it also becomes selective in its perception, perceiving insofar as possible only those elements consistent with the pattern of self already formed.

The structure of self appears to change primarily under conditions which permit a greater differentiation of the phenomenal or perceptual field. When the self is not under threat, and feels securely accepted, then the organization of self is not perceived as final. Denied sensory and visceral experience may not only be admitted to awareness, but incorporated into the structure of self. Experience which has been distorted may be reperceived and the basic sensory data more adequately differentiated and assimilated into the concept of self. These processes tend to occur since less tension is experienced when the pattern of self is constructed out of the undistorted totality of sensory experience. The changes which occur in portions of the self-structure in the ways just mentioned tend to alter in some degree the whole organizational *Gestalt* of the self.

The self is related to behavior in a significant way, in that all behavior which is perceived as being in the realm of conscious control is consistent with the concept of self. If there are exceptions, they are accompanied by marked distress. Consequently when the concept of self is changed, alteration in behavior is a predictable concomitant. The new behavior will be consistent with the new structure of self.

How would a conceptual framework of this sort contain the research evidence which we have reviewed concerning the emotionalized self-regarding attitudes? They would appear to have a definite relationship to the structure of the self as we have defined it. A positive emotional tone toward the self seems to exist when the self-structure is firmly organized, and a negative feeling about the self exists when the organization of self is threatened by experiences which are vaguely or clearly seen as inconsistent with that structure. Thus, both the integrated individual and the person who is well organized on what might be termed a defensive basis, who completely shuts certain experiences out of awareness, will tend to have positive self-regarding attitudes. The emotionalized attitudes toward the self may be significant primarily of the state of organization of the self, firmness and consistency of organization being associated with positive self-feelings, whereas to the degree that the self is experienced as threatened or lacking in structural firmness, negative self-attitudes exist. In therapy we tend to get the individual who feels threatened, who vaguely senses inconsistencies, and who, after a process of partial disorganization of the self, rebuilds a self-structure more congruent with his basic experience and thus increases in positive self-feeling. Thus our theoretical formulation would hold that feelings about the self tend to be more a measure of the quality of self-organization than a measure of basic adjustment.

Our theory would also relate to the ways in which the self is perceived, some of these self-perceptions seeming to have a relationship to basic integration. When the self is seen as being able to permit all experience to enter awareness, then self-integration and self-confidence develop on the foundation of a fluid and adaptable self-organization. One client puts this realization thus: "You must even let your own experience tell you its own meaning; the minute *you* tell it what it means . . . you are at war with yourself." It is this permissiveness of the self toward all experiences and impulses, accepting them without denial or distortion, which appears to be the measure of sound personality integration.

Perhaps these preceding paragraphs begin to suggest the ways in which a theory developed out of concepts regarding the self might bring together into a coherent system the varied sorts of research evidence summarized in this paper. It would make comprehensible the wide fluctuations in self-regarding attitudes which occur in therapy as denied and distorted experiences are admitted to awareness, disturbing the organization of self. It would provide a rationale for the fact that the individual at the conclusion of therapy feels more comfortable, that he is more nearly his "real self," that he experiences himself as more unified, as all sensory and visceral experiences are perceived more nearly in their own terms. It would enable us to conceptualize the fact that behavior and attitudes other than self-attitudes change with the organization of self. In thus endeavoring to provide a meaningful theory of therapeutic change, it is believed that a significant ontribution would be made to general theory regarding personality. It ould also be a theory which could be stated in terms of operational efinitions and thus put to experimental test. This could play a useful art in forwarding the science of personality study.

Bibliography

1. Aidman, T. Changes in self perception as related to changes in perception of one's environment. Master's thesis, Univ. of Chicago, 1947. Digest presented to American Psychological Association, Boston, 1948.
2. Assum, A. L., and Levy, S. J. Analysis of a nondirective case with followup interview. *J. abnorm. soc. Psychol.*, 1948, 43, 78–89.
3. Axline, V. M. Nondirective therapy for poor readers. *J. consult. Psychol.*, 1947, 11, 61–69.
4. Bartlett, M., and staff. Data on the Personal Adjustment Counseling Program for Veterans. Report of the Personal Adjustment Counseling Division, Advisement and Guidance Service, Office of Vocational Rehabilitation and Education, Veterans Administration, 1948.
5. Bills, R. E. An investigation of the effects of individual and group play therapy on the reading level of retarded readers. Presented to American Psychological Association, Boston, 1948.
6. Carr, A. C. An evaluation of nine nondirective psychotherapy cases by means of the Rorschach. *J. consult. Psychol.*, 1949, 13, 196–205.
7. Combs, A. W. Case of Edith Moore. In W. U. Snyder (Ed.), *Casebook of nondirective counseling.* Boston: Houghton Mifflin, 1947. Pp. 268–311.
8. Combs, A. Follow-up of a counseling case treated by the nondirective method. *J. clin. Psychol.*, 1945, 1, 145–154.
9. Cowen, E. L. A qualitative and quantitative follow-up study of thirty-two cases counselled by nondirective methods. Unpublished master's thesis, Syracuse Univ., 1948.
10. Curran, A. *Personality factors in counseling.* New York: Grune & Stratton, 1945.
11. Haigh, G. Defensive behavior in client-centered therapy. *J. consult. Psychol.*, 1949, 13, 181–189.
12. Hoffman, A. E. A study of reported behavior changes in counseling. *J. consult. Psychol.*, 1949, 13, 190–195.
13. Hogan, R. The development of a measure of client defensiveness in a counseling relationship. Doctor's dissertation, Univ. of Chicago, 1948.
14. Kasin, E. S. An exploratory comparison of personality descriptions obtained from nondirective interviews and the Thematic Apperception Test. Master's thesis, Univ. of Chicago, 1948.
15. Kauffman, P. E. An investigation of the relationship of two methods of measuring changes in verbatim protocols of counseling interviews. Unpublished master's thesis, Ohio State Univ., 1948.
16. Kauffmann, P., and Raimy, V. C. Two methods of assessing therapeutic progress. *J. abnorm. soc. Psychol.*, 1949, 44, 379–385.
17. Kessler, C. Semantics and non-directive counseling. Master's thesis, Univ. of Chicago, 1947.
18. Lipkin, S. The client evaluates nondirective psychotherapy. *J. consult. Psychol.*, 1948, 12, 137–146.
19. Muench, G. A. An evaluation of nondirective psychotherapy by means of the Rorschach and other tests. *Appl. Psychol. Monogr.*, No. 13, Stanford Univ. Press, 1947.

20. Raimy, V. C. The self-concept as a factor in counseling and personality organiza-
     tion. Doctor's dissertation, Ohio State Univ., 1943. Digest published in *J. consult
     Psychol.*, 1948, *12*, 153–163.
21. Raskin, N. J. An analysis of six parallel studies of therapeutic process. *J. consult
     Psychol.*, 1949, *13*, 206–220.
22. Reader, N. An investigation of some personality changes occurring in individuals
     undergoing client-centered therapy. Unpublished doctoral dissertation, Univ. of
     Chicago, 1948.
23. Rogers, C. R., Kell, B., and McNeil, H. The role of self-understanding in the pre
     diction of behavior. *J. consult. Psychol.*, 1948, *12*, 174–186.
24. Rogers, N. Changes in self concept in the case of Mrs. Ett. *Personal Counselor*
     1947, *2*, 278–291.
25. Rogers, N. Measuring psychological tensions in non-directive counseling. *Persona
     Counselor*, 1948, *3*, 237–264.
26. Seeman, J. A study of the process of nondirective therapy. *J. consult. Psychol.*
     1949, *13*, 157–168.
27. Sheerer, E. T. An analysis of the relationship between acceptance of and respect
     for self and acceptance of and respect for others in ten counseling cases. *J. consult
     Psychol.*, 1949, *13*, 169–175.
28. Snyder, W. U. An investigation of the nature of nondirective psychotherapy
     J. gen. Psychol., 1945, *33*, 193–223.
29. Snyder, W. U. A comparison of one unsuccessful with four successful nondirec
     tively counseled cases. *J. consult. Psychol.*, 1947, *11*, 38–42.
30. Stock, D. An investigation into the interrelations between the self-concept and
     feelings directed toward other persons and groups. *J. consult. Psychol.*, 1949, *13*
     176–180.
31. Strom, K. A re-study of William U. Snyder's "An investigation of the nature of
     non-directive psychotherapy." Master's thesis in progress, Univ. of Chicago, 1948
32. Thetford, W. N. The measurement of physiological responses to frustration before
     and after nondirective psychotherapy. Paper presented to American Psychologica
     Association, Boston, 1948.
33. Zimmerman, J. Modification of the discomfort-relief quotient as a measure of
     progress in counseling. Master's thesis in progress, Univ. of Chicago, 1948.

A THEORY OF HUMAN MOTIVATION *

(A. H. MASLOW

I. *Introduction*

In a previous paper (13) various propositions were presented which would
have to be included in any theory of human motivation that could lay
claim to being definitive. These conclusions may be briefly summarized a
follows:

* From A. H. Maslow, "A Theory of Human Motivation," *Psychol. Rev.*, 50, 370–
396. Reprinted by permission of the author and the Managing Editor, the American
Psychological Association.

1. The integrated wholeness of the organism must be one of the foundation stones of motivation theory.

2. The hunger drive (or any other physiological drive) was rejected as a centering point or model for a definitive theory of motivation. Any drive that is somatically based and localizable was shown to be atypical rather than typical in human motivation.

3. Such a theory should stress and center itself upon ultimate or basic goals rather than partial or superficial ones, upon ends rather than means to these ends. Such a stress would imply a more central place for unconscious than for conscious motivations.

4. There are usually available various cultural paths to the same goal. Therefore conscious, specific, local-cultural desires are not as fundamental in motivation theory as the more basic, unconscious goals.

5. Any motivated behavior, either preparatory or consummatory, must be understood to be a channel through which many basic needs may be simultaneously expressed or satisfied. Typically an act has *more* than one motivation.

6. Practically all organismic states are to be understood as motivated and as motivating.

7. Human needs arrange themselves in hierarchies of prepotency. That is to say, the appearance of one need usually rests on the prior satisfaction of another, more prepotent need. Man is a perpetually wanting animal. Also no need or drive can be treated as if it were isolated or discrete; every drive is related to the state of satisfaction or dissatisfaction of other drives.

8. *Lists* of drives will get us nowhere for various theoretical and practical reasons. Furthermore any classification of motivations must deal with the problem of levels of specificity or generalization of the motives to be classified.

9. Classifications of motivations must be based upon goals rather than upon instigating drives or motivated behavior.

10. Motivation theory should be human-centered rather than animal-centered.

11. The situation or the field in which the organism reacts must be taken into account but the field alone can rarely serve as an exclusive explanation for behavior. Furthermore the field itself must be interpreted in terms of the organism. Field theory cannot be a substitute for motivation theory.

12. Not only the integration of the organism must be taken into account, but also the possibility of isolated, specific, partial or segmental reactions.

It has since become necessary to add to these another affirmation.

13. Motivation theory is not synonymous with behavior theory. The motivations are only one class of determinants of behavior. While behavior is almost always motivated, it is also almost always biologically, culturally and situationally determined as well.

The present paper is an attempt to formulate a positive theory of motivation which will satisfy these theoretical demands and at the same time conform to the known facts, clinical and observational as well as experimental. It derives most directly, however, from clinical experience. This theory is, I think, in the functionalist tradition of James and Dewey, and is fused with the holism of Wertheimer (19), Goldstein (6), and Gestalt Psychology, and with the dynamicism of Freud (4) and Adler (1). This fusion or synthesis may arbitrarily be called a "general-dynamic" theory.

It is far easier to perceive and to criticize the aspects in motivation theory than to remedy them. Mostly this is because of the very serious lack of sound data in this area. I conceive this lack of sound facts to be due primarily to the absence of a valid theory of motivation. The present theory then must be considered to be a suggested program or framework for future research and must stand or fall, not so much on facts available or evidence presented, as upon researches yet to be done, researches suggested perhaps, by the questions raised in this paper.

II. *The Basic Needs*

The "physiological" needs. The needs that are usually taken as the starting point for motivation theory are the so-called physiological drives. Two recent lines of research make it necessary to revise our customary notions about these needs, first, the development of the concept of homeostasis and second, the finding that appetites (preferential choices among foods) are a fairly efficient indication of actual needs or lacks in the body.

Homeostasis refers to the body's automatic efforts to maintain a constant, normal state of the blood stream. Cannon (2) has described this process for (1) the water content of the blood, (2) salt content, (3) sugar content, (4) protein content, (5) fat content, (6) calcium content, (7) oxygen content, (8) constant hydrogen-ion level (acid-base balance) and (9) constant temperature of the blood. Obviously this list can be extended to include other minerals, the hormones, vitamins, etc.

Young in a recent article (21) has summarized the work on appetite in its relation to body needs. If the body lacks some chemical, the individual will tend to develop a specific appetite or partial hunger for that food element.

Thus it seems impossible as well as useless to make any list of fundamental physiological needs for they can come to almost any number one might wish, depending on the degree of specificity of description. We can not identify all physiological needs as homeostatic. That sexual desire, sleepiness, sheer activity and maternal behavior in animals are homeostatic, has not yet been demonstrated. Furthermore, this list would not include the various sensory pleasures (tastes, smells, tickling, stroking) which are probably physiological and which may become the goals of motivated behavior.

In a previous paper (13) it has been pointed out that these physiological drives or needs are to be considered unusual rather than typical because they are isolable, and because they are localizable somatically. That is to say, they are relatively independent of each other, of other motivations and of the organism as a whole, and secondly, in many cases, it is possible to demonstrate a localized, underlying somatic base for the drive. This is true less generally than has been thought (exceptions are fatigue, sleepiness, maternal responses) but it is still true in the classic instances of hunger, sex, and thirst.

It should be pointed out again that any of the physiological needs and the consummatory behavior involved with them serve as channels for all sorts of other needs as well. That is to say, the person who thinks he is hungry may actually be seeking more for comfort, or dependence, than for vitamins or proteins. Conversely, it is possible to satisfy the hunger need in part by other activities such as drinking water or smoking cigarettes. In other words, relatively isolable as these physiological needs are, they are not completely so.

Undoubtedly these physiological needs are the most prepotent of all needs. What this means specifically is, that in the human being who is missing everything in life in an extreme fashion, it is most likely that the major motivation would be the physiological needs rather than any others. A person who is lacking food, safety, love, and esteem would most probably hunger for food more strongly than for anything else.

If all the needs are unsatisfied, and the organism is then dominated by the physiological needs, all other needs may become simply non-existent or be pushed into the background. It is then fair to characterize the whole organism by saying simply that it is hungry, for consciousness is almost completely preempted by hunger. All capacities are put into the service of hunger-satisfaction, and the organization of these capacities is almost entirely determined by the one purpose of satisfying hunger. The receptors and effectors, the intelligence, memory, habits, all may now be defined simply as hunger-gratifying tools. Capacities that are not useful for this purpose lie dormant, or are pushed into the background. The urge to write poetry, the desire to acquire an automobile, the interest in American history, the desire for a new pair of shoes are, in the extreme case, forgotten or become of secondary importance. For the man who is extremely and dangerously hungry, no other interests exist but food. He dreams food, he remembers food, he thinks about food, he emotes only about food, he perceives only food and he wants only food. The more subtle determinants that ordinarily fuse with the physiological drives in organizing even feeding, drinking or sexual behavior, may now be so completely overwhelmed as to allow us to speak at this time (but *only* at this time) of pure hunger drive and behavior, with the one unqualified aim of relief.

Another peculiar characteristic of the human organism when it is dominated by a certain need is that the whole philosophy of the future tends also to change. For our chronically and extremely hungry man, Utopia can be defined very simply as a place where there is plenty of food. He tends to think that, if only he is guaranteed food for the rest of his life, he will be perfectly happy and will never want anything more. Life itself tends to be defined in terms of eating. Anything else will be defined as unimportant. Freedom, love, community feeling, respect, philosophy, may all be waved aside as fripperies which are useless since they fail to fill the stomach. Such a man may fairly be said to live by bread alone.

It cannot possibly be denied that such things are true but their *generality* can be denied. Emergency conditions are, almost by definition, rare in the normally functioning peaceful society. That this truism can be forgotten is due mainly to two reasons. First, rats have few motivations other than physiological ones, and since so much of the research upon motivation has been made with these animals, it is easy to carry the rat-picture over to the human being. Secondly, it is too often not realized that culture itself is an adaptive tool, one of whose main functions is to make the physiological emergencies come less and less often. In most of the known societies, chronic extreme hunger of the emergency type is rare, rather than common. In any case, this is still true in the United States. The average American citizen is experiencing appetite rather than hunger when he says "I am hungry." He is apt to experience sheer life-and-death hunger only by accident and then only a few times through his entire life.

Obviously a good way to obscure the "higher" motivations, and to get a lopsided view of human capacities and human nature, is to make the organism extremely and chronically hungry or thirsty. Anyone who attempts to make an emergency picture into a typical one, and who will measure all of man's goals and desires by his behavior during extreme physiological deprivation is certainly being blind to many things. It is quite true that man lives by bread alone—when there is no bread. But what happens to man's desires where there *is* plenty of bread and when his belly is chronically filled?

At once other (and "higher") needs emerge and these, rather than physiological hungers, dominate the organism. And when these in turn are satisfied, again new (and still "higher") needs emerge and so on. This is what we mean by saying that the basic human needs are organized into a hierarchy of relative prepotency.

One main implication of this phrasing is that gratification becomes as important a concept as deprivation in motivation theory, for it releases the organism from the domination of a relatively more physiological need, permitting thereby the emergence of other more social goals. The physiological needs, along with their partial goals, when chronically gratified cease to exist as active determinants or organizers of behavior. They now exist only in a potential fashion in the sense that they may emerge again to dominate the organism if they are thwarted. But a want that is satisfied is no longer a want. The organism is dominated and its behavior organized only by unsatisfied needs. If hunger is satisfied, it becomes unimportant in the current dynamics of the individual.

This statement is somewhat qualified by a hypothesis to be discussed more fully later, namely that it is precisely those individuals in whom a certain need has always been satisfied who are best equipped to tolerate deprivation of that need in the future, and that furthermore, those who have been deprived in the past will react differently to current satisfactions than the one who has never been deprived.

The safety needs. If the physiological needs are relatively well gratified, there then emerges a new set of needs, which we may categorize roughly as the safety needs. All that has been said of the physiological needs is equally true, although in lesser degree, of these desires. The organism may equally well be wholly dominated by them. They may serve as the almost exclusive organizers of behavior, recruiting all the capacities of the organism in their service, and we may then fairly describe the whole organism as a safety-seeking mechanism. Again we may say of the receptors, the effectors, of the intellect and the other capacities that they are primarily safety-seeking tools. Again, as in the hungry man, we find that the dominating goal is a strong determinant not only of his current world-outlook and philosophy but also of his philosophy of the future. Practically everything looks less important than safety (even sometimes the physiological needs which being satisfied, are now underestimated). A man, in this state, if it is extreme enough and chronic enough, may be characterized as living almost for safety alone.

Although in this paper we are interested primarily in the needs of the adult, we can approach an understanding of his safety needs perhaps more efficiently by observation of infants and children, in whom these needs are much more simple and obvious. One reason for the clearer appearance of the threat or danger reaction in infants, is that they do not inhibit this reaction at all, whereas adults in our society have been taught to inhibit it at all costs. Thus even when adults do feel their safety to be threatened we may not be able to see this on the surface. Infants will react in a total fashion and as if they were endangered, if they are disturbed or dropped suddenly, startled by loud noises, flashing light, or other unusual sensory stimulation, by rough handling, by general loss of support in the mother's arms, or by inadequate support.[1]

In infants we can also see a much more direct reaction to bodily illnesses of various kinds. Sometimes these illnesses seem to be immediately and *per se* threatening and seem to make the child feel unsafe. For instance, vomiting, colic or other sharp pains seem to make the child look at the whole world in a different way. At such a moment of pain, it may be postulated that, for the child, the appearance of the whole world suddenly changes from sunniness to darkness, so to speak, and becomes a place in

---

[1] As the child grows up, sheer knowledge and familiarity as well as better motor development make these "dangers" less and less dangerous and more and more manageable. Throughout life it may be said that one of the main conative functions of education is this neutralizing of apparent dangers through knowledge, *e.g.*, I am not afraid of thunder because I know something about it.

which anything at all might happen, in which previously stable things have suddenly become unstable. Thus a child who because of some bad food is taken ill may, for a day or two, develop fear, nightmares, and a need for protection and reassurance never seen in him before his illness.

Another indication of the child's need for safety is his preference for some kind of undisrupted routine or rhythm. He seems to want a predictable, orderly world. For instance, injustice, unfairness, or inconsistency in the parents seems to make a child feel anxious and unsafe. This attitude may be not so much because of the injustice *per se* or any particular pains involved, but rather because this treatment threatens to make the world look unreliable, or unsafe, or unpredictable. Young children seem to thrive better under a system which has at least a skeletal outline of rigidity, in which there is a schedule of a kind, some sort of routine, something that can be counted upon, not only for the present but also far into the future. Perhaps one could express this more accurately by saying that the child needs an organized world rather than an unorganized or unstructured one.

The central role of the parents and the normal family setup are indisputable. Quarreling, physical assault, separation, divorce or death within the family may be particularly terrifying. Also parental outbursts of rage or threats of punishment directed to the child, calling him names, speaking to him harshly, shaking him, handling him roughly, or actual physical punishment sometimes elicit such total panic and terror in the child that we must assume more is involved than the physical pain alone. While it is true that in some children this terror may represent also a fear of loss of parental love, it can also occur in completely rejected children, who seem to cling to the hating parents more for sheer safety and protection than because of hope of love.

Confronting the average child with new, unfamiliar, strange, unmanageable stimuli or situations will too frequently elicit the danger or terror reaction, as for example, getting lost or even being separated from the parents for a short time, being confronted with new faces, new situations or new tasks, the sight of strange, unfamiliar or uncontrollable objects, illness or death. Particularly at such times, the child's frantic clinging to his parents is eloquent testimony to their role as protectors (quite apart from their roles as food-givers and love-givers).

From these and similar observations, we may generalize and say that the average child in our society generally prefers a safe, orderly, predictable, organized world, which he can count on, and in which unexpected, unmanageable or other dangerous things do not happen, and in which, in any case, he has all-powerful parents who protect and shield him from harm.

That these reactions may so easily be observed in children is in a way a proof of the fact that children in our society feel too unsafe (or, in a word, are badly brought up). Children who are reared in an unthreatening, loving family do *not* ordinarily react as we have described above (17). In such

hildren the danger reactions are apt to come mostly to objects or situa-
ons that adults too would consider dangerous.[2]

The healthy, normal, fortunate adult in our culture is largely satisfied in
is safety needs. The peaceful, smoothly running, "good" society ordinarily
akes its members feel safe enough from wild animals, extremes of tem-
erature, criminals, assault and murder, tyranny, etc. Therefore, in a very
al sense, he no longer has any safety needs as active motivators. Just as
sated man no longer feels hungry, a safe man no longer feels endangered.
f we wish to see these needs directly and clearly we must turn to neurotic
r near-neurotic individuals, and to the economic and social underdogs. In
etween these extremes, we can perceive the expressions of safety needs
nly in such phenomena as, for instance, the common preference for a job
ith tenure and protection, the desire for a savings account, and for insur-
nce of various kinds (medical, dental, unemployment, disability, old age).

Other broader aspects of the attempt to seek safety and stability in the
orld are seen in the very common preference for familiar rather than un-
miliar things, or for the known rather than the unknown. The tendency
o have some religion or world-philosophy that organizes the universe and
he men in it into some sort of satisfactorily coherent, meaningful whole is
lso in part motivated by safety-seeking. Here too we may list science and
hilosophy in general as partially motivated by the safety needs (we shall
ee later that there are also other motivations to scientific, philosophical or
eligious endeavor).

Otherwise the need for safety is seen as an active and dominant mobilizer
f the organism's resources only in emergencies, e.g., war, disease, natural
atastrophies, crime waves, societal disorganization, neurosis, brain injury,
hronically bad situation.

Some neurotic adults in our society are, in many ways, like the unsafe
hild in their desire for safety, although in the former it takes on a some-
hat special appearance. Their reaction is often to unknown, psychological
angers in a world that is perceived to be hostile, overwhelming and threat-
ning. Such a person behaves as if a great catastrophe were almost always
mpending, i.e., he is usually responding as if to an emergency. His safety
eeds often find specific expression in a search for a protector, or a stronger
erson on whom he may depend, or perhaps, a Fuehrer.

The neurotic individual may be described in a slightly different way with
ome usefulness as a grown-up person who retains his childish attitudes
oward the world. That is to say, a neurotic adult may be said to behave

---

[2] A "test battery" for safety might be confronting the child with a small exploding
recracker, or with a bewhiskered face, having the mother leave the room, putting him
pon a high ladder, a hypodermic injection, having a mouse crawl up to him, etc.
Of course I cannot seriously recommend the deliberate use of such "tests" for they might
ery well harm the child being tested. But these and similar situations come up by
he score in the child's ordinary day-to-day living and may be observed. There is
o reason why these stimuli should not be used with, for example, young chimpanzees.

"as if" he were actually afraid of a spanking, or of his mother's disapprova or of being abandoned by his parents, or having his food taken away fror him. It is as if his childish attitudes of fear and threat reaction to a dar gerous world had gone underground, and untouched by the growing up an learning processes, were now ready to be called out by any stimulus tha would make a child feel endangered and threatened.[3]

The neurosis in which the search for safety takes its clearest form is i the compulsive-obsessive neurosis. Compulsive-obsessives try frantically t order and stabilize the world so that no unmanageable, unexpected or ur familiar dangers will ever appear (14). They hedge themselves about wit all sorts of ceremonials, rules and formulas so that every possible contingenc may be provided for and so that no new contingencies may appear. The are much like the brain injured cases, described by Goldstein (6), wh manage to maintain their equilibrium by avoiding everything unfamilia and strange and by ordering their restricted world in such a neat, disc plined, orderly fashion that everything in the world can be counted upor They try to arrange the world so that anything unexpected (dangers) car not possibly occur. If, through no fault of their own, something unexpecte does occur, they go into a panic reaction as if this unexpected occurrenc constituted a grave danger. What we can see only as a none-too-stron preference in the healthy person, e.g., preference for the familiar, become a life-and-death necessity in abnormal cases.

The love needs. If both the physiological and the safety needs are fairl well gratified, then there will emerge the love and affection and belongin ness needs, and the whole cycle already described will repeat itself with th new center. Now the person will feel keenly, as never before, the absenc of friends, or a sweetheart, or a wife, or children. He will hunger for affe tionate relations with people in general, namely, for a place in his grou and he will strive with great intensity to achieve this goal. He will want t attain such a place more than anything else in the world and may eve forget that once, when he was hungry, he sneered at love.

In our society the thwarting of these needs is the most commonly foun core in cases of maladjustment and more severe psychopathology. Love an affection, as well as their possible expression in sexuality, are generall looked upon with ambivalence and are customarily hedged about wit many restrictions and inhibitions. Practically all theorists of psychopatho ogy have stressed thwarting of the love needs as basic in the picture c maladjustment. Many clinical studies have therefore been made of th need and we know more about it perhaps than any of the other need except the physiological ones (14).

One thing that must be stressed at this point is that love is not synon mous with sex. Sex may be studied as a purely physiological need. Ord

---

[3] Not all neurotic individuals feel unsafe. Neurosis may have at its core a thwa ing of the affection and esteem needs in a person who is generally safe.

narily sexual behavior is multi-determined, that is to say, determined not only by sexual but also by other needs, chief among which are the love and affection needs. Also not to be overlooked is the fact that the love needs involve both giving *and* receiving love.[4]

The esteem needs. All people in our society (with a few pathological exceptions) have a need or desire for a stable, firmly based, (usually) high evaluation of themselves, for self-respect, or self-esteem, and for the esteem of others. By firmly based self-esteem, we mean that which is soundly based upon real capacity, achievement and respect from others. These needs may be classified into two subsidiary sets. These are, first, the desire for strength, for achievement, for adequacy, for confidence in the face of the world, and for independence and freedom.[5] Secondly, we have what we may call the desire for reputation or prestige (defining it as respect or esteem from other people), recognition, attention, importance or appreciation.[6] These needs have been relatively stressed by Alfred Adler and his followers, and have been relatively neglected by Freud and the psychoanalysts. More and more today however there is appearing widespread appreciation of their central importance.

Satisfaction of the self-esteem need leads to feelings of self-confidence, worth, strength, capability and adequacy of being useful and necessary in the world. But thwarting of these needs produces feelings of inferiority, of weakness and of helplessness. These feelings in turn give rise to either basic discouragement or else compensatory or neurotic trends. An appreciation of the necessity of basic self-confidence and an understanding of how helpless people are without it, can be easily gained from a study of severe traumatic neurosis (8).[7]

The need for self-actualization. Even if all these needs are satisfied, we may still often (if not always) expect that a new discontent and restlessness will soon develop, unless the individual is doing what he is fitted for. A musician must make music, an artist must paint, a poet must write, if he is to be ultimately happy. What a man *can* be, he *must* be. This need we may call self-actualization.

[4] For further details see (12) and (16, Chap. 5).

[5] Whether or not this particular desire is universal we do not know. The crucial question, especially important today, is "Will men who are enslaved and dominated, inevitably feel dissatisfied and rebellious?" We may assume on the basis of commonly known clinical data that a man who has known true freedom (not paid for by giving up safety and security but rather built on the basis of adequate safety and security) will not willingly or easily allow his freedom to be taken away from him. But we do not know that this is true for the person born into slavery. The events of the next decade should give us our answer. See discussion of this problem in (5).

[6] Perhaps the desire for prestige and respect from others is subsidiary to the desire for self-esteem or confidence in oneself. Observation of children seems to indicate that this is so, but clinical data give no clear support for such a conclusion.

[7] For more extensive discussion of normal self-esteem, as well as for reports of various researches, see (11).

This term, first coined by Kurt Goldstein, is being used in this paper in a much more specific and limited fashion. It refers to the desire for self-fulfillment, namely, to the tendency for him to become actualized in what he is potentially. This tendency might be phrased as the desire to become more and more what one is, to become everything that one is capable of becoming.

The specific form that these needs will take will of course vary greatly from person to person. In one individual it may take the form of the desire to be an ideal mother, in another it may be expressed athletically, and in still another it may be expressed in painting pictures or in inventions. It is not necessarily a creative urge although in people who have any capacities for creation it will take this form.

The clear emergence of these needs rests upon prior satisfaction of the physiological, safety, love and esteem needs. We shall call people who are satisfied in these needs, basically satisfied people, and it is from these that we may expect the fullest (and healthiest) creativeness.[8] Since, in our society, basically satisfied people are the exception, we do not know much about self-actualization, either experimentally or clinically. It remains a challenging problem for research.

The preconditions for the basic need satisfactions. There are certain conditions which are immediate prerequisites for the basic need satisfactions. Danger to these is reacted to almost as if it were a direct danger to the basic needs themselves. Such conditions as freedom to speak, freedom to do what one wishes so long as no harm is done to others, freedom to express one's self, freedom to investigate and seek for information, freedom to defend one's self, justice, fairness, honesty, orderliness in the group are examples of such preconditions for basic need satisfactions. Thwarting in these freedoms will be reacted to with a threat or emergency response. These conditions are not ends in themselves but they are *almost* so since they are so closely related to the basic needs, which are apparently the only ends in themselves. These conditions are defended because without them the basic satisfactions are quite impossible, or at least, very severely endangered.

If we remember that the cognitive capacities (perceptual, intellectual, learning) are a set of adjustive tools, which have, among other functions, that of satisfaction of our basic needs, then it is clear that any danger to them, any deprivation or blocking of their free use, must also be indirectly threatening to the basic needs themselves. Such a statement is a partial

---

[8] Clearly creative behavior, like painting, is like any other behavior in having multiple determinants. It may be seen in "innately creative" people whether they are satisfied or not, happy or unhappy, hungry or sated. Also it is clear that creative activity may be compensatory, ameliorative or purely economic. It is my impression (as yet unconfirmed) that it is possible to distinguish the artistic and intellectual products of basically satisfied people from those of basically unsatisfied people by inspection alone. In any case, here too we must distinguish, in a dynamic fashion, the overt behavior itself from its various motivations or purposes.

solution of the general problems of curiosity, the search for knowledge, truth and wisdom, and the ever-persistent urge to solve the cosmic mysteries.

We must therefore introduce another hypothesis and speak of degrees of closeness to the basic needs, for we have already pointed out that *any* conscious desires (partial goals) are more or less important as they are more or less close to the basic needs. The same statement may be made for various behavior acts. An act is psychologically important if it contributes directly to satisfaction of basic needs. The less directly it so contributes, or the weaker this contribution is, the less important this act must be conceived to be from the point of view of dynamic psychology. A similar statement may be made for the various defense or coping mechanisms. Some are very directly related to the protection or attainment of the basic needs, others are only weakly and distantly related. Indeed if we wished, we could speak of more basic and less basic defense mechanisms, and then affirm that danger to the more basic defenses is more threatening than danger to less basic defenses (always remembering that this is so only because of their relationship to the basic needs).

The desires to know and to understand. So far, we have mentioned the cognitive needs only in passing. Acquiring knowledge and systematizing the universe have been considered as, in part, techniques for the achievement of basic safety in the world, or, for the intelligent man, expressions of self-actualization. Also freedom of inquiry and expression have been discussed as preconditions of satisfactions of the basic needs. True though these formulations may be, they do not constitute definitive answers to the question as to the motivation role of curiosity, learning, philosophizing, experimenting, etc. They are, at best, no more than partial answers.

This question is especially difficult because we know so little about the facts. Curiosity, exploration, desire for the facts, desire to know may certainly be observed easily enough. The fact that they often are pursued even at great cost to the individual's safety is an earnest of the partial character of our previous discussion. In addition, the writer must admit that, though he has sufficient clinical evidence to postulate the desire to know as a very strong drive in intelligent people, no data are available for unintelligent people. It may then be largely a function of relatively high intelligence. Rather tentatively, then, and largely in the hope of stimulating discussion and research, we shall postulate a basic desire to know, to be aware of reality, to get the facts, to satisfy curiosity, or as Wertheimer phrases it, to see rather than to be blind.

This postulation, however, is not enough. Even after we know, we are impelled to know more and more minutely and microscopically on the one hand, and on the other, more and more extensively in the direction of a world philosophy, religion, etc. The facts that we acquire, if they are isolated or atomistic, inevitably get theorized about, and either analyzed or organized or both. This process has been phrased by some as the search for "meaning." We shall then postulate a desire to understand, to systematize, to organize, to analyze, to look for relations and meanings.

Once these desires are accepted for discussion, we see that they too form themselves into a small hierarchy in which the desire to know is prepotent over the desire to understand. All the characteristics of a hierarchy of prepotency that we have described above, seem to hold for this one as well.

We must guard ourselves against the too easy tendency to separate these desires from the basic needs we have discussed above, i.e., to make a sharp dichotomy between "cognitive" and "conative" needs. The desire to know and to understand are themselves conative, i.e., have a striving character, and are as much personality needs as the "basic needs" we have already discussed (19).

III. Further Characteristics of the Basic Needs

The degree of fixity of the hierarchy of basic needs. We have spoken so far as if this hierarchy were a fixed order but actually it is not nearly as rigid as we may have implied. It is true that most of the people with whom we have worked have seemed to have these basic needs in about the order that has been indicated. However, there have been a number of exceptions.

1. There are some people in whom, for instance, self-esteem seems to be more important than love. This most common reversal in the hierarchy is usually due to the development of the notion that the person who is most likely to be loved is a strong or powerful person, one who inspires respect or fear, and who is self confident or aggressive. Therefore such people who lack love and seek it, may try hard to put on a front of aggressive, confident behavior. But essentially they seek high self-esteem and its behavior expressions more as a means-to-an-end than for its own sake; they seek self-assertion for the sake of love rather than for self-esteem itself.

2. There are other, apparently innately creative people in whom the drive to creativeness seems to be more important than any other counter-determinant. Their creativeness might appear not as self-actualization released by basic satisfaction, but in spite of lack of basic satisfaction.

3. In certain people the level of aspiration may be permanently deadened or lowered. That is to say, the less prepotent goals may simply be lost, and may disappear forever, so that the person who has experienced life at a very low level, i.e., chronic unemployment, may continue to be satisfied for the rest of his life if only he can get enough food.

4. The so-called "psychopathic personality" is another example of permanent loss of the love needs. These are people who, according to the best data available (9), have been starved for love in the earliest months of their lives and have simply lost forever the desire and the ability to give and to

receive affection (as animals lose sucking or pecking reflexes that are not exercised soon enough after birth).

5. Another cause of reversal of the hierarchy is that when a need has been satisfied for a long time, this need may be underevaluated. People who have never experienced chronic hunger are apt to underestimate its effects and to look upon food as a rather unimportant thing. If they are dominated by a higher need, this higher need will seem to be the most important of all. It then becomes possible, and indeed does actually happen, that they may, for the sake of this higher need, put themselves into the position of being deprived in a more basic need. We may expect that after a long-time deprivation of the more basic need there will be a tendency to reevaluate both needs so that the more prepotent need will actually become consciously prepotent for the individual who may have given it up very lightly. Thus, a man who has given up his job rather than lose his self-respect, and who then starves for six months or so, may be willing to take his job back even at the price of losing his self-respect.

6. Another partial explanation of *apparent* reversals is seen in the fact that we have been talking about the hierarchy of prepotency in terms of consciously felt wants or desires rather than of behavior. Looking at behavior itself may give us the wrong impression. What we have claimed is that the person will *want* the more basic of two needs when deprived in both. There is no necessary implication here that he will act upon his desires. Let us say again that there are many determinants of behavior other than the needs and desires.

7. Perhaps more important than all these exceptions are the ones that involve ideals, high social standards, high values and the like. With such values people become martyrs; they will give up everything for the sake of a particular ideal, or value. These people may be understood, at least in part, by reference to one basic concept (or hypothesis) which may be called "increased frustration-tolerance through early gratification." People who have been satisfied in their basic needs throughout their lives, particularly in their earlier years, seem to develop exceptional power to withstand present or future thwarting of these needs simply because they have strong, healthy character structure as a result of basic satisfaction. They are the "strong" people who can easily weather disagreement or opposition, who can swim against the stream of public opinion and who can stand up for the truth at great personal cost. It is just the ones who have loved and been well loved, and who have had many deep friendships who can hold out against hatred, rejection or persecution.

I say all this in spite of the fact that there is a certain amount of sheer habituation which is also involved in any full discussion of frustration tolerance. For instance, it is likely that those persons who have been accustomed to relative starvation for a long time, are partially enabled thereby to withstand food deprivation. What sort of balance must be made between these two tendencies, of habituation on the one hand, and of past satisfaction breeding present frustration tolerance on the other hand, remains to be worked out by further research. Meanwhile we may assume that they are both operative, side by side, since they do not contradict each other. In respect to this phenomenon of increased frustration tolerance, it seems probable that the most important gratifications come in the first two years of life. That is to say, people who have been made secure and strong in the earliest years, tend to remain secure and strong thereafter in the face of whatever threatens.

Degrees of relative satisfaction. So far, our theoretical discussion may have given the impression that these five sets of needs are somehow in a step-wise, all-or-none relationship to each other. We have spoken in such terms as the following: "If one need is satisfied, then another emerges." This statement might give the false impression that a need must be satisfied 100 per cent before the next need emerges. In actual fact, most members of our society who are normal, are partially satisfied in all their basic needs and partially unsatisfied in all their basic needs at the same time. A more realistic description of the hierarchy would be in terms of decreasing percentages of satisfaction as we go up the hierarchy of prepotency. For instance, if I may assign arbitrary figures for the sake of illustration, it is as if the average citizen is satisfied perhaps 85 per cent in his physiological needs, 70 per cent in his safety needs, 50 per cent in his love needs, 40 per cent in his self-esteem needs, and 10 per cent in his self-actualization needs.

As for the concept of emergence of a new need after satisfaction of the prepotent need, this emergence is not a sudden, saltatory phenomenon but rather a gradual emergence by slow degrees from nothingness. For instance, if prepotent need A is satisfied only 10 per cent then need B may not be visible at all. However, as this need A becomes satisfied 25 per cent, need B may emerge 5 per cent, as need A becomes satisfied 75 per cent need B may emerge 90 per cent, and so on.

Unconscious character of needs. These needs are neither necessarily conscious nor unconscious. On the whole, however, in the average person, they are more often unconscious rather than conscious. It is not necessary at this point to overhaul the tremendous mass of evidence which indicates the crucial importance of unconscious motivation. It would by now be expected, on a priori grounds alone, that unconscious motivation would on the whole be rather more important than the conscious motivation. What we have called the basic needs are very often largely unconscious although they may, with suitable techniques, and with sophisticated people become conscious.

Cultural specificity and generality of needs. This classification of basic needs makes some attempt to take account of the relative unity behind the superficial differences in specific desires from one culture to another. Certainly in any particular culture an individual's conscious motivational content will usually be extremely different from the conscious motivational content of an individual in another society. However, it is the common experience of anthropologists that people, even in different societies, are much more alike than we would think from our first contact with them, and that as we know them better we seem to find more and more of this commonness. We then recognize the most startling differences to be superficial rather than basic, e.g., differences in style of hairdress, clothes, tastes in food, etc. Our classification of basic needs is in part an attempt to account for this unity behind the apparent diversity from culture to culture. No claim is made that it is ultimate or universal for all cultures. The claim is made only that it is relatively *more* ultimate, more universal, more basic, than the superficial conscious desires from culture to culture, and makes a somewhat closer approach to common-human characteristics. Basic needs are *more* common-human than superficial desires or behaviors.

Multiple motivations of behavior. These needs must be understood *not* to be *exclusive* or single determiners of certain kinds of behavior. An example may be found in any behavior that seems to be physiologically motivated, such as eating, or sexual play or the like. The clinical psychologists have long since found that any behavior may be a channel through which flow various determinants. Or to say it in another way, most behavior is multi-motivated. Within the sphere of motivational determinants any behavior tends to be determined by several or *all* of the basic needs simultaneously rather than by only one of them. The latter would be more an exception than the former. Eating may be partially for the sake of filling the stomach, and partially for the sake of comfort and amelioration of other needs. One may make love not only for pure sexual release, but also to convince one's self of one's masculinity, or to make a conquest, to feel powerful, or to win more basic affection. As an illustration, I may point out that it would be possible (theoretically if not practically) to analyze a single act of an individual and see in it the expression of his physiological needs, his safety needs, his love needs, his esteem needs and self-actualization. This contrasts sharply with the more naive brand of trait psychology in which one trait or one motive accounts for a certain kind of act, *i.e.*, an aggressive act is traced solely to a trait of aggressiveness.

Multiple determinants of behavior. Not all behavior is determined by the basic needs. We might even say that not all behavior is motivated. There are many determinants of behavior other than motives.[9] For instance, one other important class of determinants is the so-called "field" determinants. Theoretically, at least, behavior may be determined completely by the field, or even by specific isolated external stimuli, as in association of ideas, or certain conditioned reflexes. If in response to the stimu-

---

[9] I am aware that many psychologists and psychoanalysts use the term "motivated" and "determined" synonymously, e.g., Freud. But I consider this an obfuscating usage. Sharp distinctions are necessary for clarity of thought, and precision in experimentation.

lus word "table," I immediately perceive a memory image of a table, this response certainly has nothing to do with my basic needs.

Secondly, we may call attention again to the concept of "degree of closeness to the basic needs" or "degree of motivation." Some behavior is highly motivated, other behavior is only weakly motivated. Some is not motivated at all (but all behavior is determined).

Another important point is that there is a basic difference between expressive behavior and coping behavior (functional striving, purposive goal seeking). An expressive behavior does not try to do anything; it is simply a reflection of the personality. A stupid man behaves stupidly, not because he wants to, or tries to, or is motivated to, but simply because he *is* what he is. The same is true when I speak in a bass voice rather than tenor or soprano. The random movements of a healthy child, the smile on the face of a happy man even when he is alone, the springiness of the healthy man's walk, and the erectness of his carriage are other examples of expressive, nonfunctional behavior. Also the *style* in which a man carries out almost all his behavior, motivated as well as unmotivated, is often expressive.

We may then ask, is *all* behavior expressive or reflective of the character structure? The answer is "No." Rote, habitual, automatized, or conventional behavior may or may not be expressive. The same is true for most "stimulus-bound" behaviors.

It is finally necessary to stress that expressiveness of behavior, and goal-directedness of behavior are not mutually exclusive categories. Average behavior is usually both.

Goals as centering principle in motivation theory. It will be observed that the basic principle in our classification has been neither the instigation nor the motivated behavior but rather the functions, effects, purposes, or goals of the behavior. It has been proven sufficiently by various people that this is the most suitable point for centering in any motivation theory.[10]

Animal- and human-centering. This theory starts with the human being rather than any lower and presumably "simpler" animal. Too many of the findings that have been made in animals have been proven to be true for animals but not for the human being. There is no reason whatsoever why we should start with animals in order to study human motivation. The logic or rather illogic behind this general fallacy of "pseudo-simplicity" has been exposed often enough by philosophers and logicians as well as by scientists in each of the various fields. It is no more necessary to study animals before one can study man than it is to study mathematics before one can study geology or psychology or biology.

We may also reject the old, naive behaviorism which assumed that it was somehow necessary, or at least more "scientific" to judge human beings by animal standards. One consequence of this belief was that the whole notion

[10] The interested reader is referred to the very excellent discussion of this point in Murray's *Explorations in Personality* (15).

of purpose and goal was excluded from motivational psychology simply because one could not ask a white rat about his purposes. Tolman (18) has long since proven in animal studies themselves that this exclusion was not necessary.

Motivation and the theory of psychopathogenesis. The conscious motivational content of everyday life has, according to the foregoing, been conceived to be relatively important or unimportant accordingly as it is more or less closely related to the basic goals. A desire for an ice cream cone might actually be an indirect expression of a desire for love. If it is, then this desire for the ice cream cone becomes extremely important motivation. If however the ice cream is simply something to cool the mouth with, or a casual appetitive reaction, then the desire is relatively unimportant. Everyday conscious desires are to be regarded as symptoms, as *surface indicators of more basic needs.* If we were to take these superficial desires at their face value we would find ourselves in a state of complete confusion which could never be resolved, since we would be dealing seriously with symptoms rather than with what lay behind the symptoms.

Thwarting of unimportant desires produces no psychopathological results; thwarting of a basically important need does produce such results. Any theory of psychopathogenesis must then be based on a sound theory of motivation. A conflict or a frustration is not necessarily pathogenic. It becomes so only when it threatens or thwarts the basic needs, or partial needs that are closely related to the basic needs (10).

The role of gratified needs. It has been pointed out above several times that our needs usually emerge only when more prepotent needs have been gratified. Thus gratification has an important role in motivation theory. Apart from this, however, needs cease to play an active determining or organizing role as soon as they are gratified.

What this means is that, *e.g.*, a basically satisfied person no longer has the needs for esteem, love, safety, etc. The only sense in which he might be said to have them is in the almost metaphysical sense that a sated man has hunger, or a filled bottle has emptiness. If we are interested in what *actually* motivates us, and not in what has, will, or might motivate us, then a satisfied need is not a motivator. It must be considered for all practical purposes simply not to exist, to have disappeared. This point should be emphasized because it has been either overlooked or contradicted in every theory of motivation I know.[11] The perfectly healthy, normal, fortunate man has no sex needs or hunger needs, or needs for safety, or for love, or for prestige, or self-esteem, except in stray moments of quickly passing threat. If we were to say otherwise, we should also have to aver that every man had all the pathological reflexes, *e.g.*, Babinski, etc., because if his nervous system were damaged, these would appear.

[11] Note that acceptance of this theory necessitates basic revision of the Freudian theory.

It is such considerations as these that suggest the bold postulation that a man who is thwarted in any of his basic needs may fairly be envisaged simply as a sick man. This is a fair parallel to our designation as "sick" of the man who lacks vitamins or minerals. Who is to say that a lack of love is less important than a lack of vitamins? Since we know the pathogenic effects of love starvation, who is to say that we are invoking value-questions in an unscientific or illegitimate way, any more than the physician does who diagnoses and treats pellagra or scurvy? If I were permitted this usage, I should then say simply that a healthy man is primarily motivated by his needs to develop and actualize his fullest potentialities and capacities. If a man has any other basic needs in any active, chronic sense, then he is simply an unhealthy man. He is as surely sick as if he had suddenly developed a strong salt hunger or calcium hunger.[12]

If this statement seems unusual or paradoxical the reader may be assured that this is only one among many such paradoxes that will appear as we revise our ways of looking at man's deeper motivations. When we ask what man wants of life, we deal with his very essence.

IV. Summary

1. There are at least five sets of goals, which we may call basic needs. These are briefly physiological, safety, love, esteem, and self-actualization. In addition, we are motivated by the desire to achieve or maintain the various conditions upon which these basic satisfactions rest and by certain more intellectual desires.

2. These basic goals are related to each other, being arranged in a hierarchy of prepotency. This means that the most prepotent goal will monopolize consciousness and will tend of itself to organize the recruitment of the various capacities of the organism. The less prepotent needs are minimized, even forgotten or denied. But when a need is fairly well satisfied, the next prepotent ("higher") need emerges, in turn to dominate the conscious life and to serve as the center of organization of behavior, since gratified needs are not active motivators.

Thus man is a perpetually wanting animal. Ordinarily the satisfaction of these wants is not altogether mutually exclusive, but only tends to be. The average member of our society is most often partially satisfied and partially unsatisfied in all of his wants. The hierarchy principle is usually empirically observed in terms of increasing percentages of non-satisfaction as we go up

12 If we were to use the word "sick" in this way, we should then also have to face squarely the relations of man to his society. One clear implication of our definition would be that (1) since a man is to be called sick who is basically thwarted, and (2) since such basic thwarting is made possible ultimately only by forces outside the individual, then (3) sickness in the individual must come ultimately from a sickness in the society. The "good" or healthy society would then be defined as one that permitted man's highest purposes to emerge by satisfying all his prepotent basic needs.

the hierarchy. Reversals of the average order of the hierarchy are sometimes observed. Also it has been observed that an individual may permanently lose the higher wants in the hierarchy under special conditions. There are not only ordinarily multiple motivations for usual behavior, but in addition many determinants other than motives.

3. Any thwarting or possibility of thwarting of these basic human goals, or danger to the defenses which protect them, or to the conditions upon which they rest, is considered to be a psychological threat. With a few exceptions, all psychopathology may be partially traced to such threats. A basically thwarted man may actually be defined as a "sick" man, if we wish.

4. It is such basic threats which bring about the general emergency reactions.

5. Certain other basic problems have not been dealt with because of limitations of space. Among these are (a) the problem of values in any definitive motivation theory, (b) the relation between appetites, desires, needs and what is "good" for the organism, (c) the etiology of the basic needs and their possible derivation in early childhood, (d) redefinition of motivational concepts, i.e., drive, desire, wish, need, goal, (e) implication of our theory for hedonistic theory, (f) the nature of the uncompleted act, of success and failure, and of aspiration-level, (g) the role of association, habit and conditioning, (h) relation to the theory of inter-personal relations, (i) implications for psychotherapy, (j) implication for theory of society, (k) the theory of selfishness, (l) the relation between needs and cultural patterns, (m) the relation between this theory and Allport's theory of functional autonomy. These as well as certain other less important questions must be considered as motivation theory attempts to become definitive.

References

1. Adler, A. *Social interest.* London: Faber & Faber, 1938.
2. Cannon, W. B. *Wisdom of the body.* New York: Norton, 1932.
3. Freud, A. *The ego and the mechanisms of defense.* London: Hogarth, 1937.
4. Freud, S. *New introductory lectures on psychoanalysis.* New York: Norton, 1933.
5. Fromm, E. *Escape from freedom.* New York: Farrar and Rinehart, 1941.
6. Goldstein, K. *The organism.* New York: American Book Co., 1939.
7. Horney, K. *The neurotic personality of our time.* New York: Norton, 1937.
8. Kardiner, A. *The traumatic neuroses of war.* New York: Hoeber, 1941.
9. Levy, D. M. Primary affect hunger. *Amer. J. Psychiat.,* 1937, 94, 643–652.
10. Maslow, A. H. Conflict, frustration, and the theory of threat. *J. abnorm. (soc.) Psychol.,* 1943, 38, 81–86.
11. ———. Dominance, personality and social behavior in women. *J. soc. Psychol.,* 1939, 10, 3–39.
12. ———. The dynamics of psychological security-insecurity. *Character & Pers.,* 1942, 10, 331–344.
13. ———. A preface to motivation theory. *Psychosomatic Med.,* 1943, 5, 85–92.
14. ———, & Mittelmann, B. *Principles of abnormal psychology.* New York: Harper & Bros., 1941.

15. Murray, H. A., et al. Explorations in personality. New York: Oxford University Press, 1938.
16. Plant, J. Personality and the cultural pattern. New York: Commonwealth Fund, 1937.
17. Shirley, M. Children's adjustments to a strange situation. J. abnorm. (soc.) Psychol., 1942, 37, 201–217.
18. Tolman, E. C. Purposive behavior in animals and men. New York: Century, 1932.
19. Wertheimer, M. Unpublished lectures at the New School for Social Research.
20. Young, P. T. Motivation of behavior. New York: John Wiley & Sons, 1936.
21. ———. The experimental analysis of appetite. Psychol. Bull., 1941, 38, 129–164.

THE ORGANIZATION OF PERSONALITY *

(H. J. Eysenck

Science, as ordinarily understood, attempts to discover general rules or laws under which individual events can be subsumed. It attempts to describe the multiform world of experience through the formulation of abstract laws and the creation of abstract categories. This process of abstraction is absolutely fundamental to science; without abstraction there can be nothing but observation of particular occurrences. But "science is not interested in the unique event; the unique belongs to history, not to science." As Whitehead puts it,

the paradox is now fully established that the utmost abstractions are the true weapon with which to control our thought of concrete fact. To be abstract is to transcend particular concrete occasions of actual happenings. The construction with which the scientist ends has the neatness and orderliness that is quite unlike the varied and multiform world of common sense, yet, since science grows out of and returns to the world of common sense, there must be a precise connection between the neat, trim, tidy, exact world, which is the goal of science, and the untidy, fragmentary world of common sense.

If, then, we would construct a science of personality, we must seek for abstract models, concepts, mathematical functions, or what have you, which will adequately represent our knowledge—meager though it be—of existing facts, and which at the same time will point forward to new facts which can verify, modify, or refute our theoretical model. What are the main facts regarding personality which must be incorporated in such a model? I believe that a rough and ready answer at least can be given to these two

* From H. J. Eysenck, "The Organization of Personality," in Theoretical Models and Personality Theory, David Krech and George S. Klein (eds.), pp. 101–116, Duke University Press, Durham, N.C., 1952. Reprinted by permission of the author and the Director, Duke University Press.

questions, and that this answer must be phrased in terms of factorial analysis.

We find most of the main elements which our model must contain in Allport's well-known definition of personality as the "dynamic organization within the individual of those psychophysical systems that determine his unique adjustment to his environment" (1). A brief discussion of these terms (differing in several important ways from Allport's) may be helpful in discovering just what it is that our model is required to represent.

1. In the first place, we have to deal with an individual's adjustment (or failure to adjust) to his environment. In other words, our universe of discourse is *human behavior*, taking this term in its broadest sense as including speech (vocal and subvocal), movement, hormonal and autonomic changes, alpha rhythms, and indeed all *objectively recordable modifications of the environment*. This interpretation is in essence identical with Wolfle's "fundamental principle of personality measurement": "An individual reveals his own personality through any change he makes upon any type of material" (26).

2. But clearly such an omnibus definition is not sufficient; it does not allow for differences in importance between different items of behavior. It is a fact that person A complains about hammer toes, that person B has hallucinations, that person C has invented a new and revolutionary scientific theory, that person D has stomach ulcers and suffers from autonomic imbalance, and that person E can ride a bicycle. But these facts are not equal in importance; some are clearly peripheral, others are more central in their import. Personality implies the organization of behavior items into some kind of hierarchy, a hierarchy which determines the importance of any given item of behavior by reference to the system of relations obtaining between this item and all others.

3. It is difficult to speak about the organization of behavioral acts; it is more usual to postulate certain psychophysical systems (instincts, drives, needs, traits, habits, attitudes, complexes, sentiments, etc.) which are believed to underlie the behavioral acts, and to apply the concept of organization to these abstractions. This is of course perfectly permissible, and indeed quite essential in any scientific discussion, provided the connection between observed behavior and hypothesized abstract concept is operationally defined and experimentally verifiable. Many concepts in common use—Freudian ones in particular—lack such definition, and cannot therefore justifiably be incorporated into what purports to be a scientific system of personality.[1]

---

[1] By this I do not mean to say that the hypotheses implied in terms like "transference," "catharsis," "narcissism," "anal and oral types," and "regression" are necessarily false. I believe that some are true and others false, but clearly my belief is irrelevant to science; science demands proof, not conviction or belief, and no acceptable proof has been forthcoming so far to substantiate the claims of the psychoanalytic

4. Our definition so far gives only a cross-sectional picture at any one moment of time; clearly personality as conceived in this definition would be a term of very limited usefulness if the organization of behavior implied in it were only temporary, and had no predictive value. Hence the term "determine" in Allport's definition; personality is conceived of as an enduring (though not necessarily unchanging) organization which enables us to make predictions regarding future behavior. As Cattell puts it, "the personality of an individual is that which enables us to predict what he will do in a given situation" (3).

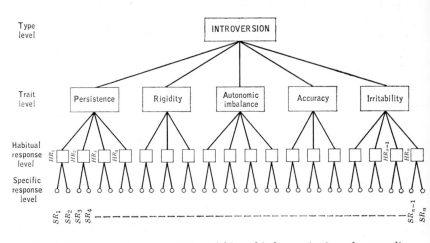

Fig. 1. Diagrammatic representation of hierarchical organization of personality.

Let us now attempt to construct a model of personality thus conceived which embodies various requirements. Figure 1 represents such an attempt. There are four main levels of organization which are recognizable in this structure. At the lowest level we have specific acts of behavior, or specific responses, labeled S.R.$_1$, S.R.$_2$, S.R.$_3$, . . . S.R.$_n$. These are items of behavior, such as responses to experiences of everyday life, or to experimental tests, which are observed once, and may or may not be characteristic of the individual.

At the second level, we have what are called habitual responses, H.R.$_1$, H.R.$_2$, H.R.$_3$, . . . H.R.$_n$. These are specific responses which tend to recur

school. A purist might even maintain, with some show of justice, that a concept of hypothesis which had no operational reference could not be regarded as "true" or "false," but merely as "meaningless." While much of modern "dynamic" theory would indeed appear to be nothing but such meaningless semantic manipulation of terms having no factual reference, it would hardly be reasonable to dismiss the whole Freudian point of view in this cavalier fashion. The difficulty appears to lie mainly in finding some agreement between psychoanalysts and psychologists as to the precise nature of the "factual referents" required.

under similar circumstances; i.e., if the test is repeated, a similar response is given, or if the life-situation recurs, the individual reacts in a similar fashion. This is the lowest level of organization; roughly speaking, the amount of organization present here can be measured in terms of reliability coefficients, i.e., in terms of the probability that on repetition of a situation behavior will be consistent.

At the third level, we have organizations of habitual acts into traits T_1, T_2, T_3, . . . T_n. These traits—suggestibility, persistence, rigidity, irritability, accuracy, honesty, perseveration, fluency, or whatever the name may be—are theoretical constructs, based on observed intercorrelations of a number of different habitual responses; in the language of factor analysis they may be conceived of as group factors.

At the fourth level, we have organization of traits into a general *type*; in our example, the *introvert*. This is also based on observed intercorrelations, this time on correlations between the various traits which between them make up the concept of the type under discussion. Thus in our example persistence, rigidity, irritability, accuracy, autonomic imbalance, and various other traits would form a constellation of traits intercorrelating among themselves, thus giving rise to a higher-order construct, the type. This level, in factorial terminology, corresponds to a general factor, or to what Thurstone calls a "second order factor." [2]

This general four-level scheme has been presented in terms of traits and types; it should be noted, however, that it is equally applicable and useful in connection with abilities (where Thurstone's "Primary Mental Abilities" would lie at the third level, and his "Second-order Factor," corresponding to Spearman's "g," would lie at the fourth level) and with social attitudes. The argument regarding the hierarchical structure of abilities is presented by Vernon in some detail (25); with respect to the structure of attitudes a series of research reports by the writer has developed this concept more concretely (7, 9, 15, 16, 17). In this paper I shall confine myself, for the sake of brevity, to a discussion of traits and types, but exactly the same arguments can be applied to other areas of personality.

This general scheme obviously implies a methodology which will enable us to isolate the hypothetical third- and fourth-level variables *uniquely* and *invariantly*. It is not sufficient, as Jung has done, to construct a system on

[2] There is in this scheme of course no assumption regarding the distribution of the population along the "trait" or "type" dimension. The stereotyped view that writers who have advocated typologies, like Jung and Kretschmer, conceive of the population as being distributed in a discontinuous, or at least bimodal, form of distribution, is not really in accord with the writings of these authors; it follows that much of the current criticism of typology based on this assumption falls to the ground. Indeed, it would be an elementary error in statistics to assume that the observed distribution of scores on a given test of extraversion-introversion, say, bore any necessary relation to the distribution of the underlying variable. Questions of distribution are meaningful only in terms of a specified metric, not in terms of raw scores on questionnaires of doubtful validity.

the basis of observation and verbal material alone; at best this suffices to give us a hypothesis which permits of being tested empirically, but it does not provide us with such a test. Nor is it sufficient, as Kretschmer has done, to elaborate tests for the measurement of the various traits hypothesized, and to show that these discriminate significantly between criterion groups —schizophrenics and manic depressives, or leptosomatic and pyknic individuals (13). What is required is a method which enables us to apply rigid tests to questions implicit in the organizational scheme presented. This method can at the present be found only in the procedures of factor analysis. These procedures are of course too technical to be discussed here; however, certain methodological features implicit in them are so often misunderstood, by opponents as well as by many practitioners, that it may be worth while to state them explicitly.

Statistical analysis, as Kendall (19) has pointed out, can be of two main kinds—analysis of *dependence*, and analysis of *interdependence*. "In the latter we are interested in how a group of variates are related among themselves, no one being marked out by the conditions of the problem as of greater prior importance than the others, whereas in the analysis of dependence we are interested in how a certain specified group (the dependent variates) depend on the others." Analysis of variance and covariance, regression and confluence analysis are examples of the former; correlational analysis, component and factor analysis are examples of the latter. The general problem of component analysis is a simple one. Given a set of observations n on each variate of a p-variate complex, that is to say, given the array of values x_{ij}, $i = 1, \ldots p; j = 1, \ldots n$, can we (1) find new variables linearly connected with the old but fewer in number which will account for the original variation, and (2) if so, what are the new variables?

Various solutions to this problem are possible, most of them being approximations to the "principal components" solution. It has, in psychology, nearly always been found possible to find new variables fewer in number than the original variation within the limits of the sampling error; the question has usually been to decide which of an infinite set of such variables to accept. Of the methods proposed to decide on this question, the best known is undoubtedly Thurstone's method of "simple structure." As this method does not seem to lead to easily acceptable solutions in the noncognitive field, the writer has proposed a rather different method, that of "criterion analysis," which appears to lead to useful results in the field of temperament, character, social attitudes, and other noncognitive areas (10).

The apparent arbitrariness with which the particular set of variables constituting a solution to the general problem of interdependence analysis is chosen has offended many psychologists who feel that there should be one and only one right solution to problems of this kind. This view does not accord with experience in other scientific fields. As the problem of finding a small number of factors to represent a large number of observations is in many ways similar to that of finding physical dimensions to represent the multiform events of physics, we may perhaps quote briefly what physicists have to say about this problem. Thus, for instance, Bridgman declares: "There is nothing absolute about dimensions—they may be anything consistent with a set of definitions which agree with the experimental facts." Or we may take the discussion of the specific case of temperature, about which there has been much discussion in physics. Temperature "is sometimes taken as an independent primary quantity (H) so that such entities as specific heat and entropy will have dimensions including (H), viz. L^2T^{-2} $(H)^{-1}$ and ML^2T^{-2} $(H)^{-1}$ respectively. The situation becomes very much simplified, however, if, in the equations relating the pressure of a gas (p) to its specific volume (volume per unit mass v) and absolute temperature (T): $pv = RT$, we define the constant R as a dimensional number. This gives T the dimensions $[ML^{-1}T^{-2}] \times [M^{-1}L^3] = L^2T^{-2}$ (an energy per unit mass) which leads to much simpler dimensions for specific heat (dimensionless) and entropy (M)" (24). Porter (23) goes so far as to say that this procedure "reveals the real dimensions of (H)." Scott Blair (24) comments on this that rather than revealing the real dimensions of (H) this procedure gives us a more convenient and effective way of expressing its dimensions and also those of a number of other entities involving temperature.

However we look at scientific concepts and models, it must be clear that dimensions and factors are not chosen by any absolute standards, but according to principles determined in their turn by usefulness, expediency, and other considerations intrinsic in the purposes of the scientist, rather than in his material. To condemn factor analysis because of a lack of "absolute" truth would mean to condemn the scientific method altogether. We may reword Bridgman's dictum slightly and say: There is nothing absolute about factors—they may be anything consistent with a set of definitions which agree with the experimental facts. The sting of this sentence is in the tail; when any considerable number of facts is known in a given field, it is usually difficult enough to find *one* set of dimensions of factors consistent with a set of definitions *and* agreeing with the experimental facts— there is seldom any opportunity to worry about the choice between a number of alternative sets of dimensions or factors. The fact that Spearman and Thurstone, starting out from very different premises, and using widely different methods, finally arrived at results which are in very good agreement illustrates this strong "determining tendency" exerted by the facts to perfection. Where there is still room for controversy, appeal to further facts still to be unearthed remains as always the only answer, and in so far as factor analysis leads to such further experimentation, it must be adjudged a fruitful and useful scientific method.

What is meant by such further experimentation may be briefly indicated by two examples. Having isolated the two factors of neuroticism and introversion-extraversion by factorial methods, and having constructed objective tests for the measurement of these dimensions (8), we attempted to apply these concepts to the study of the aftereffects of prefrontal lobotomy. The hypotheses investigated were based on the view that a factor denotes some underlying unitary personality process, and that a change in this process should be manifested in responses to all the tests used to define and measure that factor. The following hypotheses were formally set up and investigated:

1. Lobotomy in patients suffering from neurotic illnesses leads to a shift on the neuroticism continuum towards the more normal end.

2. Lobotomy in neurotic patients leads to a shift from the introverted towards the extraverted end on the introversion-extraversion continuum.

3. The same shifts, but in a much attenuated form, would be expected to occur in psychotic patients. Investigations by Petrie (20, 21, 22) of neurotic and Crown (5, 6) of psychotic patients have lent strong support to all these hypotheses.

Another hypothesis arose from the consideration that neuroticism is often believed to be an inherited predisposition, and that evidence regarding this proposition could be obtained by experimental studies on monozygotic and dizygotic twins. These studies, dealing with the inheritance of a *factor* rather than with the influence of heredity on the variance of a single test, have indeed shown that it is the factor *as a whole* which is inherited, thus disproving the view that a factor is nothing but a mathematical artifact (12). Other examples could be given of this tendency of factorial work to lead on to further experimentation, but these two must suffice for the present.

Many other objections are often brought forward against factor analysis, but these usually rest on a mistaken view of what the essential implications of this method really are. Another group of objections relates to specific findings; thus it may be said that a certain investigator discovered a certain cluster containing "the following hodge-podge: special acuities and pulchritude, combined with drive, but having some negative relation to empathy and to spatial facility" (1). Such objections are usually well founded as far as the specific example goes; they are obviously irrelevant as far as the usefulness of the method itself is concerned. Factor analysis is not a sausage machine into which any amount of rubbish can be thrown in the hope that ultimately meaningful results will emerge. Like all other mathematical tools, it demands a high degree of scientific competence and a thorough comprehension of a general problem before it can be used to advantage. That some of its devotees fall lamentably short of this ideal no one would deny; that their mistakes and failures should be used to discredit the method itself is hardly reasonable.

One set of objections occurs so frequently and has grown so much in volume in recent years that a few lines at least must be devoted to it. Factorial methods, it is said, leave out of account the fact that an individual's personality is something unique, something that cannot be analyzed into small pieces, is indeed an organismic whole which must be studied as such. This idiographic view—to use a term suggested by Windelband—has a certain appeal for most psychologists who have to deal with people because its main proposition is so obviously true. It is quite undeniably true that Professor Windelband is absolutely unique. So is my old shoe. Indeed, any existing object is unique in the sense that it is unlike any other object. This is true as much in the physical sciences as it is in the biological, sociological, and psychological sciences. But what precisely is this uniqueness? To some, it appears to be some mystical quality, something *sui generis*, distinguishing qualitatively between any two individuals. To the scientist, on the other hand, the *unique individual is simply the point of intersection of* a number of quantitative variables. There are some 340,000 discriminable color experiences, each of which is absolutely unique and distinguishable from any other. From the point of view of descriptive science, however, they can all be considered as points of intersection of three quantitative variables, hue, tint, and chroma. A combination of perfectly general, descriptive variables is sufficient to enable any individual to be differentiated from any other through specification of his position on each of these variables in a quantitative form. Many writers "seem unable to see that one individual can differ quantitatively from another in many variables, common variables though they may be, and still have a unique personality" (1). Quite on the contrary, the very notion of "being different from" implies at the same time the idea of direction and the idea of amount—in other words, two unique individuals cannot meaningfully be said to be different from each other unless they are being compared along some quantitative variable. Uniqueness, therefore, is not in any sense a concept antagonistic to science; it follows from the methods used in science to describe individual events in terms of common variables.

The second claim made by the idiographically minded is related to the necessity of studying individuals as wholes, rather than by means of any analytic method. A brief investigation of the methods used by those who favor such a "global" study will reveal that their procedure is hardly commensurate with their claims. A new nomenclature does not disguise the fact that the same "analytic" concepts have been taken over into this vaunted "study of the whole personality." To take but two examples: The Rorschach supposedly is able to diagnose a patient's "intellectual level," his "degree of maturity," his "creative or imaginative capacities," his "degree of control," and many other traits or abilities taken over directly from the workshop of the "nomothetic" psychologist. The Thematic Apperception Test is scored in terms of "Need" and "Press," a veritable palimpsest in which the original writing of McDougall, Shand, and a host of hoary Scottish philosophers is still plainly visible. It is difficult to see any great difference in these new "total" methods, unless it be that reliabilities are usually low, validities are assumed rather than demonstrated, and justification is in terms of philosophical argument rather than of empirical demonstration. It is plainly impossible to study the "whole personality" all at once, just as it is impossible to study the "whole universe"; parts of "sub-wholes" have to be analyzed out of the total complex of features and studied separately. Only when this task has been completed can we hope to study the interaction, organization, or structure of these parts. The organization of personality is not an act of faith; it is an object of empirical study.

In spite of their inconclusive nature, the objections raised by the idiographically minded do face us with a problem which factor analysts have not always considered with sufficient care. We have a model of personality, as it were, which determines our hypotheses; we have a method of analysis which we believe capable of providing us with the required proof; but what of the data needed before we can use this powerful method? Clearly, no method is capable of improving on data which are themselves worthless; yet psychologists have often carried out refined statistical procedures on data whose reliability and validity were more than doubtful. In general, I believe that certain types of data are unlikely to give results of sufficient accuracy to vouchsafe the laborious analyses required by the factorial approach; I do not believe that questionnaires or ratings are likely to provide the evidence which we require to construct an objective science of personality. Admittedly, data are easily gathered in this fashion; however, this ease of collection would appear to be inversely related to their psychological value. Cattell's work (3) is partly vitiated by this reliance on ratings; however, his awareness of the necessity to provide more objective data and to link them with the factors isolated from the ratings shows a promise that in due course we will understand better than we do now the complex interactions between rater and rates which form the basis of so many analyses (4). In any case, Cattell has attempted to forestall criticism by careful consideration of the categories to be rated. Other writers, however, have been less aware of the pitfalls involved in this type of work, and have used categories which can hardly be considered to represent modern thought. Burt's (2) analyses of ratings carried out in terms of McDougall's scheme of instincts lose most of their psychological interest through this use of an outmoded theory, and must be regarded more as exercises in statistical theory than as contributions to psychological knowledge.

The only type of data which in my view is likely to give trustworthy results is what I have called "objective performance tests." Elsewhere I have discussed at length possible classifications of psychological tests, the respective strengths and weaknesses of questionnaires, of so-called projective methods, of psychometric tests, and of the various other types which can be distinguished. If I may quote briefly:

There is one tentative generalization which, while it cannot be regarded as firmly established, may yet provide an heuristic hypothesis to serve as a basis for structuring the very confused field of modern psychological tests. It is widely agreed that personality rests on a firm hereditary basis, but is also subject to great alterations through social and other environmental influences. It would appear, by and large, that personality tests of the objective performance type are related rather more closely to the inherited pattern of a person's conative and affective traits; tests of conditioning, of suggestibility, of autonomic imbalance, of sensory dysfunctioning and of motor expression appear so closely bound up with the structural properties of the nervous system and with the body build and the sensory equipment of a person that the likelihood of hereditary determination can hardly be gainsaid. On the other hand, tests employing unstructured material would appear to reflect more the historical aspects of a person's life history and be subject to day-to-day fluctuations of mood and outlook. If we may use an anology from physics we might say that tests of this type deal with problems of hysteresis rather than with those of structure (11).

Evidence for this proposition will be found in the article from which this brief summary has been quoted and in several experimental studies reported elsewhere (8, 12, 14). They all lend support to the view that objective performance tests are more likely than any other type to provide the required data for our purposes.

When we come to the application in practice of the scheme outlined here, and of the method discussed, we find that there are two main ways of proceeding. We may start with a *tabula rasa,* as it were, and attempt to encompass the whole "personality sphere" in our analysis. This, roughly, is what Cattell has attempted in a series of studies published over the past six years or so. Or we may take existing theories regarding personality organization, such as Jung's theory of extraversion-introversion, or Kretschmer's theory of schizothymia-cyclothymia, and devise experimental and statistical tests to see whether deductions made from these theories can be verified. This is the method the present writer has followed in the main. In the long run, both methods should be expected to give identical results, and already marked similarities are beginning to emerge where the territory covered has overlapped at all.

The method advocated here may be illustrated by means of a concrete problem, viz., that of psychiatric diagnosis. If we confine ourselves for the moment to the main classifications, "neurosis" and "psychosis," we find the following distinct theories, all of which are explicitly or implicitly held by large numbers of psychiatrists and psychoanalysts.

1. The two classes represent one general dimension of "psychosexual regression," so that the psychotic has regressed most, the neurotic much less, and the normal, who presumably forms the pole opposite to the psychotic, not at all. We thus postulate a single continuum ranging from normal through neurotic to psychotic.

2. Neurosis and psychosis are separate and distinct disease-processes, quite independent one of the other; both are conceived as quantitative variables continuous with the normal, and representing extremes of their respective variates.

3. Mental disorders are qualitatively different from normal mental states, and therefore something *sui generis*, discontinuous with normality. This would be the view of those psychiatrists who believe in the genetic determination of mental disease through one or two distinct genes (as opposed to the multi-factorial theory of inheritance).

In practice, many psychiatrists will be found to hold not one of these views, but to combine points from all three, incompatible though they are, talking at one time in terms of one theory, at other times in terms of another. Even psychiatric textbooks usually fail to face squarely the problem thus presented, and adopt several contradictory theories at different stages of their discussion.

Two points are involved in this problem: (1) Continuity or discontinuity? (2) Do psychosis and neurosis constitute one or two dimensions? The method of "criterion analysis" was originally devised to answer the first of these two problems, and it has been shown that both neurosis (10) and psychosis (14) are continuous with normality. The second question has also received an answer in factorial terms: it appears that neurosis and psychosis constitute two separate dimensions (12). However, this problem can be attacked by means of procedures other than factor analysis, and as these other procedures permit of a test of significance which is more accurate than the customary approximations used in factor analysis, I will state the conclusion in nonfactorial terms.[3]

Four tests (tests M, N, O, P from the U.S.E.S. General Aptitude Test Battery) were given to fifty normals, fifty nondeteriorated psychotics, and fifty neurotics. The four scores were condensed into the two canonical variates that give the best discrimination of the three groups in two dimensions; the first variate, Y_1 and Y_2 were calculated, the latent roots were tested for significance, using Bartlett's test; both roots were significant at the $P = .001$ level. It follows from this that two dimensions are necessary and sufficient to account for the observed test data. Inspection of the scatter diagram shows that Y_1 carries the entire discrimination between normals and psychotics, and Y_2 discriminates between neurotics, and normals and psychotics. This result, therefore, strongly reinforces the conclusion derived from our factorial studies that neurosis and psychosis must be conceived as lying in two dimensions, not along one single dimension as posited by Freudians.

These results are important in two ways for the construction of an adequate model of personality. In the first place they lend experimental sup-

[3] The analysis to be described was performed by A. Lubin, Senior Statistician in the Psychology Laboratory (19a). For the conclusions drawn, I am myself responsible.

port, hitherto missing, to the frequent assumption that so-called abnormal, clinical cases of neurosis and psychosis can be used to furnish a guide to the structure of normal personality. This is permissible only on the assumption of *continuity*, and the proof that such continuity exists supplies an essential basis to the theories of Jung, Kretschmer, and others who make the abnormal field their point of departure.

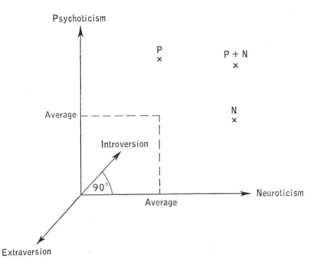

FIG. 2. Diagrammatic representation of three dimensions: psychoticism, neuroticism, introversion-extraversion.

In the second place, we now have the beginnings of a rational system of psychiatric diagnosis. Patients can be diagnosed as neurotic *or* psychotic only on the basis of an assumption of qualitative, noncontinuous differences. But if our results give an accurate picture of reality, the question "Is this patient neurotic or psychotic?" becomes as unreasonable as the question "Is this patient intelligent or tall?" Two orthogonal vectors, like neuroticism and psychoticism, generate a plane on which the position of an individual has to be indicated by reference to *both* vectors; we can only describe an individual by giving both his I.Q. and his height, or by giving both his degree of neuroticism and of psychoticism. This is illustrated in Fig. 2. The ordinate and the abscissa respectively represent the factors neuroticism and psychoticism; the average person, in each case, is assumed to lie roughly at the center of these two variates. Representing an individual's position in two-dimensional space, therefore, position A would indicate the average person's standing, P would indicate the position of the average psychotic, N that of the average neurotic, and P + N that of a person suffering from both a neurotic and a psychotic illness. All other positions on the plane thus generated are possible locations for a given individual, and it will be seen that *mixed cases* are more likely than *pure cases*—we are more likely to find individuals in the plane of the diagram than on the ordinate or on the abscissa. This preponderance of mixed cases of course agrees well with clinical experience. Diagnosis, on this showing, should consist in the accurate determination of an individual's position on the plane, rather than, as is now usual, in a simple either-or judgment.

The picture is of course much more complicated than this. In addition to the two factors depicted in the diagram, we have many others which presumably play this part in determining the nature of the illness. The only one of these to be operationally defined in terms of objective tests is extraversion-introversion (8). Thus the person who is high on neuroticism and introversion would be seen clinically as a patient suffering from dysthymic disorders (anxiety, reactive depression, obsessional features); the person who is high on neuroticism and extraversion would be seen clinically as a patient suffering from hysterical (or possible psychopathic) symptoms. Schizothymia-cyclothymia is another possible dimension, although experimental work here has not yet proceeded far enough to isolate it or to indicate its relation to the other dimensions described (14). The possibilities are, roughly, these: (1) Schizothymia-cyclothymia as a dimension may not exist at all; (2) it may coincide with extraversion-introversion, the extraverted psychotic showing manic-depressive symptoms; (3) it may exist as a separate dimension, in which case it would of course have projections on the other dimensions already isolated; (4) it may coincide with the psychotic dimension, indicating merely different degrees of severity of the illness. These hypotheses must of course be tested systematically before we can know how to incorporate schizothymia-cyclothymia into our model.

It is not hypothesized that these are the only dimensions into which personality can be analyzed, and along which measurement should take place; to take but one example, there is the case of intelligence (operationally defined in terms of Thurstone's second-order factor), which is more or less orthogonal to all the dimensions so far discussed. In due course, other dimensions will no doubt be isolated and measured, and much prospecting has already been done by Cattell (3) into possible lines of progress. But regardless of the actual number of independent dimensions which our picture of personality may require, it is clear that categorical diagnoses of the "either-or" kind are not warranted by the experimental findings; what is required is a separate assessment and measurement of each dimension in turn. It is not claimed that more than a beginning has been made in this complex, time-consuming, and difficult proceeding; it is believed, however, that results to date are fully in agreement with the general model of personality on which our procedures have been predicted.

Summary

A hierarchical model of personality organization has been presented which is believed capable of representing the majority of experimentally determined facts regarding personality structure. The method of factorial analysis, with particular stress on the method of "criterion analysis," has been suggested to be best suited to help in the solution of the problems which arise in relating experimental facts to this model. A number of criticisms of the factorial method have been discussed, and its relation to concepts like "uniqueness" and "wholeness" has been clarified. Lastly, an example has been given of the application of the theoretical concepts and practical methods advocated here to the problem of psychiatric diagnosis.

References

1. Allport, G. W. *Personality: A psychological interpretation.* New York: Henry Holt, 1937.
2. Burt, C. "The analysis of temperament." *Brit. J. med. Psychol.* 1937, 17, 158–188.
3. Cattell, R. B. *Description and measurement of personality.* New York: World Book, 1946.
4. Cattell, R. B., and Saunders, D. R. "Inter-relation and matching of personality factors from behavior rating, questionnaire, and objective test data." *J. soc. Psychol.,* 1950, 31, 243–260.
5. Crown, S. "An experimental study of psychological changes following prefrontal lobotomy." *J. gen. Psychol.* To appear.
6. Crown, S. "Psychological changes following prefrontal leucotomy." A review. *J. ment. Sci.* To appear.
7. Eysenck, H. J. "General social attitudes." *J. soc. Psychol.,* 1944, 19, 207–227.
8. Eysenck, H. J. *Dimensions of personality.* London: Kegan Paul, 1947.
9. Eysenck, H. J. "Primary social attitudes: I. The organization and measurement of social attitudes." *Int. J. opin. & attit. Res.,* 1947, 1, 49–84.
10. Eysenck, H. J. "Criterion analysis—an application of the hypothetico-deductive method to factor analysis." *Psychol. Rev.,* 1950, 57, 38–65.
11. Eysenck, H. J. "Personality tests: 1944–1949." In G. W. T. H. Fleming (ed.), *Recent progress in psychiatry.* London: Churchill, 1951.
12. Eysenck, H. J. *The scientific study of personality.* London: Routledge, 1952.
13. Eysenck, H. J. "Cyclothymia-schizothymia as a dimension of personality: I. Historical." *J. Personal.,* 1950, 19, 123–153.
14. Eysenck, H. J. "Cyclothymia-schizothymia as a dimension of personality. II: Experimental." *J. Personal.* To appear.
15. Eysenck, H. J. "Primary social attitudes and the 'Social Insight' test." *Brit. J. Psychol.,* 1951, 40, 114–122.
16. Eysenck, H. J. "Primary social attitudes as related to social class and political party." *J. Sociol.,* 1951, 2, 198–209.
17. Eysenck, H. J., and Crown, S. "An experimental study in opinion-attitude methodology." *Int. J. opin. & attit. Res.,* 1949, 3, 47–86.
18. Guilford, J. P. "Unitary traits of personality and factor theory." *Amer. J. Psychol.,* 1936, 48, 673–680.
19. Kendall, M. G., and Smith, B. B. "Factor analysis." *J. roy. stat. Soc.,* 1950, 12, 60–94.

19a. Lubin, A. "Some contributions to the testing of psychological hypotheses by means of statistical multivariate analysis." Ph.D. diss. Univ. London, 1951.

20. Petrie, A. "A preliminary report of changes after prefrontal leucotomy." *J. ment Sci.,* 1949, 95, 449–455.

21. Petrie, A. "Personality changes after prefrontal leucotomy. Report 2." *Brit. J. med Psychol.,* 1949, 22, 200–207.

22. Petrie, A. "Clinical aspects of leucotomy." *Proceed. roy. Soc. Med.,* 1950, 42, 39

23. Porter, A. W. *The method of dimensions.* London: Methuen, 1933.

24. Scott-Blair, G. W. *Measurements of mind and matter.* London: Dennis Dobson 1950.

25. Vernon, P. E. *The structure of human abilities.* London: Methuen, 1950.

26. Wolfle, H. "A fundamental principle of personality measurement." *Psychol. Rev.* 1949, 56, 273–276.

❨ section 4

The Process of Adjustment

The readings in this section have been chosen to present a broad sample of material pertaining to the process of adjustment. They include such subjects as the factors which influence adjustment, the typical stresses and problems which an individual in our society faces, and some of the patterns of adjustment which have been described in the psychological literature. The readings here have been divided into three groups.

A. The determinants of adjustment

The first group of readings reports on some of the variables which generally are considered significant in determining adjustment patterns. Whenever the topic of causative factors of behavior is approached, the question of the relative importance of heredity and environment usually is raised. The influences of hereditary and environmental variables on behavior are, however, so complex and interdependent that we cannot meaningfully separate one from the other. While we may note differences among infants at birth, we are unable to determine the extent of the hereditary influence apart from that of the prenatal environment. Infants with the same hereditary potential may differ markedly as a function of variations, deficiencies, and mishaps in the maternal condition while the child is *in utero*. Because of the difficulty in isolating hereditary factors, most investigators of the determinants of personality focus on environmental factors which lend themselves more readily to research.

The readings which follow on the determinants of adjustment were selected to present a representative picture of current thinking and therefore deal chiefly with environmental influences. The first selection, which has been taken from the *Fact-finding Report of*

237

the Midcentury White House Conference on Children and Youth,
edited by Witmer and Kotinsky, deals with some of the differences
among infants which frequently are associated with heredity. The
contributors to the Conference refer to these factors as "congenital," by which they mean those stable characteristics of the
infant which either are present at or soon after birth or which
appear to be "independent of the environment and the particular
experiences of the child." The factors included should be considered a function of the interplay between the forces of heredity
and those of the prenatal environment rather than of heredity
alone. Included in the discussion are differences between infants in
vigor, general sensitivity, vulnerability to physiological disturbance,
and intelligence. Also considered are some of the ways in which
differences in these characteristics may influence personality development and adjustment.

While extensive data on the relationships between infantile characteristics and subsequent adjustment is lacking, it seems reasonable to attribute some influence to the characteristics present at
birth. The effect of such characteristics, however, is extremely
complex and we should not expect to find a one-to-one relationship
between the description of the infant and adult adjustment. The
adjustment of the adult who as an infant was vulnerable to physiological disturbance will be determined by numerous factors other
than this predisposition. The significance of infantile characteristics
lies in the influence they have in promoting experiences from which
the individual learns specific modes of adjustment. The differences
between infants appear to constitute a significant foundation for
the differential experiences which follow, and it is these later experiences which most research investigators have looked to in order
to explain and predict the nature of an individual's adjustment.

Each of the next three selections deals with one of a group of
environmental factors important in the development of adjustment
patterns. The excerpt from Linton's classic book *The Cultural
Background of Personality* presents a theoretical discussion concerning the significance of cultural forces on the determination of personality and summarizes some of the general conclusions which have
been reached by cultural anthropologists. Linton's major thesis is
that the personality characteristics which predominate in a given culture, which he refers to as *the basic personality type,* can be explained best by the hypothesis that each culture promotes a commonality of experience among its members which in turn leads
to the learning of similar attitudes, values, and ways of behaving.
It follows from this same theoretical formulation that adjustment
techniques will differ from culture to culture, and that the specific

adjustment patterns which predominate in a given culture are related to the experiences which that culture defines for its members through its institutions, child-rearing practices, direct teaching, etc.

As Linton indicates, while individual cultures promote basic similarities in their members, they also stimulate differences among members as a function of variations *within* the specific culture. The variations that can be found within a culture also provide a basis for studying the effects of environmental influences on personality and adjustment. The second reading in this section reports on a research project utilizing this approach. Dividing our culture into groups based on class structure (determined by an index of ecological area of residence, occupation, and education), Hollingshead and Redlich present findings which indicate significant relationships between social class and the incidence of psychiatric disorders. The enthusiasm of the authors for relating social concepts to particular adjustment patterns seems warranted. As they point out, however, it is important to go beyond showing that statistical relationships exist between social class and mental illness; we must seek the specific ways in which social conditions function to influence the adjustment of individuals. The final report by Hollingshead and Redlich on this project, entitled *Social Class and Mental Illness* (John Wiley & Sons, Inc., New York, 1958), suggests that this will be a very fruitful approach to understanding ways in which social factors promote problems and patterns of adjustment.

The final selection on the determinants of adjustment deals with those experiences centering about family life. Stagner begins by commenting on the high degree of importance of the family structure on the development of personality and then considers a number of specific variables descriptive of family relationships which are especially relevant to the study of adjustment. Three groups of variables are considered in turn: First, those dealing with the nature of the relationship between the child and his parents; second, those involving the manner in which the parent attempts to influence and control the behavior of the child; and third, those concerning the characteristics of the parent which constitute a model for the child. The study of the influence of the family on the individual appears to be particularly valuable for understanding how adjustment problems and techniques develop. We may anticipate that the considerable amount of current research effort relating to family experience will result in better methods of predicting and controlling adjustment.

INDIVIDUAL DIFFERENCES IN INFANCY *

(Helen L. Witmer and Ruth Kotinsky

The Influence of Congenital Characteristics

All who have had the opportunity of watching many children of like ages have been impressed with the high degree of individuality which each one shows. Even as newborn infants they differ not only in such physical characteristics as weight and height but also in the manner in which they react to events. Some, when put to the breast or given the bottle for the first time, begin to suck vigorously almost at once; they "know what to do." Others suck weakly at first, lose their hold upon the nipple, and learn gradually. Some squall at the slightest provocation; others cry only in extremity. Some squirm and thrash about energetically and move even while asleep; others show less bodily activity and of a more gentle variety. Some, while sleeping or eating, are disturbed by the slightest noise; others remain imperturbed under the same circumstances. Some seem fragile, others robust. This does not begin to exhaust the list of observable differences among infants but it will suffice to illustrate the point that the behavior of infants shows much variability.

It is a curious fact that all investigators in the child-development field have registered their awareness of such differences, yet most have directed their scientific inquiry toward what children have in common. Clinical psychiatrists, on the other hand, have tended to stress the uniqueness of each individual, practically to the exclusion of any systematic comparison among children. A few recent studies have attempted to bridge the gap between these two approaches. Psychological and medical research workers have begun to turn their attention to sources of variability in the development of children, and some clinicians, notably psychoanalytic research workers, are studying child development in a more general and more systematic manner.[1]

At present, however, factual, tested knowledge concerning individual

* From Helen L. Witmer and Ruth Kotinsky, *Personality in the Making*, pp. 35–48, Harper & Brothers, New York, 1952. Reprinted by permission of Dr. Witmer and the publisher.

[1] See, for example, various studies by Rene Spitz, such as "Hospitalism: An Inquiry into the Genesis of Psychiatric Condition in Early Childhood," *Psychoanalytic Study of the Child*, Vols. I and II (1945, 1946), International Universities Press; "The Role of Ecological Factors in Emotional Development in Infancy," *Child Development*, Vol. 20 (1949). Also, R. A. Spitz and K. M. Wolf, "Environment versus Race as an Etiological Factor in Psychiatric Disturbances in Infancy," *Journal of Nervous and Mental Diseases*, May, 1946; "The Smiling Response: A Contribution to the Ontogenesis of Social Relations," *Genetic Psychology Monograph*, No. 34, 1946.

differences among children is so scarce that there is doubt of the wisdom of including it in this report. On the other hand, the topic is of such importance and has such impressive practical implications that a speculative discussion seems better than none at all.

The material presented in this section will be confined to personality characteristics that appear to be congenital. It is important to remember, however, that there is no sure way of knowing whether or not a given trait is of this kind. The assumption that a trait is congenital is made under two kinds of conditions: (1) differences in the behavior of infants were noted so soon after birth that experience could not reasonably be held accountable for their presence; in addition, these characteristics proved stable, i.e., the personality attribute noted in earliest infancy continued to characterize the individual in later life. (2) Personality characteristics, which may not have become apparent until a later point in development, were noted in some children and not in others, quite independent of the environment and the particular experiences of the child. It is reasoned that since such traits apparently do not differ under different cultures, with different family constellations, with different interpersonal relationships, etc., they must be intrinsic to the organism.

In the following analysis we shall first describe some of the congenital differences in children and then consider whether and how the course of healthy personality development may be affected by them.

Activity and vigor. Those who work with young infants know that some are more active than others. All babies move their bodies, and babies generally are more restless and active when they are hungry and uncomfortable than when they are content and satisfied. Yet some will rarely be altogether quiet; their movements are vigorous and tend to involve all or most of the body. Others move delicately and with less intensity. The former group are likely to impress one as vigorous and animated, the latter as either delicate or placid. Moreover, beyond the age of two or three weeks, the active ones are likely to register their response to stimulation from without by an increase in bodily activity. When they are spoken to or when a noise attracts their attention, they kick and wriggle with excitement. The more quiet babies often do just the opposite. If a toy is shown them or they are played with in some other way, they are likely to decrease or even cease movement; they respond to the stimulation with a still, absorbed kind of attention.

Dr. Margaret Fries, a psychoanalytic research worker, has given special attention to this kind of difference among infants.[2] In connection with her

[2] Margaret Fries, "Factors in Character Development, Neuroses, Psychoses and Delinquency," *American Journal of Orthopsychiatry*, Vol. VII (1937); with B. Lewis, "Interrelated Factors in Development," *American Journal of Orthopsychiatry*, Vol. VIII (1938); "Psychosomatic Relations between Mother and Infant," *Psychosomatic Medicine*, Vol. VI (1945).

work in a large metropolitan hospital she observed infants during the first days and weeks of life and was especially impressed with the great differences she noted in regard to their activity level. She continued to observe the same children as they grew older and to assess their degree of activity. She concluded that markedly active infants are likely to be markedly active at later ages as well, and that children who are relatively quiet as newborns tend to remain relatively inactive individuals in later childhood.

More important than the mere stability of this characteristic is Dr. Fries's observation that the interests and needs of children who are from the beginning markedly active, medium active, or low in activity are different. On the basis of case studies she showed that if a relatively inactive youngster happens to be born into a family of active, outgoing individuals it is possible that personality difficulties may arise from this discrepancy. She reasoned that energetic, outgoing parents are likely to expect active behavior from a child and may require of him responses that he is not constitutionally equipped to make. Similarly, more placid and reflective families can be distressed by the enormous energy an active child displays, and consider as aggressive and "naughty" ways of behaving which are quite normal and necessary to the active child. Dr. Fries is of the opinion that healthy personality development will be advanced if parents, doctors, educators, and the like, learn to recognize the child's congenital predisposition in this respect and adapt their ways of handling each child accordingly.

As is true of most studies, Dr. Fries's findings are tentative and not conclusive. Other investigators have questioned whether activity level remains constant and whether it is a constitutional trait.[3] All are agreed, however, that infants do differ in activity and that their needs and satisfactions vary accordingly. It is therefore also agreed—and this is of importance to our problem here—that the most beneficial way of dealing with a particular child (with the aim of helping him to develop his personality optimally) will depend in part upon whether he is very active or markedly placid.

Sensitivity: general. The processes by which an infant first becomes aware of the world in which he is to live and of his own place in it are of great importance to his development. These early experiences, like all experience to all of us, come to him through his sense organs. He hears, he feels, he sees, he smells. He feels sensations that arise from within, such as painful muscular contractions signifying hunger. And he receives innumerable sensations that come from outside himself, such as the touch of his mother's hand, vibrations as the buggy is pushed, the breeze, sunlight, and bath water on his skin. The sight of things and people alters strangely as people come close and withdraw, and as he is rolled from one position to

[3] See, for example, Lillian E. Malcove, "Margaret E. Fries' Research in Problems of Infancy and Childhood," *The Psychoanalytic Study of the Child*, Vol. I (1945), International Universities Press.

another, lifted and put down again. Everything he learns of his environment, and everything he does in response to it, occurs through the medium of perception.

Perceptual processes are of special importance for the very earliest phases of development for an additional reason. The immature individual, especially during the first year of life, is, in general, somewhat more fragile and easily disturbed than he will be later on. Even adults can be made nervous by excessive perceptual stimulation, such as continued loud noises, overly bright illumination, violent motion, etc. Adults however, are sturdy enough to tolerate sharp stimulation with minor discomfort or, at worst, temporary interruption of normal functioning. Moreover, they are seldom helpless; they can protect themselves by moving away from heat or cold, by turning the head or closing their eyes against intense visual stimuli. Small babies, however, cannot protect themselves in the face of unpleasant perceptual sensations; once they perceive, they cannot help but respond. Consequently, continued and overly intense perceptual stimulation is not infrequently the cause of severe fatigue, tension, and distress in infants, and may possibly lead to real disturbance in development.

It is known that adults differ greatly in acuteness of perception. The hearing of some people is keener than that of others. Some detect fine nuances in the shading of colors, and others make only grosser visual distinctions. Some can judge distances and weights with greater precision than can others, and some seem generally more responsive to all sorts of sensory stimulation. Among artists, for instance, one finds a high proportion of especially sensitive persons, using "sensitive" in the physiological meaning of the word.

Scientifically minded pediatricians and psychologists have noted that even during the first few weeks of life babies differ from one to another in respect to what may be called "generalized sensitivity." Some startle at even slight sounds, other startle only when the stimulus sound is a very loud one. If a lamp is turned on or sunlight hits the face, some babies merely blink, other grimace, whimper, or even cry. Some have to be moved very gently or else will be upset; others are not bothered by being moved rapidly, swung about, bounced, or even tossed in father's arms. A little later, yet still during the first few months, some babies seem much more aware than others of nuances of color and of brightness. Similarly, some seem to react earlier and more strongly to the differences between familiar and unfamiliar persons.

Observing such behavior differences one receives the distinct impression that the world is a very different place for the less sensitive babies than for the highly sensitive ones. The imperturbable, robust baby, it would seem, faces a somewhat simpler problem in orienting himself to the outer world. He perceives and responds to only the stronger stimulations. The lesser ones—small noises, vibrations, changes in light and temperature—

seem barely to be noticed or responded to. At the other extreme, the very sensitive infant is almost continuously flooded with strong sense impressions to which he must respond. For him there are fewer periods of quiescence. Perceptual stimulations of relatively great intensity may be overwhelming and temporarily quite upsetting to him, whereas the same stimulation may be well tolerated by less sensitive babies.

It has been thought that perceptual sensitivity is related to many characteristics of personality and temperament, although no conclusive studies have yet been carried out. Many students of child development have speculated as to whether sensitivities of this sort are inborn or acquired and what role they play in personality development. It is only very recently, however, that scientific inquiry has directed itself to the perceptual functioning of young children.[4] In presenting this material here we raise questions for further research. We do so in the belief that a workable theory of personality development requires knowledge of this sort, and that the factor of perceptual sensitivity is important for the care and practical management of children.

Such sensitivity, in and of itself, does not, we believe, bear a direct relationship to intelligence or even to the capacity for good adjustment. It seems probable, however, that many of the babies commonly called "nervous" are also highly sensitive. But under circumstances that provide protection from too much harsh stimulation (and most mothers protect their babies from extreme heat and cold, from too much handling, too much noise, etc.) highly sensitive babies develop in as healthy and wholesome a fashion as do other babies. Their behavior and their needs may in some respects be different from those of other babies but they are altogether normal. "Tough-skinned" babies, by the same token, may in earliest infancy seem a little less aware of things about but they, too, soon respond alertly and adequately to their world as they experience it. Throughout this discussion it should be kept in mind that the individual differences referred to are all encountered among entirely healthy, normal, well-developing children.

Sensitivity: specific. In addition to variation in generalized sensitivity, people also differ in particular perceptual spheres. Some adults, for instance, are described as "visual-minded," by which is meant that they are keenly aware of visual impressions and that visual images play an especially large role in their memory and imagination. Similarly, some people are markedly more sensitive to smell or temperature or pain or sound than they are to the other sense impressions. Such evidence as exists strongly suggests that differences in the relative sensitivity of some perceptual spheres over others

    [4] P. Bergman and Sibylle Escalona, "Unusual Sensitivities in Very Young Children," *Psychoanalytic Study of the Child*, Vols. III, IV (1949), International Universities Press: Albrecht Peiper, *Die Eigenart der kindlichen Hirntätigkeit*, Georg Thieme, Leipzig, 1949.

exist in earliest infancy as well. Some babies respond more strongly to sound than to sight or motion; for some, touch (which is an important sense to all babies) may be the outstandingly sensitive area of perception.

What bearing does this have on personality development? Like generalized sensitivity, its importance lies in the way in which the outer world presents itself to the child. The degree of generalized sensitivity influences how much of the sounds and sights and motions that surround him the baby will perceive, and how intensively he will perceive it. Differential sensitivities influence the kind of sense impressions that will play the relatively largest role in the child's experience of his environment and orientation to it.

It may well be, for instance, that some babies first recognize mother as distinct from all other persons primarily by the way in which she touches, holds, and moves them. The firmness of her grasp, the tempo and rhythm of her movement may be the important clues by which the kinesthetically minded baby recognizes her. To a baby predominantly sensitive in the auditory sphere, the sound of her voice may be an outstanding clue, and to a visually sensitive baby it may be her contours, her size, and her coloring that are most important.

It follows logically (and observations seem to support the notion) that different degrees of sensitivity in various perceptual spheres are among the factors that determine the important sources of pleasure, as well as of pain and discomfort, for the young child. One child more keenly aware of sound than other perceptions, for instance, will experience the pleasures of being fed, cuddled, and played with, in association with the sounds which occur incidental to these situations. He is more likely to be influenced by music than are most children, and sudden or loud noises will frighten him more readily.

For the sake of clarity, this description oversimplifies the real state of affairs. Except for children with severe physical handicaps, such as blindness or deafness, all kinds of perception in combination help to define the child's experience for him. At the same time, the most characteristic components and individual flavor of his experience will vary with variously distributed sensitivities. Also, a child is not either sensitive or robust; rather, there are an infinite number of gradations in sensitivity within each child and among children. And last, the way in which a child uses his perceptual apparatus depends to some extent on the stimulation he receives. Ours is a visually oriented culture. Especially after the first six months or so, children's toys, the manner of their teaching, and the experiences most typically provided for them have such strong visual components that visual clues will be important in the learning of all children, even those whose natural preference would be another modality. One might put it that the experiences we typically provide for children are especially well adapted to those at least moderately sensitive in the visual sphere, and that they may impose a slightly more difficult task upon those children who spontaneously emphasize other channels of perception.

Tempo and rhythm. It is generally true of people that some are quick and others slower in everything they do. Some are "slow but sure," others fast and precise, or fast and erratic. Most people can be said to have a characteristic rhythm to their activities, which may range from staccato to largo. Common sense, with justice, associates this characteristic with personality traits. We describe one person as "sharp as lightning," and a slower harmonious pace is often associated with good nature and warmth. Great literature, which remains one of the best storehouses of psychological wisdom, offers many examples for this popular conception; for instance, one might think of Don Quixote and of Falstaff.

A number of studies have thrown some light on tempo differences among infants, especially in regard to bodily functions such as sleep, movement, eating, digestion, and elimination.[5] There have not been systematic studies of this aspect of personality in its totality. Observed facts suggest, however, that a child's pace is likely to be fairly general, i.e., infants who eat and digest rapidly are also infants who tend to move quickly. Characteristic tempo and movement are among the things which unify most or all aspects of functioning in a given child, permeating all his behavior.

More definite statements await further research. We mention this source of variability in the behavior of young children because, if further study confirms our expectation that tempo differences characterize infants at birth and tend to remain characteristic of the individual through life, then this factor will influence the child's response to the demands we make of him. Skill in adapting techniques to the child's natural mode of functioning will make a significant difference in the amount of frustration imposed on children in the course of rearing them. In this way all aspects of personality development can be seen as related to this factor of characteristic tempo.

Bodily resilience and vulnerability. The younger the child, the more does his whole bodily apparatus function as one closely related unit. Respiration, circulation, the nervous system, the digestive system, and the rest have so little independence of one another that a change in one of these body systems is likely to bring on a simultaneous change in the functioning of all the others. If a baby cries, for instance, he is seen to flush (circulation), his breathing becomes shallow and more rapid (respiration), his hands become fisted, the entire body tenses (muscle tonus), and other functions are also either prevented from taking place or temporarily altered. In addition, the human child is born in a state of relatively great physio-

[5] See Nancy Bayley, "Mental Growth in Young Children," *Yearbook National Society for the Study of Education,* Vol. 39 (II), 1940; also, Nancy Bayley, "Consistency and Variability in the Growth of Intelligence from Birth to Eighteen Years," *Journal of Genetic Psychology,* No. 75, 1949.

logical immaturity. All his bodily functions are more vulnerable, more easily upset, than they will be after he has had a year or two in which to grow and consolidate them. Many sorts of necessary protections, such as temperature regulations, which later become automatic, self-regulating physiological mechanisms, are not established in the young baby. Thus, if the responsible adults fail to feed the child and keep him warm and to protect him from noxious influences, the child will die.

Medical observation and research have shown that this is not true in quite the same way for all infants. More important for our purpose is the fact that within the same baby some body systems may be relatively more resistant and others relatively more vulnerable. All infants, of course, may contract an infection on exposure or may acquire a digestive disorder as the result of improper feeding. Over and beyond this obvious fact, however, many babies seem to have characteristic bodily reactions to a great variety of disturbing causes. In response to an inoculation, for instance, or to a common cold or to a marked and sudden change in routine, some babies characteristically develop a fever, others a digestive disorder, others a skin irritation or a feeding or sleeping disorder. It is as though one part of the physiological apparatus, in many babies at least, is a relatively weak spot. This particular body system is the one most likely to show a reaction to any disturbance that may occur in the functioning of the entire organism. It is also this particular body system that is most vulnerable to noxious influences from the environment and hence is the channel through which physiological disturbance is most easily brought on.

While the fact that such differences exist very early in life is well established, the cause and effect of these differences are just beginning to attract scientific inquiry. This aspect of the child's development has become especially important to research workers in the field of psychosomatic medicine. In brief, it has been posited that psychological experience and personality characteristics are related to physiological traits.[6] In certain disease categories, adults suffering from the given physical ailment, such as arthritis, gastric ulcers, and allergies, have been found to have important personality characteristics in common. Certain kinds of personality organization have even been dubbed as the "typical diabetic" or the "typical arthritic" personality. Scientists are by no means agreed in the interpretation of these findings. The gaps in knowledge are so great that it seems wise to do no further than to acknowledge the fact that psychological experience is not isolated from bodily functioning but, on the contrary, very closely linked with it. Certain unitary principles of organization, or at least corresponding modes of functioning, exist on the physiological and on the emotional level.

It is not easy to assess the significance of different strengths and weaknesses in various body systems for personality development. This source of

[6] See, for example, numerous articles in *Psychosomatic Medicine*.

congenitally present variability in the behavior of infants has been included in the present analysis for the promise it holds of adding to our understanding in the future. Its present applicability to the task of aiding healthy personality development is close to nil. Two points of view, which do not contradict one another, are advanced by those engaged in studying such matters. Both relate bodily functioning to personality development.

The first of these proposes that congenitally given physiological characteristics predispose simultaneously toward the development of certain somatic illnesses rather than others and to certain kinds of personality characteristics rather than others. Such an assumption implies that if an infant shows more than ordinary skin sensitivity (as well as some other bodily characteristics, and only if there is no specific external cause to bring on the skin irritability) this is likely to mean that he will be predisposed toward developing allergies and eczema rather than other ailments. Such an infant would also, according to this speculation, be more likely to show the psychological traits typically associated with allergies. In other words, one would expect him to show the "allergic personality," whether or not he had occasion actually to develop allergies. This statement is a legitimate speculation, but as yet no empirical evidence has been collected that is sufficient to attest to the validity of such a notion or to prove it false.

The second point of view, also not scientifically established as yet, is more limited in scope but better supported by established fact. Psychoanalytic investigation has shown that as the child develops, different body zones and body systems come to be of special importance at successive developmental stages. Specific biological or physiological needs characterize each phase of development, and to a considerable degree the child's wellbeing and developmental progress depend upon his opportunities to satisfy these needs. Since some body systems are more vulnerable than others, this vulnerability may be thought to be of especial psychological significance at that point in the child's development at which the body system in question is of special dynamic importance. For instance, in very early life, during the phase in which the chief problem is that of developing trust, pleasures derived from sucking and other mouth activities appear to be especially important to the child. Most respiratory disturbances affect mouth functions; they interfere with easy breathing and often irritate portions of the mouth and throat. One might speculate that proneness to develop respiratory difficulties is somewhat more disturbing to the wellbeing of a child at this early age than later, when the child has moved on to a developmental phase in which the mouth is of less importance in the total economy of the organism.

One can also consider the possible effect of such a lifelong tendency to overreact with one part of the body upon the child's total development. The mere fact of repeated skin irritations, for instance, probably makes the skin and the sense of touch more important to the child than they would otherwise be. Whether or not normal developmental sequences are affected when certain bodily sensations are especially intense remains to be learned. Some psychological case studies of children who did experience such focusing of attention and painful experience on certain parts of the body suggest that this may occur. If a disruption, or perhaps modification, of normal developmental events due to such concentration of sensation in a certain body part exists, then this may help to explain some of the seemingly unreasonable emotional reactions that children sometimes show to illness and to medical care.

Intellectual endowment. Child psychologists have devoted more attention to the problem of "intelligence" than to any other aspect of development, and viewpoints about it have changed with scientific advance. Prior to 1930, it was generally held by psychologists concerned with the measurement of intelligence that the degree of intellectual endowment was a fixed characteristic of the organism and that, while adverse influences might prevent a child from realizing his abilities to the full, the degree of intellectual ability a child possessed could not be altered by education or other means. Since that time important discoveries have somewhat altered these ideas.

About 1930, considerable data were amassed that seemed to show that intelligence is but one function among many that make up a living, changing personality, and that environmental influences do alter the degree of intellectual capacity.[7] One of the most convincing arguments for this point of view was the following. It had long been known that feeble-minded parents produce more feeble-minded offspring than do parents of normal intelligence. Feeble-mindedness was therefore thought to be transmitted by heredity. Experiments were then conducted which so arranged things that children of feeble-minded parents were placed in foster homes at a very early age. It was found that these children, in large proportion, made good developmental progress and, well into school age, showed no signs of mental retardation. The high frequency of mental retardation among the offspring of retarded parents therefore seemed attributable to the kind of life experience that feeble-minded parents provided for their children. Other studies appeared to indicate that the I.Q. can be raised by means of nursery school and other kinds of enriching experience.[8] It was therefore concluded that the intellectual differences between high and low economic groups are explainable on the basis of the limitations or advantages in education and other important conditions of life that necessarily accompany these groups. Some investigators went so far as to believe that mental abilities are almost

[7] The best summary of studies suggesting that environmental influences alter intellectual ability is to be found in the Proceedings of the 1929 White House Conference. A brief summary of this same material is also given in George Stoddard and Elizabeth Wellman, *Child Psychology*, The Macmillan Company, New York, 1934.

[8] Studies tracing in detail the effect of nursery-school attendance, and the like, have in large proportion appeared as publications in the "Monograph Series" of the Iowa Child Welfare Research Station.

entirely a function of experience, provided there is no definite damage to, or abnormality in, the nervous system.

Since 1930, scientific thinking on this matter has become more sophisticated. Psychologists no longer argue in terms of either one kind of cause or the other, but in terms of complicated interrelations among many factors. There is no doubt that barren, limiting, and in other ways unfavorable early experience can stunt intellectual growth and permanently damage mental competence, just as it can stunt physical growth and cause irrevocable damage to bone and tissue. On the other hand, there is no doubt that wide differences in intellectual ability exist—ranging from feeblemindedness to genius—among children whose environment is neither bad enough to retard normal developmental progress nor so superior as to explain the extraordinary ability of the highly gifted. Many carefully conducted studies have shown that intellectual functioning (which need not be identical with intellectual capacity) changes with changes in the experience and especially in the emotional state of the person. In fact many authorities feel that it is quite false to think of intellect as apart from feelings and from personality as a whole. We begin to see that such intellectual abilities as abstract thinking, memory, and even mechanical skill have a great deal to do with a person's fears and hopes, with the degree to which he is under emotional stress, and with the ways he has devised of getting along in spite of the dissatisfactions and obstacles to fulfillment that every human being must accept.[9]

Intellectual ability, accordingly, is viewed very differently now than in 1930. Psychologists have learned enough about the conditions under which adults and children make a success of living to know that intellect as such is not as all-important as it was once thought to be. They have developed a wholesome skepticism of their instruments of measurements; they recognize that intelligence tests do not capture all that should be included in the concept of intelligence and that they barely touch upon such qualities as capacity for wisdom or creative power.

When intellectual ability is regarded as but one facet of the whole personality, its importance in the context of all else that is known about development increases, just as its importance as a single element decreases. A formulation of current thinking about intellectual differences, which is compatible with the facts presently known but which may be changed as new facts come to light, might read as follows: Children probably are born with differing potentialities for intellectual development. Some are so constituted that if their experience provides nourishment and stimulation of the right sort they can exceed the great majority in intellectual achievement. The intellectual development of the others will also depend upon their opportunities for learning but no amount of encouragement will

[9] Rapaport, Schafer, and Gill, *Diagnostic Psychological Testing*, Vol. I (1945), Chicago Year Book Publishers, Inc., Chicago; also Vol. II (1946).

enable them to go beyond a relatively fixed level of achievement that falls below that of the most highly talented. Not only the absolute level of attainment that a person may reach but also his particular pattern of mental functioning and the way he uses and molds his intelligence are influenced to a high degree by the influences to which he is exposed during the early years of life and to some extent by the influences which affect him throughout life. Not improbably, no human being ever realizes all his potentialities for intellectual achievement.

It is self-evident that level and kind of intellectual endowment have a significant influence upon the course of personality development. Even with the handicap of subnormal intelligence and the hazard of genius omitted, it would still be difficult to say "the more intellect the better" from the point of view of healthy personality development. One element that makes for adequacy in personality functioning at any age is that the person feels reasonably competent to meet the demands and exigencies that confront him. The life demands that face American children are, however, widely different. A high order of abstract intelligence may present genuine obstacles to harmonious personality development to the child of an economically underprivileged rural family whose environment may not provide scope and depth for the development of his faculties and leave him restless and dissatisfied. A child of good average endowment born into a family of scholars may fall so short of meeting the exceedingly high intellectual standards of his milieu that the development of a real sense of initiative or industry or an acceptable identity is almost impossible for him.

Adult life in our society offers an almost infinite variety of ways in which different kinds and degrees of mental ability can productively be used. If we could free ourselves from ideas about the greater desirability of certain kinds of mental ability and could provide all children with the kinds of experience and teaching they need for the optimal development of their capacities, most of the variations in degree and kind of intellect could cease to be a source of discouragement and hopeless ambition to children and parents.

THE RÔLE OF CULTURE
IN PERSONALITY FORMATION *

⟮ RALPH LINTON

One of the most important scientific developments of modern times has been the recognition of culture. It has been said that the last thing which a dweller in the deep sea would be likely to discover would be water. He would become conscious of its existence only if some accident brought him to the surface and introduced him to air. Man, throughout most of his history, has been only vaguely conscious of the existence of culture and has owed even his consciousness to contrasts between the customs of his own society and those of some other with which he happened to be brought into contact. The ability to see the culture of one's own society as a whole, to evaluate its patterns and appreciate their implications, calls for a degree of objectivity which is rarely if ever achieved. It is no accident that the modern scientist's understanding of culture has been derived so largely from the study of non-European cultures where observation could be aided by contrast. Those who know no culture other than their own cannot know their own. Until very recent times even psychologists have failed to appreciate that all human beings, themselves included, develop and function in an environment which is, for the most part, culturally determined. As long as they limited their investigations to individuals reared within the frame of a single culture they could not fail to arrive at concepts of human nature which were far from the truth. Even such a master as Freud frequently posited instincts to account for reactions which we now see as directly referable to cultural conditioning. With the store of knowledge of other societies and cultures which is now available, it is possible to approach the study of personality with fewer preconceptions and to reach a closer approximation of the truth.

It must be admitted at once that the observation and recording of data on personality in non-European societies is still fraught with great difficulty. It is hard enough to get reliable material in our own. The development of accurate, objective techniques for personality study is still in its infancy. Such appliances as the Rorschach tests and Murray's thematic apperception tests have proved their value, but those who have worked with

* From Ralph Linton, *The Cultural Background of Personality*, pp. 125–146, D. Appleton-Century Company, Inc., New York, 1945. Reprinted by permission of Appleton-Century-Crofts, Inc.

them would be the first to recognize their limitations. In the present state of our knowledge we still have to rely very largely upon informal observations and upon the subjective judgments of the observer. To complicate matters still further, most, although by no means all, of the information which we have on personality in non-European societies has been collected by anthropologists who had only a nodding acquaintance with psychology. Such observers, among whom I include myself at the time that I did most of my ethnological field work, are seriously handicapped by their ignorance of what to look for and what should be recorded. Moreover, there is a lamentable lack of comparative material on the various non-European societies which have been studied. The rapidity with which primitive societies have been acculturated or extinguished during the last hundred years has led to the development of a particular pattern of anthropological investigation. Since there were always far more societies available for study than there were anthropologists to study them and since most of these societies had to be investigated immediately or not at all, each investigator sought a new and unknown group. As a result, most of the information which we have has been collected by one investigator per society. The disadvantages of this are obvious in any case, but especially so in connection with personality studies. In a field where so much depends upon the subjective judgment of the observer and upon the particular members of the society with whom he was able to establish intimate contacts, the personality of the observer becomes a factor in every record. It is to be hoped that with the increasing number of anthropologists and the dwindling number of unstudied societies this pattern of exclusiveness will be broken down and that personality studies will benefit accordingly.

In spite of this frank recognition of difficulties and limitations which only time can remove, certain facts seem to be well established. All anthropologists who have come to know the members of non-European societies intimately are in substantial agreement on certain points. These are: (1) Personality norms differ in different societies. (2) The members of any society will always show considerable individual variation in personality. (3) Much of the same range of variation and much the same personality types are to be found in all societies. Although anthropologists base these conclusions on informal observations, they seem to be substantiated by the results of certain objective tests. Thus Rorschach series from different societies reveal different norms for such series as wholes. They also reveal a wide range of individual variation within each series and much overlapping between series. Even without this evidence, the consensus of opinion on the part of those who should be in a position to know cannot be dismissed lightly. In the absence of more complete and accurate information it seems justifiable to accept these conclusions as facts and to take them as the starting point for our investigation of the rôle of culture in personality formation.

That the norms for personality differ in different societies will scarcely be doubted by anyone who has had experience of societies other than his own. In fact the average individual tends to exaggerate rather than minimize such differences. The only question likely to be raised in this connection is whether a given society should be thought of as having a single personality norm or as having a series of different personality norms each of which is associated with a particular status group within the society. Any difficulty in reconciling these two points of view will disappear when one sees them in proper perspective. The members of any society will always be found to have a long series of personality elements in common. These elements may be of any degree of specificity, ranging from simple overt responses of the sort involved in "table manners" to highly generalized attitudes. Responses of the latter type may underlie a wide range of more specific responses in the individual. Similarly, value-attitude systems which are shared by the members of a society may be reflected in several different forms of status-linked overt behavior. Thus the men and women within a society may share the same attitudes with respect to feminine modesty or masculine courage, although the behavior linked with these attitudes will necessarily be different for each sex. For the women the common modesty attitudes will be expressed in particular patterns of dress or conduct, for the men in more generalized responses of approval or disapproval for particular costumes or conduct. These common personality elements together form a fairly well-integrated configuration which may be called the *Basic Personality Type* for the society as a whole. The existence of this configuration provides the members of the society with common understandings and values and makes possible the unified emotional response of the society's members to situations in which their common values are involved.

It will also be found that in every society there are additional configurations of responses which are linked with certain socially delimited groups within the society. Thus, in practically all cases, different response configurations are characteristic for men and for women, for adolescents and for adults, and so on. In a stratified society similar differences may be observed between the responses characteristic of individuals from different social levels, as nobles, commoners and slaves. These status-linked response configurations may be termed *Status Personalities*. They are of the utmost importance to the successful functioning of the society, since they make it possible for its members to interact successfully on the basis of status cues alone. Thus even in dealings between complete strangers, simple recognition of the social positions of the two individuals involved makes it possible for each to predict how the other will respond to most situations.

The status personalities recognized by any society are superimposed upon its basic personality type and are thoroughly integrated with the latter. However, they differ from the basic personality type in being heavily weighted on the side of specific overt responses. The weighting is so pronounced that it might even be questioned whether status personalities can be said to include any value-attitude systems distinct from those included in the basic personality. However, I feel that it is legitimate to distinguish between *knowledge* of a particular value-attitude system and *participation* in such a system. A status personality will rarely include any value-attitude system which is unknown to the members of other status groups, although it might come to do so under conditions of extreme intergroup hostility. On the other hand, it may very well include value-attitude systems in which the members of other status-groups do not participate. Thus free men may know and allow for the attitudes of slaves without actually sharing them. In any case, it is the specific, overt responses which give status personalities most of their social significance. As long as the individual develops these responses, he can function successfully in the status whether he shares the associated value-attitude systems or not. Informal observation leads us to believe that such cases are fairly numerous in all societies. The specific response patterns of a status personality are presented to the individual in simple, concrete terms which make it easy to learn them. Social pressure toward their assumption is constant, and adherence to them is socially rewarded and deviation from them punished. Even the internal conflicts which may arise during the assumption of a specific response pattern which is at variance with one of the individual's value-attitude systems are not too disturbing. Although they may be vigorous at first, they tend to diminish and finally disappear as the response becomes automatized and unconscious.

Every society has its own basic personality type and its own series of status personalities differing in some respects from those of any other society. Practically all societies tacitly recognize this fact, and many of them have explanations for it. Our own society has, until very recent times, based its explanation on biological factors. Differences in basic personality type have been regarded as due to some linkage between race and personality. Status personality differences have been re-referred to sexual factors, in the case of male and female statuses, or to heredity. The latter explanation is not too familiar to Americans, since it is one of our culture patterns to ignore the existence of status personalities other than those which are sex-linked, but it is an integral part of European culture. Folk tales inherited from the days of a rigidly stratified society bristle with incidents in which the child of noble ancestry reared by low-rank foster parents is immediately recognized by his real relatives on the basis of his noble personality. These biological explanations are a good example of the sort of culturally transmitted "knowledge." . . . They have been passed on in our society for many generations, and it is only recently that anyone has had the temerity to subject them to the tests of scientific investigation. Such an investigation really has to deal with three distinct problems: (1) In how far is personality determined by physiological factors? (2) In how far are such physiological determinants hereditary? (3) What is the probability of such hereditary determinants becoming so widely diffused in a society as to affect its basic personality type, or, in stratified societies, its status personalities?

We have already seen that the personality is primarily a configuration of responses which the individual has developed as a result of his experience. This experience, in turn, derives from his interaction with his environment. The innate qualities of the individual will influence strongly the sort of experience which he derives from this interaction. Thus a particular environmental situation may result in one sort of experience for a strong child and a quite different sort for a weak one. Again, there are many situations which will result in one sort of experience for an intelligent child and another sort for a dull one. However, it is also obvious that two children of equal intelligence or strength may derive quite different experience from different situations. If one of them is the brightest member of his family and the other the dullest member of his, their experience and the resulting response configurations will be quite different. In other words, although the innate qualities of the individual influence personality development, the sort of influence which they exert will be largely conditioned by environmental factors. Everything which we now know of the processes of personality formation indicates that we must substitute for the old formula of nature versus nurture, a new formula of nature plus or minus nurture. There seems to be abundant evidence that neither innate abilities nor environment can be regarded as constantly dominant in personality formation. Moreover, it appears that different combinations of the two may produce closely similar results as far as the developed personality is concerned. Thus any combination of innate and environmental factors which places the individual in a secure and dominant position will result in the development of certain basic attitudes; any combination which exposes him to insecurity and a subordinate position will result in the development of others.

It seems safe to conclude that innate, biologically determined factors cannot be used to account for personality configurations as wholes or for the various response patterns included within such configurations. They operate simply as one among several sets of factors responsible for the formation of these. However, the personality configuration consists of more than response patterns. It includes certain features of all-over organization which are vaguely referred to as the individual's temperament. The current definitions of this term imply that these features are innate and physiologically determined, but it is still uncertain in how far this is really the case. We do not know, for example, whether such a feature as nervous instability is really innate or a result of environmental influences or, as seems most probable, a product of the interaction of innate and environmental factors. Until this question can be answered it seems safest to leave temperament out of the discussion, while recognizing that such an omission must leave our conclusions incomplete.

In addition to response patterns and "temperamental" factors, every personality configuration includes the ability to carry on various psychological processes. It might be safer to speak of abilities, since there is plenty of evidence that a given individual may differ markedly in his facility with respect to different processes. Thus low intelligence may be linked with extraordinary ability in certain forms of learning and memory. That there are also individual differences with respect to particular abilities no one will question, although these differences seem to be a matter of degree rather than of kind. Thus all individuals are capable of some measure of learning and of thought, but they differ widely in their facility with respect to these processes. While facility can be increased by training and practice, the observed differences seem to be too great to be accounted for on this basis alone. Thus it may be questioned whether any amount of training would enable the average individual to memorize the entire Bible or to equal many of the recorded feats of lightning calculators. We are forced to conclude that there are certain innate factors which set upper limits to the possible development of particular psychological abilities and that these factors vary from one individual to another. We may also assume that such factors have some sort of physiological basis, although we still have no clear idea of what this basis may be.

To sum up, it appears that physiological factors cannot be held accountable for the developed response patterns which compose the bulk of the personality but that they may be responsible, in part, for the individual's psychological abilities. This brings us at once to our second problem: "In how far are such physiological determinants hereditary?" Unfortunately we are unable to solve this problem on the basis of our present knowledge or techniques. There is no way in which we can analyze out the psychological abilities of the individual in their "pure" state. We can only judge them by their overt manifestations, and these are always influenced by past experience. The unsatisfactory results obtained when even the best intelligence tests are applied to groups with different culture backgrounds brings this out clearly. This makes it impossible to establish the innate abilities of individuals in the terms required for a real genetic study. We can never tell in how far the apparent intelligence level of any individual is due to heredity or to opportunity. If we grant that psychological abilities have a physiological basis, it seems highly probable that at least some of the physiological factors involved are affected by heredity. At the same time, such evidence as we have on the occurrence of various levels of psychological ability seems to indicate that these are not inherited directly. Their appearance in individuals of known heredity cannot be predicted in the same simple mathematical terms as that of, say, eye color. In view of the almost infinite series of individual gradations in these abilities, it would be surprising if they were inherited directly. The most probable explanation seems to be that the physiological factors which are responsible for a particular level of ability result from certain highly complex combinations of genes and that in heredity these combinations do not move as units.

Even if this explanation is correct, it does not rule out the possibility that the basic personality type for a society may, in certain cases, be influenced by hereditary factors. The members of any society normally tend to intermarry among themselves. If the society is able to maintain its isolation for a long enough period, all its members will come to have much the same heredity. The length of time required to arrive at this condition will depend both upon the size of the original group from which the society's members are descended and on the homogeneity of this group's ancestry. The larger the original group and the more heterogeneous its origins, the longer the time required to establish a homogeneous heredity in its descendants. When the genes required to produce a particular combination are present in the bulk of a society's members, the chances of the combination appearing among their offspring is greatly increased. There is thus an excellent possibility that a small, long-isolated population may come to include a large proportion of individuals who stand at a particular level of psychological ability. Even in closely inbred societies there is always a considerable range of individual variation, so that the stupidest member of an intelligent group might well be duller than the most intelligent member of a stupid one. However, the basic personality type for any society is a matter of averages, and these averages may differ from one society to another as a result of hereditary factors. For the reasons already stated, such hereditary differences in psychological abilities would be especially likely to occur in small "primitive" societies of the sort with which anthropological studies have, for the most part, concerned themselves.

The foregoing discussion of the possibility of hereditary differences in the psychological norms for various societies may seem unnecessarily detailed. However, there is strong disagreement on this point even among anthropologists. One group takes it for granted that there are marked differences in the inherited abilities of most societies, while the other flatly denies the possibility of such differences. Apparently neither group has troubled to examine its position in the light of modern knowledge of genetics. The truth almost certainly lies somewhere between the two extremes. Small, long-isolated societies probably do differ in their inherited psychological potentialities. On the other hand, the members of most large societies, and indeed of all civilized ones, are so heterogeneous in their heredity that any physiological explanation of the observed differences in the personality norms for such societies is quite untenable. The genetic differences between, for example, the French and the Germans are so much smaller than the differences in their personality norms that it is ridiculous to try to account for the latter on a genetic basis. Even the most racialistic Germans have had to introduce the mystic concept of a Nordic soul capable of incarnation in a Mediterranean or Alpine body to bolster their concepts of racial superiority.

American anthropologists, led by the late Dr. Boas, were among the first to recognize the inadequacy of hereditary physiological factors as an explanation of the differing personality norms for various societies. Unfortunately, in their eagerness to combat doctrines of racial inequality and to emphasize the essential unity of our species they overlooked one important point. The processes of scientific advance, aside from the simple gathering of facts, are primarily processes of substitution. When accumulating knowledge renders one explanation of a particular phenomenon untenable, a new and better explanation has to be developed. It is not enough simply to point out that the previously accepted explanation was wrong. It is a readily observable fact that the personality norms for different societies do differ. Instead of accepting this frankly and attempting to account for it, certain anthropologists have contented themselves with trying to minimize the extent and importance of such differences. They have mustered the evidence to show that the differences which they are willing to admit cannot be due to racial factors, but they have done little to develop any better explanation. The belief that the differences in personality norms for various societies are due to innate hereditary factors is deeply rooted in the popular mind. It cannot be eradicated unless science is prepared to offer a better explanation. To believe that all human groups have the same psychological potentialities without trying to account for their very obvious differences in overt behavior and even in value-attitude systems, calls for a degree of faith in scientific authority of which few individuals are capable. Even general statements that the observed differences are due to cultural factors remain unconvincing as long as they are not accompanied by explanations of what these factors may be and how they operate.

Our discussion of the possible rôle of hereditary factors in determining the personality norms for various societies should have made it clear that these factors are quite inadequate to account for many of the observable differences. The only alternative is to assume that such differences are referable to the particular environments within which the members of various societies are reared. As has been pointed out elsewhere, the environmental factors which appear to be most important in connection with personality formation are people and things. The behavior of the members of any society and the forms of most of the objects which they use are largely stereotyped and can be described in terms of culture patterns. When we say that the developing individual's personality is shaped by culture, what we actually mean is that it is shaped by the experience which he derives from his contact with such stereotypes. That it actually is shaped by such contacts to a very large extent will hardly be doubted by anyone familiar with the evidence; however, the literature on the subject seems to have largely ignored one important aspect of the shaping process.

The influences which culture exerts on the developing personality are of two quite different sorts. On the one hand we have those influences which derive from the culturally patterned behavior of other individuals *toward* the child. These begin to operate from the moment of birth and are of paramount importance during infancy. On the other hand we have those influences which derive from the individual's observation of, or instruction in, the patterns of behavior characteristic of his society. Many of these patterns do not affect him directly, but they provide him with models for the development of his own habitual responses to various situations. These influences are unimportant in early infancy but continue to affect him throughout life. The failure to distinguish between these two types of cultural influence has led to a good deal of confusion.

It must be admitted at once that the two types of influence overlap at certain points. Culturally patterned behavior directed toward the child may serve as a model for the development of some of his own behavior patterns. This factor becomes operative as soon as the child is old enough to observe and remember what other people are doing. When, as an adult, he finds himself confronted by the innumerable problems involved in rearing his own children, he turns to these childhood memories for guidance. Thus in almost any American community we find parents sending their children to Sunday School because they themselves were sent to Sunday School. The fact that, as adults, they greatly prefer golf to church attendance does little to weaken the pattern. However, this aspect of any society's patterns for child-rearing is rather incidental to the influence which such patterns exert upon personality formation. At most it insures that children born into a particular society will be reared in much the same way generation after generation. The real importance of the patterns for early care and child-training lies in their effects upon the deeper levels of the personalities of individuals reared according to them.

It is generally accepted that the first few years of the individual's life are crucial for the establishment of the highly generalized value-attitude systems which form the deeper levels of personality content. The first realization of this fact came from the study of atypical individuals in our own society and the discovery that certain of their peculiarities seemed to be rather consistently linked with certain sorts of atypical childhood experiences. The extension of personality studies to other societies in which both the normal patterns of child-rearing and the normal personality configurations for adults were different from our own only served to emphasize the importance of very early conditioning. Many of the "normal" aspects of European personalities which were accepted at first as due to instinctive factors are now recognized as results of our own particular patterns of child care. Although study of the relations between various societies' techniques for child-rearing and the basic personality types for adults in these societies has barely begun, we have already reached a point where certain correlations seem to be recognizable. Although a listing of all these correlations is impossible in a discussion as brief as the present one, a few examples may serve for illustration.

In societies in which the culture pattern prescribes absolute obedience from the child to the parent as a prerequisite for rewards of any sort, the normal adult will tend to be a submissive individual, dependent and lacking in initiative. Even though he has largely forgotten the childhood experiences which led to the establishment of these attitudes, his first reaction to any new situation will be to look to someone in authority for support and direction. It is worth noting in this connection that there are many societies in which the patterns of child-rearing are so effective in producing adult personalities of this type that special techniques have been developed for training a few selected individuals for leadership. Thus, among the Tanala of Madagascar, eldest sons are given differential treatment from birth, this treatment being designed to develop initiative and willingness to assume responsibility, while other children are systematically disciplined and repressed. Again, individuals who are reared in very small family groups of our own type have a tendency to focus their emotions and their anticipations of reward or punishment on a few other individuals. In this they are harking back unconsciously to a childhood in which all satisfactions and frustrations derived from their own fathers and mothers. In societies where the child is reared in an extended family environment, with numerous adults about, any one of whom may either reward or punish, the normal personality will tend in the opposite direction. In such societies the average individual is incapable of strong or lasting attachments or hatreds toward particular persons. All personal interactions embody an unconscious attitude of: "Oh well, another will be along presently." It is difficult to conceive of such a society embodying in its culture such patterns as our concepts of romantic love, or of the necessity for finding the one and only partner without whom life will be meaningless.

Such examples could be multiplied indefinitely, but the above will serve to show the sort of correlations which are now emerging from studies of personality and culture. These correlations reflect linkages of a simple and obvious sort, and it is already plain that such one-to-one relationships between cause and effect are in the minority. In most cases we have to deal with complex configurations of child-training patterns which, as a whole, produce complex personality configurations in the adult. Nevertheless, no one who is familiar with the results which have already been obtained can doubt that here lies the key to most of the differences in basic personality type which have hitherto been ascribed to hereditary factors. The "normal" members of different societies owe their varying personality configurations much less to their genes than to their nurseries.

While the culture of any society determines the deeper levels of its members' personalities through the particular techniques of child-rearing to which it subjects them, its influence does not end with this. It goes on to shape the rest of their personalities by providing models for their specific responses as well. This latter process continues throughout life. As the individual matures and then ages, he constantly has to unlearn patterns of response which have ceased to be effective and to learn new ones more appropriate to his current place in the society. At every step in this process, culture serves as a guide. It not only provides him with models for his changing rôles but also insures that these rôles shall be, on the whole, compatible with his deep-seated value-attitude systems. All the patterns within a single culture tend to show a sort of psychological coherence quite aside from their functional interrelations. With rare exceptions, the "normal" individual who adheres to them will not be required to do anything which is incompatible with the deeper levels of his personality structure. Even when one society borrows patterns of behavior from another, these patterns will usually be modified and reworked until they become congruous with the basic personality type of the borrowers. Culture may compel the atypical individual to adhere to forms of behavior which are repugnant to him, but when such behavior is repugnant to the bulk of a society's members, it is culture which has to give way.

Turning to the other side of the picture, the acquisition of new behavior patterns which are congruous with the individual's generalized value-attitude systems tends to reinforce these systems and to establish them more firmly as time passes. The individual who spends his life in any society with a fairly stable culture finds his personality becoming more firmly integrated as he grows older. His adolescent doubts and questionings with respect to the attitudes implicit in his culture disappear as he reaffirms them in his adherence to the overt behavior which his culture prescribes. In time he emerges as a pillar of society, unable to understand how anyone can entertain such doubts. While this process may not make for progress, it certainly makes for individual contentment. The state of such a person is infinitely happier than that of one who finds himself compelled to adhere to patterns of overt behavior which are not congruous with the value-attitude systems established by his earliest experiences. The result of such incongruities can be seen in many individuals who have had to adapt to rapidly changing culture conditions such as those which obtain in our own society. It is even more evident in the case of those who, having begun life in one culture, are attempting to adjust to another. These are the "marginal men" whose plight is recognized by all who have worked with the phenomenon of acculturation. Lacking the reinforcement derived from constant expression in overt behavior, the early-established value-attitude systems of such individuals are weakened and overlaid. At the same time, it seems that they are rarely if ever eliminated, still less replaced by new systems congruous with the cultural milieu in which the individual has to operate. The acculturated individual can learn to act and even to think in terms of his new society's culture, but he cannot learn to feel in these terms. At each point where decision is required he finds himself adrift with no fixed points of reference.

In summary, the fact that personality norms differ for different societies can be explained on the basis of the different experience which the members of such societies acquire from contact with their cultures. In the case of a few small societies whose members have a homogeneous heredity, the influence of physiological factors in determining the psychological potentialities of the majority of these members cannot be ruled out, but the number of such cases is certainly small. Even when common hereditary factors may be present, they can affect only potentialities for response. They are never enough in themselves to account for the differing content and organization which we find in the basic personality types for different societies.

SOCIAL CLASS AND PSYCHIATRIC DISORDERS *

〖 AUGUST B. HOLLINGSHEAD AND FREDERICK C. REDLICH [1]

Introduction

The research reported here grew out of the work of a number of men, who, during the last half-century, have demonstrated that the social environment in which individuals live is connected in some way, as yet not fully explained, to the development of mental illness (1). Medical men have approached this problem largely from the viewpoint of epidemiology (2). Sociologists, on the other hand, have analyzed the question either in terms of ecology (3), or of social disorganization (4). Neither psychiatrists nor sociologists have carried on extensive research into the question we are concerned with, namely, interrelations between the class structure and the development of mental illness. However, a few sociologists and psychiatrists have written speculative papers in this area (5).

The present research, therefore, was designed to discover whether a relationship does or does not exist between the class system of our society and

* From August B. Hollingshead and Frederick C. Redlich, "Social Class and Psychiatric Disorders," in *Interrelations between the Social Environment and Psychiatric Disorders*, Milbank Memorial Fund, 1953, 195–207. Reprinted by permission of Dr. Hollingshead and the publisher.

[1] Adapted from a paper read at the annual meeting of the American Sociological Society held in Atlantic City, September 5, 1952, for the 1952 annual meeting of the Milbank Memorial Fund. The research reported here is supported by a grant from the National Institute of Mental Health of the United States Public Health Service to Yale University under the joint direction of Dr. F. C. Redlich, Chairman, Department of Psychiatry, and Professor August B. Hollingshead, Department of Sociology.

mental illnesses. Five general hypotheses were formulated to test some dimension of an assumed relationship between the two. These hypotheses were stated positively; they could just as easily have been expressed either negatively or conditionally. They were phrased as follows:

1. The *prevalence* of psychiatric disorders is related significantly to the class structure.
2. The *types* of psychiatric disorders are connected significantly to the class structure.
3. The type of *psychiatric treatment* is associated with an individual's position in the class structure.
4. The *psycho-dynamics* of psychiatric disorders are correlative to an individual's position in the class structure.
5. *Mobility* in the class structure is neurotogenic.

Each hypothesis is linked to the others, and all are subsumed under the general theoretical assumption of a functional relationship between stratification in society and the prevalence of particular types of mental disorders among given social classes or strata in a specified population. Although our research was planned around these hypotheses, we have been forced by the nature of the problem of mental illness to study *diagnosed* prevalence of psychiatric disorders, rather than *true* or *total* prevalence. This point should be kept in mind, when we present some of our preliminary findings.

Methodological Procedure

The question of how these hypotheses are being tested leads us to a brief discussion of methodological procedures. In the first place, the research is being done by a team of four psychiatrists,[2] two sociologists,[3] and a clinical psychologist.[4] The data are being assembled in the New Haven urban community, which consists of the city of New Haven and surrounding towns of East Haven, North Haven, West Haven, and Hamden. This community had a population of some 250,000 persons in 1950.[5] The New Haven community was selected because the community's structure has been studied intensively by sociologists over a long period. In addition, it is served by a private psychiatric hospital, three psychiatric clinics, and twenty-seven practicing psychiatrists, as well as state and Veterans Administration facilities.

Four technical operations had to be completed before the hypotheses could be tested. Briefly these operations were: (1) the delineation of the class structure of the community; (2) selection of a cross-sectional control of the community's population; (3) the determination of who was receiving

---

[2] Drs. F. C. Redlich, B. H. Roberts, L. Z. Freedman, and Leslie Schaffer.

[3] August B. Hollingshead and J. K. Myers.

[4] Harvey A. Robinson.

[5] The population of each component was as follows: New Haven, 164,443; East Haven, 12,212; North Haven, 9,444; West Haven, 32,010; Hamden, 29,715; and Woodbridge, 2,822.

psychiatric care; and (4) the stratification of both the control sample and the psychiatric patients.

August B. Hollingshead and Jerome K. Myers took over the task of delineating the class system. Fortunately, Maurice R. Davie and his students had studied the social structure of the New Haven community in great detail over a long time span (6). Thus, we had a large body of data we could draw upon to aid us in blocking out the community's social structure.

Stated categorically, the community's social structure is differentiated *vertically* along racial, ethnic, and religious lines; each of these vertical cleavages, in turn, is differentiated *horizontally* by a series of strata or classes. Around the socio-biological axis of race two social worlds have evolved: A Negro world and a white world. The white world is divided by ethnic origin and religion into Catholic, Protestant, and Jewish contingents. Within these divisions there are numerous ethnic schisms. The Irish hold aloof from the Italians, and the Italians move in different circles from the Poles. The Jews maintain a religious and social life separate from the gentiles. The *horizontal* strata that transect each of these vertical divisions are based upon the social values that are attached to occupation, education, one's place of residence in the community, and associations.

The vertically differentiating factors of race, religion, and ethnic origin, when combined with the horizontally differentiating ones of occupation, education, place of residence, and so on, produce a social structure that is highly compartmentalized. The integrating factors in this complex are twofold. First, each stratum of each vertical division is similar in its cultural characteristics to the corresponding stratum in the other divisions. Second, the cultural pattern for each stratum or class was set by the "Old Yankee" core group. This core group provided a cultural model that has shaped the status system of each sub-group in the community. In short, the social structure of the New Haven community is a parallel class structure within the limits of race, ethnic origin, and religion.

This fact enabled us to stratify the community, for our purposes, with an *Index of Social Position.*[6] This *Index* utilizes three scaled factors to determine an individual's class position within the community's stratificational system: (1) ecological area of residence; (2) occupation; and (3) education. Ecological area of residence is scaled into a six point scale; occupation and education are each scaled on a seven point scale. To obtain a social class score on an individual, we must know his address, his occupation, and the number of years of school he has completed. Each of these factors is given a scale score, and the scale score is multiplied by a factor weight determined by a standard regression equation. The factor weights are as follows: Ecological area of residence—5; occupation—8; and education—6. Then the

[6] A detailed statement of the procedures used to develop and validate this *Index* will be described in a forthcoming monograph on this research tentatively titled *Psychiatry and Social Class*, August B. Hollingshead and Frederick C. Redlich.

three factor scores are summed. The resultant score is taken as an index of this individual's position in the community's social class system.

This *Index* enabled us to delineate five *main* social class strata within the horizontal dimension of the social structure. These principal strata or classes may be characterized as follows:

Class I. This stratum is composed of wealthy families whose wealth is often inherited and whose heads are leaders in the community's business and professional pursuits. Its members live in those areas of the community generally regarded as the best; the adults are college graduates, usually from famous private institutions, and almost all gentile families are listed in the New Haven *Social Directory*, but few Jewish families are listed. In brief, these people occupy positions of high social prestige.

Class II. Adults in this stratum are almost all college graduates; the males occupy high managerial positions, many are engaged in the lesser ranking professions. These families are well-to-do, but there is no substantial inherited or acquired wealth. Its members live in the "better" residential areas; about one-half of these families belong to lesser ranking private clubs, but only 5 per cent of Class II families are listed in the New Haven *Social Directory*.

Class III. This stratum includes the vast majority of small proprietors, white-collar office and sales workers, and a considerable number of skilled manual workers. Adults are predominantly high school graduates, but a considerable percentage have attended business schools and small colleges for a year to two. They live in "good" residential areas; less than 5 per cent belong to private clubs, but they are not included in the *Social Directory*. Their social life tends to be concentrated in the family, the church, and the lodge.

Class IV. This stratum consists predominately of semi-skilled factory workers. Its adult members have finished the elementary grades, but the older people have not completed high school. However, adults under thirty-five have generally graduated from high school. Its members comprise almost one-half of the community; and their residences are scattered over wide areas. Social life is centered in the family, the neighborhood, the labor union, and public places.

Class V. Occupationally, Class V adults are overwhelmingly semi-skilled factory hands and unskilled laborers. Educationally most adults have not completed the elementary grades. The families are concentrated in the "tenement" and "cold-water flat" areas of New Haven. Only a small minority belong to organized community institutions. Their social life takes place in the family flat, on the street, or in the neighborhood social agencies.

The second major technical operation in this research was the enumeration of psychiatric patients. A Psychiatric Census was taken to learn the number and kinds of psychiatric patients in the community. *The Psychiatric Census was limited to residents of the community who were patients of a psychiatrist or a psychiatric clinic, or were in a psychiatric institution on December 1, 1950.* To make reasonably certain that all patients were included in the enumeration, the research team gathered data from all public and private psychiatric institutions and clinics in Connecticut and nearby states, and all private practitioners in Connecticut and the metropolitan New York area. It received the cooperation of all clinics and institutions, and of all practitioners except a small number in New York City. We are convinced that we have data on at least 98 per cent of all individuals who were receiving psychiatric care on December 1, 1950.

Forty-four pertinent items of information were gathered on each patient by a team composed of a sociologist and a psychiatrist, and placed on a schedule. Sociological data were collected by the sociologists, and psychiatric data by the psychiatrists. The schedule included such psychiatric items as symptomatology and diagnosis; onset of illness and duration; referral to the practitioner and the institution; the nature and intensity of treatment. On the sociological side, we were interested in age, sex, occupation, education, religion, race and/or ethnicity, family history, marital experiences, and so on.

The third technical research operation was the selection of a control sample from the normal population of the community. The sociologists drew a 5 per cent random sample of households in the community from the 1951 New Haven *City Directory*. This directory covers the entire communal area. The names and addresses in it were compiled in October and November, 1950, a period very close to the date of the Psychiatric Census. Therefore, there were comparability of residence and date of registry between the two population groups. Each household drawn in the sample was interviewed, and data on the age, sex, occupation, education, religion, and income of family members, as well as other items necessary for our purposes were placed on a schedule. This sample is our Control Population.

Our fourth basic operation was the stratification of the psychiatric patients and of the control population with the *Index of Social Position*. As soon as these tasks were completed, the schedules from the Psychiatric Census and the 5 per cent Control Sample were edited and coded, and their data were placed on Hollerith cards. The analyses of these data are in process.

Selected Findings

Before we discuss our findings relative to Hypothesis 1, we want to reemphasize that our study is concerned with *diagnosed* or *treated* prevalence rather than *true* or *total* prevalence. Our Psychiatric Census included only psychiatric cases under treatment, diagnostic study, or care. It did not include individuals with psychiatric disorders who were not being treated on December 1, 1950, by a psychiatrist. There are undoubtedly many individuals in the community with psychiatric problems not being treated by psychiatrists who escaped our net. If we had *true* prevalence figures, many findings from our present study would be more meaningful, perhaps some of our interpretations would be changed, but at present we must limit ourselves to the data we have. With this, caveat in mind, we shall turn to a discussion of our findings relative to our hypotheses.

Hypothesis I. To recapitulate, Hypothesis I, as revised by the nature of the problem, stated: *The diagnosed prevalence of psychiatric disorders is related significantly to an individual's position* in the class structure. A test of this hypothesis involves a comparison of the normal population with the psychiatric population. If no significant difference between the distribution of the normal population and the psychiatric patient population by social class is found, Hypothesis I should be abandoned as untenable. However,

TABLE 1. DISTRIBUTION OF NORMAL AND PSYCHIATRIC POPULATION
BY SOCIAL CLASS

Social class	Normal population [1]		Psychiatric population	
	No.	Per cent	No.	Per cent
I	358	3.1	19	1.0
II	926	8.1	131	6.7
III	2,500	22.0	260	13.2
IV	5,256	46.0	758	38.6
V	2,037	17.8	723	36.8
Unknown [2]	345	3.0	72	3.7
Total	11,422	100.0	1,936	100.0

P < .001 X^2 = 408.16

[1] These figures are preliminary, they do not include Yale students, transients, institutionalized persons, and refusals.

[2] The unknown cases were not used in the calculation of X^2. They are (1) individuals drawn from the sample and (2) psychiatric cases whose class level could not be determined because of paucity of data.

if a significant difference is found between the two populations by class, Hypothesis I should be entertained until more conclusive data are assembled. Pertinent data for a limited test of Hypothesis I are presented in Table 1. The data included in Table 1 show the number of individuals in the normal population and the psychiatric population by class level. What we are concerned with in this test is how these two populations are distributed by class.

When we analysed these population distributions by the use of the chi square method, we found a *very significant* relation between social class and treated prevalence of psychiatric disorders in the New Haven community. A comparison of the percentage distribution of each population by class readily indicates the direction of the distortion of psychiatric cases. For example, Class I comprises 3.1 per cent of the community's population, but only 1.0 per cent of the psychiatric cases. Class V, on the other hand, includes 17.8 per cent of the community's population, but it contributed 36.8 per cent of the psychiatric patients. The chi square tests shows that these differences are far beyond the limits of chance even at the .001 level of probability. On the basis of our data Hypothesis I clearly should be accepted as tenable.

Hypothesis II. Hypothesis II postulated a significant connection between the *type* of psychiatric disorder and social class. This hypothesis involves a test of the ideas that there may be a functional relationship between an individual's position in the class system and the type of psychiatric disorder that he may present. This hypothesis depends, in part, on the question of

TABLE 2. DISTRIBUTION OF NEUROSES AND PSYCHOSES BY SOCIAL CLASS
(Based on the Psychiatric Census)

Social class	Neuroses		Psychoses	
	No.	Per cent	No.	Per cent
I	10	52.6	9	47.4
II	88	67.2	43	32.8
III	115	44.2	145	55.8
IV	175	23.1	583	76.9
V	61	8.4	662	91.6
Total	449		1,442	

P < .001 X^2 = 296.45

diagnosis. Our psychiatrists based their diagnoses on the classificatory system developed by the Veterans Administration (7). For the purposes of this paper, we grouped all cases into two categories: the neuroses and the psychoses. The results of this grouping by social class are given in Table 2.

A study of Table 2 will show that there is a distinct inverse relationship between neuroses and psychoses by social class. The neuroses are concentrated at the higher levels, and the psychoses at the lower end of the class structure. Our team advanced a number of different theories to explain the sharp differences between the neuroses and psychoses by social class. One assumption was that the low percentage of neurotics in the lower classes was a direct reaction to the cost of psychiatric treatment. But as we accumulated data in a series of case studies, for tests of Hypotheses IV and V, we became skeptical of this simple interpretation. Our detailed case records indicate that the social distance between psychiatrist and patient may be more potent than economic considerations in determining the character of psychiatric intervention. This question requires further research.

The high concentration of psychotic patients in the lower strata is probably the product of a very unequal distibution of psychotics in the general population. To test this idea, Hollingshead selected schizophrenics for special study. Because of the severity of this disease the probability is that few schizophrenics are not receiving some kind of psychiatric care. This diagnostic group comprises 44.2 per cent of all patients, and 58.7 per cent of

the psychotics, in our study. Ninety-seven point six per cent of these schizophrenic patients had been hospitalized at one time or another, and 94 per
cent were hospitalized at the time of our census. When we analyse these
patients in terms of their class level we find that there is a highly significant
inverse relationship between social class and schizophrenia.

Hollingshead decided to determine, on the basis of our data, what the
probability of the prevalence of schizophrenia by social class might be in

TABLE 3. COMPARISON OF THE DISTRIBUTION OF THE NORMAL POPULATION
WITH SCHIZOPHRENICS BY CLASS, WITH AN INDEX OF PROBABLE PREVALENCE

Social class	Normal population (5 per cent sample)		Schizophrenics		Index of prevalence
	No.	Per cent	No.	Per cent	
I	358	3.2	6	.7	22
II	926	8.4	23	2.7	33
III	2,500	22.6	83	9.8	43
IV	5,256	47.4	352	41.6	88
V	2,037	18.4	383	45.2	246
Total	11,077	100.0	847	100.0	

the general population. To do this he used a proportional index to learn
whether or not there were differentials in the distribution of the general
population, as represented in our control sample, and the distribution of
schizophrenics by social class. If a social class exhibits the same proportion
of schizophrenia as it comprises of the general population, the index for
that class will be 100. If schizophrenia is disproportionately prevalent in a
social class the index will be above 100; on the other hand, if schizophrenia
is disproportionately low in a social class the index will be below 100. The
bias for or against the probability of schizophrenia in a given social class
is given in the last column of Table 3.

The fact that the Index of Prevalence in Class Level I is only one-fifth as
great as it would be if schizophrenia was proportionately distributed in
this class, and that it is two and one-half times as high in Class Level V as
we might expect on the basis of proportional distribution, gives further
weight to the tenability of Hypothesis II. The fact that the Index of Prevalence is 11.2 times as great in Class V as in Class I is a remarkable finding.

Hypothesis III. Hypothesis III stipulated that the type of psychiatric
treatment a patent receives is associated with his position in the class
structure. A test of this hypothesis involves a comparison of the different
types of therapy being used by psychiatrists on patients in the different
social classes. We encountered many forms of therapy, but they were
grouped under three main types; psychotherapy, organic therapy, and custodial care. The patient population, from the viewpoint of the principal

type of therapy received, was divided roughly into three main types; psychotherapy, organic therapy, and custherapy; 31.7 per cent received organic treatments of one kind or another; and 36.3 per cent received custodial care without treatment. When we analyzed these types of therapy by class a distinctly significant increase occurred in the percentage of cases who received no treatment, other than custodial care, as one moved from the higher to the lower classes. The same finding applies to organic treatment.

TABLE 4. DISTRIBUTION OF THE PRINCIPAL TYPES OF THERAPY
BY SOCIAL CLASS

Social class	Psychotherapy		Organic therapy		No treatment	
	No.	Per cent	No.	Per cent	No.	Per cent
I	14	73.7	2	10.5	3	15.8
II	107	81.7	15	11.4	9	6.9
III	136	52.7	74	28.7	48	18.6
IV	237	31.1	288	37.1	242	31.8
V	115	16.1	234	32.7	367	51.2

P < .001 X² = 336.58

Psychotherapy, on the other hand, was concentrated in the higher classes. Within the psychotherapy category there were sharp differences between the types of psychotherapy administered to the several classes. For example, psychoanalysis was limited to Class I and II, whereas patients in Class V who received any psychotherapy were treated by group methods in the state hospitals. The number and percentage of patients who received each type of therapy is given in Table 4.

The data of Table 4 shows very definitely that Hypothesis III should be retained.

At the moment we do not have data available for a test of Hypotheses IV and V. These hypotheses will be put to a test as soon as we complete work on a series of cases now under close study. Preliminary materials give us the impression that they too will come out positively.

Conclusions and Interpretations

This study was designed to throw new light upon the question of how mental illness is related to social environment. It approached this problem from the perspective of social class to determine if an individual's position in the social system was associated significantly with the development of psychiatric disorders. It proceeded on the theoretical assumption that if mental illnesses were distributed randomly in the population, then the hypotheses we phrased to test the idea that psychiatric disorders are connected in some functional way to the class system would not be found to be statistically significant.

The data we have assembled demonstrate conclusively that mental illness, as measured by diagnosed prevalence, is not distributed randomly in the population of the New Haven community. On the contrary, psychiatric difficulties of so serious a nature that they reach the attention of a psychiatrist are distributed in highly significant ways along social class lines. In addition, types of psychiatric disorders, and the ways patients are treated are strongly associated with social class position.

The objective statistical tests of our hypotheses indicate that there are definite connections between particular types of social environments in which people live, as measured by the social class concept, and the emergence of particular kinds of psychiatric disorders, as measured by psychiatric diagnosis. They do not tell us: (1) what these connections are; nor (2) do they tell us how they are functionally connected to a particular mental illness in a given individual. They do indicate, however, that we are proceeding on promising and safe ground. The next step, we believe, is to turn from the strictly statistical approach to an intensive study of the social environments associated with particular social classes, on the one hand, and of individuals in these environments who do or do not develop mental illnesses, on the other hand. Currently the research team is engaged in this next step, but we are not ready to make a formal report of our findings.

References

1. For example, see: Rosanoff, A. J.: Report of a Survey of Mental Disorders in Nassau County, New York. New York: National Committee for Mental Hygiene, 1916; Stern, Ludwig: Kulturkreis und Form der Geistigen Erkrankung (Sammlung Zwanglosen Abhandlungen aus dem Gebiete der Nerven-und-Geitesdrankheiten), X, No. 2, Halle a. S:C. Marhold, 1913, 1–62; Sutherland, J. F.: Geographical Distribution of Lunacy in Scotland. British Association for Advancement of Science, Glasgow, Sept. 1901; White, William A.: Geographical Distribution of Insanity in the United States. Journal of Nervous and Mental Disease, XXX (1903), 257–279.

2. For example, see: Braatoy, Trygve: Is It Probable that the Sociological Situation Is a Factor in Schizophrenia? Psychiatrica et Neurologica, XII (1937), 109–138; Gerard, Donald L. and Siegel, Joseph: The Family Background of Schizophrenia. The Psychiatric Quarterly, 24 (January, 1950), 47–73; Hyde, Robert W. and Kingsley, Lowell V.: Studies in Medical Sociology, I: The Relation of Mental Disorders to the Community Socio-economic Level. The New England Journal of Medicine, 231, No. 16 (October 19, 1944), 543–548; Hyde, Robert W. and Kingsley, Lowell V.: Studies in Medical Sociology; II: The Relation of Mental Disorders to Population Density. The New England Journal of Medicine, 231, No. 17 (Oct. 26, 1944), 571–577; Hyde, Robert W. and Chisholm, Roderick M.: Studies in Medical Sociology, III: The Relation of Mental Disorders to Race and Nationality. The New England Journal of Medicine, 231, No. 18 (Nov. 2, 1944), No. 3; Malamud, William and Malamud, Irene: A Socio-psychiatric Investigation of Schizophrenia Occurring in the Armed Forces. Psychosomatic Medicine, 5 (Oct. 1943), 364–375; Malzberg, B.: Social and Biological Aspects

of Mental Disease, Utica, N.Y. State Hospital Press, 1940; Roth, William F and Luton, Frank H.: The Mental Health Program in Tennessee: Statistical Report of a Psychiatric Survey in a Rural County. *American Journal of Psychiatry*, 99 (March, 1943), 662–675; Ruesch, J. and others, Chronic Disease and Psychological Invalidism. New York: American Society for Research in Psychosomatic Problems, 1946; Ruesch, J. and Others, Duodenal Ulcer—A Socio-psychological Study of Naval Enlisted Personnel and Civilians, Berkeley and Los Angeles: University of California Press, 1948; Ruesch, Jurgen; Jacobson, Annemarie; and Loeb, Martin B.: Acculturation and Illness. *Psychological Monographs: General and Applied*, 62, No. 5, Whole No. 292, 1948 (American Psychological Association, 1515 Massachusetts Ave., N.W., Washington 5, D.C.); Tietze, C.; Lemkau, Paul; and Cooper, M.: A Survey of Statistical Studies on the Prevalence and Incidence of Mental Disorders in Sample Populations. *Public Health Reports*, 1909–27, 58 (Dec. 31, 1943); Tietze, C.; Lemkau, P.; and Cooper, Marcia: Schizophrenia, Manic Depressive Psychosis and Social-Economic Status. *American Journal of Sociology*, XLVII (Sept. 1941), 167–175.

3. Faris, Robert E. L. and Dunham, H. Warren: Mental Disorders in Urban Areas. Chicago: University of Chicago Press, 1939; Dunham, H. Warren: Current Status of Ecological Research in Mental Disorder, *Social Forces*, 25 (March 1947), 321–326; Felix, R. H. and Bowers, R. V.: Mental Hygiene and Socio-environmental Factors. The Milbank Memorial Fund Quarterly, XXVI (April 1948), 125–147; Green, H. W.: Persons Admitted to the Cleveland State Hospital, 1928–1937, Cleveland Health Council, 1939.

4. Faris, R. E. L.: Cultural Isolation and the Schizophrenic Personality. *American Journal of Sociology*, XXXIX (Sept. 1934), 155–169; Faris, R. E. L.: Reflections of Social Disorganization in the Behavior of a Schizophrenic Patient. *American Journal of Sociology*, I (Sept. 1944), 134–141.

5. For example, *see*: Davis, Kingsley: Mental Hygiene and the Class Structure. *Psychiatry* (February 1938), 55–56; Parsons, Talcott: Psychoanalysis and the Social Structure. *The Psychoanalytical Quarterly*, XIX, No. 3 (1950), 371–384; Dollard, John and Miller, Neal: Personality and Psychotherapy. New York: McGraw-Hill, 1950; Ruesch, Jurgen: Social Technique, Social Status, and Social Change in Illness. Personality in Nature, Society, and Culture. Edited by Clyde Kluckhohn and Henry A. Murray, New York: Alfred A. Knopf, 1949, 117–130; Warner, W. L.: The Society, the Individual and His Mental Disorders. *American Journal of Psychiatry*, 94, No. 2 (September, 1937), 275–284.

6. Davie, Maurice R.: The Pattern of Urban Growth. Studies in the Science of Society, edited by G. P. Murdock, New Haven, 1937, 133–162; Kennedy, Ruby J. R.: Single or Triple Melting-pot Intermarriage Trends in New Haven, 1870–1940. *American Journal of Sociology*, 39 (January 1944), 331–339; McConnell, John W.: *The Influence of Occupation Upon Social Stratification*. Unpublished Ph.D. thesis, Sterling Memorial Library, Yale University, 1937; Myers, Jerome K.: Assimilation to the Ecological and Social Systems of a Community. *American Sociological Review*, 15 (June 1950), 367–372; Minnis, Myra: The Relationship of Women's Organizations to the Social Structure of a City. Unpublished Ph.D. thesis, Sterling Memorial Library, Yale University, 1951.

7. *Psychiatric Disorders and Reactions*, Veterans Administration, Technical Bulletin 10A–78, Washington, October 1947.

THE SIGNIFICANCE OF THE FAMILY
FOR ADJUSTMENT *

(Ross Stagner

The family has a unique place in the development of the individual. First, it is the one group which is common to virtually all human experience. With a very small minority of exceptions, every child is born into a family group and lives in a family for a considerable period of time. Second, the child has his earliest experiences in a family setting, and his interpretation of these experiences will bias all his later perceptions. When he encounters some novel relationship in adult life, he is likely to act on the basis of some apparent similarity to an experience of childhood. Quite unconsciously one's treatment of a business executive, a politician, or an employee may be based upon transference of an attitude from some family situation.

The parents, of course, play a very important role in the child's development. They give affection and dispense discipline. They reward and punish. They encourage certain traits and discourage others, acting either on personal prejudice or as agents of the culture, indoctrinating the values of the larger group. Furthermore, they serve as models which the child imitates. When there is a discrepancy between parental instruction and parental behavior, the child is prone to follow the latter. Thus the parents are major determinants of the hopes, fears, and expectancies of the child.

Love Relationships

The child has no innate tendency to love the parent, and it is unlikely that mother love or father love is innately determined. In the nature of the situation, however, the child should soon come to react positively to the parents, because they are sources of food and comfort. On the parental side, there is strong cultural pressure to manifest love and affection for the child, even if inwardly the parent recognizes that the child is unwanted. In the process of caring for the child's physical needs, the parent is likely also to have a variety of pleasant experiences and to develop a real affection if none was present before.

* From Ross Stagner, *Psychology of Personality*, 2d ed., pp. 345–354, McGraw-Hill Book Company, Inc., New York, 1948. Reprinted by permission of the author and the publisher.

Adequate manifestations of affection are important to the personal integrity of the infant. The concept of security stresses the idea that the child's perception of his universe should be friendly. If he encounters too much unpleasantness, he will evolve a view of life as threatening and hazardous. If, on the other hand, he receives adequate care, cuddling, and attention, he will look upon people as sources of gratification and will see the world as a safe and interesting place to explore.

The study of individual differences in infant development, as related to the amount of affection provided by the mother, for example, encounters many difficulties. Parents are prone to give interviewers or observers the culturally approved answers and performances. Few mothers will openly express dislike of their babies.

The study of orphans, however, makes possible a comparison of children reared in a family setting with others receiving no care except the formalized procedures of an institution. Various investigators have found that the institutional situation is likely to have destructive effects on personal integrity. Ribble (1944) has been especially emphatic about this. Reporting on studies of a series of 600 infants, she asserts that lack of adequate cuddling, stroking, and close physical contact with some adult constitutes a serious handicap. Some of the infants so deprived, she notes, react with marked negativism, others with exaggerated regression. The negativistic symptoms include refusal to suck, vomiting, breath holding, and constipation. The regressive reaction is sometimes even more alarming; a kind of stupor develops, peripheral circulation is poor, and nutrition is very unsatisfactory. Both of these unfavorable reactions have been successfully treated by introducing a foster mother, who regularly strokes, caresses, and fondles the child.

A close relationship between this reaction during infancy and personality at adolescence is suggested by the work of Goldfarb (1943, 1944). This investigator compared two series of adolescents: one group which had been orphaned and placed in institutions prior to the age of eighteen months, the other composed of children who had not been institutionalized until later. The groups which had been placed in the impersonal environment in infancy showed marked symptoms of emotional deprivation; as adolescents they were relatively apathetic and immature. There seemed reason to doubt that they would ever recover from this early lack of affection. Once the expectancy is established in the child's mind that people are cold, indifferent, and unloving, it will be difficult or impossible to replace this by a different attitude.

Infant feeding and personality. The feeding experiences of the infant are likely to be much more important than are his sexual experiences. One naturally wonders whether breast feeding and weaning are demonstrably related to later personality characteristics. The evidence seems contradictory. Peterson and Spano (1941) report that they could find no connection between such experiences and personality at either nursery school or adolescent levels. Hill (1937) reports that his cases show some relationship, and Maslow and Szilagyi-Kessler (1946) show a definite but curvilinear relationship.

The Maslow data are based on reports obtained on college students from their mothers. Reported length of breast feeding was related to scores on a questionnaire measure of security feeling. Highest security was found for those breast fed over a year and those not breast fed at all. Minimum security scores were made by those who were breast fed a rather short time. The authors suggest that the mothers who could not nurse their children gave an excess of caressing and affection to try to compensate for this deprivation. The mothers were mostly foreign born and may be assumed to have felt guilty regarding failure to nurse the child in the traditional manner.

This would suggest that the manner of feeding and caring for the child is more important to security than is breast feeding itself. The infant reacts readily to minimal stimuli of muscular tension, tone of voice, and other expressions of the mother. Dislike for nursing or rejection of the baby may easily be communicated in a manner entirely unconscious and virtually unobservable.

The Oedipus complex. The theory of the Oedipus complex was evolved from studies of adults. It has become plain, however, from studies of children, that there are many instances in which boys become overly attached to their mothers, girls to their fathers. For instance, a little girl of four is heard to say to her father, "Maybe mama will die, then I could marry you and keep house for you." The persistence of such attitudes beyond the fifth year, however, is considered psychologically undesirable; at this age most children begin to give up the attitude of rivalry toward the parent of like sex, and instead adopt the mechanism of identification. At this time the little girl begins to become more feminine in her manner, whereas the boy shifts in the direction of the active, rowdy, aggressive pattern which is socially expected of him.

More important than the relative frequency of this emotional relationship is the problem of its effect upon the personality when it is not successfully resolved. While numerous case studies suggest that mental health is impaired by persistence of the Oedipus complex, single cases are always confused by a number of possible alternative explanations. Stagner and Krout (1940), however, devised a statistical approach which eliminates any bias of the investigators for or against the Freudian theory. They reported that

Boys who wanted to be like father do not worry frequently—but girls who wanted to be like father do. Boys who wanted to be like father have few feelings of remorse, no thoughts of suicide, and think life is definitely worth living

. . . Boys who wanted to be like mother . . . are likely to have feelings of re-morse, dizzy spells, and suspicions of enmity.[1]

The mechanism of identification with the like-sex parent is obviously a basic step in the process of developing in accordance with social expecta-tions. Females in our society are expected to show certain personality traits; a girl who persists in trying to follow the masculine pattern is subject to criticism and disapproval. A boy who is effeminate in his behavior is often an object of ridicule and sarcasm. The occurrence of a family constellation, therefore, in which the child becomes excessively devoted to the parent of the opposite sex and tends toward identification with this parent, is prog-nostic of poor adjustment in later life. A freshman girl who came to our attention because she scored unusually high on the Bernreuter scale for neurotic tendency described her family as follows:

Our family is not a close unit. My father and I have always been close pals.
. . I think Dad is an ideal man. . . . (Mother) is extremely nervous. . . .
We are rather antagonistic toward each other. I rarely confide in anyone, and if
did confide in Mother, I feel that she would not be in harmony with my ideas.

Further questioning elicited the fact that her home was something of a battleground, with each parent vying for her affection with favors of one sort or another. The girl looked upon herself definitely as a rival to her mother. While she had not identified with her father, she showed marked symptoms of insecurity and instability. The same pattern in a boy is indicated in the following autobiographical excerpt:

Yes, I have felt particularly bitter toward him (father) already. The reason lies in his former quarrels with my mother. When some point of difference arose, my mother would invariably before long break into a spell of bitter crying, which would culminate in a period of nervous illness. . . . When I was younger I would simply slink off to bed. . . . I know now that if I ever feel that way again at the age I am now I will not hesitate to interfere physically against him in these matters.

While the excessive affection for the mother is more disguised in this instance, it is obvious that here, too, we have a case of persisting attach-ment. This boy also made a very high score for neurotic tendency on the Bernreuter.

In contrast to these cases of maladjusted personalities who exemplify persistence of the Oedipus relationship, we may cite an instance of an unusually well-adjusted college man, both by Bernreuter test score and personal observation. In this case, the normal shift to identification with the father is clearly apparent:

I think that my strongest attachment in my childhood was to my father. Our interests have always been pretty much the same, i.e., we have enjoyed

[1] Stagner and Krout (1940), p. 351. Reprinted by permission of the American Psychological Association.

fishing, hunting, hiking, and talking as well as working together. He has been the best pal that I have ever had and I was with him much more than with any of my boy friends. . . . When our work was done, we played together. The idea and judgment of us both was considered when we made plans for the things that we did together.

Overprotection. One of the functions of parents is that of protecting the child against physical harm and other potential dangers. The mother who is herself emotionally well adjusted is likely to be able to provide just the proper amount of protection: warning of dangers and preventing the child from entering very dangerous situations, yet allowing the child some freedom to experience and learn his powers and limitations for himself.

When the protective behavior of the parent becomes excessive, it is likely to prevent the child from developing self-reliance and independence of thought and action. While overprotection is generally associated with an apparent excess of affection, it may actually be a disguised manifestation of dislike for the infant. A mother who rejects her baby may feel guilty for having such thoughts and, by the mechanism of reaction formation, go to an extreme in fondling and protecting. Such overprotecting behavior actually hampers and frustrates the child and so, in a way, seems unconsciously to fulfill the mother's original tendency.

It seems generally agreed [Symonds (1939), Newell (1936), Bonney (1941)] that overprotected children manifest emotional immaturity, shyness, and withdrawal from difficult situations. Having developed no confidence in their own abilities, they are likely to lean on adults or stronger playmates for advice and control.

Rejection by parents. The personality of the child can be disturbed by excessive affection (if it involves overprotection and interference with normal development), by persistence of the Oedipus complex beyond its usual time, or by withholding of affection. For most cases labeled "rejection," the actual treatment is likely to be indifference and denial of affection, rather than an active attitude of dislike for the child. In some instances, however, we get this extreme response: e.g., when the child is illegitimate, or was born before the mother was ready for children, or represents a tie binding her to a disliked husband. Various studies of rejection by parents seem agreed that the result is likely to be an aggressive, suspicious, destructive child. The following case, abstracted from a detailed report by Hewitt and Jenkins (1945), is illustrative, if perhaps extreme:

Robert is a fourteen-year-old white boy of illegitimate birth. . . . The chief complaint was made by the mother who states that "Robert is the meanest devil God ever gave any mother for a son." Robert has been known to the juvenile court authorities since the age of nine years. At that time his mother filed a complaint, stating that he had removed the clothing from his smaller sister on two occasions. He had frequently displayed temper tantrums and fits of jealousy of this baby sister seven years younger than himself. . . . Since the age of eight years he had been openly antagonistic toward his mother, even kicking and striking her. . . . Robert . . . was also caught smoking and called his mother numerous vulgar insulting names. . . . He broke a window, ran upstairs, and asserted he was going to jump out and kill himself. When his mother grabbed him, he choked the baby. Two weeks later he ran away again, but returned home without being noticed and took $3.50 from his mother's purse and a dollar bill from his father's suit. . . .

The mother has said that she hunted for things that would hurt her husband's feelings, and finally felt most successful in using Robert. The father and his sister both state that the mother hated Robert from the first, never complimented or praised him, never kept her promises to him. At Christmas time she showed a great partiality toward the other children in the gifts she purchased, and when the father gave things to Robert, he had to conceal their real value from her. For the past six years the mother has taunted Robert and told the relatives that her husband is not the boy's father.[2]

To this extreme degree of rejection the boy's reaction of aggressiveness does not seem excessive. The amount of insecurity and frustration imposed upon him is certainly unusual. That this kind of treatment normally leads to aggressive behavior, if not actual delinquency, is confirmed by the work of FitzSimons (1935), Newell (1936), Symonds (1939), and Bonney (1941).

The manner in which the child perceives his parents (as accepting him or rejecting him, loving or disliking, tender or harsh) may be expected to transfer to his interpretation of society in general. The relationship to the parent serves as a prototype for relationships with industry, government, religion, and other institutions. . . .

Authority and Discipline

The parents are under social pressure to conform to the standards of the culture in various respects and to impose conformity upon their children. The child must learn to respect the taboos of the community and to accept its moral imperatives; in other words, his Super-Ego must be patterned according to the local standards. The second major relationship between parent and child, therefore, is the authority-discipline function of the family.

Firm authority exercised by the parents does not necessarily involve insecurity feelings for the child; in fact, we have some reason to think that a firm, consistent pattern of discipline, suitably intermingled with manifestations of affection, gives maximum security. Inconsistency of discipline may arouse feelings of insecurity because the child feels that he is punished arbitrarily according to the passing mood of the parent.

Parental personality and authority. While the culture imposes certain requirements on the parents, the manner of carrying out these functions differs widely in different families. Some fathers follow the strictly dictatorial tradition of the patriarchy, whereas others attempt to allow the child

[2] Hewitt and Jenkins (1945), pp. 37–41. Reprinted by permission.

a proper amount of practice in self-determination. Unfortunately, the studies available indicate that most parents exercise more rigid authority than psychologists consider advisable for good personality development in the offspring. Stogdill (1931) reports his study as follows:

The test employed has disclosed a definite attitude which may be said to be characteristic of the parent group. The parental attitude differs to a marked degree from that of the mental hygienist group.

The chief characteristics of parental attitudes as distinguished from those of the mental-hygienist group are: (A) greater insistence on observance of moral taboos; (B) greater insistence on parental authority; (C) greater insistence on adherence to group standards and social customs; (D) relative indifference to the effect that such insistence may have upon the child's emotional and mental adjustment to life.[3]

It appears, then, that the undesirable practices with regard to discipline are likely to center around the parent's own personality; viz., the fact that the parent has unsolved emotional complexes related to moral taboos, which prevent him from dealing intelligently with such problems; that the parent has feelings of inferiority or at least a need for dominance, and the act of dominating the child fills this need; and that the parent has identified himself with his group, hence lays emotional stress upon the child's conformity with the standards and customs of the group. These conclusions could be reached on other evidence than that of Stogdill, but his study gives neat confirmation of the general thesis that the parent's treatment of the child is largely determined by his own personality traits.

The effects of such treatment upon the child's personality have been the object of numerous investigations. All of them seem to agree that the trend is for excessive authority and certain types of discipline to be detrimental. Anderson (1940) compared pupils' reports of their own parents with classmates' judgments of pupil personality. Pupils who described their parents as nagging, criticizing, and punishing them strictly were rated by their fellows as quarrelsome, disobedient, and nervous. Lewis (1945) administered a questionnaire test to elementary school children and compared the results with teachers' ratings of parent attitudes. Children with desirable personality patterns were significantly more likely to come from homes with more liberal attitudes toward child care and training.

The results of these studies are subject to numerous exceptions. In individual case work one often encounters an adolescent who not only has been unharmed by an authoritarian home atmosphere, but accepts it, believes it was good for him, and will undoubtedly perpetuate it. The decisive factor apparently is the way in which the child perceives the discipline. Stogdill (1931) comments that college students who "resent having been punished" by their parents and those who feel that their parents were "too moralistic" favor more freedom for children. But a group who simply said they were

[3] Stogdill (1931), p. 13.

"severely punished" favor *less* freedom for children, *i.e.*, they have adopted the parental pattern.

Parents as Models

The family is a learning situation, and much of the learning is related to the aspects that we have already described, *viz.*, affection and discipline. A third feature must be noted, as well. This relates to the fact that the parent is also a model, a pattern which may be imitated by the child—or which may be rejected, in which case the child may strive for a completely different pattern.

Patterson (1943b) has reported on observations of 117 mothers and their children. The mothers took the Bernreuter Personality Inventory; the children were studied by nursery-school ratings, the Brown inventory for children, and other devices. Generally speaking, the results are inconclusive. The correlations obtained were not significant, but they were generally in the expected direction: for example, high neurotic scores of mothers were positively related to jealousy, excitability, and sensitivity of children.[4]

The same inconclusive but positive trend is found in comparisons of adolescents with their parents. Hoffeditz (1934) and Sward and Friedman (1935) correlated scores on the Bernreuter inventory for fairly large groups of subjects. In no case are the data such as to indicate close parallels between parent and child.

Hoffeditz collected Bernreuter inventory scores for 100 fathers, 100 mothers, 111 sons, and 145 daughters. Since more than one child is found in most of the families, she computed not only the direct correlation of each parent with each child, but also the correlation of the average of the two parents with the average of the children.

Table 1 summarizes the individual parent-child correlations. It indicates only very low relationships on these traits. However, it is notable that the father-son correlation is each time higher than the mother-son correlation; The mother-daughter coefficient similarly is greater than that for fathers and daughters. The same general tendency is reported by Sward and Friedman, who found that children correlated with like-sex parents .29, .31, .31 and .11,[5] while cross-sex parents correlated .16, .24, .27 and .05. These findings seem to support our general view on the importance of identification.

---

[4] The complexity of interpretation of such studies may be noted here. At least three mechanisms might be postulated to account for this correlation: (1) the mother is sensitive to emotional situations, and the child has inherited the same physiological mechanism; (2) the mother's excessive responsiveness to emotional stimuli has often upset the child, changing the child's threshold in the direction of greater sensitivity; and (3) the child is simply imitating. At present we have no convincing data as to which of these is correct or whether all three are involved.

[5] For groups respectively of Jewish boys, Jewish girls, gentile boys, and gentile girls.

Hoffeditz computed the correlation of the average of the parents with the average of the children for the 100 families studied. These correlations for the three trait measures, N, S, and D, were respectively .28, .21 and .29. Each of these is higher than any of the coefficients reported in Table 1 for the corresponding trait measure. This suggests that a more definite relationship is predictable for a group of children and a group of parents than for any individual parent and child. All such correlations are, of course, reduced by the fact that the child is molded not only by parents, but also by teachers, friends, and playmates.

TABLE 1. PARENT-CHILD SIMILARITIES ON THE BERNREUTER INVENTORY

Scale		Mothers	Sons	Daughters
N (emotionality)	Fathers	.16	.06	.23
	Mothers	. . .	.01	.27
S (self-sufficiency)	Fathers	.09	.20	.09
	Mothers	. . .	.05	.16
D (dominance)	Fathers	.15	.19	.20
	Mothers	. . .	.02	.28

Parent-child clusters in attitudes. Newcomb (1937) correlated attitudes toward the church, war, and communism for a large number of parents and children. The correlations of parents with their children were as follows: church, .63; war, .44; and communism, .56. These correlations are considerably higher than those reported for the more general traits of personality reported in the preceding paragraphs. It is likely that attitudes on specific questions are handed down in much more direct fashion, by what amounts in many cases to deliberate instruction on controversial topics. The personality traits are less subject to such indoctrination.

Newcomb then attempted to see if children agreeing with their parents on one attitude agreed on others also. By selecting cases arbitrarily he raised the parent-child correlation on the church from .63 to .96; for this group the correlation on communism was raised from .56 to .62 (only slight increase). When the selection was done so as to raise the communism correlation to .96, agreement as to attitude toward the church was raised from .63 to .74. Thus we see some tendency for children agreeing on communism to conform also on religious attitude. The coefficients on attitude to war were not changed by these manipulations, presumably indicating that it was unrelated to the church-communism cluster.

Another device used by Newcomb was to select certain parents whose attitudes on church and communism were highly correlated (favorable to religion, unfavorable to communism) and then compute the church-communism correlation in the children. This selected group of children showed a correlation of .60 on these two attitudes, while in the whole group the two had correlated only .43. It thus appears that when parents have highly consistent attitudes, the same sort of consistency is more likely to appear in the children.

Newcomb's data appear to justify the conclusion that there is a tendency, albeit small, for children who are in close agreement with parents on one attitude to be somewhat closer than the average on other attitudes; and for parents whose attitudes are internally consistent to have children whose attitudes reflect this consistency to some extent. All these processes are entirely in harmony with the view that the child receives suggestions from the parent which are important, even if not always decisive in determining his attitudes.

References

Anderson, J. P. "A Study of the Relationships between Certain Aspects of Parental Behavior and Attitudes and the Behavior of Junior High School Pupils." *Teach. Coll. Contr. Educ.*, 1940, No. 809.

Bonney, M. E. "Parents as Makers of Social Deviates." *Social Forces*, 1941, 20, 77–87.

FitzSimons, M. J. "Some Parent-Child Relationships as Shown in Clinical Case Studies." New York: Teachers College, Columbia University, 1935.

Goldfarb, W. "Effects of Early Institutional Care on Adolescent Personality." *J. exp. Educ.*, 1943, 12, 106–129.

Goldfarb, W. "Effects of Early Institutional Care on Adolescent Personality: Rorschach Data." *Amer. J. Orthopsychiat.*, 1944, 14, 441–447.

Hewitt, L. E. and R. L. Jenkins. *Fundamental Patterns of Maladjustment: The Dynamics of Their Origin.* Springfield, Ill.: State of Illinois, 1946.

Hill, J. "Infant Feeding and Personality Disorders." *Psychiat. Quart.*, 1937, 11, 356–382.

Hoffeditz, E. Louise. "Family Resemblances in Personality Traits." *J. soc. Psychol.*, 1934, 5, 214–227.

Lewis, W. D. "Influence of Parental Attitudes on Children's Personal Inventory Scores." *J. genet. Psychol.*, 1945, 67, 195–201.

Maslow, A. H. and I. Szilagyi-Kessler. "Security and Breast-feeding." *J. abnorm. soc. Psychol.*, 1946, 41, 83–85.

Newcomb, T. M. and G. Svehla. "Intra-family Relationships in Attitude." *Sociometry*, 1937, 1, 180–205.

Newell, H. A. "A Further Study of Maternal Rejection." *Amer. J. Orthopsychiat.* 1936, 6, 357–401.

Patterson, C. H. "Note on Bernreuter Personality of Mothers and Some Measures of Child Personality." *J. soc. Psychol.*, 1943, 17, 89–92.

Peterson, C. H. and F. L. Spano. "Breast Feeding, Maternal Rejection, and Child Personality." *Character and Pers.*, 1941, 10, 62–66.

Ribble, M. "Infantile Experience in Relation to Personality Development." In Hunt, J. McV. *Personality and the Behavior Disorders.* New York: The Ronald Press Company, 1944.

Stagner, R. and M. H. Krout. "Correlational Study of Personality Development and Structure." *J. abnorm. soc. Psychol.*, 1940, 35, 339–355.

Stogdill, R. M. "Parental Attitudes and Mental Hygiene Standards." *Ment. Hyg.*, 1931, 15, 813–827.

Sward, K. and M. B. Friedman. "Family Resemblance in Temperament." *J. abnorm. soc. Psychol.*, 1935, 30, 256–261.

Symonds, P. M. *Psychology of Parent-Child Relationships.* New York: D. Appleton-Century Company, Inc., 1939.

B. Dynamics of adjustment

The papers which follow discuss various ways in which the process of adjustment has been conceptualized. While the authors of these papers frequently differ in their theoretical orientations and specific ideas concerning adjustment, they adopt the general view that man's behavior is a dynamic process resulting from the interplay of forces impinging on him. They base their ideas on the assumption that man is a changing, modifiable organism. The personality characteristics and behavior man displays are the result of the continuous interaction of internal and external stimulation. Conflicts and frustrations are viewed as inevitable, and in order to resolve them, man learns or adopts different modes of thinking, believing, and acting. In this group of readings the adjustment process is analyzed, and some of the methods, techniques, and styles of adjustment which are typical in our culture are considered.

Anxiety is usually regarded as central to an understanding of the process of adjustment, and it is this topic which the first paper discusses. Basowitz et al. summarize many of the ideas associated with the concept of anxiety and describe the part this phenomenon plays in both well-adjusted and maladjusted behavior. When the individual lacks effective methods of handling anxiety, maladjustment occurs. He may lack techniques to offset anticipated danger and consequently will continue feeling anxious; or he may use inappropriate methods which themselves promote further conflict and anxiety. Mowrer in his article entitled "Neurosis: A Disorder of Conditioning or Problem Solving?" expounds on the importance of developing adequate methods for dealing with conflicts and frustrations in order to achieve a satisfactory adjustment. He contrasts his point of view that maladjustment constitutes a disorder in problem solving with that of other investigators who emphasize the part conditioning plays in the development of maladjustments. For Mowrer adjustment occurs by the same process as in other types of problem solving, i.e., by trial and error which results in the learning of effective methods for dealing with the dangers, anxieties, and conflicts of everyday life.

Horney adopts the position that conflict is the basis of maladjustment and specifies the importance of conflicts associated with the individual's interactions with others. She refers to a *basic conflict* underlying all maladjustment which involves the individual's ambivalences about the role he wishes to play with others. Where the individual overemphasizes one style of relating to others (for example, a highly aggressive attitude) at the expense of other possible modes of interacting, the basis for increased conflict and friction are present. Adjustment, according to Horney, develops from a harmonious, flexible style of interacting with others. Similarly, the paper by Shyne on the psychology of Alfred Adler analyzes the adjustment process in terms of the individual's relationships and methods of coping with his environment. Especially important in Adler's thinking is the individual's view of his own adequacy and his particular methods of attempting to exert his influence over others. Maladjustment results from the person's efforts to overcompensate for strong feelings of inferiority by attempting to dominate and control others. On the other hand, Adler's position equates adjustment with the ability to evaluate oneself realistically and to develop social relations which are beneficial to others and not merely designed for purposes of self-aggrandizement.

In recent years considerable attention has been devoted to the various methods of adjustment or patterns of behavior characteristic of individuals and groups when dealing with conflict and frustration. Since Freud's description of the "ego defenses," increasing emphasis has been placed on the classification of specific styles of adjusting and the motivations and purposes underlying them. The study of characteristic methods of dealing with conflict and anxiety is especially relevant to an understanding of the adjustment process. On the one hand, defensive techniques enable the individual to maintain a sense of equilibrium and mitigate the anxiety and discomfort he would experience without them. On the other hand, some defensive maneuvers appear to result in negative consequences which in turn give rise to additional stress and anxiety for the individual. It follows then that the relationship between adjustment and defense mechanisms is a complex one depending on numerous factors such as the frequency of the occurrence of a particular method of defense, the situations in which it occurs, and the reactions of others to it. For example, an individual's tendency to retreat into fantasy whenever he encounters frustration may enable him to maintain a sense of composure and balance under adverse conditions. But a frequent or intense withdrawal into fantasy, or its occurrence at inappropriate times, or the intolerance of others for this type of reaction may promote further difficulty for the individual rather than aid him.

The three readings in this group describe typical mechanisms and patterns of adjustment. In the selection on defense mechanisms, Coleman clearly defines and illustrates common reactions to embarrassing, unpleasant, or conflict situations. By such techniques as rationalizing, denying, or projecting, unpleasantnesses are alleviated and our sense of harmony restored. In fact, the occasional service of such responses in alleviating anxiety reactions and discomfort is a valuable aid to adjustment. These techniques, however, are only palliative and do not deal with the source of the discomfort. For this reason the frequent occurrence of defensive techniques is usually interpreted as indicative of a relatively intense area of conflict with which the individual seems unable to cope directly.

The next two papers describe styles or patterns of adjustment, discuss conditions which influence the development of such characteristics, and indicate some of the purposes which they serve for the individual. The excerpt taken from Fromm's book *Man for Himself* describes variations in what the author refers to as the *nonproductive personality*. For Fromm the truly healthy individual has developed a sense of identity which enables him to actualize his abilities and potentials so that he is in effect a productive member of society. The nonproductive character orientations, however, are those in which the individual has not learned to relate to others in a way which will enable him to fulfill his basic needs and potentials. Instead he continues to seek adjustments by ineffective styles of behavior which serve to increase the frustrations and conflicts he experiences. In addition, Fromm pays a great deal of attention to the role culture plays in promoting adjustment. The final paper by Riesman describes three personality patterns characteristic of individuals as they conform to their society. Each mode of conforming, whether it is by following tradition, adhering to the expectations of others, or deciding independently how one should behave, represents the individual's efforts to satisfy his needs in his particular society.

ANXIETY *

⟦ Harold Basowitz, Harold Persky, Sheldon J. Korchin, and Roy R. Grinker

The problem of anxiety occupies a central position in the theory of psychopathology and psychosomatic dysfunctions. Stated briefly, anxiety is the signal of danger which mobilizes the human organism's resources at all

* From Harold Basowitz, Harold Persky, Sheldon J. Korchin, and Roy R. Grinker, *Anxiety and Stress*, pp. 1–8, McGraw-Hill Book Company, Inc., New York, 1955. Reprinted by permission of Dr. Basowitz and the publisher. Slightly edited.

levels of functioning in the interests of conservation, defense, and self-preservation. Yet it is also the sign of disorganization which in larger quantities leads only to further disturbance and regression of functioning. At all levels of anxiety there are various combinations in degrees of loss of homeostatic control, and attempts at mastery to regain control.

Although the central position of anxiety in psychological dysfunction has been long recognized, our present understanding of the problem is not much more complete than Freud's (1936) final sentence on the subject, '*non liquet.*" Freud early recognized the importance of anxiety and first formulated it to be a result of a blocking of sexual drives and the conversion of libido into noxious substances. This transformation hypothesis was not verified, clinically or experimentally. With the development of ego psychology it was postulated that anxiety is the signal recognized by the conscious or preconscious ego as an indicator of present or future dangers. This in turn initiates various psychological and behavioral maneuvers in an attempt to preserve the integrity of the person and to maintain homeostasis. Many of the psychiatric and psychosomatic syndromes, as well as basic personality types, are thus viewed as chronic defenses against anxiety. However, the consequence of anxiety need not be neurosis but may be integrated and healthy behavior. In response to the threat, signaled by anxiety, the organism may mobilize and intensify its capacities toward a higher level of functioning, learning, and new forms of adjustment.

Although anxiety has the important role of signaling danger and leading to protective defense, it may also, in greater intensity and in the absence of adequate defense mechanisms, be the symptom of disturbance and itself be the end product of a breakdown of integration. In this state, in which anxiety is discharged unabated and defense is no longer possible, we speak of a *free anxiety* and clinically of an *anxiety state.* Thus, anxiety has two functional roles in our conception of psychopathology—first, as the precursor of the defensive and adjustive processes, and, secondly, as the consequence of their breakdown. It has been pointed out often that the state of affairs which anxiety (qua signal) warns against is the release of the terrible uncontrolled anxiety (qua symptom) itself. Thus, in Goldstein's view (1939, 1951) anxiety is the signal that catastrophe is imminent, and catastrophe is the state in which all integrated behavior collapses and only anxiety remains. As Rapaport (1954) states, affects such as anxiety, when released from control through the processes of psychological regression, are liberated in formidable intensities, but minimal ranges.

As a signal within the ego, anxiety develops at the time when ego functions have matured and object relationships are possible. As a discharge phenomenon, it is related to early trauma and later in life becomes an automatic response to situations threatening the organism's internal equilibrium. This form of anxiety often strains many psychosomatic functions to degrees beyond their physiological or homeostatic range, hence may lead to irreversible regressive or diseased states. Although psychoanalytic theory postulates a dualistic concept of anxiety—signal and automatic response—a monistic concept has also been suggested. According to this view anxiety may be traced in a continuum from a signal to a traumatic state from the frame of reference of the ego and its control. Thus, regression of the ego results in increasing amounts of anxiety from signal, to preparation for action, to traumatic state, associated with corresponding transitions from the most to the least degrees of ego control.

As Freud pointed out, anxiety has a central and crucial position in body-mind relationships for it is a feeling state associated with physiological changes and their perceived effects. It has an important role in organismic economy as the agent and consequence of adaptive and disordered behavior. Defenses against anxiety or reactions to it at various ages result in symptoms grouped as special psychiatric syndromes; and the physiological components are especially important in the development of psychosomatic disturbances. We believe that anxiety may be studied as a phenomenon in its own right as a psychological process, although its social, physiological, neurological and biochemical concomitants, causes, or effects are intimately and complexly related. The total field of anxiety requires the study of basic psychosomatic-social relations. However, the study of anxiety as such is the study of feeling states and requires psychological methods. But such a study is not concerned with anxiety which would be present if certain psychological defenses were removed, nor is anxiety as a feeling measurable by physiological indices which may be sequentially or concomitantly related to it. Instead, anxiety as an affect must be defined as a conscious, reportable dread of impending and unlocalized disaster.

In the normal, intact, and well-functioning individual, many relations among psychophysiological systems may be unobservable or unmeasurable. In the state of anxiety, however, the very intensity of the disruption may bring into view and make available to scientific inquiry processes central to all organismic functioning, normal as well as pathological. Thus, our interest in the understanding of normal human biology also leads us to the "experiment" provided by those conditions in which "exploded" views of psychological and psychosomatic processes may be available. Nonetheless we recognize the danger inherent in this logic because what is observable in the disrupted state may not correspond to the nature of organismic functioning under more quiescent and normal conditions. A similar caution was made by Goldstein in his study of the brain-injured, i.e., that the isolated part processes visible in the cortically damaged may be quite different qualitatively from the homologous processes of the normal. But just as the study of neurosis, as well as brain injury, has provided otherwise unobtainable understanding of personality organization, so we expect that the study of the anxiety state will similarly contribute to our understanding of normal functioning. Thus, we study anxiety because its study promises increasing knowledge of the problems of neurosis and because of the conviction that knowledge so gained will necessarily contribute to general personality and psychosomatic theory.

A Definition of Anxiety

Within the limits of this book anxiety is defined as the conscious and reportable experience of intense dread and foreboding, conceptualized as internally derived and unrelated to external threat. Differentiation is not always possible between the fear response to actual and real danger and the anxiety response so often characterized as "objectless." Similarly, we cannot always differentiate the reactions against or accompanying fear from those associated with anxiety. States of fear are conceived as temporary, more related to external events, and preparatory to appropriate behavior of the organism; anxiety is more usually derived from internal psychological problems and therefore is chronically present, leading to more serious, long-lasting somatic and psychological changes.

Under certain conditions which seem to be associated with usual or minimal quantities of danger, the organism reacts overwhelmingly as though it were confronted with a life or death situation. Here anxiety exists even though there is a nucleus of cause for fear. Anxiety then is a reaction which signifies an internal meaningfulness to the person experiencing it, and the subject tends to attribute the meaningfulness to reality (*Grinker and Robbins, 1954*).

Hence it is difficult to establish sharp distinctions between fear and anxiety.

We may first classify anxiety into certain categories. Alertness characterizes all living beings for it is a derivative of protoplasmic irritability and animal vigilance, necessary for self-preservation. The state of apprehension is an increase of alertness to prepare for special anticipated tasks or those which currently confront the individual. This feeling is associated with an increased speed and efficiency of psychological performance and with activation of physiological preparedness, some of which is perceived by the involved person. Free anxiety is pathological or neurotic and corresponds to the subjective, consciously experienced, reportable dread mentioned above. It is to some degree facilitative and in other ways destructive to psychosomatic functions. At any rate, there is a notable increase and recognition of somatic participation in this stage.

In a still larger conceptual scheme we may extend this continuum to include psychodynamic states of a more primitive nature closely allied to the earliest experiences of the person. Thus anxiety may still further increase in intensity and painfulness during agitation or panic. This exposes to some degree the narcissistic core as threshold levels of disappointment are reached. These are based on past experiences of lack of infantile satisfaction or deficiencies in care or nutriment. This form of anxiety may be associated with diffuse or global expressions of primitive physiological precursors of rage as the final attempt at attaining substances or relief from tension analogous to the apparent rageful crying of the infant. Ultimately, further regression and hopelessness result in psychological retardation, dryness, slowing of all visceral processes, apathy, and death.

From the psychological frame of reference anxiety cannot be conceived apart from the total ego organization. In addition to changes in ego control already mentioned, there is always to some degree a weakening of ego boundaries. The "objectlessness" of the anxiety state may reflect an inability of the organism to distinguish self from object. It is for this reason, and not only because the object itself may be unconscious, that the person experiences being enveloped by a threatening world in which he cannot distinguish dangerous from safe, relevant from irrelevant, real from unreal. Paralleling the dissolution of ego boundary is a corresponding restriction of time perspective. The immediacy of the present is so great that future and past decrease in significance as guides to behavior. Apprehension is concerned with coming events; in free anxiety these are uniformly dangerous, immediate, and interminable.

As we have stated, anxiety should be studied by psychological means and categorized according to the previously mentioned levels and to states of ego organization expressed in degrees of anxiety proneness or type and rigidity of defenses. Within such qualifications, anxiety may be quantified. Then simultaneous measures of overt total behavior or performance in a specified task, psychological functions such as perception, decision, memory, etc., physiological actions of somatic musculature, cardiovascular and respiratory systems indicative of action or for its preparation, and indices of biochemical functions all in some manner measure various aspects of anxiety.

Anxiety as a warning signal can be measured whether the signal is cued off psychologically through perception of a meaningful symbol evoking memories of past experiences or through transcription of physiological signals into symbols of significance to the organism. It is possible to measure the intensity of the signal before disintegrative effects take place by purely psychological means: introspection by the subject, identification processes by the observer.

The psychological symbol which sets off anxiety cannot be measured except by the resultant effects. It has meaning to the self or it does not. It reaches threshold level or not. The effective cue sets off the signal which can be estimated in terms of the reportable feelings. Yet these feelings are only partly signal processes, measurable as signals only in lesser degrees of anxiety. In greater degrees of anxiety what is measurable consists of a complex process. In addition to the signal there is the state of the organism's equilibrium—the measure of its position in its homeostatic range; the direction in which it is moving; the vast array of part cyclic processes in preparation, action, or disruption and their time-space relations; and finally the responses utilized.

Because of the many meanings of the term *anxiety*, in both common and scientific parlance, the term *free anxiety* was introduced to characterize the type of anxiety referred to [here] (Grinker and Spiegel, 1945). For brevity we will use the term anxiety throughout . . . but restrict its meaning to the conscious and reportable emotional state already discussed. In this usage a concept such as "unconscious" anxiety is impossible, although in the past it has been used to refer to that status of the patient in which a change in defense mechanisms, or a removal of a neurotic symptom, would result in the visible production of anxiety. We hold here that a patient cannot be called anxious if he is presently without affect, whatever his condition *might* be should his status change. Similarly, the physiological concomitants of anxiety, for example, such things as sweating, pupillary dilation, cardiovascular changes, etc., may accompany but do not themselves define a condition of anxiety.

Certainly the conscious, painful, present affective state is part of the total organismic condition and the study of the coordinate changes in psychological and physiological functions is vital for our understanding of anxiety. It is the hope of the present research to contribute to this goal. But for conceptual clarity the term anxiety is restricted to the description of the emotional experience and will not be used to describe the correlate changes.

Anxiety may be considered essentially a human function because it is associated with the capacity for delayed reaction, choice of action, self-reflection of motivation, and the capacity for the projection of the self into the future. It follows from the definition that anxiety may be present only in man, who has evolved a form of self-reflective consciousness. However, all living structures possess the property of irritability necessary to respond to stimuli in the service of perpetuating life and the maintenance of integration. In more evolved animals this irritability is organized into integrated systems which maintain alertness preparatory to action—vigilance (Liddell, 1950). Anxiety as a feeling state involving both somatic and psychological participation is conceived as an extension of irritability and vigilance.

The Arousal of Anxiety—The Concept of Stress

In general, anxiety may be aroused by any condition which threatens the integrity of the organism. For May (1950) "anxiety is the apprehension cued off by a threat to some value which the individual holds essential to his existence as a personality." From this viewpoint, any stimulus may have cue value, provided that it implies a threat to an essential value. Since these are largely determined through individual experience and learning and the threat-forewarning cues are similarly individual products, it follows that a wide variety of stimuli may arouse anxiety and these may be measured only as reaching or not reaching threshold levels.

Thus, any stimulus may in principle arouse an anxiety response because of the particular meaning of threat it may have acquired for the particular individual. However, we distinguish a class of stimuli which are *more likely* to produce disturbance in most individuals. The term *stress* has been applied to this class of conditions. Thus we can conceive a continuum of stimuli differing in meaning to the organism and in their anxiety-producing consequences. At one end are such stimuli or cues, often highly symbolic, which have meaning only to single or limited numbers of persons and which to the observer may appear as innocuous or trivial. At the other end are such stimuli, here called stress, which by their explicit threat to vital functioning and their intensity are likely to overload the capacity of most organisms' coping mechanisms.

Anxiety has been defined in terms of an affective response; stress is the stimulus condition likely to arouse such response. Ultimately we can truly speak of a *stress situation* only when a given response occurs, but for schematic purposes as well as consistency with common usage, we may use the term stress to designate certain kinds of stimulating conditions without regard for response. Such stimuli are called stress because of their assumed or potential effect, although we well know that in any given case the organism's adaptive capacity, threshold, or previous learning may preclude any disturbance of behavior.

In the discussion thus far on stress, we have referred primarily to the psychological level. Stress is, of course, an appropriate and certainly an important concept in the total study of biological as well as psychological phenomena. Moreover, the essential definition of stress remains the same regardless of the level of functioning to which it is referred. Stress is the threat to the fulfillment of basic needs, the maintenance of regulated (homeostatic) functioning, and to growth and development. The response will differ, depending on level, and ranges from cellular changes to individual and social phenomena such as panic and anomie. Our interest [here] is primarily on the psychological affective response of anxiety and the changes in psychological, physiological, and biochemical functions related to it as they are evoked by stress. But the study of stress in its pan-human aspects is a basic part of psychosomatic research.

References

Freud, S.: *The Problem of Anxiety*, W. W. Norton & Co., Inc., New York, 1936.

Goldstein, K.: *The Organism*, American Book Company, New York, 1939.

Goldstein, K.: "On Emotions: Considerations from the Organismic Point of View," *J. Psychol.*, 31:37, 1951.

Grinker, R. R., and F. P. Robbins: *Psychosomatic Case Book*, The Blakiston Division, McGraw-Hill Book Co., Inc., New York, 1954.

Grinker, R. R., and J. P. Spiegel: *Men under Stress*, The Blakiston Division, McGraw-Hill Book Co., Inc., New York, 1945.

Liddell, H. S.: "The Role of Vigilance in the Development of Animal Neurosis," in Hoch, P. H., and J. Zubin: *Anxiety*, Grune & Stratton, Inc., New York, 1950.

May, R.: *The Meaning of Anxiety*, The Ronald Press Co., New York, 1950.
Rapaport, D.: "On the Psychoanalytic Theory of Affects," *Internat. J. Psycho-Analysis*, 34:1, 1954.

NEUROSIS: A DISORDER OF CONDITIONING OR PROBLEM SOLVING? *

⟮ O. H. MOWRER

I. The Two-factor Conception of Learning

It will be useful, as background for the discussion which follows, to make explicit the distinction intended by the two terms, "conditioning" and "problem solving," as used in the title of this paper. There is an ever-growing recognition that neurosis and its treatment are learning phenomena, but traditional learning principles and concepts have not provided a fully satisfactory framework for dealing with clinical problems, either theoretically or practically. One of the reasons for this, it appears, is that the two types of learning designated here as conditioning and problem solving have not been precisely enough defined or their functional inter-relatedness sufficiently understood.

The distinction which will be emphasized here takes as its point of departure the fact that there are, in all higher organisms, two great response systems: one behavioral and the other physiological. The behavioral responses, commonly characterized as "voluntary," are mediated by the central nervous system acting upon the striate, or skeletal, musculature; whereas, the physiological responses are mediated by the autonomic nervous system acting upon smooth muscles and glands, and are commonly characterized as "involuntary." These two great systems are analogous, in their functioning to the action units and the supply units for an army: one does the organism's work and the other keeps the organism serviced.

Both of these response systems can be modified by "experience," *i.e.*, both of them are amenable to change through learning, but the type of change, the type of learning is very different in the two cases. The behavioral system is especially designed for problem solving. It starts with a problem, a drive, a need, and keeps the organism performing a varying succession of acts, until one of them achieves the desired result. If the environment is reasonably consistent, this response, the "successful" one, will soon become

* From O. H. Mowrer, "Neurosis: A Disorder of Conditioning or Problem Solving?" *Annals of the New York Academy of Sciences*, 56, 2, 273–288. Reprinted by permission of the author and the Managing Editor, *Annals of the New York Academy of Sciences*.

the response which the organism regularly makes whenever the same need
or problem recurs. By a process variously called selective learning, problem
solving, trial-and-error or, more properly, trial-error-and-success, the organism thus is enabled to modify its behavior in the direction of greater
efficiency and, in general, improved chances of survival. The most familiar
laboratory demonstrations of this kind of learning are those of E. L. Thorndike.

The physiological system, on the other hand, in so far as it is amenable
to learning, presents a very different picture. In general, physiological responses, as responses, are invariant. The heart, for example, may beat rapidly or slowly, but the only thing it can do is to beat; in contrast, let us say,
to an arm, which can do an almost infinite variety of things. The beating
of the heart, however, like various other physiological responses, can perform one very remarkable feat: it can "change its problem," in the sense
of being activated by different stimuli. The "adequate" stimulus for increased heart beat is a metabolic depletion state of some sort, such as that
produced by exercise. It may come about, however, that some initially
neutral stimulus regularly precedes the physiologically adequate stimulus
and, when this happens, it is not uncommon to find the heart accelerating
to the neutral stimulus, or "signal," alone. The heart is still just beating,
but it is now beating faster in response to a new stimulus, in anticipation
of the occurrence of the original, "physiologically adequate" one. This kind
of learning is the familiar one which Pavlov called conditioning and made
famous by demonstrations involving the salivary response. It is sometimes
alternatively called associative shifting, sign learning, or stimulus substitution, in contrast to the response substitution which is characteristic of solution learning.

These two types of learning, solution learning and sign learning, or the
learning of means and the learning of meanings, have been recognized for
a very long time and are loosely referred to, respectively, as "habits" and
"attitudes." The distinction between them, however, has never been drawn
with the requisite degree of clarity nor has the functional significance of
each with respect to the other been systematically developed. For a long
time Thorndike and his followers placed a quite unnecessary limitation
upon their concept of solution learning by restricting their experiments to
problems involving only such primary drives as hunger and thirst. Pavlov
likewise failed to stress the motivational implications of conditioning. He
spoke, for example, of the conditioning of the salivary response but paid
no attention to its appetitive concomitants. He did not see—indeed, his
systematic biases were such as to compel him to ignore—what is now coming to be generally recognized; namely, that perhaps the most important
feature of conditioning is that it is a mechanism whereby new drives, i.e.,
the "emotions," are brought into existence and on the basis of which living
organisms engage in some of their most energetic problem-solving behavior.

If, for example, an initially neutral stimulus is associated once or twice with a noxious stimulus, such as an electric shock, the neutral stimulus alone will, to be sure, later produce a rapid pulse and other physiological changes. The psychologically more significant fact, however, is that this stimulus, or danger signal (probably through the mediation of physiological reactions, although this is not yet fully established) causes the organism to be afraid and thus prompts it to engage in behavior which may have the highly useful function of averting the impact of the noxious stimulus proper.

The anticipatory or avoidance reactions that living organisms may develop under the foregoing circumstances have often been mis-called "conditioned responses." In the interests of a spurious kind of "objectivity," the intervening variable of fear (Brown and Farber, 1951)[1] has been ignored, with the result that many known experimental facts could not be accounted for and the gap between learning theory and clinical problems was widened rather than spanned (Mowrer, 1950).[10] Although Freud did not regard himself as a learning theorist, this is an error he never made. From the outset, he saw those items of behavior which we call "symptoms" as acts, or "habits," which serve to eliminate or reduce the inner state of anxiety, not as direct reflexive reactions to conditioned stimuli or signals in the external environment. In the laboratory situation, we now have growing reason to believe that the defensive behavior prompted by a danger signal is really a form of problem solving, based upon, but distinct from the real conditioned response, namely fear.

In short, then, we may say that living organisms can be problemed or driven in two ways: by primary drives, such as hunger and thirst, which are the products of the organism's own metabolism; and by secondary drives, such as appetite and fear, which are produced by the mechanism of conditioning. Once an organism has a drive, be it primary or secondary, its problem-solving machinery is put into action. The fact that living organisms are thus impelled to find solutions not only to metabolic but also to emotional needs, which, in general, may be said to foreshadow metabolic needs, undoubtedly represents an enormous step forward in terms of biological adaptation and survival, but it also has potentialities for evil as well as good, as will be shown later.*

II. The Freudian Conception of Neurosis and Its Treatment

We are now in a position to look at some of the prevailing views regarding the nature of neurosis and see whether they make of it a disorder of conditioning or a disorder of problem solving. Since Freud is clearly the most influential figure in this field, it will be appropriate to examine his approach first and in greatest detail.

* For further discussion of two-factor learning theory and its implications, see Mowrer (1950, 1951, 1952).[10-14]

Careful study of Freud's works shows that for him neurosis was both a disorder of conditioning and a disorder of problem solving. Neurosis for Freud was, first of all, a disorder of conditioning, in that he believed that, in every instance of this malady, one of the central problems was the "over-severity" of the superego. This over-severity, one would suppose, would trace back to the over-severity of parents in their disciplinary role or perhaps to accidental trauma of some sort. Clinically, Freud knew, however, that in many instances one finds this apparent superego severity without being able to establish either an excess of disciplinary zeal on the part of parents or other traumata (Freud, 1933).[6] Although Freud could never fully account for this discrepancy to his own satisfaction, he continued to assume, nevertheless, that the neurotic has, in some way, acquired too much fear and that one of the major objectives of therapy is to ease the intensity of this emotion.

Freud also saw, however, that, in one sense, neurosis is a disorder of problem solving. He posited that, when a conflict is created between any "instinctual" impulse, such as hostility or sex on the one hand, and an excess of fear of the kind just described on the other, some individuals will solve this problem, not normally, healthily, integratively, but by denying, dissociating, repressing one of the elements in the conflict; and, in Freud's mind, there was very little question about the direction of the repression. In his *New Introductory Lectures* (1933),[6] as on many other occasions, Freud has said, "We can say that repression is the work of the superego" (p. 98), which is tantamount to saying that the discipline-inspired fears triumph over sex, aggression, and other biological forces which may have gotten the child into trouble with his socializers.

In Freud's view, repression is a poor solution to conflict, and he believed and taught that the therapist, by interpretation and any other resources at his command, should oppose and try to undo repression and help the patient replace it by other mental habits, notably those of association and synthesis. This reversal of the dissociative strategy has the effect, as Freud pointed out, of reactivating the original conflict, a service which the patient does not wholeheartedly welcome and to which he reacts with "resistance" and "negative transference." With the previously submerged id forces now made conscious, however, the patient will discover that his old fears of retaliation for gratifying these impulses are unrealistically strong, and he can thus find his way to a normal life adjustment. So goes the Freudian argument.

Logical as this theory sounds and widely as it has been accepted, it has not brought the hoped-for results. How it commonly works out in practice is well illustrated by Lucy Freeman's (1951) [5] . . . published story of her own psychoanalysis. It is manifestly impossible here to give anything like a comprehensive account of this book, but the general picture can be quickly outlined. This book, first of all, is entitled "Fight against Fears," and we soon discover that much of the five years she was in analysis was spent trying to neutralize the fears which had supposedly been instilled in her in childhood. The following excerpts show how central was the accent upon this campaign.

On page 59, we find an incident described and a way of thinking that is typical:

> I recalled [in analysis] one afternoon on the lawn in front of our bungalow when I had been racing around the grass. I dashed over to the nurse.
> "I'd like a drink of water," I panted.
> "Go away," she ordered. "Can't you see I'm talking to my sister?"
> "But I'm thirsty."
> "Go away!" Crack! She slapped my face.
> I burst into tears. "I'll tell my father on you," I sobbed (not mother, but father).
> "You tell and I'll kill you," she threatened. "My sister and I will kill you."
> I dried my tears quickly, too terrified to say a word. A few weeks later I saw the two women packing valises. I ran to Mother, asked what had happened.
> "They're leaving," she said. "We fired them. They were fresh."
> I am lost, I thought. They have been fired and they will think I told and now they *will* kill me. I ran and hid in the bedroom until they left. For weeks I trembled lest they steal back at night and kill me.
> As I told this to John [the analyst], I started to cry. "I didn't tell on them," I sobbed, half in fear, half in rage.
> All through the years the frightened, lonely part of me expected the wicked sisters to return to do murder. I understood now why Henry James's *The Turn of the Screw* held such morbid interest for me. I, too, fought the ghost of a wicked governess.

In the face of this history of overly severe and traumatic conditioning, what did the analysis do? On page 280, Miss Freeman tells us:

> Analysis was like being wrapped in a protective cocoon of gentleness, permitted to find a safety I never knew. It was an experience through which I lived, comparable to growing up again. It was like receiving painless injections of love and trust which gave me the strength to accept myself.

But, to paraphrase the title of Bettelheim's recent book, we must ask: "Was love enough? Did the analyst's warmth and reassurance and acceptance achieve the desired result?" After four years of analysis, it clearly had not. The patient at this point contemplated leaving analysis but became depressed and was obsessed by thoughts of suicide. She says: "The anxiety, rather than disappearing, was being eased. Underneath torment still raged."

Another year, and the analysis finally ended, but the book which Miss Freeman has produced is not a reassuring one. It gives us the picture of a young woman who, while highly intelligent and capable (witness her record on the staff of the New York Times), is still fighting an unwon battle —angry, pessimistic, unhappy, and confused. While she wishes to believe that her analysis was a great and helpful experience, we find, repeatedly, wistful comments such as these:

> Some things are written in this book ten times but not written once in my heart because I still do not possess the courage to accept them any deeper than the intellect. But I keep trying (p. 280).

How typical, we must ask, was Miss Freeman's experience with psychoanalysis? The author of this paper can supply a parallel report: During his early adult life, he spent more than five years in Freudian analysis with three different analysts, and still he had not learned what he needed to know; and more to the point, statistically, are the decidedly unglowing reports of a number of investigators (Hyman, 1936; [7] Jameison and McNeil, 1938; [8] Eysenck, 1952 [4]).

Surely anyone but the most complacent must wonder how it is that a system of thought which seems so brilliant and so sound should leave in its wake, when put to the therapeutic test, such tragic disappointment and waste!

III. Ubiquity of the Mal-conditioning Hypothesis

In the preceding section, it has been pointed out that, formally, the Freudian conception of neurosis implies that this type of psychopathology involves both a disorder of conditioning and a disorder of problem solving. However, we have also seen that, in common practice, the accent falls most heavily upon the assumption that the neurotic is a person who, above all else, has been harshly, severely, traumatically treated and that there is, in such a person, an unrealistic residue of fear ["shadow fears," Dollard (1942) [2] has called them] which it is the analyst's task to banish and thus release the instinctual forces which have been denied expression and gratification by this excess of apprehension.

Review of the relevant literature shows that, despite marked differences in phraseology, essentially the same emphasis is common to many otherwise divergent schools of psychotherapeutic thought. In an area which is today often characterized as "chaotic," it is a little surprising to find how really very widespread is the acceptance of this particular hypothesis, which, for sake of conciseness in the title of this section, has been called the *mal-conditioning hypothesis*. But the very prevalence of this hypothesis and the generally unsatisfactory nature of both theory and practice in the field should perhaps make us all the more ready to re-examine and, if need be, discard it.

Fortunately, for present purposes, Dr. E. J. Shoben, Jr., has already published an extremely thoughtful paper in which the generality of the mal-conditioning hypothesis has been extensively documented; and Dr. Shoben does this in a theoretical frame of reference which immediately articulates with that of the present paper. First of all, Shoben [17] takes the position that the two-process conception of learning which has been summarized in Section I is the most defensible one. He says:

> Thus, it would seem that among current approaches to learning a two-factor theory, holding that adaptive, skeletal-muscle responses are acquired according to the reinforcement principle whereas anticipatory, emotional responses are acquired according to the contiguity principle, has the greatest explanatory power as of the present moment (Shoben, 1948, p. 138).

In the preceding section, it has been pointed out that implicit in the Freudian point of view is the assumption that the therapist must (1) provide, in terms of the patient-therapist relationship, a new and more benign emotional climate for the patient and must (2), by means of interpretations, help the patient to come to see how self-defeating is the strategy of repression, and thus open the way to him for more constructive and satisfying conflict resolutions. In other words, the Freudian position holds that neurosis is, in part, a matter of mal-conditioning (over-severity of the super-ego) and, in part, a matter of mal-functional problem solving (repression). Shoben's emphasis, however, in keeping with that of numerous other writers whom he cites, is decidedly upon the first of these. He says:

> The hypothesis here suggested as rationalizing the counseling process in terms of learning theory is that psychotherapy is essentially a form of reconditioning according to the contiguity principle. The argument runs like this: When a patient comes to a clinician, he is typically ridden by anxieties, that is, his habit structures are characterized by a number of well established S-R bonds between various stimuli and those visceral reactions called fear or anxiety. Typically, too, . . . he has built up a number of defenses [symptoms], according to the principle of reinforcement, against these anxieties. These defenses are usually somewhat nonintegrative in the sense of *ultimately* breeding further anxiety, guilt, or insecurity. Clinical experience has shown that a direct attack on these defenses is of practically no avail; it is this which has led to the dropping out of such counseling techniques as advice, persuasion, exhortation, and so forth. The basic job is somehow to get rid of the anxieties supporting the defenses, accounting in large measure for the client's "unhappiness," and acting as a barrier to his acquiring more integrative modes of behavior. In their scientifically somewhat crude, empirical, cut-and-try way, psychotherapists have found that this task can best be accomplished when the patient (a) is provided with a warm, friendly, permissive relationship and (b) is encouraged to talk about his anxiety and the situations in which he experiences and has experienced them.
> The reconditioning hypothesis can now be stated somewhat more explicitly. The chief function of the conversational-content aspect of counseling consists in the symbolic reinstatement of the stimuli which produce and have produced the anxiety from which the client suffers. Through his words to the therapist, the patient, on a symbolic level, again "lives through" the stimulus situations which were painful for him and to which his visceral anxiety responses have become connected. The relationship aspect of counseling, on the other hand, is a stimulus situation which evokes a feeling of pleasure, acceptance, and security —a non-anxiety response. The therapeutic process consists in the establishment of a bond between the symbolically reproduced stimuli which evoke and have

evoked anxiety and the non-anxiety response of comfort and confidence made to the counseling relationship.

This formulation is in some ways quite analogous to the now famous reconditioning experiment of Mary Cover Jones (1924) with the boy Peter. . . .

The meaning of this experiment is that a new S-R bond was formed between the stimulus (rabbit) which evoked fear and the response of "comfort" or "pleasantness" made to the stimulus of the lunch situation with all its various cues. . . .

It is suggested, then, that the counselor has two functions of about equal importance: providing the client with a warm and accepting relationship which elicits feelings of comfort and security, and helping the client to uncover and discuss those situations which produce anxiety in him. By properly pairing these stimulus complexes, the therapist effects a diminution in his patient's anxiety through reconditioning (Shoben, 1948, pp. 139–141).[17]

Shoben's paper was published three years before Miss Freeman's book appeared and could not, therefore, have been influenced by it, and it seems unlikely that either Miss Freeman or her analyst ever saw Shoben's paper, yet the parallelism is striking. Miss Freeman regarded her analysis as a "fight against fears" and perceived her analyst as providing "a protective cocoon of gentleness . . . safety I never knew . . . painless injections of love and trust." Surely, the equivalents for a journalist of the more academic formulations of Shoben!

Nor is the near-identity of these two documents a coincidence. It is not possible, here, at all fully to document the generality of this conception of and therapeutic approach to neurosis, but reference can be made to at least one other work to show how uniform is this thinking in the minds of many writers. In their recent book, "Personality and Psychotherapy: An Analysis in Terms of Learning, Thinking, and Culture," Dollard and Miller (1951),[3] like Shoben, take the position that neurosis and its treatment are learning phenomena and, although they do not explicitly adopt a two-factor conception of learning, they state that their position is not incompatible therewith (p. 42). The point of view which they then take with respect to neurosis and therapy, specifically, is summarized in the following excerpts:

In the neurotic, strong fear motivates a conflict that prevents the occurrence of the goal responses that normally would reduce another drive, such as sex or aggression. . . .

Because the conflicting responses prevent the drive-reducing goal responses from occurring, the drives (such as sex and aggression) build up and remain high. This state of chronic high drive is described as misery. At the same time, the high drives tend to evoke the approaches (or other incipient acts) that elicit the fear. Thus the neurotic is likely to be stimulated by both the frustrated drives and the fear. Finally, the state of conflict itself may produce additional strong stimuli, such as those of muscular tension, which contribute to the misery.

Fear or guilt also motivate the repression of verbal and other cue-producing responses. The fact that certain thoughts arouse fear motivates stopping them, and the reduction in fear reinforces the stopping. . . .

Since the verbal and other cue-producing responses are the basis for the higher mental processes, the repression of these responses makes the neurotic stupid with respect to the specific function of the responses that are repressed. One of the functions of the cue producing responses is to aid in discrimination. When they are removed by repression, it is harder for the patient to differentiate the situations in which he has been punished from similar ones in which he has not. Interference with such discriminations greatly retards the extinction of unrealistic fears and thus helps to perpetuate the vicious circle of fear, repression, stupidity, lack of discrimination, and persistence of unrealistic fear (pp. 222–224).

In a chapter entitled, "Teaching the patient to discriminate: the role of the past and the present," Dollard and Miller say:

Most generally stated, the problem is to keep the patient's behavior up to date, to keep it in accord with current conditions of life. In order to modernize the neurotic patient he must frequently learn to try out new responses appropriate to new conditions and, in order to get him to try out these responses, he must clearly see that the conflicts and repressions from which he suffers are not justified by the current conditions of reward and punishment. He must further learn that the conditions in the past which produced these conflicts are sharply dissimilar from those of the present, thanks to age-grading and often original mistraining. He must notice that many of his current habits are similar to those which he had in childhood and were learned in childhood under childhood conditions.

As a result of noting these similarities and differences, the patient becomes convinced that his neurotic behavior is functionally obsolete and this conviction gives him the courage which he has not had, to try new responses. If he tries such responses and, if they are rewarded, the neurotic impasse is broken up and the patient begins to learn anew (p. 305).

The mechanism of extinction is always available for the reduction of the anxiety gradient. If the patient can be induced to try making a sex response while afraid and if he finds that he is not punished, extinction will do its work. It may, however, be very difficult to get the patient to "try" making the formerly punished and now inhibited sex responses if the anxiety gradient remains unchanged. It is at this point that the principle of discrimination can mercifully enter (p. 307).

The role of the therapist is elaborated by Dollard and Miller in these words:

Repression interferes with the neurotic's higher mental processes and prevents him from using these effectively in solving his emotional problems. This repression was learned in a social situation in which fear, shame, or guilt were attached to certain spoken words and generalized from them to thoughts. In therapy a new type of social situation is created, the opposite of that responsible for the learning of repression. In this new type of social situation the patient is urged to say whatever comes into his mind and to be especially sure to resist suppressing those words that he finds himself afraid, ashamed, or reluctant to say. As the patient says words that provoke fear or shame, the therapist does not punish him or show any signs of disapproval; he remains warm and accepting. In this way, the fear, shame, and guilt attached to talking about tabooed topics are extinguished. This extinction generalizes from speaking to thinking.

It also generalizes from the painful but not completely repressed topics that are discussed to similar topics that could not be discussed because they were repressed. As the drives motivating repression are weakened by such generalization, it becomes possible to talk about these additional topics that had been weakly repressed, and another cycle of extinction and generalization is initiated. Thus repression is gradually unlearned under permissive social conditions that are the opposite to the punitive ones under which it was learned.

The therapeutic situation which Freud hit upon after considerable trial and error is arranged so that anxiety can be steadily weakened by extinction. As anxiety is reduced, the repressed sentences gradually become articulate. This situation is different from that of childhood in that it is vastly more permissive of free speech and free naming of emotional factors. The constricting conditions of childhood learning are reversed (pp. 240–41).

As is apparent from the foregoing excerpts, Dollard and Miller's position is remarkably similar to that of Shoben: Neurosis arises because of excessive and unrealistic fears, and the chief aim of therapy is to banish these fears, by extinction and/or counter-conditioning.

An even more extreme case for the mal-conditioning theory of neurosis could be made by citing some of the writings of Carl Rogers and his school. From the Rogerian point of view, neurosis is always a product of an inimical environment impinging upon an individual whose basic trends are toward psychological health and normality. Therapy consists of providing the patient with an emotional climate of complete respect, acceptance, understanding, and warmth, in which the "will to health," now unopposed by baleful environmental influences, can bring about a restoration of the personality to normal functioning. However, Rogers has eschewed any attempt to cast his thinking into learning-theory terms, and it is perhaps unfair to make a translation which he himself has consistently avoided.* It can be said, nevertheless, that there is nothing palpably inconsistent between his approach and the hypothesis that the basic problem in neurosis is mal-conditioning, and that its treatment consists essentially of providing the patient with an opportunity for self-corrective experience—or, in learning terms, extinction and counter-conditioning.

Space does not permit, nor does the argument require, that we here continue to pile up, as might easily be done, further and further evidence of the ubiquity of the mal-conditioning hypothesis.† It is surprising enough that we find it a common feature of such otherwise diverse schools of

* Perhaps the nearest approach to such a translation is to be found on pages 209–210 of Rogers's book, Client-centered Therapy (1951).[16]

† Since the above was written the author has listened to an address by a psychiatrist of international renown in which false fears and guilts were identified as the central problem of neurosis and a process called "desensitization" was put forward as the therapy of choice. For purposes of illustration a nurse was referred to who consulted this physician professionally. It appears that, among other problems, she suffered from conflict and shame connected with masturbation. Therapy consisted of "desensitizing" the patient with respect to her fear and guilt in this connection.

thought as those of Freud and Rogers; but it could be easily shown that this hypothesis is a central element in many other approaches to the field of neurosis and therapy, including such "fringe" schools as those of Korzybski's "general semantics" and Hubbard's "dianetics." Of course, it goes without saying that the mal-conditioning hypothesis is the keystone of the more explicitly Pavlovian's psychiatric approaches (Pavlov, 1941).[15] This investigator and his immediate associates were, to be sure, somewhat more inclined to see neurosis as involving actual organic impairment of, or damage to, cortical structures, rather than as a purely functional state which might yield to psychological methods; but even so, mal-conditioning is still seen as the essential pre-condition of neurosis.

This hypothesis is therefore all but universal today. Again we must ask: How can any assumption be so widely subscribed to when the consequences that flow from its practical applications are so discouraging? Surely, this is an enigma which has not caused us as much puzzlement and concern as it rightly should!

IV. Neurosis as a Perversity of Problem Solving

In the preceding sections, we have seen how pervasive is the view that the basic problem in neurosis is one of mal-conditioning. It is also apparent that the therapeutic accomplishments, not to mention preventive measures, which have been based upon this kind of reasoning are, today, far from gratifying. In the present section, an attempt will be made, therefore, to outline an alternative hypothesis which gives promise of being more adequate therapeutically and of leading to a more comprehensive and internally consistent type of theory.*

This approach starts in agreement with two of Freud's most basic postulates: (1) that psychoneurotic symptoms are habits which serve to "bind" anxiety and related affects, and (2) that anxiety, in its neurotic sense, can be understood only by positing an intrapsychic process which Freud called *repression*, which Rogers has called *denial of feeling*, Sullivan called *selective inattention*, and which Janet, Prince, and others have called *dissociation*. Beyond this point, there is a sharp divergence from Freudian theory. As indicated in Section II, Freud took the position that repression is the "work of the superego," *i.e.*, that in the neurotic, the superego is so strong, so harsh, so tyrannical that it compels the ego to deny certain id forces, notably those of sex and aggression, access to consciousness, and overt implementation. On the basis of his own experience as a human being and as a psychotherapist, the present writer believes that the actual situation is very often, perhaps quite regularly, the reverse of that posited by Freud. The neurotic, it seems, is not a person whose superego has overwhelmed

* For discussion of the paradoxes inherent in Freudian theory, see Mowrer (1950, 1951, 1952).[10-14]

the ego and raised impenetrable barriers against the id. Rather is the neurotic a person whose ego has remained, in certain important respects, essentially infantile, which is to say id-dominated, and in whom conflicts between forces of id and superego have been resolved by repudiation and repression, not of the id as Freud and many others have supposed, but of the superego itself.* According to this alternative view, symptoms are the disguised and dislocated expression of denied guilt and self-reproach, not of repressed sexuality, aggression, or any other biological impulses. Neurosis, in short, is thus seen as a problem, not of repudiated instincts, but of repudiated ideals.

It is not possible here to review the many considerations which have forced the writer to abandon the currently popular Freudian doctrine, in which he was trained, and to adopt a different one. Some of these considerations have been elaborated elsewhere (Mowrer, 1950) [10] and others are discussed in a volume now in press (Mowrer, 1952).[14] In the present paper, the most that can be done is to give a highly synoptic account of the genesis and dynamics of neurosis as seen from this revised point of view and to indicate briefly some of its therapeutic implications.

In order to make what is to follow now maximally clear and to avoid the possible appearance of irrelevance, it will be useful, first, to present the two points of view as compactly, as dramatically, and as contrastingly as possible. As already indicated, the mal-conditioning hypothesis holds that neurosis is, basically, something that happens or is done to the afflicted individual. The alternative view holds that neurosis is more a matter of what the individual is doing, by way of misdirected problem-solving devices, to and for himself. Many writers in this field state or imply that neurosis is something that is imposed from without. The alternative position holds that neurosis is less an imposition than an "invention" and that, in the most meaningful sense, its point of origin is internal rather than external. Neurosis is thus an expression, not of excessive conditioning, but

* There is a remarkable inconsistency in Freudian thinking in this connection. According to Freud's own stated position, the id is a pure "pleasure economy," which recognizes neither the logic of sacrifice nor the strategy of postponement ("Pinocchio" being one of its classical personifications). By contrast, the superego, one would suppose, should be based upon the "reality principle," i.e., it should represent the soundest inductions of past generations regarding strategies which work best in the long run, i.e., the realistic, the moral, the integrative ways of life. Now, let us ask, in all candor, which of these components of personality would be the more likely to initiate an action such as repression. That in those instances where the id has gained dominion over the ego, the strategy of repression should be turned against the superego seems in no way remarkable; but that the superego, which is the racial embodiment of the reality principle, should itself institute and sponsor a process so short sighted and unrealistic as repression seems most improbable. Sensing this and related paradoxes, some writers have tried to draw a distinction between the "true conscience" and the "archaic superego," but this is a palpable piece of patchwork and does not get at the root source of the difficulty.

of problem-solving skills and techniques which, under sway of the primitive pleasure principle, are directed toward the prevention of conditioning and the avoidance of discipline which, in the long run, are to the individual's decided advantage.

By the same token, therapy is not so much a matter of extinction of false fears as it is of helping the individual to learn the advantage of exposing himself to the real consequences of his actions, *i.e.*, in a word, to expose himself to the advantages of being consistent, responsible, rather than trying to avoid events which, without neurotic self-protectiveness, would surely impinge upon him.

The foregoing statements, in their brevity, are necessarily abstract. Let us now try to give them more substance and specificity.

We start with the assumption that every child, in the course of normal familial life, will experience conflicts between his own wishes, drives, desires and those of others. Having, by the age of two or three, become relatively fluent in the symbolic operations called language, children almost invariably discover the possibility of deception. They find that by introducing a discrepancy between their behavior and the verbal reports thereof, they can often avoid conflicts with others. They discover, in short, that in this way they can, so to say, have their cake and eat it too. They can do forbidden things and avoid punishment, and they can fail to do prescribed things and yet, by giving an affirmative report, enjoy the social advantages of having done them. This type of experimentation with deception is attempted, now somewhat playfully, now more intently, by almost every child—every intelligent child—; and parents, with almost equal universality, attempt to discourage such behavior. By precedent, by precept, and by punishment, they try to inculcate the trait of honesty, of consistency between word and deed. By the time most children are of school age, they have been powerfully conditioned on this score, *i.e.*, parental values have been sufficiently "introjected," so that when a child violates the canons of realistic reporting—when, in a word, he *cheats*—he experiences pangs of conscience.

Surely nothing could be more commonplace or obvious than what has just been said, but it leads to some implications which, in the writer's judgment, have not been properly noted and evaluated. Once the stage of development has been reached in which a child, upon misrepresenting the truth, feels inwardly uncomfortable, there may be any one of several outcomes. These are as follows:

1. Following a lapse from truthfulness, the child may get caught in his would-be deception and be forced to face the consequences he was trying to avoid. The psychological effects of untruthfulness are thus, so to say, self-liquidating and are of little further interest, at least as far as any specific incident is concerned.

2. The child, due to the inadequacy of his earlier training, may have so

feeble a conscience that he is troubled only passingly by deception, or not at all, and this behavior may then become an established part of his life style, to the extent that it is objectively practicable. Here again, whatever the social repercussions may be, the psychological picture is not very interesting. It is essentially that of the "confirmed liar," the exploiter, the swindler, the criminal psychopath.

3. The child may find himself so disturbed by a "bad conscience" following untruthfulness that he finally decides that the consequences of honesty, whatever they are, will be less intolerable than those of continued deception, and thus be prompted to "confess." Once more, the psychological implications of such a course of action are relatively uninteresting.

4. Only in a fourth and final sequence, do we pick up a trail which promises to lead us toward a better understanding of the genesis and meaning of neurosis. It may well happen that a child who has violated his parents' injunctions with respect to honesty may feel guilty, but not guilty enough to drive him to rectify matters spontaneously, and let us further suppose that he is not objectively "found out." Under these circumstances, the accusing, admonishing voice of conscience may continue to bother the child so persistently that, in ultimate exasperation and desperation, he, like Pinocchio, decides that the only solution is to kill this "talking cricket," once and for all. As others have found before him, conscience-killing is not the easiest thing in the world to bring about; but by a determined campaign of rationalization, forced "forgetting," fault-finding in others, and more rationalization, the youthful sufferer may at length achieve a state where "nothing bothers" him; i.e., like Pinocchio, he may finally reach the "Land of Boobies." Here, his relief and self-felicitation may be profound, but they are not likely to be permanent. Soon the dread "donkey's ears" begin to grow; soon, that is to say, the repudiated sense of responsibility and self-criticism begins to return, but now, we say, as "symptoms." Strictly speaking, what comes first is anxiety, which Pinocchio feels acutely at the sight of the growing ears and tail. Then come the symptoms, properly speaking, i.e., the efforts to counteract and control the anxiety.

It may be that the strategy of repression will work for a relatively long time. Conceivably, in some instances, it works perpetually. But in most cases, repression, like the pleasure initially experienced in the Land of Boobies, is not a dependable thing and, when repression fails and there is a return or a threatened "return of the repressed," the terror of neurosis is the outcome.

Perhaps, the foregoing account will seem too fanciful, too much a fairy tale to carry any conviction. Then let us take the case of a *real* boy, Charlie M. Early in the summer of his ninth year, Charlie persuaded another boy to enter into mutual masturbation and other forms of sex play with him in an unused garage. These activities continued for several weeks, during which time Charlie M. found himself in conflict between the attraction of the garage rendezvous and the teaching of his Catholic mother that he should regularly go to confession. Suffice it to say that it was the attendance at confession that suffered, but Charlie did not let his family know that he was being remiss in this connection. After a time, the sex play stopped, but the deception continued. Now "too afraid" to confide in anyone, as Charlie reported some fifteen years later in therapy, he continued through-out grammar school and high school to *pretend* to his family that he went regularly to confession when, in point of fact, he went not at all.

Shortly after Charlie was eighteen and just out of high school, his father died, or was killed, under very unusual circumstances; and soon thereafter the boy began to experience anxiety, phobias, and obsessional trends. How-ever, these were not sufficiently developed to prevent him from attending and successfully completing college. In college, Charlie met and married a very attractive and intelligent young woman with a Protestant back-ground. After his graduation, he and his bride went for a visit to the city where Charlie's mother and brothers and sisters were now living. Here, they were met by a reception which the young wife, at least, had no reason to anticipate. Feeling that this hussy had lured their faithful son and brother away from the Church and was now living with him in unholy union, Charlie's family immediately set out to drive her out of his life and to restore him to a state of grace.

After a few hours of apparently pretty savage treatment, the young wife decided that she had better leave and Charlie went with her. Thus did they retreat from the intolerable situation into which Charlie's deceit and evasion over the years had plunged the woman of his choice; but within a few months his symptoms were sufficiently intensified so that he could no longer hide them from his wife, and she was instrumental in helping him get into therapy.

Charlie's story could be told, with unimportant variations, many times over; but this will not be necessary here. Taken alone, the foregoing ac-count once again raises, and surely also gives us a pointed answer to the question: Is neurosis a disorder of conditioning or of problem solving? Where, in Charlie's case, was the excessive conditioning? Where the paren-tal over-severity? If his parents had failed to instill in him any ideal of honesty and sense of responsibility for the welfare of others, he would not, to be sure, have developed a neurosis; he would, instead, have been a frank psychopath. Surely, then, their error was one not of excess but of omission! Charlie's father and mother had many unsolved problems of their own, and they disagreed, as parents, upon many basic issues, including those of religion and child discipline. So their youngest son paid the price, in his neurosis, for having been insufficiently practiced in the art of solving prob-lems courageously and integratively, rather than by deception and disso-ciation.

During the course of his therapy, Charles succeeded in giving his mother and siblings a correct account of his life and of the circumstances of his defection from the Church, with dramatic improvement, not only in his and his wife's relationship, but also in the relationship with his family. At last report, there was no mention of symptoms, and he was apparently moving rapidly forward in consolidating what had previously been a faltering masculine identification. Here, in the span of 46 interviews, by proceeding on the assumption that neurosis is basically a disorder of problem solving rather than conditioning, it was possible to achieve a therapeutic outcome which we do not see in Lucy Freeman after five years of therapy based upon the contrary belief. This discrepancy is one which we cannot continue to ignore.

V. Summarizing Comments and Observations

The fifth and final section of this paper affords an opportunity to comment briefly upon some of the views previously expressed or implied at the Conference on which this monograph is based, and to summarize and re-emphasize the central thesis of the foregoing pages. Other papers have repeatedly suggested an argument which may be phrased as follows: Neurosis involves conflict. We need to study this phenomenon experimentally. This we cannot readily do in human beings. Therefore, let us produce conflicts in other organisms and call the observed results neurosis. Dr. Beach called our attention to the dangers in such a procedure. "Let us be very cautious," Beach said. "Perhaps," he warned, "what we call 'neurosis' in animals is something quite different from neurosis in human beings."

Now I venture to suggest that the difficulty goes still deeper. Even those who work most intimately with human beings in this connection appear, in one very important respect, to have over-simplified matters considerably.* Yes, to be sure, neurosis *does* involve conflicts; and we soon discover that these conflicts often take the form of a struggle between biologically given forces, or what Freud called the *id*, and the socially conditioned elements of the personality, commonly termed conscience or superego; but beyond this a number of inferences have been drawn and translated into operations of doubtful validity. The three most important of these may be formulated as follows:

1. Since neurosis involves an id—superego conflict and, since the id is biologically given, instinctually fixed, essentially immutable, then the task of treatment is to weaken the superego part of the conflict. This therapeutic approach is, so to say, a *subtractive* one.

2. Since, in terms of the same argument, a superego excess is likely to lead to neurosis, then the prophylactic lesson is this: Let parents and others who are in charge of children err in the direction of too little rather than too much training in morality and like matters.

* Cf. Mowrer (1952): "Learning Theory and the Neurotic Fallacy." [13]

3. Since, without social injunctions and tabus, there would be no neurosis in human beings, then the socially prescribed way of life holds within it grave dangers and one can afford to take it rather lightly. Indeed, to do otherwise is to invite neurosis.

All of this I believe involves a basic and surprisingly obvious error. The royal road to mental health can hardly be that of eliminating or even substantially reducing the conflict which the young human animal experiences between his own wishes and those of others. Such a conflict is inevitable, and to take seriously the proposal that we attack the problem of neurosis by analyzing away or, in some other manner, dissolving the interests and concerns of others (as well as our *own* best interests in the long run) is, in my judgment, to reject, basically, the whole human enterprise. This I am not personally prepared to do, nor does it seem in the least necessary, in order to achieve our fondest objectives in this connection.

Is not the key to neurosis and its effective treatment and prevention more likely to be found along the lines of helping the young, the immature, the neurotic to learn ways of resolving these inevitable conflicts integratively, constructively, characterfully, instead of in ways which, in the long run, will be both personally self-defeating and socially objectionable and burdensome? Integrative psychotherapy, which aims at personal strength and happiness through unifying the various existing parts of personality, rather than by analyzing away, extinguishing, sedating, or surgically removing enough of them to alleviate conflicts, is still in its early development, but it holds high promise.

One concluding observation: "Culture" and "society" are often doubly damned. Not only do they harmfully oppose the "instincts"; they are not even internally consistent, we are told. Let us get down to specifics here. Certainly, every psychotherapist is constantly being impressed by the extent to which neurotics have come from homes in which there was "social," or "cultural," conflict; i.e., homes in which there has been considerable marital disharmony, disagreement between the two principal culture-bearing agents; *viz.*, the father and the mother. This disharmony, this conflict, we are told, *makes* a conflict in the child and forthwith establishes neurosis.

Is there not a more discerning way of viewing the same facts? In keeping with what has been said before, would it not be more accurate to put the matter like this? Every child, in the best-ordered homes in the best-ordered society, is going to experience conflict; severe, painful, fateful conflict; this cannot be avoided. Where the damage is done is in those homes where marital disharmony, demoralization, neglect, and other circumstances permit the child to adopt and persevere in solutions to his basic conflicts that will predispose him to social and/or psychic pathology, instead of providing a more consistent and concerned type of training, that will enable him to find integrative rather than destructive solutions to his problems. This suggestion has been developed at some length in the preceding section and need not be again elaborated.

Finally, we should anticipate an objection which is almost certain to be raised on the basis of what has been said here. No doubt, it will be pointed out that the foregoing discussion carries the implication that human beings have some sort of "choice" between neurosis and normality; and choice, personal freedom, and responsibility, we will surely be reminded, are concepts which are thoroughly out-moded and scientifically disreputable. What does "science" mean in the realm of psychology, we will be asked, if it does not mean that all our thoughts, feelings, and actions are determined by forces outside and beyond the control of the self, the ego, the conscious "me"?

It is only fair and proper that this question should be raised, and it deserves a considered and detailed rejoinder. Unfortunately, the most that can be said here is that normal human beings, *i.e.*, persons who have kept their problem-solving capacities intact and have not perverted and abused them, do indeed have freedom and choice and responsibility in a very real and recognized way; whereas the neurotic, in the interest of immediate psychic comfort, has, quite literally, sacrificed, traded, sold his freedom of choice in order to be relieved of responsibility and guilt. It is therefore hardly surprising that, in our professional approaches to neurosis and its treatment and prevention, we have fallen considerably short of our goals. We have, it seems, made some of the same mistakes in ideology and strategy which the neurotic himself makes. But a more detailed and fully documented consideration of this important matter must be deferred until another time.*

Bibliography

1. Brown, J. S. & I. E. Farber. 1951. Emotions conceptualized as intervening variables —with suggestions toward a theory of frustration. Psychol. Bull. 48: 465–495.
2. Dollard, J. 1942. Victory over Fear. Reynal, Hitchcock. N.Y.
3. Dollard, J. & N. E. Miller. 1950. Personality and Psychotherapy. McGraw-Hill. N.Y.
4. Eysenck, H. J. 1952. The effects of psychotherapy: an evaluation. J. Consult. Psychol. 16: 319–324.
5. Freeman, L. 1951. Fight against Fears. Crown. N.Y.
6. Freud, S. 1933. New Introductory Lectures on Psychoanalysis. Norton. N.Y.
7. Hyman, H. T. 1936. The value of psychoanalysis as a therapeutic procedure. J. Am. Med. Assoc. 108: 326–329.
8. Jameison, G. R. & E. E. McNeil. 1938–1939. Some unsuccessful reactions with psychoanalytic therapy. Am. J. Psychiat. 95: 1421–1428.
9. Jones, M. C. 1924. A laboratory study of fear: the case of Peter. 31: 308–315.
10. Mowrer, O. H. 1950. Learning Theory and Personality Dynamics. Ronald Press. N.Y.

* Cf. Mowrer (1952): "Learning Theory and the Neurotic Fallacy," [14] particularly the sections on "The neurotic fallacy and its professional acceptance" and "Conformity, consistency, and confession, with special reference to freedom and responsibility."

11. Mowrer, O. H. 1951a. Two-factor learning theory: summary and comment. Psychol. Rev. 58: 350–354.
12. Mowrer, O. H. 1951b. Anxiety theory as a basis for distinguishing between counseling and psychotherapy. Concepts and Programs of Counseling. P. 7. R. F. Berdie, Ed. Univ. Minnesota Press. Minneapolis.
13. Mowrer, O. H. 1952b. Learning theory and the neurotic fallacy. Am. J. Orthopsychiat. 22: 679–689.
14. Mowrer, O. H. 1953. Psychotherapy—Theory and Research. Ronald Press. N.Y. (In press.)
15. Pavlov, I. P. 1941. Conditioned Reflexes and Psychiatry. W. H. Gantt, Trans. International Pub. Co. N.Y.
16. Rogers, C. 1951. Client-centered Therapy. Houghton Mifflin. Boston.
17. Shoben, E. J. 1948. A learning theory interpretation of psychotherapy. Harvard Educ. Rev. 18: 129–145.

THE BASIC CONFLICT *

(KAREN HORNEY

Conflicts play an infinitely greater role in neurosis than is commonly assumed. To detect them, however, is no easy matter—partly because they are essentially unconscious, but even more because the neurotic goes to any length to deny their existence. What, then, are the signals that would warrant us to suspect underlying conflicts? In . . . examples cited . . . their presence was indicated by two factors, both fairly obvious. One was the resulting symptoms—fatigue in the first case, stealing in the second. The fact is that every neurotic symptom points to an underlying conflict; that is, every symptom is a more or less direct outgrowth of a conflict. We shall see gradually what unresolved conflicts do to people, how they produce states of anxiety, depression, indecision, inertia, detachment, and so on. An understanding of the causative relation here helps direct our attention from the manifest disturbances to their source—though the exact nature of the source will not be disclosed.

The other signal indicating that conflicts were in operation was inconsistency. In the first example we saw a man convinced of a procedure being wrong and of injustice done him, making no move to protest. In the second a person who highly valued friendship turned to stealing money from a friend. Sometimes the person himself will be aware of such inconsistencies; more often he is blind to them even when they are blatantly obvious to an untrained observer.

* From Karen Horney, *Our Inner Conflicts*, pp. 34–37 and 40–47, W. W. Norton & Company, Inc., New York, copyright, 1945. Reprinted by permission of the publisher. Slightly edited.

Inconsistencies are as definite an indication of the presence of conflicts as a rise in body temperature is of physical disturbance. To cite some common ones: A girl wants above all else to marry, yet shrinks from the advances of any man. A mother oversolicitous of her children frequently forgets their birthdays. A person always generous to others is niggardly about small expenditures for himself. Another who longs for solitude never manages to be alone. One forgiving and tolerant toward most people is oversevere and demanding with himself.

Unlike the symptoms, the inconsistencies often permit of tentative assumptions as to the nature of the underlying conflict. An acute depression, for instance, reveals only the fact that a person is caught in a dilemma. But if an apparently devoted mother forgets her children's birthdays, we might be inclined to think that the mother was more devoted to her ideal of being a good mother than to the children themselves. We might also admit the possibility that her ideal collided with an unconscious sadistic tendency to frustrate them.

Sometimes a conflict will appear on the surface—that is, be consciously experience as such. This would seem to contradict my assertion that neurotic conflicts are unconscious. But actually what appears is a distortion or modification of the real conflict. Thus a person may be torn by a conscious conflict when, in spite of his evasive techniques, well-functioning otherwise, he finds himself confronted with the necessity of making a major decision. He cannot decide now whether to marry this woman or that one or whether to marry at all, whether to take this or that job, whether to retain or dissolve a partnership. He will then go through the greatest torment, shuttling from one opposite to the other, utterly incapable of arriving at any decision. He may in his distress call upon an analyst, expecting him to clarify the particular issues involved. And he will necessarily be disappointed, because the present conflict is merely the point at which the dynamite of inner frictions finally exploded. The particular problem distressing him now cannot be solved without taking the long and tortuous road of recognizing the conflicts hidden beneath it.

In other instances the inner conflict may be externalized and appear in the person's conscious mind as an incompatibility between himself and his environment. Or, finding that seemingly unfounded fears and inhibitions interfere with his wishes, a person may be aware that the crosscurrents within himself issue from deeper sources.

The more knowledge we gain of a person, the better able we are to recognize the conflicting elements that account for the symptoms, inconsistencies, and surface conflicts—and, we must add, the more confusing becomes the picture, through the number and variety of contradictions. So we are led to ask: Can there be a basic conflict underlying all these particular conflicts and originally responsible for all of them? Can one picture the structure of conflict in terms, say, of an incompatible marriage, where an endless variety of apparently unrelated disagreements and rows over friends, children, finances, mealtimes, servants, all point to some fundamental disharmony in the relationship itself? . . .

Proceeding now to evolve my own position, I see the basic conflict of the neurotic in the fundamentally contradictory attitudes he has acquired toward other persons. Before going into detail, let me call attention to the dramatization of such a contradiction in the story of Dr. Jekyll and Mr. Hyde. We see him on the one hand delicate, sensitive, sympathetic, helpful, and on the other brutal, callous, and egotistical. I do not, of course, mean to imply that neurotic division always adheres to the precise line of this story, but merely to point to a vivid expression of basic incompatibility of attitudes in relation to others.

To approach the problem genetically we must go back to what I have called basic anxiety,[1] meaning by this the feeling a child has of being isolated and helpless in a potentially hostile world. A wide range of adverse factors in the environment can produce this insecurity in a child: direct or indirect domination, indifference, erratic behavior, lack of respect for the child's individual needs, lack of real guidance, disparaging attitudes, too much admiration or the absence of it, lack of reliable warmth, having to take sides in parental disagreements, too much or too little responsibility, overprotection, isolation from other children, injustice, discrimination, unkept promises, hostile atmosphere, and so on and so on.

The only factor to which I should like to draw special attention in this context is the child's sense of lurking hypocrisy in the environment: his feeling that the parents' love, their Christian charity, honesty, generosity, and so on may be only pretense. Part of what the child feels on this score is really hypocrisy; but some of it may be just his reaction to all the contradictions he senses in the parents' behavior. Usually, however, there is a combination of cramping factors. They may be out in the open or quite hidden, so that in analysis one can only gradually recognize these influences on the child's development.

Harassed by these disturbing conditions, the child gropes for ways to keep going, ways to cope with this menacing world. Despite his own weakness and fears he unconsciously shapes his tactics to meet the particular forces operating in his environment. In doing so, he develops not only ad hoc strategies but lasting character trends which become part of his personality. I have called these "neurotic trends."

If we want to see how conflicts develop, we must not focus too sharply on the individual trends but rather take a panoramic view of the main directions in which a child can and does move under these circumstances. Though we lose sight for a while of details we shall gain a clearer perspective of the essential moves made to cope with the environment. At first a rather chaotic picture may present itself, but out of it in time three main

[1] Karen Horney, *The Neurotic Personality of Our Time*, W. W. Norton, 1937.

lines crystallize: a child can move *toward* people, *against* them, or *away from* them.

When moving *toward* people he accepts his own helplessness, and in spite of his estrangement and fears tries to win the affection of others and to lean on them. Only in this way can he feel safe with them. If there are dissenting parties in the family, he will attach himself to the most powerful person or group. By complying with them, he gains a feeling of belonging and support which makes him feel less weak and less isolated.

When he moves *against* people he accepts and takes for granted the hostility around him, and determines, consciously or unconsciously, to fight. He implicitly distrusts the feelings and intentions of others toward himself. He rebels in whatever ways are open to him. He wants to be the stronger and defeat them, partly for his own protection, partly for revenge.

When he moves *away from* people he wants neither to belong nor to fight, but keeps apart. He feels he has not much in common with them, they do not understand him anyhow. He builds up a world of his own—with nature, with his dolls, his books, his dreams.

In each of these three attitudes, one of the elements involved in basic anxiety is overemphasized: helplessness in the first, hostility in the second, and isolation in the third. But the fact is that the child cannot make any one of these moves wholeheartedly, because under the conditions in which the attitudes develop, all are bound to be present. What we have seen from our panoramic view is only the predominant move.

That this is so will become evident if we jump ahead now to the fully developed neurosis. We all know adults in whom one of the attitudes we have sketched stands out. But we can see, too, that his other tendencies have not ceased to operate. In a predominantly leaning and complying type we can observe aggressive propensities and some need for detachment. A predominantly hostile person has a compliant strain and needs detachment too. And a detached personality is not without hostility or a desire for affection.

The predominant attitude, however, is the one that most strongly determines actual conduct. It represents those ways and means of coping with others in which the particular person feels most at home. Thus a detached person will as a matter of course use all the unconscious techniques for keeping others at a safe distance because he feels at a loss in any situation that requires close association with them. Moreover, the ascendant attitude is often but not always the one most acceptable to the person's conscious mind.

This does not mean that the less conspicuous attitudes are less powerful. It would often be difficult to say, for instance, whether in an apparently dependent, compliant person the wish to dominate is of inferior intensity to the need for affection; his ways of expressing his aggressive impulses are merely more indirect. That the potency of the submerged tendencies may be very great is evidenced by the many instances in which the attitude accorded predominance is reversed. We can see such reversal in children, but it occurs in later life as well. Strickland in Somerset Maugham's *The Moon and Sixpence* would be a good illustration. Case histories of women often reveal this kind of change. A girl formerly tomboyish, ambitious, rebellious, when she falls in love may turn into a compliant, dependent woman, apparently without ambition. Or, under pressure of crushing experiences, a detached person may become morbidly dependent.

Changes like these, it should be added, throw some light on the frequent question whether later experience counts for nothing, whether we are definitely channeled, conditioned once and for all, by our childhood situation. Looking at neurotic development from the point of view of conflicts enables us to give a more adequate answer than is usually offered. These are the possibilities: If the early situation is not too prohibitive of spontaneous growth, later experiences, particularly in adolescence, can have a molding influence. If, however, the impact of early experiences has been powerful enough to have molded the child to a rigid pattern, no new experience will be able to break through. In part this is because his rigidity does not leave him open to any new experience: his detachment, for instance, may be too great to permit of anyone's coming close to him, or his dependence so deep-rooted that he is forced always to play a subordinate role and invite exploitation. In part it is because he will interpret any new experience in the language of his established pattern: the aggressive type, for instance, meeting with friendliness, will view it either as a manifestation of stupidity or an attempt to exploit him; the new experience will tend only to reinforce the old pattern. When a neurotic does adopt a different attitude it may look as if later experiences had brought about a change in personality. However, the change is not as radical as it appears. Actually what has happened is that combined internal and external pressures have forced him to abandon his predominant attitude in favor of the other extreme—but this change would not have taken place if there had been no conflicts to begin with.

From the point of view of the normal person there is no reason why the three attitudes should be mutually exclusive. One should be capable of giving in to others, of fighting, and of keeping to oneself. The three can complement each other and make for a harmonious whole. If one predominates, it merely indicates an overdevelopment along one line.

But in neurosis there are several reasons why these attitudes are irreconcilable. The neurotic is not flexible; he is driven to comply, to fight, to be aloof, regardless of whether the move is appropriate in the particular circumstance, and he is thrown into a panic if he behaves otherwise. Hence when all three attitudes are present in any strong degree, he is bound to be caught in a severe conflict.

Another factor, and one that considerably widens the scope of the conflict, is that the attitudes do not remain restricted to the area of human relationships but gradually pervade the entire personality, as a malignant tumor pervades the whole organic tissue. They end by encompassing not only the person's relation to others but also his relation to himself and to life in general. If we are not fully aware of this all-embracing character, the temptation is to think of the resulting conflict in categorical terms, like love *versus* hate, compliance *versus* defiance, submissiveness *versus* domination, and so on. That, however, would be as misleading as to distinguish fascism from democracy by focusing on any single opposing feature, such as their difference in approach to religion or power. These are differences certainly, but exclusive emphasis upon them would serve to obscure the point that democracy and fascism are worlds apart and represent two philosophies of life entirely incompatible with each other.

It is not accidental that a conflict that starts with our relation to others in time affects the whole personality. Human relationships are so crucial that they are bound to mold the qualities we develop, the goals we set for ourselves, the values we believe in. All these in turn react upon our relations with others and so are inextricably interwoven.[2]

My contention is that the conflict born of incompatible attitudes constitutes the core of neurosis and therefore deserves to be called *basic*. And let me add that I use the term *core* not merely in the figurative sense of its being significant but to emphasize the fact that it is the dynamic center from which neuroses emanate. This contention is the nucleus of a new theory of neurosis. . . . Broadly considered, the theory may be viewed as an elaboration of my earlier concept that neuroses are an expression of a disturbance in human relationships.[3]

THE CONTRIBUTIONS OF ALFRED ADLER *

(ANN W. SHYNE

An attempt is here made to draw together, from the writings of Alfred Adler, the main tenets of individual psychology, in order to bring into focus certain positive contributions which seem to have a real place in

[2] Since the relation to others and the attitude toward the self cannot be separated from one another, the contention occasionally to be found in psychiatric publications, that one or the other of these is the most important factor in theory and practice, is not tenable.

[3] This concept was first presented in *The Neurotic Personality of Our Time* and elaborated in *New Ways in Psychoanalysis* and *Self-analysis*.

* From Ann W. Shyne, "The Contribution of Alfred Adler to the Development of Dynamic Psychology," *Amer. J. Orthopsychiat.*, 12, 352–360. Reprinted by permission of the author and the Editor, *American Journal of Orthopsychiatry*.

the total configuration of dynamic psychology. Adler has not given a complete picture of the formation of the personality nor answered all of the questions of psychopathology. However, he has offered a theory of personality organization and disorganization which, though hardly of universal applicability, may be useful in understanding particular cases. He has indicated a way of bridging the gap between pedagogy and psychiatry. By his emphasis on social and environmental factors he foreshadowed the rapprochement of sociology and psychiatry. It would seem unfortunate that the valuable aspects of his work should be lost because of his failure to present a system acceptable in its totality.

Associated with Freud for several years, Adler came increasingly to disagree with Freud in regard to the fundamental idea of the libido as the motivating force in the neuroses. Despite his rupture with Freud, Adler incorporated, with modifications, some of Freud's basic concepts in his own thinking. He accepted the principle of psychic determinism of mental phenomena, but laid considerably more stress than did Freud on the relation of somatic factors to mental functioning, in his theory of organ inferiority. Like Freud, Adler stressed the early years of life as determinant of the personality and life pattern of the individual, but instead of looking to libidinal frustrations for the source of later anomalies, he saw in the child's feeling of inferiority the foundation of his goal in life and manner of striving toward that goal.

Early writings. One of Adler's earliest papers is *Die Aggressiontrieb im Leben und in den Neurose,* published in 1906, in which he repudiated the sexual etiology of mental phenomena, in favor of the concept of the aggressive drive for power as the determinant (4). The following year he published *Studie über Minderwertigkeit der Organe,* translated in 1917 as *A Study of Organ Inferiority and Its Psychical Compensation* (10). This is probably the best of Adler's writings from the point of view of logic and of adherence to clinical observation. He starts with the premise that an adequate etiology in organic disease is lacking. In renal diseases, for example, predispositions, poisons, and infections are inadequate to explain causation, for the question is not answered of why some persons are predisposed to such diseases, and why the presence of pathogenic organisms results in disease in some cases and not in others. Adler postulates the concept of a constitutional inferiority of the involved organ as the key to an understanding of disease causation.

Adler regards inferiority of the sexual organ as the inevitable accompaniment of an organ inferiority. The fact that no organ inferiority occurs without a corresponding inferiority of the "sexual apparatus" accounts for the mistaken idea of a sexual basis for the psychoneuroses, for this inferiority may lead to sexual promiscuity, masturbation, or other sexual anomalies. He contends that it is erroneous to regard these manifestations of a fundamental organ inferiority as of primary importance.

The presence of organ inferiority is difficult to determine because of the fact of compensation through hyperfunction of the defective organ, through the increased action of another organ, or through the compensatory activity of the central nervous system. The attention of the psyche tends to be directed to the inferior organ, and the psychic energy is concentrated on making up for the defect. It is in the vicissitudes of compensation for organ inferiority that neuroses and psychoses have their source.

Compensation may result in a satisfactory adjustment. Overcompensation is common, and may lead either to special achievement with the defective organ, or gross maladaptation. For example, the individual with defective hearing may become a musician or he may, on the contrary, develop paranoia with auditory hallucinations; in either case the psyche has attempted to compensate for the inferiority of the auditory organ by heightening its acuity. If the inferiority is not adequately compensated, psychic tension results, which may be manifested in emotional display or neurotic symptoms. Any defect offers an obstacle to the development of capacity for appropriate psychological reactions and modifies the character structure.

The fictive goal. Individual psychology interprets the individual as a unit organism or dynamic whole moving through a definite life pattern toward a definite goal. Psychic life can be interpreted only in terms of motion, and movement implies a goal. Particular drives do not have goals, but take their direction from the final purpose of the individual-as-a-unity. The goal is established in the first years of life and determines the life pattern or "style of life" of the individual. This goal affects the concept the individual holds of the universe, for both perception and memory are purposive, serving the goal of the personality.

Psychic life, according to Adler, is a complex of aggressive and security-finding activities whose final purpose is to guarantee the continued existence of the human organism and to enable him securely to accomplish his development (11, ch. I). The individual demands not only security from danger, but a sense of superiority. The striving for superiority is not an inborn biological instinct, but an embryonic core where its possibilities of development must be present (3, ch. III). The striving is always in a positive direction, every movement always aiming toward the goal of perfection. This concept makes untenable the idea of a death instinct, the regressive striving toward an inorganic state (9, ch. III).

The ultimate goal of this striving is perfection, omnipotence. Because of the impossible level at which the goal is set, Adler speaks of it as "fictive." The normal as well as the abnormal individual pursues such an objective, but his method and tenacity in pursuing the goal are different. The normal individual is influenced by his goal of superiority, but does not let the search for an unattainable ideal dominate his whole life, while the neurotic becomes somewhat remote from reality in his concentration on a fictitious aim.

An underlying feeling of inferiority stimulates this drive toward superiority. The relative status of the individual's sense of inferiority and his social feeling determines his attitude and behavior in relation to his goal. Because of the earlier development of the child's mental than his physical capacities, he is able to perceive his weakness and general lack of ability, and inevitably feels a sense of inferiority in relation to adults and to the physical environment. The feeling is normal and the child's effort to compensate for his weakness is the very basis of his educability. If this feeling is not exaggerated by untoward circumstances, and if it is balanced by social feeling, it will lead to courage, objectivity, adaptation to the community, all of which Adler describes as "striving on the useful side of life."

The concept of social feeling was elevated from a role of little importance in Adler's early writings to a dominant position in the later formulations of individual psychology. By social feeling is meant not merely the sense of belonging to a group, but the ability to subordinate egocentric wishes to the needs of the community, the willingness to contribute without thought of reward (22). Communal life is essential to the preservation of the species, and at least a germ of social feeling has become part of man's racial inheritance.

The degree of social feeling tends to bear an inverse relation to the degree of inferiority feeling, for the latter conduces to preoccupation with the self and egocentric behavior. There is, therefore, a certain conflict between individuation and social feeling. However, the antagonism of the two trends normally appears as only a transitional phase in the development of the individual to a level at which individualism and social feeling are synthesized. Normality implies an equilibrium between ego feeling and social feeling, while neurosis implies a lack of sufficient social feeling to maintain this equilibrium.

Development of feelings of inferiority and social feeling. The principal factors are five: organ inferiority, environmental pressures, parental attitudes, sex, and position in the family constellation. At first Adler implied the existence of some form of *organic inferiority* underlying every inferiority reaction, but he later modified this, positing organ inferiority as only one of several motivations of an inferiority complex, and changing his emphasis from the fact of organic deficiency to the reaction of the individual to such defect. Organic inferiority is a loose term, including unattractiveness, obesity, small stature, as well as specific structural or functional deviations. The feeling of inadequacy with which the child reacts to this defect may shape his character and whole way of life.

The child is of necessity faced with *environmental pressures* and obstacles when his technique of adjustment is immature. If the child meets with unreasonable demands prematurely, his sense of helplessness and inferiority will be increased. Economic deprivation, crowded housing conditions, the necessity of gainful work in childhood, all lessen the child's sense of security and may eventuate in an attitude of hostility to the world and in criminal behavior.

The *parental attitudes* toward the child are of extreme importance both in the development of inferiority feelings and of social feeling. The pampered child, for whom all obstacles are removed by his elders, is not equipped for life, is not able to face realities and cope with difficulties. The intensification of the child's inferiority feeling comes either when the parents cease to let him have his own way, or when he faces the outside world, as in the school situation. He may resort to night terrors or other manifestations of anxiety to gain attention and solicitude, and so overcome his sense of inferiority. In the case of the unwanted or neglected child, the sense of inferiority is increased, the hostility of the world exaggerated. The result may be delinquent behavior, or an evasion of responsibilities as a precaution against anticipated failure.

The child begins life in an almost parasitic relationship to the mother. We see the first evidence of social feeling when he begins to realize his importance to his mother, for this enhances his self-esteem and makes him able to subordinate his strivings to her wishes. The mother, and to some degree the father, has the responsibility of assisting the child toward independence and interesting him in contact with others. Any treatment of the child which increases his inferiority feelings, whether a pampering, neglectful, nagging or authoritarian attitude, impedes his progress toward independence and interferes with the development of social feeling. The indulgent mother gives the child no incentive to seek other relationships. The neglectful mother deprives the child of the self-confidence necessary to reach out for other contacts.

Individual psychology gives considerable attention to *sex*, but sexual strivings are treated as secondary to ego strivings. The importance of sex revolves about the concept of the dominant role of the male in respect to the female. Men have come to occupy a privileged position in our society, and the idea of the inferiority of women has become deeply imbedded in our thought processes. Dominance, success, goodness, are identified with the masculine, and submission, failure and badness are equated with the feminine. From an early age the child sees the privileges and prerogatives of the male. It is important that the child understand his sexual role and be encouraged to accept it. Otherwise the girl child is inclined to reject her sex, striving to be a boy and reacting with frustration and discouragement when puberty impresses her sex upon her. In adulthood she may revolt, adopting either the role of the masculine type who enters the professional world, rejects heterosexual relationships and seeks to dominate in every situation, or of the extremely submissive type who uses her neurotic symptoms to demonstrate her helplessness and throw the entire burden upon the male.

The counterpart of this "masculine protest" in the boy is a fear lest he not fill adequately the masculine role. The goal of being a complete man seems unattainable. Doubting his ability to achieve and dominate, the boy may seek a dependent role in marriage or in homosexual relationships. The homosexual is regarded as having a strong sense of inferiority, and insufficient social feeling to face the problems of life and try to establish normal social relationships. He retreats from difficulties and chooses a role in which success seems more sure (7, ch. 14). To a large extent, the far-reaching problems resulting from the inferior-superior relationship of the sexes can be dissipated by proper training in the family.

Adler stresses the *birth order* of the child as a decisive factor in determining his personality and pattern of life. For example, the only child tends to be overprotected, and is consequently unequipped to handle obstacles. He is inclined to tyrannize his environment by his helplessness. In adulthood he continues to search for the love and admiration he received in childhood, and is ill-prepared for an adult love relationship of reciprocal affection and mutual dependence. The eldest child gains a sense of inner security from his position, but the experience of being dethroned by a younger child may have untoward effects. For the second child, the elder sibling will serve as an effective stimulus to effort, but the wish to be first, which can never be fulfilled, may lead to inordinate striving along useless channels. The relative ages and the proportion of boys and girls in the family affect the child. There are too many variables for rigid patterns to be drawn, but Adler contends that the probable development of the child can be predicted from his position in the family, and that knowledge of the position of the individual contributes to an understanding of his pattern of life and to an explanation of his character traits.

Summing up these developmental factors, we may say that by the age of five, the pattern of life and the form taken by the psychic goal are established. This goal is always a striving toward perfection to overcome weakness and inferiority. Whether it takes the form of purely egocentric striving to dominate by degrading others, or whether the striving is directed to overcoming weaknesses through a courageous facing of the problems of life and through positive contribution to the social welfare, is determined by the relative strength of inferiority and social feelings. This in turn rests upon the total childhood situation and the child's attitude toward it.

The neurotic character. The individual relates himself to the outside world according to his own interpretation of himself and of the problems of life adjustment. Character traits are manifestations of his pattern of life, means of escaping from a feeling of inferiority to the fictitious goal of superiority. The individual in whom the striving for superiority is balanced by a well-developed social feeling makes the most socially accept able type of adjustment and shows a minimum of egocentric traits. Where there is a lack of social feeling, aggressive or dependent traits emerge. The extreme case of the aggressive mode of life is the delinquent or criminal, who regards other persons only as beings to be exploited for his own benefit (17). If the individual meets with difficulties in direct striving, he may shift to roundabout methods, showing non-aggressive character traits such as seclusiveness and timidity, in which the drive for power is expressed through isolation from others and retreat from problems. This evasion of problems and retreat from life may vary from a self-protective attitude, which does not interfere markedly with the life adjustment, to the extreme form of a severe neurosis, psychosis, or the complete with- drawal or suicide.

No line can be drawn between normality and neurosis. In the neurosis no phenomenon is found which may not occur in the normal person under conditions of stress (20). The difference between normality and neurosis lies in the use to which symptoms are put and the degree to which they dominate the life adjustment. Adler defines the neurosis as an automatic exploitation by the patient of symptoms which originate in some shocking experience (21). The neurosis is a device for maximizing ego consciousness through the circumvention of problems rather than through the straightforward tackling of them. It serves as an alibi for evading life problems, and as an excuse for the absence of achievement. The neurosis magnifies actual attainments, a minor achievement assuming greater im- portance when it is made in spite of the handicap of neurotic illness. It is used to dominate the environment, as is seen in the anxious child who gains his mother's attention through night terrors, or in the neurotic wife whose inability to go anywhere without her husband keeps him in constant attendance upon her.

The neurosis is part of the purposive adaptation of the individual. In itself it is a logical method of attaining the end sought. Adler stresses the fact that it is not the method which is false, but the goal, for the neurotic regards all human relations as struggles for supremacy and directs his maximum effort toward absolute superiority.

"All neurotic symptoms are safeguards of persons who do not feel ade- quately equipped . . . for the problems of life" (20). Individual psy- chology has not answered clearly the question of the choice of symptoms in the particular case, though the relation of symptoms to organ inferiorities has been stressed (13). Some attempt has been made to differentiate the dynamics of the various clinical types of neurosis. The neurotic, Adler writes, experiences tension because of his inability to solve major problems. In the anxiety neuroses and phobias, the effect of the tension is emotional, and in the case of hysteria the effect is in the motor sphere. In the obsessive- compulsive the tension affects the individual intellectually (20). The compulsive neurotic preserves the illusion of power by substituting a self-imposed compulsion for the external compulsion imposed by the demands of society from which he seeks to emancipate himself (7, ch. XV–XVI).

It may be appropriate to comment at this point on the Adlerian interpretation of sexual symptoms and preoccupations. The neurotic, because of his insecurity and his desperate efforts to find a frame of reference which will give some security, is inclined even more than the normal person to classify and schematize. He interprets everything in the light of the conflict of success and failure, the opposition of masculinity and femininity. Because of the equation of dominance-submission with sex, sexual symptoms become a suitable medium for the expression of the striving for superiority.

Treatment. Adler has not outlined his methods of therapy in any detail. He states the role of the therapist as: first, to point out to the patient his lack of cooperative power; second, to reveal his inferiority complex and goal of perfection as erroneous; and third, to awaken courage, optimism, cooperation (4, p. 404). The two case histories he has published (1), (2) are Adler's analyses of cases from records prepared by others, and are of interest in understanding the application of the principles of individual psychology to the interpretation of life histories, rather than for the light which they throw on methods of treatment.

Treatment has been carried out along the channels of medical pedagogy and of individual psychotherapy. In child guidance clinics the child and the parents are interviewed by the psychiatrist who sizes up the problem and offers some interpretation and advice. Clinic assistants, comparable to psychiatric social workers, may then work with the parents and the child helping them to carry through his recommendations. Efforts are directed largely to change of the environmental situation through education of the parents or removal of the child from the home. A series of these clinic cases is presented in *The Pattern of Life* (6).

Psychotherapy is not attempted with children under fifteen years of age (13). Treatment of adults follows in some respects the procedure of psychoanalysis, though there are fundamental divergences. On the basis of a full history the psychiatrist offers the patient some interpretation of his problem at an early stage in treatment. An investigation is made of early recollections as these are considered an important clue to the individual's style of life. Dream analysis is one aspect of the study of the patient. Adler describes the dream as a sort of metaphorical solution of a problem that the individual can not solve in reality. It is concerned not with satisfaction of unfulfilled wishes from the past, but with the future, preparing the individual emotionally for the solution of a problem (8, p. 228 ff.). Inhibition of the higher psychic functions in sleep accounts for the symbolic devices of the dream and makes its ideational content less reliable than its emotional content. As the emotional attitude of the patient toward his problems is more clearly expressed in the dream than in waking life, the dream in the context of the case history may throw considerable light on the patient's attitude toward life.

After the psychiatrist has gained an understanding of the patient in his life situation, he presents to him the principles of individual psychology, interpreting his style of life in the light of these principles. Insight will cause the patient to relinquish his false goal and his neurotic pattern of pursuing it, for his symptoms can no longer serve their purpose when he understands their meaning. Treatment is complete when symptoms disappear and the patient's changed attitude shows in his ceasing to evade problems. The facility with which the individual psychologist arrives at an understanding of a case, and the ease with which he brings the patient to an acceptance of his interpretation, tend to arouse skepticism in those not already convinced of the principles of individual psychology. The very paucity of concepts makes possible this seeming dexterity, as there is no problem of choosing among a variety of interpretations. That the Adlerian psychology clarifies the dynamics of every case is certainly open to question, but it seems to supply the key to an understanding of some cases.

The theories of the individual psychologists have carried their interest beyond the individual case into the field of social action. Adler frequently points to the influence of cultural factors, especially the inequality of the sexes and the competition motif of industrial life, in personal maladjustment, and stresses the need of cultural change to decrease the incidence of such maladjustment.

Summary and conclusion. Adler rejected the concept of the libido as the motivating force in the neuroses and substituted the theory of the inferiority feeling, with the concomitant striving for power and the equilibrating factor of social feeling, as the principal dynamics in personality organization and disorganization. The intensity of the inferiority feeling and its role in the life of the individual are dependent on constitutional and environmental factors, including organic inferiority, economic deprivation, parental attitudes, the sex of the individual, and his position in the family. The neurosis is an adaptive technique used in striving for superiority. Treatment is directed toward showing the patient the genesis of his feeling of inferiority and the fallacy of seeking absolute superiority, and toward helping him to reorient his goal in a more social direction.

Eclecticism is less common in contemporary psychology than enthusiastic acceptance or complete rejection of a psychological system. Crookshank has compared individual psychology with the movements initiated by Confucius and Socrates (8). Few would go to this extreme, but certain Adlerian concepts might with profit be incorporated into psychological thinking. The concept of the dynamics of the inferiority complex is, in some cases, illuminating. Adler has exerted a constructive influence in the educational field, bringing to the attention of the pedagogue psychological factors in training and personality development. His emphasis on the probable necessity of social change for attaining the better adjustment of the individual personality is an interesting contribution.

Antagonism among different schools of psychology is a factor in the uncertain status of the science, for, until there is common agreement on a fundamental body of theory and fact within a science, those outside its borders are not impressed with its validity. Salvaging the valuable aspects of such work as Adler's might strengthen the theoretical structure of dynamic psychology.

Bibliography

1. Adler, Alfred. *The Case of Mrs. A.: The Diagnosis of a Life Style.* C. W. Daniel Co., Ltd., London, 1931.
2. ———. *The Case of Miss R.: The Interpretation of a Life Story.* Greenberg Publisher, Inc., New York, 1929. (Preface by Friedrich Jensen)
3. ———. *The Education of Children.* Greenberg Publisher, Inc., New York, 1930.
4. ———. "Individual Psychology," ch. XXI of *Psychologies of 1930*, edited by Carl Murchison. Clark University Press, Worcester, 1930.
5. ———. *The Neurotic Constitution.* Moffatt, Yard, New York, 1921.
6. ———. *Pattern of Life.* Cosmopolitan Book Corp., New York, 1930. (Introduction by W. Beran Wolfe)
7. ———. *Practice and Theory of Individual Psychology.* Harcourt, Brace and Co., Inc., New York, 1924.
8. ———. *Problems of Neurosis.* Cosmopolitan Book Corp., New York, 1930. (Preface by F. G. Crookshank)
9. ———. *Social Interest.* G. P. Putnam's Sons, New York, 1939.
10. ———. *Study of Organ Inferiority and Its Psychical Compensation.* Nervous and Mental Disease Pub. Co., New York, 1917.
11. ———. *Understanding Human Nature.* Greenberg Publisher, Inc., New York, 1928. (Preface by W. Beran Wolfe)
12. Crookshank, F. G. *Individual Psychology and Nietzsche.* C. W. Daniel Co., Ltd., London, 1933.
13. Wexberg, Erwin. *Individual Psychology.* Cosmopolitan Book Corp., New York, 1929.
14. Adler, Alfred. "Fundamental Views of Individual Psychology." *Internat. J. Individ. Psychol.,* 1 (1): 5, 1935.
15. ———. "Mass Psychology." *Internat. J. Individ. Psychol.,* 3 (2): 111, 1937.
16. ———. "Prevention of Delinquency." *Internat. J. Individ. Psychol.,* 1 (3): 3, 1935.
17. ———. "Prevention of Neurosis." *Internat. J. Individ. Psychol.,* 1 (4): 3, 1935.
18. ———. "Psychiatric Aspects regarding Individual and Social Disorganization." *Am. J. Sociol.,* 42: 773, 1937.
19. ———. "A School Girl's Exaggeration of Her Own Importance." *Internat. J. Individ. Psychol.,* 3 (1): 3, 1937.
20. ———. "Structure of Neurosis." *Internat. J. Individ. Psychol.,* 1 (2): 3, 1935.
21. ———. "What is a Neurosis?" *Internat. J. Individ. Psychol.,* 1 (1): 9, 1935.
22. Driekurs, R. "Introduction to Individual Psychology." *Internat. J. Individ. Psychol.,* 3: 320, 1937.
23. Frenschel, R. "Friedrich Nietzsche and Individual Psychology." *Internat. J. Individ. Psychol.,* 1 (4): 87, 1935.

24. Krausz, Erwin O. "Homosexuality as a Neurosis." *Internat. J. Individ. Psychol.*, 1 (1): 30, 1935.
25. Seif, Leonard. "Neurosis and Weakness of Will." *Internat. J. Individ. Psychol.*, 1 (3): 79, 1935.
26. White, William A. "The Adlerian Concept of the Neurosis." *J. Abnorm. Psychol.*, 12: 168, 1917.

TYPES OF ADJUSTIVE REACTIONS *

《 JAMES C. COLEMAN

Adjustive reactions can best be understood in terms of the total personality organization of the individual and his specific life situation. The particular adjustive reaction that occurs will vary widely depending upon these two sets of factors. However, even the most divergent attempts at adjustment follow certain basic dynamic principles and can be understood as attempts to cope with actual or perceived stress in such a way as to maintain psycho-biological integrity by satisfying basic needs.

General Patterns

In general the individual deals with his adjustive problems by either attack, withdrawal, or compromise, complicated by various ego defense mechanisms and by varying degrees of emotional involvement.

Attack, aggression, hostility. In attack behavior we attempt to remove or surmount the obstacles through increased effort or a variation in mode of approach. We have seen that biological frustration leads to various compensatory or corrective activities such as the release of stored energy to allow increased activity by the organism in an attempt to meet the need and restore equilibrium. This increased tension and variant activity is apparently the primary origin of aggressive or attack-type behavior (Schilder [1]). In primitive form it is seen in the restless behavior of the infant deprived of food; such behavior is at first relatively uncoordinated and generalized, but as motor and intellectual abilities increase, the individual learns to evaluate and deal directly with an ever-increasing variety of specific obstacles.

Despite these improvements in efficiency, only a small number of stress situations can be adequately dealt with by means of direct aggression. This

* From James C. Coleman, *Abnormal Psychology and Modern Life*, pp. 78–96, Scott, Foresman and Company, Chicago, 1950. Reprinted by permission of the author and the publisher.

[1] Schilder, Paul. *Goals and Desires of Man.* New York: Columbia University Press, 1942.

means that in infancy, as well as later in life, direct attack may be un- successful, the frustration continues, and the irritation, pain, and unpleas- antness connected with it become attached to the objects or persons viewed as obstacles and sources of frustration. Such conditions, of course, lead to the arousal of emergency emotional reactions, particularly hostility. Thus aggressive reactions, which at first involve only a tendency toward increased activity and variation in mode of attack, may eventually be reinforced by hate or hostility (Cushing and Cushing [2]).

Attack behavior may be primarily constructive or destructive in nature. With hostility there is a tendency to destroy as well as attack; hence we find that where hostility is extremely intense, attack behavior may be primarily destructive. For example, an individual who feels unwanted, un- justly treated, and deprived of opportunities afforded to others may build up intense resentment and hostility which may be manifested in hostile, aggressive activities, perhaps of a delinquent or criminal nature. Stealing, destroying property, setting fires, sexual misbehavior, and assault frequently represent attack patterns involving defiant hostile reactions of this sort.

The way in which hostility is discharged is very important in personality dynamics. For example, it may be expressed directly in overt behavior (physical or verbal), in fantasies (in which the individual may machine- gun or otherwise attack and destroy his enemies), or in competitive sports and other activities; or it may be discharged internally through the visceral organs. Although hostility is ordinarily directed toward external objects and persons viewed as sources of frustration, it may be evoked by personal limi- tations and mistakes and directed toward the self in terms of self-recrimina- tion, self-punishment, and even self-mutilation and suicide.

Where the hostility is felt toward more powerful persons—authority figures—the individual may inhibit any actual outward manifestations. However, such hostile tensions may build up to high levels of intensity and become extremely difficult to manage; for we may not only view hostility as morally wrong, particularly if it is directed toward parents or siblings, but we know from unpleasant experience that overt hostile acts toward others lead to retaliation in the form of punishment and frustration. So, as we shall see, such hostility may come to be expressed in various deviant but "safe" ways.

Flight, withdrawal, fear. Simple withdrawal is the second fundamental type of reaction to stress. Many animals seem capable of fairly well-coordi- nated withdrawal or flight reactions shortly after birth, but the human infant is relatively helpless for a long period and is unable to execute any well-coordinated withdrawal reaction. However, he is able to withdraw a bodily part from a painful stimulus such as a hot object and as Watson has demonstrated, he may on the occasion of sudden, unexpected stimuli tend

[2] Cushing, J. G. N. and Cushing, Mary McK. "A Concept of the Genesis of Hostil- ity." *Bulletin of the Menninger Clinic,* 13, 94–99, 1949.

to curl up into a ball, which appears to be sort of a primitive fear reaction.

As the growing infant learns to associate certain objects and situations with frustration and hurt, he may avoid instead of attacking them. His action tendency to withdraw in the face of such dangerous situations is typically reinforced by emotional processes involving fear. With time, his fears involve a wide range of real and imagined dangers as well as being usually induced by any strong, sudden, unexpected stimulation. And in a related way his withdrawal behavior becomes more complicated; in addition to mere physical withdrawal, he may withdraw in various psychological ways: he may inhibit dangerous internal desires, or consciously suppress them, or abandon goals, or restrict the situations to which he reacts, or even become emotionally passive.

So just as simple aggression becomes complicated by hostility we find simple withdrawal or flight reactions becoming complicated by fear. In both cases the individual's action tendencies are reinforced by mobilization of reserve resources, with a high degree of psychobiological tension demanding discharge. But here again social living provides few situations in which such mobilized energy can be utilized in direct physical action. Taking final examinations, being interviewed for jobs, excessive competition, cannot ordinarily be met by direct physical withdrawal. Rather the individual is forced to face the dangerous situation despite fears and anticipated frustration. It is of interest here to note that Shaffer found, in a study of fear in aerial combat, that situations permitting no adjustive response, such as "being fired upon when you have no chance to shoot back," were the most frequently reported causes of increased fear (Shaffer [3]). On the other hand, he found that engaging in some effective activity was frequently conducive to reducing fear, even though such activities did not make possible the avoidance of the real danger.

Anxiety is very similar to fear, involving the same general pattern of emergency physiological changes and arising in connection with anticipated frustration or hurt. However, it differs from fear in certain essential respects. Fear is usually related to some immediate concrete situation, whereas the stress giving rise to anxiety is usually vague and ill-defined. Often the individual is unaware of what is causing his anxiety. Likewise, fear involves a definite action tendency of flight whereas anxiety is more in the nature of diffuse apprehension not leading to any action tendency. Thus anxiety seems to be a sort of preliminary or primitive fear reaction which mobilizes energy reserves to meet some threat, but in which neither the threat nor the appropriate direction of response is clearly discernible by the individual. Perhaps this feeling of vagueness and uncertainty adds to the unpleasantness of anxiety; in any event anxiety is one of the most painful and intolerable of all conscious experiences.

[3] Shaffer, Laurance. "Fear and Courage in Aerial Combat." *J. consult. Psychol.,* 11 137–143.

Compromise, substitution. Since most situations cannot be dealt with successfully by either direct attack or withdrawal, it usually becomes necessary to work out some sort of compromise. This represents our most common method of dealing with conflicts. Such compromises may mean accepting substitute goals or lowering one's aspirations or internal ethical or reality restraints. An individual faced with starvation may compromise with his conscience and steal "just this one time" because of the special

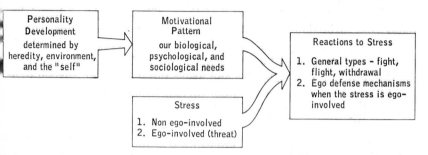

Fig. 1. Personality development determines motivational patterns. Motivational pattern and stress jointly determine reactions to stress, which will include ego defensive mechanisms if the stress is ego-involved.

nature of the conditions, or he may resort to eating worms, bugs, spiders, and even human flesh, or he may revise his ethical standards. Often, too, we resort to symbolic satisfactions under conditions of severe frustration. Thus a soldier may gain some substitutive satisfaction out of pin-up pictures or out of wish-fulfilling daydreams. In fact, Masserman [4] has shown that under frustration, the individual becomes increasingly willing to accept substitutive goals—both symbolic and nonsymbolic ones. Hate, fear, and other emotional reactions may, of course, also reinforce or be involved in compromise reactions, as well as in attack or withdrawal reactions.

Ego Defense Mechanisms

As we have noted, the self is the integrating core of the personality and any threat to its worth or adequacy is a threat to the individual's very center of existence. Consequently various psychological defenses are gradually built up around the self which are designed to protect it from insult and to enhance it as much as possible. These are then called into play when we find ourselves in an ego-involved stress situation, in which threat to the integrity or worth of the self is present. The "we won today" of the football fan may help him to achieve some measure of importance by "identifying" himself with a successful team; the student who flunks a test may "project"

[4] Masserman, Jules H. *Principles of Dynamic Psychiatry.* Philadelphia: W. B. Saunders Company, 1946.

the blame for his performance onto the poor quality of instruction and the unfairness of the test; the person who feels guilty about his unethical business dealings may "rationalize" that others would take similar advantage of him if they were smart enough. In more extreme cases an individual may insist that his failure is due to the fact that other people are working against him, or a person with unacceptable sexual fantasies may insist that others are making immoral sexual advances toward him.

All of us use these ego defense mechanisms to some extent. They are essential for softening failures, alleviating guilt, preserving internal harmony, and maintaining our feelings of personal worth and adequacy. At the same time they perform a vital function in protecting us from the intolerable anxiety aroused by threats to the value of the self. Failure, guilt, inferiority are all self-devaluating and hence threatening and anxiety-arousing. The protection of the self from overwhelming devaluation and thus from anxiety is the very essence of the defensive functions of these mechanisms.

Thus we must consider these mechanisms as normal adjustive reactions unless they are used to such an extreme degree that they actually interfere with the maintenance of self-integrity instead of aiding it. In a sense, the self, like a nation devoting its major energies to armaments, may break down under the very load of its defensive activities. In addition, these mechanisms, as necessary as they are, have certain drawbacks. They are not usually adaptive in the sense of realistically coping with the adjustment problems. The individual who continually rationalizes away his mistakes is not apt to profit from them on subsequent occasions. In this sense these mechanisms may be said to involve a high degree of self-deception and reality distortion. Also they operate on relatively unconscious levels and hence are not subject to normal conscious checks and evaluations. In fact, the individual usually resents having his attention called to them, for once they become conscious they do not serve their defensive purposes as well.

But whether or not they lead to adjustive behavior, they can be understood in the light of the *purpose* for which they are used, which is to protect the integrity and worth of the ego. Thus it is only as we conceive of an active, striving "self" that they make sense. Only in this framework are we able to understand our ability to change "facts" to fit our needs and evaluations and utilize these mechanisms to protect ourselves from anxiety.

With this brief introduction, let us now turn to a consideration of the more important of these ego defense mechanisms.

Denial of reality. We manage to evade many disagreeable realities by ignoring or refusing to acknowledge them. Very few of us, for example, accept the full inevitability of death. Of course, we act as if we were quite resigned to the idea, but the full realization of the actual physical decay of our bodies is usually mercifully obscured by vague feelings of our omnipotence—everybody else dies but not us—and by various religious and philosophical convictions about continuation of life after death. This tendency to avoid or deny unpleasant reality is exemplified in a great many of our everyday activities. We turn away from unpleasant sights, we refuse to discuss unpleasant topics, we ignore or deny criticism, we refuse to face our real problems, and even in old age we are prone to deny to ourselves the evidence of physical and mental decline. Proud parents are notoriously blind when it comes to the defects of their offspring. One mother, whose nine-year-old son had been diagnosed by several psychologists and psychiatrists as mentally deficient, developed the firm belief that her son was a member of a new species which matured at a slower rate and would in the long run achieve a higher level of mental development. The common sayings, "None is so blind as he who will not see" and "Love is blind," perhaps exemplify even more clearly our tendency to ignore things which are not compatible with our desires and wishes.

By means of this mechanism of ignoring or denying unpleasant reality we do protect ourselves from a great deal of traumatic stress. But like the proverbial ostrich who buries his head in the sand when danger approaches, we may fail to take cognizance of many things which are essential for effective adjustment.

Fantasy. Not only do we often deny unpleasant reality, but we also tend to construct the world in fantasy as we would like it to be. We fall for various half-baked get-rich-quick schemes, we accept flattery eagerly, and we are highly susceptible to selling techniques based on telling us what we want to hear about the merchandise.

Fantasy grows essentially out of mental images associated with need gratification. It is stimulated by frustrated desires, for in fantasy the person achieves his goals and gratifies his needs, albeit in substitute fashion. Such fantasies may take many forms. Starving men commonly have mental images of food; the merchant beginning his first business venture has fantasies of wealth and success.

Of course, fantasy imaginings may be either productive or nonproductive. Productive fantasy is used constructively in the solution of immediate problems, as in creative imagination, whereas nonproductive fantasy is merely a wish-fulfilling activity, compensating for lack of achievement rather than stimulating or promoting achievement.

Two common varieties of wish-fulfilling fantasy are the "conquering hero" and the "suffering hero." The first imagines himself a great and courageous soldier, an athlete, a surgeon, or some other remarkable figure who performs the most incredible feats and wins the admiration and respect of all, the essential idea being that he is rich, powerful, and respected —the fulfillment of wished-for status. James Thurber used this theme as the basis for his "Secret Life of Walter Mitty" (Thurber [5]). Hostility is

[5] Thurber, James. "The Secret Life of Walter Mitty." In *A Treasury of Laughter.* (Louis Untermeyer, ed.) New York: Simon and Schuster, 1946.

frequently dissipated safely and conveniently through conquering-hero fantasies in which the individual destroys or punishes all who stand in his way. Most students report fantasies involving the physical injury or destruction of others, such as fisticuffs, shooting, machine-gunning, and even running over people in tanks; undoubtedly all these act as safety valves for the release of hostility.

The suffering hero does not have to admit any personal inferiority because he imagines himself suffering from some terrible affliction, handicap, or visitation from unjust fate. If others only knew about his difficulties and realized how nobly and with what courage he has carried on, they would accord him the sympathy and admiration he deserves. Thus inferior accomplishments are explained away without any threat to the individual's feeling of adequacy or basic worth.

As Ruch [6] has pointed out, many of our fantasies are ready-made for us in the form of movies, soap operas, magazine stories, and books in which we escape from our own status and identify ourselves in fantasy with the hero or heroine, bravely facing and surmounting their problems with them, and sharing in their adventures and triumphs.

The ability to escape temporarily from unpleasant reality into a more pleasant fantasy world has considerable adjustive value. It may add the dash of excitement and interest which enables us to bear up under an otherwise drab and uninteresting existence, or our fantasy achievements and their rewards may spur us on to greater efforts toward our goals in real life. We often return to work with increased vigor and enthusiasm after seeing a movie. However, wish-fulfilling fantasies are divorced from reality and thus present a danger for adequate personality adjustment. For it may become increasingly easy to retreat to a dream world when the going gets tough. Particularly under conditions of extreme frustration are our fantasies apt to get out of hand. For example, at the concentration camps of Dachau and Buchenwald, it was found that "The longer the time a prisoner had spent in camp, the less true to reality were his daydreams; so much so that the hopes and expectations of the old prisoners often took the form of eschatological or messianic hopes." (Bettelheim,[7] p. 443)

Compensation. Compensatory reactions are defenses against feelings of inferiority and inadequacy growing out of real or imagined personal defect or weaknesses as well as out of our inevitable actual failures and setbacks. Such defensive reactions may take many forms. In the case of a physical handicap the individual may attempt to overcome his handicap directly through increased effort and persistence. Demosthenes, the great orator, had to overcome his early stuttering, and Theodore Roosevelt waged a valiant fight against early ill health and became noted for his physical daring

[6] Ruch, Floyd L. *Psychology and Life.* (3d ed.) Chicago: Scott, Foresman, 1948.
[7] Bettelheim, Bruno. "Individual and Mass Behavior in Extreme Situations." *J. abnorm. soc. Psychol.*, 38, 417–452.

ng and robustness. Many great athletes have had to overcome initial de-
ormities or injuries which would have been incapacitating for most people.
Compensatory reactions of this type may be a deciding factor in success,
s biographers are quick to point out. However, failures probably overwhelmingly outnumber successes in such efforts, and the increased effort
nd striving may make the eventual failure more bitter.

More commonly, compensatory reactions are more indirect; there is an
ttempt to substitute for the defect in some way or to draw attention away
rom it. The physically unattractive boy or girl may develop an exception-
lly pleasing personality, the puny boy may turn from athletics to scholas-
ics, the mediocre nobody may become the Grand Imperial Potentate of
ome secret order. A whole science of dress has developed which centers
round the concealing of undesirable physical features and the emphasiz-
ng of desirable ones. The short girl is made to look tall, the fat girl thin,
he colorless one glamorous.

Unfortunately, not all compensatory reactions are desirable or useful.
The individual who feels insecure and rejected may show off to try to get
more attention and raise his status in the eyes of others and himself. The
boy who feels inferior and unpopular may become the local bully; the per-
on who feels unloved and frustrated may eat too much, or resort to exces-
ive fantasy satisfactions. Many people brag about their illustrious ancestors
nd exaggerate their own accomplishments, while others resort to criticism
r innuendoes in an attempt to cut others down to their own size. In ex-
reme cases the individual may engage in antisocial behavior or develop
marked eccentricities in an attempt to get some attention and evidence of
nterest and concern from others.

Compensatory reactions are greatly stimulated by our highly competitive
ociety. We constantly compare ourselves with others and too often meas-
ire our worth and that of others largely by status, achievements, and pos-
essions. Such social values lead to the development of strong psychological
motivation toward at least average, and if possible superior, achievement.
n meeting these conditions, compensatory reactions may be of great adjus-
ive value but where they result in increased anxiety or become exaggerated
r take antisocial forms, they hinder rather than help us.

Identification. The growing child soon realizes that his evaluation by
thers is to a large extent dependent upon his family and other group mem-
erships. The position of his father, the size of his house, the importance
f his relatives all help to determine his personal prestige and status. Exag-
erating the strength, importance, and money of his father early becomes a
ommon means of enhancing his own prestige.

This mechanism of identification is expanded in later life to include a
wide variety of situations and persons and enables the individual to expe-
ience vicarious achievements, feelings of adequacy, and other satisfactions
hrough his various identifications. Not only does society evaluate him in

terms of his various group identifications, but he comes to evaluate himsel in the light of them. College students bask in the reflected glory of thei football teams—"we" won today. Fraternity and sorority members enjo the social prestige of their groups, adults identify themselves with thei occupations, the size of their homes, their membership in exclusive clubs the size of their bank accounts and cars. Parents identify themselves witl the accomplishments of their children. Most employees identify themselve with the power and prestige of the companies for which they work. By s doing the individual takes unto himself some of the desirable attributes o the groups and institutions with which he identifies himself.

We are probably all prone to a certain amount of fantasy identificatio in which we gain vicarious satisfaction through identifying ourselves witl the leading characters in novels, movies, and radio serials. As we hav noted, such identifications enable us to share in the adventures and tr umphs of our heroes. It is interesting to note that in those rare pictures i which the hero dies, members of the audience slump down in their seat and figuratively or symbolically die themselves. Such identifications, particu larly in the form of "hero worship," may play an important role in shapin the personality development of the child, who strives to be like his hero i dress and manner.

Most people identify themselves with the hero or winner and thu achieve increased feelings of adequacy or worth. However, some identifica tions are consistently with the loser or with the villain. Such negative iden tifications may be based upon the acceptance of undesirable models suc as gangsters, which are common in slum areas, or upon strong guilt feelings leading to a need for punishment, or upon suppressed asocial tendencies

In general, individuals tend to associate themselves with others who ar most like themselves or who possess the qualities which they most desire The athlete identifies himself with the athletic hero, the scholar with th great scientist, the co-ed with the glamorous cinema beauty. Of course where there is compensatory identification, the meek, timid individual ma become the great and brave detective, or the uneducated man the renowne scholar and scientist. However, all such identifications have to conform t the individual's ego values.

Identifications are of great value in enhancing our feelings of adequac and worth and in the reduction of frustrations through fantasy identif cations with the adventures and achievements of our heroes. We all us identifications. But like the other ego defense mechanisms it is potentiall dangerous. We see identification in extreme form in certain psychotic reac tions, with a loss of personal identification and the firm belief that one i some famous person such as Jesus Christ or Abraham Lincoln.

Introjection (*internalization*). Introjection is, in a way, a primitive form of identification, in which the individual internalizes the threatening situ ation. This is exemplified early in life when the child gradually learns an accepts as his own, various social regulations and value attitudes. He can then control his own behavior in the light of his internalized values, and protect himself from possible infractions of regulations and thus avoid social retaliation and punishment. If the individual's only restraints were based on reality considerations, he would be continually in danger of getting caught and being punished by society. But by internalizing society's values and using them to guide and control his own behavior he can protect himself from frustration and punishment.

Bettelheim,[8] in his report of his experiences at the German concentration camps of Dachau and Buchenwald, tells of the gradual breakdown of previous values under the insidious camp experiences and the development and internalization of new norms—Nazi norms:

A prisoner had reached the final stage of adjustment to the camp situation when he had changed his personality so as to accept as his own the values of the Gestapo. . . . Practically all prisoners who had spent a long time in the camp took over the Gestapo's attitude toward the so-called unfit prisoners. . . . So old prisoners were sometimes instrumental in getting rid of the unfit, in this way making a feature of Gestapo ideology a feature of their own behavior. This was one of the many situations in which old prisoners demonstrated toughness and molded their way of treating other prisoners according to the example set by the Gestapo. That this was really a taking-over of Gestapo attitudes can be seen from the treatment of traitors. Self-protection asked for their elimination, but the way in which they were tortured for days and slowly killed was taken over from the Gestapo.

Old prisoners who seemed to have a tendency to identify themselves with the Gestapo did so not only in respect to aggressive behavior. They would try to arrogate to themselves old pieces of Gestapo uniforms. If that was not possible, they tried to sew and mend their uniforms so that they would resemble those of the guards. The length to which prisoners would go in these efforts seemed unbelievable, particularly since the Gestapo punished them for their efforts to copy Gestapo uniforms. When asked why they did it they admitted that they loved to look like the guards.

The identification with the Gestapo did not stop with the copying of their outer appearance and behavior. Old prisoners accepted their goals and values, too, even when they seemed opposed to their own interests. It was appalling to see how far formerly even politically well-educated prisoners would go in this identification. . . . When old prisoners accepted Nazi values as their own they usually did not admit it, but explained their behavior by means of rationalizations. (Bettelheim,[9] pp. 447, 448, 449)

Similarly, as Sherif and Cantril [10] point out, many lighter Negroes internalize the color values of the white world and look upon darker Negroes as inferior and exclude them from the "upper class" social groupings.

[8] *Ibid.*

[9] *Ibid.* Selection is reprinted here by permission of the Managing Editor, the American Psychological Association.

[10] Sherif, M. and Cantril, H. *The Psychology of Ego-involvements.* New York: Wiley, 1947.

Introjection, or internalization, is thus a defensive reaction which seem
to follow the general idea: if you can't defeat your enemies, join them
Apparently it is preferable, from an ego-defensive point of view, to be goo
or bad oneself rather than to be continually at the mercy of good or ba
objects or forces from without.

Projection. Projection is a defensive reaction by means of which we (1)
transfer the blame for our own shortcomings, mistakes, and misdeeds to
others, and (2) attribute to others our own unacceptable impulses, thoughts
and desires.

Projection is perhaps most commonly evidenced in our tendency to
blame others for our own mistakes. The student who fails an examination
may feel sure the examination was unfair, the erring husband may blame
his moral lapse on the girl "who led me on." "It wasn't my fault, he hit me
first" or "If I hadn't taken advantage of him he would have taken advan
tage of me," and so it goes. Fate and bad luck are particularly overworke
objects of projection. Even inanimate objects are not exempt from blame
The tennis player who misses the ball may look at his racquet with a puz
zled expression as if there must be a hole in it, and the basketball playe
who slips may return to inspect the imaginary slippery spot. A three-year
old boy who falls off his hobby horse may attack it with blows and kicks

Such projections help to maintain our feelings of adequacy and self
esteem in the face of failure, and probably develop from our early realiza
tion that placing the blame on others for our own mistakes helps us to
avoid social disapproval and punishment. And as we internalize society'
value attitudes, such projections protect us from self-devaluation. In ex
treme cases, however, the individual may become convinced that his fail
ures and difficulties are not his fault while at the same time they seem to
follow some sort of pattern which cannot be entirely attributed to bad luc
or chance. It seems to him that other persons or forces are systematicall
working against him. Out of such initial ideas delusions of persecution ma
develop, involving the supposed plots and conspiracies of his enemies.

In other projective reactions we attribute to others our own unacceptabl
impulses, desires, wishes, and thoughts. In an elementary way this is ev
denced by our tendency to see others in the light of our own personalit
make-up. If we are honest, we tend to think others are too, whereas if w
are deceitful we are prone to attribute this characteristic to others. Indi
viduals who are tempted to be dishonest or to lapse morally are quick t
detect similar tendencies in others. This, of course, may enable the indi
vidual to justify his proposed behavior since others have the same tend
encies. Or he may be quick to condemn such tendencies in others, thereb
in a way protecting himself from such moral lapses. Often the individua
may ascribe ethically unacceptable desires and impulses to others while h
remains totally unaware of their internal origin. The individual with home
sexual leanings may accuse other males of attempting to seduce him. It i

common for mental patients who are obsessed by ethically unacceptable sexual ideas to accuse others of "pouring filth into their minds." Thus the individual protects himself against facing his own dangerous and unacceptable impulses by attributing them to others instead.

Rationalization. Rationalization has two major defensive values: (1) it helps us to justify what we do and what we believe, and (2) it aids us in softening the disappointment connected with unattainable goals.

Typically, rationalization involves thinking up logical, socially approved reasons for our past, present, or proposed behavior. With a little effort we can soon justify to ourselves the absolute necessity of purchasing a new car, of going to a show instead of studying, or even marrying someone with whom we are not in love. Carrying matters a step further, we may find it equally easy to justify most selfish and antisocial behavior. "Why should we yield the right of way to an oncoming motorist? He wouldn't yield it to us if he could help it, so why should we show him any consideration either?" "Suppose we did misrepresent the facts in making a sale—the other fellow has to learn sometime not to be so gullible and this provided a cheap lesson." "Yes, we did cheat on the test, but so would everyone else if he thought he could get away with it." One of the most notorious bootleggers and gangsters of American history sincerely insisted that he was being persecuted by the government when all he was trying to do was bring people the "lighter pleasures" of life. Thus we justify our behavior and protect our adequacy and self-esteem. For were we to face the real reasons or motivations for our behavior, we might feel ashamed and guilty. Of course, many rationalizations such as these, where we laud our own motives and condemn the other fellow's, overlap with the use of projection.

In a similar way we may justify our political, religious, and economic beliefs and prejudices. "Why should we worry about the unemployed? If they had any initiative they would go out and find a job! And anyway they are too lazy to work even if a job were offered to them." Similarly, a wealthy landowner in Italy who received an income from 700 peasants who tilled his estate and permitted him to live in luxury was not at all interested in helping to improve their terribly wretched farming and housing conditions. "We aren't concerned with production," he said. "We collect rents. Anyway, the peasants are retrograde. If we built clean, good homes, they'd only dirty them." (*Time* [11])

In protecting ourselves from the disappointment of unattainable goals, we often resort to two additional types of rationalization—the so-called "sour grapes" and "sweet lemon" mechanisms. The "sour grapes" mechanism is based upon the fable of the fox, who, unable to reach clusters of luscious grapes, decided that they were sour and not worth having anyway. A new automobile may not be worth having because it costs more than it is worth, the insurance on it is exorbitant, it would lead to increased driv-

[11] *Time*, May 30, 1949, p. 22.

ing, which isn't worth while in view of the high cost of gasoline and the
increased possibility of accidents, and anyway if people don't like you well
enough to enjoy riding in your old car, they aren't worth having as friends.
Similarly, we may view business success as requiring more effort than it is
worth or point out that the girl we couldn't get talks too much and will
probably lose her figure at an early age.

The "sweet lemon" attitude is in a sense an extension of sour grapes.
Not only is the unattainable not worth while, but what we have is remarkably satisfactory. Not only are the disadvantages of a new car obvious but
the many virtues of our old one would make such an exchange extremely
silly. We find comfort in our poverty, for money is the root of all evil and
would probably distort our political and economic views. Such sweet-lemon
mechanisms may involve more generalized pollyanna attitudes so that
"every dark cloud has a silver lining" and "everything happens for the
best."

Frequently, of course, it is difficult to tell where the objective consideration of facts and problems leaves off and rationalization begins. Rather
conclusive indications of rationalization are (1) hunting for reasons to
justify our behavior or beliefs, (2) being unable to recognize inconsistencies and rationalizing them away, and (3) becoming emotional when
our rationalizations are questioned. The questioning of our rationalizations,
of course, is a threat to the defenses we have managed to construct against
self-devaluation and would, if we were to permit our defenses to be destroyed, lead to the arousal of anxiety. For we would be faced with threats
to our needs without any adequate defenses with which to protect ourselves.

Even the young child soon learns to justify questionable behavior by
advancing reasons for it which he has learned are socially approved. And
as he internalizes the value attitudes of society he follows the same procedures in justifying his behavior to himself. In this way rationalization
becomes an important adjustive reaction in helping us to avoid unnecessary
frustrations and to maintain a reasonable degree of self-integrity in a dangerous world. The price of this defensive reaction, however, is self-deception, for we accept reasons for our behavior which are not the true ones. As
a result we are less likely to profit from our errors, but may instead spend
our energy in trying to justify them or in proving that they weren't errors
or misdeeds at all. When used to an extreme degree, rationalization may
lead to the development of false beliefs or delusions which are maintained
despite contradictory objective evidence.

Repression. Repression is a defensive reaction by means of which painful
or dangerous thoughts and desires are excluded from consciousness. It has
often been referred to as selective forgetting, but it is more in the nature of
selective remembering. For although the material is denied admission to
consciousness, it is not really forgotten. For example, the soldier who has

seen his best friend killed by shrapnel may find this experience so terribly painful and disruptive to ego values that it must be excluded from consciousness if he is to maintain his ego-integrity. As a result he becomes "amnesic" for the battle experience. However, by means of hypnosis or sodium amytal interviews, the repressed experience may be brought into consciousness.

It is of value dynamically to distinguish repression from *inhibition* and *suppression*. Early in life we learn the necessity for inhibiting the overt expression of various desires in order to avoid social disapproval and punishment, and, as we internalize ethical attitudes, to avoid lowered self-esteem and guilt feelings. Such inhibitions operate on a relatively conscious level, e.g., an individual may be tempted to seduce his best friend's wife, but inhibits any overt action. Suppression differs from inhibition in that the individual consciously "puts the idea out of mind" and thinks of other things. Repression, however, takes place without the individual's awareness. Now the dangerous and immoral thought is spontaneously and unconsciously excluded from consciousness.

Repression is by no means always complete: often desires and thoughts are only partially excluded from consciousness. Vague feelings of unworthiness, insecurity, and guilt often indicate incomplete repression. Also with continued frustration, the repressed desires may increase in strength and threaten to break directly through repression defenses into consciousness and overt action. Such threats lead to arousal of anxiety and to the implementation of existing ego defenses by means of other defense mechanisms such as projection and rationalization.

Furthermore, dangerous wishes continue to play a part in the actual motivation of behavior, even though the repressive defenses may successfully prevent their direct expression. Although they are refused admission to consciousness, their continued operation is frequently revealed in dreams, reverie, jokes, and slips of the tongue and under the influence of alcohol or drugs. Here they manage to escape ego defenses and find expression in behavior or consciousness (Freud [12]).

In helping the individual to control dangerous desires and in minimizing the disruptive effects of painful experiences, repression plays a vitally important and often valuable role. Like other defensive reactions, however, repression is self-deceptive and may be used to an exaggerated degree or to protect the individual from desires or problems that could better be met by a realistic facing and "working through" than by evasion. Since the repression of dangerous desires not only requires considerable energy but also

[12] Freud, Sigmund. *The Psychopathology of Everyday Life*. London: Ernest Benn, Ltd., 1948; Freud, Sigmund. *Wit and Its Relation to the Unconscious*. New York: Moffatt, Yard, 1916; Freud, Sigmund. *General Introduction to Psychoanalysis*. (new ed.) New York: Garden City. 1949.

interferes with a stable and healthy personality integration, a more realisti
facing of problems whenever possible would appear more conducive t
long-range mental health.

Reaction formation. Reaction formation refers to the development o
conscious attitudes and behavior patterns which are the opposite of variou
suppressed or repressed wishes and impulses. Dynamically speaking, it in
volves the erection of obstacles or barriers to assist in repressing these dan
gerous desires and in preventing them from being carried out in over
behavior.

Usually reaction formation can be easily recognized by its extreme anc
intolerant characteristics, which are out of all proportion to the importanc
of the situation. The most militant crusaders against vice are often fighting
their own repressed impulses as well as condemning the outcome of sucl
impulses in others. Self-appointed protectors of the public's morals whc
voluntarily devote their lives to reading obscene literature, attending bur
lesque shows, and investigating the younger generation and who obses
sively condemn homosexuality, alcohol, and other alleged vices are usuall
found to have dangerously strong impulses in the same direction them
selves. By making such activities their "duty" they both partially satisf
their repressed desires and at the same time hold them in check by thei
energetic condemnations.

In everyday behavior, reaction formation may take the form of being
excessively polite to a person we don't like—so much so that we make hin
uncomfortable—of developing a "don't care" attitude to conceal feeling
of rejection and a craving for affection, of assuming an air of bravado when
one is fearful, and of developing a puritanical attitude toward sexual anc
other pleasures. Extreme solicitousness over someone's health may concea
repressed hostility and even an actual wish for his death. The individua
may develop various exaggerated fears, as for example of syphilis, whicl
may help him to keep his dangerous impulses in check. Reaction formatior
in extreme form is well illustrated by excerpts from an interesting and self
diagnostic letter which Masserman received from a "kind-hearted" anti
vivisectionist:

. . . I read [a magazine article] . . . on your work on alcoholism [cf. Exp. 16
. . . I am surprised that anyone who is as well educated as you must be to hol
the position that you do would stoop to such a depth as to torture helples
little cats in the pursuit of a cure for alcoholics. . . . A drunkard does not wan
to be cured—a drunkard is just a weak minded idiot who belongs in the gutte
and should be left there. Instead of torturing helpless little cats why not tortur
the drunks or better still exert your would-be noble effort toward getting a bil
passed to *exterminate* the drunks. They are not any good to anyone or them
selves and are just a drain on the public, having to pull them off the street
jail them, then they have to be fed while there and it's against the law to fee
them arsenic so there they are. . . . If people are such weaklings the world i
better off without them. . . . My greatest wish is that you have brought hom
to you a torture that will be a thousand fold greater than what you have, an

are doing to the little animals. . . . If you are an example of what a noted psychiatrist should be I'm glad I am just an ordinary human being without a letter after my name. I'd rather be just myself with a clear conscience, *knowing I have not hurt any living creature*, and can sleep without seeing frightened, terrified dying cats—because I know they must die after you have finished with them. No punishment is too great for you and I hope I live to read about your mangled body and long suffering before you finally die—and I'll laugh long and loud. (Masserman [13])

Reaction formation, like repression, has adjustive value in helping us to maintain socially approved behavior and to avoid facing our unacceptable desires with the consequent self-devaluation that would be involved. To all intents and purposes we are pure—it is the other fellow who has the vices. But because this mechanism, too, is self-deceptive, it often results in exaggerated and rigid fears or beliefs which may complicate the individual's adjustive reactions and may lead to excessive harshness or severity in dealing with the lapses of others.

Displacement. Displacement refers to the shift of emotion, symbolic meaning, or fantasy from a person or object toward which it was originally directed to another person or object. Typically it involves the discharge of aroused emotions toward neutral or less dangerous objects. A child who has been spanked or thwarted by his mother may kick his little sister or a young playmate, or he may break up his toys. Many times a minor situation may act as a sort of trigger which releases the pent-up emotional feelings in a torrent of displaced anger and abuse surprising to everyone involved and out of all proportion to the immediate incident. A young housewife had been upbraided by her husband for not being more efficient and later in the day lost a bridge tournament to a disliked social rival. On her way home she was stopped by a traffic policeman for speeding. That was the final straw and she loosed a torrent of abuse on the poor fellow ranging from such questions as "Haven't you anything better to do than spy on innocent women?" to blaming him for the generally sad traffic condition of the city which he should have been working on instead of wasting his time persecuting busy civic-minded citizens for barely exceeding the speed limit.

Through a process of symbolic association or spread, displacement may become extremely complex and deviant. Swearing is commonly used as a means of discharging pent-up feelings. "Beating" a disliked rival at bridge or golf may symbolically represent his destruction. Destructive criticism and vindictive gossip are frequently only disguised methods of expressing hostility. Repressed fears of murdering a hated husband may be displaced to all sorts of dangerous weapons such as guns, knives, or poison. Such apparently irrational fears or phobias act as additional defenses by protecting

[13] Masserman, *op. cit.* Reprinted here by permission from Dr. Masserman and the publisher, W. B. Saunders Company.

the individual from situations in which his dangerous impulses might be carried out in action. Frequently displacement is combined with projection, as in Nazi Germany, where the blame for all the country's ills was projected upon the Jews and the Communists, and pent-up feelings of frustration and hosility were displaced upon these two groups.

Displacement is of considerable adjustive value because it enables the individual to discharge dangerous emotional tensions without risking loss of love and possible retaliation, and without the necessity of even recognizing the person at whom such feelings were originally directed. In this way it enables the individual to avoid the conflict of ambivalent feelings toward some powerful or loved person. By displacing his pent-up hostility on his wife, the little clerk maintains relatively pure feelings, consciously, of respect and cordiality toward his domineering boss. The boy who displaces his hostility onto his toys or playmates can maintain relatively pure feelings of love toward the mother who has just punished or frustrated him. Similarly the husband with considerable hostility toward his wife because of her sloppy housekeeping can wholeheartedly love her by displacing the blame both for her behavior and for his hostility onto his mother-in-law. In such instances displacement is often accompanied by repression (particularly where hostility is directed toward some loved person such as the mother) and this combination is an extremely potent ego defense.

Unfortunately, however, displacements can become too deviant, and they can result in the persistent avoidance of situations which could be more efficiently handled by a more direct approach, e.g., displacing hostility and blame onto one's mother-in-law may make it possible to maintain the marriage but unless a more direct and realistic approach to the wife's sloppy housekeeping is worked out, this behavior may show little improvement. In general it is much more healthful to face and work through hostility-arousing situations whenever this is feasible, rather than to avoid them through displacement.

Emotional insulation. In emotional insulation the individual reduces the tensions of need and anxiety by withdrawing into a sort of shell of passivity.

As a result of previous frustrations and disappointments, we all learn to protect ourselves not only by lowering our level of aspiration but by restricting emotional involvement in the attainment of our goals. This reaction is well expressed in the common saying "I didn't dare to even hope" (that a particular desired event would come about). Similarly, the boy who has been terribly disappointed in his first great love may be very careful not to allow himself to become so emotionally involved on subsequent occasions. In fact, he may find it very difficult or impossible to "let himself go" in the sense of entering into intimate affectional relationships. Many individuals who have been badly bruised by life's blows become cold, detached, and aloof and are often unable to either give or receive normal affection. Many times they seem highly self-sufficient, but privately such persons usually complain of intense feelings of inadequacy, loneliness, and tension. In more extreme conditions of long-continued frustration, as in chronic unemployment or prison confinement, many persons lose hope, become resigned and apathetic, and adapt themselves to a restricted way of living with an extremely low level of aspiration. Such "broken" individuals protect themselves from the bitter hurt of sustained frustration and disappointment by giving up and becoming disinterested and passive.

Another method of insulating ourselves emotionally is to avoid competitive activities or situations in which we might not compare favorably with others. Many people will not engage in sports such as bowling or ping-pong unless they feel that they excel in them. In this way they protect themselves from the unpleasantness and devaluation that might result from doing less well than others. This may be carried to the point of choosing both a vocation and leisure interests which are as noncompetitive and impersonal as possible.

Permitting ourselves to become emotionally involved in life's affairs does involve certain "calculated risks." For example, the giving of affection to other people does expose us to possible hurt in that they may reject us or may be taken from us by death. Ordinarily, of course, we operate on the assumption that the rewards of emotional involvement are worth the risks, even though, if we are realistic, we all know that we shall experience some disappointments in life.

Used to a mild degree, emotional insulation is an important means of defense against disappointment and hurt. Unfortunately, when used in more marked degree, it reduces the individual's healthy vigorous participation in life's problems and leads to shallowness and blunting of affect.

Isolation. This defense mechanism involves some measure of emotional insulation by distorting or cutting off the affective charge which normally accompanies hurtful situations. The hurt concerning Mother's death is reduced by saying that she lived a "full" life or that she died mercifully without pain. Catastrophes are interpreted within the framework of "It is the Will of the Lord!" Cynicism becomes a convenient means of withdrawing emotional support from our ideals. Guilt feelings over unethical behavior may be reduced by emphasizing the cultural relativity of our ideas of right and wrong. Often the glib admission that "we should work harder" or that "we should be less selfish and more interested in the welfare of others" seems to cut off a good deal of the guilt that normally accompanies unethical behavior without, however, leading to any positive action.

In such isolation reactions, rationalization and other ego defense mechanisms may play a prominent role, but it is the cutting off of the normal affective charge by means of "intellectualization" that we are primarily concerned with here.

Emotional conflicts may also be reduced through the process of isolating certain attitudes and dimensions of the personality. The confirmed believer in democracy may also believe firmly in racial discrimination. The ruthless and dishonest businessman may be a kind father and a pillar of the church. Such contradictory beliefs and attitudes are maintained in "logic-tight compartments" of the mind without emotional conflict. Of course the individual may resort to rationalization to make such incompatible values seem more consistent, but the essential process seems to be one of unconscious isolation in which one attitude is dissociated or segregated from the other. A passage from Sheila Cousins,[14] a London prostitute, well illustrates this type of dissociative or isolation reaction. She writes,

> The act of sex I could go through because I hardly seemed to be taking part in it. It was merely something happening to me, while my mind drifted inconsequentially away. Indeed, it was scarcely happening even to me; it was happening to something lying on a bed that had a vague connection with me, while I was calculating whether I could afford a new coat or impatiently counting sheep jumping over a gate. (pp. 150–151)

In this way situations which would ordinarily give rise to strong emotional conflicts are kept, as it were, in isolated ego positions. In more extreme cases, we may find the isolation or dissociation of entire sections of the ego, as in multiple personality or certain psychotic reactions where the patient looks up from scrubbing the floor to tell you in a sort of detached way that he is a multimillionaire.

Regression. Regression is a defensive reaction involving a retreat, in the face of stress, to the use of reaction patterns which were appropriate at an earlier level of development. It involves a modification of behavior in the direction of more primitive, infantile modes of behavior. When a new addition to the family has seemingly undermined his status, a child may revert to bed-wetting, baby talk, thumb-sucking, and other infantile behavior which once brought him parental attention. The frustrated adult may return to the temper tantrums which were useful during childhood; the bride may run home to mother at the first sign of trouble. Perhaps regression is best typified by the tendency of the aged to live more and more in the pleasures of the past. In fact, regression has been called the "old oaken bucket" delusion because of its emphasis on the superior joys of "the good old days."

Regression can be readily understood if we remember the child's gradual shift from a position of helplessness and dependency on the parents to one of independent action and responsibility. This developmental process from dependency to independency is by no means an easy accomplishment, and it is common for all of us in the face of adult difficulties to yearn for the carefree and sheltered days of infancy and childhood. Consequently it is not surprising that in the face of severe stress we may retreat

[14] Cousins, Sheila (pseud.). *To Beg I Am Ashamed.* New York: Vanguard Press, Inc., 1938.

rom adult reaction patterns to a less mature level of adjustment. Of ourse, we might expect something akin to regression to occur merely on he basis of the frequent failure of more recently learned reactions to bring atisfaction: in looking for other, more successful modes of adjustment it vould be only natural that we should try out discarded patterns which previously brought satisfaction. However, regression is a more compre- iensive reaction than merely trying out older modes of response when new ones have failed. For in regression the individual retreats from reality to a ess demanding personal status—one which involves *lowered aspiration* and nore readily accomplished satisfactions. This point is well illustrated by 3ettelheim's [15] reference to a general "regression to infantile behavior" een in nearly all the prisoners at Dachau and Buchenwald.

The prisoners lived, like children, only in the immediate present; . . . they became unable to plan for the future or to give up immediate pleasure satis- actions to gain greater ones in the near future. . . . They were boastful, telling ales about what they had accomplished in their former lives, or how they suc- ceeded in cheating foreman or guards, and how they sabotaged the work. Like children they felt not at all set back or ashamed when it became known that hey had lied about their prowess. (p. 443)

The collapse of adult attitudes under the strain of frustration or conflict s a very common form of ego breakdown and underlies a great deal of psychopathology. In its most dramatic form, it is seen in mentally ill adults vho show extreme regression to infantile levels of behavior so that they are unable to wash, dress, or feed themselves or take care of their eliminative needs. In some cases they even curl up in a position similar to that of the etus in the womb.

The defensive nature of the reaction is readily apparent in this severe ase.

A seventeen-year-old girl was brought to a psychiatric clinic by her mother with the complaint that for the preceding five months her behavior had be- come increasingly destructive and irrational. The history revealed that after the patient was about four years old her parents had begun to quarrel violently, making her early environment extremely contentious and unstable.

At about this age she first developed various neurotic traits: nail-biting, temper-tantrums, enuresis and numerous phobias. When the patient was seven the mother refused further sexual relations with the father and left the marital bed, but the patient continued to sleep with the father until she was thirteen. At this time the mother suspected that the patient was being incestuously seduced, obtained legal custody of the girl and moved away with her to a separate home. The patient resented this, quarreled frequently with her mother, became a disciplinary problem at home and at school and acquired a police record for various delinquencies. Three years later, at the patient's insistence, she and her mother paid an unexpected visit to the father and found him living with a girl in questionable circumstances. In a violent scene, the mother de-

[15] Bettelheim, *op. cit.* Selection is reprinted here by permission of the Managing Editor, the American Psychological Association.

nounced the father for unfaithfulness and, again contrary to the patient's wishes, took her home. There the patient refused to attend school and rapidly became sullen, withdrawn, and non-communicative. During her mother's absence at work she would throw the house into disorder, destroy clothes her mother had made for her, and throw her mother's effects out of the window. During one of these forays she discovered a photograph of herself at the age of five, which, incidentally, was so poorly lighted and faded that, for one detail, it did not show her eyebrows. Using this as a pattern, she shaved off her own eyebrows, cut her hair to the same baby bob, and began to affect the facial expression and sitting posture of the pictured child. When brought to the hospital her general behavior was correspondingly childish; she was untidy and enuretic, giggled incessantly or spoke in simple monosyllabic sentences, spent most of her time on the floor playing with blocks or paper dolls, and had to be fed, cleaned, and supervised as though she were an infant. In effect, she appeared to have regressed to a relatively desirable period in life antedating disruptive jealousies and other conflicts; moreover, she acted out this regression in unconsciously determined but strikingly symbolic patterns of eliminating the mother as a rival and regaining the father she had lost in her childhood. (Masserman,[16] case of Dr. John Romano)

Sublimation. Sublimation, as it has been traditionally conceived, involves the acceptance of a socially approved substitute goal for a drive whose normal channel of expression or normal goal is blocked. The girl who fails to marry may find a substitute sexual outlet in nursing or becoming a masseuse. The individual with sadistic impulses may become a surgeon.

There is considerable doubt as to whether any real process of sublimation actually takes place. For example, can a desire as basic as the sexual desire actually be sublimated? Kinsey [17] finds evidence of repression but hardly any evidence of sublimation in sexual behavior. Apparently sublimation, in so far as it does occur, is based upon the utilization of general bodily energy in constructive activities which indirectly reduce the tension built up around frustrated sexual or other drives. Also, constructive activities keep the individual too busy to dwell on the frustration. Thus even though sublimation is limited in its scope, it does have a great deal of individual and social value in producing socially approved activity when strong drives are frustrated.

Undoing. This is a defensive reaction designed to negate or annul some disapproved thought, impulse, or act. It is as if the individual has spelled a word wrong and used an eraser to clear the paper and start over. Apologizing for wrongs committed against others, penance, repentance, and being punished are all forms of undoing.

Undoing apparently develops out of our early training in which we are made to apologize or to make some restitution, or are punished in some way

16 Masserman, *op. cit.* Reprinted here by permission from Dr. Masserman and the publisher, W. B. Saunders Company.

17 Kinsey, Alfred C. *Sexual Behavior in the Human Male.* Philadelphia: W. B. Saunders Company, 1948.

SUMMARY CHART OF EGO DEFENSE MECHANISM

enial of reality	Protects self from unpleasant reality by refusal to perceive it
antasy	Gratification of frustrated desires in imaginary achievements
ompensation	Covering up weakness by emphasizing desirable trait or making up for frustration in one area by overgratification in another
dentification	Increasing feelings of worth by identifying self with person or institution of illustrious standing
ntrojection	Incorporation of external values and standards into ego structure so individual is not at their mercy as external threats
rojection	Placing blame for difficulties upon others or attributing one's own unethical desires to others
ationalization	Attempting to prove that one's behavior is "rational" and justifiable and thus worthy of self and social approval
epression	Preventing painful or dangerous thoughts from entering consciousness
eaction formation	Preventing dangerous desires from being expressed by exaggerating opposed attitudes and types of behavior and using them as "barriers"
Displacement	Discharging pent-up feelings, usually of hostility, on objects less dangerous than those which initially aroused the emotions
motional insulation	Withdrawal into passivity to protect self from hurt
solation	Cutting off affective charge from hurtful situations or separating incompatible attitudes by logic-tight compartments
egression	Retreating to earlier developmental level involving less mature responses and usually a lower level of aspiration
ublimation	Gratification of frustrated sexual desires in substitutive nonsexual activities
ndoing	Atoning for and thus counteracting immoral desires or acts

ommensurate with our socially disapproved behavior. Once the apology r restitution or punishment has taken place, our misdeed is negated and ve can start over with a clean slate and with renewed parental approval nd affection. In this sequence of events, we also learn that repentance,)enance, or restitution may enable us to avoid more serious punishment. 'or example, by returning Johnny's toys with considerable alacrity, we may void being spanked, although we may of course be scolded. By saying we re sorry and offering to do something to make up for our misdeed, we may scape punishment and rejection.

Since we have all been taught that evil and wrongdoing inevitably lead o punishment, we have all developed various methods of atoning for or undoing our misdeeds—methods designed to avoid or ameliorate the punishment that would otherwise accrue. The unfaithful husband may bring his wife presents, the unethical businessman may give huge sums of money to charitable organizations, the rejecting mother may buy her child toys.

Sometimes we feel that the only atonement for our misdeeds is punishment itself, and we may confess them in order that we may be punished and thereby pay for and erase our sins. Not infrequently people who have committed crimes years earlier will confess to the police in order to regain their self-esteem and security. Where sins seem so great to the individual that he sees no hope of undoing or atoning for them, he may suffer such intense guilt, anxiety, and self-devaluation that suicide seems the only way out.

Since undoing is fundamental to the maintenance of ethical human relations, as well as to our self-esteem, it is one of our most valuable ego defenses. Particularly in combination with rationalization and projection is it a potent ego defense against self-devaluating guilt feelings. . . . however, in . . . psychotic patterns, undoing is subject to exaggerated and unhealthy usage.

In the preceding discussion we have dealt with the major ego defense mechanisms. It is worth re-emphasizing that these defense mechanisms are learned adjustive reactions, that they function in both individual and group behavior, that they operate on relatively habitual and unconscious levels, and that they involve self-deception and reality distortion. However these mechanisms are essential for the maintenance of ego integrity and we all use them in various degrees and patterns. Consequently they may be considered quite normal and desirable except in cases where they are used to an extreme degree, at the expense of the ultimate adaptive efficiency and happiness of the individual.

THE NONPRODUCTIVE
CHARACTER ORIENTATIONS *

《 Erich Fromm

(a) The Receptive Orientation

In the receptive orientation a person feels "the source of all good" to be outside, and he believes that the only way to get what he wants—be it something material, be it affection, love, knowledge, pleasure—is to re-

* From Erich Fromm, *Man for Himself*, pp. 62–73, Rinehart & Company, Inc., New York, 1947. Reprinted by permission of the author and of Rinehart & Company, Inc., New York, Publishers.

ceive it from that outside source. In this orientation the problem of love is almost exclusively that of "being loved" and not that of loving. Such people tend to be indiscriminate in the choice of their love objects, because being loved by anybody is such an overwhelming experience for them that they "fall for" anybody who gives them love or what looks like love. They are exceedingly sensitive to any withdrawal or rebuff they experience on the part of the loved person. Their orientation is the same in the sphere of thinking: if intelligent, they make the best listeners, since their orientation is one of receiving, not of producing, ideas; left to themselves, they feel paralyzed. It is characteristic of these people that their first thought is to find somebody else to give them needed information rather than to make even the smallest effort of their own. If religious, these persons have a concept of God in which they expect everything from God and nothing from their own activity. If not religious, their relationship to persons or institutions is very much the same; they are always in search of a "magic helper." They show a particular kind of loyalty, at the bottom of which is the gratitude for the hand that feeds them and the fear of ever losing it. Since they need many hands to feel secure, they have to be loyal to numerous people. It is difficult for them to say "no," and they are easily caught between conflicting loyalties and promises. Since they cannot say "no," they love to say "yes" to everything and everybody, and the resulting paralysis of their critical abilities makes them increasingly dependent on others.

They are dependent not only on authorities for knowledge and help but on people in general for any kind of support. They feel lost when alone because they feel that they cannot do anything without help. This helplessness is especially important with regard to those acts which by their very nature can only be done alone—making decisions and taking responsibility. In personal relationships, for instance, they ask advice from the very person with regard to whom they have to make a decision.

This receptive type has great fondness for food and drink. These persons tend to overcome anxiety and depression by eating or drinking. The mouth is an especially prominent feature, often the most expressive one; the lips tend to be open, as if in a state of continuous expectation of being fed. In their dreams, being fed is a frequent symbol of being loved; being starved, an expression of frustration or disappointment.

By and large, the outlook of people of this receptive orientation is optimistic and friendly; they have a certain confidence in life and its gifts, but they become anxious and distraught when their "source of supply" is threatened. They often have a genuine warmth and a wish to help others, but doing things for others also assumes the function of securing their favor.

(b) The Exploitative Orientation

The exploitative orientation, like the receptive, has as its basic premise the feeling that the source of all good is outside, that whatever one wants to get must be sought there, and that one cannot produce anything oneself. The difference between the two, however, is that the exploitative type does not expect to receive things from others as gifts, but to take them away from others by force or cunning. This orientation extends to all spheres of activity.

In the realm of love and affection these people tend to grab and steal. They feel attracted only to people whom they can take away from somebody else. Attractiveness to them is conditioned by a person's attachment to somebody else; they tend not to fall in love with an unattached person.

We find the same attitude with regard to thinking and intellectual pursuits. Such people will tend not to produce ideas but to steal them. This may be done directly in the form of plagiarism or more subtly by repeating in different phraseology the ideas voiced by others and insisting they are new and their own. It is a striking fact that frequently people with great intelligence proceed in this way, although if they relied on their own gifts they might well be able to have ideas of their own. The lack of original ideas or independent production in otherwise gifted people often has its explanation in this character orientation, rather than in any innate lack of originality. The same statement holds true with regard to their orientation to material things. Things which they can take away from others always seem better to them than anything they can produce themselves. They use and exploit anybody and anything from whom or from which they can squeeze something. Their motto is: "Stolen fruits are sweetest." Because they want to use and exploit people, they "love" those who, explicitly or implicitly, are promising objects of exploitation, and get "fed up" with persons whom they have squeezed out. An extreme example is the kleptomaniac who enjoys things only if he can steal them, although he has the money to buy them.

This orientation seems to be symbolized by the biting mouth which is often a prominent feature in such people. It is not a play upon words to point out that they often make "biting" remarks about others. Their attitude is colored by a mixture of hostility and manipulation. Everyone is an object of exploitation and is judged according to his usefulness. Instead of the confidence and optimism which characterizes the receptive type, one finds here suspicion and cynicism, envy and jealousy. Since they are satisfied only with things they can take away from others, they tend to overrate what others have and underrate what is theirs.

(c) The Hoarding Orientation

While the receptive and exploitative types are similar inasmuch as both expect to get things from the outside world, the hoarding orientation is essentially different. This orientation makes people have little faith in anything new they might get from the outside world; their security is based upon hoarding and saving, while spending is felt to be a threat. They have surrounded themselves, as it were, by a protective wall, and their main aim is to bring as much as possible into this fortified position and to let as little as possible out of it. Their miserliness refers to money and material things as well as to feelings and thoughts. Love is essentially a possession; they do not give love but try to get it by possessing the "beloved." The hoarding person often shows a particular kind of faithfulness toward people and even toward memories. Their sentimentality makes the past appear as golden; they hold on to it and indulge in the memories of bygone feelings and experiences. They know everything but are sterile and incapable of productive thinking.

One can recognize these people too by facial expressions and gestures. Theirs is the tight-lipped mouth; their gestures are characteristic of their withdrawn attitude. While those of the receptive type are inviting and round, as it were, and the gestures of the exploitative type are aggressive and pointed, those of the hoarding type are angular, as if they wanted to emphasize the frontiers between themselves and the outside world. Another characteristic element in this attitude is pedantic orderliness. The hoarder will be orderly with things, thoughts, or feelings, but again, as with memory, his orderliness is sterile and rigid. He cannot endure things out of place and will automatically rearrange them. To him the outside world threatens to break into his fortified position; orderliness signifies mastering the world outside by putting it, and keeping it, in its proper place in order to avoid the danger of intrusion. His compulsive cleanliness is another expression of his need to undo contact with the outside world. Things beyond his own frontiers are felt to be dangerous and "unclean"; he annuls the menacing contact by compulsive washing, similar to a religious washing ritual prescribed after contact with unclean things or people. Things have to be put not only in their proper place but also into their proper time; obsessive punctuality is characteristic of the hoarding type; it is another form of mastering the outside world. If the outside world is experienced as a threat to one's fortified position, obstinacy is a logical reaction. A constant "no" is the almost automatic defense against intrusion; sitting tight, the answer to the danger of being pushed. These people tend to feel that they possess only a fixed quantity of strength, energy, or mental capacity, and that this stock is diminished or exhausted by use and can never be replenished. They cannot understand the self-replenishing function of all living substance and that activity and the use of one's powers increase strength while stagnation paralyzes; to them, death and destruction have more reality than life and growth. The act of creation is a miracle of which they hear but in which they do not believe. Their highest values are order and security; their motto: "There is nothing new under the sun." In their relationship to others intimacy is a threat; either remoteness or possession of a person means security. The hoarder tends to be suspicious and to have a particular sense of justice which in effect says: "Mine is mine and yours is yours."

(d) The Marketing Orientation

The marketing orientation developed as a dominant one only in the modern era. In order to understand its nature one must consider the economic function of the market in modern society as being not only analogous to this character orientation but as the basis and the main condition for its development in modern man.

Barter is one of the oldest economic mechanisms. The traditional local market, however, is essentially different from the market as it has developed in modern capitalism. Bartering on a local market offered an opportunity to meet for the purpose of exchanging commodities. Producers and customers became acquainted; they were relatively small groups; the demand was more or less known, so that the producer could produce for this specific demand.

The modern market * is no longer a meeting place but a mechanism characterized by abstract and impersonal demand. One produces for this market, not for a known circle of customers; its verdict is based on laws of supply and demand; and it determines whether the commodity can be sold and at what price. No matter what the *use value* of a pair of shoes may be, for instance, if the supply is greater than the demand, some shoes will be sentenced to economic death; they might as well not have been produced at all. The market day is the "day of judgment" as far as the *exchange value* of commodities is concerned.

The reader may object that this description of the market is over simplified. The producer does try to judge the demand in advance, and under monopoly conditions even obtains a certain degree of control over it. Nevertheless, the regulatory function of the market has been, and still is, predominant enough to have a profound influence on the character formation of the urban middle class and, through the latter's social and cultural influence, on the whole population. The market concept of value, the emphasis on exchange value rather than one use value, has led to a smiliar concept of value with regard to people and particularly to oneself. The character orientation which is rooted in the experience of oneself as a

---

* Cf., for the study of history and function of the modern market, K. Polanyi's *The Great Transformation* (New York: Rinehart & Company, 1944).

commodity and of one's value as exchange value I call the marketing orientation.

In our time the marketing orientation has been growing rapidly, together with the development of a new market that is a phenomenon of the last decades—the "personality market." Clerks and salesmen, business executives and doctors, lawyers and artists all appear on this market. It is true that their legal status and economic positions are different: some are independent, charging for their services; others are employed, receiving salaries. But all are dependent for their material success on a personal acceptance by those who need their services or who employ them.

The principle of evaluation is the same on both the personality and the commodity market: on the one, personalities are offered for sale; on the other, commodities. Value in both cases is their exchange value, for which use value is a necessary but not a sufficient condition. It is true, our economic system could not function if people were not skilled in the particular work they have to perform and were gifted only with a pleasant personality. Even the best bedside manner and the most beautifully equipped office on Park Avenue would not make a New York doctor successful if he did not have a minimum of medical knowledge and skill. Even the most winning personality would not prevent a secretary from losing her job unless she could type reasonably fast. However, if we ask what the respective weight of skill and personality as a condition for success is, we find that only in exceptional cases is success predominantly the result of skill and of certain other human qualities like honesty, decency, and integrity. Although the proportion between skill and human qualities on the one hand and "personality" on the other hand as prerequisites for success varies, the "personality factor" always plays a decisive role. Success depends largely on how well a person sells himself on the market, how well he gets his personality across, how nice a "package" he is; whether he is "cheerful," "sound," "aggressive," "reliable," "ambitious"; furthermore what his family background is, what clubs he belongs to, and whether he knows the right people. The type of personality required depends to some degree on the special field in which a person works. A stockbroker, a salesman, a secretary, a railroad executive, a college professor, or a hotel manager must each offer different kinds of personality that, regardless of their differences, must fulfill one condition: to be in demand.

The fact that in order to have success it is not sufficient to have the skill and equipment for performing a given task but that one must be able to "put across" one's personality in competition with many others shapes the attitude toward oneself. If it were enough for the purpose of making a living to rely on what one knows and what one can do, one's self-esteem would be in proportion to one's capacities, that is, to one's use value; but since success depends largely on how one sells one's personality, one experiences oneself as a commodity or rather simultaneously as the seller

and the commodity to be sold. A person is not concerned with his life
and happiness, but with becoming salable. This feeling might be compared to that of a commodity, of handbags on a counter, for instance, could
they feel and think. Each handbag would try to make itself as "attractive"
as possible in order to attract customers and to look as expensive as possible in order to obtain a higher price than its rivals. The handbag sold for
the highest price would feel elated, since that would mean it was the most
"valuable" one; the one which was not sold would feel sad and convinced
of its own worthlessness. This fate might befall a bag which, though
excellent in appearance and usefulness, had the bad luck to be out of date
because of a change in fashion.

Like the handbag, one has to be in fashion on the personality market
and in order to be in fashion one has to know what kind of personality is
most in demand. This knowledge is transmitted in a general way throughout the whole process of education, from kindergarten to college, and
implemented by the family. The knowledge acquired at this early stage
is not sufficient, however; it emphasizes only certain general qualities like
adaptability, ambition, sensitivity to the changing expectations of other
people. The more specific picture of the models for success one gets elsewhere. The pictorial magazines, newspapers, and newsreels show the pictures and life stories of the successful in many variations. Pictorial advertising has a similar function. The successful executive who is pictured in a
tailor's advertisement is the image of how one should look and be, if one
is to draw down the "big money" on the contemporary personality market.

The most important means of transmitting the desired personality pattern to the average man is the motion picture. The young girl tries to
emulate the facial expression, coiffure, gestures of a high-priced star as the
most promising way to success. The young man tries to look and be like
the model he sees on the screen. While the average citizen has little contact with the life of the most successful people, his relationship with the
motion-picture stars is different. It is true that he has no real contact with
them either, but he can see them on the screen again and again, can write
them and receive their autographed pictures. In contrast to the time when
the actor was socially despised but was nevertheless the transmitter of the
works of great poets to his audience, our motion-picture stars have no
great works or ideas to transmit, but their function is to serve as the link
an average person has with the world of the "great." Even if he can no
hope to become as successful as they are, he can try to emulate them; they
are his saints and because of their success they embody the norms for
living.

Since modern man experiences himself both as the seller and as the
commodity to be sold on the market, his self-esteem depends on conditions
beyond his control. If he is "successful," he is valuable; if he is not, he is
worthless. The degree of insecurity which results from this orientation can

hardly be overestimated. If one feels that one's own value is not constituted primarily by the human qualities one possesses, but by one's success on a competitive market with ever-changing conditions, one's self-esteem is bound to be shaky and in constant need of confirmation by others. Hence one is driven to strive relentlessly for success, and any setback is a severe threat to one's self-esteem; helplessness, insecurity, and inferiority feelings are the result. If the vicissitudes of the market are the judges of one's value, the sense of dignity and pride is destroyed.

But the problem is not only that of self-evaluation and self-esteem but of one's experience of oneself as an independent entity, of one's *identity with oneself.* . . . the mature and productive individual derives his feeling of identity from the experience of himself as the agent who is one with his powers; this feeling of self can be briefly expressed as meaning "*I am what I do.*" In the marketing orientation man encounters his own powers as commodities alienated from him. He is not one with them but they are masked from him because what matters is not his self-realization in the process of using them but his success in the process of selling them. Both his powers and what they create become estranged, something different from himself, something for others to judge and to use; thus his feeling of identity becomes as shaky as his self-esteem; it is constituted by the sum total of roles one can play: "*I am as you desire me.*"

CHARACTER AND SOCIETY *

⟪ DAVID RIESMAN

What is the relation between social character and society? How is it that every society seems to get, more or less, the social character it "needs"? Erik H. Erikson writes, in a study of the social character of the Yurok Indians, that ". . . systems of child training . . . represent unconscious attempts at creating out of human raw material that configuration of attitudes which is (or once was) the optimum under the tribe's particular natural conditions and economic-historic necessities." [1]

From "economic-historic necessities" to "systems of child training" is a long jump. Much of the work of students of social character has been devoted to closing the gap and showing how the satisfaction of the largest "needs" of society is prepared, in some half-mysterious way, by its most

* From David Riesman, *The Lonely Crowd*, pp. 19–42, Anchor ed., Doubleday & Company, Inc., New York, 1953, reprinted by arrangement with Yale University Press, New Haven. Reprinted by permission of the author and publisher.

[1] "Observations on the Yurok: Childhood and World Image," *University of California Publications in American Archaeology and Ethnology*, XXXV (1943), iv.

intimate practice. Erich Fromm succinctly suggests the line along which this connection between society and character training may be sought: "In order that any society may function well, its members must acquire the kind of character which makes them *want* to act in the way they *have* to act as members of the society or of a special class within it. They have to *desire* what objectively is *necessary* for them to do. *Outer force* is replaced by *inner compulsion*, and by the particular kind of human energy which is channeled into character traits." [2]

Thus, the link between character and society—certainly not the only one, but one of the most significant, and the one I choose to emphasize in this discussion—is to be found in the way in which society ensures some degree of conformity from the individuals who make it up. In each society, such a mode of ensuring conformity is built into the child, and then either encouraged or frustrated in later adult experience. (No society, it would appear, is quite prescient enough to ensure that the mode of conformity it has inculcated will satisfy those subject to it in every stage of life.) I shall use the term "mode of conformity" interchangeably with the term "social character"—though certainly conformity is not all of social character: "mode of creativity" is as much a part of it. However, while societies and individuals may live well enough—if rather boringly—without creativity, it is not likely that they can live without some mode of conformity—even be it one of rebellion.

My concern in this book is with two revolutions and their relation to the "mode of conformity" or "social character" of Western man since the Middle Ages. The first of these revolutions has in the last four hundred years cut us off pretty decisively from the family- and clan-oriented traditional ways of life in which mankind has existed throughout most of history; this revolution includes the Renaissance, the Reformation, the Counter-Reformation, the Industrial Revolution, and the political revolution of the seventeenth, eighteenth, and nineteenth centuries. This revolution is, of course, still in process, but in the most advanced countries of the world, and particularly in America, it is giving way to another sort of revolution—a whole range of social developments associated with a shift from an age of production to an age of consumption. The first revolution we understand moderately well; it is, under various labels, in our texts and our terminology; this book has nothing new to contribute to its description, but perhaps does contribute something to its evaluation. The second revolution, which is just beginning, has interested many contemporary observers, including social scientists, philosophers, and journalists. Both description and evaluation are still highly controversial; indeed, many are still preoccupied with the first set of revolutions and have not invented the categories

[2] "Individual and Social Origins of Neurosis," *American Sociological Review*, IX (1944), 380; reprinted in *Personality in Nature, Society and Culture*, edited by Clyde Kluckhohn and Henry Murray (New York, Alfred A. Knopf, 1948).

for discussing the second set. In this book I try to sharpen the contrast between, on the one hand, conditions and character in those social strata that are today most seriously affected by the second revolution, and, on the other hand, conditions and character in analogous strata during the earlier revolution; in this perspective, what is briefly said about the traditional and feudal societies which were overturned by the first revolution is in the nature of backdrop for these later shifts.

One of the categories I make use of is taken from demography, the science that deals with birth rates and death rates, with the absolute and relative numbers of people in a society, and their distribution by age, sex, and other variables, for I tentatively seek to link certain social and characterological developments, as cause and effect, with certain population shifts in Western society since the Middle Ages.

It seems reasonably well established, despite the absence of reliable figures for earlier centuries, that during this period the curve of population growth in the Western countries has shown an S-shape of a particular type (as other countries are drawn more closely into the net of Western civilization, their populations also show a tendency to develop along the lines of this S-shaped curve). The bottom horizontal line of the S represents a situation where the total population does not increase or does so very slowly, for the number of births equals roughly the number of deaths, and both are very high. In societies of this type, a high proportion of the population is young, life expectancy is low, and the turnover of generations is extremely rapid. Such societies are said to be in the phase of "high growth potential"; for should something happen to decrease the very high death rate (greater production of food, new sanitary measures, new knowledge of the causes of disease, and so on), a "population explosion" would result, and the population would increase very rapidly. This in effect is what happened in the West, starting with the seventeenth century. This spurt in population was most marked in Europe, and the countries settled by Europeans, in the nineteenth century. It is represented by the vertical bar of the S. Demographers call this the stage of "transitional growth," because the birth rate soon begins to follow the death rate in its decline. The rate of growth then slows down, and demographers begin to detect in the growing proportion of middle-aged and aged in the population the signs of a third stage, "incipient population decline." Societies in this stage are represented by the top horizontal bar of the S, again indicating, as in the first stage, that total population growth is small—but this time because births and deaths are low.

The S-curve is not a theory of population growth so much as an empirical description of what has happened in the West and in those parts of the world influenced by the West. After the S runs its course, what then? The developments of recent years in the United States and other Western countries do not seem to be susceptible to so simple and elegant a summing up. "Incipient population decline" has not become "population decline" itself, and the birth rate has shown an uncertain tendency to rise again, which most demographers think is temporary.[3]

It would be very surprising if variations in the basic conditions of reproduction, livelihood, and survival chances, that is, in the supply of and demand for human beings, with all it implies in change of the spacing of people, the size of markets, the role of children, the society's feeling of vitality or senescence, and many other intangibles, failed to influence character. My thesis is, in fact, that each of these three different phases on the population curve appears to be occupied by a society that enforces conformity and molds social character in a definably different way.

The society of high growth potential develops in its typical members a social character whose conformity is insured by their tendency to follow tradition: these I shall term *tradition-directed* people and the society in which they live *a society dependent on tradition-direction*.

The society of transitional population growth develops in its typical members a social character whose conformity is insured by their tendency to acquire early in life an internalized set of goals. These I shall term *inner directed* people and the society in which they live *a society dependent on inner-direction*.

Finally, the society of incipient population decline develops in its typical members a social character whose conformity is insured by their tendency to be sensitized to the expectations and preferences of others. These I shall term *other-directed* people and the society in which they live one *dependent on other-direction*.

Let me point out, however, before embarking on a description of these three "ideal types" of character and society, that I am not concerned here with making the detailed analysis that would be necessary before one could prove that a link exists between population phase and character type. Rather, the theory of the curve of population provides me with a kind of shorthand for referring to the myriad institutional elements that are also—though usually more heatedly—symbolized by such words as "industrialism," "folk society," "monopoly capitalism," "urbanization," "rationalization," and so on. Hence when I speak here of transitional growth or incipient decline of population in conjunction with shifts in character and conformity, these phrases should not be taken as magical and comprehensive explanations.

My reference is as much to the complex of technological and institutional factors related—as cause or effect—to the development of population as to the demographic facts themselves. It would be almost as satisfactory

---

[3] The terminology used here is that of Frank W. Notestein. See his "Population— The Long View," in *Food for the World*, edited by Theodore W. Schultz (University of Chicago Press, 1945).

or my purposes, to divide societies according to the stage of economic development they have reached. Thus, Colin Clark's distinction between the "primary," "secondary," and "tertiary" spheres of the economy (the first refers to agriculture, hunting and fishing, and mining; the second to manufacturing; the third to trade, communications, and services) corresponds very closely to the division of societies on the basis of demographic characteristics. In those societies which are in the phase of "high growth potential," the "primary" sphere is dominant (for example, India); in those that are in the phase of "transitional" growth, the "secondary" sphere is dominant (for example, Russia); in those that are in the phase of "incipient decline," the "tertiary" sphere is dominant (for example, the United States). And of course, no nation is all of a piece, either in its population characteristics or its economy—different groups and different regions reflect different stages of development, and social character reflects these differences.

High Growth Potential: Tradition-directed Types

The phase of high growth potential characterizes more than half the world's population: India, Egypt, and China (which have already grown immensely in recent generations), most preliterate peoples in Central Africa, parts of Central and South America, in fact most areas of the world relatively untouched by industrialization. Here death rates are so high that if birth rates were not also high the populations would die out.

Regions where the population is in this stage may be either sparsely populated, as are the areas occupied by many primitive tribes and parts of Central and South America; or they may be densely populated, as are India, China, and Egypt. In either case, the society achieves a Malthusian bargain with the limited food supply by killing off, in one way or another, some of the potential surplus of births over deaths—the enormous trap which, in Malthus' view, nature sets for man and which can be peaceably escaped only by prudent cultivation of the soil and prudent uncultivation of the species through the delay of marriage. Without the prevention of childbirth by means of marriage postponement or other contraceptive measures, the population must be limited by taking the life of living beings. And so societies have "invented" cannibalism, induced abortion, organized wars, made human sacrifice, and practiced infanticide (especially female) as means of avoiding periodic famine and epidemics.

Though this settling of accounts with the contradictory impulses of hunger and sex is accompanied often enough by upheaval and distress, these societies in the stage of high growth potential tend to be stable at least in the sense that their social practices, including the "crimes" that keep population down, are institutionalized and patterned. Generation after generation, people are born, are weeded out, and die to make room for others. The net rate of natural increase fluctuates within a broad range, though without showing any long-range tendency, as is true also of societies in the stage of incipient decline. But unlike the latter, the average life expectancy in the former is characteristically low: the population is heavily weighted on the side of the young, and generation replaces generation far more rapidly and less "efficiently" than in the societies of incipient population decline.

In viewing such a society we inevitably associate the relative stability of the man-land ratio, whether high or low, with the tenacity of custom and social structure. However, we must not equate stability of social structure over historical time with psychic stability in the life span of an individual: the latter may subjectively experience much violence and disorganization. In the last analysis, however, he learns to deal with life by adaptation, not by innovation. With certain exceptions conformity is largely given in the "self-evident" social situation. Of course nothing in human life is ever really self-evident; where it so appears it is because perceptions have been narrowed by cultural conditioning. As the precarious relation to the food supply is built into the going culture, it helps create a pattern of conventional conformity which is reflected in many, if not all, societies in the stage of high growth potential. This is what I call tradition-direction.

A *definition of tradition-direction*. Since the type of social order we have been discussing is relatively unchanging, the conformity of the individual tends to be dictated to a very large degree by power relations among the various age and sex groups, the clans, castes, professions, and so forth—relations which have endured for centuries and are modified but slightly, if at all, by successive generations. The culture controls behavior minutely, and, while the rules are not so complicated that the young cannot learn them during the period of intensive socialization, careful and rigid etiquette governs the fundamentally influential sphere of kin relationships. Moreover, the culture, in addition to its economic tasks, or as part of them, provides ritual, routine, and religion to occupy and to orient everyone. Little energy is directed toward finding new solutions of the age-old problems, let us say, of agricultural technique or "medicine," the problems to which people are acculturated.

It is not to be thought, however, that in these societies, where the activity of the individual member is determined by characterologically grounded obedience to traditions, the individual may not be highly prized and, in many instances, encouraged to develop his capabilities, his initiative and even, within very narrow time limits, his aspirations. Indeed, the individual in some primitive societies is far more appreciated and respected than in some sectors of modern society. For the individual in a society dependent on tradition-direction has a well-defined functional relationship to other members of the group. If he is not killed off, he "belongs"—he is not "surplus," as the modern unemployed are surplus, nor is he expendable as the unskilled are expendable in modern society. But by very virtue of his "belonging," life goals that are *his* in terms of conscious choice appear to shape his destiny only to a very limited extent, just as only to a limited extent is there any concept of progress for the group.

In societies in which tradition-direction is the dominant mode of insuring conformity, relative stability is preserved in part by the infrequent but highly important process of fitting into institutionalized roles such deviants as there are. In such societies a person who might have become at a later historical stage an innovator or rebel, whose belonging, as such, is marginal and problematic, is drawn instead into roles like those of the shaman or sorcerer. That is, he is drawn into roles that make a socially acceptable contribution, while at the same time they provide the individual with a more or less approved niche. The medieval monastic orders may have served in a similar way to absorb many characterological mutations.

In some of these societies certain individuals are encouraged toward a degree of individuality from childhood, especially if they belong to families of high status. But, since the range of choice, even for high-status people, is minimal, the apparent social need for an individuated type of character is also minimal. It is probably accurate to say that character structure in these societies is very largely "adjusted," in the sense that for most people it appears to be in tune with social institutions. Even the few misfits "fit" to a degree; and only very rarely is one driven out of his social world.

This does not mean, of course, that the people are happy; the society to whose traditions they are adjusted may be a miserable one, ridden with anxiety, sadism, and disease. The point is rather that change, while never completely absent in human affairs, is slowed down as the movement of molecules is slowed down at low temperature; and the social character comes as close as it ever does to looking like the matrix of the social forms themselves.

In western history the Middle Ages can be considered a period in which the majority were tradition-directed. But the term tradition-directed refers to a common element, not only among the people of precapitalist Europe but also among such enormously different types of people as Hindus and Hopi Indians, Zulus and Chinese, North African Arabs and Balinese. There is comfort in relying on the many writers who have found a similar unity amid diversity, a unity they express in such terms as "folk society" (as against "civilization"), "status society" (as against "contract society"), "*Gemeinschaft*" (as against "*Gesellschaft*"), and so on. Different as the societies envisaged by these terms are, the folk, status, and *Gemeinschaft* societies resemble each other in their relative slowness of change, their dependence on family and kin organization, and—in comparison with later epochs—their tight web of values. And, as is now well recognized by students, the high birth rate of these societies in the stage of high growth potential is not merely the result of a lack of contraceptive knowledge or techniques. A whole way of life—an outlook on chance, on children, on the place of women, on sexuality, on the very meaning of existence—lies between the societies in which human fertility is allowed to take its course and toll and those which prefer to pay other kinds of toll to cut down on fertility by calculation, and, conceivably, as Freud and other observers have suggested, by a decline in sexual energy itself.

Transitional Growth: Inner-directed Types

Except for the West, we know very little about the cumulation of small changes that can eventuate in a breakup of the tradition-directed type of society, leading it to realize its potential for high population growth. As for the West, however, much has been learned about the slow decay of feudalism and the subsequent rise of a type of society in which inner-direction is the dominant mode of insuring conformity.

Critical historians, pushing the Renaissance ever back into the Middle Ages, seem sometimes to deny that any decisive change occurred at all. On the whole, however, it seems that the greatest social and characterological shift of recent centuries did indeed come when men were driven out of the primary ties that bound them to the western medieval version of tradition-directed society. All later shifts, including the shift from inner-direction to other-direction, seem unimportant by comparison, although of course this latter shift is still under way and we cannot tell what it will look like when—if ever—it is complete.

A change in the relatively stable ratio of births to deaths, which characterizes the period of high growth potential, is both the cause and consequence of other profound social changes. In most of the cases known to us a decline takes place in mortality prior to a decline in fertility; hence there is some period in which the population expands rapidly. The drop in death rate occurs as the result of many interacting factors, among them sanitation, improved communications (which permit government to operate over a wider area and also permit easier transport of food to areas of shortage from areas of surplus), the decline, forced or otherwise, of infanticide, cannibalism, and other inbred kinds of violence. Because of improved methods of agriculture the land is able to support more people, and these in turn produce still more people.

Notestein's phrase, "transitional growth," is a mild way of putting it. The "transition" is likely to be violent, disrupting the stabilized paths of existence in societies in which tradition-direction has been the principal mode of insuring conformity. The imbalance of births and deaths puts pressure on the society's customary ways. A new slate of character structures is called for or finds its opportunity in coping with the rapid changes—and the need for still more changes—in the social organization.

A definition of inner-direction. In western history the society that emerged with the Renaissance and Reformation and that is only now vanishing serves to illustrate the type of society in which inner-direction is the principal mode of securing conformity. Such a society is characterized by increased personal mobility, by a rapid accumulation of capital (teamed with devastating technological shifts), and by an almost constant *expansion:* intensive expansion in the production of goods and people, and extensive expansion in exploration, colonization, and imperialism. The greater choices this society gives—and the greater initiatives it demands in order to cope with its novel problems—are handled by character types who can manage to live socially without strict and self-evident tradition-direction. These are the inner-directed types.

The concept of inner-direction is intended to cover a very wide range of types. Thus, while it is essential for the study of certain problems to differentiate between Protestant and Catholic countries and their character types, between the effects of the Reformation and the effects of the Renaissance, between the puritan ethic of the European north and west and the somewhat more hedonistic ethic of the European east and south, while all these are valid and, for certain purposes, important distinctions, the concentration of this study on the development of modes of conformity permits their neglect. It allows the grouping together of these otherwise distinct developments because they have one thing in common: *the source of direction for the individual is "inner" in the sense that it is implanted early in life by the elders and directed toward generalized but nonetheless inescapably destined goals.*

We can see what this means when we realize that, in societies in which tradition-direction is the dominant mode of insuring conformity, attention is focused on securing external *behavioral* conformity. While behavior is minutely prescribed, individuality of character need not be highly developed to meet prescriptions that are objectified in ritual and etiquette—though to be sure, a social character *capable* of such behavioral attention and obedience is requisite. By contrast, societies in which inner-direction becomes important, though they also are concerned with behavioral conformity, cannot be satisfied with behavioral conformity alone. Too many novel situations are presented, situations which a code cannot encompass in advance. Consequently the problem of personal choice, solved in the earlier period of high growth potential by channeling choice through rigid social organization, in the period of transitional growth is solved by channeling choice through a rigid though highly individualized character.

This rigidity is a complex matter. While any society dependent on inner-direction seems to present people with a wide choice of aims—such as money, possessions, power, knowledge, fame, goodness—these aims are ideologically interrelated, and the selection made by any one individual remains relatively unalterable throughout his life. Moreover, the means to those ends, though not fitted into as tight a social frame of reference as in the society dependent on tradition-direction, are nevertheless limited by the new voluntary associations—for instance, the Quakers, the Masons, the Mechanics' Associations—to which people tie themselves. Indeed, the term "tradition-direction" could be misleading if the reader were to conclude that the force of tradition has no weight for the inner-directed character. On the contrary, he is very considerably bound by traditions: they limit his ends and inhibit his choice of means. The point is rather that a splintering of tradition takes place, connected in part with the increasing division of labor and stratification of society. Even if the individual's choice of tradition is largely determined for him by his family, as it is in most cases, he cannot help becoming aware of the existence of competing traditions—hence of tradition as such. As a result he possesses a somewhat greater degree of flexibility in adapting himself to ever changing requirements and in return requires more from his environment.

As the control of the primary group is loosened—the group that both socializes the young and controls the adult in the earlier era—a new psychological mechanism appropriate to the more open society is "invented": it is what I like to describe as a psychological gyroscope.[4] This instrument, once it is set by the parents and other authorities, keeps the inner-directed person, as we shall see, "on course" even when tradition, as responded to by his character, no longer dictates his moves. The inner-directed person becomes capable of maintaining a delicate balance between the demands upon him of his life goal and the buffetings of his external environment.

This metaphor of the gyroscope, like any other, must not be taken literally. It would be a mistake to see the inner-directed man as incapable of learning from experience or as insensitive to public opinion in matters of external conformity. He can receive and utilize certain signals from outside, provided that they can be reconciled with the limited maneuverability that his gyroscope permits him. His pilot is not quite automatic.

Huizinga's *The Waning of the Middle Ages* gives a picture of the anguish and turmoil, the conflict of values, out of which the new forms slowly emerged. Already by the late Middle Ages people were forced to live under new conditions of awareness. As their self-consciousness and their individuality developed, they had to make themselves at home in the world in novel ways. They still have to.

Incipient Decline of Population: Other-directed Types

The problem facing the societies in the stage of transitional growth is that of reaching a point at which resources become plentiful enough or are utilized effectively enough to permit a rapid accumulation of capital. This

---

[4] Since writing the above I have discovered Gardner Murphy's use of the same metaphor in his volume *Personality* (New York, Harper, 1947).

rapid accumulation has to be achieved even while the social product is being drawn on at an accelerated rate to maintain the rising population and satisfy the consumer demands that go with the way of life that has already been adopted. For most countries, unless capital and techniques can be imported from other countries in still later phases of the population curve, every effort to increase national resources at a rapid rate must actually be at the expense of current standards of living. We have seen this occur in the U.S.S.R., now in the stage of transitional growth. For western Europe this transition was long-drawn-out and painful. For America, Canada, and Australia—at once beneficiaries of European techniques and native resources—the transition was rapid and relatively easy.

The tradition-directed person, as has been said, hardly thinks of himself as an individual. Still less does it occur to him that he might shape his own destiny in terms of personal, lifelong goals or that the destiny of his children might be separate from that of the family group. He is not sufficiently separated psychologically from himself (or, therefore, sufficiently close to himself), his family, or group to think in these terms. In the phase of transitional growth, however, people of inner-directed character do gain a feeling of control over their own lives and see their children also as individuals with careers to make. At the same time, with the shift out of agriculture and, later, with the end of child labor, children no longer become an unequivocal economic asset. And with the growth of habits of scientific thought, religious and magical views of human fertility—views that in an earlier phase of the population curve made sense for the culture if it was to reproduce itself—give way to "rational," individualistic attitudes. Indeed, just as the rapid accumulation of productive capital requires that people be imbued with the "Protestant ethic" (as Max Weber characterized one manifestation of what is here termed inner-direction), so also the decreased number of progeny requires a profound change in values —a change so deep that, in all probability, it has to be rooted in character structure.

As the birth rate begins to follow the death rate downward, societies move toward the epoch of incipient decline of population. Fewer and fewer people work on the land or in the extractive industries or even in manufacturing. Hours are short. People may have material abundance and leisure besides. They pay for these changes however—here, as always, the solution of old problems gives rise to new ones—by finding themselves in a centralized and bureaucratized society and a world shrunken and agitated by the contact—accelerated by industralization—of races, nations, and cultures.

The hard enduringness and enterprise of the inner-directed types are somewhat less necessary under these new conditions. Increasingly, *other people* are the problem, not the material environment. And as people mix more widely and become more sensitive to each other, the surviving traditions from the stage of high growth potential—much disrupted, in any case, during the violent spurt of industrialization—become still further attenuated. Gyroscopic control is no longer sufficiently flexible, and a new psychological mechanism is called for.

Furthermore, the "scarcity psychology" of many inner-directed people, which was socially adaptive during the period of heavy capital accumulation that accompanied transitional growth of population, needs to give way to an "abundance psychology" capable of "wasteful" luxury consumption of leisure and of the surplus product. Unless people want to destroy the surplus product in war, which still does require heavy capital equipment, they must learn to enjoy and engage in those services that are expensive in terms of man power but not of capital—poetry and philosophy, for instance.[5] Indeed, in the period of incipient decline, nonproductive consumers, both the increasing number of old people and the diminishing number of as yet untrained young, form a high proportion of the population, and these need both the economic opportunity to be prodigal and the character structure to allow it.

Has this need for still another slate of character types actually been acknowledged to any degree? My observations lead me to believe that in America it has.

A *definition of other-direction.* The type of character I shall describe as other-directed seems to be emerging in very recent years in the upper middle class of our larger cities: more prominently in New York than in Boston, in Los Angeles than in Spokane, in Cincinnati than in Chillicothe. Yet in some respects this type is strikingly similar to *the* American, whom Tocqueville and other curious and astonished visitors from Europe, even before the Revolution, thought to be a new kind of man. Indeed, travelers' reports on America impress us with their unanimity. The American is said to be shallower, freer with his money, friendlier, more uncertain of himself and his values, more demanding of approval than the European. It all adds up to a pattern which, without stretching matters too far, resembles the kind of character that a number of social scientists have seen as developing in contemporary, highly industrialized, and bureaucratic America: Fromm's "marketer," Mills's "fixer," Arnold Green's "middle class male child."[6]

It is my impression that the middle-class American of today is decisively different from those Americans of Tocqueville's writings who nevertheless strike us as so contemporary, and much of this book will be devoted to discussing these differences. It is also my impression that the conditions

[5] These examples are given by Allan G. B. Fisher, *The Clash of Progress and Security* (London, Macmillan, 1935).

[6] See Erich Fromm, *Man for Himself*; C. Wright Mills, "The Competitive Personality," *Partisan Review*, XIII (1946), 433; Arnold Green, "The Middle Class Male Child and Neurosis," *American Sociological Review*, XI (1946), 31. See also the work of Jurgen Ruesch, Martin B. Loeb, and co-workers on the "infantile personality."

I believe to be responsible for other-direction are affecting increasing numbers of people in the metropolitan centers of the advanced industrial countries. My analysis of the other-directed character is thus at once an analysis of the American and of contemporary man. Much of the time I find it hard or impossible to say where one ends and the other begins. Tentatively, I am inclined to think that the other-directed type does find itself most at home in America, due to certain unique elements in American society, such as its recruitment from Europe and its lack of any feudal past. As against this, I am also inclined to put more weight on capitalism, industrialism, and urbanization—these being international tendencies—than on any character-forming peculiarities of the American scene.

Bearing these qualifications in mind, it seems appropriate to treat contemporary metropolitan America as our illustration of a society—so far, perhaps, the only illustration—in which other-direction is the dominant mode of insuring conformity. It would be premature, however, to say that it is already the dominant mode in America as a whole. But since the other-directed types are to be found among the young, in the larger cities, and among the upper income groups, we may assume that, unless present trends are reversed, the hegemony of other-direction lies not far off.

If we wanted to cast our social character types into social class molds, we could say that inner-direction is the typical character of the "old" middle class—the banker, the tradesman, the small entrepreneur, the technically oriented engineer, etc.—while other-direction is becoming the typical character of the "new" middle class—the bureaucrat, the salaried employee in business, etc. Many of the economic factors associated with the recent growth of the "new" middle class are well known. They have been discussed by James Burnham, Colin Clark, Peter Drucker, and others. There is a decline in the numbers and in the proportion of the working population engaged in production and extraction—agriculture, heavy industry, heavy transport—and an increase in the numbers and the proportion engaged in white-collar work and the service trades. People who are literate, educated, and provided with the necessities of life by an ever more efficient machine industry and agriculture, turn increasingly to the "tertiary" economic realm. The service industries prosper among the people as a whole and no longer only in court circles.

Education, leisure, services, these go together with an increased consumption of words and images from the new mass media of communications. While societies in the phase of transitional growth begin the process of distributing words from urban centers, the flow becomes a torrent in the societies of incipient population decline. This process, while modulated by profound national and class differences, connected with differences in literacy and loquacity, takes place everywhere in the industrialized lands. Increasingly, relations with the outer world and with oneself are mediated by the flow of mass communication. For the other-directed types political events are likewise experienced through a screen of words by which the events are habitually atomized and personalized—or pseudo-personalized. For the inner-directed person who remains still extant in this period the tendency is rather to systematize and moralize this flow of words.

These developments lead, for large numbers of people, to changes in paths to success and to the requirement of more "socialized" behavior both for success and for marital and personal adaptation. Connected with such changes are changes in the family and in child-rearing practices. In the smaller families of urban life, and with the spread of "permissive" child care to ever wider strata of the population, there is a relaxation of older patterns of discipline. Under these newer patterns the peer-group (the group of one's associates of the same age and class) becomes much more important to the child, while the parents make him feel guilty not so much about violation of inner standards as about failure to be popular or otherwise to manage his relations with these other children. Moreover, the pressures of the school and the peer-group are reinforced and continued—in a manner whose inner paradoxes I shall discuss later—by the mass media: movies, radio, comics, and popular culture media generally. Under these conditions types of character emerge that we shall here term other-directed. To them much of the discussion in the ensuing chapters is devoted. *What is common to all the other-directed people is that their contemporaries are the source of direction for the individual—either those known to him or those with whom he is indirectly acquainted, through friends and through the mass media. This source is of course "internalized" in the sense that dependence on it for guidance in life is implanted early. The goals toward which the other-directed person strives shift with that guidance: it is only the process of striving itself and the process of paying close attention to the signals from others that remain unaltered throughout life.* This mode of keeping in touch with others permits a close behavioral conformity, not through drill in behavior itself, as in the tradition-directed character, but rather through an exceptional sensitivity to the actions and wishes of others.

Of course, it matters very much who these "others" are: whether they are the individual's immediate circle or a "higher" circle or the anonymous voices of the mass media; whether the individual fears the hostility of chance acquaintances or only of those who "count." But his need for approval and direction from others—and contemporary others rather than ancestors—goes beyond the reasons that lead most people in any era to care very much what others think of them. While all people want and need to be liked by some of the people some of the time, it is only the modern other-directed types who make this their chief source of direction and chief area of sensitivity.[7]

---

[7] This picture of the other-directed person has been stimulated by, and developed from, Erich Fromm's discussion of the "marketing orientation" in *Man for Himself*

It is perhaps the insatiable force of this psychological need for approval that differentiates people of the metropolitan, American upper middle class, whom we regard as other-directed, from very similar types that have appeared in capital cities and among other classes in previous historical periods, whether in Imperial Canton in eighteenth- and nineteenth-century Europe, or in ancient Athens, Alexandria, or Rome. In all these groups fashion not only ruled as a substitute for morals and customs, but it was a rapidly changing fashion that held sway. It could do so because, although the mass media were in their infancy, the group corresponding to the American upper middle class was comparably small and the elite structure was extremely reverberant. It can be argued, for example, that a copy of *The Spectator* covered its potential readership more thoroughly in the late eighteenth century than *The New Yorker* covers its readership today. In eighteenth- and nineteenth-century English, French, and Russian novels, we find portraits of the sort of people who operated in the upper reaches of bureaucracy and had to be prepared for rapid changes of signals. Stepan Arkadyevitch Oblonsky in *Anna Karenina* is one of the more likeable and less opportunistic examples, especially striking because of the way Tolstoy contrasts him with Levin, a moralizing, inner-directed person. At any dinner party Stepan manifests exceptional social skills; his political skills as described in the following quotation are also highly social:

Stepan Arkadyevitch took in and read a liberal newspaper, not an extreme one, but one advocating the views held by the majority. And in spite of the fact that science, art, and politics had no special interest for him, he firmly held those views on all subjects which were held by the majority and by his paper, and he only changed them when the majority changed them—or, more strictly speaking, he did not change them, but they imperceptively changed of themselves within him.

Stepan Arkadyevitch had not chosen his political opinions or his views; these political opinions and views had come to him of themselves, just as he did not choose the shapes of his hats or coats, but simply took those that were being worn. And for him, living in a certain society—owing to the need, ordinarily developed at years of discretion, for some degree of mental activity—to have views was just as indispensable as to have a hat. If there was a reason for his preferring liberal to conservative views, which were held also by many of his circle, it arose not from his considering liberalism more rational, but from its being in closer accord with his manner of life. . . . And so liberalism had become a habit of Stepan Arkadyevitch's, and he liked his newspaper, as he did his cigar after dinner, for the slight fog it diffused in his brain.

Stepan, while his good-natured gregariousness makes him seem like a modern middle-class American, is not fully other-directed. This gregariousness alone, without a certain sensitivity to others as individuals and as a source of direction, is not the identifying trait. Just so, we must differentiate

---

pp. 67–82. I have also drawn on my portrait of "The Cash Customer," *Common Sense*, XI (1942), 183.

the nineteenth-century American—gregarious and subservient to public opinion though he was found to be by Tocqueville, Bryce, and others—from the other-directed American as he emerges today, an American who in his character is more capable of and more interested in maintaining responsive contact with others both at work and at play. This point needs to be emphasized, since the distinction is easily misunderstood. The inner-directed person, though he often sought and sometimes achieved a relative independence of public opinion and of what the neighbors thought of him, was in most cases very much concerned with his good repute and, at least in America, with "keeping up with the Joneses." These conformities, however, were primarily external, typified in such details as clothes, curtains, and bank credit. For, indeed, the conformities were to a standard, evidence of which was provided by the "best people" in one's milieu. In contrast with this pattern, the other-directed person, though he has his eye very much on the Joneses, aims to keep up with them not so much in external details as in the quality of his inner experience. That is, his great sensitivity keeps him in touch with others on many more levels than the externals of appearance and propriety. Nor does any ideal of independence or of reliance on God alone modify his desire to look to the others—and the "good guys" as well as the best people—for guidance in what experiences to seek and in how to interpret them.

The three types compared. One way to see the structural differences between the three types is to see the differences in the emotional sanction or control in each type.

The tradition-directed person feels the impact of his culture as a unit, but it is nevertheless mediated through the specific, small number of individuals with whom he is in daily contact. These expect of him not so much that he be a certain type of person but that he behave in the approved way. Consequently the sanction for behavior tends to be the fear of being *shamed*.

The inner-directed person has early incorporated a psychic gyroscope which is set going by his parents and can receive signals later on from other authorities who resemble his parents. He goes through life less independent than he seems, obeying this internal piloting. Getting off course, whether in response to inner impulses or to the fluctuating voices of contemporaries, may lead to the feeling of *guilt*.

Since the direction to be taken in life has been learned in the privacy of the home from a small number of guides and since principles, rather than details of behavior, are internalized, the inner-directed person is capable of great stability. Especially so when it turns out that his fellows have gyroscopes too, spinning at the same speed and set in the same direction. But many inner-directed individuals can remain stable even when the rein forcement of social approval is not available—as in the upright life of the stock Englishman isolated in the tropics.

Contrasted with such a type as this, the other-directed person learns to respond to signals from a far wider circle than is constituted by his parents. The family is no longer a closely knit unit to which he belongs but merely part of a wider social environment to which he early becomes attentive. In these respects the other-directed person resembles the tradition-directed person: both live in a group milieu and lack the inner-directed person's capacity to go it alone. The nature of this group milieu, however, differs radically in the two cases. The other-directed person is cosmopolitan. For him the border between the familiar and the strange—a border clearly marked in the societies depending on tradition-direction—has broken down. As the family continuously absorbs the strange and so reshapes itself, so the strange becomes familiar. While the inner-directed person could be "at home abroad" by virtue of his relative insensitivity to others, the other-directed person is, in a sense, at home everywhere and nowhere, capable of a rapid if sometimes superficial intimacy with and response to everyone.

The tradition-directed person takes his signals from others, but they come in a cultural monotone; he needs no complex receiving equipment to pick them up. The other-directed person must be able to receive signals from far and near; the sources are many, the changes rapid. What can be internalized, then, is not a code of behavior but the elaborate equipment needed to attend to such messages and occasionally to participate in their circulation. As against guilt-and-shame controls, though of course these survive, one prime psychological lever of the other-directed person is a diffuse *anxiety*. This control equipment, instead of being like a gyroscope, is like a radar.[8]

C. *Psychopathology*

The final group of readings in this section also deals with specific patterns of adjustment but those described here generally are considered pathological or deviant in nature. The study of the abnormal or pathological is extremely important to an understanding of the adjustment process. By focusing our attention on the abnormal, we hope to develop methods by which maladjusted behavior can be decreased and adjusted behavior increased. Those members of our society who behave in ways which seem atypical, ineffective, or disturbed enable us to learn about the conditions likely to lead to adjustment difficulties.

[8] The "radar" metaphor was suggested by Karl Wittfogel.

The initial steps in the study of psychopathology are those of distinguishing between the normal and abnormal and classifying the abnormal into distinctive groups. This procedure is referred to as *diagnosis*. However, in order for diagnoses to be useful in helping us prevent and alleviate adjustment difficulties, the specific groupings or classifications should be based on more than the differential descriptions of the ways people behave. We wish our diagnostic terms to be more than mere labels which sort individuals into groups. An ideal diagnosis should do the following: (1) provide us with a description of the difficulty; (2) give us an understanding of the factors which led up to it; (3) predict the consequences or future course of the difficulty; and (4) inform us of methods by which we can remedy, control, or alter these consequences.

Our present diagnostic terms hardly approach this ideal. All of the problems associated with research methods, terminology, and personality theory make it a difficult task. Of particular significance in the area of psychopathology is the designation of meaningful concepts. In no other area of psychological inquiry have the difficulties of developing clear and useful concepts been highlighted to such an extent. Numerous investigations have found that the agreements between diagnoses made by different workers are extremely low. Too often the specific diagnosis made by a psychiatrist, psychologist, or social worker will depend more on his own theoretical and personal predilections than on the patient's condition. Even when different workers agree, the diagnostic classification provides little or no information about treatment techniques likely to be effective. Methods of treatment which are beneficial for many pathological conditions are not necessarily related to a given diagnosis. Our present diagnostic terms also encourage overgeneralizing from the observations we make and oversimplifying the individual's condition. The tendency to overgeneralize and to assume that one basic factor or entity determines pathological behavior promotes serious limitations in our efforts to deal with these conditions.

Many of the problems associated with our diagnostic efforts can be traced to historical influences. Since early times man has attempted to explain behavior by postulating that one basic, all-influencing force compels us to act in a given way. Whether this force was attributed to a mystical being or to some internal factor, it represented man's attempt to explain everything about himself in one easy sweep, i.e., with one basic idea. As science progressed, the notion was introduced that all psychological characteristics, including feelings, thoughts, actions, are centered in the brain. Consequently it was thought that psychological disturbances must be aused by disturbances in the brain. This formulation, originally roposed by Hypocrates and expanded in the last century by Craepelin, undoubtedly represented advanced thinking over the mystical connections drawn between behavior pathology and witchcraft. It should be noted, however, that attributing pathology to rain disturbance continues to involve the belief that one factor—in this case one part of the body—can explain all psychological characteristics of man. In addition the brain hypothesis attempts to explain psychopathology solely on the basis of anatomy and physiology and in so doing, models itself along the lines of medicine's approach to disease. This approach equates a psychological disturbance with a state of disease and assumes that this condition is the result of an anomaly in the structure of the organism which causes a specific pattern of symptoms. Kraepelin attempted to classify pathology by seeking and labeling a unique feature of each condition. His classifications and the disease-entity logic on which they are based constitute the major approach to formal diagnosis today and often lead to ignoring the significance of motives, conflicts, experience, and learning in psychopathology.

Our present diagnostic concepts for psychopathology involve no systematic scheme of classification. Sometimes diagnostic terms represent a summary description of the individual's behavior (*depression, obsessive-compulsive, anxiety neurosis*); sometimes they are differentiated on the basis of an hypothesized cause (*psychosomatic illness, involutional melancholia, alcoholism*); and sometimes a term is used chiefly because it has become linked traditionally with the intensity of disturbance or with one or two predominant characteristics (*schizophrenia, manic-depressive psychosis, epilepsy*). In almost every case our terms fall short of the ideal and can hardly deserve to be called diagnostic concepts. For the most part diagnosticians today use the formal classifications of disorders as rough, summary descriptions of the individual's most apparent difficulty. In actual practice they have found it more fruitful to evaluate the individual patient's condition by considering the particular adjustment problems he is having, his typical approach to them, and the consequences of his actions. In other words, in order to make a useful diagnosis of an individual's adjustment difficulties, it is essential to consider a complex of variables rather than a single one which the disease-entity approach suggests.

The three papers comprising this group of readings were selected to present a description of some of the diagnostic classifications which are commonly used in the field of psychopathology today. The first two papers deal with rather classical diagnostic concepts and categories pertaining to adults and are divided into the traditional breakdown of *neuroses* and *psychoses*. The selection taken from White's text *The Abnormal Personality* includes a discussion of anxiety states, phobias, obsessions, dissociated conditions, and hysteria. This is followed by a delineation of the more disturbed psychotic conditions in the selection by J. F. Brown from his book *The Psychodynamics of Abnormal Behavior*.

The last article, written by Jenkins and Glickman, differs from the others in two respects. First, it deals with the behavioral disturbances of children; and second, it reports on an effort to order and describe disturbances by utilizing statistical techniques. Those factors are isolated statistically which represent clusters of traits in disturbed children. As the authors point out, these clusters should not be viewed as "entities" since there is no implication or reason to believe that two children falling within the same group have experienced the same historical influences or are likely to develop along similar lines in the future. The clusters represent descriptive classifications of behavior rather than labels for "mental disease." The statistical approach to ordering pathological behavior into meaningful syndromes recently has been applied to adult disorders as well, and this method appears to offer promise in the study of deviant behavior.

The three papers in this group by no means cover all of the classifications in the area of psychopathology. Not included are the psychosomatic conditions (*ulcers, hypertension, allergies,* etc.), abnormal conditions related to disorders of the central nervous system (*general paresis, Huntington's chorea, multiple sclerosis,* etc.), pathological states associated with specific deviant behaviors (*drug addiction, alcoholism, sexual deviations,* etc.), and intellectual retardation (*cretinism, mongolism, microcephaly,* etc.). Descriptions of these can be found in any standard text in abnormal psychology.

NEUROTIC PATTERNS OF BEHAVIOR *

⟨ ROBERT W. WHITE

Anxiety States

On first thought, it might seem that anxiety states constitute a refutation of the whole anxiety theory of neurosis. If a neurosis, with all its elaboration and all its cost to the personality, comes into existence to prevent

* From Robert W. White, *The Abnormal Personality*, pp. 281–310, edited. The Ronald Press Company, New York, 1948. Reprinted by permission of the author and the publisher.

nxiety, how can one of its symptoms be the very anxiety it is supposed to revent? . . . The function or purpose of dreams is to preserve sleep, but ometimes the dream is unsuccessful and does not achieve its purpose. imilarly, a neurosis can sometimes be unsuccessful, with the result that nxiety breaks through all defenses and appears in its undisguised form as ar bordering on panic.

Partial failure of defenses. Anxiety attacks can be considered as represent-ig a partial failure of adequate defenses. Even in the face of highly dis-uieting fear, the patient does not produce defenses sufficient to bind and appress his fear. The situation is not, however, equivalent to a total ollapse with regression to the condition of a terrified child. Such collapse nd regression were sometimes seen in men who were exposed to prolonged evere combat stress.[1] They bear little resemblance to the anxiety states nat occur in civilian neuroses. These take a less sweeping form: the atient is panic-stricken but not disintegrated; from time to time he is ooded by terror, but he struggles with it, brings it somehow under control, esumes his daily life until another attack breaks through, gets himself to doctor's office if the attacks continue. The anxiety attacks are temporary ruptions of panic. Defenses are insufficient to prevent the eruptions, but ne person fights them and stamps them down.

It is characteristic that the patient is not aware of any reason for his error. He may feel that he is going insane, that he is trapped amidst angerous forces, or that something dreadful but unnameable is going to appen. The diffuseness and indefiniteness of the danger are the most rying features of the attack. The cartoonist Steig represents this by draw-ig a little gesticulating demon on the end of a stick attached to the back f a person's head—whichever way the victim turns, the demon is out here behind him, never in sight.[2] This circumstance indicates that part f the defense is being maintained. Repression still effectively prevents the atient from remembering the childhood danger situations or from be-oming aware of the danger-linked impulses in himself. It is, then, only he anxiety that escapes from control and breaks through the defenses. ven at their worst, anxiety attacks represent only a partial failure of efenses. Neither the primitive defenses of childhood nor the adult pro-ective organization give way completely. . . .

hobias

A phobia can be defined as a morbid dread of an object, act, or situation. The word "morbid" differentiates it from a normal fear, and is inserted to

---

[1] For examples see W. McDougall, *Outline of Abnormal Psychology,* New York, Chas. Scribner's Sons, 1926, pp. 285–292; and R. R. Grinker & J. P. Spiegel, *War Neuroses,* New York, McGraw-Hill–Blakiston, 1945, pp. 4–14.

[2] Steig, W., *About People,* New York, Random House, 1939, drawing entitled "Anxiety," p. 105.

indicate that we speak of phobia only when the thing that is feared offe
no actual danger. When a patient shows great fear of something that is i
fact perfectly harmless, we have to assume that the real threat lies som
where else. The phobic object is serving as a symbol or a distant remind
of some danger that is extremely real to the patient, even though its orig
may have been in childhood.

Phobias cannot readily be classified. They have sometimes been name
according to the object or situation that is feared. At one time medic
writers favored attaching Greek prefixes to indicate every possible objec
of morbid dread. A few of these fancy names, such as claustrophob
(morbid dread of closed or constricted spaces), have become harmless
lodged in the scientific vocabulary. In older medical literature there wer
literally hundreds of them: for instance, melissophobia (morbid dread c
bees), gephryophobia (morbid dread of crossing water), parthenophob
(morbid dread of virgins), homilophobia (morbid dread of sermons). Th
list becomes endless because there is really nothing that cannot be a
object of morbid dread. Lest the reader became a victim of onomatophob
(morbid dread of names), he should be assured that this pretentious vocal
ulary is now largely obsolete.

Phobia as a defense. If a phobic patient comes in contact with th
object of his fear, he is thrown into a severe anxiety attack. To this exten
phobias resemble anxiety states; there is at times a break-through of pani
The phobia, however, offers one great advantage over diffuse anxiety. Th
patient can arrange to avoid contact with his phobic object. It is impossibl
to escape from danger when it is felt to be everywhere around you. Th
focusing of danger upon a single external object or situation immediatel
restores the possibility of constructive action, even if this consists of n
more than keeping away from the threat.

The dynamics of phobia are neatly illustrated in the following incident.
A boy of ten, who suffered from various neurotic difficulties, was brough
for treatment to a child guidance clinic. Mother and child sat clos
together in the waiting room until the boy was asked to go into the psy
chiatrist's office while the mother went elsewhere to talk to the socia
worker. After a visible attempt at self-control, the boy began to cry, sayin
"I'm just scared and I don't know what it is." Plainly he was experiencin
diffuse anxiety at separation from his mother and at being in a strang
room with an as yet strange man. After a while the child spied a brief-cas
and said, suspiciously, "What's in that—what's behind it?" It was sug
gested that he go and investigate, which he did while muttering, "Mayb
there is a gun." Discovering that the brief-case held no threatening content
made it possible for the young patient to smile and relax for the first time
It is quite clear that localizing the fear on a definite object constituted

[3] Allen, F. H., *Psychotherapy with Children*, New York, W. W. Norton & Co.
1942, pp. 169–171.

tep in overcoming his anxiety. It restored his mobility; instead of remain-
ng frozen to his chair, he became free to avoid the brief-case or to investigate it. His choice of the second alternative completed the overcoming
of his fear.

Channels of displacement. The mechanism at work in the formation of
phobias is displacement. Anxiety is displaced in order to find a less terrify-
ng and more avoidable object. It makes one feel less helpless to be afraid
of a brief-case than to be just plain afraid. Displacement is particularly
serviceable when the source of danger is an impulse or need that has been
linked with anxiety in childhood history. There is no escape from an
internal impulse or need, but if the fear can be focalized on an outside
object the chances of avoidance seem much better. Displacement must be
presumed to occur along associative channels. We examined the general
operation of this process when studying Diven's experiment.[4] In that investigation the anxiety response was conditioned to the word *barn*, which
served as a signal for painful electric shock. It became conditioned also to
contiguous words in the word list and to words that bore a meaningful
relation to barn in the sense of having rural associations. We saw that this
generalization occurred even when the subjects were not conscious that
barn was the true danger signal. Associative connections served as effective
guides for generalization, even when the subject was unaware of the whole
process. Going back to an example used earlier . . . the woman who was
afraid to go alone on the street lest she faint—it is easy to see that sexual
desires and the idea of finding a partner on the street might have been
linked together in half-conscious revery or in dreams forgotten upon awakening. Links of this kind are constantly recovered during psychoanalytic
treatment. Associative channels are thus prepared which serve as avenues
for displacement when sexual pressure increases and its associated anxiety
and guilt threaten to overwhelm the patient. So far as the patient's awareness is concerned, she knows only that she feels suddenly faint on the street.
It is most frightening, so she does not run the risk of going on the street
again.

Phobias are only partially explained, however, by pointing out the general
fact of channeling along associative lines. They are not fully explained even
when we allow for very personal meanings and even symbolisms that are
peculiar to the individual patient. Just as in normal thinking we call up
ideas that are relevant and appropriate to our present need, so the phobic
patient fastens upon associations that neatly substitute for his real source
of threat. If a phobic patient had been terrified by something that happened in a barn, he would not, in a fashion analogous to Diven's normal
subjects, become vaguely uneasy about everything rural. He would come
down hard on a single item, such as hay. Panic would seize him at the sight

[4] Diven, K., "Certain Determinants in the Conditioning of Anxiety Reactions,"
Journal of Psychology, 1937, Vol. 3, pp. 291–308.

or smell of hay. This would keep him out of barns and out of the country without constantly making him think of barns. The whole trouble would be safely concentrated on hay.

A remarkable example of the process of displacement is to be found in Freud's case of the five-year-old boy, Hans.[5] This case was an important milestone, not only for its demonstration of childhood sexual interests, but also for its untangling of the roundabout lines of association that made a path from nuclear fear to phobic symptom. The child was in the midst of the Oedipus conflict, and his nuclear fear was of the angry punishment he anticipated from his father because of his possessive feelings and actions toward his mother. His fear did not present itself in this form, but rather in the form of a phobia of horses on the street. This was an avoidable threat, whereas the father could not be avoided. The connecting lines passed through all kinds of childhood scenes, fantasies, and ruminations. Hans played with his father, who pretended to be a horse; he saw a horse with a black muzzle that reminded him of his father's mustache; he played with other children, pretending that he was a horse, and fell down in the course of the play; he saw a horse fall down and struggle with its feet. All these and many other elements entered the associative tissue, until at last he was in panic at seeing horses on the street and hearing the sound of their feet. With the achievement of this symptom he was no longer afraid of his father.

Expansion of the phobic system. From what has been said it might seem that the formation of a phobia was an ideal solution to all problems of neurotic anxiety. It would indeed be a perfect scheme if the phobia could only be prevented from expanding. Internal dangers, especially those linked with strong recurrent needs, will not let the patient off so easily. The danger continues to be present. The patient avoids the phobic situation but cannot thus achieve full peace of mind. Before long some other situation is felt to be dangerous, and the patient has two phobias. In the end he has had to keep employing his phobic mechanism so extensively that he is back in the state of being more or less afraid of everything.

Not all phobias expand indefinitely. Sometimes a phobic system becomes stabilized and serves fairly well as an enduring defense. The tendency to expand, however, is a very natural consequence of the displaced or substitutive character of the phobic symptom. Avoiding the phobic object does not usually mean taking any effective action against the real threat. The fundamental problem remains unsolved and the phobic mechanism does not really bind the anxiety.

Ross describes a case in which a man became phobic for the number 13.[6]

[5] Freud, S., "Analysis of a Phobia in a Five-year-old Boy," 1909, reprinted in *Collected Papers*, International Psychoanalytic Press, 1925, Vol. 3, pp. 149–289.

[6] Ross, T. A., *The Common Neuroses*, 2d ed., Baltimore, William Wood & Co., 1937, pp. 219–223.

The real fear proved to be that he would recall some juvenile sexual esca-
pades with a superstitious maid who believed in the bad luck associated
with 13. This chapter in his history had been repressed as his personality
developed along lines of superiority and morality. The case illustrates par-
icularly well the expansion of a phobia. The patient began by staying in
bed on the thirteenth day of the month so that he would not come in con-
act with calendars and newspaper dates. Soon he discovered that "twenty-
seventh" contained thirteen letters, and he was condemned to bed two
days each month. He next began going to work by a roundabout route to
avoid the thirteen-letter sign, "Peter Robinson," that hung prominently on
he direct route. Presently he experienced uneasiness when people said,
"Oh, good morning," or when they said, "Good afternoon" without the
"Oh" that would have given the greeting a safe fifteen letters. He began
hopping over the thirteenth step in a flight, counting his own footsteps,
counting the streets he passed, until finally he had time for nothing but
avoiding the number thirteen. One laughs over the case, but the patient
was not fencing with will-o'-the-wisps. His phobic defenses later broke
down. He remembered the sexual adventures and became exposed to deep
sources of anxiety. As a result he was for some weeks deeply depressed and
dangerously suicidal. His recovery from this still worse state occurred at the
cost of reinstating a good part of the phobia.

Obsessional Neurosis

There are two names for the symptom syndrome to which we now turn
our attention. Some workers prefer the designation *obsessional neurosis,*
others prefer *compulsion neurosis.* Sometimes it is proposed to subdivide
the syndrome into conditions dominated by obsessional thoughts and conditions in which compulsive actions predominate. The underlying processes
are probably too similar to justify the separation.

Characteristics of the symptoms. An obsession is an idea or desire which
forces itself persistently into the patient's mind in what he experiences as
an irrational fashion. A compulsion is an act actually carried out, which
similarly forces itself upon the patient. Obsessive ideas and compulsive acts
are often closely linked: for instance, the obsession that there may be dangerous germs on one's hands leads to the compulsion of handwashing.
Minor obsessions and compulsions are familiar in everyone's experience.
We keep wondering whether we turned off the gas burner, or we knock
on wood after mentioning our good fortune. These everyday phenomena
resemble neurotic obsessions and compulsions to the extent that they are
sensed as irrational. We know they are foolish, but they seem to have a
little push of their own and it is easier to let them have their way. In neurotic obsessions and compulsions, this quality is greatly magnified. The
ideas and acts are like foreign bodies, forcing themselves upon the patient

yet experienced as no part of the self. Moreover, they often betray that they are working in the service of defense. If the patient tries to stop his obsessive ruminations or his compulsive rituals, he is plunged into an attack of anxiety.

Obsessional symptoms occur in great variety. The patient's mind may be full of thoughts about infection and disease, making it necessary for him to wash his hands a hundred times a day and to take precautions that would put a modern hospital to shame. He may have rituals in regard to dressing or going to bed which make these actions laborious and time-consuming He may be troubled by intrusive blasphemous thoughts when he is trying to concentrate on his prayers. Orderliness may become the demon in his life committing him to an endless task of straightening, arranging, recording and filing. Particularly trying are obsessions concerning harmful and violent acts: the patient is invaded by ideas of burning the house down, cutting his wife's throat, strangling his children, throwing himself in front of a truck The danger that such acts will be carried out is small to the vanishing point but the patient has no feeling of control over them and constantly fear that he will turn them into realities. The lives of obsessional patients are easily reduced to ineffectiveness and misery. Their energies are tied up in symptoms, and they are filled with doubt, vacillation, uneasiness, and helplessness. Occasionally an attack of anxiety breaks through.

Close scrutiny of the contents of obsessive symptoms shows that they can be classified under two headings: (1) Part of the symptoms give expression to aggressive and sexual impulses. Murderous hostility, destructiveness dirtiness, and sexual urges in a crude and violent form reveal themselves in the content of obsessional thoughts. It is as if the suppressed *antisocial impulses* returned in this guise to plague the patient. (2) The rest of the symptoms give expression to *self-corrective tendencies.* Orderliness, rituals cleanliness, propitiatory acts, self-imposed duties, and punishments all testify to the patient's need to counteract and set right his antisocial tendencies. Guilt feelings are his almost constant companions. Perhaps he reads in the paper about a murder that was committed many miles away. So strong is his guilt that he becomes obsessed with the idea that he committed the murder and deserves terrible punishment. The division of the symptoms into these two classes, *antisocial impulses* and *self-corrective tendencies,* gives an immediate insight into the nature of the underlying conflict. Nowhere is the Freudian concept of the super-ego more applicable. The childish conception of evil joins battle with the childish conception of righteousness and punishment.

Obsessional symptoms sometimes have a sudden onset, but very often they make their appearance gradually. In this neurosis it is not easy to draw the line between focal symptoms and a gradually developed neurotic trend. When the symptoms develop gradually, it is almost always the self-corrective ones that make the first appearance. The symptom picture is first occu-

ied by derivatives of the defensive process. Only later do signs of the
anxiety-linked impulses creep into the scene.

Distinctive features of obsessional neurosis. Although the obsessional
syndrome frequently overlaps with others, especially with phobias, it has a
number of characteristics which roughly differentiate it from the other
patterns.

1. The elements of the underlying conflict are more fully represented
in consciousness than is the case in any other neurotic syndrome. The anti-
social tendencies and the self-punitive tendencies can be read in the patient's obsessions and compulsions. The representation in consciousness is
of course somewhat peculiar, falling far short of a frank recognition of one's
tendencies. There is much symbolizing and disguising, and in any event
the patient does not experience the tendencies as a part of his ego. They
have a peculiar status. The patient knows that his obsessions and compulsions are inside him; he does not use projection and attribute them to external forces. Yet they feel to him like foreign bodies, not part of the tissue of
the self. They intrude themselves from unknown parts of his mind. Apparently the mechanism of repression plays a less drastic part in obsessional
neurosis. Its place is taken by this semi-detachment of the impulses from
the self.

2. Secondary defenses are very highly developed. The struggle between
anxiety-linked impulses and defensive processes is carried on in the realm
of intellect. In this realm it is possible to make an extensive use of displacement. The patient finds himself ruminating on the philosophical
implications of the dichotomy between love and hate rather than perceiving that he has certain hateful impulses toward someone whom he loves.
The treatment of obsessional patients is often badly delayed by this tendency. The patient raises theoretical objections to the physician's way of
conducting the treatment and tries to get into a long argument on basic
assumptions. We shall shortly give an example of the mechanisms of isolation and undoing, which also play a part in the patient's intellectual
defenses.

3. Overt anxiety is moderately well avoided. There is an undercurrent
of uneasiness, but acute anxiety attacks are infrequent. Obsessional neurosis is not as successful as hysteria, however, in doing away with anxiety.

4. It seems generally agreed that aggressive impulses occupy an unusually
large place in the obsessional patient's basic conflicts. Sexuality is by no
means excluded, but hostility is so predominant that it may be considered
the central issue.

5. Certain character traits appear to be particularly common among
obsessional patients. These patients seem to favor a certain pattern of neurotic trends. Generally they show a great interest in orderliness and cleanliness, which they carry to extremes. They are also conscientious and idealistic;
they want to be never angry, always kind and considerate of others. All of

these traits are socially desirable if not carried to extreme lengths, but their force in the patients suggests a strong reaction formation against aggressive destructive, messy tendencies. Two other traits often appear in the pattern stubbornness and stinginess. For all their idealistic outlook the patients do not want to be hurried or directed, and they hate to have others make demands on them. The whole pattern of traits suggests that the crucial childhood difficulties had to do with giving up autonomy, submitting to adult demands, and coping with the anger that resulted from parental interference. Strict Freudians refer to this pattern as indicating fixation at the anal sadistic stage of libidinal development. . . .

Dissociated Conditions

We turn now to a group of disorders generally classed with hysteria, but characterized by peculiarities especially in the realm of memory. Whether we are dealing with a brief amnesia, a more extended fugue, or a fully developed double or multiple personality, the central feature of the disorder is a loss of personal identity. The patient forgets who he is and where he lives. He loses the symbols of his identity and also the memories of his previous life that support a continuing sense of selfhood. The phenomenon is familiar through newspaper reports of cases of amnesia. Perhaps the patient is so confused by the loss of memory that he approaches a police officer to ask for help. In other cases—these are the ones technically called *fugue*.—he may go on for quite a while functioning as an adequate new person perhaps with a new name. There are reports of cases in which a patient has remained in a fugue state for months and even years. Conceivably, such a change might be permanent, but we would have no access to such cases

It is a little unfortunate that the term *amnesia* has been captured by the press for just this particular type of memory disorder. Literally, *amnesia* means any kind of pathological forgetting, whether caused by drugs, brain injuries, old age, or psychogenic factors. The cases we are considering here represent a particular type of amnesia, the forgetting of personal identity. This particular pattern seems to be wholly psychogenic in character. The forgetting is somehow connected with neurotic conflict and represents an attempt to do something about that conflict.

Amnesia for personal identity. We begin with an example reported by McDougall, remarkable for its transparency.[7] A color-sergeant was carrying a message, riding his motorcycle through a dangerous section of the front All at once it was several hours later, and he was pushing his motorcycle along the streets of a coastal town nearly a hundred miles away. In utter bewilderment he gave himself up to the military police, but he could tell absolutely nothing of his long trip. The amnesia was ultimately broken by

[7] McDougall, W., *Outline of Abnormal Psychology*, op. cit.

the use of hypnosis. The man then remembered that he was thrown down by a shell explosion, that he picked up himself and his machine, that he started straight for the coastal town, that he studied signs and asked for directions in order to reach this destination.

It is clear, in this case, that the amnesia entailed no loss of competence. The patient's actions were purposive, rational, and intelligent. The amnesia rested only on his sense of personal identity. The conflict was between fear, suddenly intensified by his narrow escape, and his duty to complete the dangerous mission. The forgetting of personal identity made it possible to give way to his impulse toward flight, now irresistible, without exposing himself to the almost equally unbearable anxiety associated with being a coward, failing his mission, and undergoing arrest as a deserter. When he achieved physical safety the two sides of the conflict resumed their normal proportions and his sense of personal identity suddenly returned.

If we try to characterize the patient's state of mind during the amnesic period, the most we can say is that he was powerfully dominated by a single motive. As far as he could recall the experience, he simply thought of nothing except reaching the town from which men embarked for home. Every action and thought was subordinated to this supreme goal. The state of mind was not unlike that of a person extremely preoccupied with an absorbing task, oblivious to other circumstances. But it went beyond this to the extent that the normal state was resumed abruptly, much like waking from a dream. It is interesting to observe the parallels between this amnesic condition and the artificially induced state of hypnosis. The hypnotized person carries out acts with a diminished feeling of voluntary participation. His sense of personal identity is in abeyance, though not lost. If he is told to act like someone else, he can do so with great vividness. The hypnotic state is so different from the normal that he issues from it with a sense of waking up, sometimes with amnesia for the hypnosis. We can say that hypnosis effects an artificial quieting of the sense of personal identity and of volition; in contrast, the color-sergeant's extreme fright effected a violent repression of all this in favor of the single-minded drive to escape.

In wartime there are many cases of amnesia and fugue which, like the preceding one, originate under traumatic conditions. In civilian life the same phenomenon occurs under less violent circumstances, but generally in connection with what amounts to an emotional crisis in the patient's life. Abeles and Schilder in a study of sixty-three cases found that "some unpleasant social conflict, either financial or familial, was significant in the immediate cause of the amnesia," although behind these immediate conflicts "deeper motives are found." [8] A more detailed report of five cases from the Menninger Clinic has the special advantage that the precipitating

[8] Abeles, M. & Schilder, P., "Psychogenic Loss of Personal Identity," *Archives of Neurology and Psychiatry*, 1935, Vol. 34, pp. 587–604.

events and the content of the amnesic period were carefully recovered in al
their personal meaning to the patient.[9] From this report we select the fol
lowing illustration.

A man of twenty-nine had developed a high ideal of independence and
manliness. He had been induced, however, to take work in his father-in
law's business, where he found himself dissatisfied and poorly paid. He wa
sometimes unable to meet family expenses, and was greatly humiliated to
be extricated by his father-in-law on these occasions. One day, again in dif
ficulties, he drove with his family to the town where his father-in-law lived
but could not bring himself to ask for the needed loan and turned the car
homeward. He became so preoccupied with the thought of finding a new
job and making money, that by the time he reached home he no longer
knew who he was nor recognized his wife and children in the car. Taken to
the hospital, he spoke only of his new job. He falsified reality to the exten
of interpreting everything in the hospital as though it were the operation
of a business firm. Two days later he emerged spontaneously into his nor
mal state, not remembering the amnesic episode. Shortly afterward he re
called the episode, including the suicidal despair that had filled him at the
thought of asking his father-in-law for more help.

In considering the case of the color-sergeant, we likened the amnesia to
an hypnotic state. This case of the business man suggests similarities to
dreams and sleepwalking. "Sleepwalking is not sharply differentiated from
fugue states, and there is a striking similarity in the psychological make-up
of persons who develop fugues and of sleepwalkers." [10] In dreams, sup
pressed wishes come to expression in hallucinatory form, but the person
does not have to accept responsibility for the foolish things he dreams. In
amnesic states and fugues, suppressed wishes come to expression in the
form of real actions, but on condition that the person lose his identity and
hence his responsibility for them. The business man desperately wanted to
get a better job and regain his sense of manliness and independence.
Hemmed in as he was by family debts and responsibilities, such a plan was
completely impracticable. When the fantasy grew too strong for him, he
could tolerate it only by forgetting his identity, thus forgetting the wife
and children whose presence made the fantasy so impracticable.

In summary it can be stated that the psychogenic loss of personal identity,
such as occurs in amnesias and fugues, represents another way of coping
with neurotic conflict. The loss of identity is a defense against intolerable
conflict when some powerful need or wish becomes uncontrollable. As is
so often true, the wish is ordinarily suppressed because the patient is what
he is, occupying a certain social position and having certain responsibilities
and obligations. When the wish is so strengthened, usually by some exter-

[9] Geleerd, E. R., Hacker, F. J. & Rapaport, D., "Contribution to the Study of
Amnesia and Allied Conditions," *Psychoanalytic Quarterly*, 1945, Vol. 14, pp. 199–220.
[10] *Ibid.*, p. 213.

nal crisis, that he can no longer keep it suppressed, his personal identity has to be ejected from consciousness. Both the patients we have described were dominated by a single wish during the amnesic period, and this is generally true of amnesic patients. It is interesting to speculate on the possible significance of an external crisis in such cases. Possibly the drastic defense of repressing personal identity can be used only under conditions of shock, when circumstances *very suddenly* build up the strength of a normally controllable need. On the other hand some workers favor the theory that amnesia and fugue occur only in a person constitutionally predisposed to such a solution. A special aptitude or a special weakness—call it whichever you like—may determine the readiness to meet crisis by repression and dissociation. . . .

Hysteria

Our discussion of hysteria can be relatively brief. Charcot's studies of hysterical symptoms, and Janet's study of the mental state in hysteria, were milestones in modern thinking about neurosis. Freud's first work, in association with Breuer, dealt with a typical if extreme case of hysteria. . . . Our present task will not be to examine new cases but rather to summarize the general facts about hysteria in so far as they are known today.

Varieties of hysterical symptoms. In addition to the amnesias, fugues, and multiple personalities considered in the last section, hysterical symptoms take a wide variety of bodily forms. On the motor side there are the *paralyses* which may include an arm, a leg, both legs, or one whole side of the body. These symptoms can be distinguished from true organic injuries by the fact that normal reflexes are retained in the paralyzed area, and that little or no muscular degeneration occurs. Sometimes the diagnosis is made still easier by the anatomical nonsense that characterizes the symptom: both hands, for instance, may be paralyzed, while the arms retain their motility, a state that could be produced organically only by a highly peculiar nerve injury in both wrists. Other motor symptoms are mutism (inability to speak), aphonia (inability to speak above a whisper, to "voice" the speech), *tremor,* and *tics* (spasmodic jerking in a small coordinated group of muscles). On the sensory side there are the many varieties of *anaesthesia.* These may accompany the paralyses, but they sometimes occur alone. Within any one sense department the anaesthesia may take a number of forms. In vision, for instance, the possibilities include total blindness, blindness in one eye, contraction of the visual field to a small focal point, blindness in the left half or right half of both eyes, and many other curious fragmentations of the visual process. Considerable attention has lately been paid to anorexia nervosa (literally "nervous loss of appetite"), which sometimes is carried so far as to endanger the patient's life. Symptoms of this kind, which mainly affect the viscera and act through the autonomic nervous system, are now generally removed from the category of hysteria and placed among the psychosomatic disorders. Another symptom is the *hysterical fit* which in some respects resembles an epileptic seizure but can generally be distinguished from it. Finally, there are sometimes *hysterical twilight state* in which the patient is confused and distressed, experience having an un real and dreamlike quality. The loss of contact with reality is less complete than would be the case in psychosis.

The more bodily forms of hysteria are sometimes given the title *conver sion hysteria*. The bodily symptoms represent a converted form of energy The force contained in impulses, which because of anxiety can be allowed no outward expression, is converted or diverted into sensory-motor chan nels in such a way as to block the functioning of some organ. This theory of converted energy was introduced by Freud, who regarded it as a highly hypothetical process difficult to understand or to verify. The interference with bodily functions is generally of an inhibitory character, and when this is true it is easy to regard the symptom as the outcome of defensive inhibi tion. In various degrees, then, hysterical symptoms can be looked upon as expressions of the defensive process and expressions of the anxiety-linked impulse. The mechanism, however, is certainly an obscure one, and it may even be quite different in different cases.

Kretschmer's study of hysterical tremor. A valuable clue to the nature of hysterical symptom formation is given in a monograph by Kretschmer.[11] Strictly speaking, it applies only to one type of symptom—hysterical tremor— originating under the traumatic conditions of combat. It would be hasty to generalize from this finding to all hysterical symptom formation, but the clue remains a useful one.

Tremor is a biologically performed component of the anxiety reaction. When stress is past, it subsides and disappears. Many men emerged from acute trauma trembling violently all over, but in most cases the tremor gradu ally subsided. In certain cases, however, the tremor did not subside; it lasted and became a permanent hysterical symptom. A wish to fall ill in order to be withdrawn from danger could readily be presumed in such cases, and Kretschmer worked out the following explanation of how a wish to fall ill, very likely unconscious, could prolong the tremor indefinitely without the patient's becoming aware of his collaboration in the process. It is generally true, Kretschmer pointed out, that reflexes can be reinforced by a voluntary diffuse tensing of the whole motor system. Thus the knee jerk can be am plified by clenching the hands and slightly tensing all the musculature. Sometimes a weak reflex can be brought above the threshold by this pro cedure. If one tries to reinforce a reflex directly, the result is a failure. Try ing to amplify the knee jerk by direct volition actually interferes with the

[11] Kretschmer, E., *Hysteria*, New York & Washington, Nervous and Mental Disease Monographs, No. 44, 1926.

reflex act and adds an entirely secondary voluntary kick. It is only the gentle diffuse hypertonicity of the muscles that facilitates reflexes.

One additional fact is of great importance. The indirect reinforcement of a reflex in no way changes the character of the reflex and is not in the least sensed as a voluntary act. The tremor patients, therefore, could be conceived as quite involuntarily sustaining their reflex tremor by keeping up a slight hypertonicity of the musculature. The aid they were giving to the tremor would not enter consciousness or stir up guilt feelings. If this unwitting aid were continued for a short while so as to prevent the tremor from subsiding, the symptom would become established as an independent habit system that would continue indefinitely. Kretschmer considered that his hypothesis was to some extent verified by the fact that treatment consisting of prolonged muscular relaxation often stopped the symptom, especially in its early stages. Relaxation counteracted the unwitting trick whereby the patient sustained his tremor.

Placement of the symptom. The crucial problem of hysterical symptom formation concerns the placement of the symptoms. How is the organ system chosen and how is the form of symptom determined? The possibilities are suggested in the following statements:

1. Kretschmer's hypothesis gives us one possibility. The symptom consists of some natural part of the anxiety reaction, unwittingly reinforced and sustained by the patient until it becomes permanent.

2. A somewhat similar process occurs when the symptom starts with a true organic injury. Unwitting prolongation turns what should be a temporary disability into a permanent thing. There are various reflex responses which tend to immobilize an injured part. The muscles of a wounded leg, for instance, will stiffen to prevent further motion and pain. If these immobilizing reflexes are prolonged by a mechanism akin to Kretschmer's, the wounded leg becomes an hysterically paralyzed leg.

3. The term *somatic compliance* has been coined to suggest that weak organs may be chosen as the site of hysterical symptoms. If a person has always been a little lame, or has had eye trouble or difficulties with his voice, the effect is to heighten the importance of that particular system in his mind. When neurotic breakdown occurs, that system is compliant to the need for symptom formation.

4. Temporary somatic compliance may exist when some organ is in a peculiar condition at a crucial moment of crisis. There was a good example of this in the Breuer case: [12] a paralysis of the right arm had its origin in the occasion when the patient, watching beside her father's sick bed, dozed and had a terrifying nightmare while her arm hung in an awkward position, "asleep" over the back of the chair. In neuroses of traumatic onset it some-

---

[12] Breuer, J. & Freud, S., *Studies in Hysteria*, translated by A. A. Brill, New York & Washington, Nervous & Mental Disease Publishing Co., 1936, pp. 26, 27.

times appears that the symptom falls on an organ system that was highly active at the moment of acute crisis. If an explosion catches the soldier in the act of firing his rifle, the symptoms may place themselves in the form of paralyzed hands, bent neck, closed eye, etc.

5. Direct connection between some organ system and the neurotic conflict may serve to choose the location. This is particularly true in what are called *occupational* neuroses—for example, mutism or aphonia in a salesman, paralysis of the fingers in a pianist, writer's cramp in a writer, or, to extend slightly the meaning of "occupation," sexual impotence in a Don Juan. In all such cases there are conflict and anxiety over carrying out the occupation successfully, and the symptom definitely prevents further activity.

6. The placement of a great many hysterical symptoms can be understood only by assuming—in some cases actually discovering—a roundabout associative or symbolic connection between the organ system and the conflict. Our study of phobias showed how extensive such possibilities might be. There is a connection between symptom and conflict, but one can grasp it only by untangling the chains of personal meaning that have been formed in the patient's mind in the course of experience, revery, and dream.

7. Anticipated *secondary* gain seems to play an especially important part in hysterical symptom formation. The gain is not consciously anticipated nor the symptom voluntarily devised, but the symptom shows an unmistakable relation to certain effects on the patient's environment. This is nicely illustrated in one of H. V. Dicks' cases.[13] A middle-aged married woman had to nurse her mother-in-law, who was paralyzed in both legs. Her husband forced her to do this, and seemed to become concerned only with his mother, forgetting his wife. One day the wife took a walk, feeling rebellious, but at the same time very anxious as she became dimly aware of angry wishes that the old lady would die. She felt faint and sat down on a park bench. A moment later she tried to rise, only to discover that both her legs were paralyzed and that she now needed as much of her husband's attention as did his mother.

The problem of predisposition. Looking back over obsessional neurosis and hysteria, considering the behavior of these two groups of patients in everyday life as well as their symptom pictures, it is hard to believe that we are dealing with uniform human beings who become what they are simply out of the force of circumstances. The cool affect, the predominant aggression, the complex thought process of the obsessional patient seem utterly foreign to hysterical personalities. It is a great mistake to suppose that a person can be born with such a strong obsessional tendency or hysterical make-up that neurosis follows as a matter of course. A nuclear neurotic process, a violent clash between impulse, anxiety, and defense, a develop-

[13] Dicks, H. V., *Clinical Studies in Psychopathology*, Baltimore, William Wood & Co., 1939, p. 93.

ment in the midst of great emotional or environmental difficulties must occur in the history of any neurosis. But, granting the necessity for a history of this sort, it seems likely that obsessional neurosis is the outcome in one kind of person, hysteria in another kind of person.

In hysterical patients it appears that aggression is a more or less secondary problem. Dependence, love, and sex are the critical things in the patient's life and in his neurosis. This in itself might still be due to circumstances, but it fits consistently with other characteristics generally assigned to the hysterical personality. Such patients tend to be impulsive, given to strong enthusiasms and passions, given also to vividness in behavior and a tendency to dramatize. They readily identify with others and care a good deal about personal relations. Compared to the complex obsessional, they are often described as childish and immature. Their ability to imagine themselves vividly in different roles appears in multiple personalities and in symptoms which copy another person's illness. In everyday life we constantly characterize one individual as cool and cerebral, another as warm and impulsive. We would not find it difficult to predict that the cool cerebral friend would become obsessive, and the warm impulsive one hysterical, if it should be their misfortune to be overtaken by neurotic breakdown. Thus again we find the theme of temperament weaving its way into our dynamic psychology of the neuroses. We know all too little about temperament, but until we know more about it we shall probably never explain the problem of the choice of neurosis.

FUNCTIONAL PSYCHOSES *

J. F. BROWN

The Schizophrenias

1. *The name of the disease and history of its differentiation.* The group of psychoses which we now call the schizophrenias was previously called "dementia praecox." Before the differentiation of dementia paralytica, these cases were generally classified with the dementias. Until the nineteenth century mania, melancholia, and dementia were the chief categories of descriptive psychiatry. While dementia paralytica was realized to be accompanied by neurological signs, it was noted that certain cases of dementia occurred almost exclusively in the years following puberty and were not accompanied by neurological signs. To these cases, Kraepelin gave the

* From J. F. Brown, *The Psychodynamics of Abnormal Behavior*, pp. 317–322 and 325–329, McGraw-Hill Book Company, Inc., New York, 1940. Reprinted by permission of the publisher. Slightly edited.

name "dementia praecox," which means literally a precocious falling away of the mind, and distinguished dementia praecox from the manic-depressive psychoses. Dementia, in contrast to amentia, means loss of mentality in individuals who previously were normal. The demented individual was one who was supposed quickly or gradually to lose his various powers of cognition and in whom the emotional reactions became quite inappropriate to the real situation. The powers of perception, attention, reasoning, memory, and association were all considered gradually to diminish. Dementia praecox became the most frequent of all mental disorders and the most tragic, because it was known to occur in very young people and was considered frequently to be an irreversible process, in which the dementia gradually increased.

Although the laity in general still uses the term dementia praecox and thinks of the disease as a precocious dementia, we know that this conception of the disease is inadequate. Bleuler * (1912) first pointed out that the name dementia praecox was a double misnomer. In the first place, the symptoms associated with dementia praecox are realized to occur in persons of all ages—even if the highest rate of incidence is between twenty and thirty years of age. In the second place, it is realized that the mental processes do not necessarily progressively diminish in their efficiency, but rather become split off from their proper relationship to social and physical reality. Thus the mental processes of the dementia praecox patient are by no means without rhyme or reason but rather follow a peculiar syntax and grammar of their own. C. G. Jung † (1909) was able to demonstrate this convincingly. Even the typically bizarre associations of the dementia praecox patient occur in a meaningful language, but it is a language different from that which the adult is accustomed to use. It is not controlled by the real social situation. In recent times, some psychiatrists and psychoanalysts have reached the point where they can make at least fairly good translations of the schizophrenic thought processes. Similarly, it is realized that the delusions and hallucinations and memory defects are definitely meaningful when one considers the life history. Previously it was thought that dementia praecox patients rarely recovered. Today we know that many do recover and recover to the extent that they are at least as well as before the overt manifestations of the sickness. For all these reasons Bleuler ‡ (1912) introduced the term *schizophrenia* to describe this disease. Schizophrenia means literally "a splitting of the mind" and describes the basic picture of the disease much more accurately than does dementia praecox. Today many psychiatrists speak of the schizophrenias, because, as we shall see, symptoms of

---

* Bleuler, E., *The Theory of Schizophrenic Negativism*, Nervous and Mental Disease Publishing Company, Washington, 1912.

† Jung, C. G., *The Psychology of Dementia Praecox*, translated by A. A. Brill, Nervous and Mental Diseases Publishing Company, Washington, 1909.

‡ Bleuler, *op. cit.*

schizophrenia occur in quite different constellations. All the schizophrenias have this in common, however. The central core of the personality, the ego, breaks with the reality principle so that the emotions are no longer appropriate to the real situation. The emotions are split off from the real situation. This split is shown in mild cases simply by shallowness of appropriate emotional response and mild ego regression and in severe cases by a complete lack of emotional response to the real environment and a deep ego regression.

2. *Incidence.* The schizophrenias are the most frequent of the major psychoses. In the United States 18.2 per cent of first admissions to mental hospitals are diagnosed as schizophrenia. Since the average hospitalization time in schizophrenia is sixteen years, close to 45 per cent of the resident population are schizophrenics. The incidence of the disease varies sharply with age. Starting in the early teens, the incidence is by far the highest between twenty and thirty, and falls rapidly thereafter. There are, however, first admissions reported as late as the seventies. The disease is more frequent in males than in females and in urban than in rural communities, and its victims tend to come from the lower but not the extremely low cultural and economic levels. Probably it occurs more frequently in some historical epochs than in others. The schizophrenic individual usually becomes sick early in life, is hospitalized, and, although he has some remissions and discharges, often must return periodically until he dies from some physical cause. Schizophrenia is in many respects the most serious of all the major diseases, but it is by no means the most fatal. In fact, schizophrenia itself does not kill anyone. Only 6 per cent of the schizophrenics recover in any year.

3a. *Symptomatology of the prodromal period.* The basic picture common to all the schizophrenias is the withdrawal of the person from reality with a splitting off of the appropriate affective charges from the cognitive processes. This withdrawal and splitting, although often not obvious to the layman, is the basic factor of the early symptomatology. An individual who previously has been *superficially*, at least, intellectually alert, socially active, and *seemingly* emotionally balanced begins to be irresponsible and inaccurate in his cognitive processes and to be indifferent toward social obligations and social pleasures. On closer analysis of past history, one usually finds that the individual has always shown a somewhat "schizoid" character, or, in other words, has never developed an integration of the cognitive and the emotional processes. The onset is usually very slow so that the individual, if he is in school, turns in slightly poorer work, or, if he is in business, does his work somewhat less efficiently. He gradually withdraws from social events of both an obligatory and a pleasurable sort and quite often shows emotionally inappropriate behavior. Along with this, he begins to develop peculiar mannerisms of posture, gait, gesture, and facial expression. What the individual is doing is gradually withdrawing from reality, because, for reasons which we shall discuss later, the real social situation has become unbearable to him. Usually at this time he suffers a great deal of anxiety. He is worried about what is going to happen to him. He may feel that he is going insane. He is depressed at the meaninglessness of life. In some cases this anxiety reaction becomes very severe and we then have what is known as the *schizophrenic panic*. In the panic, the individual suffers acute fear concerning everything in his life situation. In this phase, the psychotic picture is quite obvious to everyone.

3b. *Symptomatology of the acute period.* The symptomatologies of the subforms in the acute period are so different that we must deal with them separately. We know that schizophrenias represent something of an entity because of the split between the emotions and the cognitive processes common to all of them. Common to all, too, is the incoherence of associations, which become more or less desultory or bizarre. In all forms there is a surface apathy so that the feelings and emotions gradually deteriorate. There are impulsive and purposeless acts; there are schizoid mannerisms and jerky inappropriate gestures. These general symptoms are the surface signs of the splitting-off process.

There are four generally recognized subforms of schizophrenia. In the first of these, *dementia praecox simplex*, there is emotional deterioration, apathy, lack of interest. The conduct is inappropriate and neglectful. Mild delusions may occur but these are rather unsystematized. Hallucinations are rare. This is primarily an adolescent form of schizophrenia. The hospitalized cases are less frequent for this than for the other forms, but such individuals are by no means rare. Many tramps, prostitutes, and petty criminals are undoubtedly suffering from the disease. Many of them make some form of economic adjustment. Similar to these is the group for which Zilboorg has adopted the term ambulatory schizophrenia. The ambulatory schizophrenic is much like the schizoid character. . . . The transition from dementia praecox simple form to the schizoid character is gradual.

In *dementia praecox hebephrenic form*, we have a much deeper and much more rapid regression. Hallucinations are frequent. Delusions are particularly fantastic, silly, and incoherent. The associations show a poverty of ideas and are made in stilted phrases. The coinage of neologisms is frequent. The hebephrenic frequently shows purposeless mannerisms and inappropriate gestures. Of special diagnostic significance is the hollow meaningless laugh with the accompanying facial grimaces. In extreme forms, the individual regresses to childhood, talks baby talk, behaves in a babyish fashion, and may even be incontinent and unable to dress himself. Hebephrenia is a relatively rare form of schizophrenia.

The most common of the subforms of schizophrenia is *dementia praecox catatonia*. Catatonics show either severe schizophrenic excitements or severe stupors. These may alternate or either form may predominate. The excitement is characterized by increased psychomotor activity, numerous impulsive and compulsive acts, and associations showing extreme incoherence verging frequently on word hash. The catatonic stupor is characterized by mutism and catalepsy. The individual apparently is psychically completely withdrawn from reality.

Dementia praecox paranoid form shows the presence of the other symptomatologies plus paranoid delusions. It is difficult to differentiate clearly between paranoia and the paranoid form of dementia praecox. Consequently, we shall handle the symptoms of the paranoid form when we speak of paranoia.

3c. *Symptomatology of the chronic period*. In *dementia praecox simplex* the acute period goes progressively into the chronic period. The split of the cognitive and emotional processes continues and may even become sharper. Very often, however, schizophrenics make enough social recovery that they may be put to work at various menial tasks under careful supervision. They become the laborers, floor scrubbers, laundry workers, and gardeners of the hospital.

The prognosis for the acute catatonic form is the best. The acute catatonic, instead of going into a chronic period, usually makes at least one very successful recovery. If the recovery is not enough to allow the patient's parole to the outside world, the individual in the chronic period may present a clinical picture very similar to that of the simplex type. There is a continued slowness of both the cognitive and the emotional processes, but the hallucinations, delusions, and bizarre motor reactions disappear almost completely. In the hebephrenic form, the acute period to a certain extent is never overcome. The hebephrenic symptoms remain quite obvious to all observers. The individual may quiet down considerably but he remains definitely psychotic. We shall have more to say in detail about the paranoid form in connection with the disease paranoia.

3d. *Symptomatology of the recovery period*. One of the most debated problems in modern descriptive psychiatry is the problem of recovery in the schizophrenias. Until recently many psychiatrists treated reports of recovered cases of schizophrenia with considerable suspicion. Even today one frequently meets a psychiatrist who says recovered schizophrenics simply do not exist. They believe reports in the literature to be cases of incorrect diagnosis. The more modern view, on the other hand, seems to be that schizophrenics, particularly the catatonics and some of the simplex type at least, make good social recoveries. There are good reasons for believing that the schizophrenic never recovers to the extent that he is as well adjusted as, say, the manic-depressive individual in his periods of remission, but there are also reasons for believing that the schizophrenic never was well adjusted, even before the acute manifestations of his disease. Certainly social recovery is frequent, although very often the individual must return to a simpler type of activity than performed before his sickness. The recovery process is to a certain extent the reversal of the prodromal period. As the individual gradually withdrew from reality, so he gradually returns to it. This also varies in the various subforms. Acute catatonia strikes almost like lightning. The recovery process in some cases at least seems to be equally rapid. The individual suddenly says, "I don't know what was wrong with me recently, but I'm all right at the present time." In the other forms, the recovery is not only rarer but takes longer.

4. *Differential diagnosis*. Practically all the symptoms of mental disease are exhibited in one form or another in the schizophrenias. Correct diagnosis is only possible on the basis of a picture of the constellation of individual symptoms which we know as the schizoid pattern. Essential to the diagnosis of schizophrenia is the demonstration of withdrawal from reality and the splitting of affect from normal cognition. The disease most frequently confused with the schizophrenias is the manic-depressive psychosis, which in its manic phase resembles excited catatonia and in its depressive phase resembles catatonic stupor. The differentiation here is relatively easy on the basis of the association process and the nature of the delusions. The catatonic delusion is much more irrational, much further from reality than is that of the manic-depressive patient. The slowing down of associations in the depressed patient is usually a matter of retardation, while in the schizophrenic one often finds complete blockage. Schizophrenia is differentiated from the neurosyphilitic psychosis, of course, on the basis of laboratory tests. The simplex form is often confused with mental deficiency or hypophrenia. If there is a history of a previous better adjustment, this possibility is ruled out. However, there are many individuals at large who to their fellow men seem simply mentally deficient but who would be found on closer examination to be suffering from schizophrenia of the simplex form. The paranoid form can usually be differentiated on the basis of the schizoid personality picture and delusions of grandeur and persecution. . . .

The Manic-depressive Psychoses

1. *Name of disease and history of its differentiation*. Through the period of the development of descriptive psychiatry in the latter part of the nineteenth century, it was realized that there were two rather basically opposed types of psychotic reaction which showed acute manifestations and later disappeared. These were called "mania" and "melancholia," which were roughly differentiated from the various dementias, and all three together considered to constitute the severe psychoses. The manic individual was known to exhibit behavior such as that associated in the popular mind with the maniac. He was known to become excited, to expend great amounts of energy, to throw prudence overboard with regard to his own safety and that of others, and to lose his social inhibitions. The whole behavior was rather similar to that of an acutely intoxicated individual except that it continued over a considerably longer period of time. The melancholic individual was

known to present almost the inverse of this picture. Instead of being able to do a great deal more than he previously could, he was able to do much less. Instead of feeling fine, he felt "rotten." Instead of feeling powerful, he felt weak. Instead of feeling guiltless, he felt guilty. Previously, we have spoken of the differentiation of the various forms of dementia from the concept of dementia. In the case of manic-depressive psychosis, we had better think of an integration. It was one of Kraepelin's * (1921) greatest services to psychiatry to show that what was known as acute mania and acute depression were in reality two aspects of a single disease form. Just as in the alcoholic, the hangover with its postalcoholic depression follows the intoxication, so in the depressed individual, the depression follows the maniacal excitement. Today we realize, although it is not always apparent on superficial observation, that there is probably no depression that is not followed by some abnormal elation and no acute mania which is not followed by some depression. Actually psychoanalytic studies have shown us that the manic phase in itself is an attempt to cover up the anxiety and fear of subsequent depression. Furthermore, in the mixed or agitated forms we have mania and depression side by side, not merely following one another. Nearly all of us suffer some fluctuation in mood. We alternate between feeling fine and up to a great deal and feeling bad and not up to much. In the manic-depressive individual such alterations of mood are highly exaggerated, so that the individual becomes psychotic in that the mood is not at all appropriate to the real life situation. Schizophrenia is primarily a psychosis where there is a split between the affective and cognitive processes so that the patient's reactions are inappropriate, while the manic-depressive psychosis leads rather to an exaggeration of emotional response. This distinction, however, is relative rather than absolute.

2. *Incidence.* The manic-depressive psychosis is the second most frequently admitted of the psychoses. About 12 per cent of the new admissions to mental hospitals are so diagnosed. Because of the higher recovery rate, however, this disease accounts for only 12 per cent of the resident population. Of these, in a given time, about 45 per cent will show symptoms of depression and about 45 per cent those of mania, and about 10 per cent will show mixed symptoms, *i.e.*, excitement and depression at the same time. The disease occurs slightly more frequently in females than in males and is slightly more frequent in economically superior groups. It occurs with greatest frequency somewhat later in life (in the fifth decade) than does schizophrenia. This is not to be taken to mean that no young person develops a manic-depressive psychosis. Actually, the first attack very often occurs in the late teens or early twenties. Even in those cases where the first hospitalization is made in the later thirties or early forties, a case history reveals extreme fluctuations of mood usually extending far back into the

* Kraepelin, E., *Manic-depressive Insanity and Paranoia*, E. and S. Livingston, Edinburgh, 1921.

lifetime of the individual. It is claimed also that the manic-depressive psychosis is a disease which affects people more intelligent than those affected by schizophrenia. This, however, must be taken with a grain of salt, because the intelligence of schizophrenics is almost impossible to determine with the standard psychometric tests, and thus the mental inferiority of the schizophrenic found in these tests may be but a symptom.

3a. *Symptomatology of the prodromal period.* In the manic-depressive psychosis, far more than in any other which we have yet studied, there is usually a definite precipitating factor. These precipitating factors are looked on, however, by modern psychiatrists very much as modern historians look on the so-called "precipitating factors" in wars. The precipitating experience is more or less simply the catalyzing factor, which brings out the psychosis already determined in the underlying dynamics of personality. The precipitating factor in the manic-depressive psychosis is usually the loss of a loved object or an extreme frustration. The loss may be that of a friend or of money or of position. The frustration may be failure to get ahead, to gain a desired position, to arrive at some type of goal. All of us become depressed, at least to a certain extent, at the loss of either money or a loved one. All of us may react with rage, and we think, justly, when we do not get something on which we have had our hearts set. The original mania or depression may be looked on as simply an exaggeration of normal reactions to loss and frustration. When the normal individual loses a loved one, he goes into a period of mourning. The world seems a poorer place and he seems a very unfortunate individual. In depression, the loss is felt, but in addition to that there are feelings of guilt and of one's own unworthiness. When the normal individual is badly frustrated, he may fly into a rage, but he does so with certain feelings of responsibility to his objective situation. The manic individual seems to lose all feelings of personal and social responsibility. Thus in the prodromal period of either the manic or the depressive attack, we have a precipitating factor—the loss or frustration—and the development of too much emotionality concerning it or the development of inappropriate emotionality. The average individual would react to the loss of a very near relative with considerable mourning but would at least be partially cheered upon hearing that the relative had left him a sizable fortune. The depressed individual cares nothing about this. He feels the world not only poorer but himself guilty and unworthy, even of receiving the money. The average individual again reacts to frustration with rage or may even go on a "bust" or "bender." He soon tires of this, however, and returns to the real situation. The manic individual may use up both his financial and his bodily resources to the extent that his family sees that he must be hospitalized. The prodromal period, then, of the manic-depressive psychosis starts with an extreme exaggeration of the rather normal responses to loss or frustration.

3b. *Symptomatology of the acute period.* The symptomatology of the acute period in the manic-depressive psychosis depends on its form. In the elated periods, besides the elation of mood we find distractibility, flight of ideas, pressure of activity, indulgence in anti-social acts without feelings of guilt or remorse. Delusions of power and potency are also frequent. In the depressed periods, besides the deep depression we find inattention to the real environment, feelings of unpleasantness, psychomotor retardation with exaggerated feelings of fatigue. Delusions when present are hypochondriachal or concerned with guilt. In a psychotic (as opposed to a neurotic) depression, some guilt feelings are always present. Both forms show different aspects (*i.e.*, the depressed or the elated) of a basic maladjustment structure. The attention is weakened, the affectivity is inappropriate, the associations are inadequate, and the motor acts are not properly integrated. In the agitated depression or the mixed manic-depressive psychosis, the symptoms of elation and depression occur side by side.

3c. *Symptomatology of the recovery period.* In the manic-depressive psychosis one does not have to speak of a chronic period in that the individual apparently recovers completely and automatically. He undoubtedly maintains his cycloid character in the period of remission of the psychosis. He may even fluctuate between near psychotic and normal levels of elation and depression. The disease is still particularly vicious because the chances of permanent recovery are small unless an individual is treated psychotherapeutically or returned to an environment relatively free from stress.

4. *Differential diagnosis.* The depressed phase of the manic-depressive psychosis is most likely to be confused with dementia praecox catatonia of the stuperous form, with the depressed type of paresis, or with severe neurotic depressions. . . . Differentiation from severe neurotic depression is indeed not always possible, and borderline cases exist between neurotic and psychotic depression. In general, the depression is called psychotic when severe and irrational guilt feelings occur with the other symptoms, neurotic when these are absent or mild. Differentiation from paresis is of course on the basis of laboratory tests and history of syphilitic involvement. Differentiation from catatonic stupor is made on the basis of the associations (retardation rather than blocking, less severe break with reality) and on the nature of the delusions. Similarly, the manic phase may be differentiated from catatonia and hebephrenia on the basis of the associations (flight of ideas rather than word hash) and the severity of the delusions (obviously deluded but the claims are at least conceivable—the manic individual often considers himself extremely wealthy, but seldom of royal birth or divine). Laboratory tests and motor symptoms again allow differentiation from expansive paresis.

COMMON SYNDROMES IN CHILD PSYCHIATRY *

⟨ R. L. Jenkins and Sylvia Glickman

The problem of diagnostic classification is a difficult one at best. Any dis-criminating thinking about disorders, their genesis or their treatment, is necessarily dependent upon the recognition of more or less clear and definite types or groupings of disorders. On the other hand, too rigid a scheme of classification tends to embalm our faulty concepts for posterity. The problem of classification is particularly difficult in child psychiatry where many problems are fluid and changeable and represent maladjust-ments rather than disorders.

Classical psychiatry suffered from too rigid a classification of disorders, of which the disease entity concepts of Kraepelin are an outstanding example. While a useful classification was evolved, it was unduly rigid, and the authority of the master was such as to perpetuate his errors beyond their reasonable span of life. The most recent offspring of psychiatry—child psychiatry—has, perhaps as a reaction, been very slow to crystallize any systematic grouping of type of problems met in children. Classification of children's problems in the statistical manual for the use of hospitals for mental disease represents an effort at logical groupings but in no sense do the entries represent or even approach clinical entities.

Jenkins and Hewitt (1), on the basis of an analysis of 500 cases examined at the Michigan Child Guidance Institute, described and sought to give a dynamic account of three more or less idealized types. While few cases fit perfectly, many verge toward them in varying degrees.

Type I. The overinhibited child, characterized by seclusiveness, shyness, apathy, worrying, sensitiveness, and submissiveness. He is given to day dreaming, feels inferior, lacks close friendships, cries easily, is overdepend-ent, easily depressed, and is discouraged with himself. He has frequent physical complaints and is prone to neurotic illness.

Type II. The unsocialized aggressive child is characterized by assaultive tendencies, initiating fights, cruelty, defiance of authority, malicious mis-chief, and inadequate guilt feelings. He is selfish, jealous, vengeful, deceit-ful, and prone to place upon others the responsibility for his own mis-conduct. He is suspicious of others, profane and obscene in language, and precociously interested in sex.

Type III. The socialized delinquent or pseudosocial child, is character-

* From R. L. Jenkins and S. Glickman, "Common Syndromes in Child Psychiatry: I. Deviant Behavior Traits," Amer. J. Orthopsychiat., 1946, 16, 244–254. Reprinted by permission of Dr. Jenkins and the Editor, American Journal of Orthopsychiatry.

ized by stealing in the company of others, furtive stealing, habitual truancy from school, staying out late at night, desertion of home, bad companions, and gang activities.

In a child guidance clinic group of children with many traits in common, the frequent occurrence of behavior syndromes will be reflected in a statistical analysis by a cluster of traits showing some degree of concomitance.

TABLE 1. MATRIX OF INTERCORRELATIONS JUVENILE PARETIC SYNDROME *

Trait	2	3	15	31	33	37	58	74	D
2		68	53	30	33	56	28	45	52
3	68		14	19	27	25	45	11	26
15	53	14		14	51	13	05	37	35
31	30	19	14		40	55	68	11	31
33	33	27	51	40		44	22	38	18
37	56	25	13	55	44		46	31	54
58	28	45	05	68	22	46		35	35
74	45	11	37	11	38	31	35		43
D	52	26	35	31	18	54	35	43	
Mean—46	29	28	34	34	41	36	31	37

Symbol Definition

2—Pupils fixed to light
3—Pupils irregular, unequal, or sluggish
15—Spinal Wassermann or Kahn test positive
31—Irritability
33—Nervousness
37—Emotional instability
58—Temper tantrums
74—Exclusion, expulsion, or suspension from school
D—Deterioration

* Figures to two decimals, decimal points omitted for correlations in all tables.

Luton Ackerson's book (2) contains intercorrelations of over 100 behavior traits. This volume furnishes a very useful source for verifying and extending this description of the common syndromes among children. The material was based on 5,000 consecutive cases referred to the Institute for Juvenile Research and is extensive enough to include the common problems met in the child guidance clinics. Since a syndrome is by definition, a group of symptoms commonly met in association with each other, examination of the intercorrelations [1] of these traits should reveal the principal

[1] For readers unfamiliar with the statistical method, the measure of the association of two traits may be expressed in a correlation coefficient which can range in value from +1 to −1. Plus 1 represents perfect association; zero represents no association, or that degree of association accounted for by chance factors; minus 1 represents perfect inverse association.

syndromes present. Dr. Ackerson has provided the material for this examination.

The authors have systematically examined the material published by Ackerson to discover all the clusters of positively correlated traits. Such a cluster constitutes a matrix, as exemplified in Table 1. He makes some use of grouping traits. In this survey only individually listed traits were used.

Criteria for the inclusion of a trait in the matrix were:

1. This trait must correlate positively with all of the other traits in the matrix. Any negative correlation was the occasion for exclusion.

2. It is necessary that the mean correlation of this trait with the other traits in the matrix meet a certain arbitrarily selected limit. This limit may be set higher in the better marked syndromes and lower in the less well marked ones. In no instance has it been set at less than .20.

3. In selecting traits for a matrix, when a choice must be made between two or more traits, that trait is selected which has the highest mean correlation with the other traits in the matrix.

4. In those instances in which a trait is present in more than one matrix, it is, of course, not distinctive of any matrix. The procedure was established that for inclusion of a trait in a matrix the mean correlation of the trait with those traits distinctive for this matrix must meet the arbitrarily established value already referred to in 2. This practice reduces the tendency of the matrices to "flow together" and preserves a larger number of syndromes.

5. At least four intercorrelated traits are required to constitute a cluster.

As a preliminary test of the workability of this method of defining syndromes, it was applied to a statistical analysis of 154 children who were examined in a child guidance clinic and who proved to have syphilis. The intercorrelations of twenty-eight symptoms or traits have been published elsewhere (3). Among these twenty-eight items we find two matrices which meet our criterion. The symptoms and traits in the first matrix in order of the magnitude of their mean intercorrelation are: (1) pupils fixed to light; (2) emotional stability; (3) deterioration; (4) temper tantrums; (5) nervousness; (6) irritability; (7) exclusion, expulsion, or suspension from school; (8) pupils irregular, unequal, or sluggish; (9) positive Wassermann or Kahn reaction of the spinal fluid. The mean correlation of the diagnosis of paresis with the traits in this cluster is .57, which is materially higher than any of the mean intercorrelations (range .46 to .28). Thus we see an example of the location and the crude definition of the syndrome, proceeding merely from the examination of a table of intercorrelations.

Even if we discard all items from the physical and laboratory examinations, we find a recognizable syndrome of behavior traits remaining with the order: (1) emotional instability; (2) temper tantrums; (3) irritable temperament; (4) deterioration; (5) nervousness; (6) exclusion, expulsion, or suspension from school, with mean intercorrelations ranging from .46 to .32. Again the diagnosis of paresis has a mean correlation with these items which is higher than any of the mean intercorrelations, in this case being

50. It is therefore demonstrably possible to locate and crudely describe the behavior which is characteristic of the juvenile paretic syndrome from the intercorrelation of behavior traits alone.

The second matrix is summarized in Table 2 and consists of the following traits and background factors: (1) truancy from school; (2) lying; (3) sexual unconventionality of parents; (4) sex delinquency (of child);

TABLE 2. DELINQUENCY—FAMILY DISORGANIZATION MATRIX

Trait	Mean intercorrelations
Lying	53
Truancy from school	51
Sex delinquency	47
Sex unconventionality of parents	42
Stealing	42
Staying out late at night	37
Bad home conditions	34
Broken home	31

(5) stealing; (6) staying out late at night; (7) bad home conditions; (8) broken home (separation, divorce, one or both parents dead). This cluster represents the delinquent child from the disorganized home. Here both the syphilis and the delinquency may be regarded to some extent as the products of a disorganized family life or perhaps of parental instability and immaturity common in disorganized homes.

Since Ackerson separated boys and girls in his statistical treatment, the two groups form a convenient check, one on the other. The boy's group includes 2,113 white boys from six to seventeen years inclusive, I.Q. 50 or above, who were or had been in the public school. The corresponding group of white girls numbers 1,118.

The Overinhibited Child

The first matrix (Table 3) represents the syndrome of the overinhibited child to whom reference has already been made. The traits found in the matrix for boys, in the order of their average intercorrelation are: (1) sensitiveness about a specific fact or episode; (2) staff notation of inferiority feelings; (3) depressed or discouraged attitude or spells of depression or discouragement; (4) unhappy or discontented attitude, appearance, or manner; (5) worry about a specific fact or episode; (6) staff notation of mental conflict; (7) staff notation of psychoneurotic trends; (8) sensitiveness; (9) seclusiveness; (10) daydreaming. Here we have the picture of the overinhibited personality with emotional conflict, psychoneurotic tendencies, and inferiority feelings. The matrix for girls is almost equally character-

TABLE 3. THE OVERINHIBITED CHILD

Trait	Mean intercorrelations	Percentage of cases
Boys		
Sensitiveness over specific fact	36	13
Inferiority feelings	34	8
Depressed or discouraged attitude	32	6
Worry over specific fact	32	4
Mental conflict	32	4
Unhappy manner	29	4
Psychoneurotic trends	28	3
Sensitiveness	27	6
Seclusiveness	27	11
Daydreaming	24	6
Limit set at	24	
Girls		
Inferiority feelings	41	4
Depressed or discouraged attitude	39	5
Sensitiveness	37	7
Sensitiveness over specific fact	35	10
Daydreaming	32	5
Crying spells	32	24
Seclusiveness	31	9
Limit set at	28	

istic: (1) staff notation of inferiority feelings; (2) depressed or discouraged attitude or spells of depression or discouragement; (3) sensitiveness; (4) sensitiveness about a specific fact or episode; (5) daydreaming; (6) crying spells; (7) seclusiveness.

The Unsocialized Aggressive Child

The second matrix (Table 4) corresponds with the unsocialized, aggressive personality as described by Jenkins and Hewitt. Traits in the matrix for boys are: (1) disturbing influence in school; (2) violence; (3) fighting; (4) quarrelsomeness; (5) destructiveness; (6) incorrigibility; (7) boastfulness; (8) teasing other children; (9) exclusion, expulsion, or suspension from school; (10) unpopularity. For girls the matrix is somewhat larger: (1) violence; (2) fighting; (3) incorrigibility; (4) temper tantrums; (5) defiant attitude; (6) disobedience; (7) disturbing influence in school; (8) rudeness; (9) quarrelsomeness; (10) exclusion, expulsion, or suspension from school; (11) lying; (12) unpopularity; (13) leading others into bad conduct; (14) destructiveness; (15) "queerness" (patient considered by others as mentally peculiar, very erratic, crazy).

Another matrix was adequately formed by our criteria for the girls, but for the boys was not differentiated from the unsocialized aggressive

TABLE 4. THE UNSOCIALIZED AGGRESSIVE CHILD

Trait	Mean intercorrelations	Percentage of cases
Boys		
Disturbing influence in school	41	13
Violence	37	8
Fighting	35	8
Quarrelsomeness	34	8
Destructiveness	33	7
Incorrigibility	32	9
Boastfulness	32	10
Teasing other children *	32	8
Exclusion from school	31	9
Unpopularity	31	4
Limit set at	30	
Girls		
Violence	47	4
Fighting	43	4
Incorrigibility	41	6
Temper tantrums	41	8
Defiant attitude	41	7
Disobedience	40	11
Disturbing influence in school	40	6
Rudeness	39	12
Quarrelsomeness	39	8
Exclusion from school	38	4
Lying	38	18
Unpopularity	37	3
Leading others into bad conduct	36	3
Destructiveness	36	4
"Queerness"	35	5
Limit set at	34	
Variant Group—Girls		
Boastfulness	42	5
Violence	41	4
Bossiness	39	6
Temper tantrums	38	8
Unpopularity	37	3
Egocentricity	36	10
Selfishness	34	5
Changeable moods	33	10
"Spoiled child"	32	9
Limit set at	32	

* Not available in correlation with girls' group.

TABLE 5. THE SOCIALIZED DELINQUENT

Trait	Mean intercorrelations	Percentage of cases
Boys		
Stealing	53	26
Truancy from home	51	16
Truancy from school	48	21
Police arrest	48	17
Staying out late at night	44	12
Associating with bad companions	42	6
"Running with a gang" *	39	5
Smoking	38	7
Loitering	37	7
Lying	36	20
Incorrigibility	36	9
Leading others into bad conduct	35	5
Limit set at	35	
Girls		
Staying out late nights	47	9
Truancy from home	44	10
Truancy from school	43	7
Police arrest	41	11
Lying	40	18
Sex delinquency	39	11
Stealing	39	13
Overinterest in opposite sex **	37	7
Incorrigibility	36	6
Associating with bad companions	35	4
Loitering	33	4
Limit set at	32	

* Not available for correlations with girls' group.
** Not available for correlations with boys' group.

syndrome to which reference has been made. This matrix includes: (1
boastfulness; (2) violence; (3) bossiness; (4) temper tantrums; (5) u
popularity; (6) egocentricity; (7) selfishness; (8) changeable moods; (9
"spoiled child." This would almost seem to be a variant of the unsocialize
aggressive personality with (as is frequent in the female sex) a greater en
phasis upon verbal aggressiveness and egocentricity than upon the aggre
siveness of assault. It should be noted that the "spoiled child" ent
represents not a staff notation but a lay description of behavior which h
a tendency to regard any egocentric, inconsiderate child as spoiled.
seems safe to assert that the major element behind this cluster of traits
doubtless not spoiling but rejection.

The Socialized Delinquent

The third matrix (Table 5) is, for the boys, essentially the traditional cture of the gang boy; the boy who is socialized within a delinquent oup: (1) stealing; (2) truancy from home; (3) truancy from school; t) police arrest; (5) staying out late at night; (6) associating with bad mpanions; (7) "running with a gang"; (8) smoking; (9) loitering; (10) corrigibility; (11) leading others into bad conduct; (12) lying. The atrix for girls includes: (1) staying out late at night; (2) truancy from ome; (3) truancy from school; (4) police arrest; (5) lying; (6) sex elinquency (coitus); (7) stealing; (8) overinterest in the opposite sex;)) incorrigibility; (10) bad companions; (11) loitering. A difference be-veen boys and girls is the lesser prominence of stealing and the greater ominence of sex in the matrix of girls. This is in keeping with the typical fferences in what are regarded as problems of delinquency in boys and rls. There is the further fact that there were so few entries of "running th a gang" for girls that correlations were not computed for this trait, hile similarly the notation, "overinterest in opposite sex," was so infre-1ent with boys that correlation coefficients were not calculated for this iit. This last reflects the acceptance of a boy's interest in girls as natural, iile a girl's interest in boys is a cause of parental and community concern.

The Brain-injured Child

The next matrix (Table 6) represents the behavior syndrome of en-phalitis or organic brain damage as we see it in children. The matrix r boys includes: (1) question of change of personality, mental status, or havior dating from a specific time or episode; (2) question or diagnosis encephalitis; (3) irritability; (4) changeable moods; (5) "queerness";) emotional instability; (7) contrariness; (8) nervousness; (9) irregular ep habits or insomnia. The corresponding matrix for girls includes: (1) stlessness; (2) question or diagnosis of encephalitis; (3) distractibility;) nervousness; (5) violence; (6) question of change of personality, ental status, or behavior dating from specific time or episode; (7) temper ntrums; (8) restlessness in sleep; (9) disturbing influence in school; 0) changeable moods.

The Schizoid Child

The last matrix (Table 7) begins for boys with: (1) absent minded-ss; (2) "queerness" (patient considered by others as mentally peculiar, ry erratic, or "crazy"); and includes: (3) seclusiveness; (4) listlessness;) inefficiency or carelessness in work, studies, play, forgetting errands, c.; (6) daydreaming; (7) lack of initiative or ambition. This has a mate-

TABLE 6. THE BRAIN-INJURED CHILD

Trait	Mean intercorrelations	Percentage of cases
Boys		
Question of change of personality	38	5
Question of encephalitis	33	1
Irritability	31	19
Changeable moods	29	10
"Queerness"	28	5
Emotional instability	25	10
Contrariness	24	4
Nervousness	24	12
Irregular sleep habits or insomnia	22	6
Limit set at	22	
Girls		
Restlessness	41	16
Question of encephalitis	41	1
Distractibility	40	9
Nervousness	39	12
Violence	38	4
Question of change of personality	38	5
Temper tantrums	38	8
Restlessness in sleep	35	12
Disturbing influence in school	35	6
Changeable moods	33	10
Limit set at	33	

rially different character from the first matrix presented, although certa
traits are common to both. This matrix has clearly a schizoid flavor.
should be noted that the average intercorrelations are not as high in th
matrix as in most of the others, indicating that this syndrome is not as we
marked as some of the others. The corresponding matrix for girls include
(1) "queerness"; (2) changeable moods; (3) depressed or discouraged at
tude or spells of depression or discouragement; (4) question of change
personality, mental status, or behavior dating from a specific time
episode; (5) daydreaming; (6) inefficiency or carelessness in work, stud
play, forgetting errands; (7) emotional instability. The inclusion of chan
of personality suggests that some in this group may be early schizophreni

Certain possibilities and limitations of this method of approach are wort
of discussion. For this method of analysis to be applicable it is necessa
to have several traits within a syndrome; for example, if less than four,
matrix meeting our criteria could not result. In this, as in other methoc
the available materials limit the construction.

The degree of selection of the population is one factor influencing t
effectiveness of the method. It will operate best with sharply contrasti

TABLE 7. THE SCHIZOID CHILD

Trait	Mean intercorrelations	Percentage of cases
Boys		
Absentmindedness	33	5
"Queerness"	30	5
Seclusiveness	29	11
Listlessness	29	7
Inefficient in work or play	29	4
Daydreaming	27	6
Lack of initiative	23	6
Limit set at	20	
Girls		
"Queerness"	40	5
Changeable moods	38	10
Depressed or discouraged attitude	38	5
Question of change of personality	36	5
Daydreaming	35	5
Inefficient in work or play	34	5
Emotional instability	34	10
Limit set at	31	

types. Probably the types defined here are more sharply outlined than they would be in a study of the general population. This again probably explains why the correlations tend to be higher with the girls, who appear to be a more highly selected group than the boys.

There is doubtless a considerable factor of random error in many of the tetrachoric correlation coefficients used in this study, and it is therefore to be expected that chance factors may somewhat alter the outline of a syndrome. It seems inconceivable that they could either create a syndrome which did not in fact exist or obliterate one which was reasonably well marked.

Summary

Examination of the material published by Dr. Ackerson from the statistical analysis of 5,000 consecutive cases of children examined at the Institute for Juvenile Research reveals five syndromes or types of deviant behavior.

1. The overinhibited child, prone to neurotic illness. This corresponds with the overinhibited child described by Jenkins and Hewitt (1).

2. The unsocialized aggressive child, corresponding with the unsocialized aggressive child described by Jenkins and Hewitt. Among the girls in Ackerson's material it is possible to differentiate another group with more

verbal aggression and general egocentricity. This is viewed as a feminin variant of the unsocialized aggressive child.

3. The socialized delinquent or child socialized within a delinquen group. This corresponds with the traditional description of the gang bo and with the socialized delinquent or pseudosocial child as described b Jenkins and Hewitt.

4. The encephalitic or brain-damaged child, corresponding with previou descriptions by Jenkins and Ackerson (4).

5. The schizoid child.

The discriminating use of these broad categories should contribute t clarification of thinking in child psychiatry.

References

1. Jenkins, R. L., M.D., and Lester Hewitt. *Types of Personality Structure Encountere in Child Guidance Clinics*. Am. J. Orthopsychiatry, *14*, 1, 1944. The description c types I, II, and III is from this source.
2. Ackerson, Luton. *Children's Behavior Problems*, Vol. II. Behavior Research Fun Monograph, University of Chicago Press, 1942.
3. Jenkins, R. L., M.D., and Myrtle Grudim, M.D., *Behavior Problems in Childre with Syphilis*. Am. J. Orthopsychiatry, *11*, 4, 1941.
4. Jenkins, R. L., M.D., and Luton Ackerson. *The Behavior of Encephalitic Childre* Am. J. Orthopsychiatry, *4*, 4, 1934.

Adjustment and Development

ne approach to the study of adjustment seeks to examine the
otives, problems, and experiences which are typical within the
rious developmental stages of life. Adjustive behavior, conse-
ently, has been studied in infancy, childhood, prepuberty, ado-
scence, maturity, and old age. The interest in each age group
ems from the desire to obtain comparative information about the
oups as well as to determine how the characteristics of one age
vel influence those of another. Each age group has certain dis-
nguishing characteristics. The conflicts and frustrations which the
fant encounters are vastly different from those of the adolescent.
he behavioral repertory at successive ages varies and results in
me modes of adjustment occurring more frequently at one level
an another. Temper tantrums in childhood give way to explora-
on in the adolescent and independent problem solving in the
lult. Another source of variation among the age groups rests in
e differential expectations which the environment imposes on
e individual during different age spans. For example, our culture
courages dependence and obedience in children, while the adult
expected to display self-direction and independence.

Many psychologists have attributed paramount importance to
rly childhood experiences because they are viewed as providing
e foundation for the nature of subsequent adjustment. The first
per describes four training situations in early childhood which
e thought to produce long-lasting effects on the personality char-
teristics of the individual. Dollard and Miller discuss some of
e typical problems and reactions of the child concerning feeding,
eanliness, sex, and hostility. They also specify some of the habits
hich are acquired in the context of experiences with each of these.
ne example of this would be the child who is repeatedly punished
by a parent. He may learn to perceive all authority figures with
e fear and anger he felt toward his parent.

The next selection pertains to the psychological characteristics
f the adolescent. Finesinger reviews some of the significant

changes that occur during this period of life, illustrating the needs, frustrations, and conflicts the adolescent experiences. Undoubtedly this period is fraught with potential trauma in our culture, but as many cultural anthropologists have noted, the transition between childhood and adulthood is not of necessity turbulent. A major source of the adolescent's distress arises from the inconsistent expectations which our culture imposes upon him. The manner in which the adolescent responds to these inconsistent expectations is determined to a large extent by the nature of his childhood experiences.

Surprisingly enough, relatively little can be found in the psychological literature which systematically outlines the typical adjustment problems and reactions of the adult as they compare with other stages of life. While there is a wealth of literature which reports clinical descriptions of adult maladjustments, well-ordered surveys are lacking. Perhaps the reason for this is that most of the problems of the adult are so common that they lose their distinctiveness. The choice of vocation, the establishment of a family, the problems of adopting the role of a parent and of maintaining effective social relationships are some of the many crucial issues which confront the adult.

The final selection is a discussion by Havighurst about the social and psychological needs of the aging. The field of geriatrics to which this paper pertains is becoming increasingly important as more people live to an older age as a function of medical advances. Special difficulties exist for this age group, not only because of the physiological changes which occur, but also because of the tendency of our society to reject the aging. After providing an account of the way in which old age "insults" the person through loss of physical attractiveness or loss of support and status, Havighurst discusses the special needs of older people or the special adjustments which they are required by reason of age to effect.

CRITICAL TRAINING SITUATIONS
IN CHILDHOOD *

JOHN DOLLARD AND NEAL E. MILLER

The culture, of course, takes a position—a traditional position—on the various needs of the child. It has a design for the feeding situation, for cleanliness training, for sex training, for the treatment of anger responses of the child; and as the society imposes its will through the acts of the parents, the child reacts in its blind emotional way. Each one of the above-mentioned training situations can produce long-lasting effects on the character and habits of the individual and each is worth a brief discussion. We are by no means sure that these four are all of the dilemmas which can produce acute emotional conflicts, but we do know that each one of them has, in known cases, done so.

The Feeding Situation: Conflicts and Attitudes

Much important learning takes place in reference to the hunger drive and the strong responses it excites. During the nursing period the child cannot "comfort" itself. It cannot, so to say, tell itself "It won't be long now," or "Only twenty minutes 'til feeding time." The hunger of the child is an urgent, incessant, and timeless pressure which, obviously, produces the most intense activation. If the child is fed when hungry, it can learn that the one simple thing it can do to get results (*i.e.*, cry) can make a difference in what happens. Learning to cry as a signal for food is one small unit in its control of the world. Such a trait could be the basis of a later tendency to be "up and doing" when in trouble, of a belief that there is always a way out of a painful situation.

Apathy and apprehensiveness. If the child is not fed when it is crying, but is instead left to "cry itself out," it can, similarly, learn that there is nothing it can do at that time to change the painful circumstances. Such training may also lay the basis for the habit of apathy and not "trying something else" when in trouble. In a second case, when drive is allowed to mount, the child can also learn that being a little bit hungry is followed by being very painfully hungry. When the child is then fed, only its most

* From John Dollard and Neal E. Miller, *Personality and Psychotherapy*, pp. 132–54, McGraw-Hill Book Company, Inc., New York, 1950. Reprinted by permission of the authors and the publisher.

violent responses are reinforced. In this case the child can learn to fea
being very hungry when it is only slightly hungry and to make th
frightened response appropriate to severe hunger when only mild hunge
exists. It is thus learning to "overreact," to be apprehensive of evil eve
when the circumstances of life seem calm. This learning occurs throug
the behavior mechanism of anticipation.

Sociability and "love." On the other hand, probably the feeding exper
ence can be the occasion for the child to learn to like to be with other
that is, it can establish the basis of sociability. When the hungry infar
is fed, some of the wonderful relaxation responses which it experiences ca
be conditioned to the stimuli of those persons who are caring for the chil
Thereafter the mere appearance of the mother can produce a momentar
feeling of well-being. The child will learn to stop crying at the sound c
her footstep, the rustle of her dress, or the sound of the tap water whic
is warming its bottle. These experiences have an intense emotional qualit
which is often attached thereafter to the word "mother" as the source c
all beneficence.

Likewise, if the child is properly held, cared for, and played with, th
blessed relaxing quality of these experiences also will attach to those wh
care for it. Since the mother or caretaker stands at the very head of th
parade of persons who become "society" for the child, it is quite importan
that she evoke such benign and positive responses in the child.

Lack of social feeling. The reverse of all this can also take place if th
child is stuffed when it is not hungry. If its food rewards are in various way
cut down and spoiled, it may not care much whether "the others" are ther
or not. It may tend to be "low in social feeling." If the child is actuall
punished for crying when it is hungry, as by being slapped, a true hunge
anxiety conflict will be created. Though this may be rare, it does un
doubtedly happen, especially when the child is overactive as a result o
gastric upset and so is able to provoke anger in the ill-disciplined parent.

One origin of fear of being alone. The child can learn another dangerou
habit in this period. It can learn to fear being alone. Teaching a child t
fear being alone is easy to do and is often done inadvertently. Let th
child get very hungry when it is alone, let it cry and not be heard o
attended to, but let the quantity of stimulation in its body from hunge
and from crying continue to rise. When the child is finally fed, these ver
strong terminal responses are reinforced and can be attached to all th
stimuli which were present during the period of its intense hunger. Thes
responses can produce stimuli of drivelike strength. Similarly response
which produce strong drives can be attached to the darkness, to the im
mobility of objects, to quietness, to absence of parental stimuli. Once th
child has inadvertently learned to "fear" darkness and quietness and im
mobility, it will also learn to escape from the darkness into the light, from
the quietness into noise, and from immobility into the presence of others

This escape may be perceived by the parents as an additional nuisance when they are expecting their hours of relaxation; the child insists on being with them even though "there is nothing wrong with it." They may then take punitive measures, forcing the child back into the dark or the quiet and creating a true conflict between fear of darkness and the newly learned fear of the irate parent. This must indeed be a very common conflict, since fear of quietness and darkness are not innate in children and yet are frequently seen.

If this fear persists into adult life, it can be an element in the character of a person who is compulsively driven to social contacts, who cannot tolerate being alone. Compulsive sociability may also involve a sacrifice in creativeness, since in order to be creative the individual must be able to tolerate a certain amount of loneliness.

Weaning. In the case of weaning also, severe traumatic circumstances may arise. If the child is suddenly changed from one type of food or mode of feeding to another, it may go on a hunger strike which the parents obstinately oppose, saying "It will eat when it gets hungry enough." Indeed it will, but in the meantime it may have learned some of the fears or the apathy already listed. If parents punish the child for its refusal to eat the new food a genuine conflict is created which in turn will have its consequences. There seems hardly anything valuable that an infant can learn by punishment under such circumstances, and parents should take the greatest pains to avoid this.

Colic and recurring hunger. The child with colic is also a sore trial to itself and its parents. One of the simplest circumstances producing "colic" is that the infant has eaten too much and must regurgitate some of the food or the gases which its digestion produces. Once it has been laboriously walked or patted into parting with food or gas it may be hungry again. Unimaginative parents, not understanding that hunger has innocently recurred, will fail to feed the child. If the mother does feed it, the child may overeat again and the cycle of gastric tension, vomiting, and hunger may recur. However, until an infant learns to make its gastric distress anticipatory and thus to check itself while eating, there is no way of avoiding these circumstances. The sequence overeating, gastric distress, vomiting, and recurring hunger seems more likely to occur with children fed on schedule since they will get much hungrier while waiting for the scheduled moment of feeding and are more likely to overeat.

If parents lose their tempers and punish the young child at any phase of this awkward kind of learning to eat just the right amount, severe conflict concerning feeding may ensue. If the infant is punished before it is burped, the result may be that it has anxiety attached to burping and regurgitating, and it is thus condemned to bear gastric tension. If it is punished after regurgitating when it is again hungry, anxiety responses will be attached to hunger stimuli. Under these conditions punishment cannot teach the infant anything that will help it along its road of development. Nevertheless this unavoidable circumstance of colic is one to test the character of the most devoted parents.

The foregoing discussion is by no means a check list of all the things that a child can learn during the first year or so of life. For example, in learning to crawl and walk the child is also learning to fear bumps. It learns not to poke its head under the table and then suddenly try to stand erect. It is learning a few words and common commands. Those interested in the somatic development of the child can consult Gesell (1940). Various specialists in pediatrics such as Spock (1946) have described the behavior problems that are most frequent among young children in the home.

Secret learning of early years. What we have attempted to do here is to show that the seemingly innocuous feeding situation can be fraught with important emotional consequences. Outsiders who cannot know what is going on in a home may see no reason to suppose that the infant is learning anything at all. Yet observant insiders may see the child becoming apathetic, apprehensive, learning to fear the dark, on the one hand, or becoming loving, sociable, and confident, on the other. It is this secret learning of the early years which must be made the object of scientific research. We are firmly of the opinion that anything that can be sensed can be scaled and thus that apathy, sociability, and fear can be scientifically treated if we but trouble to study the child in the home—where these habits are being learned.

Early conflicts unlabeled, therefore unconscious. The young child does not notice or label the experiences which it is having at this time. It cannot give a description of character traits acquired during the first year of life nor yet of its hardships, fears, or deep satisfactions. What was not verbalized at the time cannot well be reported later. An important piece of history is lost and cannot be elicited by questionnaire or interview. Nevertheless, the behavioral record survives. The responses learned occur and may indeed recur in analogous situations throughout life. They are elicited by unlabeled cues and are mutely interwoven into the fabric of conscious life. The fact that different children learn different things during this period undoubtedly accounts for some of the variability between children which is often attributed to innate factors.

2. Cleanliness Training Can Create Conflicts

If the child has come safely and trustfully through the early feeding and weaning experience it may learn for the first time in its cleanliness training that the culture patterns lying in wait for it have an ugly, compulsive aspect. No child may avoid this training. The demands of the training system are absolute and do not take account of individual differences in learning ability. The child must master cleanliness training or forfeit its place in the ranks of socially acceptable persons. Freud describes the culture's task as building within the personality of the child the psychic dams of loathing and disgust (Freud, 1930, p. 40) for urine and feces and particularly for the latter. The attempt to construct these inward barriers immediately puts the child in a conflict situation.

Observation of children within the home indicates that children begin with the same naïve interest in their feces and urine that they have in the other parts and products of their bodies. Development of the ability to grasp and finger objects makes it possible for the young child to handle and play with fecal material. The morning will arrive in every nursery when the astonished parents will observe their beloved child smearing feces over his person, his hair, and his immediate environment with gurgling abandon. This may be the first occasion for sharp, punishing exhortations, for angry rousing, for the awakening of anxiety in connection with fecal materials. On pain of losing the parents' love and so exposing itself to the high drives and tensions which occur when they do not support it, and on further pain of immediate punishment, the child must learn to attach anxiety to all the cues produced by excretory materials—to their sight, smell, and touch. It must learn to deposit the feces and urine only in a prescribed and secret place and to clean its body. It must later learn to suppress unnecessary verbal reference to these matters, so that, except for joking references this subject matter is closed out and excluded from social reference for life.

Difficulty of cleanliness learning. Cleanliness training is difficult because culture must work a reversal of a strong innate connection between a cue and a response. The swelling bladder or bowel produces a strong drive stimulus which at a certain strength releases the urethral sphincter or touches off the evulsion response in the anus. To meet cultural demands this sequence must be rearranged. The connection between bowel stimulus and the evulsion response must be weakened. The child must learn to suppress the evulsion response to the bowel drive-stimulus alone. It must then insert other responses in the sequence. At first it must learn to call to the parents. It must later learn to insert walking, unbuttoning, and sitting on the toilet chair while it is still suppressing the urgent evulsion response. Only to a new pattern of cues—the bowel stimulus, the cues of the proper room, the sense of freedom of clothes, the pressure of the toilet seat on the child's thighs—may the evulsion response occur without anxiety.

In short, this response occurs not only to the pressure of the primary drive involved but also to the complex stimulus pattern just named. If one can once get the child to order the responses correctly, the strong tension reduction produced by defecation will reinforce the responses to the pattern of cues enumerated. The real problem, therefore, is getting the child to suppress the naïve evulsion response and to insert a considerable series of responses into the sequence before evulsion.

We do not revel in the details of this analysis but offer the detaile analysis because we believe it is impossible to understand the difficulty (the learning involved unless one sees all the new units which must b learned. For instance, buttoning and unbuttoning is a difficult habit f(small children to learn and may hold up the perfect learning of the sequenc for some time. The child, however, is not really trained until it can carr out the whole sequence by itself.

Learning without verbal aids. The difficulties which produce conflict i this learning arise chiefly from the fact that the child must accomplish in a period of life when it has to learn mainly without verbal aids, that i by trial and error. Learning cleanliness control by trial and error is a slo and vexing business. The child must learn to wake up in order to go to th toilet, though sleep seems good. It must learn to stop its play even whe social excitement is strong. It must learn to discriminate between th different rooms of the house—all this by crude trial and error. In this cas("trial" means urinating or defecating in an inappropriate place, and "erroɪ means being punished for the act so that anxiety responses are attache(to the cues of this place. In the trial-and-error situation this must b repeated for each inappropriate place—bed, living room, dining roon kitchen, "outside."

The function of this training is to attach anxiety responses to the def(cation drive so that they win out over the immediate evulsion responsɛ These anxiety responses also motivate and cue off the next responses i the series, such as calling to the parents, running to the bathroom, uɪ buttoning the clothes, and the like. When accomplished by trial-and-errɔ means, this training necessarily takes considerable time, perhaps severɛ years in all, in which child and parent are under severe pressure.

Strong emotions aroused in cleanliness training. Learning cleanliness no mere behavioral routine. It arouses strong emotions—perhaps as stron as are ever evoked in the child again. Anger, defiance, stubbornness, an fear all appear in the course of such training. Fear may generalize to th toilet itself and excite avoidance responses in the very place where th child is expected to "go." Unable to discriminate between the safe and th unsafe place, the child may try "not to defecate at all." This behavior i perfectly automatic, but it may seem willful to the parents, and they ma particularly resent the final loss of control after the protracted attempt t inhibit defecation. Once hit on, this response would be strongly reinforce and tend to become habitual since the drive reduction after prolonge withholding would be much more intense than after a normal period o withholding. When "losing control," instead of deliberately relaxing, i strongly rewarded, the habit of "losing control" should become anticipɛ tory and thus prolong the problem of cleanliness training. In other word: great strictness at early ages may block rather than advance the child i his cleanliness learning.

Learning to escape from sight of parents. The child may become, from the parents' standpoint, furtive by the following means: When it is punished for a cleanliness error by the parent, anxiety is attached to the sights and sounds produced by that parent. In order to escape that anxiety the child may attempt to escape from the parental presence and attempt to keep to a minimum the amount of time it spends near the parent. This state of affairs has the disadvantage that the child is escaping from one of its natural teachers. It may learn to speak less well than it might because it simply does not remain near those people who could teach it to speak. Infliction of punishment may also arouse anger toward the inflicting agent. The child may attempt struggling with the parents, biting them, or slapping at them and, in turn, be punished for this behavior. Thus, an anger-anxiety conflict is learned.

Excessive conformity and guilt. Again, the child may get the impression that it is pursued by an all-seeing, punishing guardian and may try making as few responses as possible—and certainly not innovating any novel responses. Its conclusion on the basis of punishments received may be that unless a response is known to be correct it should not be risked. Thus may be laid the characterological basis of the excessively timid, conforming individual. Similarly, the child may not be able to discriminate between parental loathing for its excreta and loathing for the whole child himself. If the child learns to adopt these reactions, feelings of unworthiness, insignificance, and hopeless sinfulness will be created—feelings which sometimes so mysteriously reappear in the psychotic manifestations of guilt.

Advantages of verbal aids. From this discussion it will be clear that the trial-and-error method of early training, with its many punishments, has much more risk attached than training carried on at a time when the child can be verbally aided to hit on the right sequence of responses in a few early trials. Once the child has acquired the words "living room," "kitchen," "bedroom," and "outside," a single punishment trial, if properly conducted, can attach anxiety to all these cues at the same time and so spare the brutal repetition of punishment. If the child has already learned to call for help when it needs help, it can much more easily learn to call for aid when it needs to defecate. If it has learned to stop various activities to the word "stop," it is much easier to get it to check the evulsion response when this is occurring to its innate stimulus. If certain promises of the parents already have reward value attached to them, the child can be aided to make the right responses by being promised simple rewards. If the child already attaches anxiety to certain instructions of the parents, these instructions can have some of the same effect as repeated, direct punishments.

In this case also the reinforcement of the act of defecation itself will fix the correct series of responses into place. This will happen whether the course of the training has been stormy or smooth. However, in the case

of the smooth, verbally aided learning there is much less danger of arousing
furious anger or of creating maladaptive habits such as retention of feces
and loss of control. Extremely strong anxiety reactions do not occur and
feelings of excessive worthlessness are less likely. The end result is the same
so far as mere cleanliness training is concerned. The difference lies in the
fact that the later, verbally aided method of getting out the response has
much less risk of violent side reactions and character distortions.

Freud's Superego. The foregoing analysis employs the thoughts and
sentences of Freud reworked from the standpoint of behavior theory. The
course of cleanliness training is unlabeled and unconscious. Any one of us
may have been through a stormy period of this kind and yet have no recollection of it. The results may show themselves in our symptoms, our most
deeply embedded "character" traits, in our dreams, in our intuitive presuppositions about life, but they will not show themselves in our verbal behavior. The record of this training will be found in no man's autobiography
and yet the fate of the man may be deeply influenced and colored by it.

The first broad strands of what Freud calls the Superego are laid down
at this time. Anxiety reactions, never labeled, are attached to stimuli
also unlabeled. When these stimuli recur later the anxiety reactions automatically recur. The resulting effect Freud has called the "Superego" or
unconscious conscience. When unconscious guilt reactions are severe, the
personality is suffused with terror. It is hard to say whether a morbid
conscience is a worse enemy of life than a disease like cancer, but some
comparison of this kind is required to emphasize the shock produced in
the witness when he sees a psychotic person being tortured by such a
conscience. Enough is known now to convince us that we should make
the humble-seeming matter of cleanliness training the subject of serious
research.

3. Conflicts Produced by Early Sex Training

Sex-anxiety conflicts seem frequently to be involved in neuroses arising
in civilian life. The recurrent appearance of sex as a conflict element does
not seem to be due to the fact that sex is the strongest of human drives.
At their highest levels, pain, hunger, and fatigue certainly outrank it.
Many strong secondary drives such as anxiety, ambition, and pride can
also be stronger than sex. Sex seems to be so frequently implicated because it is the most severely attacked and inhibited of primary drives. Even
though relatively weaker, sex can exert a strong pressure which produces
great activation in the organism and great misery if blocked for long
periods. In no other case is the individual required to wait so many years
while patiently bearing the goading drive.

Source of first sex conflict—the masturbation taboo. Erection of the
penis can be observed in male infants as a reflexive response to interrupted
feeding or to urethral drive pressure (Halverson, 1938). At the age of a

year the child is able to grasp an object quite perfectly. The sensitivity of the genital and the ability to prehend make masturbation possible. It seems likely also that there is some kind of reward associated with masturbating. On the basis of his observations, Kinsey *et al.* (1948) believes that small boys acquire the capacity for orgasm long before they become able to ejaculate; similarly an experiment by Sheffield, Wulff, and Backer (1950) demonstrates that sexual responses short of ejaculation can serve to reinforce learning in the albino rat. It is certainly a fact that, if unchecked, children do learn to masturbate and that they sometimes obstinately persist even when quite severe sanctions are applied.

The sight of a child masturbating evokes intense anxiety in the adults of our culture and they promptly apply sanctions, ranging from persistently removing or jerking the child's hand away from its genital to slapping and spanking it. The result is to set up in the child the same sex-anxiety conflict which the adults have. As in other cases, masturbatory conflicts established in the first years of life are invariably unconscious. A vague negative feeling, a tendency to withdraw, an unease is established at the act, sight, or thought of masturbatory behavior. These conflicts differ for different individuals in many ways and for many reasons. Some individuals may be caught in the act more often than others; some may be punished more severely than others; some may have stronger innate sex drive than others. Some may have had more time to learn the habit before being caught and punished and may thus have a stronger appetite for this behavior than other persons. Some may, so to say, scare easier than others because they already have strong anxieties established in the cleanliness-training situation. Such anxieties generalize easily from urethral to the genital stimuli. Often both are called "nasty" and the cue produced by the common verbal response helps to mediate generalization of fear. In this case it is easy to train the individual out of the masturbatory habit, since the fear does not have to be learned but only generalized to the sex stimuli.

Parents don't notice effects of taboo. The imposition of a masturbation taboo can have important effects on the child's life. There may be immediate and direct changes in behavior. . . . When behavior changes occur it seems quite surprising that parents do not notice them as results of conflict over masturbation. The fact that they do not so notice is, however, easily explained. Intimate as their contact is with the child they may yet be very poor observers of cause and effect. Most of the young child's emerging life is mysterious to parents anyway. They may further have particular avoidances against noticing matters and connections which arise in the sexual sphere. Likely, they believe themselves to have been sexless in childhood and can do no less than believe the same in respect to their children. Whether correctly evaluated by parents or not, the masturbatory taboo is the first of the important sex taboos, and it sets up a sex-anxiety conflict in each of us.

Sex typing of personality. The sexual development of the child cannot be understood without understanding the forceful training in sex typing which it receives. The unspecialized or less specialized human being, the infant, is identified as boy or girl and its relationship with others is defined in terms of sex type. Sex typing is a strictly conventional arrangement that varies from society to society (Mead, 1949). Our own society is strongly organized around sex specialization of personality. This begins with male and female names, clothes, play patterns, toys, and continues throughout life by defining specialized sex roles for man and woman. The ultimate love object of the child is defined as a member of the opposite sex. The nascent sexual reactions of the child are directed toward stimuli of the opposite sex. The child is led to expect eventual sex rewards from persons of the opposite sex.

The taboo on homosexuality. Training in sex typing has the indirect effect of imposing a vigorous taboo on homosexuality. Homosexual objects are not presented, are treated by neglect or, if need be, vigorously condemned. The errors children make while learning sex typing are the source of much amusement to adults. The little girl declares she is going "to marry mommie" when she grows up or the little boy states he will marry his admired older brother. Children are carefully corrected and trained into making the appropriate distinctions. Furthermore, it seems probable that parents, already sex-typed, help to develop this turning toward the opposite sex by themselves "favoring" the child of the opposite sex.

Students of sexual abnormalities have suspected that the failure to define sharply the sex type is a factor in producing perverse sex adjustment (Henry, 1948). Thus, if a boy child were ardently desired, the parents might fail to impose sharp feminine sex typing on the girl who actually arrived. Or, in the opposite case, a mother who prefers her son to remain her "baby" may make him effeminate when she should be emphasizing his masculine character. Such inversions of social sex typing cannot directly produce a sexual perversion since sex responses must be attached to same-sex cues before a perverse sex appetite can exist; but they might tend to confuse the child about what its socially expected sex goals were and thus contribute to deviation.

After sex typing has been imposed and well learned, the child is in about this net position: masturbation has been tabooed, and it cannot give itself sex rewards by this means; sex behavior between siblings has been suppressed; on the other hand, a new channel, though a long one, has apparently been opened through the fact of sex typing. The child is vaguely led to expect something rewarding in the general direction of the opposite sex. These two circumstances set up the situation of the Oedipus complex.

How fear is attached to heterosexual approach responses. The anxiety which adolescents, and often adults, show at the prospect of heterosexual contact must be explained. It does not arise by chance. It arises rather in the family situation which is the child's most important early learning situation. The first definition of sexual responses is learned in relation to parents and siblings and only later transferred to others. Freud calls this the Oedipus situation.

We will illustrate from the case of the boy child, where the matter seems to be clear, and rehearse and paraphrase the familiar facts discovered by Freud. The boy child turns to his mother in fact or thought in the hope of getting sex rewards when he can no longer get them by himself. He expects sex rewards partly by generalization (Miller, 1948b; von Felsinger, 1948) of expectation of reward—that is, by analogy to the many rewards the mother has already given him—and partly from the fact that by sex typing he has learned to expect sex rewards from a woman and his mother is the woman at hand. Doubtless some of the anxiety already learned in connection with masturbation generalizes to the sex impulse when it begins to show itself toward family women.

A new source of anxiety appears, however; that is, fear of the father. The five-year-old boy knows his father is the head of the house, the symbolic source of punishments and discipline. He also knows that his father is the husband of his mother and has some unique relationship to her. This rivalry of the father does not exist merely in the boy's mind. It is often made very concrete in the father's behavior. The father may complain that the little boy sleeps in the mother's bed when he is already "too old" for such behavior. The father may object to the fact that the child or children sop up so much of the mother's time and leave so little to him. The father may impose certain restrictions about entering the parents' room which leave the child with a mystery on his hands. Whenever the male child makes emotional demands on the mother, the father may become more critical of him in other and more general respects, saying that the boy talks too much, that he does not work enough, and so forth. If the boy reacts with fear toward his father as a rival, it is because the father, consciously or unconsciously, is acting in a way that seems fearsome and rivalrous. The child is usually unable to discriminate between opposition on ground of sexual leanings and that evoked by its other claims on the mother. The whole thing may be played out as a kind of dumb show. The heterosexual strivings of the boy toward the mother may be behaviorally real and active but not labeled in the boy's mind. On the other hand, the opposition of the father, though active and effective, may be oblique and unconscious.

Often the mother herself rejects the claims of the boy. She has anxiety at any overtly sexual responses from the child, stops fondling him, and may suddenly and inexplicably change from being loving and approving to being horrified, disgusted, and disapproving.

In this case there is less need for the father to be harsh and hostile. But if the mother does not reject and does not clearly show her separate loyalty and adherence to the father, a great burden is placed upon him to maintain his control of his wife. The mother, for example, may use the seeming need of the child as a way of escaping from her husband and from the sexual conflicts which she has in regard to him. She may favor and cozen the son while avoiding her husband, and unconsciously this may seem to the father like a genuine kind of preferment. The father may then react by very actively arousing the boy's fears.

Specific genital anxiety. If the boy's motives are sexual, the increased threat from the father produces anxiety which is directly attached to the sexual motives and interpreted as a sexual threat. This is one way in which castration anxiety may become an important factor in the boy's life even though the father never threatens castration in so many words. The boy has learned that the punishment often fits the crime.

There are other and less ghostly sources of the castration threat. Very often it has been specifically associated with the masturbation taboo—*i.e.*, that if the boy plays with his penis, the penis will be cut off. The threat may appear in the fables of childhood which are told so eagerly. One of the authors as a six-year-old boy was permitted to participate in an after-dark session of older boys. They were telling the tale of how Bill Smith, a prominent citizen of the town, had come home and surprised his wife in bed with her lover. Smith thereupon pulled out a spring-labeled jackknife (demonstration of length and viciousness of same by boy telling the story) and proceeded to unman the lover. Such a story does not remain, however, as a mere "fable." It is taken to heart and has the effect of teaching straight-out castration fear to sex motives.

The castration idea may occur in still another way; that is, as an inference from the lack of penis in the girl. The parents do not explain the different nature of the girl's genital. The uninstructed boy may assume that the girl once had an external genital but has been deprived of it, perhaps as a punishment. There is no doubt that this inference is often made. The authors have repeatedly heard it in those in-family situations where children are first questioning their elders about sexual matters. It is further surprising in the history of adults how often the idea of bodily damage occurs in relation to sex "sins." Castration fear has been shown clinically to be connected with fears of bodily damage, especially in the cases of heart and brain, to aversion to crippled people, and to avoidance of women in their genital aspect. Castration fear is frequently escaped by approaching the bachelor girl (who has no husband or father at her side) or by recourse to women of lower class or racial status (whose normal protectors are not allowed to function).

In any case, and engendered by whatever of these several means or combination of them, the sex conflict takes a new twist when it is worked out within the family. Anxiety which was once attached only to the masturbation impulse is now attached to the heterosexual approach situation. If this anxiety is made very strong it can produce a certain relief in the intensity of the conflict. This is the so-called "resolution" of the Oedipus complex. When anxiety is greatly dominant over approach tendencies, the conflicted individual stays far from his goal and but few of the acquired elements in the sexual appetite are aroused. Thus, that part of the intensity of the conflict which is produced by appetitive sex reactions is missing, and the conflict is therefore lessened. However, this conflict should and does recur when the individual is placed near his goal object and cannot easily escape, as frequently happens in adolescence. Then again the full strength of the sex reactions is pitted against the terror of sexual injury. Marriage evidently seems to some adults a similar situation—that of being held close to a feared goal—and they make the blind escape responses which would be expected.

Heterosexual conflict not labeled. If the prior intimidation of the person has been very great, and if the mother's stand is correct, much less fear need be imposed by the father. If sex appetite is weak rather than strong, there is much less pressure from the child's side and less anxiety need be imposed to counteract it.

All these events are but poorly labeled at the time they occur. The culture is niggardly about giving names to sexual organs, sexual feelings, or the fears attached to them. The child is therefore not able to make a logical case for itself and, so to say, "put it up to the parents." Furthermore, repression sets in in two ways: Children are frequently forbidden to talk to others about their sexual reactions. Such sentences or thoughts as do occur tend to make the conflict keener both by arousing sex appetites and by cueing off the anxiety attached to them. The child is pained when it tries to think about sexual things and relieved when it stops. The result is repression. This repression has one unfortunate consequence for science. When the individual is later interviewed he is not able, promptly and freely, to give account of these matters. The renaming and mental reestablishment of these bygone events can thereafter only be made through the weary work of psychotherapy.

Science is not the only loser. The individual himself has lost his opportunity to use higher mental activities in solving the conflicts involving sex and authority. There are many ways in which the person can be victimized. A sexual perversion may lurk behind the blank surface of repression. The individual may never again be able cheerfully and amiably to accept a measure of authority exerted over him. Acute anxiety may be attached to his heterosexual impulses and when the time comes that society expects, almost requires, that he marry, he may be unable to do so. Even though he is able to get over the line into marriage, he may find the years of his marital life haunted and poisoned by constant, unconscious anxiety. In this case, the individual has automatically generalized to all women the anxiety proper only to the incest situation. He has failed to discriminate, as a free mental life would enable him to do, between the tabooed sexual feelings and objects of childhood and the relative freedom permitted to adults. To every authoritarian figure in his life he generalizes the intense anxiety that he once experienced when attempting to rival his father in the sexual field. Only when higher mental processes are restored can the individual make those discriminations which allow him to proceed freely and constructively with his life as an adult.

4. Anger-Anxiety Conflicts

At this point we are more interested in the connection between angry emotions and fear than we are in the problem of how angry feelings are aroused in the child. We assume, however, as before (Dollard *et al.*, 1939) that anger responses are produced by the innumerable and unavoidable frustration situations of child life. In the frustration situation, new and strong responses are tried out. Some of these have the effect of inflicting pain on other people. Society takes a special stand toward such anger responses, generally inhibiting them and allowing them reign only in a few circumstances (self-defense, war, etc.). Many of these attack, or "put through the act," responses produce strong stimuli, and these we recognize as the emotion of anger. Lift the veil of repression covering the childhood mental life of a neurotic person and you come at once upon the smoking responses of anger.

Patriarchal code on child's anger. Parents intuitively resent and fear the anger and rage of a child, and they have the strong support of the culture in suppressing its anger. Direct punishment is probably used much more frequently when the child is angry and aggressive than in any other circumstance. More or less without regard to what the child is angry about, fear is attached to the stimuli of anger. The virtuous chastisement of the rebellious child is an age-old feature of our patriarchal culture. According to the old Connecticut Blue Laws, a father could kill a disobedient son (Blue Laws of Connecticut, 1861, Section 14, p. 69). Even though this code was never exercised in this extreme in recent times, it shows the complete freedom to punish which was once culturally allowed parents. As the domestic representative of the patriarch in his absence, the mother is free to punish children "in their own interest."

How fear is attached to anger cues. We have already noted the situation of early cleanliness training as one tending to produce angry confusion in the small child. At earliest ages the cultural practice seems to be that of extinguishing anger rather than punishing it; that is, the child is segregated, left to "cry and thresh it out." However, parents' motivation to teach the child cleanliness training is so strong that they frequently also use punishment, especially in the case of what they interpret as stubborn or defiant behavior. Anxiety responses therefore become attached not only to the cues produced by the forbidden situation but also to the cues produced by the emotional responses which the child is making at the time. It is this latter connection which creates the inner mental or emotional conflict. After this learning has occurred, the first cues produced by angry emotions may set off anxiety responses which "outcompete" the angry emotional responses themselves. The person can thus be made helpless to use his anger even in those situations where culture does permit it. He is viewed as abnormally meek or long-suffering. Robbing a person of his anger completely may be a dangerous thing since some capacity for anger seems to be needed in the affirmative personality.

Other frustrations producing anger. The same state of affairs can prevail and be additionally reinforced as a result of the frustrations occurring in the sex-training situation. If the child is punished for masturbating it may react with the response of anger. The parent may not notice the provocative circumstance but see only that the child has become mysteriously "naughty." Its naughtiness may be punished and the connection between anger and fear be strengthened.

Parental rejection or desertion may likewise produce anger in the child. If the child feels secure only when the parents are present, it may react with fear when the parents leave or when they threaten to leave again. When the parents return, the child may make excessive claims, want unusual favors, "be clingy." To these demanding and possessive gestures on the part of the child the parent may react with unintelligent punishment, thus again teaching the child to fear.

The new tasks involved in growing up impose many frustrations on the child. Giving up long-standing privileges may arouse rage. Being forced to try out new responses, such as putting on its own clothes or tying its own shoe laces, can anger the child. If it screams, lunges, slaps at the parent in these circumstances, punishment is the almost inevitable answer, and the connection between anger and fear is additionally strengthened.

Sibling rivalry. Rivalry between siblings is a constant incitement to anger, and such rivalry occurs in every household, without exception, where there are siblings of younger ages. The occasions for rivalry seem innumerable. Siblings may compete for evidences of parental love. If the parent disappoints a child, that child may "take it out" on the luckier brother or sister. Younger children may anger older ones by being allowed to assume too quickly privileges which the older have long waited and worked for. Older children may tease and torment younger ones in retaliation. Sometimes the younger child is resented merely for existing and for having displaced the older one and alloyed its satisfaction in being the unique child.

The younger children may enjoy privileges which the older have been forced to abandon and thus create some degree of unconscious resentment. Younger children may tyrannize over older ones by too freely playing with or even destroying their toys and precious objects. Parents should intervene and prevent such behavior but often they do not, and the older child revenges himself in roundabout ways. Younger children may resent the privileges enjoyed by the older and attempt to punish older siblings for their greater freedom. These angry displays result in punishment of the one or the other child by the parents—and sometimes of both. The younger children tend to "catch it" more from the older, and the older children more from the parents. Though parents may mitigate these angry relationships between siblings by just rules which are honestly enforced, there seems no way to take all the hostile strain out of such relations.

Mental limitations. Small children confront an unintelligible world. Many of their frustrations result from this fact. They do not have the mental units to be patient and foresightful. They do not know how to comfort themselves while waiting. They cannot live in the light of a plan which promises to control the future. Since so much is frustrating to them that is later bearable, they are especially prone to anger. They want to know "Why isn't the circus here today?" "Why do I have to wait 'til my birthday to get a present?" "Why does Daddy have to go to work just when it's so much fun to play with him?" Living in the present and being unable to reassure themselves about the future, young children resort to anger at these inevitable frustrations. Adults experience the hostile or destructive behavior of young children as a nuisance, do not understand its inevitability, and frequently punish aggressive responses.

Devious aggression. If anger must be abandoned as a response in a frustrating situation, other responses will be tried out such as pleading for what one cannot take by force or submitting to frustrations which can only be worsened through opposition. Devious forms of aggression are particularly likely to occur in this case. The individual can be punished for direct anger responses but it is much harder to catch him at roundabout aggression. He may learn to lie in wait and take revenge by hastening and sharpening punishment which his opponent has invoked in some other way. Gossip, deceit, creating dangerous confusion about agreements and life relationships may all be indirect modes of angry reaction.

Anger conflict unlabeled. As in the case of sex-anxiety conflicts, the anger-anxiety conflict is likely to be poorly labeled. Verbal skills are at a low level when much of this training is going on. Repression of the language describing anger-anxiety conflicts may occur because conflict is thus, momentarily at least, reduced. As a result, the individual cannot, in later life, be selectively angry, showing anger in just those social situations in which it is permitted and rejecting anger where it is not.

The overinhibited person. Inhibition of anger may occur in two different degrees. The overt, or some of the overt, responses of direct aggression may be inhibited. Some such inhibitions must occur if a child is to live in our culture. The process may, however, go farther and the emotion of anger itself be throttled. If the response-produced drives of anger evoke intense fear, the individual may be incapable of a normal life. The victim loses the core of an affirmative personality. He may be unable to compete as is demanded by our society in school or business spheres. He may be additionally shamed because he cannot bring himself to fight. He may depend unduly on others, waiting for them to give him what is everyone's right to take. Such a child cannot be a self-maintaining person because he cannot produce any anger responses at all, let alone those which are "legitimate and proper."

Since many outlets for anger are permitted adults which are not permitted to children, the person who is overtrained to inhibit anger may seem childish in that he is still following the age-graded code of childhood and is unable to embrace the freer standards of adulthood. One of the chief tasks of psychotherapy, in the case of unduly inhibited persons, is to enable them to name and describe their angry feelings so that they may extinguish undue fear and begin to learn a proportionate self-assertiveness.

Frustrated Mobility Aspirations Produce Aggression

There is little doubt that adults can be in conflict concerning their mobility strivings and that these conflicts can lead to pathological results in behavior (Ruesch, Loeb, et al., 1946). The conflict could be described somewhat as follows: In order to be strong and safe, or stronger and safer, the person wants to identify with and possess the symbols of a social group above that of his original family. In order to make this transition, however, certain prescribed routes must be followed. The person must have a talent which brings him in touch with and makes him useful to the group into which he wants entry. This talent could be intellectual, could be a facility for making money, could be beauty, could be an exceptionally loving and understanding personality. If an individual has the wish to change position but does not have such a talent or does not enjoy it to a sufficient degree, he may find it impossible to make the transition. He may find himself unable to establish the contacts which will enable him to learn the rituals of behavior of the superordinate group. He may gradually come to know that, though "the promised land" is in sight, he will never enter it. Meanwhile the group he is trying to leave punishes him for being "different" and the group he tries to enter rejects him as presumptuous. The realization, conscious or unconscious, that his campaign has failed may serve as a severe frustration and produce varying types of aggressive and compensatory behavior. The resentment of the person who fails of mobility is likely to be severely punished and thus to create an acute anger-fear conflict.

Mobility conflicts which are unconscious. Except in one circumstance, which we shall come to in a moment, it does not seem likely that conflicts such as the one just described are engendered in early childhood. The conflict may nevertheless be unconscious. This unconsciousness of the elements of an adult conflict can arise because the mobile person gets little help from his society in labeling his behavior. He is not told what he is trying to do, and he has no clear understanding of what the techniques are. If he hits on the means of mobility, it is, from his point of view, a matter of luck or accident. He is ordinarily not permitted to think that different social classes exist because the social beliefs which protect the class system forbid this recognition. Usually the mobile individual sees himself only as rising in some value such as "wealth" or occupation but he does not realize that his real mobility will be founded on a complex set of behavioral adaptations and changes in taste and outlook. Usually, therefore, the mobile person does not know what is happening to him while it is happening, does not know how he failed if he fails, and does not know until "afterward" how he succeeded if he succeeds. This is a set of conditions which is bound to baffle and to arouse a confusion of angry, rebellious, apathetic, and submissive responses.

Children of a mixed-class marriage. The one circumstance that we can see under which difference in social class can have an effect on a small child is the case where the child is born of a mixed-class marriage. If the mother is superordinate, she might in some ways "look down" on the father, apologize for him, and limit his usefulness as a model to her male child. Such a mother may be unduly "ambitious" for her children, attempting to speed them over the landscape of childhood instead of allowing them to find their natural pace through it. She may get satisfaction in imposing early cleanliness training because it seems to her like a guarantee of the future precocity of the child. She may inculcate the sex taboos strongly because she feels that the "goodness" of the child in this respect will keep it out of "bad company" and aid its development in the schools. She may handle its angry tendencies severely in the hope of making it amenable and yet urge it to highly competitive performance outside the home. One would predict that this kind of family training would give a special coloring to the circumstances which ordinarily produce conflict in small children (Davis and Havighurst, 1947; Warner, 1949, pp. 70–72).

A child in a class-stable family with parents matched from the class standpoint would not ordinarily discover in the early years of life that there is any group "above" its parents. During the formative period these parents would play their august roles, majestic in their competence and authority so far as the child could see. It would only be later in life, perhaps first during school days, that the child would learn that there are any people who look down upon it or its parents. Undoubtedly such knowledge would have some kind of effect on the career of the child, but we cannot say what the possible outcomes might be. We can be sure, however, that the evaluation put on the self and the family by the surrounding society will be a fact of importance in the developmental history of every child.

References

Blue Laws of Connecticut. Capital Laws. Code of 1650, Section 14, Duane Rulison, Philadelphia, 1861.

Davis, Allison, and Havighurst, Robert, *Father of the Man*, Houghton Mifflin, Boston, 1947.

Dollard, John, Doob, L. W., Miller, N. E., and Sears, R. R., *Frustration and Aggression*, Yale University Press, New Haven, 1939.

Freud, Sigmund, *Three Contributions to the Theory of Sex*, 4th ed., Nervous and Mental Disease Publishing Company, Washington, D.C., 1930.

Gesell, Arnold, *The First Five Years of Life*, Harper, New York, 1940.

Halverson, H. M., "Infant sucking and tensional behavior," *J. gen. Psychol.*, 53:365–430, 1938.

Henry, G. W., *Sex Variants*, 1-vol. ed., Hoeber-Harper, New York, 1948.

Kinsey, A. C., Pomeroy, W. B., and Martin, C. E., *Sexual Behavior in the Human Male*, Saunders, Philadelphia, 1948.

Mead, Margaret, *Male and Female*, Morrow, New York, 1949.

Miller, N. E., "Theory and experiment relating psychoanalytic displacement to stimulus response generalization," *J. abnorm. soc. Psychol.*, 43:155–178, 1948b.

Ruesch, Jurgen, Loeb, M. B., *et al.*, *Chronic Disease and Psychological Invalidism: A Psychosomatic Study*, American Society for Research in Psychosomatic Problems, New York, 1946.

Sheffield, F. D., Wulff, J. J., and Backer, Robert, 1950. "Reward Value of Sexual Stimulation without Ejaculation" (in preparation).

Spock, Benjamin, *Baby and Child Care*, Pocket Books, New York, 1946.

von Felsinger, John, "The Effects of Ovarian Hormones on Learning," Ph.D. dissertation, Yale University, New Haven, 1948.

Warner, W. L., and Associates, *Democracy in Jonesville*, Harper, New York, 1949.

PSYCHOLOGICAL FACTORS
IN ADOLESCENT BEHAVIOR *

(Jacob E. Finesinger

The acceleration in growth characteristic of adolescence is not the only aspect of development that merits consideration. At the same time that this is taking place, profound changes in feelings, attitudes, intellect, and

* From Jacob E. Finesinger, "The Needs of Youth: The Physiological and Psychological Factors in Adolescent Behavior," *Psychiatry*, 7, 1, 45–57. Pp. 50–57 reprinted by special permission of the author and The William Alanson White Psychiatric Foundation, Inc.

general behavior are in process. Before adulthood and maturity are reached, the child goes through processes which result eventually in emancipation from the family, the development of a heterosexual life [1] and the selection of a vocation.[2] Of the multiplicity of factors determining these changes in adjustment, the child himself may be aware of only certain ones, while others he does not sense or he misunderstands. In the normal, these processes go along in a fairly coördinated way. The emotional life shows spurts in the direction of new interests and attitudes which come to the fore for longer or shorter periods, but which eventually amalgamate into a pattern of behavior characteristic of the person. Feelings of which the child only had previous glimpses in earlier days assert themselves. These feelings are, at times, precipitous and bring with them reëvaluation of the family organization and of other more impersonal situations. The growth of sex desires bring about the necessity for adjustment between the personal needs and the social system.[3] The normal child undergoes periods of greater sensitivity, greater conscious conflict and upheaval.[4] The difficulty in the resolution of these new trends in some persons results in pathological or asocial behavior.[5] An incidence of neurotic symptoms, or psychiatric disturbances,[6] and of delinquency marks the attempts of the less fortunate and the less stable in integrating these new elements.

Students of this period of life agree almost unanimously that during adolescence the person tends to become more introspective.[7] The interest shifts from the outside world to the self. Observations and learning which heretofore have been directed toward objects in the attempt to understand external reality become focused more critically upon the person. Whether this shift in focus is due to a greater consciousness of the developing body or other factors is not known. The interest in one's body and in one's feel-

[1] Williams, Frankwood E., *Adolescence: Studies in Mental Hygiene*; New York, Farrar and Rinehart, 1930 (xi and 279 pp.).

[2] Hollingworth, Leta S., *The Psychology of the Adolescent*; New York, Appleton, 1929 (227 pp.).

[3] Zachry, Caroline B., Emotional Problems of Adolescence. *Bull. Menninger Clin.* (1940) 4:63–73.

[4] Frank, Lawrence K., General Considerations: Certain Problems of Puberty and Adolescence. *J. Pediatrics* (1941) 19:294–301.

[5] Howard, Edgerton McC., An Analysis of Adolescent Adjustment Problems. *Mental Hygiene* (1941) 25:363–391.

[6] Richards, Esther L., Following the Hypochondriacal Child for a Decade. *J. Pediatrics* (1941) 18:528–537.

Reckless, Walter C., Juvenile Delinquency and Behavior Patterning. *J. Educational Sociol.* (1937) 10:493–505.

Oltman, Jane E., and Friedman, Samuel, A Psychiatric Study of One Hundred Criminals. *J. N. and M. Disease* (1941) 93:16–41.

[7] Lohbauer, Hans L., Die Entwicklung der Fähigkeit zur Selbstwahrnehmung in Kindesalter. *Zeitschr. f. Angewandete Psych.* (1928) 31:1–65.

Note also reference footnote 1.

ings necessarily brings with it comparisons with other persons with whom one has contact. These comparisons in some persons emphasize the awkwardness and the clumsiness of the adolescent. They stimulate feelings of restlessness and of impatience with oneself in the growing process. The adolescent strives to attain an objective appraisal of himself and to fit himself into the changing reality about him. Most adolescents resolve this problem by attaining a transient but definite distortion of their position and rôle in the world. At times these comparisons result in feelings of inferiority, and, at times, in feelings of superiority. The difficulty in obtaining a consistent appraisal of oneself makes it difficult to face this self directly and realistically. The result is that the person assumes poses, clichés, and mannerisms which are transient and necessary, but bring about difficulties in adjustment. They tend to emphasize old insecurities carried over from childhood.[8]

In an attempt to resolve the turmoil, the child battles with reality either directly or through flight. The direct attack results in rebellion against socially accepted behavior. Yet, down deep, the feelings of insecurity continue to mount. The significance of feelings and emotions are denied and substituted by a bravado which is only too apparent to the outside world. At the same time, an outlet is found in the more idealistic and mystic aspects of life. Adolescence is the great period for ideals to flourish. Religious conversions,[9] the sentimental dramatizations toward perfection, concern with the ultimate, and the need for reform are some of the ways of dealing with an uncomfortable reality. These developments are normal. The unusual person in this period of life is the one who has not struggled with these personal issues.

One pertinent aspect of the rebellion of adolescents is directed against the immediate family. In early childhood children believe in the omniscience of their parents. As they grow older an adjustment takes place, the child handles this by recourse to phantasy. In adolescence this problem once more comes to the fore. At this period some children directly rebel against parents by ignoring parental authority. This specific type of rebellion, although no different in essence from other types of rebellion, is of special importance because it stirs up latent difficulties in the parent. The net result often is that the parents are unable to be of any practical help to adolescents in assisting them in solving their current problems. As a result of the interaction the adolescent is often alienated. Thus, the child

[8] Mead, Margaret, Back of Adolescence Lies Early Childhood. *Childhood Education* (1941) 18:58–61.

[9] Starbuck, Edwin Diller, *The Psychology of Religion*; New York, Scribner's, 1911 (xx and 423 pp.).

Brenman, Margaret, Minority-group Membership and Religious, Psychosexual and Social Patterns in a Group of Middle-class Negro Girls. *J. Social Psychol.* (1940) 12:179–196.

loses whatever stabilizing forces the parents might exert upon him. As a result of this alienation, the child seeks social contact with gangs, which, in some instances, eventually lead to delinquency.[10]

The developments of the person in the direction of emancipation from the family are worthy of note. Here again the experience and attitude of the parents as well as those of the child play a rôle. It seems that children, who in earlier childhood, and during the latent period, escaped the need for great dependence upon the parental organization, have a much easier time during adolescence. The difficulties in emancipation, seen so clearly in adults as well, centers about the affect of guilt. Either through conscious or unconscious guilt, children and adolescents, as well as adults, are inhibited in respect to their capacity for independent activity. The reasons why emancipation does not take place are confused in the mind of the adolescent with plausible rationalizations. On the one hand, there is the need for freeing oneself not only from the parental influence and abode, but also from parental ideologies. This need is balanced and often overcome by other feelings, such as the need for security and protection found in the home setting. The need for economic dependence, the need for following the whims of the parents, and the fears of parental displeasure are all used as rationalizations for a fundamental dependence. Children, in whose lives the guilt motif plays a significant rôle, find greater difficulty in working through their emancipation. In some few persons the guilt associated with the more unsublimated sexual behavior is instrumental in bringing about reactions of anxiety and panic. These may reach such intensity as to require psychiatric help.

The development of the primary sex glands and the secondary sex characteristics also cast their shadow upon the feelings and attitudes of the adolescent. Here one encounters varied reactions. Some adolescents, especially those whose development is on the precocious side, tend to be solely preoccupied with the sexual topic directly. The pre-adolescent child, as well as the younger child, is conscious of sex differences in a simple and direct way. There is no undue emphasis on specific reproductive functions. However, the development of the sex glands with the resultant concentration on specific sexual feelings and activities differentiate the attitude of the adolescent from that of the younger child. Children who approach adolescence with attitudes and taboos picked up as the result of personal inhibitions plus the environmental rigidity in respect to sex topics are thrown into intense conflict. The resolution of this conflict is generally handled either in the direct rebellion against parental standards, or in flight from the reality conflict. In the normal, one can see an inkling of the processes involved. In the young patient both horns of the dilemma assert themselves

[10] Freud, Anna, *The Ego and the Mechanisms of Defense*; London, The Hogarth Press, 1937 (x and 196 pp.)—in particular, Chapter XI.
Aichorn, August, *Wayward Youth*; New York, Viking, 1935 (xii and 236 pp.).

n clean-cut precision. The adolescent either talks loose sex, may even act loose sex, or may flee the problem by idealizing the opposite sex.

In sharp contrast to the idealized object of sexual phantasy is the stark reality of menstruation, masturbation, and nocturnal emissions. Unless reasonably prepared for the occurrence of these natural functions, most children have sharp conflicts about these processes. The adolescent feels the need and gives way to masturbation with mixed feelings. The physical joy in these new discoveries is short-lived and followed by the guilt of having done something wrong and dirty. This guilt is at times associated with the direct need for punishment. Often it manifests itself in feelings of mild depression and weakness. Often it is associated with ideas of having hurt oneself irreparably and of being a marked person whose crime is visible to the outside world through acneiform eruptions or through "bags" under the eyes. Attempts at handling the masturbation impulse in compulsive people may become part of a complex ritual in which emphasis is placed upon the need for touching or avoidance of other objects directly associated with or symbolic of genital activity. The current attitudes and mores of many parents, who may have had similar problems in their own adolescence, often reënforce the guilt instead of alleviating it. The normal adolescent after puberty is able to shift the emphasis from the pure unadulterated genital satisfaction to other aspects of the sex drive which have more points of contact with his total self, interests, and goals. The resulting socialization, whether it be with the same sex or the opposite sex, is as a rule associated with a let-up in the acute and overwhelming need for masturbation. Little by little the sex drive takes its place as one in the mosaic of functions constituting the activity of the person.

The less fortunate find greater difficulties in developing a well-integrated mode of reaction. In some instances this is due to disharmonies in development [11] with the typical adolescent preoccupation about these disharmonies. In other instances this is due to unusual and morbid concern over the specific sex functions and urges thrust upon the adolescent. Truancy, stealing, and destructiveness are often manifestations of an extreme aggressiveness associated with worries over masturbation and erection. The aggressive child runs into social difficulties. The sensitive child withdraws from the situation into himself. When attempts at obtaining understanding are thwarted, he gets moody, unhappy, and resentful at unfair treatment and lack of understanding. He is both afraid and ashamed to discuss his internal worries and finds small comfort from his awkwardness, laziness, belligerency, sensitivity, and self-consciousness. In extreme cases guilt in connection with masturbation and homosexual experiences lead to states of emotional turmoil and panic. In other patients the same conflict is associated with symptoms of withdrawal from reality, marked preoccupation with body

[11] Thom, Douglas A., Psychologic Aspects of Adolescence. J. Pediatrics (1941) 19:392–402.

functions in a hypochondriacal setting. Often such distortions of reality are found that the psychiatrist is inclined to think of ominous diagnoses. Luckily, many of these "adolescent storms" abate with maturing years and with understanding and supportive treatment on the part of the doctor.

The physical needs of the adolescent are on the whole the easiest to meet. Well-balanced diets, sufficient vitamins, are not difficult to prescribe. Considerable progress has been made in recent years in the treatment of glandular dyscrasias. Many workers are at present concerned with the problems of endocrinology. That these efforts have already borne fruit is indicated not merely by the great increase of information obtained by new methods of investigation, but even some of the gross glandular disturbances have been treated successfully. Much remains to be learned, but the field has been opened widely by new contributions. One can reasonably hope that even the milder glandular disturbances will be helped by researchers in endocrinology.

At present it seems that the needs presenting the greatest difficulty in supplying are those associated with the emotional development. The problems and conflicts of the adolescent often inhibit him not only in his social adjustment, but even may prevent him from obtaining the necessary requirements for proper growth. No matter how bountiful and complete a diet is presented to the growing person, it is of no value if the adolescent refuses to eat or regurgitates most of the food and vitamins which he does eat. Adolescents develop food fads and precious methods of eating which, as a rule, can be traced back to earlier difficulties, which in turn may be the child's way of expressing hostility, fear, and the need for domination over the parents. The compulsive child may refuse meat on account of distorted attitudes toward killing animals for food. He may refuse vegetables on account of squeamish associations with dirt. The adolescent girl may refuse all food not only because she prefers to stay slim, but because eating certain foods and gaining weight are associated with repressed taboo phantasies of oral impregnation and pregnancy. Often the vomiting in hysteria is associated with similar phantasies. In severe psychiatric disturbances food is not eaten out of fear that it may be poisoned. In anorexia nervosa,[12] a psychiatric disturbance which must be differentiated from the pituitary disorder of Simmond's cachexia,[13] one finds the most bizarre type of eating disturbances. This disorder begins in young girls during adolescence, and food is not eaten presumably for the sake of slimming. However, even after the desired weight has been attained, the patient still refuses to eat. This leads to a profound state of inanition, which in some cases leads to death due to starvation. In other patients with anorexia nervosa the period of starvation

[12] Rahman, Lincoln; Richardson, Henry B.; and, Ripley, Herbert S., Anorexia Nervosa with Psychiatric Observations. *Psychosom. Med.* (1939) 1:335–365.

[13] Richardson, Henry B., Simmonds' Disease and Anorexia Nervosa. *Arch. Int. Med.* (1939) 63:1–28.

followed by a period of overeating and gorging of food. These patients ften have bizarre appetites and will only eat highly spiced food or delicaies, such as nuts, pickles, and specially choice morsels. The ætiology of this isturbance is at present unknown, and symptomatic treatment is of only ight value.

The fact that obesity and increase in weight are found in Froehlich's ndrome and in hypothyroidism [14] has led many physicians to treat this isturbance in adolescents by glandular therapy. In a study on obesity in elation to puberty Bruch [15] has shown that obese children are advanced in rowth of stature and maturation, and that early development in puberty is ne rule of obese girls and is not uncommon for obese boys. However, there nothing in the study which justifies the assumption that obesity in childood is associated with hypogenitalism or delayed puberty. The fact that bese children show acceleration in growth rather than retardation, which the case in hypofunction of the thyroid and pituitary, indicates that the nyroid and pituitary are not involved, and hence glandular therapy is not idicated. Bruch is inclined to believe that the overeating and inactivity, hich go hand in hand with a marked retardation in social and emotional evelopment, indicates a disturbance in the general behavior of the person. he behavior of these children has been influenced by the environment, hich is characterized by an overprotective and oversolicitous attitude on he part of the parents.[16] The child resolves his conflicts by overeating as source of comfort and enjoyment. Treatment in these cases involves not nly changes in diet but direct help in dealing with the adolescent's peronal difficulties. In this group of adolescents the emphasis is again on the esolution of personal difficulties and conflicts.

The great need of the adolescent is for understanding and acceptance. hese are much more effective when given indirectly and subtly. No amount f verbalization that all is tolerated can make up for the subtle indications of isapproval betrayed by parents and teachers. The adolescent as well as the hild is much more sensitive to attitudes and feelings indicated by behavior han he is to verbal formulation. In other words, any approach toward understanding and helping the adolescent attain his maturity with the minimum f discomfort and maladjustment might focus first in the attitude of the arents, teachers, and psychiatrists. Until they can frankly face and accept he realities of adolescent behavior and present reasonable attitudes toward he adolescent, their value as therapeutic agents is strictly limited. The eed is paramount for strict objectivity on the part of parents and educators. ariations of adolescent behavior and the multifarious problems presented

[14] Schultz, Frederic W., What to Do about the Fat Child at Puberty. *J. Pediatrics* 1941) 19:376–381.

[15] Bruch, Hilde, Obesity in Relation to Puberty. *J. Pediatrics* (1941) 19:365–375.

[16] Bruch, Hilde, and Touraine, Grace, Obesity in Childhood: V. The Family Frame f Obese Children. *Psychosom. Med* (1940) 2:141–206.

are to be accepted in an impersonal yet understanding way. One must avoid measuring the behavior of others by a personal yardstick, which, to be sure, is the result of one's own personality and experience, but as such is limited to the experience of one person. It is essential to divorce oneself from one's own personal conflicts and the resolution of these conflicts. Otherwise one fails before the battle has even been joined.

The problems of adolescence must be recognized as being realistic problems, in which the adolescent is consciously battling for light and understanding. By the use of cynicism and superiority in personal contacts one merely adds to the adolescent's defenses and reënforces his wall of isolation. By pointing out the adolescent's difficulties in a critical way, his conflicts are merely intensified, and in most situations heap up more and more guilt and insecurity where more than enough already exists. The need is primarily for a good positive relationship in living and working with the adolescent.[1] This type of relationship gives security and enables the person to express himself and at least impart the conscious aspect of his conflicts. No matter what subsequent task parents, educators, or psychiatrists may have, effective contact cannot be made without good interpersonal relations. The subsequent approaches depend more specifically upon the presenting problems, and these must be assessed for the individual person. Reassurance to the adolescent that the disharmonies are the usual and expected thing, some encouragement and clarification of the underlying insecurities, some insight into the behavior of other persons and their needs, all are of value. In some instances a better understanding [18] of the family setting and the relationship between the adolescent and his intimates clarifies some sources of conflict.

The basic emotional need of the adolescent is one for security.[19] Just as in younger children, the feeling of belonging to the family and acceptance by the family and the group plays an important rôle in maintaining the person's sense of security. Patterns of behavior are developed in light of the special adjustments of the person in respect to feelings of security. These patterns, first developed in connection with intimates in the family, are carried along to other social contacts. The special problems of adolescence put additional strain upon persons whose adjustment is tentative. The adolescent is groping toward an integration of his various drives, which at times are at loggerheads with each other. He legitimately demands recognition of himself as an independent human being.[20]

[17] Ruggles, Arthur M., *These Adolescents: Their Right to Grow Up*; Norman, Oklahoma, Coöperative Books, 1940 (36 pp.).

[18] Goddard, Henry Herbert, *Juvenile Delinquency*; New York, Dodd and Mead, 192 (120 pp.).

[19] Williams, Frankwood E., *Can Youth Be Coerced? Mental Hygiene of Normal Childhood*; Buffalo, Mental Hygiene Council, 1927 (59 pp.).

[20] Garrison, Karl Claudius, *Psychology of Adolescence*; New York, Prentice-Hall 1940 (xix and 477 pp.).

More specific approaches in dealing with these difficulties are, generally speaking, of two kinds. One approach deals with attempts at getting at the basic conflicts with which the person is struggling and which he is attempting to modify. This approach usually leads to an exploration into the history and emotional development of the person which carries back into early childhood. Attempts are made at giving the person some understanding or insight into the development of his patterns and into their historic and current rôle in his life. The most standardized approach of this kind is psychoanalysis, which obviously had best be left in the hands of the specialists.

Fortunately many adolescent difficulties respond to simpler types of approach. These approaches are concerned with giving the person a broad picture of his current situation and some information about his specific modes of reaction. This is coupled with reassurance that his problems, both specific and general, are usual and the expected thing in adolescence. More specifically reassurance and a plausible explanation can be advanced for his inferiorities, his guilt feelings in connection with sex and other topics. In addition, suggestions as to methods of sublimating the pressing drives and helping the adolescent make use of his reactions, defenses though they may be, in a way which will be socially useful and bring with it the approbation rather than the censure of the group.[21]

The sex topic presents a major source of difficulty both to the child and the parent. Sex education begins much earlier than adolescence, and the information and attitudes of the child depend so much upon those of the parents. The ideal situation is one in which children are given what sex information they indicate that they need.[22] Information beyond the needs and capacity of the child is rejected by a return to earlier phantasies of the mechanics of sex activity. If this information can be imparted with the same casual ease that other facts of growth and human functioning are given, a great deal of the persistent curiosity is avoided. This information can include the facts of reproduction, of sexual intercourse, menstruation, erection, nocturnal emissions, or even later, facts about venereal diseases. It is always best to ascertain first just what the adolescent actually knows. By doing this one often is able to find certain misconceptions, which can be corrected and another source of worry in this way can be eliminated. Above all it is of paramount importance to reassure the adolescent in reference to guilt feelings no matter with what aspect of sex life they are associated.

So much emphasis has been placed upon the personal aspects of the adolescent's life and his relationship with his intimates because these adjustments are considered fundamental to any type of program for youth. One would believe that if the adolescent were well adjusted in respect to his

[21] Plant, James S.: The Warp and Woof of Mental Hygiene. Mental Hygiene (1941) 5:25–29.

[22] Mohr, George J., Sexual Education of the Adolescent. J. Pediatrics (1941) 19:387–91.

personal and emotional needs he could be able to handle them as they arose. This view emphasizes the importance of allowing the adolescent to work out the solution of his problems in his own way. Parents and educators would do well in encouraging the adolescent to assume the responsibility for decisions and plans. This involves not only the articulation of the needs, but also planned realistic attempts at satisfying them.

The fact that the physical, glandular, and emotional development characteristic of the adolescent have their beginnings years before the onset of puberty has certain other implications. The needs for emotional, educational, and social adjustment also existed long before puberty. Specific outlets for these needs during the earlier periods of development are essential. Both the adjustment and the maladjustment of the adolescent in many persons can be traced back to earlier years. The development of patterns of emotional response, educational interests, attitudes toward the opposite or the same sex antedate puberty. The ideal status is one in which adequate behavior in response to personal needs merges almost imperceptibly from one period of development into the next.

The adolescent is in need of activities of various kinds [23] to divert him from his introspective tendencies. Some children attempt this through rebellion and asocial activity. In these persons compensatory intellectual [24] and manual activity directed in personally and socially useful channels would be indicated. Educators have long been concerned with this need. The most successful type of education is that which has the development of the person and his life work as its goal. Inspirational teaching is to be avoided. Teaching can be directed toward the exploitation of existing interests and the development of new interests in light of the capacity of the person. This often involves dealing with the interference of parents who attempt to fit children into occupations and careers either below or above their capacity. The results are no better whether the coercion on the part of the parents results from ignorance, sentimental attachment to their own vocation, or personality maladjustment. Education is not only a preparation for adult life; it is an experience in itself. At present, vocational guidance can be given only along general lines.

The social needs of the adolescent must also be considered. This is especially true for the person who tends to withdraw from reality. The adolescent needs encouragement in making social contacts, especially with members of the opposite sex. Environmental situations can be arranged in

[23] Britt, Steuart Henderson, and Janus, Sidney Q., Toward a Social Psychology of Human Play. *J. Social Psychol.* (1941) 13:351–384.

Boynton, Paul L., The Relationship of Hobbies to Personality Characteristics of School Children. *J. Experimental Education* (1940) 8:363–367.

Boynton, Paul L., The Relationship between Children's Tested Intelligence and Their Hobby Participations. *J. Genetic Psychol.* (1941) 58:353–362.

[24] Cutts, Norma E., and Moseley, Nicholas, *Practical School Discipline and Mental Hygiene*, Boston, Houghton Mifflin, 1941 (324 pp.).

vhich the person can meet in a natural way sufficient numbers of the oppo-
ite and same sex of his own age, with diverse interests but similar needs.
)ancing, athletic, social and literary clubs, and innumerable other resources
an be made available for handling this need. Self-control, consideration
nd social adaptation can best be taught on the basis of economics, psy-
hology, and hygiene.

In adolescents the need for sublimation is apparent. The ideal type of
ublimation is that which leads directly into vocational training and into
he life work of the adult. The exact type of activity indicated must depend
pon the specific person, the specific setting, and the problem at hand.[25]
\t present, it would seem wise to emphasize the importance of the emo-
ional needs. The ultimate goal is the adjustment of the person and his
eeds to the social group and its demands. The solution is neither through
cense nor through suppression. Too much guilt makes for neurosis; too
ttle makes for delinquency. The fact that most children attain maturity
nd adulthood successfully does not mean that even they might not have
een spared anxieties, frustrations, disappointments, and guilt feelings.[26]
n the physical, psychological, and psychiatric fields there is still much to
e learned about the adolescent. One can reasonably hope that more accu-
ate knowledge of the behavior of the adolescent will ultimately lead to a
etter personal and social adjustment.

OCIAL AND PSYCHOLOGICAL NEEDS
)F THE AGING *

ROBERT J. HAVIGHURST

n considering the needs of older people it is well, first, to remember that
lder people have the needs that are common to all people, and, second,
hat they have special needs due to the fact that they are old people.

The needs which are common to all people are: (1) emotional security
nd affection, met by receiving love and by living in a world where things
re predictable and come out usually in a favorable or at least tolerable

[25] Williams, Frankwood E., The Importance of Social Relationships in the Develop-
ent of the Personality and Character of the Adolescent. Mental Hygiene (1930)
4:901–906.

[26] Frank, Lawrence K., Freedom for the Personality. Psychiatry (1940) 3:341–349.

* From Robert J. Havighurst, "Social and Psychological Needs of the Aging," Ann.
mer. Acad. pol. soc. Sci., 279, 11–17. Reprinted by permission of the author and the
diter, Annals of the American Academy of Political and Social Science.

way; (2) social recognition and status, met by receiving respect from people who count in one's world; (3) a sense of worth and self-respect, met by living up to one's ideals; (4) adequate food, clothing, shelter, and health.

Whenever these common needs are not met as well as people have grown accustomed to expect, there is a social problem. If we have a social problem of old age today, it is because these needs are not being met adequately in the lives of many older people.

Why are these needs not met as well for older people as they are for middle-aged people in our society? The reasons lie in the fact that both the human body and the human society systematically "insult" the person as he grows older and make it difficult for him to meet his needs.

How Old Age Insults the Person [1]

Loss of physical attractiveness. Most of us, men as well as women, learn to place a high value upon our beauty and our strength. At the very least we value highly our physical and mental vigor, our ability to do a hard day's work. In addition, most of us value our manliness or womanliness—the things that make us attractive to the other sex. Against these values the advancing years wage war. They rob a woman of her ability to have children, usually before she is fifty. Many women interpret this as a sign that they have lost much of their worth as women. Men do not fare much better. Already in the forties most of them lose much of their hair, grow fat in awkward places, and have to wear bifocal glasses. Both sexes lose the smooth skin that they value highly as a sign of youth. Then as the years go on there is a real decrease of enjoyment of the physical aspects of love between the sexes, and finally the external sense organs of hearing and sight begin to lose their acuity.

These insults to the self usually strike us in vulnerable places. We express it by saying that we do not like to grow older—but what we really mean is that we have invested a great deal of emotional capital in our physical attractiveness, and this investment is going bad on us.

Loss of supporting persons. As if this were not enough to do to us, advancing years also rob us of the people who could best reassure us that we are still attractive people, worthy to be loved. Death of husband or wife and loss of old friends, leave us without emotional support just when we most need it.

Loss of status. In spite of inevitable loss of physical attractiveness due to middle age, most of us get along very well with the status and prestige and

---

[1] The writer wishes to acknowledge his indebtedness to Dr. Jack Weinberg for the concept of the insults due to aging. See Weinberg's "Mental Health Needs of the Aged" in *Proceedings of the National Conference of Social Work, 1948* (New York: Columbia University Press, 1949), pp. 403–409.

ower of middle age. At this age we are usually at the peak of our ability
) work, we are as well off financially as we shall ever be. More people look
p to us than ever before. Then we begin to lose these things. Younger
eople come along and take the lead away from us in our social and civic
rganizations. We are no longer in line for promotion in our business. And
he crowning blow of all may come in the form of forced retirement from
ork at a time when we need more than ever to have the assurance that we
ill count for something in the world. In addition, to some people old age
neans economic dependency. They are no longer able to support them-
lves, and must take a status of old-age pensioner which many of them
ave thought to be an unworthy status.

Loss of useful and respected roles. The status-giving roles begin to dis-
ppear. We lose our hold on work, the principal status-giving role for men
i middle age. A woman who has become the mother of an attractive group
f sons and daughters, sees them depart from the home, and one day she
nds that people have forgotten what a fine mother she has been. Leader-
iip roles in civic and political and social life are taken over by younger
eople. There is left the custom of respecting older people for what they
nce were, not for what they are. A few specific roles of older people be-
ome available, and have some value, such as those of grandparent, world
aveler, village sage. But these are usually poor substitutes for the roles we
ave lost.

Lessening of physical health and vigor. When we have asked people in
neir sixties what they feared most about old age, a great many of them
ave said they were afraid their bodies would fail them and they would
ecome helpless. At the very least they must anticipate a decreased physi-
il vigor, but this could be tolerable if it were a slow, predictable change.
Vhat undermines emotional security is the fear that one may suffer a heart
:tack which will leave one an invalid, or that a crippling arthritis may
ome on, or that cancer may develop insidiously.

Developmental Needs of Older People

The aging body conspires with society's youth-favoring attitudes and
ractices to create a set of special needs of older people. Because these
eeds are part of the process of human development, it is well to call them
levelopmental needs" and to regard them in somewhat the same positive
ght with which we regard the developmental needs of youth and middle
lulthood.

These developmental needs pose learning problems that are fully as com-
lex as any problems faced during a lifetime. In fact, later maturity requires
tore learning of most people than they have had to achieve since their
trly adulthood. They meet more new and strange and difficult situations
: older people than they have met as middle-aged people.

Later maturity is, then, a period of learning, rather than a period when learning is past. It is a period of facing new and unsolved problems, rather than a period of floating gently on the surface of familiar solutions to familiar problems. Everybody during the age period from 60 to 75 experiences several of the following developmental needs:

Adjustment to death of spouse. Often in our research we hear a man or woman say, "I hope when my wife (husband) dies I can go too. Life won't be worth while after that." This expresses the fear that a man or woman has, after living forty or fifty years with a marital partner, of having to face life without the partner. A man and wife become so thoroughly wedded that they work out a single life pattern which cannot go on when one of them drops out.

Getting along without one's spouse is usually a woman's task in the United States, because men die younger than women, and women tend to marry older men. The average woman becomes a widow before she is 70. The average man does not lose his wife until he is 85.

If a woman loses her husband, she may have to move from her house to a smaller place, she may have to learn about business matters, and, above all, she has to learn to be alone. A man has the same adjustment to make to loneliness, and he may have to learn to cook, to keep house, and to keep his clothes in order.

The solutions of this task run through the range of living on alone in the old home, moving into a small home, living in a rooming house, moving in with brothers or sisters, living with children, remarrying, going to an old people's home. Every solution requires unlearning of old ways and learning of new ways, at a time when learning comes harder than it did in earlier years.

Adjustment to loss of employment and reduced income. In the American society a job is the axis of life for most men and for many women. If the occupation goes, the individual feels that he does not count, that he is not a worthy member of society. Yet the occupation must be abandoned by the great majority of people, whether they be professional or manual workers, sometime between 60 and 70. Half of American men quit work by the age of 65.

Some people fill up the vacuum created by retirement in their lives with a useful and interesting leisure-time activity; others find a part-time job which keeps them busy and happy; too many fret and mope over their forced inactivity.

When retirement also means a serious reduction in income, another adjustment problem appears—that of reducing expenditures—which often means a narrowing of contacts. For instance, an elderly lady feels that she must drop out of the church ladies' circle because she cannot pay her dues. An old man must drop out of his lodge just at a time when he has increased leisure.

Affiliation with the age group of elders. Try as one may to keep young nd to avoid being classed with the "elders," the day must come to everyone vhen he says to himself, "I'm not as young as I used to be. I'd better *be* ny age." This day is brought on by the fact that the costs of continued articipation in the middle-age group rise more rapidly than the gains. The osts consist of fatigue due to the too rapid tempo of middle life; embarrassment at being unable to keep up, physically and financially and vocaionally, with the middle-age group; and a feeling of being ignored or pushed side by younger people.

Over against these costs are the rewards of participation in the older-age roup, such as a more comfortable tempo of life; ease of finding companionhip among other people who have leisure time; availability of positions of restige and leadership in organizations of older people.

Adjustment to decrease of physical vigor. The human body ages in almost very one of its cells and cellular systems. The cells gradually lose their elf-repairing properties. They slow down in their nutritional processes. The enses lose their acuity. In at least a third of the people, heart disease comes n slowly and cuts down their ability to do hard work. The individual must earn a new way of life that is in harmony with his decreased strength and ealth.

Making satisfactory physical living arrangements. The high incidence of eart disease and "rheumatism" in older people makes physical exertion lifficult or dangerous for many of them, and argues against stair climbing nd heavy housework. There is increasing danger from falls, due to the inreasing brittleness of bones and their slow mending rates. A decreasing bility to masticate foods, with an increasing need for a good diet, makes ood selection and preparation of food necessary. Decreasing metabolic bility of the body makes it difficult for older people to keep warm, and equires good heating facilities.

The principal values that older people look for in housing, according to tudies of this matter, are: quiet, privacy, independence of action, nearness o relatives and friends, residence among own cultural group, cheapness, loseness to transportation lines and communal institutions—libraries, hops, motion pictures, churches, and so forth.

These values vary for different people. Most older people tend to cling o established housing arrangements until they become very unsatisfactory. 'et residential mobility is high, especially among the very old. Thus, living n in the familiar quarters one has known for years is not the most common olution of the problem. The older person has to decide whether to: live n in a large and increasingly burdensome house or find a smaller and more nanageable place; live on alone in the old house after death of the spouse r find smaller and more convenient quarters; live alone or with one or nore other people; stay in the community where he has lived as an adult r move to a place with a better climate.

Group Needs of Older People

If older people are to meet their developmental needs in satisfying ways they must have a certain minimum of help, in the form of attitudes and services, from the community in which they live. As a group, older people have the following needs:

Satisfactory social roles, which bring social recognition and self-respect It lies within the power of the individual to create for himself some of the satisfying social roles, such as those of friend, member of a social clique constructive user of leisure time, informed citizen, active church member and therefore the individual is responsible to that degree for his own happiness. But some significant social roles are denied to many older people by the community. For example, the role of worker may be denied through the practice of arbitrary retirement or prejudice against hiring older workers. Since to most people work has certain personal satisfactions as well as the purely economic meaning, the assurance of economic security does not take the place of the worker's role.

A chance to earn a living, or economic security. Older people need economic security, but under existing conditions relatively few of them can live in reasonable comfort on their own lifetime savings. Hence they need work if they are able to work, or a system of pensions which gives them reasonable economic security.

Social and recreational facilities. Just as the community provides recreational facilities and leadership to meet the needs of youth, so it should meet the needs of older people with analogous facilities through municipal recreation departments, churches, schools, and clubs. At a minimum, the older people require meeting places, equipment for games, leadership for group recreation, and instructions in arts and crafts.

Health services. The one set of eventualities that few older people can prepare for is the chance of ill health with need for expensive services. This need is not met by a comfortable pension or modest savings or the willingness of grown children to help when they have families of their own to support. For older people there should be a guaranteed health service to which they can turn as a matter of right. Whether this is financed through an insurance company or through a public-supported fund is not here an issue.

Ways of Meeting Personal Needs

When the community has done its share toward meeting the needs of older people, the main burden still falls upon the individual himself. He must learn a way of life appropriate to his years and his strength. He must erect his own defenses against the insults of aging.

In general, the individual has a choice of two kinds of defense—the irrational and the rational.

Irrational defenses. If one has great difficulty in meeting one's developmental needs due to the insults and deprivations of aging, one is quite likely to adopt certain defenses which seem to other people to be irrational. There are several types:

MEMORIES AND FANTASIES. Since the present is uncomfortable and the future does not seem to promise much, it is natural for the self to turn to the past and dwell on the pleasures and triumphs of bygone days. Why think about today's fading beauty when one can live over in retrospect the parties and the dances when one was the most beautiful, the most charming of persons? Why worry about the complaints that are being made about one's work today when one can remember the days when one was the most productive and successful of workers? And if the reality of yesterday was not rosy enough, one can add color in one's fantasies. One can imagine that one had a dozen beaux and all handsome and dashing, instead of the one or two plain and conservative boys that came around for Saturday night dates. One can imagine that one had a fine, profitable business and many civic responsibilities, instead of the struggling little shop that was always on the verge of bankruptcy.

REGRESSION TO INFANCY. When the present reality becomes very unpleasant, one can rediscover a long-forgotten solace—that of becoming an infant again. Usually this is outgrown about the age of eight or ten, when a boy or girl becomes independent enough and mature enough to take the bad things of life without crying in mother's lap. Then, fifty or sixty years later, the long-forgotten way of escaping from hard reality may come back to one. As an elderly person one may revert to infantile behavior. One may become dependent for feeding and dressing upon another person. One may go to bed and stay there as much as possible. If one is denied the normal adult sexual outlets, particularly if one is a man, one may revert to infantile sexual behavior.

LOSS OF HEARING, SIGHT, AND MEMORY. Since the present is becoming uncomfortable, one may commence to shut it out by becoming "hard of hearing," "forgetful," and dim-sighted. This is not to say that people do not actually suffer a decrease of hearing and of visual acuity, and brain damage which possibly results in forgetfulness. But the actual biological changes of aging are not always responsible for the changes in older people in the behavior of hearing, seeing, and remembering. Sometimes an older person gets a reputation for being hard of hearing, and people converse in his presence in ordinary tones about things they do not want this person to hear. Just then the elderly person is likely to hear what is being said, and people complain, "He hears what he shouldn't hear." If it is convenient to forget an appointment or to overlook a task one does not wish to do, an older person may forget such things and yet remember events of yesteryear with clear fidelity.

HALLUCINATIONS. Sometimes a woman who has lost her husband or a man who has lost his wife will go on talking to the absent loved one. Why not? It is a pleasure to have someone to talk to. So why not go on talking to the people one loved? If one listens carefully, one may hear them reply; and so a person living alone may converse a great deal with absent persons. Then when someone—a son or daughter—notices this, that person becomes disturbed and goes to a doctor and says: "My old mother (father) is having hallucinations." Yet when a child discovers what we call an imaginary playmate, which often happens with only children or first children, and carries on long conversations with that imaginary person, the parents are often quite proud, and they say, "My, what a good imagination that child has!"

These are some of the irrational but natural defenses that a self may muster to meet the insults of old age. They are not morally wrong, but they are not particularly useful. At best, they tend to be an escape from reality.

Rational defenses. On the other hand, there are some rational, or positive, defenses, which actually make for a happier and more highly approved life.

GOOD CARE OF ONE'S BODY. It is possible for most people to retain a good proportion of their adult vigor and physical attractiveness if they make an effort. A person can see his doctor for a medical examination once or twice a year. He can eat a balanced diet containing adequate amounts of protein and plenty of minerals and vitamins. It seems possible that older people will more and more take medicines of certain hormones, to keep themselves vigorous and alert.

A man as well as a woman can pay attention to grooming. Older people should dress more carefully than younger ones, because they can thereby make better use of their physical attractiveness. There are few women, for example, who do not have the possibility of attractive hair as they grow older. Few men have the advantage of a magnificent head of white or gray hair, but they can dress carefully, select neckties with care, and perhaps add little affectations such as pocket handkerchiefs and gaily colored socks.

NEW FRIENDS. When one's old friends disappear, one can find new ones. One can join new social groups. If husband or wife dies, one can marry again.

INTERESTS IN CIVIC AND COMMUNITY AFFAIRS. Who can make a better citizen, ideally, than a man or woman with time for study of civic problems and for community service, and with the wisdom of maturity? Older persons can read more thoroughly, can explore into complex political and economic problems more clearly, and should vote more intelligently than younger people.

NEW LEISURE-TIME ACTIVITIES AND HOBBIES. When the extra time gained from retirement or reduction of hours at work gives the opportunity, person can do things which he wanted to do during middle age but for which he could not find the time. Travel is one possibility, arts and crafts are another, so are gardening, reading, collecting, and other pursuits.

RELEASE OF ONE'S CHILDREN. Sometime during middle age, parents should let their children free and expect that henceforth their relations will be on the basis of mutual respect and mutual consideration, and no longer on the emotional basis of a dominant parent and a dependent child. Once this has been accomplished, a parent is in a position to make whatever arrangements are appropriate for living with or not living with grown children, for supporting grown children or being supported by them or being financially independent of them. Too many parents go into their later years quite unprepared to meet their grown children on a grown-up basis.

AVOIDANCE OF REMINISCENCE. An insidious habit is that of telling stories about the olden days as a means of "entertaining" younger people. It is so obviously enjoyable to an old-timer to recall and recount events of great importance that occurred before his listeners were born that he must be warned against and almost prohibited from engaging in this pleasant vice. Young people simply are not interested, unless they are very young. A good rule to follow is to tell stories of the past only to people under eight years old or to people one's own age. Another good rule is to listen to other people's reminiscences two hours for every hour one asks them to listen.

Conclusion

The conclusion is inescapable that the individual, if he is to be reasonably happy and secure in his later years, must himself find rational and practicable ways of meeting his needs. No one else can do it for him. One's old age is what one makes it. But in modern America the community must carry the responsibility of creating conditions that make it possible for the great majority of older people to lead the independent and emotionally satisfying lives of which they are capable.

Psychotherapy

The basic goal in the treatment of adjustment difficulties is the alteration of the patient's behavior. The behavior to be changed may involve both the overt actions of the individual, such as his manner of interacting with others, and internal characteristics, such as the individual's self-perception or conflicting attitudes and motives. Numerous methods of effecting changes in behavior are employed in the treatment of adjustment problems. Some of these are chemotherapy (tranquilizing drugs, sedatives, stimulants, etc.), physical therapy (sports, physical exercise, etc.), psychosurgery (lobotomies and various other surgical operations on the brain), and electroshock therapy. The interest here is in the use of psychological approaches to the treatment of adjustment problems and these are called psychotherapy. Because of the wide variety of techniques which are based on the application of psychological principles and which are referred to as psychotherapy, it is extremely difficult to define the term in more than a broad fashion. In general, psychotherapy refers to a controlled interaction between a person seeking psychological assistance and another person who is professionally trained to provide it. The goal is to bring about a more effective adjustment on the part of the individual seeking aid. Usually psychotherapy is associated with talking, since most of the interaction between the persons involved is of a verbal nature. As will be described, however, some psychotherapeutic techniques stress a planned program of physical activity in the context of which the interaction between patient and therapist takes place.

Psychotherapies may be classified in numerous ways. Sometimes the types of therapy are identified on the basis of the theoretical ideas underlying them (psychoanalytic therapy, client-centered therapy, Adlerian therapy); sometimes by the particular group of people or type of problem for which the approach was designed (child guidance therapy, marriage counseling); sometimes by the methods employed (play therapy, dance therapy); and sometimes by the goal which the therapy establishes (supportive therapy, reconstructive therapy). The readings which follow were selected as a sample of the various therapeutic approaches in common use. In addition they illustrate the thinking underlying the three major theoretical approaches which have influenced psychotherapy the most: psychoanalysis, phenomenological theory or client-centered therapy, and learning theory.

The first paper by Axline presents one approach to psychotherapy with children. The focus here is on the play activities of the child, and the interaction between child and therapist which is portrayed is consistent with the general point of view of Rogers and the client-centered group. The therapist attempts to establish a warm, permissive atmosphere wherein the child feels free to examine his feelings, motivations, and desires without the fear of rejection and hostility from the therapist. With patience and understanding the therapist reflects back to the child the feelings which the child expresses and, through this process, hopes to help the child develop a more positive set of attitudes toward himself and toward others.

The next paper illustrates another approach which is based on a theoretical position concerning the development of personality characteristics. Meyer utilizes one of the major principles of learning theory—primary stimulus generalization—in designing therapeutic techniques which he uses in treating two phobic patients. His paper is of particular interest because it attempts to test the fruitfulness and effectiveness of using concepts and procedures which have been largely derived from experimental work with animals in altering complex human behavior.

Durkin's paper was chosen to provide an illustration of both group psychotherapy and the application of psychoanalysis to a treatment situation. The practice of group psychotherapy, wherein one therapist interacts with a number of patients at the same time, initially became popular because of the limited number of therapists available and the costliness of individual therapy. Since the Second World War, however, many of the special attributes of this procedure have been recognized. These attributes include the experiences the group situation provides the individual in social interaction, the opportunity to compare one's own problems with those of others, the development of supportive and constructive relationships, etc. The reader will note that Durkin utilized a psychoanalytic orientation in conceptualizing her patients' problems and the interactions occurring between the group members.

The three preceding papers described therapeutic efforts which take place in a relatively controlled environment. The time, place, and purpose are stipulated and the therapeutic experience itself is divorced from the ordinary activities of the everyday life of the patients. Another approach to altering behavior is called milieu therapy. The paper by Goldsmith, Schulman, and Grossbard gives an account of a treatment setting in which the resources of the total environment are integrated into the therapeutic program for the patient. The ordinary life events of the patients are consciously and deliberately manipulated to help them effect a better adjustment. The paper reports on some experiences using milieu therapy with disturbed children. There is growing utilization of this procedure in hospitals, schools for the retarded, foster homes, prisons, and recreational and work camps.

Considering the variety of techniques and approaches of psychological treatments in use, it is reasonable to inquire about the general effectiveness of psychotherapy in producing desired behavioral change. Bindra considers the difficulties which inhere in efforts to demonstrate the effects of psychotherapy. He suggests that evidence for the success of psychotherapy with neuroses has not yet been demonstrated and offers an orientation toward research which might be fruitful.

PLAY THERAPY *

(Virginia M. Axline

What do we mean by "play therapy"? It is just another play experience for the child? Or is it something uniquely different? And if it is different why is that so? What happens to the child as a possible result of the play therapy experience? In other words what are the dynamics of play therapy? And what are the implications of it?

Let us take a brief excerpt from a play therapy experience. Mary Ann is four and a half. This is the second time she has been in the playroom with the therapist. For the first half of the period she has been playing with the sand and the water. She has been as she states it "cooking soup and birthday cakes." She chatters as she plays. Anything she says is accepted. She talks sense and nonsense. She laughs and she pouts and she is very serious and she jokes. She keeps a wary eye on the therapist and

* From Virginia M. Axline, "Some Observations on Play Therapy," *J. consult Psychol.*, 12, 209–216. Reprinted by permission of the author and the Managing Editor, the American Psychological Association.

without comment seems to be summing up the situation and the relationship as she feels her way along. Then she decides to paint. She looks at the paints on the easel. She looks at the therapist. "I shall paint," she announces. The therapist accepts this new interest of Mary Ann's—asks, "The easel paints or the finger paints?" thus pointing out the other kind of paint she had not recognized. Mary Ann points expansively to the jar of yellow finger paint. "That kind!" she announces decisively. "All right," the therapist says. "I'll show you how they are used." She wets the special finger-painting paper and places it on the table. Mary Ann sits down eagerly. The therapist spoons out some paint. "Where do you want it?" she asks—indicating *where?* on the paper. Mary Ann points to a spot in the middle. "There!" she says. The therapist places it on the designated spot and says "When you want some more tell me." "Okay!" says Mary Ann. She touches the blob of paint with the tip of her finger. She laughs. Then she puts in two fingers and three and four and then her hand—then the other hand, then her arms, then she squeezes it through her hands and rubs it over her hands and arms.

All this time her expression changes from curiosity, to wonderment, to cautious experimentation, to enjoyment, to abandonment. She laughs. She talks about what she is doing. She indicates when she wants more paint. She says she'll put it on her face—she'll become "a dirty little girl." She dabs her face gingerly. Then she rubs it on, laughing. Then she declares that she will show her mother that she is a *dirty* little girl. The therapist accepts every thing she says and does. Then Mary Ann decides when the time is up that she will wash off her hands—then her arms and just leave it on her face to show her mother what a dirty little girl she is. But the last minute, before she leave the room she climbs up to the sink again and asks the therapist to take it off her face, too. She'll go out and be "a clean girl for mommy."

When she meets her mother she says cautiously, "I painted!" "You did?" replies her mother. "Did you have a good time?" "Yes," Mary Ann says. "Could I see what you painted?" her mother asks. "Yes," Mary Ann replies leading her mother back to the playroom. "I got some on me," Mary Ann says then adds very quickly, "but I took it off. I'm *clean* girl now." "I see," her mother says. "You got it on yourself, but you washed it off." "Umhm," says Mary Ann and grins at the therapist.

Mary Ann had had a very happy time in the playroom; but when her mother asks her if she wants to stay on in the playroom alone while she talks to the therapist, Mary Ann says "No." She had seen a playground nearby and wants to go there. Although she likes the playroom very much when the therapist is in there with her and talks about coming each time and talks about what fun it was each week after she leaves she doesn't want to stay in there alone. Now why? Is it because she prefers the company of other children? Sometimes she is alone on the playground. And she does not express the choice of the playground on her way *to* the play-room. What is it about the play therapy experience that makes it a signifi-cant experience for the child? What happens, psychologically, that brings about the changes we can observe? What are these changes?

In this brief excerpt we can see the fluctuating attitudes. The desire to be "a dirty little girl" which was carried out in the playroom. The expressed desire to go out and show mother "a dirty little girl," the gradual dissipa-tion of the desire, the cautious sharing of this experience with the mother, the grin in the therapist's direction that seemed to convey the attitude "You know *me*," with an absence of any concern about how it had been accepted by the therapist—a feeling of self-freedom.

Does this seem to imply that Mary Ann was experiencing her real self more completely in the playroom and perhaps learning to know herself a little better? Was she differentiating between "This is what I *like* to do" and "This is what I think I'm *expected* to do"?

If we take a completely recorded series of play therapy contacts we can see a pattern in them—a decrease of negative feelings and an increase of positive feelings towards the self and toward others. We can see the child emerge from restriction of his behavior to more relaxed spontaneous be-havior. We can see the child leave one track and become a more complete individual and this occurs in a very interesting manner.

Take seven-year-old Joey for example. His play was all hostile aggression —enemies, spies, the powerful giant, the unknown—treachery that sneaked up on him. Did his play indicate that he felt insecure? that he could not trust people? that he could not cope with the situation because he didn't understand himself and his world?

He was referred for play therapy because he seemed to be "a very dis-turbed child." Reports from his teachers, his mother, and the psychologist who gave him the Rorschach and the TAT all contributed evidence that he was seriously disturbed. Although he seemed very intelligent he was not doing satisfactory school work. He would not associate with other children. At school and at home he stood apart from the others and stared at them through half-closed glazed eyes that they all said "glittered with hatred." It was there in the playroom, too. The play was intense at the beginning of the series,—hostile, hateful, full of destructive impulses—full of in-security—full of defensiveness.

Joey came in once a week for a 45 minute period. It was interesting to note the stiffness of his walk, the mechanical jerkiness of his motions, the detached glance toward the therapist—remote—intangible—cold—and the gradual disappearance of this kind of behavior as the weeks went by.

"We will have another fight," he would announce during the first few contacts. "There will be killing and murder." And there was—very em-phatic repeated attacks upon his victims because he wanted to be sure they died.

Then there was a noticeable let down of tensions when the therapist would announce the time was up. He would discuss with her his current plans—or references to his home situation—such as "I have *lots* of toys at home. Mother says we should *be very grateful* for all the things she does for us," and "I like it on Sundays. We go away—out to the Dunes. And there are caves there and I have secret hiding places. Nobody knows about them but me. And I can get away from my mother there," and again, "There is no doubt about it. Mother is the *boss* in *our* house," and "The thing I liked best that I got for my birthday was a light for my new bicycle. I like it best—but mother says it isn't any good. She says it was a foolish thing to give a seven-year-old boy because I couldn't ever go out riding my bicycle at night. But I *like* it better than anything I ever got." (Incidentally, "Mother" had given him the bicycle for his birthday.)

The hostility begins to wane. The glazed look disappears in the playroom, in the schoolroom, at home. The violent temper tantrums disappear at home. He seems more relaxed and happier and a sense of humor creeps into his play and his conversation. In the playroom his facial expression is quite happy. His eyes twinkle when he looks at the therapist. He moves away from the soldiers and the battle ground a bit. He asks if he can bring his younger sister.

This hostile, aggressive, tense behavior had been typical of Joey for over a year. What changed it during the eight play therapy contacts? His mother reports that he is much happier at home, that he is gaining weight, that he eats better, that he is much less tense and aggressive, that his reading is improving. What has happened to Joey?

What Are the Dynamics of Therapy?

What are the dynamics of play therapy? That is a question that we are interested in answering at least partially. We do not have the answer. All we have are the verbatim records of play therapy cases, concomitant reports from parents, schools, and in some cases physicians, and follow up studies to determine how lasting and effective are the changes in behavior that seem to be brought about by the play therapy experiences. We can only take this material, study it and formulate hypotheses for further testing and examination.

Let us look at a sample case.

Billy was five years old. He was attending kindergarten and was threatened with expulsion when he was referred for play therapy. His behavior was described as follows: Billy is very odd. He has nothing to do with other children. He will not talk to any one. He crawls around the room on his hands and knees—close to the wall. When another child comes close to him he hides his face in his arms and rolls up in a ball. He never participates in any of the school activities. He cannot listen to a story. The only directions he follows are the ones "Time to go for recess" and "Time to go home." Billy was not like this when he entered kindergarten six months ago. He had very little to offer then, but he did speak occasionally and he did not crawl around like a baby. This extreme regressive behavior has been in operation for several weeks. Last week the school gave him a Stanford-Binet test. This was his second test during the time he has been in this school. Results on the first test were 65. Results on the second test were 68.

The mother came in for a preliminary interview. She expressed her concern about Billy's behavior and her fear that he might be mentally defective. She cited evidence that indicated to her that he was of normal intelligence and evidence that indicated to her that he was feebleminded. She said that until he was three years old he had shown signs of being normal—that he had developed slowly but steadily. Then when he was three years old he had suddenly stopped talking, stopped walking, had regressed completely to an infantile stage—wouldn't play with any other child. She broke down and cried—said she had taken him to a doctor and had been told that the child was feebleminded, but that she would not and could not accept it. She said she was determined to prove the doctor was wrong and had devoted all the time she had to Billy—and worked and played with him by the hour. Gradually he picked up again—talked, walked, ate better, seemed all right. At three she had been able "to teach him his colors, his alphabet, how to work puzzles, how to cut out pictures and paste them, how to count to twenty, how to print his name." She had *proved* that he was all right! It had been a nerve-wracking experience for just before he had stopped talking and regressed so suddenly she had been taken to the hospital for an emergency operation and had been quite ill. Then when she had come back home and found that Billy had become like he was—she had thought it was some brain disease. She had been panicky. Once again she broke down and wept bitter tears and explained between her sobs that she had a brother who was feebleminded and she was afraid Billy had inherited it! It was a tragic story. The mother was in complete conflict about Billy. She firmly believed he was all right. She firmly believed that the tests were correct. She could not accept either part of her ambivalence completely.

It was decided that a series of play therapy contacts would be undertaken on a tentative basis to determine whether or not it seemed helpful. The physician's examination gave him a clear bill of health. The psychometrician's report at the University gave him an I.Q. of 68.

Then Billy came in—blank stare, drooping figure, dragging shuffling gate. He went back to the playroom, stood in the middle of the room and looked straight ahead. The therapist explained to him that he might play with any of the toys in the room if he wanted to. Then the therapist sat down by the sandbox and let Billy go on from there. He stood there for a long ime. Finally he dropped down on his knees beside the sandbox and lifted the sand through his hands. That was all he did during the 45 minute period. When time was up he dragged out after the therapist. The second week he seemed more alert as he walked back to the playroom. He knelt down beside the sand and played in the sand again—then selected one of the little cars and pushed it around. He looked more often at the therapist but said nothing. During the third contact he played with the cars and the sand, made a few comments about what he was doing. The therapist replied each time he spoke. He seemed much more alert. When he came in for a fourth contact there was a decided change in his appearance, walk and behavior. He no longer dragged his feet. His eyes were more alert. He talked more to the therapist. His mother said there was a noticeable change at home. He was talking more, seemed less tense—the regressive behavior was disappearing. During the fifth week the school principal called the mother and asked her what was happening to Billy. He was behaving differently—still not joining in group activities and not doing any of his "kindergarten work" but walking around, talking a little, seeming happier, and occasionally speaking to some one else. The teacher reported to the mother that he was listening to stories now, or at least to part of the stories.

The sixth, seventh, eighth, ninth, tenth week came and went and Billy's behavior continued to improve. He talked more and more to the therapist. His play became more complex and imaginative. He interrupted it quite often to jump around the room, fling his arms wide and call out quite happily that "This is fun!" Any casual observer could now notice marked changes in Billy. He was bright-looking, walked with a quick firm step, talked freely in the waiting room, played happily and constructively in the playroom. The mother was quite pleased with the changes in him. She reported some interesting observations. She remarked at one time that the father said he could always tell when Billy had been to the clinic because he was so much more spontaneous in his behavior, that he was so much more interested in things, seemed sharper and more observing, seemed so much happier and even his gestures and physical behavior were free and easy. At this time they took Billy out west to visit his grandmother. His mother said she had purposely not mentioned the fact that he had been receiving any kind of treatment because she wanted to see if the grandmother would notice any changes in Billy since the six months had elapsed since she had seen him. The mother reported later that the grandmother had immediately noticed big changes in Billy and had remarked about it. The school became sufficiently curious to give him another Binet. He received a score of 96 on that test.

The mother also reported these differences in his behavior—more self-assertion at home—more rejection of help—more show of temper—a stubborn streak if anyone tried to show him how he should do something—wanting to do things *his* way. Not staying so close to her—going out and edging up to the other children in the neighborhood—"But," the mother said, "the teacher has given Billy such a bad reputation and has said so many times to the other children 'Billy can't do things like other children so let him alone'—that the other children call him 'Silly-Billy' and 'Dummy' and 'Crazy-Like-A-Fox.'" She said when they did that it hurt his feelings and he came in and seemed unhappy.

She also reported at one time during the therapy that Billy had suddenly become quite impatient if things didn't go together just right and would cry out for help and demand that they do something. This shortness of patience and temper over his inability to construct something was a new type of behavior and she wondered about this display of frustration and irritability. The therapist also wondered about it because it coincided exactly with a period of three weeks when in the playroom he was trying to build a bridge across the sandbox with an odd assortment of blocks and was having considerable difficulty in engineering this structure so that it would have firmness and balance enough to run cars over. He had an uncanny eye for space factors and would look at it and level it off with amazing ingenuity. The child would spend the entire 45-minute period working over this complex structure, week after week. Why, then, was he so short-tempered at home during this time? Why did he express quick frustration when things did not go just right? Why did he not try at home to work things out as he did in the playroom? The fourth week of the bridge construction saw its completion. He had solved the problem—could run cars across it without knocking it down—and he viewed his achievement with a great deal of delight and satisfaction. The mother reported a sudden disappearance of the impatience and frustration at home. The therapist—interested in a study of concomitant behavior of the child at home while under therapy—asked the mother if she would make some notes about Billy's behavior each week and bring them in. The mother agreed. The next week she said she didn't have it ready. The second week she said, "Here it is!—But I don't think it's much help. I wrote down—not how Billy is changing, but how *my attitude toward him* is changing and how *that* seems to be influencing him. When I studied him to write down my report I tried to figure out what he had in mind, how things really looked to him. And I gave up. I could only write down how I felt." That in itself seems to be a valuable little document. Later on in the therapy it was decided to finish off the treatment with a series of group therapy experiences. The first time a little five-year-old girl was added. Billy accepted her quite graciously. They sized up one another and in a few minutes were playing together and soon talking together.

This gives an example of observable results of a therapeutic experience. It is not a rare example. It is rather typical of the changes that occur during therapy. The follow-up studies indicate that the child not only maintains the gains, but continues on to more and more mature behavior in keeping with his age.

What, now, seems to be the dynamics of this situation? What seems to have happened to Billy? In contrast to the case of Joey there was very little emotional release play. Occasionally "something happened to the school bus" or "something happened to the doll family," but it was always gently done and with a sense of humor.

What, in this particular case, seems to have changed? There have been physical changes. He has gained weight, sleeps better, has a good appetite. He looks more alert, smiles more often, moves with more freedom and spontaneity, walks with more decision. His behavior has changed. He has taken more initiative, is more independent, is happier, talks quite freely, is beginning to edge-up to groups and to participate a bit in group activities. He is "harder to manage" because is not so readily pushed around. His play is becoming more imaginative and he laughs freely and seems to enjoy himself.

Has his attitude toward himself changed? The answer seems to be "Yes." He has more confidence in himself, draws upon the resources within himself. He seems to feel more adequate to cope with the situations he meets —at least he is willing to try. He *wants* to do things for himself now. He wants to go out on his own.

Would we seem to be justified in saying that there is obvious emotional relaxation, a new feeling of security within himself, an achievement of psychological independence, and increased use of the capacities within him, and a belief in that capacity to help the self? And if this is so, what brought it about? The change is the mother's attitude toward the child? The experience of learning to know himself and of gaining a belief in his ability to cope with his life situations by experiencing such complete acceptance and freedom to do it his own way that he grew in self-confidence? Do we know, from the material that has been presented here what has caused the difficulty? Does that seem to be necessary?

It is interesting to notice that in this kind of therapy only the present attitudes and feelings and behavior are utilized.

There is no going back into causes. It is definitely working with the present organization of the child's personality and going on from there.

Does play therapy increase the child's feeling of adequacy to cope with increased self-understanding? Do we have sufficient evidence to pose this hypothesis: *The child behaves as he perceives himself in relation to others, and dependent upon his present feelings of adequacy to cope with the situation?*

It seems to me that the child's perception is based upon his past and present experiences and upon his present feelings of adequacy or inadequacy to cope with the situation. His emotional reaction seems to be the expressive measurement of the degree of deviation between his feelings of ability to cope adequately and a realistic perception of himself and the factors in his environment. Therefore, it seems important to try to perceive things as the child perceives them.

Perhaps the play therapy experience frees the child from the chains of the past experiences and gives him a safety zone in which he can operate. Perhaps it prevents rigid "attitudinal habits" from forming and creates an attitude of "adjustability" rather than a feeling of "adjustment."

Perhaps this type of treatment conveys to the child in a way that he understands that whatever comes out is *him*—as he sees it—and avoids the confusion caused by mixing the way things appear to him and the perceptions of others. Perhaps that is a necessary part of the treatment—and once he gets himself lined up, then he can be free to see how things look to others.

Various types of treatment are effective. It seems important, in order to further our study of the personality and of behavior, to find out *why different* types of treatment are effective—to seek some common element in all therapies. And again we ask: Is behavior caused by the way the individual perceives himself in relation to others, and dependent upon his feelings of adequacy to cope with the situation? If the individual learns to know himself does that bring about the feeling of security within himself? Does knowing the self better bring about a feeling of self-adequacy? Could this be the element that is common to all therapies?

It is a real challenge to examine closely the rich verbatim material that comes spontaneously from the clients—to observe the behavior as objectively as possible—to follow up the cases from every possible angle—to try and discover more about human behavior.

The research that is done in this field is important and the implications are far reaching. It is very important that we keep an open and scientific attitude toward our studies and eliminate any defensiveness or restrictiveness in the work we do.

In all probability we will be asking ourselves for a long time to come, what are the dynamics of therapy? and of human behavior? And how can our findings be utilized constructively in our educational procedures and in bringing about more adequate solutions to social problems?

It is enough of a job to keep us busy for a long time to come—hoping that some day we can answer little seven year old Jacky's question, "What *is* it? What *is* it? In here I just spill out all over myself." He plunges his arms down deep in the sand, looks up at the therapist with a grin. He reaches over to a nearby table and runs his hand through the thick oozy black finger paint with which he has been working. It is still wet and he smears it on his face and rubs his face down in the white sand and it sticks to his face. He casts an oblique look at the therapist. He smiles quite happily and stretches out full length in the sand.

"You sure ain't no don't person," he observes with a sigh. And he can relax and be himself as long as he is in the playroom.

Billy, One Year Later

One year after the termination of Billy's play therapy experience, he and his mother returned for a follow-up interview with the therapist. Billy recognized the therapist, smiled, spoke to her, called her by name. "I wanted to come back and see you once more," he said. He skipped down the hall to the playroom, stopped just inside the door and looked all around the room with a big smile on his face. "Same place," he said. "Same room, same toys, same us." He ran across the room and opened the cupboard doors. He laughed. He ran back to the sandbox and stood there looking at it with a grin on his face. "Well!" he exclaimed. He turned and looked at the therapist. "You know I thought these walls were so much higher than they really are—I didn't think then I could ever reach the top. I didn't think *anybody* could. Now, I think even I could—with a ladder." He knelt down and looked at the sandbox. "Last time when I came here," he said, "I remember I tried and tried to build a bridge across that box." He sighed. "Now I wouldn't try to build a bridge out of things that weren't meant to build bridges with." He ran over to the doll house—selected the removable front and quickly spanned the sandbox. "See?" he said, "See how I'd do it now? And now cars can run across it, too." He ran a little car across the bridge. It "fell off." "Down into the waters," he cried. "It fell off. Something happened to it. *I* pushed it in." He picked up one of the wooden dolls and walked it across the bridge, "accidentally" knocked it in, picked it out and then hit it with his fist and knocked it in the water. "I *knocked* him in myself," he said. "If I feel like it, I'll knock him in. He just won't fall!"

These are just a few of the incidents that occurred during the follow-up interview. Do they seem to throw any additional light on the significance of a play therapy experience for a child?

The mother reports an excellent adjustment to a new school situation where there were 48 children in the first grade. She reported that he had learned to read and write and count as well as the best children in the group. She said he was a happy, relaxed child—still a little shy in a large group, but expressing himself quite vividly and spontaneously. The Binet I.Q. at the end of the year and at the time of the follow-up was 105.

AN APPLICATION OF LEARNING PRINCIPLES

TO PSYCHOLOGICAL TREATMENT *

⟨ Victor Meyer [1]

This paper is presented as an illustration of the possibility of applying experimental method and some of the principles available in psychological theories of learning to the treatment of psychiatric symptoms. As such, it is somewhat similar to an earlier study by Jones (7). It differs from the latter, however, in that it demonstrates the importance of individual differences in personality structure and the manner in which such differences dictate modifications of therapeutic techniques.

The treatments to be described were based mainly on the principle of primary stimulus generalisation (5). According to this principle, a conditioned reaction is not only evoked by the original conditioned stimulus but also, to some degree, by a series of stimuli more or less similar to the original one. The more dissimilar the new stimulus, the less intense is the conditioned reaction.

Many phobic patients display anxiety so intense when presented with certain environmental situations that they are not amenable to any therapeutic approach. However, the generalisation principle suggests that the presentation of an environmental situation which resembles the original one but evokes a reduced amount of anxiety can be exploited therapeutically. In such a situation, one can attempt to substitute an adaptive normal reaction for the original unadaptive anxiety response. A graded continuum of similar situations can then be employed, moving towards the original one, so that the original unadaptive response can be eliminated. This is essentially one of the methods advocated by Jersild and Holmes (6) for the treatment of children's fear, and its theoretical basis has been elaborated by such writers as Guthrie (4) and Wolpe (8). The latter, among others, has demonstrated the usefulness of these techniques in experiments

* From Victor Meyer, "Case Report: The Treatment of Two Phobic Patients on the Basis of Learning Principles," *J. abnorm. soc. Psychol.*, 55, 261–267. Reprinted by permission of the author and the Managing Editor, the American Psychological Association.

[1] Thanks are due Dr. D. Hill, Dr. D. A. Pond, and Dr. J. D. Dewsbery, consultants to the Bethlem Royal and Maudsley Hospitals, for their permission, encouragement, and assistance in carrying out the treatment. A debt is also acknowledged to Dr. M. B. Shapiro, Mr. H. Gwynne Jones, and Mr. J. Inglis for offering valuable suggestions.

on animals and has applied them successfully in the treatment of a series of psychiatric patients (9).

Summary of Case Histories

For the purposes of this paper, a complete case history of each patient is not essential. A brief summary of the psychiatric notes will suffice.

Case 1. The patient, a married woman of 48 years, was admitted to the hospital for investigation of suspected temporal lobe epilepsy. Apart from blackouts, she complained of an excessive fear of going out.

No family history of psychiatric disorder or epilepsy was reported. The birth and developmental milestones seemed normal. She left school at the age of 15 and had a successful work history up to the time of her illness. Her marriage was fairly satisfactory, but there were no children. Before her illness, she was described as quick-tempered but a good mixer, cheerful, hardworking, and conscientious.

Her blackouts started at the age of 28 during pregnancy. Since then, she had suffered 18 blackouts. They all followed physical exertion or emotional upset and were usually preceded by an aura of dull sensation in the chest. She usually lost consciousness, fell limp, and hurt herself on several occasions. On recovery she vomited and felt "horrible."

At the age of 44 she began having peculiar "feelings." These consisted of epigastric sensations, followed by a "horrible" sensation of being about to fall. These episodes occurred frequently when she was about to go out or when she was outside on her own. Occasionally, when she was unable to control these feelings, she tended to panic and then to suffer one of her blackouts.

As a result of these symptoms, she developed a strong fear of going out on her own, of traveling on public conveyances and of having sexual intercourse for fear of an attack. From the age of 46 she refused to go out unaccompanied. Shortly before the admission to the hospital, she was occasionally unable to go out with friends or even with her husband. She gradually became more and more anxious, depressed (entertaining suicidal thoughts), and fearful. Losing confidence, she resigned from a responsible job and stopped caring for her home. She continued working until admission, but needed to be accompanied all the way to and from work. On admission she was pleasant, sociable, cooperative, rational, and well oriented.

The results of all investigations were negative with respect to temporal lobe epilepsy. Except for some mild abnormalities shown on the air-encephalogram, all the tests contraindicated organic involvement. In view of the possibility that the attacks might be of cardiac origin, she was referred to cardiologist. He could find no abnormalities in the cardiovascular system.

The patient was diagnosed as exhibiting a phobic state with blackouts of unknown nature and was referred to the Psychology Department for the symptomatic treatment of her phobias.

Case 2. A man of 42 years was admitted to the hospital for investigation of blackouts. He also suffered from excessive tension and various fears mainly related to entering enclosed and crowded spaces.

Two instances of psychiatric disorder were reported in the family history: His mother had a "nervous breakdown," and his elder brother experienced difficulty in going out alone. The patient's early development and childhood seemed normal. He left school at the age of 14 and worked successfully as a precision grinder. He had been happily married and had two children. Before his illness he was described as undemonstrative and timid, but affectionate as a father and husband.

At the age of 22 he had several fainting attacks on parades when serving in the armed forces. Following these, he developed episodes of apprehension which usually occurred in crowded places. He felt tense, flustered and experienced an urge to run away in a panic. Strange or crowded places and feelings of boredom were associated with the onset of these episodes. The presence of a friend and strong interest tended to prevent their development. Up to the age of 38, he could preserve control and avert panic. After that time, control became more tenuous. On four occasions episodes of panic terminated in fainting attacks. As a result, he became worried about himself and sharply curtailed his social activities. Shortly before admission to the hospital, he had a feeling of apprehension in a barber's shop, panicked, mounted his bicycle and shortly afterwards collapsed. After this accident he refused to ride the bicycle and would not go out. He became anxious, tense, and depressed.

He was treated by his own physician with phenobarbitone with very little success. On examination for possible temporal lobe epilepsy, the results were negative. When admitted to the hospital, he appeared very tense and anxious, but rational, well oriented, and cooperative. He was reluctant to talk about himself and needed much encouragement.

Like the first case, he was referred to the Psychology Department for symptomatic treatment of a phobic state.

Treatment

Case 1. The patient was interviewed twice with the aim of getting detailed information about her phobic symptoms. The rationale of the treatment was then explained and discussed with her. During this time the experimenter (E) endeavored to establish good rapport. According to the theory outlined, this is essential since E becomes part of the various environmental situations during treatment and, by establishing an effective relationship, he becomes a reassuring stimulus, tending to reduce anxiety.

No exact record of each treatment session was kept and, therefore, some of the description lacks precision. Since the most likely place for the abnormal behavior to occur was a door leading to the "outside" and the "outside" itself, the hospital roof garden, which has walls but no ceiling, was selected as a starting point for treatment. On the first occasion, the subject (S) entered the garden with E. She only reported mild "thumping in the stomach" throughout this session. Next day she reported feeling perfectly well and volunteered to enter the garden on her own. When she had gone twice on her own without any signs of the symptoms recurring, the place of treatment was changed to the main hospital garden. She went out several times with E on successive days, then was required to go out on her own to meet E, and then to seek and find him. Since S appeared rather dependent on E's presence, other staff members of the ward were asked to participate in the treatment without S's knowledge of prearrangement by E. She went out with various nurses and patients for walks in the garden. Similar expeditions took place during the evening. Not more than two sessions (30 minutes each) were given each day. When asked to go into the garden on her own, she did without any difficulty. From that point, she was encouraged to take frequent walks into the garden during the daytime and the evenings.

The next stage consisted of E's taking walks with the patient outside the hospital grounds. These started in back streets and were gradually extended into the main street; the distance covered increased gradually day by day. She also went out with other people. Eventually, she was able to set out on her own to meet E and others outside. She was taken out at least three times when feeling "upset." She took four bus rides accompanied by E and frequently volunteered to go shopping with other patients. After two weeks (16 sessions) of this treatment, she was able to make short expeditions on her own without difficulty.

She spent the subsequent 16 days going for walks with E and other people and on her own. Short trips on buses were included, and at least three times she went out on her own in the evening. She spent three weekends at home but was instructed to go out on her own only if she felt confident. She managed to take three short walks near her house. On the last day of treatment she traveled some three miles away from the hospital and back. During the whole treatment, she never reported any symptoms except occasional mild thumping in the stomach. Her behavior on the ward improved. According to the psychiatrist in charge and the nursing staff, she had very few "upsets" and was more cheerful. She felt confident and eager to be discharged.

The treatment took about five weeks, and the patient claimed to have enjoyed it. When she was discharged, her relatives and friends were told that she should be encouraged to go out on her own provided she felt confident and not upset. It was planned that she should be seen once every two weeks in the outpatient department for follow-up purposes and, if necessary, to modify management.

FOLLOW-UP. For nearly five months the patient worked regularly and was unaccompanied when visiting the hospital. She took occasional solitary walks and was able to do her shopping. Each working day she was met at the station by a friend who traveled with her to the factory; on the return journey she was met by her husband. She managed to get to the station on her own, and on two occasions when the friend failed to meet her, she experienced no difficulties. A month after discharge from the hospital, she developed an acute chest pain for which she was treated by her doctor. Also, while on a bus with some friends, she had one of her blackouts without any warning and was unconscious for about 45 minutes. Despite these difficulties and worries, she continued to work and to go out on her own. At the end of the fourth month, she increased the frequency of her un-accompanied expeditions, and for the first time in two years attended ade-quately to her housework. She also went to work on her own seven times in succession when her friend was on vacation. She reported occasional feelings of anxiety, but she never panicked and was able to ward off the attacks by thinking about treatment and handling a mascot (a piece of candy) which she kept throughout the treatment. The last time she was seen, she felt cheerful, confident about going out on her own, and practi-cally cured of "unreasonable fears."

Three days after the last interview, the patient died following one of her sudden blackouts when travelling with friends. The cause of her death was attributed to left ventricular failure; postmortem examination demonstrated heart disease.

Case 2. Two extensive interviews with this patient indicated that his anxiety was not associated with any specific stimulus but was more gen-eralised and might depend on a variety of factors. For this reason, a modified technique was adopted, aimed at enabling S, by a process of conditioning, to cope efficiently with his anxiety no matter where it arose. First, a course of systematic desensitisation was given, based on Wolpe's (9) relaxation techniques. This form of treatment failed, since the patient reported that he could not evoke any increased anxiety by thinking about stressful situ-ations. He remained tense and anxious throughout the sessions, but re-ported no changes in feeling; GSRs similarly indicated no disturbances.

The conditioning of anxiety-relief responses was then attempted by means of a technique similar to that described by Wolpe (9). An induc-torium with a maximum inflow of 6 volts was applied to two fingers; the strength of the current was controlled by turning a knob. The patient was told to say aloud "calm yourself" when the shock became unbearable. As soon as the patient said this, E switched off the current. Wolpe has re-ported that many of his patients experienced relief from anxiety in disturb-ng situations when they used these words associated with the release from hock-induced tension.

Since it appeared that S was most likely to manifest his symptoms in a rowded cinema, it was decided to initiate a procedure similar to that used vith the first patient. It was planned to visit the local cinema at a time vhen it was usually relatively empty and then gradually delay visits, going ater and later each day until eventually the visit would be made at a time vhen the cinema is commonly quite full. The effect of boredom was also aken into account since the patient saw at least part of the same picture ach day. During the first week, the patient received 5 or 6 electrical con- litioning trials immediately before visiting the cinema with E. After some hirty to forty minutes, both S and E returned to the hospital, where 5 or 6 urther conditioning trials were given.

After seven days of this treatment, there was no change in S's behavior.)uring most of the visits to the cinema, he reported feelings of tension and n urge to leave. Following a weekend at home, he said that he still felt lepressed, anxious, and tense, and although the "calm yourself" technique lelped him slightly, he considered that he was generally unimproved by he treatment.

In every respect, the patient's reactions to the treatment differed from hose manifested by Case 1. Whereas Case 1 reacted very quickly to the reatment and a good rapport was easily established, Case 2 remained aloof nd detached.

At this stage, Case 2 was reconsidered. A plausible hypothesis was de- ived from Franks's study (2) concerning the conditionability of extraverts nd introverts and from Eysenck's theory of anxiety and hysteria (1). From hese ideas, it seemed to follow that Case 1 would condition better and xtinguish less rapidly than Case 2. Similarly, both cases should be more leurotic than average, and Case 1 should be more introverted than Case 2. These inferences were supported by the patient's scores on Franks's eye- link conditionability measure and on the Maudsley Personality Inventory.)n the theory [2] that inhibitory drugs decrease conditionability and heighten atiation effects, Case 2 was given 10 milligrams of dexedrine (excitant) for our days. As soon as the effects of the drug became apparent, he was sub- nitted each day to the same treatment procedure as during the previous veek.

Throughout this second stage of treatment, the patient felt cheerful and elaxed and enjoyed going to the cinema. At no time did he display any ymptoms. On the second day, he was left alone in the cinema. On the last lay, he managed to stay alone in a crowded cinema without any difficulty.

[2] There is some evidence to support this theoretical position. Unpublished studies t Maudsley Hospital on amobarbital sodium and dexamphetamine sulfate by Franks and Trouton, and on arecoline and methyl atropine by Franks, Laverly, and Trouton have ielded results consistent with the notions applied therapeutically in the present study.

During the following weekend he went home but took 10 milligrams of dexedrine each day. He traveled alone on buses, rode his bicycle, and went to a cinema with his wife. He reported no feelings of disturbance. On his return from the weekend, the dosage of dexedrine was reduced by 2.5 milligrams a day with an equivalent amount of placebo substituted without the patient's knowledge. The conditioning procedure and the visits to the cinema on his own continued daily after the administration of the drug and the placebo. On the fourth day, he received 10 milligrams of placebo only. During this stage of treatment, he gradually became tense and anxious and reported feeling slightly depressed. After each treatment session, however, he said that he felt better temporarily and at no time did he feel tense and anxious in the cinema.

During the next weekend at home, he was given one placebo tablet for the Saturday and none for the Sunday. He coped with traveling and riding his bicycle, but felt somewhat tense and anxious. He maintained that the cause of these symptoms was the fear that the treatment might fail and that he might have to stay in the hospital. He expressed a strong desire to leave, saying that he had not felt this desire before the treatment started. He also claimed that his present anxiety and tension had a "different quality since he could find a reason for these feelings."

The first day after his return from this weekend, he was given a final test. He had to travel on a bus some three miles away from the hospital, return, and then visit, unaccompanied, another very crowded cinema. He reported that before the bus ride he felt tense and worried, but on his return, he had recovered, regained his confidence, and felt cheerful. He also enjoyed the cinema and reported that he "never felt better."

The rationale of the treatment was explained to him and every step of the treatment (except the substitution of placebo) was discussed with him. After the final test he was discharged.

FOLLOW-UP. It was planned to see the patient once every two weeks. He kept his first appointment only, reporting considerable improvement in travelling and in visiting crowded places. He had also gained confidence in himself and in relation to strangers and his superiors. He still occasionally got his "queer feelings" of worry, strain, and fear of fainting, but these were very mild and not very disturbing. The only difficulty he experienced was when riding his bicycle, but he continued to cycle to and from work. Two weeks later he sent a letter, saying that he could not keep the appointment since he was in financial difficulties. Apart from these difficulties, he was managing very well and had mastered his fear of cycling completely. He could cope easily with any uncomfortable feelings he experienced.

Three months later he sent another letter, informing E that he was progressing very well. He had taken his children to the coast for a holiday, cycled to and from work without any difficulty, and visited cinemas regularly.

Discussion

This paper attempts to demonstrate the application of some aspects of learning and the personality theory to the symptomatic treatment of psychiatric patients. At present, the experimental findings are not completely consistent, and the theories themselves are in early stages of development. The available findings, however, suggest rational experimental techniques for symptomatic treatment.

It cannot be strongly maintained that a mere stay in the hospital could account for the recovery from the symptoms, since both patients stayed in hospital well over a month prior to treatment, and according to their verbal account and the observation of their behavior in stressful situations, there was no indication of any improvement. In the present state of knowledge, however, it cannot be argued with any degree of assurance that the improvement of these patients' long-standing phobic symptoms was due to the treatment given. Even if there was sufficient evidence to maintain that the treatment was responsible for the improvement, so many relevant factors were uncontrolled that one would not know which aspect of the treatment was relevant and which irrelevant. These relationships can only be established by more extensive and well-controlled research.

Moreover, the usual objections made against symptomatic treatment on a priori grounds lack force. It seems plausible to argue, as Jones (7) has, that "Much evidence points to the fact that neuroticism is largely a constitutional defect for which no effective radical therapy is yet available. The individual of neurotic constitution in certain environmental circumstances develops certain symptoms. The rational therapeutic approach is then to treat the symptoms and to modify the environment so as to avoid their recrudescence or the development of fresh symptoms. The more specific the treatment, the more likely may be its success."

Several implications of theoretical and practical interest emerge from this study: (1) Since both cases manifested blackouts of an unknown nature, particularly Case 1, the phobic symptoms presented were not certainly known to be functional in origin. The treatment, however, was oriented towards a functional analysis of the disorder. (2) It would be desirable to know whether, following a course of treatment like that described, the neurotic reactions are eliminated or merely overshadowed by a stronger normal reaction. Although Wolpe (8) provides some evidence that neurotic reactions in cats can be eliminated, the question must remain open on the present evidence. (3) Although on clinical grounds Case 1 was regarded as an hysterical personality and Case 2 as a dysthymic, objective psychological tests indicated the reverse. It seems likely, moreover, that the etiology of the phobic states must have been quite different in the two cases. One would like to know how two patients showing such a considerable difference in conditionability came to develop more or less similar patterns of abnormal behavior. (4) The results obtained during the course of treatmen are consistent with Eysenck's theory (1) concerning the dynamics of anxi ety and hysteria. They also indicate, in accordance with Eysenck's view that for the purpose of treatment, adequate regard must be paid to th importance of certain individual differences as related to the disorders pre sented. (5) The use of drugs may facilitate and speed up successful treat ment of this type, and this theory of individual differences may give ; rational basis for the selection of drugs.

Summary

The treatment of two phobic patients has been described. Case 1 mani fested an excessive fear of going out on her own; Case 2 displayed disablin, symptoms in the form of an excessive fear of going into enclosed an crowded places. Both cases had blackouts of unknown nature.

The treatment program for both cases was mainly based on the principl of primary stimulus generalisation. Owing to the more "diffuse" nature o the anxiety displayed by Case 2, an additional simple conditioning tech nique was employed.

Case 1 responded to the treatment immediately and an improvement in her general behavior was observed. The effects of treatment persisted fo nearly five months, when the patient died of left ventricular failure.

Case 2 failed initially to respond to treatment. An attempt was made to account for this failure in terms of Eysenck's theory of anxiety and hysteria From the theory, inferences were made with respect to the patient's be havior on objective psychological tests; the results were consistent with the inferences. The treatment was modified according to the theory and the patient responded as expected. Four months after discharge from the hos pital, the patient seemed to be managing well and to feel much improved.

References

1. Eysenck, H. J. A dynamic theory of anxiety and hysteria. *J. ment. Sci.*, 1955, *101*, 28–51.
2. Franks, C. M., & Laverley, S. G. Sodium amytal and eyelid conditioning. *J. ment. Sci.*, 1955, *101*, 654–663.
3. Franks, C. M. Conditioning and personality: a study of normal and neuroti subjects. *J. abnorm. soc. Psychol.*, 1956, *52*, 143–150.
4. Guthrie, E. R. *The psychology of learning.* New York: Harper, 1935.
5. Hull, C. L. *Principles of behavior.* New York: Appleton, 1943.
6. Jersild, A. T., & Holmes, F. B. Methods of overcoming children's fears. *J. Psychol.*, 1935, *1*, 75–104.
7. Jones, H. G. The application of conditioning and learning techniques to the treat ment of a psychiatric patient. *J. abnorm. soc. Psychol.*, 1956, *52*, 414–419.
8. Wolpe, J. Experimental neurosis as learned behavior. *Brit. J. Psychol.*, 1952, *43*, 243–268.
9. Wolpe, J. Reciprocal inhibition as the main basis of psychotherapeutic effects. *Arch. Neurol. Psychiat.*, 1954, *72*, 205–226.

THE THEORY AND PRACTICE
OF GROUP PSYCHOTHERAPY *

Helen E. Durkin

John Levy's Relationship Therapy as we have crystallized, developed, and applied it to groups, is direct interpretative therapy. It is geared to go as deep as but no deeper than the patient's needs and capacities indicate. It is not meant to be palliative, nor to strengthen the patient's repressions.

In the course of a lifetime, people build up various defenses against certain unacceptable instinctual drives, such as hostility. When these defenses are not working well, they become anxious and develop neurotic symptoms (which are danger signals like any symptoms of a physical disease) or they experience general anxiety. This often brings them to the psychotherapist for help. In treatment, they make another attempt to keep away the unbearable drives. Their defenses become *resistances*, and the therapist must dissolve them one by one until the basic drives can be reached, re-evaluated, and handled in a more mature way. This process will strengthen the patient's ego and bring about a real character change.

The Relationship Therapy is a transference therapy, psychoanalytically oriented. Like any such therapy, it is based on the premise that, sooner or later, the patient will bring into his relationship with the therapist the full range of his emotions—his fears, resentments, demandingness, tenderness, and so on. He will express them in the characteristic attitudes and patterns which, under pressure of his early familial experiences, he has built up to defend his ego. For example, as a child, the patient may have been afraid to show his resentment to a tyrannical father. He may have discovered that one way to escape his dilemma and find temporary relief was to run away—physically or symbolically. He will do the same in the treatment situation as soon as resentment is aroused toward the therapist (as a person of authority). Unless the therapist is keenly alert to the first signs of approaching hostile feelings and brings them into the open, he is likely to lose this patient.

Let us examine another similar but more complex example. I was working with a young man who had felt rejected by his mother, toward whom he had a strong attachment. His frustration filled him with rage, but he

* From Helen E. Durkin, "The Theory and Practice of Group Psychotherapy," *Ann. N.Y. Acad. Sc.*, 49, 6, 889–901. Reprinted by permission of the author and the Managing Editor, *Annals of the New York Academy of Sciences*.

dared not be angry lest he lose the little he got from her. Both his eroti
and his hostile feelings had caused him so much pain that he tried to avoi
them. He had started psychotherapy twice and twice he had run away from
his woman therapist as soon as he became aware of her as a woman. He le￼
enraged notes behind accusing her of seducing him. It was a kind of trip￼
defense. He projected his erotic feelings on to her, thus getting rid of hi
anxiety about them. Then he converted his rage at expected frustratio￼
into righteous indignation at her bad behavior. Finally, he rid himself o
the whole anxiety-producing situation by running away. His people, how
ever, insisted on treatment and he was sent back, this time to me. As
expected, he entered treatment easily, talked with apparent frankness an￼
soon claimed improvement. When he expressed inordinate gratitude, I saic
"You know, when you feel so grateful to me, you are apt to become ver
fond of me, and if this happens you are going to be pretty upset. You ma
even want to run away." He denied it, but stammered and blushed fur￼
ously. I went on, "Patients have all kinds of disturbing feelings toward thei
therapists. But it is different in treatment from outside, and you will find i
is good to talk about these feelings here. This is the way I help people.￼
The boy managed to stay and, instead of running away, he eventually de
scribed how he would like to marry me. Again I warned him that, on findin￼
that I have to be impersonal, he would be angry with me and want to leave
Again he was able to stick it out and I was soon listening to a descriptio￼
of how he would like to murder me—with an ice pick. Treatment scene￼
are seldom as dramatic as this, perhaps never in a group, but the principl￼
is the same.

As you can see, the pivot on which this therapy moves is the analysis o￼
every implication of interpersonal attitudes as they near the threshold o￼
consciousness (whether positive or negative). Trivial as these first evidence
of irrational feelings may seem, they are the clues to the patient's ego de
fenses and, in treatment, these defenses become the resistances. Dissolvin￼
the resistance at the earliest possible moment speeds up treatment.

Each patient has any number of such defensive patterns, and, as th￼
therapist exposes one after another of them, the patient gradually come￼
face to face with the unbearable impulses which were originally behin￼
them. Recognizing them in the controlled interpersonal setting helps hin￼
to become aware that they have little bearing on the immediate situation￼
and to discover their real meanings and sources. Once that has happened
he becomes free to relate himself to people in a more realistic way.

Modification of the feelings of guilt derived from identification with ￼
permissive therapist and the catharsis of dammed-up feeling are a part o￼
therapeusis, but we feel that the greatest change in the patient comes from
the gradual dawning of insight within himself as he is helped to recogniz￼
how inappropriate his neurotic attitudes are. He catches himself in the act

s it were. The essence of the treatment, therefore, is in the living experi-
nce of the relationship.

Since we see our patients only once or twice a week, we do not let them
truggle alone with the anxiety they must experience as they become aware
f their instinctual drives. We help them to verbalize the anxiety-ridden
eelings as these reach the threshold of awareness instead of waiting until
he patient is fully conscious of them. This requires skilful timing; for inter-
reting too soon will *give* him the insight which should *come* from within
nd will make an intellectual process of treatment. It may succeed only in
trengthening his resistance. Waiting too long to interpret, on the other
and, will increase the patient's anxiety between visits when the therapist
; not available for help. It would also increase the length of treatment
onsiderably.

These are the principles of therapy, and they remain the same whether
sed with individuals or with groups, with adults or with children. In the
roup, the therapist finds himself handling many relationships at once; the
eelings of the four or five women (or children) toward one another and
oward himself. These start as surface reactions but gradually develop into
ransferences. The same kinds of defenses and resistances display them-
elves as occur in individual treatment, and, if one uses a transference
herapy like this one, much the same kind of treatment process takes place
s in individual therapy.

There are, in addition, many intra-group impacts of which the therapist
nust be constantly aware and which he must handle. Some women, for
nstance, express one kind of feeling or another more easily than others and
ct as catalytic agents for a time. Others will take over, as it were, when
ther kinds of emotion come up. Although the patient-therapist transfer-
nce may not become as intense as in individual therapy (sometimes it
loes), the subjective attitudes of the other patients serve rather quickly to
ring into being what we might term secondary transferences.

For example, Mrs. B. may display attitudes that remind Mrs. A. of her
nother or, for that matter, of her father. This may arouse tender or resent-
ul feelings toward Mrs. B. which will be expressed in Mrs. A.'s usual pat-
erns. The therapist must interpret such relationships just as he does when
hey apply to himself, and he must also handle the feelings of the recipient
f such transferences. Among such feelings will almost certainly be sibling
ivalry, for the group naturally tends to enhance this feeling, which comes
ut more quickly and realistically than in individual treatment. If the theraist has a tendency to steer away from socially unacceptable feeling, the
roup will soon develop a sewing circle character. If he sits by, passively but
ermissively, some superego modification and some catharsis will occur. If
e interprets skilfully, timing his comments so that the patients themselves
ecome aware of their conflicts and anxieties, real character change is pos-

sible in the group, as in individual treatment. To reach this goal, the thera pist encourages all emotional expressions, however socially unacceptable He helps to bring them out by repeatedly bringing to light the undercur rents of feelings as he senses them behind the factual productions of th patients.

The nature of his comments, as well as his timing, must be geared to th patients' level, psychologically, educationally, and socially, so that they ca accept and assimilate what he says. If what he says is too strong for th patients' weak egos (if he deals narcissistic blows), treatment will be vitiated It follows inevitably, then, that if the therapist's own drives enter into hi work beyond the point at which he can recognize and control them, he wil create trouble instead of bringing relief. Supervision during training wil control this possibility. There is another safeguard, however: such a thera pist would soon find himself without any patients—certainly without an groups.

Perhaps the best way of illustrating the method is to try to show it i action by describing a particular group. In order to simplify this too ambi tious undertaking, I shall try to follow some of the more illuminating mc ments in the progress of a particular patient, Mrs. S., within her group bringing in the others just enough to show the kind of interaction that take place.

The group I have chosen to discuss consisted of four women who me once weekly. They were mothers whose children were also in treatment a the New Rochelle Child Guidance Center. One patient is an attractiv woman of about thirty-four who came because her older child, a girl o seven, suffered from extreme shyness, enuresis, nail-biting, and general irr tability. The mother is a neat, modestly dressed woman whose most notice able characteristic was an almost constant artificial smile which gave he face a mask-like quality.

On the day of our initial meeting, Mrs. S. was the first to arrive and immediately began to complain about her husband and his mother. Sh spoke stiffly and without feeling, as if reciting a lesson. Her husband, sh said, like his mother, never praised but often criticized her, especially fo being extravagant. She felt this was unfair because she had always had t be thrifty by necessity. Although her mother and her aunts had been har up, they were always generous and did not stint with praise. In spite of he righteous indignation, however, she felt that, somehow or other, the whol thing was her fault anyway, perhaps because she was no good as a house keeper or a mother and did not know how she could ever improve. Sinc we are, on the whole, passive during the first interview, my only commen was an attempt to help her feel I understood the way she felt. I interprete not the material, but the undercurrents of feeling, saying only, "I get th impression you have been trying for a long time to keep your chin up." Sh burst into tears, and spoke with less tension after that.

When the other group members came in, Mrs. S. went right on address-
ng herself to me alone for a minute. Then she apologized for taking too
much time. She was not ready yet for an interpretation of the sibling rivalry
he revealed, nor of her need for approval. I waited for an occasion when it
was so clear that she herself would see it.

For the rest of the hour the women talked about their children's be-
avior, as they usually do before they have accepted the idea that they
hemselves are patients. Mrs. S. listened for the most part, but occasion-
lly she gave an example of similar behavior—however, always choosing it
rom her own childhood.

Since first interviews are usually revealing as a kind of forecast of things
o come, it is a good idea to ask, "What does this all add up to?"

1. Mrs. S.'s artificial, tense manner seemed to indicate that she was
truggling to keep an overwhelming anxiety out of sight.

2. What she said seemed to imply, "I am a child, and I'll be good and
ell you what you want to know, but please be kind and approve of me."

3. Her disturbance over being criticized made me guess that she used
pproval and praise to cover up some deep-seated anxiety and warned me
hat she would want praise from me, too, which would serve to build up her
lefenses; that she had come for treatment for that very purpose and that
when it was not forthcoming she would feel criticized, rejected, angry, and
nxious.

4. Her disregard of the other women at the beginning and her quick
pology for it revealed her strong drive to keep the therapist (as a mother
erson) to herself and that one of the first things to handle, as often hap-
ens in a group, would be sibling rivalry.

5. Her use of examples from her own childhood confirmed the feeling
hat she still regarded herself as a child. What had prevented her assuming
dult responsibilities would be left to find out. It might also shed light on
he deep sense of inadequacy expressed in her inability to cope with house-
old and parental duties.

Since Mrs. S. had not been aggressive enough to keep the floor at the
irst meeting, I was not surprised when she came late the next time. We
ind it a useful rule to comment on such evidences of hidden feeling. I said,
"I think it was a little harder for you to come this time." She denied it,
referring to the silly use of this interpretation in the social-work school she
attended for a while. I did not press the point because we feel that arguing
with a patient implies self-defense and might make her feel aggression or
resentment is not acceptable. She might, then, shut off future display of it,
whereas we want her to feel free to express any feeling whatever. I said only,
"You must have been disappointed in the group last time because you had
so much to say and so little chance to say it," whereupon she answered,
"Well, I did have a lot I wanted to talk about." I knew all the women
would be experiencing rivalry at this time, so I said, looking around, "Natu-

rally, every one of you would prefer to be seeing me alone." I could tell b
their expressions I had hit home. I said this to relieve them of the need t
hide this aggressive feeling, and so to pave the way for later, more explici
expression and interpretation of sibling rivalry. The immediate result in th
second interview was that, when Mrs. S. spoke again about her husband
she could include the other women instead of looking at me alone. Month
later, when one of the women told how jealous her two boys and husban
were of her ministrations, I compared it to their group situation. By thi
time, they had become aware of their rivalry and could see it in this nev
sense.

    Mrs. S. was early for the third interview and announced that she ha
made an inexcusable display of herself the week before, when she "blew up'
at me. I said that apparently she had felt criticized by me. She said, "
always felt criticized at school when they made that interpretation," an
she told us about a teacher who had told a girl to stay away altogether a
long as she felt so resistant that she was always late. I said, "I have an ide
you are afraid I might send you away too." Mrs. S. nodded, her eyes fillin
with tears, as she told us how she had always felt on the fringe of her famil
as a child—lonely and lost. She seemed freer now and dropped the stiff
artificial manner. When she talked about her husband and mother-in-lav
again, she gave vent to strong resentment.

    Apparently, she gained some relief from this tirade, for she soon reporte
that she was getting along much better with her husband. She had, for th
first time, been able to confide in him her feelings about his mother and h
had actually taken her part and had been much sweeter to her. She als
made him see how she felt about treatment, to which he had been antago
nistic. Such immediate results from the first six weeks or so of treat
ment are not at all rare, for the first layers of anxiety are lifted off. Some
times the exigencies of the case lead us to terminate treatment at thi
time, but if the patient needs it, can profit by it, and we have time, w
go on.

    Mrs. L., a thin, determined-looking woman, who expressed aggressio
under a usually pleasant, soft-spoken manner, was the woman in the grouj
who had the greatest impact on the treatment of Mrs. S. She was of a lowe
socio-economic and educational level but had, at the beginning, much mor
self-confidence. She was typical of many of our group mothers who com
only because we insist on it. She saw no relation between her son's anti
social behavior and herself, for had she not always "beaten her brains out'
to teach him right from wrong? She said the school principal "had a nerve'
blaming her. Very soon she made the demand mothers of this kind alway
make for advice about handling her son. I said I knew that she and some
of the others would probably be disappointed because I do not give advice
Experience had shown that it was best not to if we were to get to the bot
tom of the trouble. We found that the children's problems were usuall

elated to the parents' emotional difficulties, so that the mothers would
alk while I listened and together we would try to find the answers.

Mrs. P., a third member of our group, had so far sat by quietly, saying
nothing. She was an untidy, withdrawn woman with a blinking tic. She was
a college woman who, because of a deep sense of inadequacy, had married
an uneducated man late in life. She was now at a complete loss as to how
to cope with her two small boys. She was not really good group material
but we had no other time for her and decided to risk it.

Now, for the first time, she took part in the discussion, quoting from
books (she was a librarian) to give Mrs. L. the advice I had withheld. I
remarked that she seemed to agree with Mrs. L. in that I should give advice.
She blushed and said "Well, no, but,—" I smiled in a friendly way and said
that here everyone was entitled to her own opinion and that all mothers
feel the same way at first. I realized I would have another set of intellectual
defenses to cope with here and, furthermore, that Mrs. P. was the kind of
patient with so little ego that I must go very slowly in tackling even her
resistance. It is best to let such women sit quietly by until, from hearing
the others express all sorts of emotions, they have gained sufficient reassurance to be able to touch on their own.

I shall omit the fourth woman from the discussion because she had least
impact on Mrs. S. and it is necessary to save space.

Gradually, the women came to talk less and less about their children's
behavior. (From then on, when they did revert to it, I would know that
some new resistance was making itself felt.) They spoke more about their
feelings toward them, their protectiveness, their feeling of responsibility
and guilt and, in the end, their resentment and hostility toward them.
Some groups are so emotionally mobile that they can even be helped to
accept their death wishes in these first months of treatment. This group
was far from ready for it. In some groups, where one or two members may
go this far while the others would be shocked by it, the therapist must be
especially careful to handle the feelings of both kinds of women.

The therapist's part in this group was to help them express these facets
of their parent-child relationships freely, to show them the meaning of
parental ambivalence and to help them see that they were not alone in their
various predicaments.

During this period, Mrs. S. was the chief catalytic agent, leading the
other women gradually to more personal problems because of her emphasis
on her own childhood. Mrs. L. responded by telling of her childhood experiences, too. She criticized her mother freely. In her characteristic way,
she showed her sibling rivalry by aggressively taking the floor most of the
hour. She complained of being snubbed and ignored by so-called friends for
whom she tried to do too much. Gradually, she began to see that she was
not just the victim of their hostility but that she herself activated it by the

chip on her shoulder. The same situation appeared to hold in her relation
ship with her son and, as a result, she began to treat him more tolerantly

Mrs. P. talked freely at this time, too, for she half lived in her childhood
fantasies anyway. Becoming aware of the meaning of some of them (her
driving competition with her mother) seemed to bring her into somewhat
closer touch with her daily life.

Since the others gave Mrs. S. little chance to talk these days, another of
her defensive patterns was high-lighted. She appeared to be listening sym
pathetically. When she finally got the floor she complained of one of her
severe headaches. She thought it was because someone had called her as she
was hurrying to get to our meeting. It was the head of a committee who
told her a long story of woe in order to convince her that she should take
over some onerous duties. Mrs. S. had listened with apparent sympathy
although she was angry. She took the job, but now felt overburdened and
inadequate. I said I had an idea she was feeling the same way about the
group lately when she sat for such long stretches listening with apparent
interest to the other women's troubles. I knew this must be frustrating to
her. Mrs. S. laughed a little and said she had also been having headaches
after our meetings lately. I tried to get her to talk about these headaches
from which she had been suffering all her life. She started talking about
them, but soon drifted off into a long story about how angry she became
when her husband insisted on taking the whole family on endless drives
and then expected dinner in a jiffy after she got home. As a matter of fact
she said, she often had headaches on Sunday. This demonstrated the feel
ing behind the headaches, and she laughed again as she put two and two
together. Then she suddenly recalled an illuminating childhood memory
When she was about nine years old, she used to go to an art class. The
other children used to make many demands on the teacher whereas she sat
in a corner not daring to ask for help, although she could never draw as well
as they. When she went home, she used to cry herself to sleep. I asked why
she thought she had just recalled this. It was easy for her to see that she
was doing something very similar here.

From that point on, Mrs. S. became a little more aggressive in the group
Soon there were several signs that her hostility toward her mother, of whom
she had said only the most complimentary things so far, was mounting
She again became anxious and resistant, even though she had been some
what prepared for the recognition of such feelings in herself by Mrs. L.'s
open, bitter criticism of her mother.

When her resistance had been broken through, Mrs. S. revealed a nega
tive transference to Mrs. L., whose overprotection of her son reminded her
of her own mother's attitude. At this time, the group was talking about
how to tell children the facts of life. Mrs. L. revealed that she could not
talk about it to her son; that she worried about whether he masturbated
sometimes she even spied on him. Mrs. S. looking angry and upset, I said

You seem to have some feelings about this, Mrs. S." In a cold, intellectual way, she said that a child's reaction to such handling could only be one of rebellion. I said, "I think you are feeling irritated at Mrs. L. for the way she treats Charles." She broke through then and said angrily, "Yes, he'll never forgive her, you know," to which I replied, "This seems to be the way you feel too; I think she reminds you of your mother." She burst out, "That's right, I'll never forgive my mother. She always pretended that sex was all romance and then one day she called us children together and told us the 'bestial side of sex' all at once. She made it sound so gruesome I never have got over it. It just about spoiled the first part of my marriage"— and as usual she cried.

From then on, her mother came in for one bout of criticism after another, until she reached a climax when she was telling us about her mother's irritating "sweetness and light" attitude when she came to take care of her grandchildren. Grandma always sidetracked them when they were going to be aggressive, and Mrs. S. felt that was at the bottom of her little girl's shyness and inability to be aggressive, just as it was at the bottom of her own inability to assert herself. Her voice rose in a crescendo as she burst out, "Pretending, pretending, that's all my life has ever amounted to—no wonder I can't manage my household, my children, or anything." She began to cry bitterly. While she was working through this hostility, her real relationship with her mother, who was visiting her, was very much disturbed. She had things out with her mother regularly. Her husband called me to ask what was going on, and I assured him that her reactions were an unavoidable part of treatment, but I felt they would soon subside and she would find a better equilibrium as a result. Fortunately, it was not long before Mrs. S. reported that she was much better able to manage her children now and that her daughter was much more aggressive than she ever had been. The incidents she told seemed to show that Mrs. S. was asserting herself in a more adult way at home. The explanation seemed to me to be that as soon as she was able to face aggressive feelings toward her mother, the need to remain a child in order to suppress her feelings of hostile rivalry toward her was greatly reduced. She could be the mother to her own children now instead of being just another guilty child with them. She was also getting on better with her mother-in-law, who no longer was the recipient of hostility meant for her mother. Her husband also apparently responded to her increased maturity, for she told us he had been so attentive she felt as if she were a bride again.

By that time, most of the women had talked a lot about their resentment toward the various members of their family, but they had not yet been able to criticize me directly. As in all matters of aggression, Mrs. L. was the leader. One morning, when they were all resistant at once, the conversation turned toward teachers. Mrs. L. (to whom I had recently had to deny information about what her son had told his therapist) said, "Teachers never tell you anything. When I want to know something, I ignore them and go straight to the principal," and Mrs. S. chipped in, "I think they ought to learn some psychology." (Note the appeal for my approval.) "They think they can handle all children the same way" (objection to group). Mrs. P complained that, at school meetings, the teacher never seemed to notice her, so that she never had a chance to talk to her about her little boy.

Enough material about their familial backgrounds had come out by this time so that I could easily show them all that this was exactly how they had felt about their mothers, persons in authority, and, more recently, about me. Each one, in her characteristic pattern, had presented a picture of her own irrational idea of my attitude toward her. I showed them each the meaning of what they had been saying. Insight was stimulated because each woman could see so clearly that what I said about the others was true, and they all laughed. Because the whole group was expressing resentment toward me at once here, it was possible for each to accept such feelings in herself at this time (security from the gang).

Following this episode, Mrs. S. expressed resentment to me more directly, but the persistent struggle of her need for approval over her emerging hostile feelings made treatment a slow, laborious process for her. The insight she gained was partial and frequently repressed again, as often happens. One episode threw into clear relief the way she used an appeal for approval as a means of defense against anxiety about hostile feelings. She was expressing resistance again one day, by talking about her dislike of doctors, when she stopped abruptly and asked me if fear could be repressed. I said, "Suppose you tell me what you mean." She told us about an operation she had undergone several years before. She had been calm beforehand and was often complimented by the day nurses. The night before the operation, however, she could not go to sleep, and one of the night nurses scolded her severely for it. Suddenly she became panicky and the next morning she insisted on calling up her doctor to ask him some questions. He told her abruptly that she was afraid. She referred to her calmness until this time. He answered harshly that she had only repressed her fears. She was angry, but helpless and more panicky than ever about the operation. She felt he had had no business making interpretations. As she talked about it I helped her see that she had been all right until someone had criticized her, as if being approved of (loved) had been a way of keeping down panic. I showed her, too, how the same pattern was working in the group. She had often tried to win my approval (this much had come out frequently and she had long since accepted it), and when I did not give it to her she became angry, panicky, and resistant.

It was clear now why Mrs. S. had come to treatment. Ostensibly, it was to learn how to handle her affairs. What she wanted, unconsciously, was to get approval from an authority so that she could continue to suppress hostility and deeper fears. It is clear, too, that had the therapist given her dvice or praise he would have strengthened her defenses and made it arder, if not impossible, to work through the anxiety-laden drives that lay ehind them.

When she was a child, her family's defensive generosity with money and raise had served to keep up her defenses, although they often wore thin nd she had actually had a nervous breakdown at college. When she mared, her husband and critical mother-in-law withheld both money and pproval, and the defenses broke down. She was both angry and filled with deep sense of inadequacy.*

When the same pattern had played itself out in treatment, the vicious ircle could be broken because the therapist neither played into her deensive patterns nor rejected her, but showed her the meaning of what she as feeling.

What had kept her in treatment so long in spite of the enormous struggle he had to undergo to face her hostility, was a deeply passive dependent rive. I was her last hope of help and she had to stick to it. (Had the theraist been punishing or masochistic, she could not have stayed.) Her passive rends had also been evident from the very beginning and, by this time, she ad gained some understanding of them. But she could not experience the ender and erotic nature of the feelings connected with the dependent rive until she was released by the expressions of resentment in a situation vhich did not bring with it the rejection or the retaliation she feared. I vill not attempt to describe the slow steps by which she became aware of vhat she called "wanting to lean." The incident in which she recognized he connection between this drive and her hostile feelings, however, is vorth recording because, without it, it is not possible to understand how he came at last to grapple with still deeper layers of anxiety.

Toward the end of our second year of work (about the 60th interview), vhen the others were complaining about their children again, Mrs. S. oined them, this time without any attempt to avoid my disapproval (hereofore, she had always worked in some compliment to me, for safety). She mplied that her little girl was worse now than when she had first brought er to the center (in spite of the fact that she had already told us that the ail-biting and enuresis had stopped). I was glad to see that hostility to the herapist was stronger now than her need to side with the mother (myself) gainst the siblings as she used to do. Here we see a decrease in dependency.

She denied my interpretation of her doubts about treatment, but the ext week she came in feeling depressed. She was worried, she said, lest she nd her husband would have to help support her aunts who were now trystop ng to live on their pensions. Using a deadly monotone, she gave the miutest details about how these aunts had helped her out financially, through ollege. Now she felt mean to begrudge them help.

---

* Her basic fears had to do with castration anxiety which had frequently been indiated, but which she had certainly not been ready to touch so far.

I had only to remind her that this tone of voice usually meant resistance and she immediately spoke in a more heartfelt way. The youngest of these aunts was very important to her because she had been the only bright spot in Mrs. S.'s life the year her sister had been sick. The rest of the family attention had been concentrated entirely on the invalid, and only this aunt had paid any attention to Mrs. S. It was possible to show her how she was struggling here with guilty feelings about being hostile to someone she wanted to lean on. I showed her, too, how she was feeling just that way toward me at this time—needing my help and feeling guilty when she was angry or resistant so that she did not want to talk in the group. She indicated her growing insight by giving examples of how this same interplay had often happened in her relationship with her mother, although she had never before known what it was all about.

The following week, Mrs. S. came in a warm friendly mood such as she had never shown before. She thanked me and said she was touched by my desire to help her. She spoke tenderly of her aunt who, she said, reminded her of her father: they both loved church music. Even now she gets a thrill whenever she hears organ music. Soon this was her theme for the hour. I was the first time she had said much about her relationship with her father and the first time that genuine tender, erotically tinged feeling came out Aunt, father, therapist seemed to be equated here.

Apparently, it had been even harder for Mrs. S. to express affection, which was choked off by such angry feelings that she feared rebuff and even retaliation. The praise her mother had offered her had merely covered up basic rejection and preference for Mrs. S.'s brother. Our patient had, therefore found herself in constant need for an expression of love, or its substitute—approval. Never satisfied, she kept asking for more, repressing the hostility which she felt might cut her off altogether. Now, at last, she could express love and she looked much happier as a result.

At the last visit before vacation, Mrs. S. expressed regret at leaving, but compared herself favorably to the year before, when she had been terrified of the summer vacation. She had an excellent summer and when she returned in the fall she seemed an entirely different patient, for she plunged with real feeling and spontaneity into some of her underlying conflicts. It was apparent that we were through the worst resistance. She tackled first her difficult, partially frigid sexual relationship with her husband, which heretofore she had declared was one thing with which she needed no help. Next, she came face to face with her inability to assume either a feminine or a masculine role (which was the real significance of her intellectual strivings). Trying to compete with men made her feel hypocritical and "hollow." She always felt she might be found out at any moment. On the other hand, being a woman always made her feel dirty and castrated. Working out some of the hidden feelings and fantasies surrounding this basic conflict gave her enormous relief, making it possible for her to express franker sexual feelings toward her husband. She has been looking radiant of late and speaks of experiencing a new *"joie de vivre"* entirely unknown to her. Her housekeeping is improving at last, and the family manages to have more fun when they are together. It seems clear that, by the end of the year, she will have worked out a much better relationship with her husband, for he seems to be responding to her own changed attitudes.

In spite of the fact that I have selected only a few of the highlights of a long, tedious process, it seems clear that treatment is not a series of beautiful insights. It is more like putting together the tiny parts of a jig-saw puzzle. The fact that there are three other women to be dealt with makes the puzzle more complex and one is frequently distracted from one by the others, but, on the other hand, they offer many clues and stimulation that would never occur in a two-way relationship. This therapy offers even the beginner a safe guide through what often seems a dense fog. If he concentrates on sensing and handling only the immediately underlying feelings that the patients are experiencing at any given time, he will succeed in gradually building up a clear picture and helping his patients to richer personalities and fuller lives.

INTEGRATING CLINICAL PROCESSES
WITH PLANNED LIVING EXPERIENCES *

(Jerome M. Goldsmith, Rena Schulman,
  and Hyman Grossbard

Psychotherapy, the deliberate intervention into the psychic life of the emotionally disturbed child, has been traditionally confined to the interviewing room. Considerable knowledge has been accumulated and many treatment techniques formulated in dealing with the disturbed child on the affective and cognitive level through the use of transference, release and play techniques, etc. Relatively little effort has been directed toward coping with the child's reality and altering his daily living experience. The emphasis has been on his reactions to reality while reality was allowed to remain relatively fixed. Obviously, the disturbed child when at home and at school forced his bewildered parent or teacher to modify his reality for him and improvise expectations and pressures and allow considerable flexibility

* From Jerome M. Goldsmith, Rena Schulman, and Hyman Grossbard, "Integrating Clinical Processes with Planned Living Experiences," *Amer. J. Orthopsychiat.*, 24, 280–289. Reprinted by permission of Dr. Goldsmith and the Editor, *American Journal of Orthopsychiatry*.

in the child's experience. The flexibility, however, was not necessarily therapeutic and more often than not was shaped in accordance with the given pressures of a given time. Nor were these modifications reduced to any scientific principles when accomplished by a social worker or psychiatrist in clinic practice. The traditional effort on the part of the clinician to modify the environment for the child was usually done in broad surgical strokes intended to change the complete milieu of the child, by removal of the child from exposure to parental attitudes, by changing his school or sending him to camp.

The psychiatric efforts in the treatment of these children ran parallel with their actual living experiences. The therapist charted the psychic experiences of the child but gave little direction to the content and nature of his daily living.

The increasing awareness of the role of living experiences and their potential therapeutic value in the treatment of disturbed children has contributed to the development of residential treatment as a specialized type of care for the disturbed child. We conceive of the residential treatment institution as a psychodynamically determined environment in which the total living experiences of the child are schematized and integrated with psychotherapy, constituting an individual and unified treatment plan. The total life of the child, including his group living experiences, relationships with adults and children, his school classes, work assignments and recreational activities, becomes part of the armamentarium of the therapist, to be used in contriving the most therapeutic experiences for each child. In the residential treatment setting, the experiential aspects of the child's life are consistent, parallel and intermeshed with the process of individual therapy. The content of the intrapsychic struggle and the working out of the dynamic problems in the interviewing room coexist with the externalization of the problems as they are reflected in the child's activities and attitudes. The projection of distorted feelings, the acting out of irrational impulses and hostilities, and the course of the changes take place against the backdrop of deliberately planned adult attitudes and reactions. The experiences of the child may be contrived and planned to diminish anxiety, to arouse anxiety, to test out increased strengths, to permit gratifications at a more infantile or more mature level.

The structure of the total setting, the particular nature of the group with which the child lives, the kinds of adults, as well as the experiences which are specifically planned for him become part of the total therapeutic intervention. Certain community norms and standards are maintained for all children whatever the level of their disturbance because their very presence is a factor in nurturing reality principles and living which even the sickest child may absorb at his own pace.

In this kind of setting, the management aspects of daily life must be based upon sound psychiatric principles. The child's life from awakening to bedtime, the rule and routines and the pattern of his daily life must be cast broadly to incorporate general therapeutic goals. Integration thus takes place in an environment which is consistent and therapeutic in all of its aspects. One cannot integrate a clinical process with an environment which is alien to it—which relies only on a rational approach taking behavior at its face value. Nor is a benign environment consisting of warmth and love with good people and nutritive experiences sufficient to be integrated into a united treatment plan.

To achieve a schematized environment which can be consistent and therapeutic in all its aspects, there must first and foremost be a common denominator in the functioning of all staff—clinical and nonclinical—beginning with the acceptance of a common formulation for the treatment of these disturbed children. The common bond, the thread which runs through the institution, must be the understanding of the nature of the child. It is this understanding which extends the clinical process into all aspects of the environmental setting. This understanding creates identification, sympathy and tolerance. It permits individualization in the handling of children by all concerned. It is this which creates the basic milieu of attitudes for and of therapy. The acceptance of the idea of unconscious motivation and general psychiatric thinking influences the personnel in the environment in their attitudes and daily handling of reality and conscious problems. The knowledge that the most disturbed behavior is unconsciously motivated and stimulated by symbolic distortions enables the staff to control their reactions to the surface behavior of children and increases their level of tolerance. This basic psychological orientation which permeates the whole staff converts the environment from one that is benign to one which is therapeutic.

Under the impact of clinical thinking the total milieu undergoes a change. The character of many of the group disciplines is modified and traditional methodologies show the influence of the clinical process. Individualization becomes the primary process and with it alters the character of the group experience. Education, recreation, and the group living programs—the traditional group disciplines focus on the individualized handling of the child within their specialized type of group care. This individualization and differentiation in the handling of children who live together in a group may seem contrary to the usual group management procedures which are based on principles of fairness, equality, group approval, group law and majority decision. Yet it is possible to retain group structure with continuous concern for the individual child and his particular needs.

In the process of individualization and the development of an individual treatment plan, one of the most perplexing problems with which one is faced in a residential treatment center is the optimum degree of flexibility and individualization that is therapeutic for the disturbed child. Proceeding with the assumption that no one clear-cut formula is possible, the pressing question is what kind of criteria can be evolved to reduce flexibility to scientific measurements. In the past, we have leaned heavily on our diagnostic understanding of our youngsters, allowing considerable leeway to the neurotic and schizophrenic and tending to limit and fence in the child with a primary behavior disorder, and particularly the one with psychopathic tendencies. We are, however, increasingly experiencing the sense of being astray when guided only by the diagnostic categories. They seem to us too general and too broad. They offer us general direction, but are not sufficiently definitive in dealing with the detailed and specific. The need for permissiveness and flexibility, for rigidity and restraint, cuts across all present diagnostic categories. Diagnosis is therefore helpful to us primarily in delineating wide circles within which we are forced to speculate and improvise. At present, forced to make decisions under reality pressures, we fall back very much on our intuitive understanding of the child, and total knowledge of his strengths and needs. We do have, however, some basic principles to which we anchor ourselves while we improvise and individualize. Paradoxically, these basic principles are contradictory. However, it is in the process of crossing and synthesizing these opposites that some pragmatic principles applicable to the specific child emerge.

The first principle that is basic to our thinking is the need for structure and a constant framework of reality in the treatment of the emotionally disturbed child, but it assumes particular meaning to special types of disturbances. With the schizophrenic youngster, whose point of gravity is disturbed, whose perception of reality is blurred and chaotic, the need of structured living is particularly therapeutic. This child, because of his disturbed sense of inner order, and feeling of chaos and destruction around him, needs an environment providing routine and simple basic patterns of living. The regularity with which certain activities are carried out, his physical needs met by an adult world, are some of the primary media through which we translate to him our interest in him, and thus lay the basis for object relationship and inner emotional security.

However, the disturbed child in spite of his great need for order and structure in living very often fights it and reacts violently to it. Partly this reaction is a manifestation of his illness, and reflects his conflict about anything that symbolizes help and his being helped through it. Moreover, it seems that structure and order, by their very nature, imply restraint and denial.

The disturbed child, in line with his other distortions of reality, will tend to interpret controls and denials as expressions of hostility directed against him. At times, the very regularity of life looms threateningly at him. Order has an impact that has a crushing quality threatening the very essence of his fragile being. Order and structure impose certain responsibilities upon him that he feels unable to meet. He cannot mobilize him self to wake up on time, nor is he able to go through other activities during accepted clock time. The recurrent question is to what extent these protestations are expressions against the prevailing system being respected, and to what extent these very structures are therapeutic to him and therefore may be imposed on him.

As stated, this problem predicates the need for delineating an orbit of movement for each child, with an outer line of demarcation beyond which he is not allowed to go. Within this line, however, a great deal of flexibility and elasticity prevails. The existence of an outer line gives him a sense of protection and security. The flexibility inside gives him a sense of not being crushed, of having some control, and that his particular needs are understood and appreciated.

One of the ways that order and structure can be made acceptable to some children is when this is not presented in an impersonal way stemming from outside authority, but rather it is cushioned and translated into human relationships. For then, in spite of the denial inherent in these limitations, there is a giving of one's personality by the one who sets the limits which is in itself compensating. This predicates a type of communication between the adult and the child which is still in the process of exploration and improvisation. The denial of the immediate concrete request of the child may be amply replaced by the adult's giving of himself and his time to the child in the process of denying it.

One can hardly exaggerate the structure inherent in group activities. Structure that stems from arbitrarily imposed routines and authoritative rules and regulations disturbs and threatens, whereas the structure that flows from group living has a certain force and sweep that is particularly therapeutic to the disturbed child. The getting up in the morning on time, when practiced by a group, often compensates the schizophrenic who is unable to mobilize himself and he is swept into activities by the motion of the group. This structure, although it has some threatening elements, seems to be more palatable to the disturbed child and can be used in treatment.

The following is illustrative: Torn by anxiety and a sense of unworthiness, Sally occasionally sinks into a depressive state. This is characterized by aimless wandering and a quality of restlessness and detachment. On one hand, she seems anxious to become involved and complains of not being loved, not being cared for, and not being able to care for anyone. She wants a dog, one she can love and trust, and by whom she can be loved and not be betrayed. She is unable to come to the class setting and mobilize herself to any activities. She is listless, and her whole behavior assumes an amorphous pattern. In addition to her psychotherapy and relationship with her therapist, she is in need of some activity with some structure in her very shapeless existence. She resists, however, any semblance of system and order, and insists on having any need or interest, meaningless as it may be to her, met immediately. She has to see her friend immediately. She has to talk with her therapist right away, and if allowed to do so, her confusion becomes even more intensified. It is then that the resident staff's responsibility is to set limits as to when she is to see and when not to see her friends, to attempt to relate Sally's activities to certain hours and some system, while at the same time giving her some time in the process to compensate her for denial and limitations set upon her. Thus, a sense of structure is established without its destructive by-product of denial and frustration.

As we talk of extending the clinical process, this means not only individualization and flexibility and understanding, but also the translation of the treatment plan into the specific programs. It also means the modification of certain techniques and methodologies. This can be illustrated in specific application to the discipline of education.

It has been almost axiomatic that with the disturbed child learning could not occur without the one-to-one relationship's being established between teacher and child. This is one of the principles encouraged by modern progressive education. With many children, however, this method must fail because of the particular nature of the child's disturbance. There is no principle, sound as it may be, which can be applied without adaptation and individualization for our disturbed children. Occasionally, we may have to accept the converse to what may be accepted practice.

Frank, a 15-year-old with a long history of stealing, truancy and severe subject retardation, had presented a lifelong pattern of self-defeat and damaged self-esteem. He was a sullen, evasive boy, with occasional flashes of wit, humor and intelligence and frequently so likable that people might wish to extend themselves to him in a spirit of friendliness. For Frank, learning was fraught with conflict and danger, not only as it related to his sense of inadequacy, but as it symbolized giving pleasure or love to his family. This was dramatically shown when Frank, painting tiles, was praised by a staff member and then picked up the tiles and smashed them violently against the floor.

For this kind of youngster, the learning situation entangled in a personal relationship with the teacher could only end in another disaster, as did all other attempts at friendliness. The principle of depersonalization must be applied in the educational approach to him. Learning, knowledge, skills and media must be separated from personalities. Approbation could only bring anger and destruction to his work. The teacher gave him his work whether it was a creative project or a workbook on fundamentals, with simple instructions and then erased himself from the picture. The choice of materials was made by the teacher with sensitivity to the boy's needs for projects which had a certain amount of framework, a limited freedom of choice, a short-term goal, where results initially could be seen within an hour. This conscious effort on the part of the teacher diminished the emotional charge in the atmosphere in terms of relationships and their echoes and left more room for learning without a personal equation. For his boy, the working out of his core problem was confined to the interviewing room with a neutral insulation of his living experiences.

The initial individualization of the child's treatment stimulates individual educational approaches for different children. Just as with Frank the educational environment had to be depersonalized, with other children learning has to be personalized. Whether the problem may stem from the meaning of learning itself, or the fears imbedded in its content, the child may be helped in his environment to meet and conquer his fears. The personalized relationship with the teacher may give a child security to enable him to take some beginning steps toward the mastery of content and goes step by step with the content of his individual treatment.

The traditional educational framework of a classroom is a teacher and a variable number of children. Reducing the number of children in the group, particularly in working with disturbed children, has been the aim of educational planning. This has been developed to achieve greater individualization. In working with the disturbed child with his complex distortions of adult relationships, our clinical thinking has led us to the conclusion that regardless of the diminished size of the groups the struggle for the teacher takes up a good part of the energies of the group and teacher whether it be 5 or 15. The teacher with these disturbed children finds herself struggling with the fringes, with the attendant loss of one part of the group. We are coming to the conclusion that the presence of a second adult in the classroom group is an important element for improved treatment and education. It provides a dual polarity around which different children can circulate. It reduces the competition for the adult whom the child actually may or may not want. It fragments the group, and enervates the struggles between the single adult and the children. We are currently working toward providing this kind of classroom situation rather than toward a further reduction in the size of class groups.

Treatment is a continuous process. The course of treatment is set and modified and interpreted continuously. The other disciplines understand the description and direction and then strike an attitude and plan using their own knowledge and techniques to effect it.

The control, dilution and regulation of personal relationships has been mentioned as an important aspect of residential treatment. Persons in the milieu in any of the nonclinical functions have always found the avenue of warm personal relationships—or what one might often more accurately term seduction—an easy way to express their individualization of the child. Since most of the children in the treatment setting arrive with a history of unsuccessful interpersonal relationships, this is an area where difficulty again arises in the child's living. The onslaught of warmth from good human beings with whom the child may live is not therapeutic in and of itself, and may even be disastrous to the child's security. The clinical staff must guide the nonclinical personnel in their first approaches to the new child.

One of the early problems in controlling relationships is the spoon-feeding of the human element, which must be controlled as to amounts, and the selection of the area in which it first takes place cannot be left to chance.

Joe, a 15-year-old homosexual, schizophrenic youngster, extremely creative, artistic, and highly intelligent, was placed in a cottage where the cottage parent was also a creative person; he became interested in the boy's painting and encouraged it. The therapist initially fostered this mutual interest in painting, and felt it might be a bridge to a real relationship. Unfortunately, Joe became too much overwhelmed by the extent of his cottage father's interest, was panicked by this much closeness, and ran away from the school. The need for a step-by-step review and regulation of such relationships becomes obvious.

The adults in the environment must know enough about the child to avoid evoking sick responses by their attitudes and activities. Harry was emerging from a withdrawn pattern of behavior into contact with the adults in his environment aside from his therapist. He became involved with a group in his class and with his teacher in some horseplay and in a discussion of mutual strengths, and he challenged his teacher to an informal wrestling match. This was a boy whose basic problem was his tremendous fear of his own aggressive impulses and who had struggled through several years of treatment to establish some repressive controls. The teacher must know enough about the nature of the child and the stage of treatment to avoid the situation where challenge had to be the inevitable result, and side-step the physical contact with its threat to this boy's still tenuous controls.

The selection of the child's experiences is based on valid treatment planning for the individual child. The boy who cannot relate to human beings and finds security in closeness to animals and comparative isolation may be assigned to the farm. A youngster with severe oral deprivation may be initially helped in part through an assignment in the kitchen where he gets satisfaction and security from the constant availability of food. Leisure-time activities should be available to provide sublimatory channels and opportunities for symbolic fulfillment.

Dick is a 16-year-old who had come to the school after a succession of car thefts and who had several times absconded with the school's vehicles. Shortly after his return from his last escapade, when the neurotic pattern of his delinquencies was emerging in treatment, he was working with our painter. He was assigned the task of painting the fence at the entrance to the grounds. He remained in this assignment for weeks, painting the 12 pickets, one foot inside the gate, one foot outside, a study in ambivalence in front of the many parked cars of our neighbors. With one foot outside the gate physically, he acted out his struggle to remain or to flee and he prolonged this struggle with many coats of paint. Such calculated risks must be part of the fabric of the institution's planning where one gambles on the strength of the ego rather than giving custody to the pathology.

The melting of differences of philosophy and approach must be the culture within which residential treatment is developed. With common understanding and orientation, the differences lie in individual functions and acceptance and willingness to play a segment of the role in each child's experience. It carries with it a need for acceptance of one's own and everyone else's function with the individual child.

Integrative devices are merely the external expression of a total approach, and orientation. But the structure and devices must be provided with efficient and continuous channels of communication. The administrators' role is one of discerning and preserving all the distinctive contributions of the individuals and disciplines in a harmonious orchestration.

In advocating the extension of the clinical process into the living situation, which involves conscious and planful participation of the nonprofessional staff in treatment, we are not unmindful of some of the pitfalls that are on this road. Translation of the clinical process in all areas implies consistency and direction emanating from a central source. The source obviously must be the clinician. This direction from another profession, if not carefully and sensitively applied, may prove inimical to the very function of other members of the team. Believing as we do in the therapeutic potentials of the reality situation, we have to recognize the significance of the roles played by those who deal with the reality experiences of the children. They cannot be converted into automatons nor should we allow them to view themselves as puppets in the hands of the clinical staff who pull the strings. We have to be careful not to translate offering direction into giving definite and detailed prescriptions which have to be carried out literally. Such an attitude on the part of the clinical staff to the nonclinical people would tend to destroy their very usefulness, for this would deprive the nonprofessional staff of the basic freedom which animates them in their activity with children.

Without freedom there would be little imagination, spontaneity and creativity—the basic essentials necessary for those who work with children. Furthermore, in order to be meaningful and therapeutic to the children, the nonclinical people have to be looked upon by the youngster as potent and independent. Any structure prescribing types of relationships that would tamper with the image assigned to them by the children would inevitably undermine the value of their relationships. Special vigilance must be maintained to protect the role and freedom of activity and movement of the nonprofessional staff.

Another question often posed when closer contact and communication between clinical and nonclinical staff is being discussed is how this would affect the natural and spontaneous functioning of nonprofessional people.

In other words, professional discipline creates a certain self-awareness which may be incompatible with natural living. Self-awareness may inhibit the normal reaction of the staff and create a somewhat sterile atmosphere. Our children, while reality ought to be modified for them to meet their therapeutic needs, should also be given opportunities to stimulate their natural growth. This involves exposure to natural limitations and pressures. They need some experience of people being angry, irritated, impatient with them.

Upon reflection, however, it seems that there is some fallacy in the very formulation of the problem. It is not an either/or situation. It is not impulsive, uncontrolled handling versus self-conscious approach. It is rather a synthesis of the two, with self-awareness and professionalization intended to eliminate or to soften the extreme reaction of the nonprofessional people to the children. While attempting to reduce the subjective handling of children, there is considerable room left for a natural interplay between adults and children to allow them sufficient normal experiences conducive to growth.

Most of the residential treatment centers have, as with us, adopted a point of view and tested it in the course of their work. Our own approach at Hawthorne is inherent in the title of this paper and the concepts which we have presented. We believe that residential treatment is created essentially out of the sum and substance of the atmosphere and attitudes of the entire staff. The methods themselves and the people are affected by the processes and changes. These changes come about over a period of time through the impact of ideas and their absorption and synthesis into the total plan. This very process is a continuous one and is basic to our approach guaranteeing continuous refinement and more accurate formulation of treatment planning. The milieu cannot be fashioned by blueprint alone but must be aged and mellowed in the process of learning by the residential treatment staff.

PSYCHOTHERAPY AND THE RECOVERY
FROM NEUROSIS *

⟨ DALBIR BINDRA

Both practically and theoretically, it is important to find out whether or to what extent psychotherapy is effective in the treatment of various behavioral disorders. This paper considers from a critical and broad viewpoint the problem of the efficacy of psychotherapy in the treatment of neurosis.

* From Dalbir Bindra, "Psychotherapy and the Recovery from Neurosis," *J. abnorm. soc. Psychol.*, 53, 251–254. Reprinted by permission of the author and the Managing Editor, the American Psychological Association.

It separates and clarifies the specific issues involved, and attempts to show what questions can or cannot be answered on the basis of available evidence.

Problem

Basically, the question is whether or not the proportion of recoveries is greater among neurotics who undergo psychotherapy than among neurotics who do not receive such therapy. Meehl, in his recent review of the literature on this subject (5), notes the lack of the type of controlled studies which would unequivocally answer this question. In the absence of adequate experimental evidence on this question, psychologists have tried to argue (e.g., 2, 3, 8) for or against the efficacy of psychotherapy on the basis of indirect evidence obtained from improperly controlled studies. In general these arguments reach one of two conclusions: "No one has yet demonstrated that psychotherapy is effective in treating neurosis," or "No one has yet demonstrated that psychotherapy is *not* effective in treating neurosis." Clearly, this question is amenable to experimental attack. With two groups of patients equated in terms of symptoms, severity of neurosis, motivation for therapy, socioeconomic status, intelligence, and the like, only one of the groups must receive psychotherapy. A comparison of the proportion of recoveries in the two groups will then indicate whether psychotherapy is effective.

Unfortunately, discussions of this rather straightforward empirical question can easily get complicated by certain theoretical preconceptions. In the thinking of many psychologists, the problem of the efficacy of psychotherapy is intimately tied up with the problem of the etiology of neurosis. The notion that life experiences play a dominant and crucial role in the onset of neurotic ailments is generally considered to support the view that psychotherapy can cure these ailments. And the view that neuroses arises primarily from organic or nonpsychological factors is considered to favor the view that psychotherapy is ineffective. No one has explicitly stated and defended this type of argument, but it is implicit in most reputable psychological discussions (e.g., 9). There is little justification, however, for this contention that etiology and therapy bear such a direct and clear-cut relation to each other. The only effective treatment of a disorder of organic origin (like cerebral palsy) may consist of some form of training or psychotherapy; on the other hand, a psychogenic disorder (like some insomnias) may be most effectively treated by medication. The mere knowledge of the etiology in these cases does not tell whether a particular treatment would be effective. Similarly, whether neurotic ailments result from psychological conflicts, environmental stresses, or some subtle chemical factors in the blood is quite irrelevant in determining the efficacy of psychotherapy in their treatment. I do not mean to imply that neurotic disorders can be identified in a way that excludes etiological concerns. Rather, the point here is simply that the effectiveness of psychotherapy is an issue that can be and should be decided without linking it with any specific conjecture about the etiology of neurotic ailments.

Clarity and explicitness are also necessary in defining neurosis. In the present discussion, *neurosis* or neurotic disorder refers to cases of persistent and gross maladjustments involving some definite, palpable, behavioral peculiarities (or symptoms) such as anorexia, phobias, compulsive acts, demonstrable anxiety attacks, hysterical blindness, impotence, amnesias, and the like. It should be noted that this rough and arbitrary definition excludes minor maladjustments defined with reference only to subjective states such as "unhappiness," "anxiety," and "tension." It is true that "anxiety," "unhappiness," and "tension" are often (though not always) reported by neurotics, but they are also frequently reported by normals. Since these states are not a *sine qua non* of persistent and gross maladjustments unless accompanied by definite symptoms of the type listed above, they are excluded from the present definition of neurosis. Some psychologists believe that both neurosis and these minor maladjustments arise from the same type of etiological factors. Even if this view is correct, it does not necessarily imply that an effective treatment of minor maladjustments would also be effective in cases of neurosis, or vice versa. The concern here is primarily with recovery from neurosis.

A General Formulation

Recovery from neurosis means nothing more than a kind of behavioral change, a change in those aspects of the patient's behavior that put him in the category of neurotics. Thus, the question of the effectiveness of psychotherapy is really a special case of the general problem of the extent to which psychotherapy can produce *personality change*. A clear formulation of this question requires a closer analysis of the concepts of "personality change" and "psychotherapy." Precise descriptions are needed of (1) the personality variables along which change is presumed to occur, and (2) the psychotherapeutic processes which are presumed to effect the change. The effect of a specified therapeutic process on a specified personality variable can then be investigated.

Personality variables can be specified easily enough. For present purposes, they can arbitrarily be categorized into five rough categories: (1) *cognitive variables*, such as general information, reasoning ability, and memory; (2) *attitude variables*, such as attitudes toward in- and outgroups, attitude toward oneself, and likes and dislikes; (3) *need variables*, such as introversion, super-ego, anxiety, and aggression; (4) *specific neurotic symptoms*, behavioral characteristics, such as hysterical or compulsive symptoms, which are used in defining persons as neurotics; (5) *personality variables (if any) that are causally related to neurotic ailments.* Intelligence tests, scales of attitudes, and "personality tests" could be used to measure changes along the first three types of personality variables. The last two categories are not at the same level of discourse as the first three, nor have they been adequately identified so far, but they are listed here to focus attention on the type of variables that are of direct concern in this discussion. Accepting this admittedly arbitrary categorization, the problem of the effect of psychotherapy on personality variables resolves itself into five separate questions. Does psychotherapy have any effect on (1) cognitive variables, (2) attitude variables, (3) need variables, (4) specific neurotic symptoms, and (5) personality variables (if any) that cause neurotic symptoms?

To answer these questions, it is necessary to specify the exact nature of psychotherapy.[1] Unfortunately, it is not possible to do so. Psychotherapy still has its mysterious aspects, and present knowledge is far from unraveling the essential nature of all that takes place in the therapist's office. But from all accounts, it appears that the therapist provides the patient with a friendly, permissive, and uncritical atmosphere, and then systematically makes use of "interpretation," suggestion, and catharsis. It is not clearly understood, however, exactly how these various processes operate in the psychotherapeutic situation. Ideally, empirical questions should be formulated in terms of specific psychotherapeutic processes. Thus, one could ask such questions as "Can suggestion change attitudes and needs?" or "Can interpretive analysis affect compulsive or hysterical symptoms?" or "Can catharsis relieve functional impotence?" Such questions, however, cannot be answered unless psychotherapy is analyzed into its component processes rather than conceived as a unitary whole. The only point here is that if knowledge of exactly how psychotherapy produces whatever effects it does produce is to be gained, then an analysis of this type must be undertaken. From the point of view of the therapist, psychotherapy may well be considered as a unitary healing device, but for the researcher it is an analyzable complex of psychological processes. For the present, however, one is forced to discuss the issues without benefit of this kind of analysis. With this handicap in mind, questions concerning the effects of psychotherapy on the various categories of personality variables may now be considered.

Effects of Psychotherapy

Inasmuch as psychotherapy involves prolonged social interaction between the therapist and the patient, it is to be expected that the psychotherapeutic

[1] This conception excludes the *incidental* "psychotherapy" that is sometimes said to have taken place when a neurotic gets some attention from a nurse or when he confides his innermost thoughts to his bartender, priest, or barber. Whether or not incidental "psychotherapy" has some of the same ingredients as psychotherapy proper (given by a qualified psychiatrist or clinical psychologist) is impossible to say until more is known about what is involved in the latter.

situation will produce change along at least some personality dimensions. It is known that interpersonal relations can affect behavior. Interests and tastes change through association with friends. Gestures of immigrants begin to conform to the typical gestures of their adopted communities (1). Exposure to conflicting social influences may contribute to behavioral disturbances in juveniles (4). Attitudes can be changed, one way or the other, simply by showing a short movie to audiences (6). In view of the abundance of naturalistic and experimental evidence of this kind, it would be strange, indeed unbelievable, if the long and intimate social interaction between the therapist and his patient did not produce some change in the patient (and, indeed, in the therapist himself). The patient is likely to learn something about the work of the therapist, to increase his vocabulary, and to change his attitudes. Since he is the focus of attention in the therapeutic situation, the patient is particularly likely to learn more about himself and to evaluate himself rather differently. Also, the change from a nagging wife, a rude boss, and critical friends to the understanding and permissive therapist is likely to facilitate these new self-evaluations, and they may be more in keeping with the therapist's direct or indirect suggestions regarding what a normal person thinks of himself.

The recent studies of Rogers, Dymond, and their collaborators (7) present direct evidence in support of these statements. They administered a number of personality tests to their patients before, during, and after psychotherapy. Comparable control data were obtained from normal subjects, who were not given therapy, and from patients who had to wait for therapy. The most impressive finding was that psychotherapy produced a significant change in self-perception or in the perception of the self-ideal. It was also found that responses of patients to the Thematic Apperception Test changed as a result of psychotherapy in the direction of greater judged personality integration and adjustment. The results on needs and changes in behavior in everyday life situations were equivocal, and no change in attitudes toward others could be attributed to the treatment. No data are presented on the changes in specific neurotic symptoms. It seems appropriate to conclude that psychotherapy has some effect on the client's attitudes toward himself. That specific psychotherapy (as well as informal interpersonal relations generally) can produce behavioral changes does not, of course, diminish the need for analyzing "psychotherapy" into its component processes, as suggested in the last section. If one could identify the specific effective agents in the psychotherapeutic situation, it would be a step toward more efficient therapeutic procedures.

These demonstrations by Rogers, Dymond, and collaborators, important as they are, do not, of course, tell anything about the efficacy of psychotherapy in the cure of neurosis. These workers have shown that the attitudes of their patients changed, and that, *on the basis of test data*, they were said to become more "mature" and "better adjusted." But this does not indicate whether psychotherapy was effective in eradicating the specific neurotic symptoms of their clients. Even if psychotherapy demonstrably alleviates some minor maladjustments involving attitudes of different kinds, the issue of the effectiveness of psychotherapy in the treatment of the basic, gross, and persistent maladjustment ("primary neurotic symptoms") still remains unanswered. A neurotic with hysterical or compulsive symptoms may well become better adjusted as a result of psychotherapy without showing any change in his primary neurotic symptoms. Even a person who loses a leg may benefit from psychotherapy inasmuch as his life-goals and attitudes may change in a way that would be more consistent with his handicap, and in this sense he may become more mature, better adjusted, and happier. However, in order to demonstrate that psychotherapy is effective in curing neurosis, it must show that it diminishes or eradicates the symptoms that constitute the neurosis, quite apart from making the patient better adjusted, mature, or happier. Such a demonstration has not yet been made. Perhaps future research will show that certain psychotherapeutic processes can be effective in the treatment of certain types of neurotic maladjustments.[2]

Even if it were demonstrated that psychotherapy can relieve neurotic ailments, there would still be no answer to the final question. Can psychotherapy produce a change in those processes or personality variables (if any) that are causally connected with neurosis? Evidence showing psychotherapy to be effective in eradicating neurotic symptoms would not indicate anything about the mechanism by which psychotherapy operated. In this connection, two types of treatments should be distinguished. One kind involves directly undoing the disease process analogous to treating streptococcal infections with penicillin. The other type of treatment is indirect and is aimed at something other than the disease process itself; an analogy is treating typhoid or tuberculosis with rest. In textbooks on psychiatry and abnormal psychology, it is generally implied that the effectiveness of psychotherapy results from directly undoing (through relearning) the processes that produce neurosis. However, there is no evidence for this belief, and there cannot be until we know the exact basis of neurosis. It is quite conceivable that, were psychotherapy shown to be effective in treating neurosis, its effectiveness could result from some indirect effects that are quite unrelated to the causes of neurosis.

In summary, available evidence suggests that psychotherapy can be effective in alleviating minor maladjustments characterized by such subjective states as "unhappiness," "anxiety," and "tension" that often accompany neurosis. But the evidence does not yet support the view that psychotherapy is effective in relieving those gross and persistent maladjustments

[2] Whether the recovery from neurosis could be more effectively produced by methods other than psychotherapy is an important question, but one that need not be raised in the present discussion.

(neuroses) that are characterized by definite, palpable symptoms. Whether it has any effect on these is a question which only future research can settle.

References

1. Efron, D., & Foley, J. P. Gestural behavior and social setting. In T. M. Newcomb & E. L. Hartley (Eds.), *Readings in social psychology*. New York: Holt, 1947. Pp. 33–40.
2. Eysenck, H. J. The effects of psychotherapy: an evaluation. *J. consult. Psychol.*, 1952, *16*, 319–324.
3. Eysenck, H. J. The effects of psychotherapy: a reply. *J. abnorm. soc. Psychol.*, 1955, *50*, 147–148.
4. Hunt, J. McV. An instance of the social origin of conflicts resulting in psychoses. In C. Kluckhohn & H. A. Murray (Eds.), *Personality in nature, society and culture*. New York: Knopf, 1948. Pp. 367–374.
5. Meehl, P. E. Psychotherapy. *Annu. Rev. Psychol.*, 1955, *6*, 357–378.
6. Peterson, R. C., & Thurstone, L. L. *Motion pictures and the social attitudes of children*. New York: Macmillan, 1933.
7. Rogers, C. R., & Dymond, Rosalind F. (Eds.), *Psychotherapy and personality change*. Chicago: Univer. of Chicago Press, 1954.
8. Rosenzweig, S. A transvaluation of psychotherapy—a reply to Hans Eysenck. *J. abnorm. soc. Psychol.*, 1954, *49*, 298–304.
9. White, R. W. *The abnormal personality*. New York: Ronald, 1948.

Pressing Problems

Throughout this volume problems relating to methodology, theory, and application have been presented and discussed. For the most part these issues have meaning and significance chiefly for persons studying psychology. However, many of the problems associated with the study of adjustment have far-reaching import and should attract the interest and concern of a wider audience than only those involved with psychology. The final section of this book is devoted to issues which are of significance to the general community, layman as well as scientist, and raises a number of questions about the relationships between psychological knowledge and various philosophical and practical questions.

One of the most perplexing problems confronting mankind today is the application of scientific knowledge. As scientific efforts lead to increased ability to predict and control events, numerous questions arise pertaining to the purposes and methods of using the power which the knowledge affords. This has been illustrated dramatically in the application of nuclear physics, which has promoted both the fear and the possible reality of mankind's annihilation from the misuse of science. In recent years attention has also been drawn to issues involved in the application of knowledge from the social sciences, particularly psychology. Advances in our understanding of and accuracy in predicting human behavior have brought us increased ability to manipulate, change, and control human beings. And as this control increases, questions arise concerning the use to which it will be placed. All members of society must be concerned with such questions as: Who exerts this control? who is being controlled? what are the purposes of the control? and perhaps most important of all, what safeguards must we invoke against its misuse? B. F. Skinner has emphasized the importance of establishing control over the controllers, pointing out that the psychological knowledge existing today makes available sufficient power to manipulate societies of men to conform to a master

scheme. His major thesis is that we must develop counterforces to
check the possibility that this power might be used in a fashion
harmful to mankind. In the first paper included in this section,
Rogers and Skinner discuss the increasing control which the advances in psychological knowledge make possible. The authors
elaborate on many of the issues involved and effectively indicate
the need for policies formulated by the general community to
guide and govern the use of psychological knowledge.

The next selection deals with the application of information
about mental health to criminal law. Sobeloff traces the major historical developments in the legal definitions of insanity and carefully examines the arguments in favor of and opposed to the
recent decision which has become known as the Durham Rule.
This decision holds that a person accused of an unlawful act should
be relieved of the responsibility for that act if it can be demonstrated that his behavior was the product of a mental disorder. In
contrast, the McNaghten Rule, which has guided most court decisions involving mental illness in the past, defined insanity by the
single symptom of knowledge of right and wrong. If the defendant
were found to be aware of the unlawful nature of his act, he was
considered legally responsible for his actions regardless of other
evidence about his state of mental health; only when it could be
demonstrated that the defendant was unaware of the nature of
his crime and was unable to distinguish between right and wrong
could a plea of innocence by reason of insanity be accepted. As
Sobeloff points out, the McNaghten Rule is based on a very limited
and often erroneous notion of mental disorder, and the Durham
decision establishes greater harmony between criminal law and
the knowledge of psychiatry and psychology.

Despite this increased congruence between legal and psychological thinking, the issues which arise from differences in the
legal and psychological approaches to crime are not resolved. While
the Durham Rule encourages the court to seek a professional evaluation of the defendant's mental health, the definitive statement
which is desired is usually difficult to formulate, and often alien
to the thinking of the practicing clinician. The definitions of
mental health and the assessment procedures used frequently do
not enable us to make a dichotomous statement about the presence
or absence of insanity as desired by the courts. Instead, the efforts
of the psychiatrist or psychologist more frequently are devoted to
determining the nature of the individual's conflicts and his typical
defenses, and such an evaluation conceptualizes insanity as different in degree rather than kind from normality. Furthermore, there
appears to be a basic difference between the view of human be-

behavior of the law official and that of the student of mental health. In seeking to determine whether or not an individual is responsible for an unlawful act, the courts assume that man's actions are self-determined or involve free will. They are concerned with the "facts" or sequence of events immediately prior to the occurrence of the crime in order to assess the defendant's willful intent. Most students of mental health, on the other hand, tend to adopt a deterministic explanation of human behavior and seek knowledge of the historical events which are considered to have *compelled* the individual to behave as he did. The psychologist's purpose is to understand what led up to the action rather than to assess personal responsibility for the act. Undoubtedly it is desirable for the courts to utilize the knowledge provided by psychiatrists and psychologists. However, the increased adoption by criminal law of a completely deterministic orientation to man may result in extremely complex and drastic changes from our present legal procedures and traditions. For example, if the courts were to adopt the same orientation as most psychologists, the concept of personal responsibility or guilt might well be abandoned and any unlawful act might be related to the individual's state of adjustment rather than to personal responsibility. Such a change in orientation involves both positive and negative consequences which are extremely important for the community to consider.

The last paper deals with the question: Who should be permitted to engage in psychological practice? This topic again raises extremely important problems which confront both the community member and the professional person. Some of the related issues are: What standards and qualifications can we establish to assure professional competence in those who treat mental disturbances? Who should determine these standards and how can they be implemented? To what extent is it necessary to exert control over the educational curricula of the various recognized workers in the field of mental health? How shall we define "psychological practice" specifically enough to determine when a person is engaging in professional services?

All professions are confronted with such questions concerning qualifications and standards, but it would seem that the disciplines working in the field of mental health are especially beset by problems. Since no sharp line can be drawn between the activities of the professionally trained worker and those which take place in many types of nonprofessional interactions between people, it is difficult to define professional practice. In addition, psychological principles are used in the activities of many groups of persons and cannot be arrogated by a select group for its exclusive use. Conse-

quently, the field of mental mealth does not have clearly defined
standards and, therefore, is quite open to charlatans and mal-
practitioners. The paper by Lebo describes the unfortunate situation whereby a large number of legally established schools provide
degrees with little or no requisite training and thus encourage
quackery. Lebo points to the threat which this practice constitutes
and offers a number of suggestions which may help the community
establish greater control over the quality of the service it receives.

THE CONTROL OF HUMAN BEHAVIOR *

《 Carl R. Rogers and B. F. Skinner

I [Skinner]

Science is steadily increasing our power to influence, change, mold—in a
word, control—human behavior. It has extended our "understanding"
(whatever that may be) so that we deal more successfully with people in
nonscientific ways, but it has also identified conditions or variables which
can be used to predict and control behavior in a new, and increasingly
rigorous, technology. The broad disciplines of government and economics
offer examples of this, but there is special cogency in those contributions of
anthropology, sociology, and psychology which deal with individual behavior. Carl Rogers has listed some of the achievements to date in a recent
paper (1). Those of his examples which show or imply the control of the
single organism are primarily due, as we should expect, to psychology. It is
the experimental study of behavior which carries us beyond awkward or
inaccessible "principles," "factors," and so on, to variables which can be
directly manipulated.

It is also, and for more or less the same reasons, the conception of human
behavior emerging from an experimental analysis which most directly chal-
lenges traditional views. Psychologists themselves often do not seem to be
aware of how far they have moved in this direction. But the change is not
passing unnoticed by others. Until only recently it was customary to deny
the possibility of a rigorous science of human behavior by arguing, either
that a lawful science was impossible because man was a free agent, or that
merely statistical predictions would always leave room for personal freedom.
But those who used to take this line have become most vociferous in expressing their alarm at the way these obstacles are being surmounted.

    * From Carl R. Rogers and B. F. Skinner, "Some Issues Concerning the Control of
Human Behavior: A Symposium," *Science, 124,* 1057–1066. Reprinted by permission
of the authors and the Editor, *Science.*

Now, the control of human behavior has always been unpopular. Any undisguised effort to control usually arouses emotional reactions. We hesitate to admit, even to ourselves, that we are engaged in control, and we may refuse to control, even when this would be helpful, for fear of criticism. Those who have explicitly avowed an interest in control have been roughly treated by history. Machiavelli is the great prototype. As Macaulay said of him, "Out of his surname they coined an epithet for a knave and out of his Christian name a synonym for the devil." There were obvious reasons. The control that Machiavelli analyzed and recommended, like most political control, used techniques that were aversive to the controllee. The threats and punishments of the bully, like those of the government operating on the same plan, are not designed—whatever their success—to endear themselves to those who are controlled. Even when the techniques themselves are not aversive, control is usually exercised for the selfish purposes of the controller and, hence, has indirectly punishing effects upon others.

Man's natural inclination to revolt against selfish control has been exploited to good purpose in what we call the philosophy and literature of democracy. The doctrine of the rights of man has been effective in arousing individuals to concerted action against governmental and religious tyranny. The literature which has had this effect has greatly extended the number of terms in our language which express reactions to the control of men. But the ubiquity and ease of expression of this attitude spells trouble for any science which may give birth to a powerful technology of behavior. Intelligent men and women, dominated by the humanistic philosophy of the past two centuries, cannot view with equanimity what Andrew Hacker has called "the specter of predictable man" (2). Even the statistical or actuarial prediction of human events, such as the number of fatalities to be expected on a holiday weekend, strikes many people as uncanny and evil, while the prediction and control of individual behavior is regarded as little less than the work of the devil. I am not so much concerned here with the political or economic consequences for psychology, although research following certain channels may well suffer harmful effects. We ourselves, as intelligent men and women, and as exponents of Western thought, share these attitudes. They have already interfered with the free exercise of a scientific analysis, and their influence threatens to assume more serious proportions.

Three broad areas of human behavior supply good examples. The first of these—*personal control*—may be taken to include person-to-person relationships in the family, among friends, in social and work groups, and in counseling and psychotherapy. Other fields are *education* and *government*. A few examples from each will show how nonscientific preconceptions are affecting our current thinking about human behavior.

Personal control. People living together in groups come to control one another with a technique which is not inappropriately called "ethical."

When an individual behaves in a fashion acceptable to the group, he receives admiration, approval, affection, and many other reinforcements which increase the likelihood that he will continue to behave in that fashion. When his behavior is not acceptable, he is criticized, censured, blamed, or otherwise punished. In the first case the group calls him "good"; in the second, "bad." This practice is so thoroughly ingrained in our culture that we often fail to see that it is a technique of control. Yet we are almost always engaged in such control, even though the reinforcements and punishments are often subtle.

The practice of admiration is an important part of a culture, because behavior which is otherwise inclined to be weak can be set up and maintained with its help. The individual is especially likely to be praised, admired, or loved when he acts for the group in the face of great danger, for example, or sacrifices himself or his possessions, or submits to prolonged hardship, or suffers martyrdom. These actions are not admirable in any absolute sense, but they require admiration if they are to be strong. Similarly, we admire people who behave in original or exceptional ways, not because such behavior is itself admirable, but because we do not know how to encourage original or exceptional behavior in any other way. The group acclaims independent, unaided behavior in part because it is easier to reinforce than to help.

As long as this technique of control is misunderstood, we cannot judge correctly an environment in which there is less need for heroism, hardship, or independent action. We are likely to argue that such an environment is itself less admirable or produces less admirable people. In the old days, for example, young scholars often lived in undesirable quarters, ate unappetizing or inadequate food, performed unprofitable tasks for a living or to pay for necessary books and materials or publication. Older scholars and other members of the group offered compensating reinforcement in the form of approval and admiration for these sacrifices. When the modern graduate student receives a generous scholarship, enjoys good living conditions, and has his research and publication subsidized, the grounds for evaluation seem to be pulled from under us. Such a student no longer *needs* admiration to carry him over a series of obstacles (no matter how much he may need it for other reasons), and, in missing certain familiar objects of admiration, we are likely to conclude that such *conditions* are less admirable. Obstacles to scholarly work may serve as a useful measure of motivation—and we may go wrong unless some substitute is found—but we can scarcely defend a deliberate harassment of the student for this purpose. The productivity of any set of conditions can be evaluated only when we have freed ourselves of the attitudes which have been generated in us as members of an ethical group.

A similar difficulty arises from our use of punishment in the form of censure or blame. The concept of responsibility and the related concepts of foreknowledge and choice are used to justify techniques of control using punishment. Was So-and-So aware of the probable consequences of his action, and was the action deliberate? If so, we are justified in punishing him. But what does this mean? It appears to be a question concerning the efficacy of the contingent relations between behavior and punishing consequences. We punish behavior because it is objectionable to us or the group, but in a minor refinement of rather recent origin we have come to withhold punishment when it cannot be expected to have any effect. If the objectionable consequences of an act were accidental and not likely to occur again, there is no point in punishing. We say that the individual was not "aware of the consequences of his action" or that the consequences were not "intentional." If the action could not have been avoided—if the individual "had no choice"—punishment is also withheld, as it is if the individual is incapable of being changed by punishment because he is of "unsound mind." In all these cases—different as they are—the individual is held "not responsible" and goes unpunished.

Just as we say that it is "not fair" to punish a man for something he could not help doing, so we call it "unfair" when one is rewarded beyond his due or for something he could not help doing. In other words, we also object to wasting *reinforcers* when they are not needed or will do no good. We make the same point with the words *just* and *right*. Thus we have no right to punish the irresponsible, and a man has no right to reinforcers he does not earn or deserve. But concepts of choice, responsibility, justice, and so on, provide a most inadequate analysis of efficient reinforcing and punishing contingencies because they carry a heavy semantic cargo of a quite different sort, which obscures any attempt to clarify controlling practices or to improve techniques. In particular, they fail to prepare us for techniques based on other than aversive techniques of control. Most people would object to forcing prisoners to serve as subjects of dangerous medical experiments, but few object when they are induced to serve by the offer of return privileges—even when the reinforcing effect of these privileges has been created by forcible deprivation. In the traditional scheme the right to refuse guarantees the individual against coercion or an unfair bargain. But to what extent *can* a prisoner refuse under such circumstances?

We need not go so far afield to make the point. We can observe our own attitude toward personal freedom in the way we resent any interference with what we want to do. Suppose we want to buy a car of a particular sort. Then we may object, for example, if our wife urges us to buy a less expensive model and to put the difference into a new refrigerator. Or we may resent it if our neighbor questions our need for such a car or our ability to pay for it. We would certainly resent it if it were illegal to buy such a car (remember Prohibition); and if we find we cannot actually afford it, we may resent governmental control of the price through tariffs and taxes. We resent it if we discover that we cannot get the car because the manufacturer is holding the model in deliberately short supply in order to push a model we do not want. In all this we assert our democratic right to buy the car of our choice. We are well prepared to do so and to resent any restriction on our freedom.

But why do we not ask *why* it is the car of our choice and resent the forces which made it so? Perhaps our favorite toy as a child was a car, of a very different model, but nevertheless bearing the name of the car we now want. Perhaps our favorite TV program is sponsored by the manufacturer of that car. Perhaps we have seen pictures of many beautiful or prestigeful persons driving it—in pleasant or glamorous places. Perhaps the car has been designed with respect to our motivational patterns: the device on the hood is a phallic symbol; or the horsepower has been stepped up to please our competitive spirit in enabling us to pass other cars swiftly (or, as the advertisements say, "safely"). The concept of freedom that has emerged as part of the cultural practice of our group makes little or no provision for recognizing or dealing with these kinds of control. Concepts like "responsibility" and "rights" are scarcely applicable. We are prepared to deal with coercive measures, but we have no traditional recourse with respect to other measures which in the long run (and especially with the help of science) may be much more powerful and dangerous.

Education. The techniques of education were once frankly aversive. The teacher was usually older and stronger than his pupils and was able to "make them learn." This meant that they were not actually taught but were surrounded by a threatening world from which they could escape only by learning. Usually they were left to their own resources in discovering how to do so. Claude Coleman has published a grimly amusing reminder of these older practices (3). He tells of a schoolteacher who published a careful account of his services during 51 years of teaching, during which he administered: ". . . 911,527 blows with a cane; 124,010 with a rod; 20,989 with a ruler; 136,715 with the hand; 10,295 over the mouth; 7,905 boxes on the ear; [and] 1,115,800 slaps on the head. . . ."

Progressive education was a humanitarian effort to substitute positive reinforcement for such aversive measures, but in the search for useful human values in the classroom it has never fully replaced the variables it abandoned. Viewed as a branch of behavioral technology, education remains relatively inefficient. We supplement it, and rationalize it, by admiring the pupil who learns *for himself*; and we often attribute the learning process, or knowledge itself, to something *inside* the individual. We admire behavior which seems to have inner sources. Thus we admire one who *recites* a poem more than one who simply *reads* it. We admire one who *knows* the answer more than one who *knows where to look it up*. We admire the *writer* rather than the *reader*. We admire the arithmetician who can do a problem in his head rather than with a slide rule or calculating machine, or in "original" ways rather than by a strict application of rules.

In general we feel that any aid or "crutch"—except those aids to which we are now thoroughly accustomed—reduces the credit due. In Plato's *Phaedus*, Thamus, the king, attacks the invention of the alphabet on similar grounds! He is afraid "it will produce forgetfulness in the minds of those who learn to use it, because they will not practice their memories. . . ." In other words, he holds it more admirable to remember than to use a memorandum. He also objects that pupils "will read many things without instruction . . . [and] will therefore seem to know many things when they are for the most part ignorant." In the same vein we are today sometimes contemptuous of book learning, but, as educators, we can scarcely afford to adopt this view without reservation.

By admiring the student for knowledge and blaming him for ignorance, we escape some of the responsibility of teaching him. We resist any analysis of the educational process which threatens the notion of inner wisdom or questions the contention that the fault of ignorance lies with the student. More powerful techniques which bring about the same changes in behavior by manipulating *external* variables are decried as brainwashing or thought control. We are quite unprepared to judge *effective* educational measures. As long as only a few pupils learn much of what is taught, we do not worry about uniformity or regimentation. We do not fear the feeble technique; but we should view with dismay a system under which every student learned everything listed in a syllabus—although such a condition is far from unthinkable. Similarly, we do not fear a system which is so defective that the student must *work* for an education; but we are loath to give credit for anything learned without effort—although this could well be taken as an ideal result—and we flatly refuse to give credit if the student already knows what a school teaches.

A world in which people are wise and good without trying, without "having to be," without "choosing to be," could conceivably be a far better world for everyone. In such a world we should not have to "give anyone credit"—we should not need to admire anyone—for being wise and good. From our present point of view we cannot believe that such a world would be admirable. We do not even permit ourselves to imagine what it would be like.

Government. Government has always been the special field of aversive control. The state is frequently defined in terms of the power to punish, and jurisprudence leans heavily upon the associated notion of personal responsibility. Yet it is becoming increasingly difficult to reconcile current practice and theory with these earlier views. In criminology, for example, there is a strong tendency to drop the notion of responsibility in favor of some such alternative as capacity or controllability. But no matter how strongly the facts, or even practical expedience, support such a change, it is difficult to make the change in a legal system designed on a different plan. When governments resort to other techniques (for example, positive reinforcement), the concept of responsibility is no longer relevant and the theory of government is no longer applicable.

The conflict is illustrated by two decisions of the Supreme Court in the 1930's which dealt with, and disagreed on, the definition of control or coercion (4, p. 233). The Agricultural Adjustment Act proposed that the Secretary of Agriculture make "rental or benefit payments" to those farmers who agreed to reduce production. The government agreed that the Act would be unconstitutional if the farmer had been *compelled* to reduce production but was not, since he was merely *invited* to do so. Justice Roberts (4) expressed the contrary majority view of the court that "The power to confer or withhold unlimited benefits is the power to coerce or destroy." This recognition of positive reinforcement was withdrawn a few years later in another case in which Justice Cardozo (4, p. 244) wrote "To hold that motive or temptation is equivalent to coercion is to plunge the law in endless difficulties." We may agree with him, without implying that the proposition is therefore wrong. Sooner or later the law must be prepared to deal with all possible techniques of governmental control.

The uneasiness with which we view government (in the broadest possible sense) when it does not use punishment is shown by the reception of my utopian novel, *Walden Two* (4a). This was essentially a proposal to apply a behavioral technology to the construction of a workable, effective, and productive pattern of government. It was greeted with wrathful violence. *Life* magazine called it "a travesty on the good life," and "a menace . . . a triumph of mortmain or the dead hand not envisaged since the days of Sparta . . . a slur upon a name, a corruption of an impulse." Joseph Wood Krutch devoted a substantial part of his book, *The Measure of Man* (5), to attacking my views and those of the protagonist, Frazier, in the same vein, and Morris Viteles has recently criticized the book in a similar manner in *Science* (6). Perhaps the reaction is best expressed in a quotation from *The Quest for Utopia* by Negley and Patrick (7):

> Halfway through this contemporary utopia, the reader may feel sure, as we did, that this is a beautifully ironic satire on what has been called "behavioral engineering." The longer one stays in this better world of the psychologist, however, the plainer it becomes that the inspiration is not satiric, but messianic. This is indeed the behaviorally engineered society, and while it was to be expected that sooner or later the principle of psychological conditioning would be made the basis of a serious construction of utopia—Brown anticipated it in *Limanora*—yet not even the effective satire of Huxley is adequate preparation for the shocking horror of the idea when positively presented. Of all the dictatorships espoused by utopists, this is the most profound, and incipient dictators might well find in this utopia a guidebook of political practice.

One would scarcely guess that the authors are talking about a world in which there is food, clothing, and shelter for all, where everyone chooses his own work and works on the average only 4 hours a day, where music and the arts flourish, where personal relationships develop under the most favorable circumstances, where education prepares every child for the social and intellectual life which lies before him, where—in short—people are truly happy, secure, productive, creative, and forward-looking. What is wrong with it? Only one thing: someone "planned it that way." If these critics had come upon a society in some remote corner of the world which boasted similar advantages, they would undoubtedly have hailed it as providing a pattern we all might well follow—provided that it was clearly the result of a natural process of cultural evolution. Any evidence that intelligence had been used in arriving at this version of the good life would, in their eyes, be a serious flaw. No matter if the planner of *Walden Two* diverts none of the proceeds of the community to his own use, no matter if he has no current control or is, indeed, unknown to most of the other members of the community (he planned that, too), somewhere back of it all he occupies the position of prime mover. And this, to the child of the democratic tradition, spoils it all.

The dangers inherent in the control of human behavior are very real. The possibility of the misuse of scientific knowledge must always be faced. We cannot escape by denying the power of a science of behavior or arresting its development. It is no help to cling to familiar philosophies of human behavior simply because they are more reassuring. As I have pointed out elsewhere (8), the new techniques emerging from a science of behavior must be subject to the explicit countercontrol which has already been applied to earlier and cruder forms. Brute force and deception, for example, are now fairly generally suppressed by ethical practices and by explicit governmental and religious agencies. A similar countercontrol of scientific knowledge in the interests of the group is a feasible and promising possibility. Although we cannot say how devious the course of its evolution may be, a cultural pattern of control and countercontrol will presumably emerge which will be most widely supported because it is most widely reinforcing.

If we cannot foresee all the details of this (as we obviously cannot), it is important to remember that this is true of the critics of science as well. The dire consequences of new techniques of control, the hidden menace in original cultural designs—these need some proof. It is only another example of my present point that the need for proof is so often overlooked. Man has got himself into some pretty fixes, and it is easy to believe that he will do so again. But there is a more optimistic possibility. The slow growth of the methods of science, now for the first time being applied to human affairs, *may* mean a new and exciting phase of human life to which historical analogies will not apply and in which earlier political slogans will not be appropriate. If we are to use the knowledge that a science of behavior is now making available with any hope of success, we must look at human nature as it is brought into focus through the methods of science rather than as it has been presented to us in a series of historical accidents.

If the advent of a powerful science of behavior causes trouble, it will not be because science itself is inimical to human welfare but because older conceptions have not yielded easily or gracefully. We expect resistance to new techniques of control from those who have heavy investments in the old, but we have no reason to help them preserve a series of principles that are not ends in themselves but rather outmoded means to an end. What is needed is a new conception of human behavior which is compatible with the implications of a scientific analysis. All men control and are controlled The question of government in the broadest possible sense is not how freedom is to be preserved but what kinds of control are to be used and to what ends. Control must be analyzed and considered in its proper proportions No one, I am sure, wishes to develop new master-slave relationships or bend the will of the people to despotic rulers in new ways. These are patterns of control appropriate to a world without science. They may well be the first to go when the experimental analysis of behavior comes into its own in the design of cultural practices.

II [Rogers]

There are, I believe, a number of matters in connection with this important topic on which the authors of this article, and probably a large majority of psychologists, are in agreement. These matters then are not issues as far as we are concerned, and I should like to mention them briefly in order to put them to one side.

Points of agreement. I am sure we agree that men—as individuals and as societies—have always endeavored to understand, predict, influence, and control human behavior—their own behavior and that of others.

I believe we agree that the behavioral sciences are making and will continue to make increasingly rapid progress in the understanding of behavior and that as a consequence the capacity to predict and to control behavior is developing with equal rapidity.

I believe we agree that to deny these advances, or to claim that man's behavior cannot be a field of science, is unrealistic. Even though this is not an issue for us, we should recognize that many intelligent men still hold strongly to the view that the actions of men are free in some sense such that scientific knowledge of man's behavior is impossible. Thus Reinhold Niebuhr, the noted theologian, heaps scorn on the concept of psychology as a science of man's behavior and even says, "In any event, no scientific investigation of past behavior can become the basis of predictions of future behavior" (9). So, while this is not an issue for psychologists, we should at least notice in passing that it is an issue for many people.

I believe we are in agreement that the tremendous potential power of a science which permits the prediction and control of behavior may be misused, and that the possibility of such misuse constitutes a serious threat

Consequently Skinner and I are in agreement that the whole question of the scientific control of human behavior is a matter with which psychologists and the general public should concern themselves. As Robert Oppenheimer told the American Psychological Association last year (10) the problems that psychologists will pose for society by their growing ability to control behavior will be much more grave than the problems posed by the ability of physicists to control the reactions of matter. I am not sure whether psychologists generally recognize this. My impression is that by and large they hold a laissez-faire attitude. Obviously Skinner and I do not hold this laissez-faire view, or we would not have written this article.

Points at issue. With these several points of basic and important agreement, are there then any issues that remain on which there are differences? I believe there are. They can be stated very briefly. Who will be controlled? Who will exercise control? What type of control will be exercised? Most important of all, toward what end or what purpose, or in the pursuit of what value, will control be exercised?

It is on questions of this sort that there exist ambiguities, misunderstandings, and probably deep differences. These differences exist among psychologists, among members of the general public in this country, and among various world cultures. Without any hope of achieving a final resolution of these questions, we can, I believe, put these issues in clearer form.

Some meanings. To avoid ambiguity and faulty communication, I would like to clarify the meanings of some of the terms we are using.

Behavioral science is a term that might be defined from several angles but in the context of this discussion it refers primarily to knowledge that the existence of certain describable conditions in the human being and/or in his environment is followed by certain describable consequences in his actions.

Prediction means the prior identification of behaviors which then occur. Because it is important in some things I wish to say later, I would point out that one may predict a highly specific behavior, such as an eye blink, or one may predict a class of behaviors. One might correctly predict "avoidant behavior," for example, without being able to specify whether the individual will run away or simply close his eyes.

The word *control* is a very slippery one, which can be used with any one of several meanings. I would like to specify three that seem most important for our present purposes. *Control* may mean: (1) The setting of conditions by B for A, A having no voice in the matter, such that certain predictable behaviors then occur in A. I refer to this as external control. (2) The setting of conditions by B for A, A giving some degree of consent to these conditions, such that certain predictable behaviors then occur in A. I refer to this as the influence of B on A. (3) The setting of conditions by A such that certain predictable behaviors then occur in himself. I refer to this as internal control. It will be noted that Skinner lumps together the first two

meanings, external control and influence, under the concept of control.
find this confusing.

Usual concept of control of human behavior. With the underbrush thu
cleared away (I hope), let us review very briefly the various elements tha
are involved in the usual concept of the control of human behavior as med:
ated by the behaviorial sciences. I am drawing here on the previous writing
of Skinner, on his present statements, on the writings of others who hav
considered in either friendly or antagonistic fashion the meanings tha
would be involved in such control. I have not excluded the science fictio
writers, as reported recently by Vanderberg (11), since they often show a;
awareness of the issues involved, even though the methods described ar
as yet fictional. These then are the elements that seem common to thes
different concepts of the application of science to human behavior.

1. There must first be some sort of decision about goals. Usually desi
able goals are assumed, but sometimes, as in George Orwell's book 1984
the goal that is selected is an aggrandizement of individual power witl
which most of us would disagree. In a recent paper Skinner suggests tha
one possible set of goals to be assigned to the behavioral technology is this
"Let men be happy, informed, skillful, well-behaved and productive" (12)
In the first draft of his part of this article, which he was kind enough t
show me, he did not mention such definite goals as these, but desired "im
proved" educational practices, "wiser" use of knowledge in government
and the like. In the final version of his article he avoids even these value
laden terms, and his implicit goal is the very general one that scientific con
trol of behavior is desirable, because it would perhaps bring "a far bette
world for everyone."

Thus the first step in thinking about the control of human behavior i
the choice of goals, whether specific or general. It is necessary to come t
terms in some way with the issue, "For what purpose?"

2. A second element is that, whether the end selected is highly specifi
or is a very general one such as wanting "a better world," we proceed b
the methods of science to discover the means to these ends. We continu
through further experimentation and investigation to discover more effec
tive means. The method of science is self-correcting in thus arriving a
increasingly effective ways of achieving the purpose we have in mind.

3. The third aspect of such control is that as the conditions or method
are discovered by which to reach the goal, some person or some group estal
lishes these conditions and uses these methods, having in one way or an
other obtained the power to do so.

4. The fourth element is the exposure of individuals to the prescribe
conditions, and this leads, with a high degree of probability, to behavio
which is in line with the goals desired. Individuals are now happy, if tha
has been the goal, or well-behaved, or submissive, or whatever it has bee
decided to make them.

5. The fifth element is that if the process I have described is put in
motion then there is a continuing social organization which will continue
to produce the types of behavior that have been valued.

Some flaws. Are there any flaws in this way of viewing the control of
human behavior? I believe there are. In fact the only element in this description with which I find myself in agreement is the second. It seems to
me quite incontrovertibly true that the scientific method is an excellent
way to discover the means by which to achieve our goals. Beyond that, I
feel many sharp differences, which I will try to spell out.

I believe that in Skinner's presentation here and in his previous writings,
there is a serious underestimation of the problem of power. To hope that
the power which is being made available by the behavioral sciences will be
exercised by the scientists, or by a benevolent group, seems to me a hope
little supported by either recent or distant history. It seems far more likely
that behavioral scientists, holding their present attitudes, will be in the
position of the German rocket scientists specializing in guided missiles.
First they worked devotedly for Hitler to destroy the U.S.S.R. and the
United States. Now, depending on who captured them, they work devot-
ally for the U.S.S.R. in the interest of destroying the United States, or
devotedly for the United States in the interest of destroying the U.S.S.R.
If behavioral scientists are concerned solely with advancing their science,
it seems most probable that they will serve the purposes of whatever individual or group has the power.

But the major flaw I see in this review of what is involved in the scientific
control of human behavior is the denial, misunderstanding, or gross underestimation of the place of ends, goals or values in their relationship to
science. This error (as it seems to me) has so many implications that I
would like to devote some space to it.

Ends and values in relation to science. In sharp contradiction to some
views that have been advanced, I would like to propose a two-pronged
thesis: (1) In any scientific endeavor—whether "pure" or applied science—
there is a prior subjective choice of the purpose or value which that scientific work is perceived as serving. (2) This subjective value choice which
brings the scientific endeavor into being must always lie outside of that
endeavor and can never become a part of the science involved in that
endeavor.

Let me illustrate the first point from Skinner himself. It is clear that in
his earlier writing (12) it is recognized that a prior value choice is necessary,
and it is specified as the goal that men are to become happy, well-behaved,
productive, and so on. I am pleased that Skinner has retreated from the
goals he then chose, because to me they seem to be stultifying values. I can
only feel that he was choosing these goals for others, not for himself. I
would hate to see Skinner become "well-behaved," as that term would be
defined for him by behavioral scientists. His recent article in the *American*

Psychologist (13) shows that he certainly does not want to be "productive" as that value is defined by most psychologists. And the most awful fate I can imagine for him would be to have him constantly "happy." It is the fact that he is very unhappy about many things which makes me prize him.

In the first draft of his part of this article, he also included such prior value choices, saying for example, "We must decide how we are to use the knowledge which a science of human behavior is now making available." Now he has dropped all mention of such choices, and if I understand him correctly, he believes that science can proceed without them. He has suggested this view in another recent paper, stating that "We must continue to experiment in cultural design . . . testing the consequences as we go. Eventually the practices which make for the greatest biological and psychological strength of the group will presumably survive" (8, p. 549).

I would point out, however, that to choose to experiment is a value choice. Even to move in the direction of perfectly random experimentation is a value choice. To test the consequences of an experiment is possible only if we have first made a subjective choice of a criterion value. And implicit in his statement is a valuing of biological and psychological strength. So even when trying to avoid such choice, it seems inescapable that a prior subjective value choice is necessary for any scientific endeavor, or for any application of scientific knowledge.

I wish to make it clear that I am not saying that values cannot be included as a subject of science. It is not true that science deals only with certain classes of "facts" and that these classes do not include values. It is a bit more complex than that, as a simple illustration or two may make clear.

If I value knowledge of the "three R's" as a goal of education, the methods of science can give me increasingly accurate information on how this goal may be achieved. If I value problem-solving ability as a goal of education, the scientific method can give me the same kind of help.

Now, if I wish to determine whether problem-solving ability is "better" than knowledge of the three R's, then scientific method can also study those two values but *only*—and this is very important—in terms of some other value which I have subjectively chosen. I may value college success. Then I can determine whether problem-solving ability or knowledge of the three R's is most closely associated with that value. I may value personal integration or vocational success or responsible citizenship. I can determine whether problem-solving ability or knowledge of the three R's is "better" for achieving any one of these values. But the value or purpose that gives meaning to a particular scientific endeavor must always lie outside of that endeavor.

Although our concern in this symposium is largely with applied science, what I have been saying seems equally true of so-called "pure" science. In pure science the usual prior subjective value choice is the discovery of truth.

But this is a subjective choice, and science can never say whether it is the best choice, save in the light of some other value. Geneticists in the U.S.S.R., for example, had to make a subjective choice of whether it was better to pursue truth or to discover facts which upheld a governmental dogma. Which choice is "better"? We could make a scientific investigation of those alternatives but only in the light of some other subjectively chosen value. If, for example, we value the survival of a culture, then we could begin to investigate with the methods of science the question of whether pursuit of truth or support of governmental dogma is most closely associated with cultural survival.

My point then is that any endeavor in science, pure or applied, is carried on in the pursuit of a purpose or value that is subjectively chosen by persons. It is important that this choice be made explicit, since the particular value which is being sought can never be tested or evaluated, confirmed or denied, by the scientific endeavor to which it gives birth. The initial purpose or value always and necessarily lies outside the scope of the scientific effort which it sets in motion.

Among other things this means that if we choose some particular goal or series of goals for human beings and then set out on a large scale to control human behavior to the end of achieving those goals, we are locked in the rigidity of our initial choice, because such a scientific endeavor can never transcend itself to select new goals. Only subjective human persons can do that. Thus if we chose as our goal the state of happiness for human beings (a goal deservedly ridiculed by Aldous Huxley in *Brave New World*), and if we involved all of society in a successful scientific program by which people became happy, we would be locked in a colossal rigidity in which no one would be free to question this goal, because our scientific operations could not transcend themselves to question their guiding purposes. And without laboring this point, I would remark that colossal rigidity, whether in dinosaurs or dictatorships, has a very poor record of evolutionary survival.

If, however, a part of our scheme is to set free some "planners" who do not have to be happy, who are not controlled, and who are therefore free to choose some other values, this has several meanings. It means that the purpose we have chosen as our goal is not a sufficient and a satisfying one for human beings but must be supplemented. It also means that if it is necessary to set up an elite group which is free, then this shows all too clearly that the great majority are only the slaves—no matter by what high-sounding name we call them—of those who select the goals.

Perhaps, however, the thought is that a continuing scientific endeavor will evolve its own goals; that the initial findings will alter the directions, and subsequent findings will alter them still further, and that science somehow develops its own purpose. Although he does not clearly say so, this appears to be the pattern Skinner has in mind. It is surely a reasonable description, but it overlooks one element in this continuing development, which is that subjective personal choice enters in at every point at which the direction changes. The findings of a science, the results of an experiment, do not and never can tell us what next scientific purpose to pursue. Even in the purest of science, the scientist must decide what the findings mean and must subjectively choose what next step will be most profitable in the pursuit of his purpose. And if we are speaking of the application of scientific knowledge, then it is distressingly clear that the increasing scientific knowledge of the structure of the atom carries with it no necessary choice as to the purpose to which this knowledge will be put. This is a subjective personal choice which must be made by many individuals.

Thus I return to the proposition with which I began this section of my remarks—and which I now repeat in different words. Science has its meaning as the objective pursuit of a purpose which has been subjectively chosen by a person or persons. This purpose or value can never be investigated by the particular scientific experiment or investigation to which it has given birth and meaning. Consequently, any discussion of the control of human beings by the behavioral sciences must first and most deeply concern itself with the subjectively chosen purposes which such an application of science is intended to implement.

Is the situation hopeless? The thoughtful reader may recognize that, although my remarks up to this point have introduced some modifications in the conception of the processes by which human behavior will be controlled, these remarks may have made such control seem, if anything, even more inevitable. We might sum it up this way: Behavioral science is clearly moving forward; the increasing power for control which it gives will be held by someone or some group; such an individual or group will surely choose the values or goals to be achieved; and most of us will then be increasingly controlled by means so subtle that we will not even be aware of them as controls. Thus, whether a council of wise psychologists (if this is not a contradiction in terms), or a Stalin, or a Big Brother has the power, and whether the goal is happiness, or productivity, or resolution of the Oedipus complex, or submission, or love of Big Brother, we will inevitably find ourselves moving toward the chosen goal and probably thinking that we ourselves desire it. Thus, if this line of reasoning is correct, it appears that some form of *Walden Two* or of *1984* (and at a deep philosophic level they seem indistinguishable) is coming. The fact that it would surely arrive piecemeal, rather than all at once, does not greatly change the fundamental issues. In any event, as Skinner has indicated in his writings, we would then look back upon the concepts of human freedom, the capacity for choice, the responsibility for choice, and the worth of the human individual as historical curiosities which once existed by cultural accident as values in a prescientific civilization.

I believe that any person observant of trends must regard something like the foregoing sequence as a real possibility. It is not simply a fantasy. Something of that sort may even be the most likely future. But is it an inevitable future? I want to devote the remainder of my remarks to an alternative possibility.

Alternative set of values. Suppose we start with a set of ends, values, purposes, quite different from the type of goals we have been considering. Suppose we do this quite openly, setting them forth as a possible value choice to be accepted or rejected. Suppose we select a set of values that focuses on fluid elements of process rather than static attributes. We might then value: man as a process of becoming, as a process of achieving worth and dignity through the development of his potentialities; the individual human being as a self-actualizing process, moving on to more challenging and enriching experiences, the process by which the individual creatively adapts to an ever-new and changing world; the process by which knowledge transcends itself, as, for example, the theory of relativity transcended Newtonian physics, itself to be transcended in some future day by a new perception.

If we select values such as these we turn to our science and technology of behavior with a very different set of questions. We will want to know such things as these: Can science aid in the discovery of new modes of richly rewarding living? more meaningful and satisfying modes of interpersonal relationships? Can science inform us on how the human race can become a more intelligent participant in its own evolution—its physical, psychological and social evolution? Can science inform us on ways of releasing the creative capacity of individuals, which seem so necessary if we are to survive in this fantastically expanding atomic age? Oppenheimer has pointed out (14) that knowledge, which used to double in millenia or centuries, now doubles in a generation or a decade. It appears that we must discover the utmost in release of creativity if we are to be able to adapt effectively. In short, can science discover the methods by which man can most readily become a continually developing and self-transcending process, in his behavior, his thinking, his knowledge? Can science predict and release an essentially "unpredictable" freedom?

It is one of the virtues of science as a method that it is as able to advance and implement goals and purposes of this sort as it is to serve static values, such as states of being well-informed, happy, obedient. Indeed we have some evidence of this.

Small example. I will perhaps be forgiven if I document some of the possibilities along this line by turning to psychotherapy, the field I know best.

Psychotherapy, as Meerloo (15) and others have pointed out, can be one of the most subtle tools for the control of A by B. The therapist can subtly mold individuals in imitation of himself. He can cause an individual to become a submissive and conforming being. When certain therapeutic principles are used in extreme fashion, we call it brainwashing, an instance

of the disintegration óf the personálity and a reformulation of the persor
along lines desired by the controlling individual. So the principles oí
therapy can be used as an effective means óf external control of humar
personality and behavior.˙ Can psychotherapy be anything else?

Here I find the developments going on in client-centered psychotherapy
(16) an exciting hint óf what a behavioral science can do in achieving the
kinds óf válues I have stated. Quite aside from being a somewhat new
orientation in psychotherapy, this development has important implications
regarding the relation óf a behavioral science to the control of human behavior. Let me describe our experience as it relates to the issues of this
discussion.

In client-centered therapy, we are deeply engaged in the prediction and
influencing of behavior, or even the control of behavior. As therapists, we
institute certain attitudinal conditions, and the client has relatively little
voice in the establishment of these conditions. We predict that if these
conditions are instituted, certain behavioral consequences will ensue in
the client. Up to this point this is largely external control, no different
from what Skinner has described, and no different from what I have discussed in the preceding sections of this article. But here any similarity
ceases.

The conditions we have chosen to establish predict such behavioral consequences as these: that the client will become self-directing, less rigid,
more open to the evidence of his senses, better organized and integrated,
more similar to the ideal which he has chosen for himself. In other words,
we have established by external control conditions which we predict will
be followed by internal control by the individual, in pursuit of internally
chosen goals. We have set the conditions which predict various classes of
behaviors—self-directing behaviors, sensitivity to realities within and without, flexible adaptiveness—which are by their very nature unpredictable in
their specifics. Our recent research (17) indicates that our predictions are
to a significant degree corroborated, and our commitment to the scientific
method causes us to believe that more effective means of achieving these
goals may be realized.

Research exists in other fields—industry, education, group dynamics—
which seems to support our own findings. I believe it may be conservatively
stated that scientific progress has been made in identifying those conditions
in an interpersonal relationship which, if they exist in B, are followed in
A by greater maturity in behavior, less dependence on others, an increase
in expressiveness as a person, an increase in variability, flexibility and
effectiveness of adaptation, an increase in self-responsibility and self-direction. And, quite in contrast to the concern expressed by some, we do not
find that the creatively adaptive behavior which results from such self-
directed variability of expression is a "happy accident" which occurs in
"chaos." Rather, the individual who is open to his experience, and self-

directing, is harmonious not chaotic, ingenious rather than random, as he orders his responses imaginatively toward the achievement of his own purposes. His creative actions are no more a "happy accident" than was Einstein's development of the theory of relativity.

Thus we find ourselves in fundamental agreement with John Dewey's statement: "Science has made its way by releasing, not by suppressing, the elements of variation, of invention and innovation, of novel creation in individuals" (18). Progress in personal life and in group living is, we believe, made in the same way.

Possible concept of the control of human behavior. It is quite clear that the point of view I am expressing is in sharp contrast to the usual conception of the relationship of the behavioral sciences to the control of human behavior. In order to make this contrast even more blunt, I will state this possibility in paragraphs parallel to those used before.

1. It is possible for us to choose to value man as a self-actualizing process of becoming; to value creativity, and the process by which knowledge becomes self-transcending.

2. We can proceed, by the methods of science, to discover the conditions which necessarily precede these processes and, through continuing experimentation, to discover better means of achieving these purposes.

3. It is possible for individuals or groups to set these conditions, with a minimum of power or control. According to present knowledge, the only authority necessary is the authority to establish certain qualities of interpersonal relationship.

4. Exposed to these conditions, present knowledge suggests that individuals become more self-responsible, make progress in self-actualization, become more flexible, and become more creatively adaptive.

5. Thus such an initial choice would inaugurate the beginnings of a social system or subsystem in which values, knowledge, adaptive skills, and even the concept of science would be continually changing and self-transcending. The emphasis would be upon man as a process of becoming.

I believe it is clear that such a view as I have been describing does not lead to any definable utopia. It would be impossible to predict its final outcome. It involves a step-by-step development, based on a continuing subjective choice of purposes, which are implemented by the behavioral sciences. It is in the direction of the "open society," as that term has been defined by Popper (19), where individuals carry responsibility for personal decisions. It is at the opposite pole from his concept of the closed society, of which *Walden Two* would be an example.

I trust it is also evident that the whole emphasis is on process, not on end-states of being. I am suggesting that it is by choosing to value certain qualitative elements of the process of becoming that we can find a pathway toward the open society.

The choice. It is my hope that we have helped to clarify the range of

choice which will lie before us and our children in regard to the behaviora
sciences. We can choose to use our growing knowledge to enslave peopl
in ways never dreamed of before, depersonalizing them, controlling then
by means so carefully selected that they will perhaps never be aware o
their loss of personhood. We can choose to utilize our scientific knowledg
to make men happy, well-behaved, and productive, as Skinner earlie
suggested. Or we can insure that each person learns all the syllabus whicl
we select and set before him, as Skinner now suggests. Or at the other enc
of the spectrum of choice we can choose to use the behavioral sciences ir
ways which will free, not control; which will bring about constructivc
variability, not conformity; which will develop creativity, not contentment
which will facilitate each person in his self-directed process of becoming
which will aid individuals, groups, and even the concept of science to be
come self-transcending in freshly adaptive ways of meeting life and it:
problems. The choice is up to us, and, the human race being what it is
we are likely to stumble about, making at times some nearly disastrou
value choices and at other times highly constructive ones.

I am aware that to some, this setting forth of a choice is unrealistic, be
cause a choice of values is regarded as not possible. Skinner has stated:

> Man's vaunted creative powers . . . his capacity to choose and our right t
> hold him responsible for his choice—none of these is conspicuous in this nev
> self-portrait (provided by science). Man, we once believed, was free to expres
> himself in art, music, and literature, to inquire into nature, to seek salvation ir
> his own way. He could initiate action and make spontaneous and capriciou
> changes of course. . . . But science insists that action is initiated by force
> impinging upon the individual, and that caprice is only another name fo
> behavior for which we have not yet found a cause (12, pp. 52–53).

I can understand this point of view, but I believe that it avoids lookin;
at the great paradox of behavioral science. Behavior, when it is examinec
scientifically, is surely best understood as determined by prior causation
This is one great fact of science. But responsible personal choice, which i
the most essential element in being a person, which is the core experienc
in psychotherapy, which exists prior to any scientific endeavor, is an equall
prominent fact in our lives. To deny the experience of responsible choic
is, to me, as restricted a view as to deny the possibility of a behaviora
science. That these two important elements of our experience appear to b
in contradiction has perhaps the same significance as the contradiction be
tween the wave theory and the corpuscular theory of light, both of whicl
can be shown to be true, even though incompatible. We cannot profitabl
deny our subjective life, any more than we can deny the objective descrip
tion of that life.

In conclusion then, it is my contention that science cannot come int
being without a personal choice of the values we wish to achieve. Anc
these values we choose to implement will forever lie outside of the scienc

which implements them; the goals we select, the purposes we wish to follow, must always be outside of the science which achieves them. To me this has the encouraging meaning that the human person, with his capacity of subjective choice, can and will always exist, separate from and prior to any of his scientific undertakings. Unless as individuals and groups we choose to relinquish our capacity of subjective choice, we will always remain persons, not simply pawns of a self-created science.

III [Skinner]

I cannot quite agree that the practice of science *requires* a prior decision about goals or a prior choice of values. The metallurgist can study the properties of steel and the engineer can design a bridge without raising the question of whether a bridge is to built. But such questions are certainly frequently raised and tentatively answered. Rogers wants to call the answers "subjective choices of values." To me, such an expression suggests that we have had to abandon more rigorous scientific practices in order to talk about our own behavior. In the experimental analysis of other organisms I would use other terms, and I shall try to do so here. Any list of values is a list of reinforcers—conditioned or otherwise. We are so constituted that under certain circumstances food, water, sexual contact, and so on, will make any behavior which produces them more likely to occur again. Other things may acquire this power. We do not need to say that an organism chooses to eat rather than to starve. If you answer that it is a very different thing when a man chooses to starve, I am only too happy to agree. If it were not so, we should have cleared up the question of choice long ago. An organism can be reinforced by—can be made to "choose"—almost any given state of affairs.

Rogers is concerned with choices that involve multiple and usually conflicting consequences. I have dealt with some of these elsewhere (20) in an analysis of self-control. Shall I eat these delicious strawberries today if I will then suffer an annoying rash tomorrow? The decision I am to make used to be assigned to the province of ethics. But we are now studying similar combinations of positive and negative consequences, as well as collateral conditions which affect the result, in the laboratory. Even a pigeon can be taught some measure of self-control! And this work helps us to understand the operation of certain formulas—among them value judgments—which folk-wisdom, religion, and psychotherapy have advanced in the interests of self-discipline. The observable effect of any statement of value is to alter the relative effectiveness of reinforcers. We may no longer enjoy the strawberries for thinking about the rash. If rashes are made sufficiently shameful, illegal, sinful, maladjusted, or unwise, we may glow with satisfaction as we push the strawberries aside in a grandiose avoidance response which would bring a smile to the lips of Murray Sidman.

People behave in ways which, as we say, conform to ethical, governmental, or religious patterns because they are reinforced for doing so. The resulting behavior may have far-reaching consequences for the survival of the pattern to which it conforms. And whether we like it or not, survival is the ultimate criterion. This is where, it seems to me, science can help— not in choosing a goal, but in enabling us to predict the survival value of cultural practices. Man has too long tried to get the kind of world he wants by glorifying some brand of immediate reinforcement. As science points up more and more of the remoter consequences, he may begin to work to strengthen behavior, not in a slavish devotion to a chosen value, but with respect to the ultimate survival of mankind. Do not ask me why I want mankind to survive. I can tell you why only in the sense in which the physiologist can tell you why I want to breathe. Once the relation between a given step and the survival of my group has been pointed out, I will take that step. And it is the business of science to point out just such relations.

The values I have occasionally recommended (and Rogers has not led me to recant) are transitional. Other things being equal, I am betting on the group whose practices make for healthy, happy, secure, productive, and creative people. And I insist that the values recommended by Rogers are transitional, too, for I can ask him the same kind of question. Man as a process of becoming—*what*? Self-actualization—for what? Inner control is no more a goal than external.

What Rogers seems to me to be proposing, both here and elsewhere (1), is this: Let us use our increasing power of control to create individuals who will not need and perhaps will no longer respond to control. Let us solve the problem of our power by renouncing it. At first blush this seems as implausible as a benevolent despot. Yet power has occasionally been foresworn. A nation has burned its Reichstag, rich men have given away their wealth, beautiful women have become ugly hermits in the desert, and psychotherapists have become nondirective. When this happens, I look to other possible reinforcements for a plausible explanation. A people relinquish democratic power when a tyrant promises them the earth. Rich men give away wealth to escape the accusing finger of their fellowmen. A woman destroys her beauty in the hope of salvation. And a psychotherapist relinquishes control because he can thus help his client more effectively.

The solution that Rogers is suggesting is thus understandable. But is he correctly interpreting the result? What evidence is there that a client ever becomes truly *self*-directing? What evidence is there that he ever makes a truly *inner* choice of ideal or goal? Even though the therapist does not do the choosing, even though he encourages "self-actualization"—he is not out of control as long as he holds himself ready to step in when occasion demands—when, for example, the client chooses the goal of becoming a more accomplished liar or murdering his boss. But supposing the therapist does withdraw completely or is no longer necessary—what about all the other forces acting upon the client? Is the self-chosen goal independent of his early ethical and religious training? of the folk-wisdom of his group? of the opinions and attitudes of others who are important to him? Surely not. The therapeutic situation is only a small part of the world of the client. From the therapist's point of view it may appear to be possible to relinquish control. But the control passes, not to a "self," but to forces in other parts of the client's world. The solution of the therapist's problem of power cannot be *our* solution, for we must consider *all* the forces acting upon the individual.

The child who must be prodded and nagged is something less than a fully developed human being. We want to see him hurrying to his appointment, not because each step is taken in response to verbal reminders from his mother, but because certain temporal contingencies, in which dawdling has been punished and hurrying reinforced, have worked a change in his behavior. Call this a state of better organization, a greater sensitivity to reality, or what you will. The plain fact is that the child passes from a temporary verbal control exercised by his parents to control by certain inexorable features of the environment. I should suppose that something of the same sort happens in successful psychotherapy. Rogers seems to me to be saying this: Let us put an end, as quickly as possible, to any pattern of master-and-slave, to any direct obedience to command, to the submissive following of suggestions. Let the individual be free to adjust himself to more rewarding features of the world about him. In the end, let his teachers and counselors "wither away," like the Marxist state. I not only agree with this as a useful ideal, I have constructed a fanciful world to demonstrate its advantages. It saddens me to hear Rogers say that "at a deep philosophic level" *Walden Two* and George Orwell's *1984* "seem indistinguishable." They could scarcely be more unlike—at any level. The book *1984* is a picture of immediate aversive control for vicious selfish purposes. The founder of *Walden Two*, on the other hand, has built a community in which neither he nor any other person exerts any *current* control. His achievement lay in his original *plan*, and when he boasts of this ("It is enough to satisfy the thirstiest tyrant") we do not fear him but only pity him for his weakness.

Another critic of *Walden Two*, Andrew Hacker (21), has discussed this point in considering the bearing of mass conditioning upon the liberal notion of autonomous man. In drawing certain parallels between the Grand Inquisition passage in Dostoevsky's *Brothers Karamazov*, Huxley's *Brave New World*, and *Walden Two*, he attempts to set up a distinction to be drawn in any society betwen conditioners and conditioned. He assumes that "the conditioner can be said to be autonomous in the traditional liberal sense." But then he notes: "Of course the conditioner has been conditioned. But he has not been conditioned by the conscious manipulation of another *person.*" But how does this affect the resulting behavior? Can we not soon forget the origins of the "artificial" diamond which is identical with the real thing? Whether it is an "accidental" cultural pattern, such as is said to have produced the founder of *Walden Two,* or the engineered environment which is about to produce his successors, we are dealing with sets of conditions generating human behavior which will ultimately be measured by their contribution to the strength of the group. We look to the future, not the past, for the test of "goodness" or acceptability.

If we are worthy of our democratic heritage we shall, of course, be ready to resist any tyrannical use of science for immediate or selfish purposes. But if we value the achievements and goals of democracy we must not refuse to apply science to the design and construction of cultural patterns, even though we may then find ourselves in some sense in the position of controllers. Fear of control, generalized beyond any warrant, has led to a misinterpretation of valid practices and the blind rejection of intelligent planning for a better way of life. In terms which I trust Rogers will approve, in conquering this fear we shall become more mature and better organized and shall, thus, more fully actualize ourselves as human beings.

References and Notes

1. C. R. Rogers, *Teachers College Record* 57, 316 (1956).
2. A. Hacker, *Antioch Rev.* 14, 195 (1954).
3. C. Coleman, *Bull. Am. Assoc. Univ. Professors* 39, 457 (1953).
4. P. A. Freund *et al.*, *Constitutional Law: Cases and Other Problems*, vol. 1 (Little, Brown, Boston, 1954).
4a. B. F. Skinner, *Walden Two* (Macmillan, New York, 1948).
5. J. W. Krutch, *The Measure of Man* (Bobbs-Merrill, Indianapolis, 1953).
6. M. Viteles, *Science* 122, 1167 (1955).
7. G. Negley and J. M. Patrick, *The Quest for Utopia* (Schuman, New York, 1952).
8. B. F. Skinner, *Trans. N.Y. Acad. Sci.* 17, 547 (1955).
9. R. Niebuhr, *The Self and the Dramas of History* (Scribner, New York, 1955), p. 47.
10. R. Oppenheimer, *Am. Psychol.* 11, 127 (1956).
11. S. G. Vandenberg, *ibid.* 11, 339 (1956).
12. B. F. Skinner, *Am. Scholar* 25, 47 (1955–56).
13. ———, *Am. Psychol.* 11, 221 (1956).
14. R. Oppenheimer, *Roosevelt University Occasional Papers* 2 (1956).
15. J. A. M. Meerloo, *J. Nervous Mental Disease* 122, 353 (1955).
16. C. R. Rogers, *Client-centered Therapy* (Houghton Mifflin, Boston, 1951).
17. ——— and R. Dymond, Eds., *Psychotherapy and Personality Change* (Univ. of Chicago Press, Chicago, 1954).
18. J. Ratner, Ed., *Intelligence in the Modern World: John Dewey's Philosophy* (Modern Library, New York, 1939), p. 359.
19. K. R. Popper, *The Open Society and Its Enemies* (Routledge and Kegan Paul, London, 1945).
20. B. F. Skinner, *Science and Human Behavior* (Macmillan, New York, 1953).
21. A. Hacker, *J. Politics* 17, 590 (1955).

THE LAW AND PSYCHOPATHOLOGY *

⟨ Simon E. Sobeloff

"Insanity and the Criminal Law" is a complicated and difficult subject, and its literature is as voluminous as it is interesting.

Let me first of all state that I speak only for myself. Proposals for improvement of criminal law and procedure are under consideration in the Department of Justice, and likely the matters which I shall touch upon here, informally and non-technically, will be given thorough consideration and the results embodied in a program for legislation which it is hoped will be presented by the department next year.

We are concerned here only with the question of criminal responsibility. We are not dealing with problems of mental capacity to contract or generally to manage one's affairs, or with the standards to be followed in civil commitment proceedings—although what will be said here necessarily has a bearing on these questions.

How far persons suffering from mental disease, mental deficiency, or other forms of mental abnormality, should be held legally responsible for breaches of the criminal law, is something that has stirred vigorous debate for a long time. As you know, in ancient times lunatics were not regarded as suffering from disease but were believed to be possessed by demons, the result of their evil passions. For this wickedness they therefore deserved to be and were beaten, kept in chains, and not uncommonly sentenced to death by burning or hanging. If acquitted, they went free, often a menace to their own and others' safety. An early formulation of a rule to determine criminal responsibility may be traced to England in the early part of the eighteenth century when it was declared that an accused might escape punishment if he could not distinguish good and evil—that is, to use the quaint language of Justice Tracy, if he "does not know what he is doing, no more than . . . a wild beast." [1]

The extreme and picturesque requirement that to qualify for immunity the accused shall know no more than a wild beast was altered and moderated somewhat about 1760.[2] The terms "right and wrong" were substituted for "good and evil," and the accused no longer needed to be reduced to a bestial level. The generally prevalent American rule stems directly from the famous McNaghten case,[3] in 1843, in which 14 out of 15 English justices agreed that: "the jurors ought to be told in all cases that

* From Simon E. Sobeloff, "From McNaghten to Durham and Beyond," *Psychiat. Quart.*, 29, 357–370. Reprinted by permission of the author and the Editor, State Hospitals Press.

every man is to be presumed to be sane, and to possess a sufficient degree
of reason to be responsible for his crimes, until the contrary be proved to
their satisfaction; and that, to establish a defence on the ground of insanity, it must be clearly proved that at the time of the committing of the
act, the party accused was labouring under such a defect of reason, from
disease of the mind, as not to know the nature and quality of the act he
was doing; or, if he did know it, that he did not know he was doing what
was wrong." [4]

This test, known familiarly as the "right and wrong test," turns on a
specified and very limited symptom of insanity, which science no longer
deems necessarily or even typically associated with most serious mental
disorders. Only the drooling idiot can be said to have no knowledge of
right and wrong, and he almost never gets into the criminal court. Judging
the issue of insanity according to the right-wrong test exclusively is like
saying as a matter of law that the only acceptable symptom in defining
appendicitis is a pain in the abdomen and that no other diagnostic symptom is valid.

In most jurisdictions this "right and wrong test" is still the law today.
Courts have adhered tenaciously to this rule despite a heavy and persistent
barrage of criticism for more than a hundred years. Almost from the
moment the McNaghten rule was born, it was strongly attacked, not only
by physicians, but also by such eminent lawyers as Sir James Fitzjames
Stephen, author of the classic "History of the Criminal Law in England." [5]
A quarter of a century ago, Mr. Justice Cardozo summed up the almost
universal judgment. "Everyone," he said, "concedes that the present definition of insanity has little relation to the truths of mental life." [6]

Mr. Justice Cardozo also said: "If insanity is not to be a defense, let us
say so frankly and even brutally, but let us not mock ourselves with a
definition that palters with reality. Such a method is neither good morals
nor good science nor good law." [7]

A present member of the United States Supreme Court, Mr. Justice
Frankfurter, recently stated in testifying before the British Royal Commission on Capital Punishment:

. . . The M'Naghten Rules were rules which the Judges, in response to
questions by the House of Lords, formulated in the light of the then existing psychological knowledge. . . . I do not see why the rules of law should
be arrested at the state of psychological knowledge of the time when they
were formulated. . . . If you find rules that are, broadly speaking, discredited
by those who have to administer them, which is, I think, the real situation,
certainly with us—they are honoured in the breach and not in the observance
—then I think the law serves its best interests by trying to be more honest
about it. . . . I am a great believer in being as candid as possible about my
institutions. They are in large measure abandoned in practice, and therefore
I think the M'Naghten Rules are in large measure shams. That is a strong
word, but I think the M'Naghten Rules are very difficult for conscientious
people and not difficult enough for people who say "We'll just juggle them"

. . . . I dare to believe that we ought not to rest content with the difficulty of finding an improvement in the M'Naghten Rules.[8]

The Royal Commission reported in 1953 that the "right and wrong" test had been objected to by experienced doctors for over 100 years as "based on an entirely obsolete and misleading conception of the nature of insanity, since insanity does not only, or primarily, affect the cognitive or intellectual faculties, but affects the whole personality of the patient, including both the will and the emotions. An insane person may therefore often know the nature and quality of his act and that it is wrong and forbidden by law, and yet commit it as a result of the mental disease." [9]

Despite unyielding resistance to any restatement of the rule, it was observed nearly 60 years ago that judges of England "generally have not hesitated so to interpret the law as to bring within its exonerating scope cases in which its narrow, literal interpretation would have had a different result." [10]

In fact, Stephen [11] is among those who insisted that if a person is prevented by mental disease from controlling his conduct he cannot be said in any true sense to "know the nature of his act," and that it is to be argued, therefore, that such a person is not criminally responsible, even under the McNaghten rule; but this strained interpretation of the rule has not appealed to the judiciary.

In a few American jurisdictions, there has been a minor modification or supplementation of the rule, so as to exempt from criminal responsibility persons suffering from irresistible or uncontrollable impulse. But the word "impulse" is unsatisfactory for it covers only a small and very special group of the mentally ill. The word "impulse" is suggestive of some sudden episode, and it is well known that in many cases the sufferer acts, not suddenly or impulsively, but coolly and with ingenious calculation. This is characteristic of many who suffer from schizophrenia or paranoid psychosis. Long and sustained brooding is characteristic of certain familiar forms of mental illness.

In 1869 the Supreme Court of New Hampshire,[12] in the Pike case, handed down a historic opinion sweeping aside the McNaghten rule. It renounced the McNaghten rule's insistence on the right-wrong test. The New Hampshire Court did not, however, adopt a new set of symptoms to ascertain insanity, for to do so would, in its view, have been as arbitrary as the old rule. The court recognized simply that an accused person is not criminally responsible if his unlawful act was the result of mental disease or mental defect. Under this decision, insanity is no longer defined as a matter of law; instead it is made a question of fact to be determined like any other fact. This determination rests upon testimony of the psychiatric expert respecting the latest knowledge of human behavior and his interpretation of such knowledge in terms of his observations of the accused.

More than 30 years before the New Hampshire Court decided the Pike case, Dr. Isaac Ray, who was consulted by Justice Doe, writer of the opinion in that case, attracted widespread attention in both the medical and legal professions by his book which is remarkable indeed for the clarity and modernity of the views therein expressed.[13]

Anybody interested in tracing the development of thought on this entire subject will find that one of the most rewarding pieces of legal literature is the opinion of Judge Somerville in the Supreme Court of Alabama, written in 1886.[14] The merit of this opinion, which reviews not only the legal but the medical knowledge of the day, is highlighted by a dissent which declares that, while the majority opinion sounds interesting and persuasive, the dissenter deems it his duty as a judge to take into account only legal authorities and that extra-legal writings cannot be considered safe guides in judicial administration.

The intervening years have brought abundant confirmation of the idea that responsibility implies reasonable integration of the total personality, which includes the emotions as well as the intellect. Medical psychology teaches that the mind cannot be split into watertight, unrelated, autonomously functioning compartments like knowing, willing and feeling. These functions are intimately related and interdependent. We know today that the external manifestations of mental disease follow no neat pattern permitting pat legal definitions suitable for universal application.

Attention is also invited to an interesting and instructive discussion by Chief Judge Biggs of the Third Circuit in *United States* v. *Baldi*,[15] who stated:

> The human mind . . . is an entity. It cannot be broken into parts, one part sane, the other part insane. The law, when it requires the psychiatrist to state whether in his opinion the accused is capable of knowing right from wrong, compels the psychiatrist to test guilt or innocence by a concept which has almost no recognizable reality.

There is nothing more futile than the search for an absolute test as a matter of law; for it is a scientific fact, which has passed into common knowledge that no such single test exists. We do not insist on a legal formula in diagnosing other diseases; why in this instance? It is a question of fact like any other, to be decided after hearing the explanations of the experts. The weight to be assigned to a single phenomenon is not to be determined by a rule of law but in a factual judgment. If the issues in a case were whether a bone was fractured, and surgeons were told they could give their diagnosis and prognosis but must disregard x-ray pictures as irrelevant, no one would think that desirable. If on an issue of whether someone had typhoid the pathologist were told that he must not consider the laboratory tests, but only one symptom, temperature, which was solemnly declared legally conclusive, who would have confidence in such testing or such procedure? While the tests psychiatrists use may lack the precision and finality often associated with the x-ray and microscope, it is scarcely arguable that the issues will be better decided if the most advanced and enlightened thought is barred from the witness stand.

Justice Doe in the New Hampshire Pike case argued that the McNaghten formula was false and should be rejected because it adopted as law a mistake of fact, and that the mistakes of science are not science and they are not law. As Justice Doe expressed it in a letter to his friend, Dr. Ray, "The theory of the common law is that it is unchangeable, that lawyers and judges may make mistakes, as well as men of science, but that the law, being the perfection of reason, does not consist of such mistakes, any more than astronomy consists of the idea that the earth is flat and that the sun passes over it." [16] This is an interesting and penetrating observation.

Again, he argues, "The mistake of our predecessors was in taking judicial notice of contemporaneous medical opinion and adopting it as law." [17] He points out that the rejection of a proven mistake does not make the law variable, but is merely a refusal to continue the according of judicial notice to a fact once it is shown not to be a fact at all. No new proposition of law is involved.

There has been much spirited discussion throughout the country since the recent decision of the Durham case,[18] in which the Court of Appeals for the District of Columbia Circuit handed down a notable opinion by Judge Bazelon in which he was joined by Judges Edgerton and Washington. The full nine-judge bench declined to review this decision which adopted in substance the 85-year-old New Hampshire rule, relieving the courts in this jurisdiction of the unbending McNaghten rule with its discredited right-wrong test.

The full merit of the New Hampshire decision and of the more recent District of Columbia opinion in the Durham case is precisely that they do not attempt to embody one set of medical theories in place of another, for even if it were possible to frame a test embodying more modern knowledge there would still be the danger that in the progress of science the new rule itself might be found inadequate. The whole point is not to restrict the test to particular symptoms, but to permit as broad an inquiry as may be found necessary according to the latest accepted scientific criteria.

Professor Whitehorn of the Johns Hopkins Medical School, in a memorandum prepared for a commission on legal psychiatry, appointed in 1948 by the Governor of Maryland, wrote:

Psychiatrists are challenged to set forth a crystal-clear statement of what constitutes insanity. It is impossible to express this adequately in words alone, since such diagnostic judgments involve clinical skill and experience which cannot wholly be verbalized. . . . The medical profession would be baffled if asked to write into the legal code universally valid criteria for the diagnosis of the many types of psychotic illness which may seriously disturb a person's responsibility, and even if this were attempted, the diagnostic criteria would have to be rewritten from time to time, with the progress of psychiatric knowledge.[19]

The court in the Durham case directs trial judges within its jurisdiction to instruct juries that where there is some evidence of mental disease or defect, in order to convict they must find two things, (1) that the accused was not suffering from a mental defect or disease, and (2) that even if he was, the criminal act was not the product of that condition, for if the jury finds that the mental disease did not cause the act, it should have no influence on the question of the defendant's guilt.

Critics of this view have not been entirely consistent. On the one hand it has been claimed by some of them that the McNaghten rule does not need to be changed, for, like the judges mentioned in the Royal Commission's Report,[20] juries have frequently exercised a so-called "moral judgment" to ameliorate the severity of the McNaghten rule. Hence, it is argued that even if the rule seems in terms to require the defendant to be held responsible, since he knew the nature of his act and that it was wrong, if the jury nevertheless recognized that a mental condition caused his act, they would likely refuse to convict. But why, we permit ourselves to ask, should we maintain a rule that must be breached in order to make it work?

On the other hand, the Durham rule has been criticized on the score of its vagueness, for it does not pronounce as a matter of law precisely what symptoms are sufficient for a finding of mental irresponsibility. This criticism seems to me without merit. The facts as to mental condition will be endless in their variety. It is for the psychiatrists, after a study of the defendant, to inform the jury of their observations and interpret them in the light of their knowledge and experience. The jury will consider the evidence of the psychiatrists as they do expert testimony in any field. No longer will they be restricted to the artificial and discredited right-wrong test. They will not be forced to ignore the question of the extent to which the defendant's lack of control over his emotions has deprived him of control over his acts, or, if you please, has overcome his will, for that is crucial in arriving at an intelligent verdict. This does not mean that the law will no longer recognize that a man has free will within normal limits of mental health. As Judge Bazelon said in the Durham case:

> The jury's range of inquiry will not be limited to, but may include, for example, whether an accused, who suffered from a mental disease or defect did not know the difference between right and wrong, acted under the compulsion of an irresistible impulse, or had "been deprived of or lost the power of his will. . . ."

Juries will continue to make moral judgments, still operating under the fundamental precept that "Our collective conscience does not allow punishment where it cannot impose blame." But in making such judgments, they will be guided by wider horizons of knowledge concerning mental life.[21]

To put it in general terms, the jury will, as heretofore, be called on to distinguish whether the act was done with evil intent (*mens rea*) for which there is criminal responsibility, or was the product of a mental condition that makes the act not one of free will, and hence not criminally punishable. The right-wrong test is not completely abandoned; it is merely dethroned from its exclusive preeminence.

Judges and lawyers boast that there is no definition of fraud; they think this is in aid of the law's effectiveness and does not weaken it. Its very vagueness is said to be a source of strength, for it renders the law more adaptable to unpredictable conditions. Or, to take another example: Is the so-called definition of negligence really a definition? What could be fuzzier than the instruction to the jury that negligence is a failure to observe that care which would be observed by a "reasonable man"—a chimerical creature conjured up to give an aura of definiteness where definiteness is not possible. Have you ever tried to imagine what goes on in the minds of jurors when they are handed such a formula? No two of them would agree on what the standard of due care is. Yet it is the best possible working rule, and we do quite well with it in specific situations. We recognize that the alternative of a fixed formula, however ingenious, is bound to prove disappointing in practice.

Every man is likely to think of himself as the happy exemplification of "the reasonable man"; and so the standard he adopts in order to fulfill the law's prescription will resemble himself, or what he thinks he is, or what he thinks he should be, even if he is not. All these shifts and variations of his personal norm will find reflection in the verdict. The whole business is necessarily equivocal. This we recognize, but we are reconciled to the impossibility of discovering any form of words that will ring with perfect clarity and be automatically self-executing. Alas, there is no magic push button in this or in other branches of the law.

To pursue the point further, consider such a term as "due process." Is there a pat definition to tell us what is "due" in due process? I had a wise teacher at law school who concluded his lecture on undue influence in his course in testamentary law by summarizing, "In short, undue influence is influence which under all the circumstances is undue." Look at such words and phrases as "reasonable," "practicable," "obscene," "unfair competition," or "cruel and unusual punishment." Such standards, found in almost every branch of the law, are the bases for judgments of law as well as fact. They are all as capable of expansion and contraction as the subjective judgment of those who interpret them. They must derive their meaning largely from the common sense of the people who apply these terms.

The concept of causality expressed in the court's use in the Durham case of the word "product" has also been criticized as leaving too much to the fact-finders' discretion, but this is no broader a discretion than courts habitually accord juries when they charge them to determine proximate cause in negligence cases.

What we ought to fear above all is not the absence of a definition but being saddled with a false definition. We must avoid the rigidity which precludes inquiry, which shuts out light and insists on concepts that are at odds with things known and acknowledged, not only by the medical profession, but by all informed men.

The McNaghten rule requires medical witnesses to testify in terms that to them are artificial and confining. A doctor can offer expert judgment when he talks of illness, disease, symptoms, and the like. When he is forced to adopt the vocabulary of morality and ethics, he is speaking in what to him is a foreign language and in an area in which he claims no expertness. If the wrong questions are asked, it should surprise no one if wrong answers are given. Is it not preferable to permit the medical witnesses sufficient latitude to describe the conditions and express their findings in terms they consider significant and meaningful?

This very day the American Law Institute is considering the proposed Model Penal Code, which submits several alternative provisions concerning mental disease or defect as excluding responsibility. Three different formulations have been presented. The first declares that "a person is not responsible for criminal conduct if . . . he lacks substantial capacity either to appreciate the criminality of his conduct or to conform his conduct to the requirements of law." [22]

Another stresses "capacity either to appreciate the criminality of his conduct or to conform his conduct to the requirements of law is so substantially impaired that he cannot justly be held responsible." [23] Note that the ultimate question to be determined by the jury is whether the accused can *justly* be held responsible for his act.

The third formulation emphasizes capacity to appreciate punishment as a restraining influence.[24]

Even if there were time, I should consider it unprofitable to burden you with the minutiae of the arguments pro and con that have been advanced concerning these several versions. The debate seems to reveal a greater degree of accord than of actual disharmony. All seem to be agreed that the McNaghten rule is obsolete. All are agreed that there are conditions, recognized as disease or defect, which in good morals should excuse the afflicted one from criminal responsibility. All concur that not every mental abnormality should be deemed sufficient to relieve of responsibility. Imposture and evasion must be prevented in the interest of society. All are likewise agreed that a person who has committed a criminal act and is found not guilty by reason of insanity should be put in detention and remain there as long as necessary to protect society. Where to draw the line between what is and what is not sufficient evidence of insanity is a matter of judgment in the particular case; it cannot be described with precision in advance. Saying that the disease must be "serious" as some insist, would not achieve the hoped-for certainty, for such terms are themselves inexact.

The same observation may be made in respect to the suggestion that the defendant should be deemed responsible if he has the capacity to respond to a single influence, namely, the threat of punishment. Psychiatrists of great eminence have declared that this is too difficult to isolate for psychiatric judgment. Moreover, this again singles out one factor and exalts it to a special legal status, when the problem needs to be considered as a whole in the light of all the circumstances.

In the comments accompanying the American Law Institute draft of a penal code, it is recommended that the concept of mental disease or defect should exclude "the case of the so-called 'psychopathic personality.'" [25] This proposed exclusion rests on the assertion that "psychopathy 'is a statistical abnormality; that is to say, the psychopath differs from a normal person only quantitatively or in degree, not qualitatively; and the diagnosis of psychopathic personality does not carry with it any explanation of the causes of the abnormality.'" To me, with all deference, this is unconvincing. The New Hampshire or Durham approach seems preferable. It makes the causes of abnormality matters of fact for the juries to determine in each case upon the basis of explanations furnished them by the psychiatric expert witnesses. Dr. Winfred Overholser of St. Elizabeths has said that "psychopathic personality" is a wastebasket classification. The very term is used in the profession in different senses to describe different things. Therefore, it is unwise to provide a blanket exclusion or blanket inclusion of that particular characterization. Indeed, in the official nomenclature of the American Psychiatric Association, the very term has been dropped as meaningless.

I note in passing that many pyromaniacs or kleptomaniacs would probably be held responsible under this American Law Institute proposal, since they are frequently termed "no more than psychopathic personalities." Many psychiatric authorities think these cases are obsessive-compulsive neurotics. Those suffering from these diseases may well not be psychotic; yet, by common agreement they often lack that degree of integration which is necessary for legal responsibility. I suspect that there will be a tendency here first to make a judgment as to what is the wise and fair disposition of the individual case and then to announce a classification accordingly, and not the other way about. Attempting to categorize cases as a matter of law according to these vague distinctions would only complicate the difficulty. Not an unbending rule, but enlightened understanding of the special facts of each case should be our aim, especially where there is a broad twilight zone.

I confess to a feeling that the niceties of these several verbalizations by the Institute or by courts will escape the jury. Any of these variations, if adopted, will probably result in something not very different from what the Court of Appeals for the District of Columbia Circuit declared as the law, when it stated:

It was the jury's function to determine from all the evidence, including the expert testimony, not only whether appellant suffered from an abnormal mental condition, but also whether the nature and extent of any condition . . . was such as to relieve him of criminal responsibility under the standards then prevailing.[26]

But whichever formulation is accepted, it is an advance, because it allows the jury to receive more light. The testimony presented to the jurors will be cast in terms that are meaningful to the witnesses and that can be more amply explained.

Much of the reluctance to change the McNaghten rule is doubtless occasioned by the fear that if the criteria for determining insanity are broadened, instances may multiply of violators escaping punishment and being released after a brief detention in a mental institution. The court in the Durham case was not unmindful of this apprehension. It pointed out that an accused person who is acquitted by reason of insanity is presumed to be insane and may be committed under the District of Columbia statute for an indefinite period. The court recommended that trial courts invoke this commitment procedure "so that the accused may be confined as long as "the public safety and . . . [his] welfare' require." [27] This is also the insistence of the American Law Institute proposals.

Let us look at a typical case. An accused person is found incompetent to stand trial; that is, he cannot fully understand the charge against him and assist in his defense. He is committed and after a period of confinement is certified to be competent to stand trial. If upon trial he is found not guilty by reason of insanity at the time of the offense, he is not necessarily entitled to release. The inquiry into mental competency to stand trial and assist in one's defense is not the same as either the question of criminal responsibility or that of whether he may safely be permitted at large after acquittal.

So experienced an authority as Dr. Manfred Guttmacher, chief medical officer of the Supreme Bench of Baltimore, assures us that "the truth of the matter is that the finding 'not guilty by reason of insanity' has not resulted in the premature release of offenders into the community. Dr. Wm. Alanson White made a study many years ago showing that, on the average, perpetrators of homicide committed to institutions for the insane spent more time in confinement than those sentenced to penal institutions."

No restatement of the rule will revolutionize the practical operation of the criminal courts in dealing with mental illness as a defense. The change which is under consideration will not spell ruin to law enforcement; neither will it bring salvation. Juries will doubtless continue to bring to bear their unscientific notions upon the scientific testimony that has been adduced before them. This is not an unmixed calamity, for juries often find ways, sometimes with the benign acquiescence of judges, to mitigate rigidities and absurdities in the law; juries, who are not very different from judges in this respect, will still tend to reflect the community sense of justice which courts cannot wholly ignore in maintaining public order. The restatement will not of itself eliminate from the courtroom unseemly conflicts between experts. This is a separate problem, but these conflicts will at least relate to things that are genuine and not fictitious.

There is no reason to fear that the proposed change will so relax the law as to weaken its sanctions or its deterrent influence. After all, commitment to a hospital for the insane for an indefinite period is no more inviting a prospect than a fixed term in jail. It is no soft and coddling disposition. Durham is a case in point. Having been declared mentally incompetent to stand trial and assist in his own defense, he was committed to a mental hospital. There is reason to believe that as a result of several years of treatment there he may be cured. If so, society's needs will have been better met than by any prison sentence, long or short.

Which offers greater protection to society—detention and treatment in a hospital, and ultimately a medical judgment that the person is not likely to offend again; or a penitentiary warden's certificate that the prisoner has served his sentence and been discharged regardless of his medical condition? It must be remembered that prison terms do expire and prisoners are released. Such release gives no assurance whatever of safety to the community. Statistics of recidivism may well temper our faith in the prison system. Detention and treatment of sick people rather than holding them to full accountability comports with our traditional concept of the dignity of the individual. It takes into due account the public safety and fully vindicates the proper interests of public justice. Let us give the new rule a chance; and as we gain in wisdom from experience, necessary refinements and revisions in practice can be made.

I conclude by suggesting that there is need for continuing research to enlarge the resources of knowledge in the problems of mental health and behavior, and for changes in court procedures as well as in the substance of the law. Means must be found to bring the legal and medical professions together on common ground. If psychiatry is to provide maximum guidance and assistance to juries, psychiatric witnesses must learn to avoid technical jargon which baffles laymen. We need better institutional facilities—perhaps of a more specialized character—to deal with the criminally insane and those who may be prevented by timely help from becoming such. Lawyers who feel a concern for improvements in legal procedures and in public justice have important work in their respective communities.

Office of the Solicitor General
Washington, D.C.

References

1. Rex v. Arnold, 16 Howard State Trials 695, 764 (1724).

2. Ferrer's case, 19 Howard State Trials 886 (1760).

3. 10 Cl. & Fin. 200, 8 Eng. Rep. 718 (1843).

4. 10 Cl. & Fin. at 210, 8 Eng. Rep. at 722.

5. 2 Stephen. 154 et seq. (1883).

6. Cardozo: What Medicine Can Do for the Law. P. 32. (1930).

7. Id.

8. Report of the Royal Commission on Capital Punishment, 1949–1953. Cmd. No. 8932 at P. 102.

9. Ibid., at P. 80.

10. Id., quoting an 1896 Report of a Committee of the Medico-Psychological Association.

11. 2 Stephen. Pp. 167 et seq. (1883).

12. State v. Pike, 49 N.H. 399 (1869).

13. Ray: A Treatise on the Medical Jurisprudence of Insanity. (First ed. 1838).

14. Parsons v. State, 81 Ala. 577, 2 So. 854 (1886).

15. Dissenting opinion, 192 F. 2d 540, 568 (C.A. 3, 1951).

16. Letter of July 22, 1868, quotd in Reik: The Doe-Ray Correspondence: A Pioneer Collaboration in the Jurisprudence of Mental Disease. 63 Yale L.J. 183, 191 (1953).

17. Id.

18. Durham v. United States, 214 F. 2d 862 (C.A.D.C., 1954).

19. Quoted in Guttmacher and Weihofen, Psychiatry and the Law. Pp. 419–420. (1952.)

20. See Ref. 10, supra.

21. 214 F. 2d at 876.

22. American Law Institute, Model Penal Code, Tentative Draft No. 4, Sec. 4.01 (1955).

23. Ibid., alternative formulations of Sec. 4.01.

24. Id.

25. Ibid., Comments Sec. 4.01, p. 160.

26. Stewart v. United States, 214 F. 2d 879, 882 (C.A.D.C., 1954).

27. 214 F. 2d at 876, fn. 57.

DEGREES FOR CHARLATANS *

⟨ DELL LEBO

Clinical psychologists have tried to meet their increasing responsibilities by taking steps to assure that only properly qualified and trained persons receive recognition as clinical psychologists. The methods of insuring proper training and qualification place importance upon a graduate degree. Most

* From Dell Lebo, "Degrees for Charlatans," Amer. Psychologist, 8, 231–234. Reprinted by permission of the author and the Managing Editor, The American Psychological Association.

frequently, at least eight years of university training must be completed before a PhD degree is conferred in clinical psychology.

With the increasing demand for the services of clinical psychologists, some schools have capitalized upon offering easily obtained degrees in psychology. Schools exist whose sole purpose appears to be the awarding of degrees for little or no effort. These degrees are offered to people of indiscriminate background for the completion of a negligible amount of study on frequently indifferent courses.

The present paper is concerned with the effect such degree-granting institutions have upon clinical psychology. These degree-granting correspondence schools are firmly and legally established. The paper is not peppered with the names of fly-by-night schools which manage to award a few degrees before going out of business. The schools to be discussed represent a serious and lasting threat to the status of clinical psychology.

All the correspondence schools attracting degree-hungry quacks make announcements indicating that students need not have any special educational background in order to enroll. They also seek to whet the appetite of potential students. For example, the "catalogue" of the Neotarian College of Philosophy devotes considerable space to saying that the possession of a doctor's degree carries with it the advantage of distinction and prestige in one's chosen field. One reads that this coveted degree may be obtained in a comparatively short time, through an easy study course, and at a very reasonable rate. Such an announcement is typical of all the degree-granting schools to be discussed in the present paper.

Types of Degrees Offered

Some correspondence schools offer such esoteric degrees in psychology that there is little danger of their being confused with the academic degrees of recognized schools. The degree of Certified Grapho Analytical Psychology, offered upon the completion of correspondence training with the International Grapho Analysis Society, Inc., would probably never be seriously confused with a bona fide degree in clinical psychology. It is also unlikely that the $50 course of Western University, designed to train technicians in such fundamental principles as chiropractic, mechanotherapy, hydro therapy, Swedish massage, divine healing, psychotherapy, and colon therapy, would be mistaken for an academic graduate course. Nor would a Western University Doctor of Chiro-Deo-Therapy be recognized as the same as a PhD in clinical psychology.

The same may be said of the now well-established mystic and semi-religious correspondence school degree of Doctor of Psychology (PsD). More than one psychologist has been able to slough off such a degree by saying that no recognized institution has ever conferred one. This is true, but the average patient cannot be expected to know it. When a patient sees a diploma behind a charlatan's desk, the diploma is assumed to be valid. When the diploma reads, as the majority of correspondence school diplomas do, something like this: "Know all men by these presents that _____ has satisfactorily and honorably completed a course of study and training in the Snow White College, and we, the Board of Trustees in accordance with the articles of incorporation under and by the authority of the State of _____, confer upon him the degree of Doctor of Psychology [signed and magnificently sealed]," it appears to be evidence of academic recognition. It does not say anything about having been by correspondence work. One could not blame a patient for being led into thinking he was consulting a qualified psychologist.

Courses leading to the Doctor of Psychology degree are offered by the following correspondence schools: College of Universal Truth, Institute of Metaphysics, Searchlight University, The College of Divine Metaphysics, and the Neotarian College of Philosophy. The PsD degree is apparently in such demand that the National Institute of Hypnology has recently offered a course leading to the degree of Doctor of Psychology in Hypnology (PsDH). It would seem that the PsD degree is as well established in some correspondence schools as the PhD is in recognized colleges. We have our Doctor of Philosophy in Psychology degree. They now have their Doctor of Psychology in Hypnology degree course.

The PsD degree course from most of the schools listed above will cost the student $100, with a 5 to 10 per cent discount for cash in advance. That is, all save the Doctor of Psychology in Hypnology degree course. This course was designed, according to the three pages of mimeographed matter supplied by the offering institution, for physicians, dentists, and all others who are qualified to receive the doctorate. Since the prospective student is told to check the course that is most applicable to his needs, it seems that the tuition fee is sufficient to qualify one for the doctorate. The Institute states that anyone completing a previous, briefer course in hypnosis is eligible to matriculate for the $150 doctor's degree. To make it even more convenient, the material of the PsDH course includes the text material of the earlier course, as well as some new material. The Doctor of Psychology in Hypnology receives ten lessons and two textbooks. There is no mention of an examination covering this reading.

The required courses of the Neotarian College of Philosophy for the Doctor of Psychology degree are representative of the type of lessons supplied by other degree-granting correspondence schools. Two courses must be completed before a diploma can be issued. They are applied metaphysics and applied psychology. The 30 mimeographed lessons of the applied metaphysics course explain "the Why of God, World, and Man." They also tell the student how to make eternal truth as simple as his ABC's. According to the prospectus, the following subjects are taken up and fully analyzed: that complex human being—you, and your personal entity; the planes of consciousness, the origin and scope of the mind's psychic powers; breathing the breath of God; thought waves carry soul-vibrations; ever active powers of mind control destiny; and "the World is but empty shadows."

In the applied psychology course the students learn that psychology is simply the science of mind. Applied psychology explains mind in its "every form of manifestation." The course is said to be written in plain and simple words. It is both easy to understand and to put into practical use in everyday life, to the great and lasting benefit of those who take it. Perhaps an example of the simplicity and practicality of the psychology course is found in the discussion of phenomena, both mental and physical, and their control through the laws of nature. For, the catalogue continues, all mental phenomena result from definite ideas. "Mental activity is always a force and is either positive or negative."

The student may receive the PsD degree from The College of Divine Metaphysics upon completing courses in practical metaphysics and the psychology of business success. The College of Universal Truth requires course work in building the healing matrix and the seven steps to self-sufficiency. They warn, further, that no work written in pencil will be accepted.

For the completion of two courses, namely, metaphysics and realization, and metaphysical healing, a diploma and the degree of Doctor of Psychology are awarded by the Institute of Metaphysics.

In spite of the freedom with which correspondence schools award PsD degrees, the clinical psychologist may feel somewhat protected. Some clinical psychologists believe that eventually all clinicians in psychology will possess a PhD. When such is the case the public should come to expect bona fide clinical psychologists to be Doctors of Philosophy. However, the College of Universal Truth, the Neotarian College of Philosophy, and Searchlight University are currently offering courses leading to the Doctor of Philosophy degree. The College of Universal Truth has the esoteric degree of Doctor of Philosophy in Metaphysics (DPhM).

The Neotarian College of Philosophy requires the completion of courses in basic philosophy, mystical Bible interpretation, applied metaphysics, metaphysical healing, and applied psychology as well as a thesis on one of the above subjects for their PhD degree. This may seem like a small course load for a doctoral student to carry. However, the college offers no other courses. The cost is $250.

One may obtain a PhD degree from Searchlight University for only $100 on the easy payment plan by completing a single course. This course *introduces* the student to philosophy and "with remarkable directness" leads him into provocative philosophic readings.

Most of the degree-granting correspondence schools schedule one lesson every week. In the present writer's experience, there has been no adherence to such a rule. They will allow the student to progress as rapidly as he wishes. A student with spare time, the ability to read and write English, and the required fee may become a PhD in a matter of weeks.

A PhD may be obtained from Western University without taking any lessons. This unique university is authorized to accept the hours of students from any educational institution. If the hours are sufficient to meet with the requirements of the board of directors a certificate, diploma, or degree will be awarded. One desiring a degree is instructed to send in copies of diplomas from other schools, or a notarized affidavit of studies and practical work. It is also necessary to write a 3,000-word thesis (approximately the length of this article) on the subject in which a diploma is desired. Written examinations of unspecified content must be passed with a grade of at least 75 per cent before a degree will be conferred.

After the hours, thesis, and examinations have been accepted, Western University will award a degree in the desired area. On one of their application blanks the degree pictured reads, in part, as follows: "Be it known that _____ having satisfactorily completed that Course of Study as prescribed and passed the required examinations, the Board of Trustees upon recommendation of the Faculty, confer the Degree of Doctor of Philosophy upon him together with all rights and privileges pertaining thereto."

The cost of Western University office expenditures is $100. If the applicant does not meet the requirements his money will be returned. There is "no charge" for the degree; it is awarded.

Need for Control of Degree-granting Correspondence Schools

When the records of Oriental University, Washington, D.C. were brought into court in 1925, it was found that 601 degrees had been conferred in a little more than two years by that correspondence institution. The degrees included 348 doctorates in chemistry, pharmacy, engineering, medicine, philosophy, and divinity (12). Educators interested in upholding standards in American universities capitalized upon the publicity of the trial. They were among the first to suggest controlling diploma mills. As early as 1926 an article appeared (8) on institutions without equipment, standards of admission, or graduation but which awarded a degree-conferring diploma. Educators have continued working for the elimination of fraud in education (3).

For some time psychologists have been concerned with psychological racketeers (5, 11). Only recently have they become slightly interested in the correspondence schools that may supply charlatans with high-sounding degrees (1, 4, 9, 10). Not only may patients be easily deceived by the holders of degrees from the types of schools mentioned, but also, the existence of such easily conferred degrees tends to undermine the respect given to earned degrees from reputable institutions. Standards in clinical psychology will be materially advanced by controlling the sources of degrees for the untrained and the unscrupulous.

Legal Recognition

It is not an easy matter to control degree-granting correspondence schools. Several of those mentioned in the present article have been in business for 30 years or more. All of them have legal recognition. That is to say, all of them are chartered or incorporated in their respective states and have been granted the full legal right to confer the degrees they offer. None of the schools treated in the present paper is fraudulent in the sense that it is not legally empowered to grant degrees.

Many of the correspondence schools cited make the most of their legal recognition. For example, The College of Divine Metaphysics stresses that it was incorporated as a religious educational institution in 1918 and has the full legal right to grant the degrees it offers. The Institute of Metaphysics and the Neotarian College of Philosophy both prominently mention that they were incorporated as religious and educational institutions under the laws of their respective states. The College of Universal Truth and the National Institute of Hypnology operate under a charter from their respective states. Western University advertises it has received a charter from its state for *all* learning.

It was once felt that an association of college and university administrators (12) or smaller regional groups (2) could take steps to solve the problem of control. It was believed that legislation sponsored by such an association could solve the problem.

However, state control is not standardized (2, 12, 13). Of the correspondence schools mentioned as advertising their legal recognition, one has been given the legal right to confer degrees by Indiana, another by Missouri. Both states now exercise adequate legal control. Another college operates in Illinois, a state which also exercises control over nonprofit colleges. One has been chartered by the State of Delaware, which is one of four states at present with the highest legal requirements for the recognition of a nonprofit degree-granting school. Delaware requires a certificate of approval in addition to a charter or license to establish a nonprofit college.

The references made by degree-granting correspondence schools to the state-conferred legal right to grant degrees are apparently intended to imply that the school is operated and controlled by the state, hence it must be a recognized school. As we have seen, this is not so. We can, however, be certain that the degree-granting correspondence colleges are "nonprofit schools," because there never is a profit. All the moneys are applied to the salaries of the "faculty" and for office expenses.

Answer to Problem

Legal recognition by means of state control does not seem to be the entire answer. Some states once exercising poor control now exercise adequate controls (2, 12, 13). Some states regarded as having adequate controls in 1938 (2) now have inadequate controls (13). Schools providing charlatans with educational degrees have been criticized and investigated by such competent groups as the United States Office of Education, the Federal Trade Commission, the Better Business Bureau, the American Association of University Professors, and the Institute of International Education. None of these groups has ever been able to substantiate its suspicions that the schools were out-and-out diploma mills (6). They have only succeeded in finding that the schools were chartered by the state in which they were established and had the legal right to grant degrees. As long as they make no claim that their degrees are state licenses to practice, they remain well within the law.

Clinical psychologists can help to end fraud in degrees in psychology by writing articles for local papers and giving talks before local groups in which they stress the requirements for a recognized degree in clinical psychology. These requirements can be contrasted with course offerings of degree-granting correspondence schools. They can encourage university and professional associations to emphasize to their state congressmen the need for effective legislation and control over correspondence schools. They can work to have state and national organizations denounce fraudulent degrees in psychology by means of resolutions and pronouncements. They can encourage psychologists to be alert and to send letters and other materials pertaining to fraudulent colleges to the Federal Trade Commission in Washington, D.C. They may write to James B. Edmonson, Chairman, Committee on Fraudulent Schools and Colleges, University of Michigan, Ann Arbor, for information on effective ways of outlawing unscrupulous institutions.

Such action will make the public aware of the existence of fraudulent degrees in psychology. State officials will be encouraged to assume more responsibility for correspondence schools that give little real service to students.

Diploma mills are already a cancerous growth on the body of education (7). Charlatans must not be allowed to eat away the structure of respect and responsibility for which clinical psychologists are working.

References

1. David, H. P. An analysis of psychologists in the classified telephone directory. *Amer. Psychologist*, 1948, 3, 133–134.
2. Dryness, E. C. How may we co-operate to secure legislation to curb diploma mills. *J. Amer. Ass. Coll. Reg.*, 1938, 13, 530–532.
3. Edmonson, J. B. Fraudulent schools and colleges. *Sch. & Soc.*, 1950, 72, 33–35.

4. Katz, S. Beware the witch doctor. *Sch. Guid. Wkr*, 1952, 7, 22–30.
5. Kirkpatrick, F. H. Psychological racketeers. *Personnel J.*, 1942, 20, 283–286.
6. Meyer, A. E. Diploma mills. *Amer. Mercury*, 1945, 61, 304–310.
7. Pencke, W. L. Degrees for sale. *J. Nat. educ. Ass.*, 1949, 38, 286–287.
8. Robertsen, D. A. Degrees for dollars. *Educ. Rec.*, 1926, 7, 11–24.
9. Shoben, E. J. Private clinicians in Los Angeles. *Amer. Psychologist*, 1948, 3, 127–132.
10. Steiner, L. R. *Where do people take their troubles?* Boston: Houghton Mifflin, 1945.
11. Yates, D. H. *Psychological racketeers*. Boston: Richard G. Badger, 1932.
12. *Diploma mills*. (Ed. Cmnt). *Bull. Amer. Ass. Coll. Reg.*, 1935, 11, 59–69.
13. *State authority with respect to the establishment and supervision of nonpublic schools and colleges*. Washington, D.C.: National Educational Association of the United States, 1951.